THE PROSE

Essays for Thinking, Reading, and Writing

ELEVENTH EDITION

Kim Flachmann

California State University, Bakersfield

Michael Flachmann

New! 2016 MLA Updates

PEARSON

Boston   Columbus   Indianapolis   New York   San Francisco
Amsterdam   Cape Town   Dubai   London   Madrid   Milan   Munich   Paris   Montréal   Toronto
Delhi   Mexico City   São Paulo   Sydney   Hong Kong   Seoul   Singapore   Taipei   Tokyo

For Laura and Raymond

Senior Editor: Brad Potthoff
Program Manager: Anne Shure
Product Marketing Manager: Ali Arnold
Field Marketing Manager: Mark Robinson
Media Producer: Elizabeth Bravo
Content Specialist: Laura Olson
Media Editor: Kelsey Loveday
Project Manager: Donna Campion

Text Design, Project Coordination, and
    Electronic Page Makeup: SPi Global
Design Lead: Beth Paquin
Cover Designer: Studio Montage
Cover Illustration: *Lisa-Blue*/Getty Images
Senior Manufacturing Buyer: Roy L. Pickering, Jr.
Printer/Binder: LSC communications/Crawfordsville
Cover Printer: Lehigh-Phoenix Color/Hagerstown

Acknowledgments of third-party content appear on page[s] 593–594, which constitute an extension of this copyright page.

PEARSON, ALWAYS LEARNING, and MYWRITINGLAB are exclusive trademarks owned by Pearson Education, Inc. or its affiliates in the United States and/or other countries.

Unless otherwise indicated herein, any third-party trademarks that may appear in this work are the property of their respective owners and any references to third-party trademarks, logos, or other trade dress are for demonstrative or descriptive purposes only. Such references are not intended to imply any sponsorship, endorsement, authorization, or promotion of Pearson's products by the owners of such marks, or any relationship between the owner and Pearson Education, Inc., or its affiliates, authors, licensees, or distributors.

Library of Congress Cataloging-in-Publication Data
The Prose reader: essays for thinking, reading, and writing / [compilers] Kim Flachmann, California State University, Bakersfield; Michael Flachmann. — Eleventh Edition.
     pages cm
  Includes bibliographical references and index.
  ISBN 978-0-13-407155-8 (alk. paper)
1. College readers. 2. English language—Rhetoric—Problems, exercises, etc. 3. Report writing—Problems, exercises, etc.   I. Flachmann, Kim, compiler. II. Flachmann, Michael, compiler.
  PE1417.P847 2017
  808'.0427—dc23

                                                                        2015032509

2   17

Student Edition ISBN 10: 0-13-467885-0
Student Edition ISBN 13: 978-0-13-467885-6
A la Carte Edition ISBN 10: 0-13-470302-2
A la Carte Edition ISBN 13: 978-0-13-470302-2

PEARSON   www.pearsonhighered.com

RHETORICAL CONTENTS

RAY BRADBURY *Summer Rituals* **54**
The description of a simple, comforting ritual—the putting up of a front-porch swing in early summer—confirms the value of ceremony in the life of a small town.

KIMBERLY WOZENCRAFT *Notes from the Country Club* **60**
Have you ever wondered what being in prison is like? Kimberly Wozencraft takes us for a no-nonsense tour of the "correctional institution" in Kentucky that was her home for more than a year.

5 Narration: *Telling a Story*   95

6 Example: *Illustrating Ideas*   143

7 Process Analysis: *Explaining Step by Step*   187

10 Definition: *Limiting the Frame of Reference*   345

---

13 Writing in Different Genres:
Combining Rhetorical Modes   514

THEMATIC CONTENTS

PREFACE TO THE INSTRUCTOR

The Prose Reader is based on the assumption that lucid writing follows lucid thinking whereas poor written work is almost inevitably the product of foggy, irrational thought processes. As a result, our primary purpose in this book, as in the first ten editions, is to help students *think* more clearly and logically—both in their minds and on paper.

Furthermore, we believe that college students should be able to think, read, and write on three increasingly difficult levels:

1. *Literal*—characterized by a basic understanding of words and their meanings;
2. *Interpretive*—consisting of a knowledge of connections between ideas and an ability to make valid inferences based on those ideas; and
3. *Critical*—the highest level, distinguished by the systematic investigation of complex ideas and by the analysis of their relationship to the world around us.

To demonstrate the vital interrelationship between reader and writer, our text provides students with prose models intended to inspire their own thinking and writing. Rhetorical strategies are introduced as methods of thinking and processing information; they provide a productive means of helping students become better writers. These essays are intended to encourage your students to improve their writing through a partnership with some of the best examples of professional prose available today. Just as musicians and athletes richly benefit from studying the techniques of the foremost people in their fields, your students will grow in spirit and language use from their collaboration with the excellent writers in this collection.

NEW IN THE ELEVENTH EDITION

- Nineteen new selections on such fascinating topics as Mars, the value of college, making friends, business communication, different ways of being smart, music, sports, virtual assault, video games, the Internet, binge drinking, social media, and gender equality are included.
- New graphic flowcharts of the reading and writing processes consisting of questions that guide the reading and writing students do in each chapter have been added for each rhetorical mode; if students actually see how a particular rhetorical mode works as they read, they are more likely to be able to manipulate and use those same features as they write.
- Two professional documented essays show MLA and APA in action (Vozza in Chapter 7 and Hanson in Chapter 10); students can refer to

these samples as they use Part III (Reading and Writing from Sources) to work on their own research papers.

- A new multigenre chapter of readings reflects the primary changes in the Outcomes for First-Year Composition approved by the Council of Writing Program Administrators; it includes one autobiography, one speech, two poems, one piece of fiction, and a creative photograph, and its purpose is to give students practice with genres besides essays as they near the end of your college writing course.

- To supplement the new multigenre additions to this text is a new category of writing assignments at the end of each chapter in Part II entitled Composing in Different Genres; it offers two writing assignments (one multimedia and one multigenre) so students can vary their responses to their readings if such projects align with your course goals.

OUR UNIQUE, DISTINGUISHING FEATURES

Special Checklists of the Reading and Writing Processes

Highlighted pages at the end of chapters 2 and 3 outline the reading and writing processes. They serve as overviews of the material your students will study in this text and are designed to be used for reference throughout the text. Students are referred to these checklists for both their reading and writing assignments in the book.

In-Text Critical Thinking Questions

This edition offers questions throughout each reading selection that will help students interact critically with the material they read as they prepare for the assignments after each essay. These questions appear at the bottom of the pages of the essays and are designed to provide a "bridge" between the personal prereading questions and the more academic questions and assignments that follow each essay. Students will understand their reading on a deeper level by filtering the content of each essay through their own experience, moving progressively toward interpretive and critical understanding. The questions are marked both in the essays and at the bottom of the pages by sequential numbers within diamonds.

Companion Internet Exercises

Two "LEARNING⏾NLINE" exercises frame each essay. The prereading material contains an Internet activity that asks students to explore on the Internet some aspect of the selection's topic. Following each essay is a writing assignment linked to the initial Learning Online exercise.

Visual Rhetoric

This edition offers 19 photographs to access our students' natural interest in visual stimuli. Because most college-age students have grown up accustomed to television, video games, and the Internet, they have the natural ability to "read" visual rhetoric. But they need to learn how to analyze it, just as they analyze words and ideas. Therefore, we include one photograph for each chapter introduction in Part II to teach critical thinking in that mode, one photograph for each set of writing assignments at the end of each chapter, and one photo as a reading selection in Chapter 13.

OUR TRADITIONAL FEATURES

Sequential Organization

The Prose Reader is still organized according to the belief that our mental abilities are logically sequential. In other words, students cannot read or write analytically before they are able to perform well on the literal and interpretive levels. Accordingly, the book progresses from selections that require predominantly literal skills (*Description, Narration,* and *Example*) through readings involving more interpretation (*Process Analysis, Division/Classification, Comparison/Contrast,* and *Definition*) to essays that demand a high degree of analytical thought (*Cause/Effect* and *Argument/Persuasion*). Depending on your curriculum and the experience of your students, these rhetorical modes can, of course, be studied in any order.

Two Tables of Contents

The Prose Reader provides two tables of contents: rhetorical and thematic. First, the book contains a Rhetorical Contents, which includes a one- or two-sentence synopsis of each selection so you can peruse the list quickly and decide which essays to assign. An alternate Thematic Contents lists selections by academic subject for instructors who prefer to teach essays in thematic clusters.

Student Writing Samples in Each Chapter

Two separate student writing samples are featured in each rhetorical introduction. The chapter introductions contain a sample student paragraph and a complete student essay that illustrate each rhetorical pattern, followed by the student writer's analysis of the most enjoyable, exasperating, or noteworthy aspects of writing that particular essay. We have found that this combination of student essays and commentaries makes the professional selections easier for students to read and even more accessible as models of thinking and writing.

Prereading Material

Each reading selection is preceded by thorough biographical information on the author and provocative prereading questions on the subject of the essay. Because students comprehend what they read most thoroughly when they understand its context, the biographies explain the real experiences from which each essay emerged, and the prereading questions ("Preparing to Read") help students focus on the purpose, audience, and subject of the essay. The prereading material also foreshadows the questions and writing assignments that follow each selection. This introductory material invites students to identify with both the author of an essay and its subject matter, thereby energizing their responses to the selections they read.

Wide Range of Essay Topics

The essays in *The Prose Reader* continue to represent a wide range of topics. As in the past, the essays in this edition were selected on the basis of five important criteria: (1) high interest level, (2) currency in the field, (3) moderate length, (4) readability, and (5) broad subject variety. Together, they portray the universality of human experience as expressed through the viewpoints of men and women, many different ethnic and racial groups, and a variety of ages and social classes.

Strong Commitment to Cultural and Gender Diversity

This edition continues its strong commitment to cultural and gender diversity. Although multicultural and gender issues have always been well represented in *The Prose Reader,* this edition includes even more essays by women and ethnic minority authors to offer a wide range of perspectives by such writers as Lewis Sawaquat, Maya Angelou, Sandra Cisneros, Richard Rodriguez, Amy Tan, Stephanie Ericsson, Amy Chua, Motoko Rich, Gloria Steinem, Robert Ramirez, Dana Gioia, Richard Wright, Emma Watson, and Jessica Anya Blau.

Expanded Chapter on Argument/Persuasion

The Argument/Persuasion chapter (Chapter 12) now includes four essays on an interesting variety of topics and two sets of opposing viewpoint essays. These essays are particularly useful for helping students refine their critical thinking skills in preparation for longer, more sustained papers on a single topic. The first four essays in Chapter 12 encourage students to grapple with provocative issues that make a crucial difference in how we all live, such as our obsession with illness, thinking and the Internet, violence and TV, and mental health. The two sets of opposing-viewpoint essays on social media and DNA testing will help your students see coherent arguments at work from several different perspectives on a single issue.

Four Types of Questions

This edition offers four progressively more sophisticated types of questions at the end of each selection. These questions are designed to help students move sequentially from various literal-level responses to interpretation and analysis; they also help reveal both the form and content of the essays so your students can cultivate a similar balance in their own writing.

1. *Understanding Details*—questions that test students' literal and interpretive understanding of what they have read;
2. *Thinking Critically*—questions that require students to analyze various aspects of the essay;
3. *Discovering Rhetorical Strategies*—questions that investigate the author's rhetorical strategies in constructing the essay;
4. *Making Connections*—questions that ask students to find thematic and rhetorical connections among essays they have read.

Prewriting Prompts

The writing assignments ("Ideas for Discussion/Writing") are preceded by "Preparing to Write" questions. These questions are designed to encourage students to express their feelings, thoughts, observations, and opinions on various topics related to their reading. Questions about their own ideas and experiences help students develop strong convictions that they can then mold into compelling essays.

Engaging Writing Assignments

The writing assignments after each essay seek to involve students in realistic situations. For instructors who like to use role-playing in their teaching, many writing assignments provide a specific purpose and audience in the essay topics. In this manner, student writers are drawn into rhetorical scenarios that carefully focus their responses to a variety of interrelated questions or problems. These assignments are designed for use inside or outside the classroom.

This edition also offers five sets of writing assignments at the end of each chapter. They provide practice in the following categories: (1) more practice in a specific rhetorical mode, (2) a focus on interesting, contemporary themes regardless of rhetorical mode, (3) an opportunity to analyze and respond to a provocative photograph, (4) a new set of assignments offering options for multimedia projects, and (5) related research assignments. These prompts give students even more opportunities to practice their writing—now in a variety of genres.

Glossary of Composition Terms

The book concludes with a glossary of composition terms. The glossary provides not only definitions of composition terms, but also examples of these terms from essays in this book, including specific page numbers. This serves as an excellent reference tool for students as they progress through the material in the text.

HOW THE TEXT WORKS

This text is divided into three sections:

Part I: Thinking, Reading, and Writing Critically
Part II: Reading and Writing Rhetorically
Part III: Reference: Reading and Writing from Sources

Part I consists of three chapters dedicated to the interaction of critical thinking, reading, and writing. It furnishes students with ideas and facts to help them discover for themselves how these skills are related.

Each chapter of **Part II** of *The Prose Reader* begins with an explanation of a single rhetorical technique as a means of processing information. These explanations are divided into six sections that progress from the effect of this technique on our daily lives to its integral role in the writing process. Featured in each introduction is a new flowchart of the reading and writing processes in that particular mode. We also include in each introduction a student paragraph and a student essay featuring each rhetorical strategy under discussion. The student essay is annotated to illustrate how a particular rhetorical mode operates and to help bridge the gap between student writing and the professional selections that follow. After each student essay, the writer has drafted a personal note with some useful advice for other student writers.

The essays that follow each chapter introduction are selected from a wide variety of well-known contemporary authors. Although each essay in this collection features a single rhetorical mode, other modes are always simultaneously at work. These selections concentrate on one primary technique at a time in much the same way a well-arranged photograph highlights a certain visual detail, though many other elements function in the background to make the picture an organic and effective whole.

Before each reading selection, we offer students a context for their reading including biographical information about the author and some prereading questions to whet the reader's appetite for the essay that follows. The prereading questions forecast not only the content of the essay but also the questions and writing assignments that follow.

The questions after each reading selection are designed as guides for thinking about the essay. These questions are at the heart of the relationship represented in this book among thinking, reading, and writing. They are divided into four interrelated sections that shepherd your students smoothly from a literal understanding of what they have just read to interpretation and finally to analysis and critical thinking.

After your students have studied the different techniques at work in a reading selection, specific essay assignments let them practice these skills in unison and discover even more details about effective communication. Four "Ideas for Discussion/Writing" topics (one of which is based on the prereading Internet exercise) are preceded by "prewriting" questions to help students focus their writing as precisely as possible.

The word *essay* (which comes from the Old French *essai,* meaning a "try" or an "attempt") is an appropriate label for these writing assignments because they all ask your students to wrestle with an idea or problem and then *attempt* to give shape to their thoughts in some effective manner. The essay lets your students demonstrates that they can assemble all the skills they have learned into a coherent piece of writing.

At the end of every chapter is a collection of essay assignments that ask your students to choose a topic in one of five categories: Practicing [a particular rhetorical mode], Exploring Ideas, Analyzing Visual Images, Composing in Different Genres (a new category of prompts in this edition), and Writing from Sources. Each of these groups of assignments lets your students demonstrate what they have learned in a slightly different way.

The final chapter in Part II (Writing in Different Genres: Combining Rhetorical Modes) aligns with the latest version of the Writing Program Administrators' outcomes for first-year composition by including selections in multiple genres. It provides selections in five different genres; one autobiography, one speech, two poems, one piece of fiction, and one photograph.

Part III of this edition provides a tabbed reference guide for writing a documented essay. It demonstrates how to approach a writing assignment based on sources by following a student through the entire process from reading a documented essay to responding to that reading by writing on a related topic. It covers finding sources, avoiding plagiarism, staying organized, documenting sources, and writing the paper itself—all from the perspective of our model student.

RESOURCES FOR TEACHERS AND STUDENTS

Available with *The Prose Reader* are three resources intended to help your students discover how to read and write analytically and respond to the world around them coherently.

Instructor's Resource Manual

First is an extensive *Instructor's Resource Manual* designed to help make your life in the classroom a little easier. It offers innovative options for organizing your course, creative teaching ideas, instructor comments on teaching the different rhetorical modes, background information on each essay, and several successful techniques for responding to student writing. In addition, it provides specific suggestions for the first day of class, a series of student essays (one for each rhetorical strategy featured in the text) followed by the student writer's comments, provocative quotations, definitions of terms that may be unfamiliar to your students, detailed answers to the questions that follow each selection, additional essay topics, and various strategies for revision. This supplement ends with an annotated bibliography of books and articles about thinking, reading, and writing. To learn more, visit www.pearsonhighered.com or ask your Pearson representative.

The Prose Reader Quiz Book

Available on the Pearson website (www.pearsonhighered.com) under "Instructional Resources" is *The Prose Reader Quiz Book*, which includes two objective quizzes on the vocabulary and content of each selection to help you monitor your students' understanding of the selections in this book. These quizzes are posted for you in Word so you can edit and print them.

MyWritingLab™ *and The Prose Reader eText*

MyWritingLab is an online practice, tutorial, and assessment program that provides engaging experiences for teaching and learning. It includes *The Prose Reader* eText, which lets students access their textbook whenever and wherever they can access the Internet.

In addition to the eText, students may use MyWritingLab to respond to the four detailed writing project prompts found at the end of each reading in *The Prose Reader*, plus the ten end-of-chapter writing assignments. Instructors can then track and respond to submissions easily—right in MyWritingLab—making the response process easy for the instructor and engaging for the student.

In the Writing Space Assignments, students will have direct access to *The Prose Reader's* checklists and flowcharts, and there they can use instructor-created peer review rubrics to evaluate and comment on other students' writing. When giving feedback on student writing, instructors can add links to activities that address issues and strategies needed for review. Instructors may link to multimedia resources in Pearson Writer, which include curated content from Purdue OWL. Paper review by specialized tutors through Smarthinking is available, as is plagiarism detection through TurnItIn.

Adaptive learning. My WritingLab offers preassessments and personalized instruction so students see improved results and instructors spend less time in class reviewing the basics.

Learning Catalytics. MyLab and Mastering with eText now provides Learning Catalytics—an interactive student response tool that uses students' smartphones, tablets, or laptops to engage them in sophisticated tasks and thinking.

MediaShare. MediaShare allows students to post multimodal assignments easily—whether they are audio, video, or visual compositions—for peer review and instructor feedback. In both face-to-face and online course settings, MediaShare saves instructors valuable time and enriches the student learning experience by enabling contextual feedback to be provided quickly and easily. Visit www.mywritinglab.com for more information.

ACKNOWLEDGMENTS

We are pleased to acknowledge the kind assistance and support of a number of people who have helped us put together this eleventh edition of *The Prose Reader*. For creative encouragement and editorial guidance at Pearson, we thank Brad Potthoff, senior acquisitions editor; Anne Shure, program manager; Amanda Norelli, editorial assistant; Ali Arnold, product marketing manager; Donna Campion, project manager; Joseph Croscup, permissions project manager; and Eric Stano, editorial director of English. We'd also like to thank Michelle Gardner, project manager at SPi-Global.

For insightful reviews leading to this eleventh edition, we are grateful to Joann F. Allen, Oral Roberts University; Martha Dawson, Florida Memorial University; Jacqueline Goffe-McNish, Dutchess Community College; Leslie Jane Harrelson, Dalton State College; Jan Alexia Holston, Bethune-Cookman University; Vickie Hunt, Northwest Florida State College; Robert Kroll, Luzerne County Community College; Guy Shebat, Youngstown State University; Marc Willis, Carl Albert State College; and Kristy Wooten, Catawba Valley Community College.

For the many reviews of previous editions whose valuable contributions have guided *The Prose Reader* through ten successful editions, we wish to thank Brenda Abbott, Bay Path College; Maureen Aitkn, University of Michigan; Martha R. Bachman, Camden County College; Christopher Belcher,

Community College of Allegheny County; Martha Bergeron, Vance-Granville Community College; Vermell Blanding, Hostos Community College; Arnold Bradford, Northern Virginia Community College, Loudoun Campus; Mickie R. Braswell, Lenoir Community College; James Brumbaugh, Lord Fairfax Community College; Melissa A. Bruner, Southwestern Oklahoma State University; Terrence Burke, Cuyahoga Community College; Judith Burnham, Tulsa Community College; Mechel Camp, Jackson State Community College; Gena E. Christopher, Jacksonville State University; Bill Clemente, Peru State College; Charles H. Cole, Carl Albert State College; Carolyn D. Coward, Shelby State Community College; Marie T. Cox, Stark State College; Hal Crimmel, Weber State University; Judith Dan, Boston University; Bill Day, Carl Albert State College; Merry Dennehy, Monterey Peninsula College; Michel L. Dodds, Calvary Bible College; Michael W. Donaghe, Eastern New Mexico University; Ellen Dugan-Barrette, Brescia College; Lewis Emond, Dean Junior College; Mary M. Ertel, Erie Community College; John Esperian, College of Southern Nevada; June Farmer, Southern Union State Community College; Marla Fowler, Albany Technical College; Geoffrey C. Goodale, University of Massachusetts at Boston; Nate Gordeon, Kiswaukee College; Lorena Horton, San Jacinto College North; Craig Howard White, University of Houston; Jay Jernigan, Eastern Michigan University; Janice Jones, Kent State University; Steve Katz, State Technical Institute; O. Brian Kaufman, Quinebaug Valley Community College; Wade King, North Dakota State College of Science; Paul Kistel, Pierce College; Jan LaFever, Friends University; Shanie Latham, Jefferson College; Amy Lawlor, Pasadena City College; Virginia Leonard, West Liberty State College; Todd Lieber, Simpson College; Pam Lieske, Kent State University; Bill Marsh, National University; Marlene Martin, Monterey Peninsula College; Beth Maxfield, Blinn College; Helen F. Maxon, Southwestern Oklahoma State University; Nellie McCrory, Gaston College; Paula Miller, Azusa Pacific University; Lyle W. Morgan II, Pittsburgh State University; Robin Morris Hardin, Cape Fear Community College; Donna Mungen, Pasadena City College; Kevin Nebergall, Kirkwood Community College; Barbra Nightingale, Broward College; Diana Nystedt, Palo Alto College; Ollie Oviedo, Eastern New Mexico University; Felicia S. Pattison, Sterling College; Arlie R. Peck, University of Rio Grande; Dianne Peich, Delaware County Community College; Teresa Purvis, Lansing Community College; Melissa Richardson, Central Texas College; Diana Roberts Gruendler, Penn State University Angela Saragusa, Brookdale Community College; M. Susan Schmidt, Carteret Community College; Nelda Sellers, Jackson State Community College; Marcia Shams, Gwinnett Technical College; Stella Shepard, Henderson State University; Leslie Shipp, Clark County Community College; Peter L. Shoughrue, Alfred State College; Alice Sink, High Point University; Barbara Smith, Iona College; Donna Smith, Odessa College; Rosie Soy, Hudson County

Community College; Matthew Stiffler, Utah State University; William F. Sutlife, Community College of Allegheny County; Brenda Tuberville, Rogers State University; Coreen Wees, Iowa Western Community College; Melanie Whitebread, Luzerne County Community College; K. Siobhan Wright, Carroll Community College; Nancy G. Wright, Austin Peay State University; Donnie Yeilding, Central Texas College; James Zarzana, Southwest State University; John Ziebell, Community College of Southern Nevada; and Melody Ziff, Northern Virginia Community College–Annandale.

Several writing instructors across the United States have been kind enough to help shape *The Prose Reader* over the course of its development by responding to specific questions about their teaching experiences with the book: Charles Bordogna, Bergen Community College; Mary G. Marshall and Eileen M. Ward, College of DuPage; Michael J. Huntington and Judith C. Kohl, Dutchess Community College; Ted Johnston, El Paso County Community College; Koala C. Hartnett, Rick James Mazza, and William H. Sherman, Fairmont State College; Miriam Dick and Betty Krasne, Mercy College; Elvis Clark, Mineral Area College; Dayna Spencer, Pittsburg State University; James A. Zarzana, Southwest State University; Susan Reinhart Schneling and Trudy Vanderback, Vincennes University; Carmen Wong, Virginia Commonwealth University; John W. Hattman and Virginia E. Leonard, West Liberty State College; Jonathan Alexander, Widener University; Jo Ann Pevoto, College of the Mainland; Anita Pandey, University of Illinois at Urbana–Champaign; Leaf Seligman, University of New Hampshire; Arminta Baldwin, West Virginia Wesleyan College; Joaquim Mendes, New York Institute of Technology; and Sandra R. Woods, Fairmont State College.

In preparing the text and the *IRM*, we owe special gratitude to the following writing instructors, who have contributed their favorite techniques for teaching various rhetorical strategies: Mary P. Boyles, Pembroke State University; Terrence W. Burke, Cuyahoga Community College; Mary Lou Conlin, Cuyahoga Community College; Ellen Dugan-Barrette, Brescia College; Janet Eber, County College of Morris; Louis Emond, Dean Junior College; Peter Harris, West Virginia Institute of Technology, Montgomery; Jay Jernigan, Eastern Michigan University; Judith C. Kohl, Dutchess Community College; Joanne H. McCarthy, Tacoma Community College; Anthony McCrann, Peru State College; Nellie McCrory, Gaston College; Alan Price, Pennsylvania State University–Hazelton; Patricia A. Ross, Moorpark College; Leslie Shipp, Clark County Community College; Rodney Simard (deceased), California State University, San Bernardino; Elizabeth Wahlquist, Brigham Young University; John White, California State University, Fullerton; and Ted Wise, Porterville College.

For student essays and writing samples, we thank Rosa Marie Augustine, Donel Crow, Dawn Dobie, Gloria Dumler, Jeff Hicks, Julie Anne Judd, Judi Koch, Dawn McKee, Paul Newberry, Joanne Silva-Newberry, JoAnn Slate, Peggy Stuckey, and Jan Titus.

For their work on this edition, we also want to thank Jessica Wojtysiak, our coauthor on the *Instructor's Resource Manual,* as well as Cody Ganger, Keith Keikiro, Tracie Grimes, Sabrina Buie, Tiffany Wong, Laura Harris, Veronica Wilson, Julie Paulsen, Robyn Thompson, Kevin Goodwin, Kristen Mercer, Carlos Tkacz, and Laraine Rosema for their dedicated efforts on many different tasks on this edition.

This book also benefits from the outstanding insights and consummate teaching of Kathryn Benander (Porterville College, Porterville, CA), Cheryl Smith (Kingsborough Community College, New York City), and Lauren Martinez, who have served as editorial consultants for multiple editions of the book. Their work, opinions, and friendship have been tremendously helpful to us over the years.

Our most important debt is to our children, Christopher and Laura, who have motivated us to be good teachers since the day they were born.

Part I

Thinking, Reading, and Writing Critically

Chapter 1

THINKING CRITICALLY

LEARNING OBJECTIVES

After completing this chapter, you will be able to do the following:
- Understand the three levels of thinking
- Use the in-text critical thinking questions successfully
- Understand the reading-writing connection

Have you ever had trouble expressing your thoughts? If so, you're not alone. Many people have this difficulty—especially when they are asked to write down their ideas. The good news is that this "ailment" can be cured. We've learned over the years that the more clearly students think about the world around them, the more easily they can express their thoughts through written and spoken language. So thinking more clearly, logically, and critically about important ideas and issues that exist in our world today will actually help your writing. In fact, to succeed in college you need to reason, read, and write about the world in increasingly complex ways, moving steadily from a simple, literal understanding of topics to interpretation and analysis.

LEVELS OF THINKING

The foundation of all successful reading and writing on the college level is critical thinking. You need to know as much as you can about this skill in order to do your best in all your classes. Inspired by the well-crafted prose models in this text and guided by carefully worded questions, you can actually raise the level of your thinking skills while improving your reading and writing abilities on three progressively more difficult levels:

1. **The literal level** is the foundation of all human understanding; it entails knowing the meanings of words, both as individual terms and in relation to one another. For someone to comprehend the sentence "You must exercise your brain to reach your full mental potential" on the literal level, for example, that person would have to know the definitions of all the words in the sentence and understand the way those words work together to make meaning.

2. **Interpretation** requires the ability to make associations between details, draw inferences from pieces of information, and reach conclusions about the material you have read. An interpretive understanding of the sample sentence in level 1 might be translated into the following thoughts: "Exercising the brain sounds a bit like exercising the body. I wonder if there's any correlation between the two. If the brain must be exercised, it is probably made up of muscles, much like the body is." None of these particular thoughts is made explicit in the sentence, but each is suggested in one way or another.

3. **Thinking critically**, the most sophisticated reasoning ability, involves a type of mental activity that is crucial for successful academic and professional work. A critical analysis of our sample sentence might proceed in the following way: "This sentence is talking to me. It actually addresses me with the word *you*. I wonder what *my* mental potential is. Will I be able to reach it? Will I know when I attain it? Will I be comfortable with it? I certainly want to reach this potential, whatever it is. Reaching it will undoubtedly help me succeed scholastically and professionally. The brain is obviously an important tool for helping me achieve my goals in life, so I want to take every opportunity I have to develop and maintain this part of my body." Students who can disassemble an issue or idea in this fashion and understand its various components more thoroughly after reassembling them are rewarded intrinsically with a clearer knowledge of life's complexities and the ability to generate creative, useful ideas. They are also rewarded extrinsically with good grades and are more likely to earn responsible jobs with higher pay because they are able to apply this understanding effectively to their professional and personal lives.

Psychological studies have shown that thinking and feeling are complementary operations. All of us have feelings that are automatic and instinctive. To feel pride after winning first place at a track meet, for example, or to feel anger at a spiteful friend is not behavior we have to study and master; such emotions come naturally to all of us. Thinking, however, is much less spontaneous than feeling; research suggests that study and practice are required for sustained mental development.

Thinking critically involves grappling with ideas, issues, and problems that surround you in your immediate environment and in the world at large. It does not necessarily entail finding fault, which you might naturally associate with the word *critical*, but rather suggests continually questioning and analyzing the world around you. Thinking critically is the highest form of mental activity that human beings engage in; it is the source of much success in college and in our professional and personal lives. Fortunately, all of us can learn how to think more critically.

Critical thinking means taking apart an issue, examining its various parts, and reassembling the topic with a more complete understanding of its details. Implied in this explanation is the ability to see the topic from several new perspectives. Using your mind in this way will help you find solutions to difficult problems, design creative plans of action, and ultimately live a life consistent with your opinions on important issues we all confront daily.

Because critical or analytical thinking is one of the highest forms of mental activity, it requires a great deal of concentration and practice. Once you have actually felt how your mind processes information at this level, however, re-creating the experience is somewhat like riding a bicycle: You will be able to do it naturally, easily, and skillfully whenever you choose.

Our initial goal, then, is to help you think critically when you are required to do so in school, on the job, or in any other area of your life. If this form of thinking becomes part of your daily routine, you will quite naturally be able to call on it whenever necessary. Because rhetorical strategies are presented in this text as ways of thinking and processing information that you can use in all your academic tasks, working with these traditional modes is an effective way to achieve this goal. With some guidance, each rhetorical pattern can give you a mental workout that prepares you for writing and critical or analytical thinking in the same way that physical exercises warm you up for various sports. Just as in the rest of the body, the more exercise the brain gets, the more flexible it becomes and the higher levels of thought it can attain. Through these various guided thinking exercises, you can systematically strengthen your ability to think analytically. We feature one strategy in each chapter so you can understand how it works before you combine it with other strategies, thus providing you with a systematic means of improving your ability to think critically about the complex world around you.

As you move through the following chapters, we will ask you to isolate each rhetorical mode—much like isolating your abs, thighs, and biceps in a weight-lifting workout—so you can concentrate on these thinking patterns one at a time. Each rhetorical pattern you study will suggest slightly different ways of seeing the world, processing information, and solving problems. Looking closely at rhetorical modes or specific patterns of thought will also allow you to discover how your mind works in that particular mode. In the same fashion, becoming more intricately aware of your thought patterns will help you improve your thinking skills as well as your reading and writing abilities. Thinking critically enables you to identify fresh insights within old ideas, generate new thoughts, and see connections between related issues. It is an energizing mental activity that puts you in control of your life and your environment rather than leaving you at the mercy of your surroundings.

Each chapter introduction provides three exercises—one of which is based on a photograph—specifically designed to help you focus on a particular pattern of thought in isolation. While you are attempting to learn what each pattern feels like in your mind, use your imagination to play with these exercises on as many different levels as possible.

IN-TEXT CRITICAL THINKING QUESTIONS

Critical thinking does not automatically occur after you complete these exercises, but rather is the result of sustained practice. With this in mind, we "coach" you through the entire reading process as you move from a literal understanding of the author's ideas to a critical approach to your reading. If this partnership is successful, you will be able to apply this level of performance to all your academic tasks in this class and throughout the curriculum.

Your approach to critical thinking in any subject must be built on a solid foundation, which is the reason that each essay in this collection is preceded by a number of questions that introduce you to the author's main ideas before you start reading. Forming some initial opinions and relating some of the ideas to your own experiences is the starting point of all good thinking.

Next, this initial engagement with the essay must be woven into and out of the reading process—without abandoning your original thoughts. To this end, critical thinking questions are furnished at the bottom of the pages you are read-ing to help you make both personal and intellectual connections with the text. These questions (marked in the text by numbers in diamonds) always start by encouraging you to interact personally with each reading selection before you analyze it. You are asked to filter the reading through your own life experiences, which will help you discover meaning by associating the reading with your own worldview. Once you begin to interact personally with the text, the questions will then take you deeper and deeper into the content of the reading. These critical thinking questions will engage you on many different levels, so the act of reading each selection will ultimately become an act of total immersion in the subject matter. These questions essentially serve as a guide through your reading, or a teacher in your head, when you use this feature productively.

To achieve these goals, the "in-text" critical thinking questions progress very consciously from personal to more academic concerns. In other words, they teach you, through carefully scaffolded prompts, how to ascend to understanding at the critical or analytical level. The questions fall quite naturally into the following progressively more difficult levels of interaction:

Making personal associations: These questions ask you to make connections with your own experiences.

Understanding definitions: These questions check your literal understanding.

Engaging curiosity: These questions stimulate your curiosity and require you to look outside yourself to generate some of your own questions.

Drawing conclusions: These questions prompt you to make some deductions from the material you have read so far.

Making connections: These questions ask you to connect ideas in your reading.

Finding evidence: These questions encourage you to find examples, statistics, data, and reasons that support your conclusions.

Analyzing your discoveries: These questions require you to step away from the reading selection and study the ideas and connections that have resulted from your reading.

Through this entire process, as we guide you to more advanced levels of reasoning, you must be willing to tolerate ambiguity at every stage of the process. This uncertainty allows you ultimately to bring together exciting ideas and make creative discoveries. This approach to your reading will also keep your mind open to new ideas and unique interpretations as you read.

Finally, these in-text questions will lead you smoothly and seamlessly to the questions following each essay. In essence, the in-text questions build a bridge to the postreading questions. So if you have reflected and taken notes on the critical thinking questions at the bottom of the pages as you were reading, you will be fully prepared for the postreading questions to take you to even higher levels of thought after reading the essay. In each case, these questions move from literal understanding of details, definitions, and concepts through interpretation to analysis of this same information. Working systematically with the in-text questions will stimulate your own opinions and thoughts, which will help support your final discoveries and analyses.

The in-text critical thinking questions prepare you for what follows so you will be ready to read, write, and discuss the topic at hand from a number of different perspectives and with various audiences and purposes in mind. These final questions, then, will spark your creativity and enable you to think more deeply about the topic. At the end of this process, your head will be filled with ideas that you will want to use in class discussions, papers, oral reports, or any other assignments you might encounter.

As you practice each of the rhetorical patterns of thought in isolation, you should be aware of building on your previous thinking skills. As the book progresses, the rhetorical modes become more complex and require a higher degree of concentration and effort. You should, therefore, keep in mind that you ultimately want to let these skills develop into a high-powered, well-developed ability to process the world around you—including reading, writing, seeing, and feeling—on the most advanced analytical level you can master.

THE READING-WRITING CONNECTION

Your approach to critical thinking will determine your potential as a reader and a writer. Continuing to refine your definition of critical thinking and your own ability to think critically is important to your progress and success as a student. With a good, clear understanding of critical thinking, you are now ready to move on to the relationship of critical thinking to reading and writing.

Part of becoming a better writer involves understanding that reading and writing are companion activities that engage people in the creation of thought and meaning—either as readers interpreting a text or as writers constructing one. Clear thinking is the pivotal point that connects these two efforts. If you learn to apply your critical thinking skills to your reading, you will naturally be able to write critically. You must process thoughts on this higher level as you read in order to produce essays of your own on this level. In other words, you must "import" your reading critically to "export" critical writing. These next two chapters explain the relationship of reading and writing and give annotated examples of these processes at work. Part I ends with Reading and Writing Inventories that will serve as a summary of these processes and a reference for your reading and writing throughout this textbook.

MyWritingLab™ Visit Ch. 1 Thinking Critically in *MyWritingLab* to test your understanding of the chapter learning objectives.

Chapter 2

READING CRITICALLY

After completing this chapter, you will be able to do the following:
- Understand the reading process
- Use the reading process to read critically

Reading critically begins with developing a natural curiosity about an essay's subject and then nurturing that curiosity throughout the reading process. It involves many different activities that work together to keep your mind active and engaged, all of which revolve around approaching your reading with an inquiring mind. To learn as much as you can from an essay, you need to read closely and deeply. That means you work in partnership with your reading material to make meaning literally interpretively, and analytically.

THE READING PROCESS

The reading process begins as soon as you get a reading assignment. It involves many different activities from getting ready to read to thinking critically about your reading. First, you should study any preliminary material you can find, then read the essay to get a general overview of its main ideas, and finally read the selection again to achieve a deeper understanding of its content. These three phases of the reading process—preparing to read, reading, and rereading—will help you develop the natural curiosity you need to be a good reader. What is especially important is establishing your own routine for reading that is comfortable for you. Once you establish your reading ritual, make sure you go through the entire process for each of your assignments. The Reading Inventory at the end of this chapter will guide you through this discovery process.

Preparing to Read

Focusing your attention is an important first stage in the reading processes. In fact, learning as much as you can about an essay and its context (the circumstances surrounding its development) before you begin reading can help you move through the essay with an energetic, active mind and then reach some degree of analysis before writing on the assigned topics. In particular, knowing where an essay was first published, studying the writer's background, and doing some preliminary thinking about the subject of a reading selection will help you establish a rhetorical context for the writer's ideas and encourage you to form some valid opinions of your own on the topic.

As you approach any essay, you should concentrate on four specific areas that will begin to give you an overview of the material you are about to read. We will use an essay by Lewis Thomas to demonstrate these techniques.

Title.   A close look at the title will usually provide important clues about the author's attitude toward the topic, his or her stand on an issue, or the mood of the essay. It can also furnish you with a sense of audience and purpose.

To Err Is Human

From this title, for example, we might infer that the author will discuss errors, human nature, and the extent to which mistakes influence human behavior. The title is half of a well-known proverb written by Alexander Pope ("To err is human, to forgive, divine"), so we might speculate further that the author has written an essay intended for a well-read audience interested in the relationship between errors and humanity. After reading only four words of the essay—its title—you already have a good deal of information about the subject, its audience, and the author's attitude toward both.

Synopsis.   The Rhetorical Table of Contents in this text contains a synopsis of each essay, very much like the following, so you can discover more specific details about its contents before you begin reading.

Physician Lewis Thomas explains how we can profit from our mistakes—especially if we trust human nature. Perhaps someday, he says, we can apply this same principle to the computer and magnify the advantages of these errors.

From this synopsis, we learn that Thomas's essay will be an analysis of human errors and of the ways in which we can benefit from those errors. The synopsis also tells us that the computer has the potential to magnify the value of our own innate errors.

Biography.   Learning as much as you can about the author of an essay will generally stimulate your interest in the material and help you achieve a deeper understanding of the issues to be discussed. It also provides a context for your reading. From the biographies in this book, you can learn, for example, whether a writer is young or old, conservative or liberal, open- or close-minded. You might also discover if the essay was written at the beginning, middle, or end of the author's career or how well versed the writer is on the topic. Such information will invariably help you reach a more thorough understanding of a selection's ideas, audience, and logical structure. If such information is not provided for other reading tasks, you might go to the Internet to learn about the author.

LEWIS THOMAS   (1913–1993)

Lewis Thomas was a physician who, until his death in 1993, was president emeritus of the Sloan-Kettering Cancer Center and scholar-in-residence at the Cornell University Medical Center in New York City. A graduate of Princeton University and Harvard Medical School, he was previously head of Pathology and dean of the New York University–Bellevue Medical Center and dean of the Yale Medical School. In addition to having written over two hundred scientific papers on virology and immunology, he authored many popular scientific essays, some of which have been collected in *Lives of a Cell* (1974), *The Medusa and the Snail* (1979), *Late Night Thoughts on Listening to Mahler's Ninth Symphony* (1983), *Etcetera, Etcetera* (1990), and *The Fragile Species* (1992). The memoirs of his distinguished career have been published in *The Youngest Science: Notes of a Medicine Watcher* (1983). Thomas liked to refer to his essays as "experiments in thought": "Although I usually think I know what I'm going to be writing about, what I'm going to say, most of the time it doesn't happen that way at all. At some point, I get misled down a garden path. I get surprised by an idea that I hadn't anticipated getting, which is a little bit like being in a laboratory."

As this information indicates, Thomas was a prominent physician who published widely on scientific topics. We know that he considered his essays "experiments in thought," which makes us expect a relaxed, spontaneous treatment of his subjects. From this biography, we can also infer that he was a leader in the medical world and that, because of the positions he has had held, he was well respected in his professional life. Last, we can speculate that he had a clear sense of his audience because he was able to present difficult concepts in clear, everyday language.

Prereading Background and Questions.   One other type of preliminary material in this text will broaden your overview of the topic and enable you to approach the essay with an active, inquiring mind. The "Preparing to Read" background information and questions following the biographies are intended to focus your attention and stimulate your curiosity before you begin the essay. They will also prepare you to form your own opinions on the essay and make predictions as you read.

Learning where, why, and how an essay was first written will provide you with a context for the material you are about to read: Why did the author write this selection? Where was it first published? Who was the author's original audience? This type of information enables you to understand the circumstances surrounding the development of the selection and to identify any topical or historical references the author makes. All the selections in this textbook were published elsewhere first—in another book, a journal, or a magazine. The author's original audience, therefore, consisted of the readers of that particular publication.

In addition, two types of questions will serve to focus your attention. The first type (Exploring Experience) asks you to begin drawing on your prior knowledge in reference to this particular topic; they ask pointed questions about your previous life experiences in preparation for this reading assignment. The second set (Learning Online) guides you to an Internet activity that will prepare you for your reading; this activity is then linked to the first writing assignment at the end of the essay.

Preparing to Read

The following essay, which originally appeared in the *New England Journal of Medicine* (January 1976), illustrates the clarity and ease with which Thomas explains complex scientific topics.

Exploring Experience: As you prepare to read this essay, take a few moments to think about the role mistakes play in our lives: What are some memorable mistakes you have made? Did you learn anything important from these errors? Do you make more or fewer mistakes than other people you know? Do you see any advantages to making mistakes? Any disadvantages?

LEARNING ⏻NLINE Most computers have games included in their operating systems. Find a game on your computer, and play it for a while. Who won? What types of mistakes did the computer make? What types of mistakes did you make? Consider your experience while reading Thomas's essay.

From the sample "Preparing to Read" material, we learn that Thomas's essay "To Err Is Human" was originally published in the *New England Journal of Medicine,* a prestigious periodical read principally by members of the scientific community. Written in 1976, the article plays on its audience's growing fascination with computers and with the limits of artificial intelligence—subjects just as timely today as they were in the mid-1970s.

The Exploring Experience questions here prompt you to consider your own ideas, opinions, or actions as a way to help you generate thoughts on the topic of errors in our lives. The Internet exercise is designed to stimulate your thinking and expand your knowledge on this and related subjects. These queries are, ideally, the last step in preparing yourself for the active role you should play as a reader.

If questions are not provided for your reading in other courses, you might generate some for yourself so you can look for the answers to them as you read. Keeping a journal to respond to these questions is an excellent idea because you will then have a record of your thoughts on various subjects related to your reading assignments.

Reading

People read essays in books, newspapers, magazines, and journals for a great variety of reasons. One reader may want to be stimulated intellectually, whereas another seeks relaxation; one person reads to keep up with the latest developments in his or her profession, whereas the next wants to learn why a certain event happened or how something can be done; finally, some people read to be challenged by new ideas, whereas others find comfort principally in printed material that supports their own moral, social, or political opinions. The essays in this textbook fulfill all these expectations in different ways. They have been chosen, however, not only for these reasons but for an additional, broader purpose: Reading them can help make you a better writer.

Every time you read an essay in this book, you will also be preparing to write your own essay based on the same rhetorical pattern. For this reason, as you read, you should pay careful attention to both the content (subject matter) and the form (language, sentence structure, organization, and development of ideas) of each essay. In this way, you will see how experienced writers use particular rhetorical modes or patterns of thought to organize and communicate their ideas. Each essay in this collection features one dominant pattern that is supported by several others. The more aware you are of each author's writing techniques, the more skillfully you will be able to apply these strategies to your own writing.

The questions before and after each essay teach you a way of reading that can help you discover the relationships of a writer's ideas to one another as well as to your own thoughts. These questions can also help clarify for you the connections among the writer's topic, his or her style or manner of expression, and your own composing process. Such an approach to the process of reading takes some of the mystery out of reading and writing and makes them manageable tasks at which anyone can become proficient.

Within each essay, at the bottom of the pages, are questions designed specifically to raise your level of thinking as you read. They provide a "bridge" between the personal prereading questions before each essay and the more broad-based academic questions and assignments that follow each essay. In other words, the questions within the essays prepare you for the thinking and processing you will be asked to do at the end of a reading assignment. These "bridge" questions actually teach you how to interact critically with your reading material, guiding you through the text as you become partners with the essay in the creation of meaning. They invite you to engage fully with your reading and bring it into your life so you will understand it both instinctively and intellectually. If you take the time to produce written responses to these questions, you will quite naturally form your own opinions and arguments in preparation for the assignments that follow each essay.

To understand your reading material on the critical level, you should be prepared to read each essay at least three times. The first reading is an overview, during which you want to get a general sense of the essay in relation to its title, purpose, audience, and publication information. You should annotate the essay with your personal reactions and make sure you understand all the author's vocabulary. You should also read the questions at the bottom of the pages, but don't answer them until your second reading.

To illustrate this process, on the following pages Lewis Thomas's essay is printed with a student's comments in the margins, showing how she interacted with the essay while reading it for the first time. The student also circled words she didn't know and put their definitions in the margins.

LEWIS THOMAS   (1913–1993)

To Err Is Human

Boy is this true

Everyone must have had at least one personal experience with a computer error by this time. Bank balances are suddenly reported to have jumped from $379 into the millions, appeals for charitable contributions are mailed over and over to people with crazy sounding names at your address, department stores send the wrong bills, utility companies write that they're turning everything off, that sort of thing. If you manage to get in touch with someone and complain, you then get instantaneously typed, guilty letters from the same computer, saying, "Our computer was in error, and an adjustment is being made in your account." 1

Last spring this happened to me

exactly

These are supposed to be the sheerest, blindest accidents. Mistakes are not believed to be part of the normal behavior of a good machine. If things go wrong, it must be a personal, human error, the result of fingering, tampering, a button getting stuck, someone hitting the wrong key. The computer, at its normal best, is infallible. 2

How can this be?

perfect

I wonder whether this can be true. After all, the whole point of computers is that they represent an extension of the human brain, vastly improved upon but nonetheless human, superhuman maybe. A good computer can think clearly and quickly enough to beat you at chess, and some of them have even been programmed to write obscure verse. They can do anything we can do, and more besides. 3

In what way?

Can this be proven?

I expected this essay to be so much more stuffy than it is. I can even understand it.

It is not yet known whether a computer has its own consciousness, and it would be hard to find out about this. When you walk into one of those great halls now built for the huge machines, and stand listening, it is easy to imagine that the faint, distant noises are the sound of thinking, and the turning of 4

Thinking Critically

To what extent do you feel computers "extend" the human brain? Can humans do anything that computers can't do? If so, what?

the spools gives them the look of wild creatures rolling their eyes in the effort to concentrate, choking
with information. But real thinking, and dreaming,
are other matters.

In what way?

good, clear comparison for the general reader

On the other hand, the evidences of something like   5
an unconscious, equivalent to ours, are all around, in
every mail. As extensions of the human brain, they
have been constructed with the same property of error,
spontaneous, uncontrolled, and rich in possibilities. ❷

so true

Mistakes are at the very base of human thought,   6
embedded there, feeding the structure like root
nodules. If we were not provided with the knack of
being wrong, we could never get anything useful
done. We think our way along by choosing between
right and wrong alternatives, and the wrong choices
have to be made as frequently as the right ones. We
get along in life this way. We are built to make
mistakes, coded for error. ❸

great image

I don't under- stand this??

I agree! This is how we learn

We learn, as we say, by "trial and error." Why do   7
we always say that? Why not "trial and rightness" or
"trial and triumph"? The old phrase puts it that way
because that is, in real life, the way it is done.

Another effective compari- son for the gen- eral reader

A good laboratory, like a good bank or a corpora-   8
tion or government, has to run like a computer.
Almost everything is done flawlessly, by the book, and
all the numbers add up to the predicted sums. The days
go by. And then, if it is a lucky day, and a lucky laboratory, somebody makes a mistake: the wrong buffer,
something in one of the blanks, a decimal misplaced
in reading counts, the warm room off by a degree and
a half, a mouse out of his box, or just a misreading of
the day's protocol. Whatever, when the results come
in, something is obviously screwed up, and then the
action can begin.

Isn't this a contradiction?

storage area for data being transferred

plan

What?

The misreading is not the important error; it   9
opens the way. The next step is the crucial one. If the
investigator can bring himself to say, "But even so,
look at that!" then the new finding, whatever it is, is

aha!

Thinking Critically

❷ How could computer errors be "rich in possibilities"?

❸ Have you ever made an error that turned out to be beneficial? What happened?

ready for snatching. What is needed, for progress to be made, is <u>the move based on error</u>.

Whenever new kinds of thinking are about to be accomplished, or new varieties of music, there has to be an argument beforehand. <u>With two sides debating</u> *(arguing)* in the same mind, *(haranguing,)* there is an amiable understanding that one is right and the other wrong. Sooner or later the thing is settled, but there can be no action at all if there are not the two sides and the *interesting* argument. <u>The hope is in the faculty of wrongness</u>, *idea* the tendency toward error. The capacity to leap across mountains of information and land lightly on the wrong side represents the highest of human endowments.   10

I believe Thomas here because of his back-ground

Could this be related to the human ability to think critically?

It may be that this is a uniquely human gift, perhaps even stipulated in our genetic instructions. [4] Other creatures do not seem to have DNA sequences for making mistakes as a routine part of daily living, certainly not for programmed error as a guide for action.   11

We are at our human finest, <u>dancing with our minds</u>, when there are more choices than two. Some-times there are ten, even twenty different ways to go, all but one bound to be wrong, and the richness of selection in such situations can lift us onto totally new ground. This process is called exploration and is based *(imperfection)* on human *(fallibility)*. If we had only a single center in our brains, capable of responding only when a correct decision was to be made, instead of the jumble of *(gullible)* different, *(credulous,)* easily *(conned)* clusters of neurons *(fooled)* that provide for being flung off into blind alleys, up trees, down dead ends, out into blue sky, along wrong turnings, around bends, we could only stay the way we are today, stuck fast.   12

Yes, but this is so frustrating

nice mental image

This is a great sentence—it has a lot of feeling

I love the phrase "splendid freedom" <u>The lower animals do not have this splendid free-dom</u>. They are limited, most of them, to absolute *(infallibility)*. Cats, for all their good side, never make mistakes. <u>I have never seen a</u> *(maladroit)* <u>clumsy, or</u> *(perfection)* blundering cat. Dogs are sometimes fallible, occasion-ally able to make charming minor mistakes, but they   13

See ¶11

look up "maladroit"

awkward

Thinking Critically

[4] Do you agree with Thomas that we are genetically programmed to make mistakes in our lives? Explain your answer.

*I like
this idea*

get this way by trying to mimic their masters. <u>Fish are flawless in everything they do</u>. Individual cells in a tissue are mindless machines, perfect in their performance, as absolutely inhuman as bees.

I never thought of mistakes this way

We should have this in mind as we become dependent on more complex computers for the arrangement of our affairs. Give the computers their heads, I say; let them go their way. If we can learn to do this, turning our heads to one side and wincing while the work proceeds, the possibilities for the future of mankind, and computerkind, are limitless. <u>Your average good computer can make calculations in an instant which would take a lifetime of slide rules for any of us</u>. Think of what we could gain from the near infinity of precise, machine-made (miscomputation) which is now so easily within our grasp. We would begin the solving of some of our hardest problems. How, for instance, should we go about organizing ourselves for social living on a planetary scale, now that we have become, as a plain fact of life, a single community? We can assume, as a working hypothesis, that all the right ways of doing this are unworkable. What we need, then, for moving ahead, is a set of wrong alternatives much longer and more interesting than the short list of mistaken courses that any of us can think up right now. We need, in fact, an infinite list, and when it is printed out we need the computer to turn itself on and select, at random, the next way to go. If it is a big enough mistake, we could find ourselves on a new level, stunned, out in the clear, ready to move again. [5,6]

14

Thomas makes our technology sound really exciting

so true

error or mistake

yes

We need to program computers to make deliberate mistakes so they can help our natural human tendency to learn thru error

So mistakes have value!

Not a contradiction after all

After you have read the essay for the first time, summarize its main ideas in some fashion. The form of this task might be anything from a drawing of the main ideas as they connect with one another to a succinct written summary. You could draw a graph or map of the topics in the essay (in much the same way that a person would draw a map of an area for someone unfamiliar with a particular route); outline the ideas to get an overview of the piece; or summarize the ideas to check your understanding of the main

---

Thinking Critically

[5] What do the author's final words mean to you: "stunned, out in the clear, ready to move again"?

[6] Why do you think Thomas ends his essay this way?

points of the selection. Any of these tasks can be completed from your original notes and underlining. Each will give you a slightly more thorough understanding of what you have read.

Finally, read the questions and assignments following the essay to help focus your thinking for the second reading. Don't answer the questions at this time; just read them to make sure you are picking up the main ideas from the selection and thinking about relevant connections among those ideas.

Rereading

The second and third readings will dramatically increase your understanding of each essay in this book. The temptation to skip these two stages of the reading process is often powerful, but these readings are crucial to your development as a critical reader in all your courses. Rereading can be compared to seeing a good movie for the second or third time: The first viewing provides you with a general understanding of the plot, the characters, the setting, and the overall artistic accomplishment of the director; during the second viewing, however, you would notice many more details and see their specific contributions to the artistic whole. Similarly, the second and third readings of an essay provide for a much deeper understanding of the essay and prepare you to analyze the writer's ideas.

Your second reading is a time to develop a deeper understanding of the author's argument or main ideas. Concentrate on reading "with the grain," as the rhetorician John Bean calls it, meaning you are essentially trying to adopt the author's reasoning in an attempt to learn how he or she thinks and came to certain conclusions. This reading will expand your reasoning capacity and stimulate new ideas.

Also during this reading, you should answer the questions at the bottom of the pages of the essay (the "bridge" questions). These questions are marked throughout the text both in the essay and at the bottom of the pages by numbers within diamonds. Then, you might ask some additional questions of your own. You will get the most out of this stage if you respond in writing. Keeping a journal to collect these responses is especially effective as you work to make this essay your own. Here are some sample student responses to the bridge questions accompanying the Thomas essay.

1. Sample response: Computers can supply us with more memory than we could ever have. Perhaps we even rely on them too much for this service. On the other hand, I think we can reason on more complex levels than the computer can.

2. Sample response: Errors on the computer, like errors made by humans, might lead to new discoveries or new insights into old theories and observations.

3. Sample response: I have made several mistakes that turned out to be beneficial: I dated a guy who turned out to be a negative force in my life, which helped me understand what it means to be happy; I followed a lead on the Internet that taught me an important lesson; and I learned a lot about myself when I discovered a mistake I made on a math test.

4. Sample response: Compared to cats and dogs, we are definitely programmed to make mistakes. We are not meant to do everything perfectly, and we learn from our mistakes—in both positive and negative ways.

5. Sample response: My guess is that Thomas means we will be stunned by our new discoveries and ready to break into the clear—like a football player running freely with the ball.

6. Sample response: This ending sounds like a new beginning ("stunned," "into the clear"), which is an effective way to end his essay and get his point across.

Then, during your third reading, you should consciously read "against the grain," actively doubting and challenging what the author is saying. Do some detective work, and look closely at the assumptions on which the essay is based: For example, how does the writer move from idea to idea? What hidden assertions lie behind these ideas? Do you agree or disagree with these assertions? Your assessment of these unspoken assumptions will often play a major role in your critical response to an essay. In the case of Thomas's essay, do you accept the unspoken connection he makes between the workings of the human brain and the computer? What parts of the essay hinge on your acceptance of this connection? What other assumptions are fundamental to Thomas's reasoning? If you accept his thinking along the way, you are more likely to agree with the general flow of Thomas's essay. If you discover a flaw in his premises or assumptions, your acceptance of his argument will start to break down.

Next, answer the questions that follow the essay. The "Understanding Details" questions will help you comprehend and remember what you have read on both the literal and the interpretive levels. Some of the questions (the literal questions) ask you to restate various important points the author makes; others (the interpretive questions) help you see relationships among the different ideas presented.

UNDERSTANDING DETAILS

Literal
1. According to Thomas, in what ways are computers and humans similar? How are they different?

Literal/
Interpretive
2. How do we learn by "trial and error"? Why is this a useful way to learn?

Interpretive
3. What does Thomas mean by the statement, "If we were not provided with the knack of being wrong, we could never get anything useful done" (paragraph 6)?

Interpretive
4. According to Thomas, in what important ways do humans and "lower" animals differ? What does this comparison have to do with Thomas's main line of reasoning?

The "Reading Critically" questions require you to analyze and evaluate some of the writer's ideas to form valid opinions of your own. These questions demand a higher level of thought than the previous set and help you prepare more specifically for the discussion/writing assignments that follow the questions.

READING CRITICALLY

Analytical
1. What is Thomas's main point in this essay? How do the references to computers help make his case?

Analytical
2. In paragraph 10, Thomas explains that an argument must precede the beginning of something new and different. Do you think this is an accurate observation? Explain your answer.

Analytical
3. Why does Thomas perceive human error as such a positive quality? What does "exploration" have to do with this quality (paragraph 12)?

Analytical
4. What could we gain from "the near infinity of precise, machine-made miscomputation" (paragraph 14)? In what ways would our civilization advance?

The "Discovering Rhetorical Strategies" questions ask you to look closely at what strategies the writer uses to develop his or her thesis and how those strategies work. The questions address important features of the writer's composing process, such as word choice, use of detail, transitions, statement of purpose, organization of ideas, sentence structure, and paragraph development. The intent of these questions is to raise various elements of the composing process to the conscious level so you can use them later in your own essays. If you are able to understand and describe what choices a writer makes to create certain effects in his or her prose, you are more likely to be able to discover the range of choices available to you as you write, and you will also become more aware of your ability to control your readers' thoughts and feelings.

DISCOVERING RHETORICAL STRATEGIES

1. Thomas begins his essay with a list of experiences most of us have had at one time or another. Do you find this an effective beginning? Why or why not?
2. Which main points in his essay does Thomas develop in most detail? Why do you think he chooses to develop these points so thoroughly?
3. Explain the simile Thomas uses in paragraph 6: "Mistakes are at the very base of human thought, embedded there, feeding the structure like root nodules." Is this comparison between mistakes and root nodules useful in this context? Why or why not? Find another simile or metaphor in this essay, and explain how it works.
4. What principal rhetorical strategies does Thomas use to make his point? Give examples of each from the essay.

A final set of questions, "Making Connections," asks you to consider the essay you have just read in reference to other essays in this book. Written so you can focus your responses on the essays you have read, the questions have you compare the writers' treatment of an idea, the authors' style of writing, the differences in their opinions, or the similarities between their views of the world. Such questions will help you see connections in your own life— not only in your reading and your immediate environment, but also in the larger world around you. These questions, in particular, encourage you to move from specific references in the selections to a broader range of issues and circumstances that affect your daily life.

MAKING CONNECTIONS

1. Kimberly Wozencraft ("Notes from the Country Club") and Joe Keohane ("How Facts Backfire") refer both directly and indirectly to learning from mistakes. Would Lewis Thomas agree with either of their approaches to this topic? In what ways do any of these authors you have read agree about the benefits of making errors? In what ways do they differ on the topic? Explain your answer.

2. Lewis Thomas, Jessica Mitford ("Behind the Formaldehyde Curtain"), and Michael Dorris ("The Broken Cord") all write about the intersection of science and humanity. Which of these authors, from what you have read, is most intrigued by the human aspect of this equation? Explain your answer.

3. According to Thomas, humans are complex organisms with a great deal of untapped potential. Maya Angelou ("New Directions") and Sarah Toler ("Understanding the Birth Order Relationship") also comment on the uniqueness of human beings. In what ways do any of these writers that you have read agree or disagree with each other on the intelligence and resourcefulness of humans? To what extent would each author argue that we use our mental capacities wisely and completely? Explain your answer.

The last stage of responding to the reading selections in this text offers you various "Ideas for Discussion/Writing" that will allow you to demonstrate the different skills you have learned in each chapter. This material includes questions to consider before you write, followed by the writing topics themselves. You will be most successful if you envision each writing experience as an organic process that follows a natural, recursive cycle of prewriting, writing, and rewriting, which we will discuss in the next chapter.

IDEAS FOR DISCUSSION/WRITING

Preparing to Write

Write freely about an important mistake you have made: How did the mistake make you feel? What (if anything) did you learn from this mistake? What did you fail to learn that you should have learned? Did this mistake have any positive impact on your life? What were its negative consequences? How crucial are mistakes in our lives?

Choosing a Topic

MyWritingLab™

1. **LEARNING ⏻NLINE** Return to the game you played in "Preparing to Read." If you could change a mistake you made in this game, what mistake would you fix? Why would you rethink this play? Write an analysis in which you reflect on this mistake, and offer an explanation of its consequences and outcomes. Then, relate the lesson you learned to a similar life experience.

2. You have decided to write an editorial for your local newspaper concerning the impact of computers on our lives. Cite specific experiences you have had with computers to help make your main point.

3. You have been invited back to your high school to make a speech to a senior English class about how people can learn from their mistakes. Write your speech in the form of an essay explaining what you learned from a crucial mistake you have made. Use examples to show these students that mistakes can be positive factors in their lives.
4. In an essay for your writing class, explain one specific human quality. Use Thomas's essay as a model. Cite examples to support your explanation.

READING CRITICALLY

Reading critically is the heart and soul of successful studying. But it requires reflection. Only when the imagination is engaged will you read critically and be productive students in our fast-paced world. Taking the time to read critically will positively affect every aspect of your life in and out of college—especially your writing ability.

Because checklists can provide a helpful method of learning and reviewing important information, we offer a series of questions on the next page that represents the reading process we have just described. All these guidelines can be used for your reading in any discipline. Keeping a continuous journal of your responses to your readings is an excellent way to improve your reading and raise your level of understanding.

MyWritingLab™ Visit Ch. 2 Reading Critically in *MyWritingLab* to complete the writing assignments and test your understanding of the chapter learning objectives.

READING CHECKLIST

Preparing to Read

Title
√ What can you infer from the title of the essay?
√ Who do you think is the author's audience? What is the principal purpose of the essay?

Synopsis
√ What is the general subject of the essay?
√ What is the author's approach to the subject?

Biography
√ What do you know about the author's age, political stance, general beliefs?
√ How qualified is the author to write on this subject?
√ When did the author write the essay? Under what conditions? In what context?

Prereading Background and Questions
√ Where was the essay first published?
√ What would you like to learn about this topic?
√ What are some of your opinions on this subject?

Reading
√ What are the essay's main ideas?
√ What words do you need to look up?
√ What are your initial reactions to the ideas in this essay?

Rereading
√ What do you agree with in this essay? What do you disagree with?
√ What assumptions underlie the author's reasoning?
√ Do you have a solid interpretive understanding of this essay? Do you understand the relationship among ideas? What conclusions can you draw from this essay?
√ Do you have an accurate analytical understanding of this essay? Which ideas can you take apart, examine, and put back together again? What is your evaluation of this material?
√ Do you understand the rhetorical strategies the writer uses and the way they work? What are the effects of these strategies?
√ How does the author achieve his or her purpose in this essay?

Chapter 3

WRITING CRITICALLY

LEARNING OBJECTIVES

After completing this chapter, you will be able to do the following:
- Understand the writing process
- Use the writing process to write critically

Writing critically involves analyzing your topic in detail and then engaging deeply in a sustained investigation of one aspect of that topic. Just as reading does, writing requires a natural curiosity about an essay's subject that will prompt your investigation. Structuring your analysis in some standard way is essential for communicating your ideas to others so that you always present a beginning, middle, and end to your discussion. To understand this structure and use it as effectively as possible, you need to learn about the writing process and then mold it to your own purposes.

THE WRITING PROCESS

The phases of the writing process mirror those of the reading process—preparing to write, writing, and rewriting. Following this format will help you develop the natural curiosity you need to write a good analytic essay. The writing process consists of identifiable "stages" that overlap in a number of unique ways. No two people write in the same way, so it is important for you to discover a writing process that is most comfortable for you.

In other words, you need to learn how to arrange these stages to produce the best writing you are capable of. Knowing each of the steps individually will help you organize them in a way that best suits your lifestyle. The Writing Inventory at the end of this chapter will also guide you through this process.

First, let's review the "Ideas for Discussion/Writing" that were introduced in Chapter 2 after the Lewis Thomas essay:

IDEAS FOR DISCUSSION/WRITING

Preparing to Write

Write freely about an important mistake you have made: How did the mistake make you feel? What (if anything) did you learn from this mistake? What did you fail to learn that you should have learned? Did this mistake have any positive impact on your life? What were its negative consequences? How crucial are mistakes in our lives?

Choosing a Topic   MyWritingLab™

1. **LEARNINGⓊNLINE** Return to the game you played in "Preparing to Read." If you could change a mistake you made in this game, what mistake would you fix? Why would you rethink this play? Write an analysis in which you reflect on this mistake, and offer an explanation of its consequences and outcomes. Then, relate the lesson you learned to a similar life experience.
2. You have decided to write an editorial for your local newspaper concerning the impact of computers on our lives. Cite specific experiences you have had with computers to help make your main point.
3. You have been invited back to your high school to make a speech to a senior English class about how people can learn from their mistakes. Write your speech in the form of an essay explaining what you learned from a crucial mistake you have made. Use examples to show these students that mistakes can be positive factors in their lives.
4. In an essay for your writing class, explain one specific human quality. Use Thomas's essay as a model. Cite examples to support your explanation.

Preparing to Write

The prewriting phase involves choosing a subject, generating ideas, selecting and narrowing a topic, analyzing an audience, and developing a purpose. Preceding the writing assignments are "Preparing to Write" questions you should respond to before trying to structure your thoughts into a coherent essay. These questions will assist you in generating new thoughts on the topics that follow and may even stimulate new approaches to old ideas. Keeping a journal in response to these questions is an excellent practice because you will then have a record of your opinions on various subjects related to the writing assignments. No matter what format you use to answer these questions, the activity of prewriting generally continues in various forms throughout the writing process.

Responses to the prewriting questions can be prompted by a number of different "invention" techniques and carried out by individuals, in pairs, in small groups, or as a class project. Invention strategies can help you generate responses to these questions and discover related ideas through the various stages of writing your papers. Because you will undoubtedly vary your approach to different assignments, you should be familiar with all the following choices available to you.

Brainstorming.   The basis of brainstorming is free association. Ideally, you should get a group of students together and bounce ideas, words, and thoughts off one another until they begin to cluster around related topics. If you don't have a group of students handy, brainstorm by yourself or with a friend. The exchange of thoughts usually starts orally but should transfer to paper when your ideas begin to settle into related categories. The act of recording your ideas becomes a catalyst for other thoughts; you are essentially setting up a dialogue with yourself or with others on paper. Then, keep writing down words and phrases that occur to you until they begin to fall into logical subdivisions or until your new ideas come to an end.

Freewriting.   Freewriting means writing to discover what you want to say. Set a time limit of about 10 minutes, and write by free association, meaning whatever comes to mind. Write about what you are seeing, feeling, touching, thinking; write about having nothing to say; recopy the sentence you just wrote—anything. Just keep writing on paper or on a computer. After you have generated some material, locate an idea that is central to your writing assignment, put it at the top of another page, and start freewriting again, letting your thoughts take shape around this central idea. This second type of preparation is called *focused freewriting* and is especially valuable when you already have a specific topic.

Journal Entries.   Journal entries are much like freewriting, except you have some sense of an audience—probably either your instructor or yourself. In a journal, anything goes. You can respond to the "Preparing to Write" questions, jot down thoughts, include articles that spark your interest, write snippets of dialogue, draft letters (the kind you never send), record dreams, or make lists. The possibilities are endless. An excellent way of practicing writing, keeping a journal is also a wonderful means of stimulating new ideas—a way of fixing them in your mind and making them yours.

Direct Questions.   This technique involves asking a series of questions useful in any writing situation to generate ideas, arrange thoughts, or revise prose. One example of this strategy is to use the inquiries journalists rely on to develop their articles:

Who: *Who played the game?*
            Who won the game?
What: *What kind of game was it?*
            What happened in the game?
Why: *Why was the game played?*
Where: *Where was the game played?*
When: *When was the game played?*
How: *How was the game played?*

If you ask yourself questions of this type on a specific topic, you will begin to produce thoughts and details that will undoubtedly be useful to you in the writing assignments that follow.

Clustering.   Clustering is a method of drawing or mapping your ideas as fast as they come into your mind. Put a word, phrase, or sentence in a circle in the center of a blank page. Then put every new idea that comes to you in its own circle, and show its relationship to a previous thought by drawing a line to the circle containing the original thought. You will probably reach a natural stopping point for this exercise in two to three minutes.

Although you can generate ideas in a number of different ways, the main principle behind the "Preparing to Write" questions in this text is to encourage you to do what is called *expressive writing* before you tackle any writing assignment. This is writing based on your feelings, thoughts, experiences, observations, and opinions. The process of answering questions about your own ideas and experiences makes you "think on paper," thereby enabling you to surround yourself with your own thoughts and opinions before you apply them to an academic question. From this reservoir, you can then choose the ideas you want to develop into an essay and begin writing about them one at a time.

As you use various prewriting techniques to generate responses to the "Preparing to Write" questions, you should know that these responses can (and probably will) appear in many different forms. You can express yourself in lists, outlines, random notes, sentences, paragraphs, charts, graphs, or pictures—whatever keeps your thoughts flowing smoothly and productively.

One of our students used a combination of brainstorming and clustering to generate the following thoughts in response to the prewriting questions for the Thomas essay:

Brainstorming

Mistakes:

happen when I'm in a hurry	*getting back on track*
make me feel stupid	*parents*
love	*corrections*
relationships	*learning from mistakes*
trip back East	*I am a better person*
pride	*my values are clear*
going in circles	*mistakes help us change*
Bob	*painful*
learned a lot about people	*helpful*
people aren't what they seem	*Valuable*

Clustering

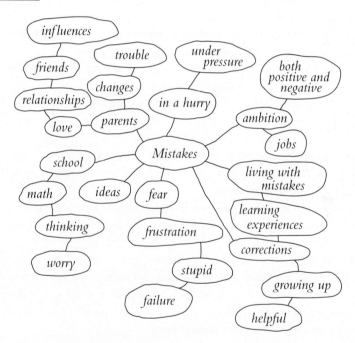

From the free-flowing thoughts you generate, you need to decide what to write about and how to limit your subject to a manageable length. Our student writer chose topic 3 from the "Choosing a Topic" list after the essay. Her brainstorming and clustering in response to the prewriting questions helped her decide to write on "A Time I Got Lost." She then generated more focused ideas and opinions in the form of a journal entry, which is printed here just as she wrote it—errors and all.

Journal Entry

The craziest mistake I think I ever made was on a trip I took recently—I was heading to the east coast from California and reached Durham, North Carolina. I was so excited because I was going to get to see the Atlantic Ocean for the first time in my life and Durham was one of my last landmarks before I reached the sea. In Durham I was going to have to change from a northeast direction to due east.

When I got there the highway was under construction. I took the detour, but got all skrewed up till I realized that I had gone the wrong direction. By this time I was lost somewhere in downtown Durham and didn't know which way was east. I stoped and asked a guy at a gas station and he explained how to get back on the east-bound highway. The way was through the middle of town. By the time I got to where I was supposed to turn right I could only turn left. So I started left and then realized I couldn't turn back the other way! I made a couple of other stops after that, and one jerk told me I "just couldn't get there from here." Eventually I found a truck driver heading toward the same eastbound highway, and he told me to follow him. An hour and forty minutes after reaching Durham's city limits I finally managed to leave going east. I felt as if I had spent an entire month there!

The thing I learned from this was just how egocentric I am. I would not have made this error if I had not been so damn cocky about my sense of direction. My mistake was made worse because I got flustered and didn't listen to the directions clearly. I find that the reason I most often make a mistake is because I don't listen carefully to instructions. This has been a problem all my life.

After I got over feeling really dum I decided this kind of thing was not going to happen again. It was too much a waste of time and gas, so I was going to be more careful of road signs and directions.

This all turned out to be a positive experience though. I learned that there are lots of friendly, helpful people. It was kind of reassuring to know that other folks would help you if you just asked.

I feel this and other mistakes are crucial not only to my life but to my personal growth in general. It is the making of mistakes that helps people learn where they are misdirecting their energies. I think mistakes can help all of us learn to be more careful about some part of our lives. This is why mistakes are crucial. Otherwise, we would continue in the same old rut and never improve.

This entry served as the foundation on which the student built her essay. Her next step was to consider *audience* and *purpose* (which are often written into the writing assignments in this text). The first of these features identifies the person or group of people you will address in your essay. The second is a declaration of your principal reason for writing the essay, which usually takes the form of a thesis statement (the statement of purpose or the controlling idea of an essay). Together these pieces of information help you make most of the decisions you are faced with as you write: what words to choose, what sentence structures to use, what order to present ideas in, which topics to develop, and which to summarize. The more you know about your audience (for example, age, educational background, likes, dislikes, biases, political persuasion, and social status) and your purpose (to inform, persuade, and/or entertain), the easier the writing task will be. In the rough draft and final draft of the essay in the section that follows, the student knew she was writing to a senior English class at her old high school to convince them that mistakes can be positive factors in their lives. This clear sense of audience and purpose helped her realize she should use fairly advanced vocabulary, call on a variety of sentence structures, and organize her ideas chronologically in order to make her point most effectively to her intended audience.

At this stage of the writing process, some people benefit from assembling their ideas in the form of an outline. Others use an outline to double-check their logic and organization after they write their first draft. Whether your outlines are informal (a simple list) or more structured, they can help you visualize the logical relationship of your ideas to one another. We recommend using a rough outline throughout the prewriting and writing stages to ensure that your work is carefully and tightly organized. Your outline, however, should be adjusted to your draft as it develops.

Writing

The writing stage asks you to draft an essay based on the prewriting material you have developed. Because you have already made the important preliminary decisions regarding your topic, your audience, and your purpose, the task of actually writing the essay should follow naturally. (Notice we did not say this task should necessarily be easy—just natural.) At this stage, you ought to look on your essay as a way of solving a problem or answering a question: The problem/question is posed in your writing assignment, and the solution/answer is your essay.

The four "Choosing a Topic" assignments that follow the prewriting questions in this text invite you to consider issues related to the essay you just read. Although they typically ask you to focus on one particular rhetorical pattern, they draw on many rhetorical strategies (as do all writing assignments in the text) and require you to support your statements with concrete evidence and examples. The assignments for the Lewis Thomas essay ("Choosing a Topic," listed earlier) emphasize the use of example, his dominant rhetorical strategy.

The following essay is our student's first-draft response to topic 3. After writing her journal entry, the student drafted a tentative thesis statement: "I know there are positive changes that can come from making a mistake because I recently had an opportunity to learn some valuable lessons from one of my errors." This statement helped the student writer further develop and organize her ideas as she focused finally on one well-chosen example to illustrate her thesis. At this point, the thesis is simply the controlling idea around which the other topics take shape; it is often revised several times before the final draft.

First Draft: A Time I Got Lost

Parents and teachers frequently pressure us to avoid committing errors. Meanwhile, our friends laugh at us when we make mistakes. With all these different messages, it is hard for us to think of mistakes as positive events. But if any of you take the time to think about what you have learned from mistakes, I bet you will realize all the good things that have come from these events. I know there are positive changes that can come from making a mistake because I recently had an opportunity to learn some valuable lessons in this way.

While traveling back east this last summer, I made the mistake of turning west on an interstate detour in order to reach the Atlantic Ocean. The adventure took me into the heart of Durham, North Carolina, where I got totally lost. I had to get directions several times until two hours later I was going in the right direction. As I was driving out of town, I realized that although I had made a dumb mistake, I had learned a great deal. Overall, the detour was actually a positive experience.

The first thing I remember thinking after I had gotten my wits together was that I had definitely learned something from making the mistake. I had the opportunity to see a new city, filled with new people—3,000 miles from my own hometown, but very much like it. I also became aware that the beach is not always toward the west, as it is in California. The entire experience was like getting a geography lesson firsthand.

As this pleasant feeling began to grow, I came to another realization. I was aware of how important other people can be in making a mistake into a positive experience. My first reaction was "Oh no, someone is going to know I made a mistake!" But the amazing part about this mistake was how supportive everyone was. The townspeople had been entirely willing to help someone they did not know. This mistake helped me learn that people tend to be nicer than I had imagined.

The final lesson I learned from getting lost in Durham was how to be more cautious about my actions so as not to repeat the same mistake. It was this internalization of all the information I gleaned from making the mistake that I see as the most positive part of the experience. I realized that in order to avoid such situations in the future I would have to be less egocentric in my decisions and more willing to listen to directions from other people. I needed to learn that my set way of doing things was not always the best way. If I had not made the mistake, I would not have been aware of my other options.

By making this mistake I learned that there is a more comprehensive manner of looking at the world. In the future, if we could all stop after making a mistake and ask ourselves, "What can I learn from this?" we would be less critical of ourselves and have a great many more positive experiences. If I were not able to make mistakes, I would probably not be able to expand my knowledge of my environment, my sense of others, and my understanding of myself.

Rewriting

The rewriting stage includes (1) revising, (2) editing, and (3) proofreading. The first of these activities, *revising,* actually starts as you are writing a draft when you change words, recast sentences, and move whole paragraphs from one place to another. Making these linguistic and organizational choices means you will also constantly be adjusting your content to your purpose (what you want to accomplish) and your audience (the readers) in much the same way you alter your speech to communicate more effectively in response to the gestures, eye movements, or facial expressions of your listeners. Revising is literally the act of "re-seeing" your essay, looking at it through your readers' eyes to determine whether or not it achieves its purpose. As you revise, you should consider matters of both content and form on the checklist at the end of this chapter.

Revising the Content
√ Does your essay have a clear, interesting title?
√ Will your statement of purpose or thesis be clear to your audience?
√ Will the introduction make your audience want to read the rest of your essay?
√ Have you included enough details to prove your main points?
√ Does your conclusion sum up your central points?
√ Will you accomplish your purpose with your audience?

Revising the Form
√ Have you organized your ideas as effectively as possible for this specific audience?
√ Do you use appropriate rhetorical strategies to support your main points?
√ Is your sentence structure varied and interesting?
√ Is your vocabulary appropriate for your topic, purpose, and audience?

After you rearrange paragraphs and check your logic, you can then remove repetitions or insert words and sentences that will serve as the transitions between sections before you turn to editing and proofreading.

Editing entails correcting mistakes in your writing so that your final draft conforms to the conventions of standard written English. Correct punctuation, spelling, and mechanics will help you make your points and will encourage your readers to move smoothly through your essay from topic to topic. At this stage, you should be concerned about such matters as whether your sentences are complete, whether your punctuation is correct, whether you have followed conventional rules for using mechanics, and whether the words in your essay are spelled correctly. Refer to the checklist at the end of this chapter for specific editing questions.

Proofreading involves reading over your entire essay, slowly and carefully, to make certain you have not allowed any errors to slip into your final draft; most college instructors don't look upon errors as kindly as Thomas does. In general, good writers try to let some time elapse between writing the final draft and proofreading it (at least a few hours, or even a day or so). Otherwise, they find themselves proofreading their thoughts rather than their words. Some writers even profit from proofreading their papers backward—a technique that allows them to focus on individual words and phrases rather than on entire sentences.

Following is the student's revised essay on making mistakes in life. This final draft (written to high school seniors, as the assignment specifies) represents the entire writing process at work. We have made notes in the margin to highlight various effective elements in her essay, some of which we have underlined for emphasis. The various rhetorical modes she draws on are listed in the margins in brackets.

Mistakes and Maturity

Catchy title; good change from first draft

Parents and teachers frequently harp on us to correct our errors. Meanwhile, our friends laugh at us when we make mistakes. With all these negative messages, most of us have a hard time believing that problems can be positive experiences. But if we take the time to think about what we have learned from various blunders, we will realize all the good that has come from these events. I know that making mistakes can have positive results because I recently learned several valuable lessons from one unforgettable experience.

Rapport with audience and point of view established

Clear, stimulating introduction for high school seniors

Revised thesis statement

Good, brief summary of complex experience (see journal entry from Preparing to Write)

While I was traveling on the East Coast last summer, I made the mistake of turning west on an interstate detour in an attempt to reach the Atlantic Ocean. This adventure took me into the center of Durham, North Carolina, where I became totally lost, bewildered, and angry at myself. I had to ask for directions several times until two hours later, when I finally found the correct highway toward the

Background information

Good details

ocean. As I was driving out of town, I realized that although I had made a "dumb" mistake, I had actually learned a great deal. Overall, my adventure had been quite positive.

[Narration]

First topic (topics are in chronological order)

Adequate number of examples

The first insight I remember having after my wits returned was that <u>I had definitely learned more about United States geography from making this mistake</u>. I had become intimately acquainted with a town 3,000 miles from home that greatly resembled my own city, and I had become aware that the beach is not always toward the west, as it is in California. I had also met some pleasant strangers. <u>Looking at my confusion as a learning experience encouraged me to have positive feelings about the mistake.</u>

[Examples]

Nice close to this paragraph

[Cause/ Effect]

Clear explanation with details

[Description]

As I relaxed and let this happy feeling grow, I came to another realization. <u>I became aware of how important other people can be in turning a mistake into a positive event.</u> Although my first reaction had been "Oh, no! Someone is going to know I'm lost," I was amazed by how supportive other people were during my panic and embarrassment. From an old man swinging on his front porch to an elementary school boy crossing the street with his bright blue backpack, I found that the townspeople of Durham were entirely willing to help someone they did not even know. <u>I realized that people in general are nicer than I had previously thought.</u>

Second topic

[Examples]

Good summary statement

Third topic

[Process Analysis]

The final lesson I learned from making this mistake was <u>how to be more cautious about my future decisions</u>. This insight was, in fact, the most positive part of the entire experience. What I realized I must do to prevent similar errors in the future was to relax, not be so bullheaded in my decisions, and be more willing to listen to directions from other people. <u>I might never have had these positive realizations if I had not made this mistake.</u>

Specific details

[Cause/ Effect]

Good summary statement

Clear transition statement

[Cause/ Effect]

Thus, <u>by driving in circles for two hours, I developed a more comprehensive way of looking at the world.</u> If I were unable to make mistakes, I probably would not have had this chance to <u>learn about my environment, improve my impressions of strangers, and reconsider the egocentric way in</u>

Good summary of three topics without being repetitive

[Process Analysis] which I act in certain situations. Perhaps there's a lesson here for all of us. Instead of criticizing ourselves unduly, if each one of us could pause after we make an error and ask, "How can I profit from this?" we would realize that mistakes can often be turned into positive events that will help us become more confident and mature.

Nicely focused concluding remark

Concluding statement applicable to all readers

As these various drafts of the student paper indicate, the essay assignments in this book encourage you to transfer to your own writing an understanding of how form and content work together. As you work through this book, the writing assignments will help you learn how to give shape to your own ideas and how to engage your readers' thoughts and feelings. In essence, they will help you recognize the control you have, through language, over your personal and academic success.

WRITING CRITICALLY

Writing critically, or analytically, will play a significant role in your life both in college and in the workplace. It is one of the few ways people have to communicate their ideas and make progress in the world. Essentially, you will write for the rest of your life—to make a point, to demonstrate your knowledge of a subject, to earn a grade, to apply for a job, to get a raise. Writing critically in these situations helps you get what you want in life, and college is the place to perfect this ability.

The guidelines presented in this chapter are summarized here in a checklist for your reference as you work through this text. We recommend that you also use this list of questions on your writing assignments in other disciplines. If you make this checklist part of your academic writing ritual, you will always have a guide for your writing assignments. As with reading, keeping a journal of your thoughts, references, and ideas for assignments is an effective way to improve your writing.

MyWritingLab™ Visit Ch. 3 Writing Critically in *MyWritingLab* to complete the writing assignments and test your understanding of the chapter learning objectives.

WRITING CHECKLIST

Preparing to Write
√ Do you understand your assignment?
√ Have you narrowed your topic adequately?
√ Who is your audience (What are their likes/dislikes? What is their educational level? Their knowledge of the subject?)
√ What is your purpose?

Writing
√ Can you express your thesis as a problem or question?
√ Is your essay a solution or an answer to that problem or question?

Revising

Revising the Content
√ Does your essay have a clear, interesting title?
√ Will your statement of purpose or thesis be clear to your audience?
√ Will the introduction make your audience want to read the rest of your essay?
√ Have you included enough details to prove your main points?
√ Does your conclusion sum up your central points?
√ Will you accomplish your purpose with your audience?

Revising the Form
√ Have you organized your ideas as effectively as possible for this specific audience?
√ Do you use appropriate rhetorical strategies to support your main points?
√ Is your sentence structure varied and interesting?
√ Is your vocabulary appropriate for your topic, purpose, and audience?

Editing and Proofreading
√ Have you written complete sentences throughout the essay?
√ Have you used punctuation correctly and effectively (check especially the use of commas, apostrophes, colons, and semicolons)?
√ Have you followed conventional rules for mechanics (capitalization, underlining or italics, abbreviations, and numbers)?
√ Are all the words in your essay spelled correctly? (Use a dictionary or a spell-checker when in doubt.)

Part II

Reading and Writing Rhetorically

Chapter 4

DESCRIPTION
Exploring Through the Senses

LEARNING OBJECTIVES

After completing this chapter, you will be able to do the following:
- Define description
- Use description to think critically
- Read descriptive essays critically
- Write and revise effective descriptive essays

All of us use description in our daily lives. We might, for example, try to convey the horrors of a recent history exam to our parents, help a friend visualize someone we met on vacation, or describe the cars in an accident for a police report. Whatever our specific purpose, description is a fundamental part of communication: We give and receive descriptions constantly, and our lives are continually affected by this simple yet important rhetorical technique.

DEFINING DESCRIPTION

Description may be defined as the act of capturing people, places, events, objects, and feelings in words so that a reader (or listener) can visualize and respond to them. Unlike narration, which traditionally presents events in a clear time sequence, description essentially suspends its objects in time, making them exempt from the limits of chronology. Narration tells a story, whereas pure description contains no action or time. Description is one of our primary forms of self-expression; it paints a verbal picture that helps the reader understand or share a sensory experience through the process of *showing* rather than *telling*. *Telling* your friends, for example, that "the campgrounds were filled with friendly, happy activities" is not as engaging as *showing* them by saying, "The campgrounds were alive with the smell of spicy baked beans, the sound of high-pitched laughter, and the sight of happy families sharing the warmth of a fire." Showing your readers helps them understand your experience through as many senses as possible.

Descriptions fall somewhere between two extremes: (1) totally objective reports (with no trace of opinions or feelings), such as we might find in a dictionary or an encyclopedia; and (2) very subjective accounts, which focus almost exclusively on personal impressions. The same horse, for instance, might be described by one writer as "a large, solid-hoofed herbivorous mammal having a long mane and a tail" (objective) and by another as "a magnificent and spirited beast flaring its nostrils in search of adventure" (subjective). Most descriptive writing, however, falls somewhere between these two extremes: "a large, four-legged beast in search of adventure."

Objective description is principally characterized by its impartial, precise, and emotionless tone. Found most prominently in technical and scientific writing, such accounts might include a description of equipment to be used in a chemistry experiment, the results of a market survey for a particular consumer product, or a medical appraisal of a heart patient's physical symptoms. In situations like these, accurate, unbiased, and easily understandable accounts are of the utmost importance.

Subjective description, in contrast, is intentionally created to produce a particular response in the reader or listener. Focusing on feelings rather than on raw data, it tries to activate as many senses as possible, thereby leading the audience to a specific conclusion or state of mind. Examples of subjective descriptions are a parent's disapproving comments about one of your friends, a professor's glowing analysis of your most recent "A" paper, or a basketball coach's critique of the team's losing effort in last night's big game.

In most situations, the degree of subjectivity or objectivity in a descriptive passage depends to a large extent on the writer's purpose and intended audience. In the case of the heart patient mentioned earlier, the person's physician might present the case in a formal, scientific way to a group of medical colleagues; in a personal, sympathetic way to the invalid's spouse; and in financial terms to a number of potential contributors in order to solicit funds for heart disease research.

The following paragraph describes one student's fond memories of visiting a farm. As you read it, notice the writer's use of subjective description to communicate to her readers the multitude of contradictory feelings she connects with this rural retreat.

> *The shrill scream of the alarm shatters a dream. This is the last day of my visit to the place I call "the farm," an old ramshackle house in the country owned by one of my aunts. I want to go out once more in the peace of the early morning, walk in the crisp and chilly fields, and breathe the sweet air. My body feels jarred as my feet hit the hard-packed clay dirt. I tune out my stiff muscles and cold arms and legs and instead focus on two herons playing hopscotch on the canal bank. Every few yards I walk toward them, they fly one over the other an almost equal distance away from me. A killdeer with its piercing crystalline cry dips its body as it flies low over the water, the tip of its wing leaving a ring to reverberate outward. The damp earth has a strong, rich, musky scent. To the east, dust rises, and for the first time I hear the clanking and straining of a tractor as it harrows smooth the soil before planting. A crop duster rises close by just as it cuts off its release of spray, the acrid taste of chemicals filtering down through the air. As the birds chatter and peck at the fields, I reluctantly return to my life in the city.*

THINKING CRITICALLY THROUGH DESCRIPTION

Each rhetorical mode in this book gives us new insights into the process of thinking by providing different options for arranging our thoughts and our experiences. The more we know about these options, the more conscious we become of how our minds operate and the better chance we have to improve and refine our communication skills.

As you examine description as a way of thinking, consider it in isolation for a moment—away from the other rhetorical modes. Think of it as a muscle you can isolate and strengthen on its own in a weight-training program before you ask it to perform together with other muscles. By isolating description, you will learn more readily what it entails and how it functions as a critical thinking tool. In the process, you will also strengthen your knowledge of how to recognize and use description more effectively in your reading, in your writing, and in your daily life.

Just as you exercise to strengthen muscles, so too will you benefit from doing exercises to improve your skill in using descriptive techniques. As you have learned, description depends to a great extent on the keenness of your senses. So, as you prepare to read and write descriptive essays, do the following tasks so that you can first learn what the process of description feels like in your own head. Really use your imagination to play with these exercises on as many different levels as possible. Also write when you are asked to do so. The combination of thinking and writing is often especially useful when you practice your thinking skills.

Jedphoto/Fotolia.

1. Imagine what you might smell, taste, hear, feel, or see in the preceding photograph. Then, using words that will create these sensory details, write a few sentences that could accompany this photograph if it were published in a newspaper or travel magazine.
2. Make a list of five descriptive words you would use to trigger each of the following senses: taste, sight, hearing, touch, and smell.
3. Choose an unusual object and brainstorm about its physical characteristics. Then brainstorm about the emotions this object evokes. Why is this object so unusual or special? Compare your two brainstorming results, and draw some conclusions about their differences.

READING AND WRITING DESCRIPTIVE ESSAYS

All good descriptions share four fundamental qualities: (1) an accurate sense of audience (who the readers are) and purpose (why the essay was written), (2) a clear vision of the object being described, (3) a careful selection of details that help communicate the author's vision, and (4) a consistent point of view or perspective from which a writer composes. The dominant impression or main effect the writer wishes to leave with a specific audience dictates virtually all the verbal choices in a descriptive essay. Although description is featured in this chapter, you should also pay close attention to how other rhetorical strategies (such as example, division/classification, and cause/effect) can best support an essay's dominant impression.

Reading Descriptive Essays

Understanding how descriptive essays work rhetorically will help you make decisions for your own writing. Here is a flowchart of questions that will guide your reading for this purpose.

Questions to Guide Your Reading

PREPARING TO READ Before you read the essays, answer the following questions:

- What assumptions can you make from the essay's **title**?
- What do you think the general **mood** of the essay will be?
- What is the essay's **purpose** and **audience**?
- What does the **synopsis** tell you about the essay?
- What can you learn from the author's **biography**?
- What do you predict the author's **point of view** toward the subject will be?

READING As you read the essays for the first time, answer the following questions:

- What is the essay's **dominant impression**?
- Is the essay predominantly **objective or subjective**?
- What **senses** does the author engage?

REREADING When you read the essays again, answer the following questions:

- What **details** support the essay's dominant impression?
- How are these details **organized**?
- How does the essay **show rather than tell** the audience about its dominant impression?
- What other **rhetorical modes** does the author use?
- How does your understanding of the essay **change** with each rereading?

Preparing to Read.   As you approach the reading selections in this chapter, you should focus first on the author's title and try to make some initial assumptions about the essay that follows: Does Ray Bradbury reveal his attitude toward his subject in the title "Summer Rituals"? Can you guess what the general mood of Kimberly Wozencraft's "Notes from the Country Club" will be? Then scan the essay to discover its audience and purpose: Why does Garrison Keillor write an essay about "hopping"? Whom is Malcolm Cowley addressing in "The View from 80"? What do you think NASA's purpose is in "Mars"? You should also read the synopsis of each essay in the Rhetorical Table of Contents (on pages iii–xi); these brief summaries will provide you with helpful information at this point in the reading process.

Next, learn as much as you can about the author and the conditions under which the essay was composed; this information is provided in the biographical statement before each essay. For a descriptive essay, the conditions under which the author wrote the essay, coupled with his or her purpose, can be very revealing: When and under what conditions did Kimberly Wozencraft write "Notes from the Country Club"? What was her intention in writing the essay? Can you determine when Malcolm Cowley's piece was written? Does it describe the author's life now or in the past? Learning where the essay was first published will also give you valuable information about its audience.

Last, before you begin to read, try to do some brainstorming on the essay's title. In this chapter, respond to the Preparing to Read questions before each essay, which ask you to begin thinking and writing about the topic under consideration. At the same time, take advantage of the Internet prompt to help you find more information on the topic you are about to consider. Then pose your own questions: What are some of the most important rituals in your life (Bradbury)? What is one of your favorite scenes (Keillor)? What would you like to learn from NASA about Mars?

Reading.   As you read each essay for the first time, jot down your initial reactions to it, and try to make connections and see relationships among the author's biography; the essay's title, purpose, and audience; and the synopsis. In this way, you will create a context or framework for your reading. See if you can figure out, for example, what Bradbury is implying about rituals in general in his essay "Summer Rituals" or why Wozencraft wrote an essay about her experiences in prison. Try to discover what the relationships are among purpose, audience, and publication information in Cowley's essay.

Also, determine at this point if the author's treatment of his or her subject is predominantly objective (generally free of emotion) or subjective (heavily charged with emotion). Or perhaps the essay falls somewhere between these two extremes.

In addition, make sure you have a general sense of the dominant impression each author is trying to convey. Such an initial approach to reading these descriptive selections will give you a foundation on which to analyze the material during your second, more in-depth reading.

To help you develop the ability to read critically, a set of questions at the bottom of the essays' pages will prompt you to make connections between ideas, apply the material to your own experiences, and draw analytical conclusions that prepare you to answer the questions after each essay and ultimately write an essay on a related topic. These questions extend the mental exercises you complete before you read each essay to the deeper thinking you must do in the activities at the end of the essays. Responding to these questions in writing is the best way to discover new, innovative ideas about your reading on any subject.

Finally, at the end of your first reading, take a look at the questions after each essay to make certain you can answer them. This material will guide your rereading.

Rereading.   As you reread these descriptive essays, notice each author's careful selection of details that support his or her dominant impression. Also try to determine how certain details add to and detract from that dominant impression and which senses the author is engaging to create this impression. Finally, determine how the writers show rather than tell their audience about the impression they are trying to make: How does Keillor create a sense of wonder in "Hoppers"? How does Cowley enable us to understand his experiences if we have never been eighty years old?

During this reading, try to find other rhetorical modes that support the description. Although the essays in this chapter describe various persons, places, or objects, all of the authors call on other rhetorical strategies (especially example and comparison/contrast) to communicate their descriptions. How do these various rhetorical strategies work together in each essay to create a coherent whole? In addition, all the authors attempt to get you to see their view of the world.

Finally, answering the questions after each essay will check your understanding of the author's main points and help you think critically about the essay in preparing for the discussion/writing assignments that follow.

For an inventory of the reading process, you may want to review the checklist at the end of Chapter 2.

Writing Descriptive Essays

Now that you see how description works in an essay, use the same features in your own writing. Here is a flowchart of questions that will guide you.

Questions to Guide Your Writing

PREPARING TO WRITE Before you start writing, answer these questions:

- What is your **purpose** or dominant impression?
- Who is your **audience**?

WRITING As you write your first draft, consider these questions:

- Is your dominant impression in your **thesis**?
- What is your **point of view** toward your subject (objective or subjective)?
- What **details** support your dominant impression?
- How did you **organize** your supporting details?
- Did you engage all five **senses**?
- How do you **show rather than tell** readers your description?

EDITING Be sure to proofread and edit your paper before turning it in.

- Are all your **sentences** complete?
- Do your words say exactly **what you mean**?
- Do you follow conventional **grammar and usage** rules?

REVISING After you write your first draft, use the following questions to revise your essay:

- Did you create the **dominant impression** you want to convey?
- Do you have a clear, consistent **point of view** toward your subject?
- Do your **details** support your dominant impression?
- Are these details **organized** to achieve your purpose?
- Which **senses** do you stimulate?
- Are you **showing rather than telling** in your description?
- Do you use **similes or metaphors** when appropriate?

Preparing to Write.   Before you choose a writing assignment, use the prewriting questions that follow each essay to help you discover your own ideas and opinions about the general topic of the essay. Next, choose an assignment or read the one assigned to you. Then, just as you do when you read an essay, you should determine the audience and purpose for your description (if these are not specified for you in the assignment). To whom are you writing? Why? Will an impartial, objective report be appropriate, or should you present a more emotional, subjective account to accomplish your task? In assessing your audience, you need to determine what they do and do not know about your topic. This information will help you make decisions about what you are going to say and how you will say it. Your purpose will be defined by what you intend your audience to know, think, or believe after they have read your descriptive essay. Do you want them to make up their own minds about summer rituals or old age, for example, based on an objective presentation of data, or do you hope to sway their opinions through a more subjective display of information? Or perhaps you will decide to blend the two techniques, combining facts and opinions to achieve the impression of personal certainty based on objective evidence. What dominant impression do you want to leave with your audience? As you might suspect, decisions regarding audience and purpose are as important to writing descriptions as they are to reading descriptions and will shape your descriptive essay from start to finish.

The second quality of good description concerns the object of your analysis and the clarity with which you present it to the reader. Whenever possible, you should thoroughly investigate the person, place, moment, or feeling you wish to describe, paying particular attention to its effect on each of your five senses. What can you see, smell, hear, taste, and touch as you examine it? If you want to describe your house, for example, begin by asking yourself a series of pertinent questions: How big is the house? What color is it? How many exterior doors does the house have? How many interior doors? Are any of the rooms wallpapered? If so, what are the colors and textures of that wallpaper? How many different shades of paint cover the walls? Which rooms have constant noises (for example, from clocks and other mechanical devices)? Are the kitchen appliances hot or cold to the touch? What is the quietest room in the house? The noisiest? What smells do you notice in the laundry? In the kitchen? In the basement? Most important, do any of these sensory questions trigger particular childhood memories? Although you will probably not use all these details in your descriptive essay, the process of generating and answering such detailed questions will help reacquaint you with the object of your description as it also assists you in designing and focusing your paper.

To help you generate some of these ideas, you may want to review the prewriting techniques introduced on pages 26–28.

Writing.   As you write, you must select details for your description with great care and precision so that you leave your reader with a specific impression. Pay special attention to the way you engage all five senses in your description. If, for instance, you want your audience to feel the warmth and comfort of your home, you might concentrate on describing the plush carpets, the big upholstered chairs, the inviting scent of hot apple cider, and the crackling fire. If, on the other hand, you want to gain your audience's sympathy, you might prefer to focus on the sparse austerity of your home environment: the bare walls, the quietness, the lack of color and decoration, the dim lighting, and the frigid temperature. You also want to make sure you omit unrelated ideas, such as a conversation between your parents you accidentally overheard. Your careful choice of details will help control your audience's reaction.

The next important quality of an effective descriptive essay is point of view, your physical perspective on your subject. Because the organization of your essay depends on your point of view, you need to choose a specific angle from which to approach your description. If you verbally jump around your home, referring first to a picture on the wall in your bedroom, next to the microwave in the kitchen, and then to the quilt on your bed, no reasonable audience will be able to follow your description. Nor will they want to. If, however, you move from room to room in some logical, sequential way, always focusing on the details you want your readers to know, you will be helping your audience form a clear, memorable impression of your home.

Your vision will become their vision. In other words, your point of view plays a part in determining the organization of your description. Working spatially, you could move from side to side (from one wall to another in the rooms we have discussed), from top to bottom (from ceiling to floor), or from far to near (from the farthest to the closest point in a room), or you might progress from large to small objects, from uninteresting to interesting, or from funny to serious. Whatever plan you choose should help you accomplish your purpose with your particular audience.

To make your impression even more vivid, you might use figurative language to fill out your descriptions. Using words figuratively means using them imaginatively rather than literally. The two most popular forms of figurative language are *simile* and *metaphor*. A *simile* is a comparison between two dissimilar objects or ideas introduced by *like* or *as*: "The rocking chairs sounded like crickets" (Bradbury). A *metaphor* is an implied comparison between two dissimilar objects or ideas and is not introduced by *like* or *as*: "Life for younger persons is still a battle royal of each against each" (Cowley). Besides enlivening your writing, figurative language helps your readers understand objects, feelings, and ideas that are complex or obscure by comparing them to those that are more familiar.

Revising.   As you reread each of your descriptive essays, play the role of your audience, and try to determine what dominant impression they will receive by the end of your reading.

For additional suggestions on the writing process, you may want to consult the Writing Checklist at the end of Chapter 3.

STUDENT ESSAY: DESCRIPTION AT WORK

In the following essay, a student relives some of her childhood memories through a subjective description of her grandmother's house. As you read it, pay particular attention to the different types of sensual details the student writer chooses to communicate her dominant impression of her grandmother's home. Notice also her use of carefully chosen details to *show* rather than *tell* us about her childhood reminiscences, especially her comparisons, which make the memory as vivid for the reader as it is for the writer.

Grandma's House

Writer's point of view or perspective — <u>My most vivid childhood memories</u> are set in my Grandma Goodlink's house, which is a curious blend of familiar and mysterious treasures. Grandma lived at the end of a dead-end street in the same house she had moved into on the first day of her marriage. That was half a century and thirteen children ago. A set of crumbly steps made of concrete mixed with gravel led up to her front door. I remember a big gap between the house and the steps, <u>as if someone had not pushed them up close enough to the house.</u> Anyone who looked into the gap <u>could see old toys and books</u> that had fallen into the crack behind the steps and had remained there, forever irretrievable.

Dominant impression

Comparison (simile)

Sight

Only a hook-type lock on the front door protected Grandma's many beautiful antiques. Her living room was set up <u>like a church or schoolroom</u>, with an <u>old purple velvet couch</u> against the far wall and two chairs immediately in front of the couch facing the same direction. <u>One-half of the couch was always buried in old clothes, magazines, and newspapers, and a lone shoe sat on top of the pile, a finishing touch to some bizarre modern sculpture.</u> To one side was an aged and <u>tuneless</u> upright piano with <u>yellowed keys</u>.

Comparison (simile)

Sight

Sight

Comparison (metaphor)

Sound

Sight

The ivory overlay was missing so that <u>the wood underneath showed through</u>, and many of the keys *Sight* <u>Sound</u> made only a <u>muffled and frustrating thump</u>, no matter how hard I pressed them. On the wall facing the piano was the room's only window, draped with <u>yellowed</u> *Sight* <u>lace curtains</u>. Grandma always left that window open.

Smell I remember sitting near it, <u>smelling the rain</u> while the curtains <u>tickled my face</u>.   *Touch*

For no apparent reason, <u>an old curtain</u> hung in the *Sight* door between the kitchen and the living room. In the kitchen, a large Formica-topped table always held at least a half-dozen varieties of <u>homemade jelly, as well</u> *Taste* <u>as a loaf of bread, gooseberry or cherry pies with the</u> <u>pits left in, boxes of cereal</u>, and anything else not requiring refrigeration, <u>as if the table served as a small,</u> *Comparison* <u>portable pantry</u>. Grandma's kitchen always <u>smelled of</u> (simile) *Smell* <u>toast</u>, and I often wondered—and still do—if she lived entirely on toast. <u>A hole had eaten through the kitchen</u> *Sight* <u>floor</u>, not just the warped yellow linoleum, but all the way through the floor itself. My sisters and I never wanted to take a bath at Grandma's house, because we discovered that anyone who lay on the floor face down and put one eye to the hole <u>could see the bathtub</u>, *Sight* which was kept in the <u>musty</u> basement because the *Smell* upstairs bathroom was too small.

The back bedroom was near the kitchen and adjacent to the basement stairs. I once heard one of my aunts call that room a firetrap, and indeed it was. The room was <u>wallpapered with the old newspapers</u> *Sight* Grandma liked to collect, and the bed was stacked high *Sight* with <u>my mother's and aunts' old clothes</u>. There was no space between the furniture in that room, only a narrow path against one wall leading to the bed. A sideboard was shoved against the opposite wall; a sewing table was pushed up against the sideboard; a short chest of drawers lay against the sewing table; and so on. But } *Sight* no one could identify these pieces of forgotten furniture without digging through the sewing patterns, half-made dresses, dishes, and books. Any outsider would just think this was a part of the room where the floor had been raised to about waist level, so thoroughly was the mass of furniture hidden.

Comparison (simile) Stepping off Grandma's sloping back porch was <u>like stepping into an enchanted forest</u>. The grass and weeds were hip level, with a tiny dirt path leading to nowhere, Comparison (simile) <u>as if it had lost its way in the jungle</u>. <u>A fancy white fence</u>, Sight courtesy of the neighbors, bordered the yard in back and vainly attempted to hold in the Sight <u>gooseberries, raspberries, and blackberries</u> that grew wildly along the side of Grandma's yard. Huge Sight <u>crabapple, cherry, and walnut trees</u> shaded the house and hid the sky. I used to stand under them and look up, pretending to be deep in a magic forest. The ground was <u>cool and damp</u> under my bare feet, even Touch in the middle of the day, and my head would fill with Smell the <u>sweet fragrance of mixed spring flowers</u> and the Sound <u>throaty cooing of doves</u> I could never find but could always hear. But, before long, the wind would shift, and the <u>musty aroma of petroleum</u> from a nearby Smell refinery would jerk me back to reality.

Grandma's house is indeed a place of wonderful memories. Just as her decaying concrete steps store the treasures of many lost childhoods, <u>her house still</u> Dominant <u>stands, guarding the memories of generations of</u> impression rephrased <u>children and grandchildren</u>.

Student Writer's Comments

Writing this descriptive essay was easy and enjoyable for me—once I got started. I decided to write about my grandmother's house because I knew it so well, but I had trouble coming up with the impression I wanted to convey to my readers. I have so many recollections of this place I didn't know which set of memories would be most interesting to others. So I began by brainstorming, forcing myself to think of images from all five senses.

After I had accumulated plenty of images, which triggered other memories I had completely forgotten, I began to write. I organized my essay spatially as if I were walking through Grandma's house room by room. I let my senses lead the way. Before I started writing, I had no idea how many paragraphs I would have, but as I meandered through the house recording my memories of sights, smells, sounds, tastes, and textures, I ended up writing one paragraph on each room, plus one for the yard. For this assignment, I wrote the three paragraphs about the inside of the house first; then, the introduction started to take shape in my head, so I got it down; and last, I wrote the paragraph on the backyard and my conclusion. At that point, my "dominant impression" came to me: This is a house that guards the memories of many generations. My grandmother has always lived in this house, and my mother has her own set of memories associated with this place too.

This focus for my paper made the revising process fairly easy, as I worked on the entire essay with a specific purpose in mind. Previously, my biggest problem had been that I had too many scattered memories and realized I had to be more selective. Once I had my dominant impression, I knew which images to keep and which to drop from my draft. Also, as I reworked my essay, I looked for ways to make my description more exciting and vivid for the reader—as if he or she were right there with me. To accomplish this, I explained some special features of my grandma's house by comparing them with items the reader would most likely be familiar with. I also worked, at this point, on making one paragraph flow into another by adding transitions that would move the reader smoothly from one group of ideas to the next. "Only a hook-type lock on the front door" got my readers into the living room. The old curtain between the kitchen and the living room moved my essay out of the living room and into the kitchen. I started my third paragraph about the indoors by saying "The back bedroom was near the kitchen and adjacent to the basement stairs" so my readers could get their bearings in relation to other parts of the house they had already been introduced to. Finally, I was satisfied that my essay was a clear, accurate description of my view of my grandma's house. My brother might have a completely different set of memories, but this was my version of a single generation of impressions organized, finally, into one coherent essay.

SOME FINAL THOUGHTS ON DESCRIPTION

Because description is one of the most basic forms of verbal communication, you will find descriptive passages in most of the reading selections throughout this text. Description provides you with the means to capture your audience's attention and clarify certain points in all of your writing. The examples chosen for the following section, however, are predominantly descriptive, the main purpose in each being to involve the readers' senses as vividly as possible. As you read through each of these essays, try to determine its intended audience and purpose, the object of the description, the extent to which details are included or excluded, and the author's point of view. Equipped with these four areas of reference, you can become an increasingly sophisticated reader and writer of descriptive prose.

RAY BRADBURY   (1920–2012)

Summer Rituals

Ray Bradbury is one of America's best-known and most loved writers of science fiction. His extensive publications include such popular novels as *The Martian Chronicles* (1950), *The Illustrated Man* (1951), *Fahrenheit 451* (1953), *Dandelion Wine* (1957), and *Something Wicked This Way Comes* (1962). He has also written dozens of short stories, poems, essays, plays, and radio and movie scripts (including the screenplay of John Huston's film version of *Moby Dick*). As a child, he escaped his strict Baptist upbringing through a steady diet of Jules Verne, H. G. Wells, and Edgar Rice Burroughs, along with Buck Rogers and Prince Valiant comic books: "I was a sucker for lies, beautiful, fabulous lies, which instruct us to better our lives as a result, but which don't tell the truth." A frequent theme in his many novels is the impact of science on humanity: "My stories are intended," he claims, "as much to forecast how to prevent dooms, as to predict them." Bradbury's more recent publications include *The Last Circus* (1981), *The Complete Poems of Ray Bradbury* (1982), *The Love Affair* (1983), *Dinosaur Tales* (1983), *A Memory for Murder* (1984), *Forever and the Earth* (1984), *Death Is a Lonely Business* (1985), *The Toynbee Convector* (1989), *A Day in the Life of Hollywood* (1992), *Quicker Than the Eye* (1996), *Driving Blind* (1998), *From the Dust Returned* (2000), *Let's All Kill Constance* (2003), and *Bradbury Speaks: Too Soon from the Cave, Too Far from the Stars* (2005). The author lived in Cheviot Hills, California, where he enjoyed painting and making ceramics. His advice to student writers was to "look for obvious answers to impossible futures."

Preparing to Read

"Summer Rituals," an excerpt from *Dandelion Wine,* describes the comfortable ceremony of putting up a front-porch swing in early summer. Focusing on the perceptions of Douglas, a young boy, the essay clearly sets forth the familiar yet deeply significant rhythms of life in a small town.

Exploring Experience: Before you read this selection, take a few moments to consider the value of ritual in your own life: Can you think of any activities that you and your family have elevated to the level of ceremonial importance? What about holidays? Birthdays? Sporting events? Spring cleaning? When do these activities take place? Do the same people participate in them every year? Why do you repeat these rituals? What purpose do they have for you? For others whom you know? For society in general?

LEARNING⏻NLINE Go to Bing Images or Google Images, and search for "summer photos." Find a picture that represents summer to you. Study the picture, and think about how you would describe the location or moment in time.

Before reading this essay, you may want to consult the flowchart on page 44.

Yes, summer was rituals, each with its natural time and place. The   1
ritual of lemonade or ice-tea making, the ritual of wine, shoes, or
no shoes, and at last, swiftly following the others, with quiet dignity, the ritual of the front-porch swing. [1]

On the third day of summer in the late afternoon Grandfather reappeared   2
from the front door to gaze serenely at the two empty eye rings in the ceiling
of the porch. Moving to the geranium-pot-lined rail like Ahab surveying
the mild day and the mild-looking sky, he wet his finger to test the wind,
and shucked his coat to see how shirt sleeves felt in the westering hours. He
acknowledged the salutes of other captains on yet other flowered porches,
out themselves to discern the gentle ground swell of weather, oblivious to
their wives chirping or snapping like fuzzball hand dogs hidden behind black
porch screens.

"All right, Douglas, let's set it up."   3

In the garage they found, dusted, and carried forth the howdah, as it   4
were, for the quiet summer-night festivals, the swing chair, which Grandpa
chained to the porch-ceiling eyelets.

Douglas, being lighter, was first to sit in the swing. Then, after a moment,   5
Grandfather gingerly settled his pontifical weight beside the boy. Thus they
sat, smiling at each other, nodding, as they swung silently back and forth,
back and forth.

Ten minutes later Grandma appeared with water buckets and brooms to   6
wash down and sweep off the porch. Other chairs, rockers and straight-
backs, were summoned from the house.

"Always like to start sitting early in the season," said Grandpa, "before the   7
mosquitoes thicken."

About seven o'clock you could hear the chairs scraping back from the   8
tables, someone experimenting with a yellow-toothed piano, if you stood
outside the dining-room window and listened. Matches being struck, the
first dishes bubbling in the suds and tinkling on the wall racks, somewhere,
faintly, a phonograph playing. And then as the evening changed the hour,
at house after house on the twilight streets, under the immense oaks and
elms, on shady porches, people would begin to appear, like those figures
who tell good or bad weather in rain-or-shine clocks. [2]

Uncle Bert, perhaps Grandfather, then Father, and some of the cousins;   9
the men all coming out first into the syrupy evening, blowing smoke, leaving the women's voices behind in the cooling-warm kitchen to set their

---

Thinking Critically

[1] How can rituals bring dignity to our lives?

[2] How does Bradbury speed up and slow down time? Mark all the time references you can
find, and examine them after you finish the essay.

universe aright. Then the first male voices under the porch brim, the feet up, the boys fringed on the worn steps or wooden rails where sometime during the evening something, a boy or a geranium pot, would fall off.

At last, like ghosts hovering momentarily behind the door screen, Grandma, Great-grandma, and Mother would appear, and the men would shift, move, and offer seats. The women carried varieties of fans with them, folded newspapers, bamboo whisks, or perfumed kerchiefs, to start the air moving about their faces as they talked.   10

What they talked of all evening long, no one remembered next day. It wasn't important to anyone what the adults talked about; it was only important that the sounds came and went over the delicate ferns that bordered the porch on three sides; it was only important that the darkness filled the town like black water being poured over the houses and that the cigars glowed and that the conversations went on and on. The female gossip moved out, disturbing the first mosquitoes so they danced in frenzies on the air. The male voices invaded the old house timbers; if you closed your eyes and put your head down against the floor boards you could hear the men's voices rumbling like a distant, political earthquake, constant, unceasing, rising or falling a pitch. ❸   11

Douglas sprawled back on the dry porch planks, completely contented and reassured by these voices, which would speak on through eternity, flow in a stream of murmurings over his body, over his closed eyelids, into his drowsy ears, for all time. The rocking chairs sounded like crickets, the crickets sounded like rocking chairs, and the moss-covered rain barrel by the dining-room window produced another generation of mosquitoes to provide a topic of conversation through endless summers ahead.   12

Sitting on the summer-night porch was so good, so easy and so reassuring that it could never be done away with. These were rituals that were right and lasting; the lighting of pipes, the pale hands that moved knitting needles in the dimness, the eating of foil-wrapped, chill Eskimo Pies, the coming and going of all the people. For at some time or other during the evening, everyone visited here; the neighbors down the way, the people across the street; Miss Fern and Miss Roberta humming by in their electric runabout, giving Tom or Douglas a ride around the block and then coming up to sit down and fan away the fever in their cheeks; or Mr. Jonas, the junkman, having left his horse and wagon hidden in the alley, and ripe to bursting with words, would come up the steps looking as fresh as if his talk had never been said before, and somehow it never had. And last of all, the children, who had been off squinting their way through a last hide-and-seek or   13

Thinking Critically

❸ How many different sound images can you find in the essay? How do these images help characterize Douglas, the young narrator? Which specific sounds are most memorable for him?

kick-the-can, panting, glowing, would sickle quietly back like boomerangs along the soundless lawn, to sink beneath the talking talking talking of the porch voices which would weigh and gentle them down. . . . ◆

Oh, the luxury of lying in the fern night and the grass night and the night   14 of susurrant, slumbrous voices weaving the dark together. The grownups had forgotten he was there, so still, so quiet Douglas lay, noting the plans they were making for his and their own futures. And the voices chanted, drifted, in moonlit clouds of cigarette smoke while the moths, like late appleblossoms come alive, tapped faintly about the far street lights, and the voices moved on into the coming years. . . .

UNDERSTANDING DETAILS

1. What are the main similarities and differences between Douglas and Grandfather in this essay? How are their views of the world the same? How are their views different?

2. From the scattered details you have read in this essay, describe Douglas's house. How large do you think the front porch is? What color is the house? How many trees and shrubs surround it? What part of your description is based on facts in the essay? What part comes from inferences you have made on your own?

3. How do the men differ from the women in this excerpt? Divide a piece of paper into two columns; then list as many qualities of each gender as you can find. (For example, the narrator hears the men's voices "rumbling" like an "earthquake"; in contrast, the women move like "ghosts," their gossip "disturbing the . . . mosquitoes.") What other descriptive differences can you find between the men and women? What conclusions can you draw from these differences?

4. How did the conversation blend with the surroundings in Bradbury's description?

READING CRITICALLY

5. A "ritual" may be briefly defined as "a customarily repeated act that expresses a system of values." Using this definition, explain why the ritual of the front-porch swing is important to Douglas's family. What feelings or implicit values lie behind this particular ritual?

6. What other rituals are mentioned in this essay? How are they related to the front-porch swing? To summer? To Douglas and his family?

7. Bradbury helps us feel the comfort, warmth, and familiarity of the scene depicted in this essay through the use of a number of original descriptive details:

Thinking Critically

◆ What is the relationship between the children's games and the adult rituals that Bradbury mentions? In what way can children's games be called "rituals"?

for example, "summer-night festivals," "yellow-toothed piano," "rain-or-shine clocks," "syrupy evening," and "foil-wrapped, chill Eskimo Pies." Find at least five other descriptive words or phrases, and explain how each enables us to identify with the characters and situations in this story. Which of the five senses does each of these details stimulate in the reader?

8. In what ways do you think Douglas was "completely contented and reassured" (paragraph 12) by the voices around him? Why did Douglas feel this contentment would last "for all time" (paragraph 12)?

DISCOVERING RHETORICAL STRATEGIES

9. Some of the author's sentences are very long and involved, whereas others are quite short. What effects do these changes in sentence length have on you as a reader? Give a specific example of a shift in length from one sentence to another, and explain its effect.

10. This descriptive essay is filled with many interesting similes (comparisons using the words *like* or *as*) and metaphors (comparisons without *like* or *as*). For example, Grandfather standing on the front porch looks *like* Ahab, the possessed sea captain from Herman Melville's epic novel *Moby Dick* (paragraph 2). Later, Bradbury uses a metaphor to focus his readers on "the night of susurrant, slumbrous voices weaving the dark together" (paragraph 14). Find at least one other comparison, either a simile or a metaphor, and explain how it works within the context of its sentence or paragraph. What type of comparison is being made (a simile or a metaphor)? What do we learn about the object being described (for example, Grandfather or the night) through its association with the other reference (in this case, Ahab or "voices weaving the dark together")?

11. What is the point of view of the author in this selection? Would the essay be more effective if it were reported from the standpoint of Douglas? Of Grandfather? Of the women? Why or why not? How does the author's point of view help Bradbury organize his description? Should the fact that Bradbury's middle name is Douglas have any bearing on our interpretation of this story?

12. Although Bradbury draws mainly on description to write this essay, what other rhetorical strategies work together to help the reader grasp the full effect of "Summer Rituals"? Give examples of each strategy.

MAKING CONNECTIONS

13. For Douglas, hanging the porch swing was an important yearly ritual. What rituals can you find in the family backgrounds of Russell Baker ("The Saturday Evening Post") and/or Michael Dorris ("The Broken Cord")? What specific meanings did these rituals have within each author's family?

14. Compare and contrast Bradbury's neighborhood with that of Robert Ramirez ("The Barrio"). Which neighborhood would you feel more comfortable in? Why would you feel comfortable there?

15. Which author's relationship with his or her parents is most like your own: Ray Bradbury's, Sandra Cisneros's ("Only Daughter"), or Russell Baker's ("The

Saturday Evening Post")? How did each of these children relate differently to his or her parents?

IDEAS FOR DISCUSSION/WRITING

Preparing to Write

List some of the most important rituals in your life: How many times a year do these rituals occur? What purpose do they serve? How do rituals help create a strong social framework in your life? In your friends' lives? In society in general?

Choosing a Topic

MyWritingLab™

1. **LEARNING⏻NLINE** Using either a photo that has special meaning for you or an image you found on the Internet in Preparing to Read, write an essay describing a moment or place suspended in time. Following Bradbury's approach to his topic, develop your narrative through concrete and consistent details.
2. Write a descriptive essay about a ritual that is significant in your life, addressing it to someone who has never experienced that particular activity. Include the people involved and the setting. Try to use all five senses in your description.
3. Choose a ritual that is part of your family life, and write an essay describing your feelings about this ceremonial event. Address it to someone outside your family. Use similes and metaphors to make your description as vivid as possible.
4. Explain to someone visiting the United States for the first time the value of a particular tradition in American society. Then help this person understand the importance of that tradition in your life.

Before beginning your essay, you may want to consult the flowchart on page 47.

KIMBERLY WOZENCRAFT   (1954–   )

Notes from the Country Club

Kimberly Wozencraft grew up in Dallas, Texas, and dropped out of college when she was 21 to become a police officer. Her first assignment after training at the police academy was a street-level undercover narcotics investigation. Like many narcotics agents, Wozencraft became addicted to drugs, which impaired her judgment and resulted in a 1981 conviction for violating the civil rights of a reputed child pornographer. After serving an eighteen-month sentence in the Federal Correctional Institution at Lexington, Kentucky, she moved to New York City, where she raised her three children. She holds a Master of Fine Arts degree from Columbia University, and her essays, poems, and short stories have appeared in a variety of publications, including *Northwest Review, Quarto, Big Wednesday, Witness, Texas Monthly, New York Newsday,* and the *Los Angeles Times.* Her first novel, *Rush,* was made into a movie in 1991 starring Jennifer Jason Leigh. In 1998, she completed two more books, *The Catch* and *Slam* (with Richard Stratton), followed by *Wanted* in 2004. Her most recent novel, *The Devil's Backbone,* was published in 2006. Wozencraft has also written for HBO and is an editor of *Prison Life* magazine, a publication concerned with the rights of the incarcerated as well as the effects of the cost of funding prisons on the American economy. Currently, she is working on a new novel and a script. Her advice to college writers is to read as much as possible. She confesses, "I used to read books late at night under the covers when I was a child."

Preparing to Read

Originally published in *Witness,* "Notes from the Country Club" was selected for inclusion in *The Best American Essays of 1988,* edited by Annie Dillard. Through carefully constructed prose, the author describes her prison environment and the anxiety caused by living for more than a year in such an alien, difficult place.

Exploring Experience: As you prepare to read this essay, take a moment to think about your own behavior in difficult situations: What kind of person do you become? How do you act toward other people? How is this behavior different from the way you usually act? How do you know when you're in a difficult situation? What do you generally do to relieve the tension? How successful are your solutions?

LEARNING◯NLINE Wozencraft's description of her experience as an undercover narcotics agent was made into a movie entitled *Rush.* To better understand her experience, go to www.mgm.com. Search for "Rush," and view photos from the film.

Before reading this essay, you may want to consult the flowchart on page 44.

They had the Haitians up the hill, in the "camp" section where they   1
used to keep the minimum security cases.[1] The authorities were
concerned that some of the Haitians might be diseased, so they
kept them isolated from the main coed prison population by lodging them
in the big square brick building surrounded by eight-foot chain-link with
concertina wire on top. We were not yet familiar with the acronym AIDS.

One or two of the Haitians had drums, and in the evenings when the rest   2
of us were in the Big Yard, the drum rhythms carried over the bluegrass to
where we were playing gin or tennis or softball or just hanging out waiting
for dark. When they really got going some of them would dance and sing.
Their music was rhythmic and beautiful, and it made me think of freedom.

There were Cubans loose in the population, spattering their guttural   3
Spanish in streams around the rectangular courtyard, called Central Park, at
the center of the prison compound. These were Castro's Boat People, guilty
of no crime in this country, but requiring sponsors before they could walk
the streets as free people.

Walking around the perimeter of Central Park was like taking a trip in   4
microcosm across the United States. Moving leftward from the main entrance,
strolling along under the archway that covers the wide sidewalk, you passed
the doorway to the Women's Unit, where I lived, and it was how I imagined
Harlem to be. There was a white face here and there, but by far most of them
were black. Ghetto blasters thunked out rhythms in the sticky evening air,
and folks leaned against the window sills, smoking, drinking Cokes, slinking,
and nodding. Every once in a while a joint was passed around, and always
there was somebody pinning, checking for hacks on patrol.

Past Women's Unit was the metal door to the Big Yard, the main   5
recreation area of three or four acres, two sides blocked by the building, two
sides fenced in the usual way—chain-link and concertina wire.[2]

Past the Big Yard you entered the Blue Ridge Mountains, a sloping grassy   6
area on the edge of Central Park, where the locals, people from Kentucky,
Tennessee, and the surrounding environs, sat around playing guitars and
singing, and every once in a while passing around a quart of hooch. They
make it from grapefruit juice and a bit of yeast smuggled out of the kitchen.
Some of the inmates who worked in Cable would bring out pieces of a black
foam rubber substance and wrap it around empty Cremora jars to make
thermos jugs of sorts. They would mix the grapefruit juice and yeast in the

---

Thinking Critically

[1] Does the first sentence catch your attention? Why or why not? How soon do you know
what kind of place the author is describing?

[2] Why do you think the prison has two different types of fences?

containers and stash them in some out-of-the-way spot for a few weeks until presto! you had hooch, bitter and tart and sweet all at once, only mildly alcoholic, but entirely suitable for evening cocktails in Central Park.

Next, at the corner, was the Commissary, a tiny store tucked inside the   7 entrance to Veritas, the second women's unit. It wasn't much more than a few shelves behind a wall of Plexiglas, with a constant line of inmates spilling out of the doorway. They sold packaged chips, cookies, pens and writing paper, toiletries, some fresh fruit, and the ever-popular ice cream, sold only in pints. You had to eat the entire pint as soon as you bought it, or else watch it melt, because there weren't any refrigerators. Inmates were assigned one shopping night per week, allowed to buy no more than seventy-five dollars' worth of goods per month, and were permitted to pick up a ten-dollar roll of quarters if they had enough money in their prison account. Quarters were the basic spending unit in the prison; possession of paper money was a shippable offense. [3] There were vending machines stocked with junk food and soda, and they were supposedly what the quarters were to be used for. But we gambled, we bought salami or fried chicken sneaked out by the food service workers, and of course people sold booze and drugs. The beggars stood just outside the Commissary door. Mostly they were Cubans, saying, "Oyez! Mira! Mira! Hey, Poppy, one quarter for me. One cigarette for me, Poppy?"

There was one Cuban whom I was especially fond of. His name was   8 Shorty. The name said it. He was only about five-two, and he looked just like Mick Jagger. I met him in Segregation, an isolated section of tiny cells where prisoners were locked up for having violated some institutional rule or another. They tossed me in there the day I arrived; again the authorities were concerned, supposedly for my safety. I was a police woman before I became a convict, and they weren't too sure that the other inmates would like that. Shorty saved me a lot of grief when I went into Seg. It didn't matter if you were male or female there, you got stripped and handed a tee shirt, a pair of boxer shorts and a set of Peter Pans—green canvas shoes with thin rubber soles designed to prevent you from running away. As if you could get past three steel doors and a couple of hacks just to start with. When I was marched down the hall between the cells, the guys started whistling and hooting, and they didn't shut up even after I was locked down. They kept right on screaming until finally I yelled out, "Yo no comprendo!" and they all moaned and said, "Another . . . Cuban," and finally got quiet. Shorty was directly across from me, I could see his eyes through the rectangular slot in my cell door. He rattled off a paragraph or two of Spanish, all of which was

---

Thinking Critically

[3] How do you feel about these prison rules? Are they appropriate for the situation, or are they too restrictive? Explain your reasoning.

lost on me, and I said quietly, "Yo no comprendo bien español. Yo soy de Texas, yo hablo inglés?" I could tell he was smiling by the squint of his eyes, and he just said, "Bueno." When the hacks came around to take us out for our mandatory hour of recreation, which consisted of standing around in the Rec area while two guys shot a game of pool on the balcony above the gym, Shorty slipped his hand into mine and smiled up at me until the hack told him to cut it out. He knew enough English to tell the others in Seg [4] that I was not really Spanish, but he kept quiet about it, and they left me alone.

Beyond the Commissary, near the door to the dining hall, was East St. Louis. The prison had a big portable stereo system, which they rolled out a few times a week so that an inmate could play at being a disc jockey. They had a good-sized collection of albums, and there was usually some decent jazz blasting out of there. Sometimes people danced, unless there were uptight hacks on duty to tell them not to. [5] 9

California was next. It was a laid back kind of corner near the doors to two of the men's units. People stood around and smoked hash or grass or did whatever drugs happened to be available and there was sometimes a sort of slow-motion game of handball going on. If you wanted drugs, this was the place to come. 10

If you kept walking, you would arrive at the Power Station, the other southern corner where the politicos-gone-wrong congregated. It might seem odd at first to see these middle-aged government mavens standing around in their Lacoste sport shirts and Sans-a-belt slacks, smoking pipes or cigars and waving their arms to emphasize some point or other. They kept pretty much to themselves and ate together at the big round tables in the cafeteria, sipping cherry Kool-Aid and pretending it was Cabernet Sauvignon. 11

That's something else you had to deal with—the food. It was worse than elementary school steam table fare. By the time they finished cooking it, it was tasteless, colorless, and nutritionless. The first meal I took in the dining room was lunch. As I walked toward the entry, a tubby fellow was walking out, staggering really, rolling his eyes as though he were dizzy. He stopped and leaned over, and I heard someone yell, "Watch out, he's gonna puke!" I ducked inside so as to miss the spectacle. They were serving some rubbery, faint pink slabs that were supposed to be ham, but I didn't even bother to taste mine. I just slapped at it a few times to watch the fork bounce off and then ate my potatoes and went back to the unit. 12

Thinking Critically

[4] What does the word "Seg" mean? What other prison slang can you find in the essay?
[5] To what extent does each location in the prison have its own ethnic identity?

Shortly after that I claimed that I was Jewish, having gotten the word from   13
a friendly New York lawyer who was in for faking some of his clients' immigration papers. The kosher line was the only way to get a decent meal in
there. In fact, for a long time they had a Jewish baker from Philadelphia
locked up, and he made some truly delicious cream puffs for dessert. They
sold for seventy-five cents on the black market, but once I had established
myself in the Jewish community, I got them as part of my regular fare. They
fed us a great deal of peanut butter on the kosher line; every time the "goyim"
got meat, we got peanut butter, but that was all right with me. Eventually I
was asked to light the candles at the Friday evening services, since none of
the real Jewish women bothered to attend. I have to admit that most of the
members of our little prison congregation were *genuine alter kokers,* but some
of them were amusing. And I enjoyed learning firsthand about Judaism. The
services were usually very quiet, and the music, the ancient intoning songs,
fortified me against the screeching pop-rock vocal assaults that were a constant in the Women's Unit. I learned to think of myself as the *shabot shiksa,*⁶
and before my time was up, even the rabbi seemed to accept me.

I suppose it was quite natural that the Italians assembled just "down the   14
street" from the offending ex-senators, judges, and power brokers. Just to the
left of the main entrance. The first night I made the tour, a guy came out of
the shadows near the building and whispered to me. "What do you need,
sweetheart? What do you want, I can get it. My friend Ahmad over there, he's
very rich, and he wants to buy you things. What'll it be, you want some smoke,
a few ludes, vodka, cigarettes, maybe some kosher salami fresh from the
kitchen? What would you like?" I just stared at him. The only thing I wanted
at that moment was out, and even Ahmad's millions, if they existed at all,
couldn't do that. The truth is, every guy I met in there claimed to be wealthy,
to have been locked up for some major financial crime. Had I taken all of them
up on their offers of limousines to pick me up at the front gate when I was
released and take me to the airport for a ride home in a private Lear jet, I
would have needed my own personal cop out front just to direct traffic.

Ahmad's Italian promoter eventually got popped for zinging the cooking   15
teacher one afternoon on the counter in the home economics classroom,
right next to the new Cuisinart. The assistant warden walked in on the
young lovebirds, and before the week was up, even the Cubans were walking
around singing about it. They had a whole song down, to the tune of
"Borracho Me Acosté a Noche."

At the end of the tour, you would find the jaded New Yorkers,⁷ sitting   16
at a picnic table or two in the middle of the park, playing gin or poker and

---

Thinking Critically

6 How does the use of foreign language here and elsewhere contribute to the tone of the essay?
7 Why do you think the New Yorkers are "jaded"?

bragging about their days on Madison Avenue and Wall Street, lamenting the scarcity of good deli, even on the kosher line, and planning where they would take their first real meal upon release.

If you think federal correctional institutions are about the business of 17
rehabilitation, drop by for an orientation session one day. There at the front of the classroom, confronting rows of mostly black faces, will be the warden, or the assistant warden, or the prison shrink, pacing back and forth in front of the blackboard and asking the class, "Why do you think you're here?" This gets a general grumble, a few short, choked laughs. Some well-meaning soul always says it—rehabilitation.

"Nonsense!" the lecturer will say. "There are several reasons for locking 18
people up. Number one is incapacitation. If you're in here, you can't be out there doing crime. Secondly, there is deterrence. Other people who are thinking about doing crime see that we lock people up for it and maybe they think twice. But the real reason you are here is to be punished. Plain and simple. You done wrong, now you got to pay for it. Rehabilitation ain't even part of the picture. [8] So don't be looking to us to rehabilitate you. Only person can rehabilitate you is you. If you feel like it, go for it, but leave us out. We don't want to play that game."

So that's it. You're there to do time. I have no misgivings about why I 19
went to prison. I deserved it. I was a cop; I got strung out on cocaine; I violated the rights of a pornographer. My own drug use as an undercover narcotics agent was a significant factor in my crime. But I did it, and I deserved to be punished. Most of the people I met in Lexington, though, were in for drugs, and the majority of them hadn't done anything more than sell an ounce of cocaine or a pound of pot to some apostle of the law.

It seems lately that almost every time I look at the *New York Times* op-ed 20
page, there is something about the drug problem. I have arrested people for drugs, and I have had a drug problem myself. I have seen how at least one federal correctional institution functions. It does not appear that the practice of locking people up for possession or distribution of an insignificant quantity of a controlled substance makes any difference at all in the amount of drug use that occurs in the United States. The drug laws are merely another convenient source of political rhetoric for aspiring officeholders. Politicians know that an antidrug stance is an easy way to get votes from parents who are terrified that their children might wind up as addicts. I do not advocate drug use. Yet, having seen the criminal justice system from several angles, as a police officer, a court bailiff, a defendant, and a prisoner, I am convinced

---

Thinking Critically

[8] Do you believe prison can rehabilitate its inmates? Why or why not?

that prison is not the answer to the drug problem, or for that matter to many other white-collar crimes. If the taxpayers knew how their dollars were being spent inside some prisons, they might actually scream out loud. [9]

There were roughly 1,800 men and women locked up in Lex, at a ratio   21 of approximately three men to every woman, and it did get warm in the summertime. To keep us tranquil they devised some rather peculiar little amusements. One evening I heard a commotion on the steps at the edge of Central Park and looked over to see a rec specialist with three big cardboard boxes set up on the plaza, marked 1, 2, and 3. There were a couple of hundred inmates sitting at the bottom of the steps. Dennis, the rec specialist, was conducting his own version of the television game show *Let's Make a Deal!* Under one of the boxes was a case of soda, under another was a racquetball glove, and under the third was a fly swatter. The captive contestant picked door number 2, which turned out to contain the fly swatter, to my way of thinking the best prize there. Fly swatters were virtually impossible to get through approved channels, and therefore cost as much as two packs of cigarettes on the black market.

Then there was the Annual Fashion Show, where ten or twenty inmates   22 had special packages of clothing sent in, only for the one evening, and modeled them on stage while the baddest drag queen in the compound moderated and everyone else ooohed and aahhed. They looked good up there on stage in Christian Dior and Ralph Lauren instead of the usual fatigue pants and white tee shirts. And if such activities did little to prepare inmates for a productive return to society, well, at least they contributed to the fantasyland aura that made Lexington such an unusual place.

I worked in Landscape, exiting the rear gate of the compound each   23 weekday morning at about nine after getting a half-hearted frisk from one of the hacks on duty. I would climb on my tractor to drive to the staff apartment complex and pull weeds or mow the lawn. Landscape had its prerogatives. [10] We raided the gardens regularly and at least got to taste fresh vegetables from time to time. I had never eaten raw corn before, but it could not have tasted better. We also brought in a goodly supply of real vodka, and a bit of hash now and then, for parties in our rooms after lights out. One guy strapped a six-pack of Budweiser to his arms with masking tape and then put on his prison-issue Army field jacket. When he got to the rear gate, he raised his arms straight out at shoulder level, per instructions, and the

---

Thinking Critically

[9] Do you think Wozencraft's opinions about the penalties for drug abuse have anything to do with the fact that she was a former drug addict?

[10] Why did most prisoners like Landscape duty?

hack patted down his torso and legs, never bothering to check his arms. The inmate had been counting on that. He smiled at the hack and walked back to his room, a six-pack richer.

I was fortunate to be working Landscape at the same time as Horace, a   24
fellow who had actually lived in the city of Lexington before he was locked up. His friends made regular deliveries of assorted contraband, which they would stash near a huge elm tree near the outer stone fence of the reservation. Horace would drive his tractor over, make the pickup, and the rest of us would carry it, concealed, through the back gate when we went back inside for lunch or at the end of the day. "Contraband" included everything from drugs to blue eye shadow. The assistant warden believed that female inmates should wear no cosmetics other than what she herself used—a bit of mascara and a light shade of lipstick. I have never been a plaything of Fashion, but I did what I could to help the other women prisoners in their never-ending quest for that Cover Girl look.

You could depend on the fact that most of the hacks would rather have   25
been somewhere else, and most of them really didn't care *what* the inmates did, as long as it didn't cause any commotion. Of course, there were a few you had to look out for. The captain in charge of security was one of them. We tried a little experiment once, after having observed that any time he saw someone laughing, he took immediate steps to make the inmate and everyone around him acutely miserable. Whenever we saw him in the area, we immediately assumed expressions of intense unhappiness, even of despair. Seeing no chance to make anyone more miserable than they already appeared to be, the captain left us alone.

Almost all of the female hacks, and a good number of the males, had   26
outrageously large derrières, a condition we inmates referred to as "the federal ass."[11] This condition may have resulted from the fact that most of them appeared, as one inmate succinctly described it, simply to be "putting in their forty a week to stay on the government teat." Employment was not an easy thing to find in Kentucky.

Despite the fact that Lexington is known as a "country club" prison,   27
I must admit that I counted days. From the first moment that I was in, I kept track of how many more times I would have to watch the sun sink behind eight feet of chain-link, of how many more days I would have to spend eating, working, playing, and sleeping according to the dictates of a "higher authority." I don't think I can claim that I was rehabilitated. If anything I

Thinking Critically

[11] What does the author mean by the term "the federal ass"?

underwent a process of dehabilitation. What I learned was what Jessica Mitford tried to tell people many years ago in her book *Kind and Usual Punishment*. Prison is a business,[12] no different from manufacturing tires or selling real estate. It keeps people employed, and it provides cheap labor for NASA, the U.S. Postal Service, and other governmental or quasi-governmental agencies. For a short time, before I was employed in Landscape, I worked as a finisher of canvas mailbags, lacing white rope through metal eyelets around the top of the bags and attaching clamps to the ropes. I made one dollar and fourteen cents for every one hundred that I did. If I worked very hard, I could do almost two hundred a day.

It's not about justice. If you think it's about justice, look at the newspapers   28 and notice who walks. Not the little guys, the guys doing a tiny bit of dealing or sniggling a little on their income tax, or the woman who pulls a stunt with welfare checks because her husband has skipped out and she has no other way to feed her kids. I do not say that these things are right. But the process of selective prosecution, the "making" of cases by D.A.s and police departments, and the presence of some largely unenforceable statutes currently on the books (it is the reality of "compliance": no law can be forced on a public which chooses to ignore it; hence, selective prosecution) make for a criminal justice system which cannot realistically function in a fair and equitable manner. Criminal justice—I cannot decide if it is the ultimate oxymoron or a truly accurate description of the law enforcement process in America.

In my police undercover capacity, I have sat across the table from an   29 armed robber who said, "My philosophy of life is slit thy neighbor's throat and pimp his kids." I believe that the human animals who maim and kill people should be dealt with, as they say, swiftly and surely. But this business of locking people up, at enormous cost, for minor, nonviolent offenses does not truly or effectively serve the interest of the people. It serves only to promote the wasteful aspects of the federal prison system, a system that gulps down tax dollars and spews up *Let's Make a Deal!*

I think about Lexington almost daily. I will be walking up Broadway to   30 shop for groceries, or maybe riding my bike in the original Central Park, and suddenly I'm wondering who's in there now, at this very moment, and for what inane violations, and what they are doing. Is it chow time, is the Big Yard open, is some inmate on stage in the auditorium singing "As Time Goes By" in a talent show? It is not a fond reminiscence or a desire to be back in the Land of No Decisions.[13] It is an awareness of the waste.

Thinking Critically

[12] In what way is prison a "business"?
[13] Why does the author refer to prison as "the Land of No Decisions"?

The waste of tax dollars, yes, but taxpayers are used to that. It is the unnecessary trashing of lives that leaves me uneasy. The splitting of families, the
enforced monotony, the programs which purport to prepare an inmate for
re-entry into society but which actually succeed only in occupying a few
more hours of the inmate's time behind the walls. The nonviolent offenders,
such as small-time drug dealers and the economically deprived who were
driven to crime out of desperation, could remain in society under less costly
supervision, still undergoing "punishment" for their crime, but at least contributing to rather than draining the resources of society.

Horace, who was not a subtle sort of fellow, had some tee shirts made up.   31
They were delivered by our usual supplier out in Landscape, and we wore
them back in over our regular clothes. The hacks tilted their heads when
they noticed, but said nothing. On the front of each shirt was an outline of
the state of Kentucky, and above the northwest corner of the state were the
words "Visit Beautiful Kentucky!" Inside the state boundary were

- Free Accommodations
- Complimentary Meals
- Management Holds Calls
- Recreational Exercise

In small letters just outside the southwest corner of the state was: "Length   32
of Stay Requirement."[14] And in big letters across the bottom:

Take Time to Do Time
F.C.I. Lexington

I gave mine away on the day I finished my sentence. It is a time-honored   33
tradition to leave some of your belongings to friends who have to stay
behind when you are released. But you must never leave shoes. Legend has
it that if you do, you will come back to wear them again.

UNDERSTANDING DETAILS

1. Draw Lexington prison, and put the names on the sections of the facility. Then
   describe each section in your own words.
2. Why was walking around the outside of Central Park "like taking a trip in
   microcosm across the United States" (paragraph 4)? Give examples to explain
   your answer.
3. Why was Wozencraft especially fond of Shorty? What secret did they share at
   the beginning of the author's prison term?

Thinking Critically

[14] In what ways do you think a sense of humor would be helpful to inmates doing time in
prison?

4. Does the author feel she was unfairly punished by being sent to prison? What had she done wrong?

READING CRITICALLY

5. What was Wozencraft's attitude toward other people in Lexington prison? Why do you think she felt this way? What types of relationships did she have with inmates and staff members?
6. Why does the author say, "If the taxpayers knew how their dollars were being spent inside some prisons, they might actually scream out loud" (paragraph 20)? What exactly is she referring to? What is she implying? Give some examples.
7. Why do you think Lexington is known as a "country club" prison? What features of the prison might have generated its nickname?
8. Wozencraft feels strongly that people who perform minor, nonviolent crimes should not be put in prison. Why does she feel this way? Who should be locked up, according to the author? From her point of view, how does rehabilitation take place?

DISCOVERING RHETORICAL STRATEGIES

9. This essay is organized predominantly as a clockwise tour of Lexington prison. How and when does Wozencraft introduce the facts about her own imprisonment and her opinions about the current American system of justice? Explain in as much detail as you can the effect of integrating the guided tour and the related facts and opinions.
10. Wozencraft uses specific prison jargon throughout this essay. In what way does this jargon add to or detract from the essay? What effect would the essay have without this jargon?
11. Wozencraft ends her essay with an explanation of "a time-honored tradition." Is this an effective ending for the piece? Why or why not?
12. Though spatial description is the dominant rhetorical strategy the author uses in this essay to accomplish her purpose, what other strategies help make the essay effective? Give examples of these strategies.

MAKING CONNECTIONS

13. If Kimberly Wozencraft, John Tierney ("A Generation's Vanity, Heard Through Lyrics"), Robert Ramirez ("The Barrio"), and/or Mary Pipher ("Beliefs About Families") were discussing the importance of belonging to a "community," which of the authors you read would argue most strongly that community is a positive force in our lives? Explain your answer.
14. Malcolm Cowley ("The View from 80"), Sandra Cisneros ("Only Daughter"), Harold Krents ("Darkness at Noon"), and Elizabeth Svoboda ("Virtual Assault") explain situations in which people feel imprisoned in much the same way Wozencraft does in her essay. In what ways does each of these authors deal with "confinement"? Have you ever felt imprisoned for any reason? Why? How did you escape?

15. What would Wozencraft, Robert Ramirez ("The Barrio"), and/or Samantha Pugsley ("How Language Impacts the Stigma Against Mental Health (And What We Must Do to Change It)") have to say about the importance of relying on other people to help endure difficult or challenging situations? How much do you rely on friends and relatives in your own life? How comfortable are you with these relationships?

IDEAS FOR DISCUSSION/WRITING

Preparing to Write

Write freely about your memories of a recent difficult or awkward situation in your life: What were the circumstances? What did you do? What did others do? How did you relate to others in this situation? Why was the situation so difficult? How did you get out of it?

Choosing a Topic

MyWritingLab™

1. **LEARNING⏻NLINE** In this essay, Wozencraft develops a descriptive narrative from personal experience. As in the movie version you viewed on the Internet in Preparing to Read, she "shows" rather than "tells" her readers about Lexington prison's attitude toward rehabilitation. Compose either an email to a friend not attending college or a brief script for a movie that describes your current educational experience. Try to show rather than tell your observations, achievements, frustrations, and unique experiences. Remember to organize your descriptions to convey a clear and consistent message.

2. Write an essay describing for your peers a difficult or awkward situation you have been in recently. Why was it awkward? Explain the specific circumstances so that your classmates can clearly imagine the setting and the difficulty or problem. Then discuss your reaction to the situation.

3. A friend of yours has just been sentenced to prison for one year. Write a letter to this person describing what you think his or her biggest adjustments will be.

4. Wozencraft describes many problems within the prison system. With these problems in mind, write a letter to the editor of your local newspaper discussing whether prisons actually rehabilitate criminals. Use examples from Wozencraft's essay to help make your point.

Before beginning your essay, you may want to consult the flowchart on page 47.

Hoppers

Best known for his creation of the Peabody Award-winning radio program *A Prairie Home Companion*, Garrison Keillor, a native of Anoka, Minnesota, began his career as a radio announcer and producer during his student days at the University of Minnesota. His show, still on the air today, features an eclectic mix of traditional jazz and folk music, supplemented by Keillor's rambling, nostalgic, and often hilarious anecdotes about the zany inhabitants of the fictitious small town of Lake Wobegon, Minnesota. Chief among its residents are Father Emil, the local priest, who blesses small animals on the lawn of Our Lady of Perpetual Responsibility Church; Dorothy, the garrulous owner of the Chatterbox Café; and Dr. Nute, a retired dentist who coaxes trout toward his fishing lure by intoning, "Open wide . . . this may sting a bit." Keillor—a tall, soft-spoken man who often performs in a tuxedo, high-top sneakers, red socks, and red suspenders—even has a pseudo-sponsor for the show: Powdermilk Biscuits, "a whole-wheat treat that gives shy people the strength to do what has to be done." Thus far, Keillor's monologues have spawned a number of short stories published in *The New Yorker*, along with several books, including *Happy to Be Here* (1982), *Lake Wobegon Days* (1985), *Leaving Home* (1987), *We Are Still Married* (1989), *Good Poems* (2002), *Homegrown Democrat* (2004), *A Christmas Blizzard* (2009), *Good Poems, American Places* (2011), and *The Keillor Reader* (2014). His first book of original poems, entitled *O, What a Luxury*, was published in 2013.

Preparing to Read

Originally published in the *New Yorker* magazine (April 11, 1988), this early essay by Garrison Keillor describes the many different ways pedestrians jump over a stream of water flowing down Seventh Avenue in New York on a beautiful spring day.

Exploring Experience: Humans come in a wide array of types. What are some of these types? What are the differences among them? What activities capture these differences? How do these various types enrich society as a whole? How do they cause problems in society?

LEARNING☺NLINE Before reading Keillor's essay, go to www.wikihow. com, and search "How to Begin People Watching." As you look at the nine steps in this article, pay special attention to step one. Consider the reasons people watch other people. Then, as you read the following essay, think about Keillor's perspective on the "hoppers" he describes.

Before reading this essay, you may want to consult the flowchart on page 44.

A hydrant was open on Seventh Avenue above 23rd Street last Friday morning, and I stopped on my way east and watched people hop over the water. It was a brilliant spring day. The water was a nice clear creek about three feet wide and ran along the gutter around the northwest corner of the intersection. A gaggle of pedestrians crossing 23rd went *hop hop hop hop hop* over the creek as a few soloists jaywalking Seventh performed at right angles to them, and I got engrossed in the dance. Three feet isn't a long leap for most people, and the ease of it permits a wide range of expression. Some hoppers went a good deal higher than necessary. [1]

Long, lanky men don't hop, as a rule. The ones I saw hardly paused at the water's edge, just lengthened one stride and trucked on across—a rather flatfooted approach that showed no recognition of the space or occasion. Tall men typically suffer from an excess of cool, but I kept hoping for one of them to get off the ground. Most of the tall men wore topcoats and carried briefcases, so perhaps their balance was thrown off. One tall man in a brown coat didn't notice the water and stepped off the curb into the fast-flowing Hydrant Creek and made a painful hop, like a wounded heron: a brown heron with a limp wing attached to a briefcase bulging full of dead fish. He crossed 23rd looking as though his day had been pretty much shot to pieces.

Short, fat men were superb: I could have watched them all morning. A typical fat man crossing the street would quicken his step when he saw the creek and, on his approach, do a little shuffle, arms out to the sides, and suddenly and with great concentration *spring*—a nimble step all the more graceful for the Springer's bulk. Three fairly fat men jiggled and shambled across 23rd together, and then one poked another and they saw the water. They stepped forward, studying the angle, and just before the point man jumped for the curb his pals said something, undoubtedly discouraging, and he threw back his head and laughed over his shoulder and threw himself lightly, boyishly, across the water, followed—boing *boing*—by the others. [2]

The women who hopped the water tended to stop and study the creek and find its narrows and measure the distance and then lurch across. They seemed dismayed that the creek was there at all, and one, in a beige suit, put her hands on her hips and glared upstream, as if to say, "Whose water *is* this? This is utterly unacceptable. I am *not* about to jump over this." But then she

---

Thinking Critically

[1] Have you ever watched people when they didn't know they were being observed? What were they doing? What was interesting about them?

[2] How does Keillor compare and contrast the ways different types of people jump over the water? What do these distinctions tell us about the personalities of the jumpers?

made a good jump after all. She put her left toe on the edge of the curb, leaned forward with right arm outstretched—for a second, she looked as if she might take off and zoom up toward the Flatiron Building—and pushed off, landing easily on her right toe, her right arm raised. The longest leap was made by a young woman in a blue raincoat carrying a plastic Macy's bag and crossing west on Seventh. She gathered herself up in three long, accelerating strides and sailed, her coat billowing out behind her, over the water and five feet beyond, almost creaming a guy coming out of Radio Shack. He shrank back as she loped past, her long black hair and snow-white hands and face right *there,* then gone, vanished in the crowd.

And then it was my turn. I waited for the green light, crossed 23rd,   5 stopped by the creek flowing around the bend of curb and heard faint voices of old schoolmates ahead in the woods, and jumped heavily across and marched after them.[3]

UNDERSTANDING DETAILS

1. What were the main differences between the jumps of the "long, lanky men" and the "short, fat men"?
2. What characterizes the "hops" of the women?
3. What details from this description are most vivid to you? Explain your answer.
4. Which specific senses are represented in this essay?

READING CRITICALLY

5. Why do you think Keillor could have watched the "short, fat men" all morning (paragraph 3)?
6. Draw a picture of the longest jump (paragraph 4). What details of this "hop" are most striking to you?
7. What was unusual about the author's jump?
8. What makes Keillor's description most interesting to you? What is its significance?

DISCOVERING RHETORICAL STRATEGIES

9. What do you think is the author's dominant impression?
10. Keillor refers to people as a "gaggle of pedestrians" in paragraph 1. What does this metaphor bring to mind for you? Is this an effective image for the essay? Explain your answer.
11. What do the words "*hop hop hop hop hop*" add to this essay?
12. How does Keillor organize his description? (See the chapter introduction for patterns of organization.)

Thinking Critically

[3] Do you suspect anyone was watching the author as he jumped? How do you think they would have described his leap over the water? How would you characterize Keillor physically based on his brief description of his own jump?

MAKING CONNECTIONS

13. Imagine that Keillor, Gloria Steinem ("The Politics of Muscle"), David Hanson ("Binge Drinking"), and/or Michael Dorris ("The Broken Cord") were having a discussion about the validity of inferring people's personality traits from their physical actions. Which author would say that this predictor was usually accurate and valid? Who would argue that people's size, shape, actions, and other physical characteristics seldom forecast personality types?

14. Keillor, Sara Gilbert ("The Different Ways of Being Smart"), Robert Ramirez ("The Barrio"), and Dave Grossman ("We Are Training Our Kids to Kill") are keen observers of the world around them. Which author's descriptions seem most vivid and realistic to you? Why?

15. How does Keillor's system of classifying the jumpers differ from similar division/classification techniques used by Karen Lachtanski ("Match the Right Communication Type to the Occasion") and Sarah Toler ("Understanding the Birth Order Relationship")? Which author's categories are most understandable? Why?

IDEAS FOR DISCUSSION/WRITING

Preparing to Write

Write freely about a scene that was interesting to you: Who was in this scene? What were the participants doing? Why were they at this location? What was happening? What senses help you describe this scene?

Choosing a Topic

MyWritingLab™

1. **LEARNING◯NLINE** After reading "Hoppers," use some information from "How to Begin People Watching" in Preparing to Read to do a little people watching of your own. Find a comfortable place where you are sure to see many different people. Using all your senses, observe others and take notes for thirty minutes. Then, write an essay describing what you noticed during this exercise.

2. You have been asked to write an article for your high school newspaper on the most memorable scene you have ever witnessed. Explore your thoughts on this topic; then write an essay that will appeal to the values and concerns of today's high school students.

3. Why do we view events so differently? When several people watch the same activity, they often see it in very different ways. How can this happen? Write an essay explaining this phenomenon.

4. In paragraph 1, Keillor indirectly compares pedestrians to geese in the phrase "a gaggle of pedestrians." Think of another comparison involving human beings that teaches us important truths about ourselves; then, using Keillor's essay as a model, write an essay that explores this comparison and leads us to new insights about our shared humanity.

Before beginning your essay, you may want to consult the flowchart on page 47.

The View from 80

Malcolm Cowley had a long and distinguished career as a literary historian, critic, editor, and poet. After receiving his bachelor's degree at Harvard, he served in the American Ambulance Corps during World War I and then pursued graduate studies in literature at the University of Montpellier in France. In 1929, he became Associate Editor of *The New Republic,* presiding over the magazine's literary department for the next fifteen years. Perhaps his most important book of literary criticism is *Exile's Return* (1934), a study of the "lost generation" of expatriate Americans living in Paris in the 1920s, which included Ernest Hemingway, Ezra Pound, F. Scott Fitzgerald, and Hart Crane. Cowley returned to the same topic in 1973 with *A Second Flowering: Works and Days of the Lost Generation.* He also published editions of such authors as Hemingway, William Faulkner, Nathaniel Hawthorne, Walt Whitman, and Fitzgerald; two collections of his own poetry, *Blue Juniata* (1929) and *The Dry Season* (1941); and numerous other translations, editions, and books of criticism. His most recent publications include *The Flower and the Leaf: A Contemporary Record of American Writing Since 1941* (1985) and *Conversations with Malcolm Cowley* (1986). When asked about the secret of his amazing productivity, Cowley replied, "Writers often speak of 'saving their energy,' as if each man were given a nickel's worth of it, which he is at liberty to spend. To me, the mind of the poet resembles Fortunatus's purse: The more spent, the more it supplies."

Preparing to Read

The following essay was originally commissioned by *Life* magazine (1978) for inclusion in a series of articles on aging. Cowley later converted the piece into the first chapter of a book with the same title: *The View from 80* (1980). Through a combination of vivid personal experience and research, the author crafted an essay that helps us experience what life is like for an eighty-year-old.

Exploring Experience: As you prepare to read Cowley's description of "the country of age," take some time to think about age in general: How many people over the age of sixty do you know? Over the age of seventy? How do they behave? Do you think these older people see themselves in the same way you see them? Do you think they consider themselves "old"? What clues remind them of their advancing age? What events and attitudes remind you of your age? In what ways will you be different than you are now when you reach the age of eighty?

LEARNING〇NLINE Visit the website of the American Association of Retired Persons (www.aarp.org), and read about some of the issues affecting the elderly. Use the left side bar on the homepage to guide your search. Keep these in mind while reading Cowley's observations about aging.

Before reading this essay, you may want to consult the flowchart on page 44.

They gave me a party on my 80th birthday in August 1978. First there were cards, letters, telegrams, even a cable of congratulation or condolence; then there were gifts, mostly bottles; there was catered food and finally a big cake with, for some reason, two candles (had I gone back to very early childhood?). I blew the candles out a little unsteadily. Amid the applause and clatter I thought about a former custom of the Northern Ojibwas when they lived on the shores of Lake Winnipeg. They were kind to their old people, who remembered and enforced the ancient customs of the tribe, but when an old person became decrepit, it was time for him to go. Sometimes he was simply abandoned, with a little food, on an island in the lake. If he deserved special honor, they held a tribal feast for him. The old man sang a death song and danced, if he could. While he was still singing, his son came from behind and brained him with a tomahawk. ◆

That was quick, it was dignified, and I wonder whether it was any more cruel, essentially, than some of our civilized customs or inadvertencies in disposing of the aged. I believe in rites and ceremonies. I believe in big parties for special occasions such as an 80th birthday. It is a sort of belated bar mitzvah, since the 80-year-old, like a Jewish adolescent, is entering a new stage of life; let him (or her) undergo a *rite de passage,* with toasts and a cantor. Seventy-year-olds, or septuas, have the illusion of being middle-aged, even if they have been pushed back on a shelf. The 80-year-old, the octo, looks at the double-dumpling figure and admits that he is old. The last act has begun, and it will be the test of the play.

To enter the country of age is a new experience, different from what you supposed it to be. Nobody, man or woman, knows the country until he has lived in it and has taken out his citizenship papers. Here is my own report, submitted as a road map and guide to some of the principal monuments.

The new octogenarian feels as strong as ever when he is sitting back in a comfortable chair. He ruminates, he dreams, he remembers. He doesn't want to be disturbed by others. It seems to him that old age is only a costume assumed for those others; the true, the essential self is ageless. In a moment he will rise and go for a ramble in the woods, taking a gun along, or a fishing rod, if it is spring. Then he creaks to his feet, bending forward to keep his balance, and realizes that he will do nothing of the sort. The body and its surroundings have their messages for him, or only one message: "You are old." Here are some of the occasions on which he receives the message:

- when it becomes an achievement to do thoughtfully, step by step, what he once did instinctively
- when his bones ache

Thinking Critically

◆ What do you think about the Ojibwa custom described by Cowley? Do you agree or disagree with the author that it conferred a "quick" and "dignified" death on decrepit older members of the tribe?

- when there are more and more little bottles in the medicine cabinet, with instructions for taking four times a day
- when he fumbles and drops his toothbrush (butterfingers)
- when his face has bumps and wrinkles, so that he cuts himself while shaving (blood on the towel)
- when year by year his feet seem farther from his hands
- when he can't stand on one leg and has trouble pulling on his pants
- when he hesitates on the landing before walking down a flight of stairs
- when he spends more time looking for things misplaced than he spends using them after he (or more often his wife) has found them
- when he falls asleep in the afternoon
- when it becomes harder to bear in mind two things at once
- when a pretty girl passes him in the street and he doesn't turn his head
- when he forgets names, even of people he saw last month ("Now I'm beginning to forget nouns," the poet Conrad Aiken said at 80)
- when he listens hard to jokes and catches everything but the snapper
- when he decides not to drive at night anymore
- when everything takes longer to do—bathing, shaving, getting dressed or undressed—but when time passes quickly, as if he were gathering speed while coasting downhill. The year from 79 to 80 is like a week when he was a boy. ❷

Those are some of the intimate messages. "Put cotton in your ears and pebbles in your shoes," said a gerontologist, a member of that new profession dedicated to alleviating all maladies of old people except the passage of years. "Pull on rubber gloves. Smear Vaseline over your glasses, and there you have it: instant aging." Not quite. His formula omits the messages from the social world, which are louder, in most cases, than those from within. We start by growing old in other people's eyes, then slowly we come to share their judgment.

I remember a morning many years ago when I was backing out of the parking lot near the railroad station in Brewster, New York. There was a near collision. The driver of the other car jumped out and started to abuse me; he had his fists ready. Then he looked hard at me and said, "Why, you're an old man." He got back into his car, slammed the door, and drove away, while I stood there fuming. "I'm only 65," I thought. "He wasn't driving carefully. I can still take care of myself in a car, or in a fight, for that matter."

My hair was whiter—it may have been in 1974—when a young woman rose and offered me her seat in a Madison Avenue bus. That message was

---

Thinking Critically

❷ List five ways you know how old you are.

kind and also devastating. "Can't I even stand up?" I thought as I thanked her and declined the seat. But the same thing happened twice the following year, and the second time I gratefully accepted the offer, though with a sense of having diminished myself.[3] "People are right about me," I thought while wondering why all those kind gestures were made by women. Do men now regard themselves as the weaker sex, not called upon to show consideration? All the same it was a relief to sit down and relax.

A few days later I wrote a poem, "The Red Wagon," that belongs in the [8] record of aging:

> For his birthday they gave him a red express wagon
> with a driver's high seat and a handle that steered.
> His mother pulled him around the yard.
> "Giddyap," he said, but she laughed and went off
> to wash the breakfast dishes.
>
> "I wanta ride too," his sister said,
> and he pulled her to the edge of a hill.
> "Now, sister, go home and wait for me,
> but first give a push to the wagon."
> He climbed again to the high seat,
> this time grasping that handle-that-steered.
>
> The red wagon rolled slowly down the slope,
> then faster as it passed the schoolhouse
> and faster as it passed the store,
> the road still dropping away.
> Oh, it was fun.
> But would it ever stop?
> Would the road always go downhill?
> The red wagon rolled faster.
> Now it was in strange country.
> It passed a white house he must have dreamed about,
> deep woods he had never seen,
> a graveyard where, something told him, his sister
> was buried.
>
> Far below
> the sun was sinking into a broad plain.
>
> The red wagon rolled faster.
> Now he was clutching the seat, not even trying to steer.
> Sweat clouded his heavy spectacles.
> His white hair streamed in the wind.

Thinking Critically

[3] Why do you think the author felt "diminished" by accepting someone else's seat on the bus?

Even before he or she is 80, the aging person may undergo another [9] identity crisis like that of adolescence.[4] Perhaps there had also been a middle-aged crisis, the male or the female menopause, but the rest of adult life he had taken himself for granted, with his capabilities and failings. Now, when he looks in the mirror, he asks himself, "Is this really me?"—or he avoids the mirror out of distress at what it reveals, those bags and wrinkles. In his new makeup he is called upon to play a new role in a play that must be improvised. André Gide, that long-lived man of letters, wrote in his journal, "My heart has remained so young that I have the continual feeling of playing a part, the part of the 70-year-old that I certainly am; and the infirmities and weaknesses that remind me of my age act like a prompter, reminding me of my lines when I tend to stray. Then, like the good actor I want to be, I go back into my role, and I pride myself on playing it well."

In his new role the old person will find that he is tempted by new vices, [10] that he receives new compensations (not so widely known), and that he may possibly achieve new virtues. Chief among these is the heroic or merely obstinate refusal to surrender in the face of time. One admires the ships that go down with all flags flying and the captain on the bridge.

Among the vices of age[5] are avarice, untidiness, and vanity, which last [11] takes the form of a craving to be loved or simply admired. Avarice is the worst of those three. Why do so many old persons, men and women alike, insist on hoarding money when they have no prospect of using it and even when they have no heirs? They eat the cheapest food, buy no clothes, and live in a single room when they could afford better lodging. It may be that they regard money as a form of power; there is a comfort in watching it accumulate while other powers are dwindling away. How often we read of an old person found dead in a hovel, on a mattress partly stuffed with bank-books and stock certificates! The bankbook syndrome, we call it in our family, which has never succumbed.

Untidiness we call the Langley Collyer syndrome. To explain, Langley [12] Collyer was a former concert pianist who lived alone with his 70-year-old brother in a brownstone house on upper Fifth Avenue. The once fashionable neighborhood had become part of Harlem. Homer, the brother, had been an admiralty lawyer, but was now blind and partly paralyzed; Langley played for him and fed him on buns and oranges, which he thought would restore Homer's sight. He never threw away a daily paper because Homer, he said, might want to read them all. He saved other things as well and the house became filled with rubbish from roof to basement. The halls were lined on

---

Thinking Critically

4 ▸ What does Cowley mean by the "identity crisis" of old age?
5 ▸ What do you think are the worst "vices" of people who are twenty years old? Forty years old?

both sides with bundled newspapers, leaving narrow passageways in which Langley had devised booby traps to catch intruders.

On March 21, 1947, some unnamed person telephoned the police to report that there was a dead body in the Collyer house. The police broke down the front door and found the hall impassable; then they hoisted a ladder to a second-story window. Behind it Homer was lying on the floor in a bathrobe; he had starved to death. Langley had disappeared. After some delay, the police broke into the basement, chopped a hole in the roof, and began throwing junk out of the house, top and bottom. It was 18 days before they found Langley's body, gnawed by rats. Caught in one of his own booby traps, he had died in a hallway just outside Homer's door. By that time the police had collected, and the Department of Sanitation had hauled away, 120 tons of rubbish, including, besides the newspapers, 14 grand pianos and the parts of a dismantled Model T Ford. [6]

Why do so many old people accumulate junk, not on the scale of Langley Collyer, but still in a dismaying fashion? Their tables are piled high with it, their bureau drawers are stuffed with it, their closet rods bend with the weight of clothes not worn for years. I suppose that the piling up is partly from lethargy and partly from feeling that everything once useful, including their own bodies, should be preserved. Others, though not so many, have such a fear of becoming Langley Collyers that they strive to be painfully neat. Every tool they own is in its place, though it will never be used again; every scrap of paper is filed away in alphabetical order. At last their immoderate neatness becomes another vice of age, if a milder one.

The vanity of older people is an easier weakness to explain and to condone. [7] With less to look forward to, they yearn for recognition of what they have been: the reigning beauty, the athlete, the soldier, the scholar. It is the beauties who have the hardest time. A portrait of themselves at twenty hangs on the wall, and they try to resemble it by making an extravagant use of creams, powder, and dyes. Being young at heart, they think they are merely revealing their essential persons. The athletes find shelves for their silver trophies, which are polished once a year. Perhaps a letter sweater lies wrapped in a bureau drawer. I remember one evening when a no-longer athlete had guests for dinner and tried to find his sweater. "Oh, that old thing," his wife said. "The moths got into it, and I threw it away." The athlete sulked, and his guests went home early.

Thinking Critically

[6] Why do you think some people accumulate junk? Do you feel that older folks collect it more often than younger ones? If so, why?

[7] What kinds of "vanity" do older people have? In what ways do people your age display vanity? How are these two types of vanity different?

But there are also pleasures of the body, or the mind, that are enjoyed by   16
a greater number of older persons. Those pleasures include some that
younger people find hard to appreciate. One of them is simply sitting still,
like a snake on a sunwarmed stone, with a delicious feeling of indolence that
was seldom attained in earlier years. A leaf flutters down; a cloud moves by
inches across the horizon. At such moments the older person, completely
relaxed, has become a part of nature—and a living part, with blood coursing
through his veins. The future does not exist for him. He thinks, if he thinks
at all, that life for younger persons is still a battle royal of each against each,
but that now he has nothing more to win or lose. He is not so much above
as outside the battle, as if he had assumed the uniform of some small neutral
country, perhaps Liechtenstein or Andorra. From a distance he notes that
some of the combatants, men or women, are jostling ahead—but why do
they fight so hard when the most they can hope for is a longer obituary? He
can watch the scrounging and gouging, he can hear the shouts of exultation,
the moans of the gravely wounded, and meanwhile he feels secure; nobody
will attack him from ambush.

Age has other physical compensations besides the nirvana of dozing in   17
the sun. A few of the simplest needs become a pleasure to satisfy. When an
old woman in a nursing home was asked what she really liked to do she
answered in one word: "Eat." She might have been speaking for many of her
fellows. Meals in a nursing home, however badly cooked, serve as climactic
moments of the day. The physical essence of the pensioners is being renewed
at an appointed hour;[8] now they can go back to meditating or to watching
TV while looking forward to the next meal. They can also look forward to
sleep, which has become a definite pleasure, not the mere interruption it
once had been.

Here I am thinking of old persons under nursing care. Others ferociously   18
guard their independence, and some of them suffer less than one might
expect from being lonely and impoverished. They can be rejoiced by visits
and meetings, but they also have company inside their heads. Some of them
are busiest when their hands are still. What passes through the minds of
many is a stream of persons, images, phrases, and familiar tunes. For some
that stream has continued since childhood, but now it is deeper; it is their
present and their past combined. At times they conduct silent dialogues with
a vanished friend, and these are less tiring—often more rewarding—than
spoken conversations. If inner resources are lacking, old persons living alone
may seek comfort and a kind of companionship in the bottle. I should judge

---

Thinking Critically

[8] How is "the physical essence of pensioners . . . renewed" during mealtime in retirement
homes? What is the significance of this activity?

from the gossip of various neighborhoods that the outer suburbs from Boston to San Diego are full of secretly alcoholic widows. One of those widows, an old friend, was moved from her apartment into a retirement home. She left behind her a closet in which the floor was covered wall to wall with whiskey bottles. "Oh, those empty bottles!" she explained. "They were left by a former tenant."

Not whiskey or cooking sherry but simply giving up is the greatest   19
temptation of age. It is something different from a stoical acceptance of infirmities, which is something to be admired.

The givers-up see no reason for working. Sometimes they lie in bed all   20
day when moving about would still be possible, if difficult. I had a friend, a distinguished poet, who surrendered in that fashion. The doctors tried to stir him to action, but he refused to leave his room. Another friend, once a successful artist, stopped painting when his eyes began to fail. His doctor made the mistake of telling him that he suffered from a fatal disease. He then lost interest in everything except the splendid Rolls-Royce, acquired in his prosperous days, that stood in the garage. Daily he wiped the dust from its hood. He couldn't drive it on the road any longer, but he used to sit in the driver's seat, start the motor, then back the Rolls out of the garage and drive it in again, back twenty feet and forward twenty feet; that was his only distraction.[9]

I haven't the right to blame those who surrender, not being able to put   21
myself inside their minds or bodies.[10] Often they must have compelling reasons, physical or moral. Not only do they suffer from a variety of ailments, but also they are made to feel that they no longer have a function in the community. Their families and neighbors don't ask them for advice, don't really listen when they speak, don't call on them for efforts. One notes that there are not a few recoveries from apparent senility when that situation changes. If it doesn't change, old persons may decide that efforts are useless. I sympathize with their problems, but the men and women I envy are those who accept old age as a series of challenges.

For such persons, every new infirmity is an enemy to be outwitted, an   22
obstacle to be overcome by force of will.[11] They enjoy each little victory over themselves, and sometimes they win a major success. Renoir was one of them. He continued painting, and magnificently, for years after he was

---

Thinking Critically

[9] The image of Cowley's friend who drove his Rolls Royce in and out of the garage every day is a metaphor for what? Find two other metaphors in this essay.

[10] Why does Cowley use the word "surrender" in this context?

[11] What does Cowley mean when he says, "Every infirmity is an enemy to be outwitted"? According to Cowley, what are some other "enemies" of age?

crippled by arthritis; the brush had to be strapped to his arm. "You don't need your hand to paint," he said. Goya was another of the unvanquished. At 72 he retired as an official painter of the Spanish court and decided to work only for himself. His later years were those of the famous "black paintings" in which he let his imagination run (and also of the lithographs, then a new technique). At 78 he escaped a reign of terror in Spain by fleeing to Bordeaux. He was deaf, and his eyes were failing; in order to work he had to wear several pairs of spectacles, one over another, and then use a magnifying glass; but he was producing splendid work in a totally new style. At 80 he drew an ancient man propped on two sticks, with a mass of white hair and beard hiding his face and with the inscription "I am still learning."

"Eighty years old!" the great Catholic poet Paul Claudel wrote in his   23
journal. "No eyes left, no ears, no teeth, no legs, no wind! And when all is said and done, how astonishingly well one does without them!"

UNDERSTANDING DETAILS

1. Name five ways, according to Cowley, that people begin to realize they are "old." How did Cowley himself learn that he was old?
2. List three vices of old age, and explain them as Cowley sees them.
3. What are three compensations of advancing age? In what ways are these activities pleasurable?
4. What does Cowley mean in paragraph 15 by "the vanity of older people"? How do older people manifest this vanity?

READING CRITICALLY

5. What does the wagon symbolize in the author's poem about aging (paragraph 8)? What purpose does this poem serve in the essay?
6. For older people, what is the value of the conversations, images, friends, relatives, and melodies that pass through their minds? How might the elderly use these distractions constructively?
7. According to this essay, what qualities characterize those people who "surrender" (paragraph 21) to old age and those who "accept old age as a series of challenges" (paragraph 21)? Why do you think Cowley has more respect for the latter group?
8. What is Cowley's general attitude toward "the country of age" (paragraph 3)? Why does he feel that way about this stage of life?

DISCOVERING RHETORICAL STRATEGIES

9. After reading this essay, try to summarize in a single word or phrase Cowley's impressions of old age. How does this dominant impression help the author organize the many different details presented in his essay?
10. Why did Cowley include the reference to the Ojibwas at the end of the first paragraph? What effect does that anecdote have on our sympathies as readers?

11. Cowley uses a number of distinct metaphors in describing old age. He equates being old, for example, with acting out a certain "role" in life. He also portrays aging as a "rite of passage," a "challenge," and an "unfamiliar country" through which we must travel. In what sense is each of these metaphors appropriate? How does each help us understand the process of growing old?

12. Cowley uses language to describe a state of being that most of us are not familiar with yet. What other rhetorical strategies does he call upon to make his descriptive essay effective? Give examples of each.

MAKING CONNECTIONS

13. What are the primary differences among the "ageism" recounted by Malcolm Cowley, the racism explained by Lewis Sawaquat ("For My Indian Daughter"), and/or the sexism described by Sandra Cisneros ("Only Daughter")? Is one of these "isms" more dangerous than the others? Have you ever experienced any of these types of prejudice?

14. Compare and contrast the weaknesses of old age depicted in Cowley's essay with those portrayed by the grandfather in Ray Bradbury's "Summer Rituals" and/or by Frank Furedi in "Our Unhealthy Obsession with Sickness." Do you know anyone in his or her eighties? How does that person act? How do you think you will behave when you are that old?

15. How is Cowley's description of the "identity crisis" many older people go through similar to the identity crisis Lewis Sawaquat ("For My Indian Daughter") suffered when he discovered his Native American heritage and/or Brent Staples ("A Brother's Murder") discovered when he became more aware of his ethnic and racial heritage? Have you ever gone through an identity crisis? How did you resolve it? Was your crisis in any way like those described by Cowley, Sawaquat, or Staples?

IDEAS FOR DISCUSSION/WRITING

Preparing to Write

Write freely about your impressions of one or more older people in your life: Who are they? What characteristics do they share? How are they different from each other? Different from you? Similar to you? How do you know they are "old"?

Choosing a Topic

MyWritingLab™

1. **LEARNING⏻NLINE** In this essay, Cowley details many of the surprises and realities of aging. What "surprises and realities" have you encountered at your current age? Write an email to your future retired self, entitled "The View from _____," describing these observations and experiences. Revisit www. aarp.org (see Preparing to Read) for ideas.

2. Cowley explains at the outset of his essay that "the country of age is a new experience, different from what you supposed it to be. Nobody, man or woman, knows the country until he has lived in it and has taken out his citizenship papers" (paragraph 3). Interview an older person to discover his or her view of "the country of age." Then write an essay for your peers describing that person's opinions.

3. In his essay, Cowley describes the signals he receives from his body and his environment that tell him he is "old." What messages did you receive when you were young that indicated you were a "child"? What messages do you receive now that remind you of your present age? How are these messages different from those you received when you were a child? Describe these signals in a well-developed essay addressed to your classmates.

4. Do you think that Americans treat their aged with enough respect? Explain your answer in detail to an older person. Describe various situations that support your opinion.

Before beginning your essay, you may want to consult the flowchart on page 47.

NASA   (1958–   )

Mars

The National Aeronautics and Space Administration (NASA), a U.S. government agency, is responsible for aeronautics and aerospace research, as well as the civilian space program. Started in 1958 by President Dwight D. Eisenhower, NASA has led most of U.S. space exploration efforts, including the Apollo missions, the Skylab space station, and the Space Shuttle. NASA is dedicated to understanding the Earth, heliophysics, and the bodies throughout the solar system. NASA has made major contributions to many fields beyond space science, from medical procedures to treat sports injuries to technology for managing salt evaporation. One of NASA's major, ongoing objectives is studying and understanding both natural and human-induced changes to the global environment. To this end, NASA works with the National Renewable Energy Laboratory, the U.S. Environmental Protection Agency, the Department of Energy, the U.S. Air Force, and various other military agencies to reduce the use of hazardous materials and processes. NASA was recognized by the Environmental Protection Agency in 2008 as the first federal agency to use gas from landfills to produce energy at one of its facilities. While conducting continuous research, such as the Mars rover missions and the New Horizons mission to Pluto, NASA supports the International Space Station, oversees the development of new space exploration related technologies, and is responsible for the Launch Services Program.

Preparing to Read

The following essay, "Mars," is NASA's description of what we currently know about Mars. This piece is vivid and informative concerning the details we know about this planet.

Exploring Experience: As you prepare to read this essay, think for a moment about your desire for new experiences: Can you imagine yourself being an astronaut? Do you like exploring new places? Do you consider yourself the adventurous type? What are the advantages of being adventurous? What are the disadvantages?

LEARNING(ʘ)NLINE Visit Nasa.gov and select the Multimedia tab at the top of the page. Search images, and on the right sidebar, under "Mission Images," select "Mars." Look through the "Latest Images." Take a few minutes to consider how you would describe this particular area. What is unique about this place, and what seems familiar?

Before reading this essay, you may want to consult the flowchart on page 44.

Mars is the fourth planet from the sun [1] and the next planet beyond Earth. It is, on average, more than 142 million miles from the sun. Mars is about one-sixth the size of Earth. Mars is known as the Red Planet. It gets its red color from the iron oxide (like rust) in its soil.

Mars is named for the ancient Roman god of war. The Greeks called the planet Ares. The Romans and Greeks associated the planet with war because its color resembles the color of blood.

Mars has two small moons. Their names are Phobos and Deimos. They are named for the sons of Ares, the Greek god of war. Phobos means "fear," and Deimos means "flight." [2]

What Is Mars Like?

Mars is very cold. The average temperature on Mars is minus 80 degrees Fahrenheit— way below freezing! [3]

Its surface is rocky, with canyons, volcanoes, dry lake beds, and craters all over it. Red dust covers most of its surface. Mars has clouds and wind just like Earth. Sometimes the wind blows the red dust into a dust storm. Tiny dust storms can look like tornados, and large ones can be seen from Earth. Mars' large storms sometimes cover the whole planet.

Mars has about one-third the gravity of Earth. A rock dropped on Mars would fall more slowly than a rock falls on Earth. A person who weighs 100 pounds on Earth would only weigh about 37 pounds on Mars because of the reduced gravity. [4]

Mars' atmosphere is much thinner than Earth's. The atmosphere of Mars contains more than 95 percent carbon dioxide and much less than 1 percent oxygen.

What Has NASA Learned About Mars?

NASA has used both spacecraft and robots to learn more about Mars. In 1965, Mariner 4 flew past Mars and became the first NASA spacecraft to take close-up images of another planet. In 1976, Viking 1 and Viking 2 were the first NASA spacecraft to land on Mars. Both spacecraft took images and collected science data on the Martian surface.

Since then, several spacecraft have orbited or landed on Mars. Scientists are particularly interested in searching for clues of water on Mars. Living

---

Thinking Critically

1. Why do you think the location of Mars is given in relation to the sun?
2. In what ways are the names of the two moons on Mars appropriate?
3. Why do you think Mars is cold?
4. How much would you weigh on Mars?

things need water to survive. So finding evidence that water exists or used to exist on Mars would mean that there could be or could have been life on the planet.

NASA's Spirit and Opportunity rovers found evidence that water once   10 flowed on Mars when they found minerals that only form in water. NASA's Mars Global Surveyor orbited the Red Planet for nine years. The orbiter found that Mars once had a magnetic field like Earth's that shielded it from deadly cosmic rays.

How Is NASA Exploring Mars Today?

Today, three NASA spacecraft are orbiting Mars. The spacecraft are using   11 scientific tools to collect information about things like climate, topography, and the kinds of minerals on Mars. They are taking pictures and continuing to search for water.

Two rovers, Opportunity and Curiosity, are working on the surface of   12 Mars. They are taking pictures and studying the planet's soil and rocks. Rovers are robots that drive around. They send the pictures and data back to Earth. NASA uses the images and information gathered by the spacecraft and rovers to learn more about Mars.

How Will NASA Explore Mars in the Future?

NASA plans to send more robots to Mars. An orbiter named MAVEN   13 started its orbit of Mars in September 2014. MAVEN studies Mars' atmosphere. NASA plans to send a lander to Mars in 2016. And a new Mars rover is planned for launch in 2020. NASA wants robots to, some day, collect Martian soil and rocks and bring them back to Earth to be studied.

After robots have explored the Red Planet and brought back soil samples,   14 NASA wants to send astronauts there. To prepare to send humans to Mars, NASA is researching new kinds of homes where astronauts can live. Scientists are studying how people living in space can grow plants for food. To find out how living in space affects humans, NASA is studying what happens to astronauts on the International Space Station. 5

UNDERSTANDING DETAILS

1. What are three differences between Earth and Mars?
2. How is spacecraft able to help us learn about Mars? Explain your answer.
3. What details suggest to scientists that life might have once existed on Mars?
4. What are the next planned stages of exploration on Mars?

Thinking Critically

5 What are researchers studying at the International Space Station?

READING CRITICALLY

5. Why are researchers so interested in finding out whether or not water existed on Mars?
6. Why would sending people to Mars be especially difficult?
7. What implicit messages do the various names for the rovers on Mars communicate?
8. What will the next robots do on Mars?

DISCOVERING RHETORICAL STRATEGIES

9. Which senses does NASA concentrate on most in this description? Choose one paragraph to analyze. In one column, write down all the senses the description arouses; in another, record the words and phrases that activate these senses.
10. What "tone" or "mood" does NASA create in this excerpt? Does it support the essay's purpose? Explain your answer.
11. What is NASA's point of view in this essay? How would the method of description change if the story were told from the vantage point of an astronaut planning to go to Mars? How does this particular point of view help the author organize the description?
12. NASA relies mostly on description to make its point. What other rhetorical modes support this description? Give examples of each of these modes from the essay.

MAKING CONNECTIONS

13. In what ways does our desire to learn more about Mars involve daring to make changes (Kanchier, "Dare to Change Your Job and Your Life in 7 Steps")? How are these two "desires" similar? How are they different?
14. In this reading selection, how does NASA feel about the notion of exploration in general? Would Harold Krents ("Darkness at Noon") and Barbara Ehrenreich ("Nickel and Dimed") agree with him? Explain your answer.
15. Compare and contrast NASA's interest in putting humans on Mars with comparable interests of Malcolm Cowley ("The View from 80"), Lewis Sawaquat ("For My Indian Daughter"), and Roni Jacobson ("A Digital Safety Net"). How are they similar? How are they different?

IDEAS FOR DISCUSSION/WRITING

Preparing to Write

Write freely about places (imaginary or real) you would like to explore: What are the common characteristics of these places? Why are you attracted to them? Do you imagine you will ever actually travel to any of these places? What types of places do not interest you?

Choosing a Topic

MyWritingLab™

1. **LEARNING⏻NLINE** In their research, NASA is trying to learn what living on Mars would be like. Use description to speculate on this question, imagining that you were sent to Mars. If you need inspiration, go back to the nasa.gov images mentioned in the Preparing to Read exercise.
2. Give a name (either real or fictitious) to a place you have just described in the prewriting exercise, and write an essay describing this place. Try to make your description as vivid and as well organized as NASA's portrait of Mars. Decide on a dominant impression, and imagine that the audience for your description is someone who has never been to this place.
3. Write an essay describing for your classmates some of the risks you have taken in your life. What characterizes these choices? Why do you think some risks are appealing to some and not to others? What makes the risks you have taken attractive to you?
4. Describe the inside of your house, apartment, or room, explaining to your class what the decorations say about you as a person. If someone in your class were to see where you live, could he or she make any accurate deductions about your political, social, or moral values based on the contents and arrangement of the place you call "home"?

Before beginning your essay, you may want to consult the flowchart on page 47.

Chapter Writing Assignments

Practicing Description

1. Write a spatial description of your home by exploring its basic sections or rooms. What does your home reveal about you as a person? About your family?

2. Think about the extent to which influences such as family, education, and community have contributed to the person you are today. Describe the kind of person you are and the sources of a few of your most important qualities.

3. Consider the health of the environment in your immediate community (air quality, noise, landscape). Describe an environmental problem you have observed. Be sure to provide specific details about the problem you are describing.

Exploring Ideas

4. Discuss a cultural icon (such as a rock star or a prominent building) and what it represents about its culture. How did this person or object become an icon in its culture? What biases or ideals does it express? How do people outside this culture view it?

5. Think about the ways people's physical surroundings (office, weather, house, apartment) affect them. Discuss one important way these surroundings have influenced someone's behavior. Provide examples in your discussion that explore the relationship between various features in your surroundings and the manner in which people react to them.

6. In your opinion, how well are elderly people treated in America? Write an essay describing the level of respect older people get in American society. Use examples of people you know to support your ideas.

Analyzing Visual Images

Rudi1976/Fotolia.

7. Look at the detail in this picture, and try to imagine what smells, tastes, sounds, textures, and sights you might experience while standing in this setting. Write a description of this scene for someone who has never been here, including all the senses that this scene evokes.

8. Look at the photograph on page 43 in the introduction of this chapter. Choose a sense besides sight (smell, hear, taste, or feel), and explain the role of this sense in this picture.

Composing in Different Genres

9. Multimedia: List the sights, sounds, smells, textures, and tastes that are appealing to you. Analyze your list, and figure out what attracts you to them. Then, create a short video that communicates a dominant impression about these senses, including the reasons you find them pleasing.

10. Multigenre: Write an imaginary conversation of two people discussing Mars: one who wants to go to Mars and the other who has no interest in the trip at all. Give details about the setting of the conversation when appropriate.

Writing from Sources

For detailed information on writing from sources, see Part III.

11. Consider the different security levels of imprisonment in the United States. What qualifies an individual for each level? What are the housing facilities and environment for each level? Research this topic, and write an essay that provides a detailed description of each type of prison.
12. How does attitude affect the aging process? Research the connection between psychological and physical health in the elderly. Then, citing evidence from your research, explain this relationship in a documented essay.

MyWritingLab™ Visit Ch. 4 Description: Exploring Through the Senses in *MyWritingLab* to complete the writing assignments and test your understanding of the chapter learning objectives.

Chapter 5

NARRATION
Telling a Story

LEARNING OBJECTIVES

After completing this chapter, you will be able to do the following:
- Define narration
- Use narration to think critically
- Read narration essays critically
- Write and revise effective narration essays

A good story is a powerful method of getting someone's attention. The excitement that accompanies a suspenseful ghost story, a lively anecdote, or a vivid joke easily attests to this fact. In reality, narration is one of the earliest verbal skills we all learn as children, providing us with a convenient, logical, and easily understood means of sharing our thoughts with other people. Storytelling is powerful because it offers us a way of dramatizing our ideas so that others can identify with them.

DEFINING NARRATION

Narration involves telling a story that is often based on personal experience. Stories can be oral or written, real or imaginary, short or long. A good story, however, always has a point or purpose. Narration can be the dominant mode (as in a novel or short story) supported by other rhetorical strategies, or it can serve the purpose of another rhetorical mode (as in a persuasive essay, a historical survey, or a scientific report).

In its subordinate role, narration can provide examples or explain ideas. If asked why you are attending college, for instance, you might turn to narration to make your answer clear, beginning with a story about your family's hardships in the past. The purpose of telling such a story would be to show your listeners how important higher education is to you by encouraging them to understand and identify with your family history.

Unlike description, which generally portrays people, places, and objects in *space,* narration asks the reader to follow a series of actions through a particular *time* sequence. Description, however, often complements the movement of narration. People must be depicted, for instance, along with their relationships to one another, before their actions can have any real meaning for us; similarly, places must be described so that we can picture the setting and understand the activities in a specific scene. The organization of the action and the time spent on each episode in a story should be based principally on a writer's analysis of the interests and needs of his or her audience.

To be most effective, narration should prolong the exciting parts of a story and shorten the routine facts that simply move the reader from one episode to another. If you were robbed on your way to work, for example, a good narrative describing the incident would concentrate on the traumatic event itself rather than on such mundane and boring details as what you had for breakfast and what chores you did prior to the attack. Finally, just like description, narration *shows* rather than *tells* its purpose to the audience. The factual statement "I was robbed this morning" could be made much more vivid and dramatic through the addition of some simple narration: "As I was walking to work at 7:30 A.M., a huge and angry-looking man ran up to me, thrust a gun into the middle of my stomach, and took my money, my new wristwatch, all my credit cards, and my pants—leaving me penniless and embarrassed."

The following paragraph written by a student recounts a recent parachuting experience. As you read this narrative, notice especially the writer's use of vivid detail to *show* rather than *tell* her message to the readers.

> I have always needed occasional "fixes" of excitement in my life, so when I realized one spring day that I was more than ordinarily bored, I made up my mind to take more than ordinary steps to relieve that boredom. I decided to go parachuting. The next thing I knew, I was stuffed into a claustrophobically small plane with five other terrified people, rolling down a bumpy, rural runway, droning my way to 3,500 feet and an exhilarating experience. Once over the jump area, I waited my turn, stepped onto the strut, held my breath, and then kicked off into the cold, rushing air as my heart pounded heavily. All I

could think was, "I hope this damn parachute opens!" The sensation of falling backward through space was unfamiliar and disconcerting until my chute opened with a loud "pop," momentarily pulling me upward toward the distant sky. After several minutes of floating downward, I landed rudely on the hard ground. Life, I remembered happily, could be awfully exciting, and a month later, when my tailbone had stopped throbbing, I still felt that way.

THINKING CRITICALLY THROUGH NARRATION

Rhetorical modes offer us different ways of perceiving reality. Narration is an especially useful tool for sequencing or putting details and information in some kind of logical order, usually chronological. Practicing exercises in narrative techniques can help you see clear patterns in topics you are writing about.

Although narration is usually used in conjunction with other rhetorical modes, we are going to isolate it here so you can appreciate its specific mechanics separate from other mental activities. If you feel the process of narration in your head, you are more likely to understand exactly what it entails and therefore use it more effectively in reading essays and in organizing and writing your own essays.

For the best results, we will once again do some warm-up exercises to make your sequencing perceptions as accurate and successful as possible. In this way, you will actually learn to feel how your mind works in this particular mode and then be more aware of the thinking strategies available to you in your own reading and writing. As you become more conscious of the mechanics of the individual rhetorical modes, you will naturally become more adept at combining them to accomplish the specific purpose and the related effect you want to create.

The following exercises, which require a combination of thinking and writing skills, will help you practice this particular strategy in isolation. Just as in a physical workout, we will warm up your mental capabilities one by one as if they were muscles that can be developed individually before being used together in harmony.

1. Write or tell the story that goes with the photo on page 98. Make this scene the beginning of your story, and then create the remainder of the plot.
2. Make a chronological list of the different activities you did yesterday, from waking in the morning to sleeping at night. Randomly pick two events from your day, and treat them as the highlights of your day. Now write freely for five minutes, explaining the story of your day and emphasizing the importance of these two highlights.

Johnnychaos/Fotolia.

3. Recall an important event that happened to you between the ages of five and ten. Brainstorm about how this event made you feel at the time it happened. Then brainstorm about how this event makes you feel now. What changes have you discovered in your view of this event?

READING AND WRITING NARRATIVE ESSAYS

Making meaning in reading and writing is a fairly straightforward process with the narrative mode. To read a narrative essay most effectively, you should spend your time concentrating on the writer's main story line and use of details. Together, these tasks will help you make meaning as you read. To create an effective story, you have some important decisions to make before you write and certain variables to control as you actually draft your narrative. During the prewriting stage, you need to generate ideas and choose a point of view through which your story will be presented. Then, as you write, the preliminary decisions you have made regarding the selection and arrangement of your details (especially important in a narrative) will allow your story to flow more easily. Carefully controlled organization, along with appropriate timing and pacing, can influence your audience's reactions in very powerful ways.

Reading Narrative Essays

Understanding how narration essays work rhetorically will help you make decisions for your own writing. Here is a flowchart of questions that will guide your reading for this purpose.

Questions to Guide Your Reading

PREPARING TO READ Before you read the essays, answer the following questions:

- What assumptions can you make from the essay's **title**?
- What do you think the general **mood** of the essay will be?
- What is the essay's **purpose** and **audience**?
- What does the **synopsis** tell you about the essay?
- What can you learn from the author's **biography**?
- What do you predict the author's **point of view** toward the subject will be?

READING As you read the essays for the first time, answer the following questions:

- What is the author's **purpose**?
- What is the story's **context**?
- What is the essay's **story line**?

REREADING When you read the essays again, answer the following questions:

- What **details** did the author choose?
- How are they **arranged**?
- How does the author control the **pace** of the story?
- How does the author **show rather than tell** the story?
- What other **rhetorical modes** does the author use?
- How does your understanding of the essay **change** with each rereading?

Preparing to Read.   As you prepare to read the narratives in this chapter, try to guess what each title tells you about its essay's topic and about the author's attitude toward that topic: Can you guess, for example, how Lewis Sawaquat feels about his daughter from his title "For My Indian Daughter" or what Maya Angelou's attitude is toward the events described in "New Directions"? Also, scan the essay and read its synopsis in the Rhetorical Table of Contents to help you anticipate as much as you can about the author's purpose and audience.

Next, the more you learn from the biography about the author and the circumstances surrounding the composition of a particular essay, the better prepared you will be to read the essay. For a narrative essay, the writer's point of view or perspective toward the story and its characters is especially significant. From the biographies, can you determine Maya Angelou's attitude toward Annie Johnson's energy and determination in "New Directions" or Sandra Cisneros's reason for writing "Only Daughter"? Also, what is Russell Baker's opinion of his mother in "The Saturday Evening Post"?

Last, before you begin to read, answer the Preparing to Read questions, and then try to generate some of your own inquiries on the general subject of the essay: What do you want to know about being a Native American (Sawaquat)? What do you think of children in general (Cisneros)? What childhood experience greatly affected your life (Baker)?

Reading.   Based on the biographical information preceding the essay and on the essay's tone, purpose, and audience, try to create a context for the narrative as you read. How do such details help you understand your reading material more thoroughly?

As you continue to read a narrative essay, simply follow the story line, and try to get a general sense of the narrative and of the author's general purpose. Is Baker trying to encourage us all to be writers or simply to help us understand why he writes? Record your initial reactions to each essay as they occur to you. Is Miller's purpose to make us feel sympathetic toward or critical of his main character?

At the bottom of the pages of these essays are questions that will help you think analytically about the topic of the essay and related subjects. They are designed to provide a "bridge" between the questions at the beginning of the essay and the more complex questions at the end. Thinking critically is a skill that can be learned if you practice it, which is what these prompts intend to help you do. If you take time to consider and respond to each inquiry, you will be ready to write in depth on the questions and writing assignments that follow each essay.

A first reading of this sort, along with a survey of the questions that follow the essay, will help prepare you for a critical understanding of the material when you read it for the second time.

Rereading.   As you reread these narrative essays, notice the author's selection and arrangement of details that created the story line. Why does Angelou organize her story one way and Cisneros another? What effect does their organization create?

Also, pay attention to the timing and the pacing of the story line. What do the long descriptions of Annie's plans add to Angelou's "New Directions"? What does the quick pace of Miller's narrative communicate?

In addition, consider at this point how the authors show rather than tell their stories and what other rhetorical strategies the authors use to support their narratives. Which authors in this chapter are most engaging? Which writers use examples to supplement their stories? Which use definitions? Which use comparisons? Why do they use these strategies?

Finally, when you answer the questions after each essay, you can check your understanding of the material on different levels before you tackle the discussion/writing topics that follow.

For a list of reading guidelines, please see the Reading Checklist at the end of Chapter 2.

Writing Narrative Essays

Now that you see how narration works in an essay, use the same features in your own writing. The flowchart on the next page provides some questions to guide you.

Preparing to Write.   First, you should answer the prewriting questions to help you generate thoughts on the subject at hand. Next, as in all writing, you should explore your subject matter and discover as many specific details as possible. (See Chapter 3 for a discussion of prewriting techniques.) Some writers rely on the familiar journalistic checklist of *who, what, when, where, why,* and *how* to make sure they cover all aspects of their narrative. If you were using the story of a basketball game at your college to demonstrate the team spirit of your school, for example, you might want to consider telling your readers *who* played in the game and/or *who* attended; *what* happened before, during, and after the game; *when* and *where* the game took place; *why* it was being played (or *why* these particular teams were playing each other or *why* the game was especially important); and *how* the winning basket was shot. Freewriting or a combination of freewriting and the journalistic questions is another effective way of getting ideas and story details on paper for use in a first draft.

Questions to Guide Your Writing

PREPARING TO WRITE
Before you start writing, answer these questions:

- What is your **purpose**?
- Who is your **audience**?
- What is your narrator's **point of view**—including person, vantage point, and attitude toward the subject?
- What is the **context** of your story?

WRITING As you write your first draft, consider these questions:

- What is your **thesis**?
- What **details** will best support this thesis?
- How can you **arrange** and **pace** these details to accomplish your purpose?
- How can you **show rather than tell** readers your story?

EDITING Be sure to proofread and edit your paper before turning it in.

- Are your **sentences** all complete?
- Do your words say exactly **what you mean**?
- Do you follow conventional **grammar and usage** rules?

REVISING After you write your first draft, use the following questions to revise your essay:

- Is your purpose clearly stated in your **thesis**?
- Does your **narrator** help you achieve your purpose?
- Do you create or imply a clear **context** for your narrative?
- Are all the **details** relevant to your purpose?
- Are they **organized** logically?
- Do you **show rather than tell** your message?

Once you have generated these ideas, you should always let your purpose and audience ultimately guide your selection of details, but the process of gathering such journalistic information gives you some material from which to choose. You will also need to decide whether to include dialogue in your narrative. Again, the difference here is between *showing* and *telling*: Will your audience benefit from reading what was actually said, word for word, during a discussion, or will a brief description of the conversation be sufficiently effective? In fact, all the choices you make at this stage of the composing process will give you material with which to create emphasis, suspense, conflict, and interest in your subject.

Next, you must decide on the point of view that will most readily help you achieve your purpose with your specific audience. Point of view includes the (1) person, (2) vantage point, and (3) attitude of your narrator. *Person* refers to who will tell the story: an uninvolved observer, a character in the narrative, or an omniscient (all-seeing) narrator. This initial decision will guide your thoughts on *vantage point,* which is the frame of reference of the narrator: close to the action, far from the action, looking back on the past, or reporting on the present. Finally, your narrator will naturally have an *attitude,* or *personal feeling,* about the subject: accepting, hostile, sarcastic, indifferent, angry, pleased, or any number of similar emotions. Once you adopt a certain perspective in a story, you should maintain it for the duration of the narrative. This consistency will bring focus and coherence to your essay.

Writing. After you have explored your topic and adopted a particular point of view, you need to write a thesis statement and to select and arrange the details of your story coherently so that the narrative has a clear beginning, middle, and end. The most natural way to organize the events of a narrative, of course, is chronologically. In your story about the school basketball game, you would probably narrate the relevant details in the order they occurred (i.e., sequentially, from the beginning of the game to its conclusion). More experienced writers may elect to use flashbacks: An athlete might recall a significant event that happened during the game, or a coach might recollect the contest's turning point. Your most important consideration is that the elements of a narrative essay follow some sort of time sequence, aided by the use of clear and logical transitions (e.g., *then, next, at this point, suddenly*) that help the reader move smoothly from one event to the next.

In addition to organization, the development of your essay with enough details is important. In this way, the details that you choose should *show* rather than *tell* your story. This approach will help your essay become interesting and believable to your readers. Furthermore, the point of view of your narrator should remain consistent throughout your essay, which will give the essay a high degree of credibility.

Revising. As you reread the narrative you have written, pretend you are a reader (instead of the writer), and make sure you have told the story from the most effective point of view, considering both your purpose and your audience.

For more advice on writing, revising, and editing, see the Writing Checklist at the end of Chapter 3.

STUDENT ESSAY: NARRATION AT WORK

The following student essay characterizes the writer's mother by telling a story about an unusual family vacation. As you read it, notice that the student writer states her purpose clearly and succinctly in the first paragraph. She then becomes an integral part of her story as she carefully selects examples and details that help convey her thesis.

A Vacation with My Mother

First-person narrator

I had an interesting childhood—not because of where I grew up and not because I ever did anything particularly adventuresome or thrilling. In fact, I don't think my life seemed especially interesting even to me at the time. But now, telling friends about my supposedly ordinary childhood, I notice an array of responses ranging from astonishment to hilarity. The source of their surprise and amusement is my mother—gracious, charming, sweet, and totally out of synchronization with the rest of the world. One strange family trip we took when I was eleven captures the essence of her zaniness.

General subject

Specific subject

Thesis statement

Narrator's attitude

My two sets of grandparents lived in Colorado and North Dakota, and my parents decided we would spend a few weeks driving to those states and seeing all the sights along the relaxed and rambling way. My eight-year-old brother, David, and I had some serious reservations. If Mom had ever driven Dad to school, we reasoned, he'd never even consider letting her drive us anywhere out of town, let alone out of California. If we weren't paying attention, we were as likely to end up at her office or the golf course as we were to arrive at school. Sometimes she'd drop us off at a friend's house to play and then forget where she had left us. The notion of going on a long trip with her was really unnerving.

Examples

Transition

How can I explain my mother to a stranger? Have you ever watched reruns of the old *I Love Lucy* with Lucille Ball? I did as a child, and I thought Lucy Ricardo was normal. I lived with somebody a lot like her. Mom wasn't a redhead (not usually, anyway), and Dad wasn't a Cuban nightclub owner, but

Narrator's vantage point — at home we had the same situation of a loving but bemused husband trying to deal with the off-the-wall logic and enthusiasm of a frequently exasperating wife. We all adored her, but we had to admit that Mom was a flaky, absent-minded, genuine eccentric.

As the first day of our trip approached, David and I reluctantly said good-bye to all of our friends. Who knew if we'd ever see any of them again? Finally, the moment of our departure arrived, and we loaded suitcases, books, games, camping gear, and a tent into the car and bravely drove off. We bravely drove off again two hours later after we'd returned home to get the purse and traveler's checks that Mom had forgotten. — Careful selection of details; Transition

David and I were always a little nervous when using gas station bathrooms if Mom was driving while Dad napped: "You stand outside the door and play lookout while I go, and I'll stand outside the door and play lookout while you go." I had terrible visions: "Honey, where are the kids?" "What?! Oh, gosh . . . I thought they were being awfully quiet. Uh . . . Idaho?" We were never actually abandoned in a strange city, but we weren't about to take any chances. — Use of dialogue; Examples

On the fourth or fifth night of the trip, we had trouble finding a motel with a vacancy. After driving futilely for an hour, Mom suddenly had a great idea: Why didn't we find a house with a good-looking backyard and ask if we could pitch our tent there? To her, the scheme was eminently reasonable. Vowing quietly to each other to hide in the back seat if she did it, David and I groaned in anticipated mortification. To our profound relief, Dad vetoed the idea. Mom never could understand our objections. If a strange family showed up on her front doorstep, Mom would have been delighted. She thinks everyone in the world is as nice as she is. We finally found a vacancy in the next town. David and I were thrilled—the place featured bungalows in the shape of Native-American tepees. — Transition; Passage of time; Example

The Native-American motif must have reminded my parents that we had not yet used the brand-new tent, Coleman stove, portable mattress, and other — Transition

<u>camping gear we had brought.</u> We headed to a national park the next day and found a campsite by a lake. It took hours to figure out how to set up the tent; it was one of those deluxe models with mosquito-net windows, canvas floors, and enough room for three large families to sleep in. It was after dark before we finally got it erected, and the night had turned quite cold. We fixed a hurried campfire dinner (chicken burned on the outside and raw in the middle) and prepared to go to sleep. That was when we realized that Mom had forgotten to bring along some important pieces of equipment—our sleeping bags. The four of us huddled together on our thin mattresses borrowed from our station-wagon floor. That ended our camping days. Give me a stucco tepee any time.

Careful selection of details — *Chronological order*

Transition

We drove through several states and saw lots of great sights along the way: the Grand Canyon, Carlsbad Caverns, mountains, waterfalls, and even a haunted house. David and I were excited and amazed at all the wonders we found, and Mom was just as enthralled as we were. Her constant pleasure and sense of the world as a beautiful, magical place was infectious. I never realized until I grew up how really childlike—in the best sense of the word—my mother actually is. She is innocent, optimistic, and always ready to be entertained.

Examples (spatial order)

<u>Looking back on that long-past family vacation, I now realize that my childhood was more special because I grew up with a mother who wasn't afraid to try anything and who taught me to look at the world as a series of marvelous opportunities to be explored.</u> What did it matter that she thought England was bordered by Germany? We were never going to try to drive there. So what if she was always leaving her car keys in the refrigerator or some other equally inexplicable place? <u>In the end, we always got where we were going—and we generally had a grand time along the way.</u>

Transition — *Narrator's attitude*

Examples

Concluding remark

Student Writer's Comments

I enjoyed writing about this childhood vacation because of all the memories it brought back. I knew I wanted to write a narrative to explain my mother, and the word *zany* immediately popped into my mind. So I knew what my focus was going to be from the outset. My prewriting started spontaneously as soon as I found this angle. So many thoughts and memories rushed into my head that I couldn't even get to a piece of paper to write them down before I lost some of them. There were way too many to put into one essay. The hardest part of writing this narrative was trying to decide what material to use and what to leave out. Spending a little more time before writing my first draft proved to be a good investment in this case. I got a clean piece of paper and began freewriting, trying to mold some of my scattered ideas from brainstorming into a coherent, readable form. During this second stage of prewriting, I remembered one special vacation we took that I thought might capture the essence of my mother—and also of my family.

My first draft was about three times the length of this one. My point of view was the innocent participant/observer who came to know and love her mother and her absent-mindedness. I had really developed my thesis from the time I got this writing assignment. I told my story chronologically except for looking back in the last paragraph when I attempted to analyze the entire experience. I had no trouble *showing* rather than *telling* because all of the details were so vivid to me—as if they had happened yesterday. But that was my main problem. I soon realized that I could not possibly include everything that was on the pages of my first draft.

The process of cranking out my rough draft made my point of view toward life with my mother very clear to me and helped me face the cutting that was ahead of me. I took the raw material of a very lengthy first draft and forced myself to choose the details and examples that best characterized my mother and what life was like growing up under the care of such a lovely but daffy individual. The sense of her being both "lovely" and "daffy" was the insight that helped me the most in revising the content of my essay. I made myself ruthlessly eliminate anything that interfered with the overall effect I was trying to create—from extraneous images and details to words and phrases that didn't contribute to this specific view of my mom.

The final result, according to my classmates, communicated my message clearly and efficiently. The main criticism I got from my class was that I might have cut too much from my first draft. But I think this focused picture with a few highlights conveys my meaning in the best possible way. I offered enough details to *show* rather than *tell* my readers what living with my mother was like, but not too many to bore them. I was also able to take the time in my essay to be humorous now and then ("David and I reluctantly said good-bye to all of our friends. Who knew if we'd ever see any of them again?" and "Give me a stucco tepee any time."), as well as pensive and serious ("I now realize that my childhood was more special because I grew up with a mother who wasn't afraid to try anything and who taught me to look at the world as a series of marvelous opportunities to be explored."). Even though I would change a few things now, I am generally happy with the final draft. It captures the essence of my mother from my point of view, and it also gave my class a few laughs. Aren't the readers' reactions the ultimate test of a good story?

SOME FINAL THOUGHTS ON NARRATION

Just as with other modes of writing, all decisions regarding narration should be made with a specific purpose and an intended audience constantly in mind. As you will see, each narrative in this section is directed at a clearly defined audience. Notice, as you read, how each writer manipulates the various features of narration so that the readers are simultaneously caught up in the plot and deeply moved to feel, think, believe, and even act on the writer's personal opinions.

LEWIS SAWAQUAT   (1935–2009)

For My Indian Daughter

Lewis Sawaquat was a Native American who worked for thirty years as a surveyor for the Soil Conservation Service of the U.S. Department of Agriculture. He was born in Harbor Springs, Michigan, where his great-great-grandfather was the last official "chief" of the region. After finishing high school, Sawaquat entered the army, graduated from Army Survey School, and then completed a tour of duty in Korea. Upon returning to America, he enrolled in the Art Institute of Chicago to study commercial art. Sawaquat's final residence was in Traverse City, Michigan, where he enjoyed gardening, swimming, walking in the woods, reading, and playing with his cat. He served as a pipe carrier and cultural/spiritual adviser to his Ottawa tribe. Toward the end of his life, he ran a consulting firm and traveled around the country speaking on Native-American issues. His daughter, Gaia, who is described in the following essay, graduated from Yale University. His advice to students using *The Prose Reader* is to "pay attention to life; there's nothing more important to becoming a writer."

Preparing to Read

"For My Indian Daughter" originally appeared in the "My Turn" column of *Newsweek* magazine (September 5, 1983) under the author's former name, Lewis Johnson. In his article, the author speaks eloquently about prejudice, ethnic pride, and growing cultural awareness, which are timely topics for all of us.

Exploring Experience: Before reading this selection, think for a few minutes about your own heritage: What is your ethnic identity? Are you content with this background? Have you ever gone through an identity crisis? Do you anticipate facing any problems because of your ancestry? If so, what do you think these problems will be? How will you handle them when they occur?

LEARNING◯NLINE To understand the context in which Sawaquat is writing, visit the "National Museum of the American Indian-Smithsonian" homepage: www.nmai.si.edu. Click the "Explore" tab, and select "Exhibitions." Then view the online exhibitions of Native-American culture, past and present.

Before reading this essay, you may want to consult the flowchart on page 99.

My little girl is singing herself to sleep upstairs, her voice mingling   1
with the sounds of the birds outside in the old maple trees. She
is two, and I am nearly 50, and I am very taken with her. She
came along late in my life, unexpected and unbidden, a startling gift.

Today at the beach my chubby-legged, brown-skinned daughter ran   2
laughing into the water as fast as she could. My wife and I laughed watching
her, until we heard behind us a low guttural curse and then an unpleasant
voice raised in an imitation war whoop.

I turned to see a fat man in a bathing suit, white and soft as a grub, ◆ as he   3
covered his mouth and prepared to make the Indian war cry again. He was
middle-aged, younger than I, and had three little children lined up next to
him, grinning foolishly. My wife suggested we leave the beach, and I agreed.

I knew the man was not unusual in his feelings against Indians. His beach   4
behavior might have been socially unacceptable to more civilized whites,
but his basic view of Indians is expressed daily in our small town, frequently
on the editorial pages of the county newspaper, as white people speak out
against Indian fishing rights and land rights, saying in essence, "Those Indians are taking our fish, our land." It doesn't matter to them that we were
here first, that the U.S. Supreme Court has ruled in our favor. It matters to
them that we have something they want, and they hate us for it. Backlash is
the common explanation of the attacks on Indians, the bumper stickers that
say, "Spear an Indian, Save a Fish," but I know better. The hatred of Indians
goes back to the beginning when white people came to this country. For
me it goes back to my childhood in Harbor Springs, Mich.

Theft

Harbor Springs is now a summer resort for the very affluent, but a   5
hundred years ago it was the Indian village of my Ottawa ancestors. My
grandmother, Anna Showanessy, and other Indians like her, had their land
there taken by treaty, by fraud, by violence, by theft. They remembered how
whites had burned down the village at Burt Lake in 1900 and pushed the
Indians out. These were the stories in my family.

When I was a boy, my mother told me to walk down the alleys in Harbor   6
Springs and not to wear my orange football sweater out of the house. This
way I would not stand out, not be noticed, and not be a target.

I wore my orange sweater anyway and deliberately avoided the alleys. I   7
was the biggest person I knew and wasn't really afraid. But I met my come-
uppance when I enlisted in the U.S. Army. One night all the men in my

---

Thinking Critically

◆ How does Sawaquat's description of the "fat man" betray the author's feelings about the
confrontation on the beach? What other words reveal the author's biases?

barracks gathered together and, gang-fashion, pulled me into the shower and scrubbed me down with rough brushes used for floors, saying, "We won't have any dirty Indians in our outfit." It is a point of irony that I was cleaner than any of them. Later in Korea I learned how to kill, how to bully, how to hate Koreans. I came out of the war tougher than ever and, strangely, white. [2]

I went to college, got married, lived in La Porte, Ind., worked as a sur-   8
veyor and raised three boys. I headed Boy Scout groups, never thinking it odd when the Scouts did imitation Indian dances, imitation Indian lore.

One day when I was 35 or thereabouts I heard about an Indian powwow.   9
My father used to attend them and so with great curiosity and a strange joy at discovering a part of my heritage, I decided the thing to do to get ready for this big event was to have my friend make me a spear in his forge. The steel was fine and blue and iridescent. The feathers on the shaft were bright and proud.

In a dusty state fairground in southern Indiana, I found white people   10
dressed as Indians. I learned they were "hobbyists," that is, it was their hobby and leisure pastime to masquerade as Indians on weekends. I felt ridiculous with my spear, and I left.

It was years before I could tell anyone of the embarrassment of this weekend   11
and see any humor in it. But in a way it was that weekend, for all its silliness, that was my awakening. I realized I didn't know who I was. I didn't have an Indian name. I didn't speak the Indian language. I didn't know the Indian customs. Dimly I remembered the Ottawa word for dog, but it was a baby word, *kahgee*, not the full word, *muhkahgee*, which I was later to learn. Even more hazily I remembered a naming ceremony (my own). I remembered legs dancing around me, dust. Where had that been? Who had I been? "Sawaquat," my mother told me when I asked, "where the tree begins to grow." [3]

That was 1968, and I was not the only Indian in the country who was feeling   12
the need to remember who he or she was. There were others. They had pow-wows, real ones, and eventually I found them. Together we researched our past, a search that for me culminated in the Longest Walk, a march on Washington in 1978. Maybe because I now know what it means to be Indian, it surprises me that others don't. Of course there aren't very many of us left. The chances of an average person knowing an average Indian in an average lifetime are pretty slim.

Circle

Still, I was amused one day when my small, four-year-old neighbor   13
looked at me as I was hoeing in my garden and said, "You aren't a real Indian, are you?" Scotty is little, talkative, likable. Finally I said, "I'm a real

---

Thinking Critically

[2] How and when did the author first acquire prejudice?

[3] Look up the meaning of the Indian word "sawaquat," and explain how it helps characterize the author's increasing familiarity with his ethnic heritage and personal identity.

Indian." He looked at me for a moment and then said, squinting into the sun, "Then where's your horse and feathers?" The child was simply a smaller, whiter version of my own ignorant self years before.◆ We'd both seen too much TV, that's all. He was not to be blamed. And so, in a way, the moronic man on the beach today is blameless. We come full circle to realize other people are like ourselves, as discomfiting as that may be sometimes.

As I sit in my old chair on my porch, in a light that is fading so the   14
leaves are barely distinguishable against the sky, I can picture my girl asleep upstairs. I would like to prepare her for what's to come, take her each step of the way saying, there's a place to avoid, here's what I know about this, but much of what's before her she must go through alone. She must pass through pain and joy and solitude and community to discover her own inner self that is unlike any other and come through that passage to the place where she sees all people are one and in so seeing may live her life in a brighter future.

UNDERSTANDING DETAILS

1. What is the principal point of this essay by Sawaquat? How many different stories does the author tell to make this point?
2. What does Sawaquat see as the origin of the hatred for Native Americans in the United States?
3. What does Sawaquat learn from his first powwow (paragraphs 9 and 10)?
4. How does Sawaquat discover his original identity? In what way does this knowledge change him?

READING CRITICALLY

5. Why does Sawaquat begin this essay with the story about his daughter on the beach? How does the story make you feel?
6. Why do thoughts about his daughter prompt Sawaquat's memories of his own identity crisis? What does the author's identity have to do with his daughter?
7. The author calls paragraphs 5–12 "Theft" and paragraphs 13–14 "Circle." Explain these two subtitles from the author's point of view.
8. Why do you think Sawaquat says that his daughter "must pass through pain and joy and solitude and community to discover her own inner self" (paragraph 14)? To what extent do we all need to do this in our lives?

DISCOVERING RHETORICAL STRATEGIES

9. Sawaquat occasionally uses dialogue to help make his points. What does the dialogue add to the various narratives he cites here?
10. Describe as thoroughly as possible the point of view of Sawaquat's narrator. Include in your answer a discussion of person, vantage point, and attitude.

Thinking Critically

◆ What important truths did the author learn about himself during this transition in his life?

11. Why do you think Sawaquat divides his essay into three sections? Why do you think he spends most of his time on the second section?

12. Although Sawaquat uses primarily narration to advance his point of view, which other rhetorical strategies help support his essay? Give examples of each.

MAKING CONNECTIONS

13. Compare the concern Lewis Sawaquat has for his daughter with that displayed between parent and child in "The Saturday Evening Post" (Russell Baker), "Mother Tongue" (Amy Tan), and/or "Battle Hymn of the Tiger Mother" (Amy Chua). Which parent do you think loves his or her child most? On what do you base this conclusion?

14. How strong is Sawaquat's attachment to his Native-American culture? Contrast the passion of his ethnic identity with that demonstrated by Sandra Cisneros ("Only Daughter"), Richard Rodriguez ("Public and Private Language"), and/or Robert Ramirez ("The Barrio").

15. What responsibilities, according to Sawaquat, should parents accept regarding the eventual happiness of their children? Would Mary Pipher ("Beliefs About Families") and/or Michael Dorris ("The Broken Cord") agree with him? Why or why not? To what extent do you agree with Sawaquat?

IDEAS FOR DISCUSSION/WRITING

Preparing to Write

Write freely about your own identity: What is your cultural heritage? How do you fit into your immediate environment? Has your attitude about yourself and your identity changed over the years? Do you know your own inner self? How do you plan to continue learning about yourself?

Choosing a Topic   MyWritingLab™

1. **LEARNING ONLINE** If you had a blog that was a forum for your ideas, what topics would you want to write about and publish? Write a narrative for your blog in which you share some personal experiences in a public arena. Using Sawaquat's essay as a model, describe specific incidents and the way they affected you. If possible, to support your story, add artwork similar to that on the Smithsonian website from Preparing to Read.

2. Write a narrative essay that uses one or more stories from your past in order to describe to a group of friends the main features of your identity.

3. Explain to your children (whether real or imaginary) in narrative form some simple but important truths about your heritage. Take care to select your details well, choose an appropriate point of view, and arrange your essay logically so that you keep your readers' interest throughout the essay.

4. Have you recently experienced any social traumas in your life that you would like to prepare someone else for? Write a letter to the person you would like to warn. Use narration to explain the situation, and suggest ways to avoid the negative aspects you encountered.

Before beginning your essay, you may want to consult the flowchart on page 102.

MAYA ANGELOU   (1928–2014)

New Directions

Maya Angelou was born Marguerite Johnson on April 4, 1928, in St. Louis, Missouri. Nicknamed "Maya" by her brother, she moved with her family to California; then, at age three, she was sent to live with her grandmother in Stamps, Arkansas, where she spent the childhood years later recorded in her autobiographical novel *I Know Why the Caged Bird Sings* (1970). After a brief marriage, she embarked on an amazingly prolific career in dance, drama, and writing. Before her death in 2014, Angelou was at various times a nightclub performer specializing in calypso songs and dances, an actress, a playwright, a civil-rights activist, a newspaper editor, a television writer and producer, a poet, and a screenwriter. She also wrote several television specials, including *Three Way Choice* (a five-part miniseries) and *Afro-Americans in the Arts,* both for PBS. Her other work includes five novels: *I Shall Not Be Moved* (1990), *Lessons in Living* (1993), *Wouldn't Take Nothing for My Journey Now* (1993), *A Brave and Startling Truth* (1995), and *Phenomenal Woman* (2000). In addition, she published *A Song Flung Up to Heaven* (2002), *Hallelujah! The Welcome Table* (2004), *Letter to My Daughter* (2008), *Great Food, All Day Long* (2010), and *Mom & Me & Mom* (2013). Angelou received numerous awards, including the Presidential Medal of Freedom in 2010 and over 50 honorary degrees. A tall, graceful, and imposing woman, Angelou was once described as conveying "pride without arrogance, self-esteem without smugness." Her advice to writers is "to write so that what you say slides through the brain and goes straight to the heart."

Preparing to Read

Taken from Angelou's book *Wouldn't Take Nothing for My Journey Now,* the following essay describes how Annie Johnson, a strong and determined woman, found "a new path" in her life.

Exploring Experience: Before you read this essay, take a moment to think about a time you changed directions: What were the circumstances surrounding this change? Why did you make the change? What did you learn from the experience? What alterations would you make if you followed this path again?

LEARNINGⓊNLINE Maya Angelou has some strong opinions on the topic of courage. To get a sense of Angelou's thoughts on this subject, go to www.youtube.com, and type "Dr. Maya Angelou/Courage" into the search field. Play the top search result, and consider how Angelou's attitudes toward courage and self-identity are evident in Annie Johnson's character.

Before reading this essay, you may want to consult the flowchart on page 99.

In 1903 the late Mrs. Annie Johnson of Arkansas found herself with two   1
toddling sons, very little money, a slight ability to read and add simple
numbers. To this picture add a disastrous marriage and the burdensome
fact that Mrs. Johnson was a Negro.❶

When she told her husband, Mr. William Johnson, of her dissatisfaction   2
with their marriage, he conceded that he too found it to be less than he
expected and had been secretly hoping to leave and study religion. He added
that he thought God was calling him not only to preach but to do so in
Enid, Oklahoma. He did not tell her that he knew a minister in Enid with
whom he could study and who had a friendly, unmarried daughter. They
parted amicably, Annie keeping the one-room house and William taking
most of the cash to carry himself to Oklahoma.

Annie, over six feet tall, big-boned, decided that she would not go to   3
work as a domestic and leave her "precious babes" to anyone else's care.
There was no possibility of being hired at the town's cotton gin or lumber
mill, but maybe there was a way to make the two factories work for her. In
her words, "I looked up the road I was going and back the way I come, and
since I wasn't satisfied, I decided to step off the road and cut me a new path."
She told herself that she wasn't a fancy cook but that she could "mix groceries well enough to scare hunger away from a starving man."

She made her plans meticulously and in secret. One early evening to see   4
if she was ready, she placed stones in two five-gallon pails and carried them
three miles to the cotton gin. She rested a little, and then, discarding some
rocks, she walked in the darkness to the saw mill five miles farther along the
dirt road. On her way back to her little house and her babies, she dumped
the remaining rocks along the path.

That same night she worked into the early hours boiling chicken and   5
frying ham. She made dough and filled the rolled-out pastry with meat. At
last she went to sleep.❷

The next morning she left her house carrying the meat pies, lard, an iron   6
brazier, and coals for a fire. Just before lunch she appeared in an empty lot
behind the cotton gin. As the dinner noon bell rang, she dropped the savors
into boiling fat, and the aroma rose and floated over to the workers who
spilled out of the gin, covered with white lint, looking like specters.❸

Most workers had brought their lunches of pinto beans and biscuits or   7
crackers, onions and cans of sardines, but they were tempted by the hot meat

---

Thinking Critically
❶ Why does Angelou describe Annie Johnson's ethnicity as "burdensome"?
❷ What specific details does the author include to indicate how hard Annie worked for success?
❸ How do these particular details affect Angelou's essay?

pies which Annie ladled out of the fat. She wrapped them in newspapers, which soaked up the grease, and offered them for sale at a nickel each. Although business was slow, those first days Annie was determined. She balanced her appearances between the two hours of activity.

So, on Monday if she offered hot fresh pies at the cotton gin and sold the   8
remaining cooled-down pies at the lumber mill for three cents, then on Tuesday she went first to the lumber mill presenting fresh, just-cooked pies as the lumbermen covered in sawdust emerged from the mill.

For the next few years, on balmy spring days, blistering summer noons,   9
and cold, wet, and wintry middays, Annie never disappointed her customers, who could count on seeing the tall, brown-skin woman bent over her brazier, carefully turning the meat pies. When she felt certain that the work-ers had become dependent on her, she built a stall between the two hives of industry and let the men run to her for their lunchtime provisions.

She had indeed stepped from the road which seemed to have been chosen   10
for her and cut herself a brand-new path. In years that stall became a store where customers could buy cheese, meal, syrup, cookies, candy, writing tablets, pickles, canned goods, fresh fruit, soft drinks, coal, oil, and leather soles for worn-out shoes.

Each of us has the right and the responsibility to assess the roads which lie   11
ahead, and those over which we have traveled, and if the future road looms ominous or unpromising, and the roads back uninviting, then we need to gather our resolve and, carrying only the necessary baggage, step off that road into another direction. ⁴ If the new choice is also unpalatable, without embarrassment, we must be ready to change that as well.

UNDERSTANDING DETAILS

1. What path is Annie Johnson following that she dislikes? How does she change this path?
2. Describe Annie physically and mentally in your own words. Use as much detail as possible.
3. Why does Annie carry stones in two five-gallon pails for three miles? What is she trying to accomplish?
4. In what ways does Annie's business grow? How does Annie's personality make this growth possible?

Thinking Critically

4 ▸ Have you ever "changed direction" in your life? How did it compare to Angelou's change? Was the change good for you? Why or why not?

READING CRITICALLY

5. Why do you think Annie succeeds in her business? What are the main ingredients of her success?

6. In what ways are the details at the beginning of this narrative essay typical of the year 1903?

7. What does Angelou mean when she says, "Each of us has the right and the responsibility to assess the roads which lie ahead, and those over which we have traveled" (paragraph 11)? In what way is this message basic to an understanding of the essay?

8. Explain the title of the essay. Cite specific details from the essay in your explanation.

DISCOVERING RHETORICAL STRATEGIES

9. Angelou writes this narrative essay in a fairly formal style, using multisyllable words (*concede* rather than *yield* or *let*) and the characters' titles with their names (Mrs. Annie Johnson instead of Annie Johnson). Why do you think Angelou presents her essay in this way? Describe the tone she maintains throughout the essay.

10. The author uses the metaphor of taking a "new road" to describe Annie Johnson's decision. Is this metaphor effective, in your opinion? Why or why not?

11. Over what period of time do you think this story took place? How does the author show her readers that time is passing in this narrative essay?

12. Angelou often ends her essays with lessons that she wants the readers to understand. How does her lesson in the last paragraph of this narrative essay affect the story? Does the story itself go with the lesson? How did you respond to having the author tell you what to think at the end of the story?

MAKING CONNECTIONS

13. In Angelou's essay, Annie Johnson cuts "a new path" for herself by selling food to factory workers. Contrast this sudden change in the direction of her life with similar "new paths" taken by Brent Staples in "A Brother's Murder," Carole Kanchier in "Dare to Change Your Job and Your Life in 7 Steps," and/or by female weightlifters in Gloria Steinem's "The Politics of Muscle." Who do you think had the most difficult transition to make? Explain your answer.

14. If Angelou, Sandra Cisneros ("Only Daughter"), Russell Baker ("The Saturday Evening Post"), and/or Harold Krents ("Darkness at Noon") were discussing the value of persistence and determination in life, which author would argue most strongly for the importance of that quality? Why? Would you agree?

15. Food or drink is an important ingredient not only in Angelou's essay, but also in those written by Ray Bradbury ("Summer Rituals"), Kimberly Wozencraft ("Notes from the Country Club"), and David Hanson ("Binge Drinking"). How is food or drink featured in these essays? Does this topic help achieve the author's purpose in each case?

IDEAS FOR DISCUSSION/WRITING

Preparing to Write

Write freely about all the major changes you have made in your life: Were most of these changes for the best? How did they benefit you? How did they benefit others? Did they hurt anyone? Do you think most people have trouble changing directions in their lives? Why or why not? How might we all improve our attitudes about change?

Choosing a Topic

MyWritingLab™

1. **LEARNINGⓊNLINE** Go online and find an entrepreneur who inspires you. Possible examples include Shawn Fanning (Napster), Ben Cohen and Jerry Greenfield (Ben & Jerry's Ice Cream), Masaru Ibuka and Akio Morita (Sony), Walt Disney (Disneyland, Walt Disney Pictures), Anita Roddick (The Body Shop), Bill Gates (Microsoft), Oprah Winfrey (*Oprah, O,* HARPO), Ted Turner (Cable News Network, Turner Network Television), Martha Stewart (Martha Stewart Omnimedia), Mark Zuckerberg (Facebook), Steve Jobs (Apple), or Howard Schultz (Starbucks). Some of these people are no longer with us, but all of them had to have courage to launch their companies. Gather enough details about the entrepreneur you choose so you can write a narrative with a clear focus. Using Angelou's essay as a model, organize your story around a central theme or message.

2. The editor of your school newspaper has asked you to write a narrative essay about an important change you made in your life. The newspaper is running a series of essays about changing directions in life, and the staff has heard that you have a story to tell. Tell your story in essay form to be printed in the school newspaper.

3. Why are major changes so difficult for us to make? Write a narrative essay for your peers to respond to this question. Use characters to dramatize your answer.

4. Decide on an important truth about life, and then write a narrative essay to support that truth. Make the details as vivid as possible.

Before beginning your essay, you may want to consult the flowchart on page 102.

KENNETH MILLER   (1960–   )

Class Act

After flirting with possible careers as a punk rock musician and cartoonist, Kenneth Miller earned his B.A. in American Studies at Wesleyan University and his M.S. in Journalism at Columbia, followed by a series of high-profile publishing jobs, including stints as an associate editor at *Rolling Stone* and as a senior editor at *People Magazine*, *Life*, and *Reader's Digest*. Currently a freelance writer based in Los Angeles who specializes in human interest, real-life adventure, crime, and entertainment features, he has published articles in *Discover*, *Elle*, *Mother Jones*, *Los Angeles Times Magazine*, *Prevention*, and other popular periodicals. His books include *Our Times: The Illustrated Encyclopedia of the 20th Century* (1995), *Pictures of the Year* (1996), and *Decades of the Twentieth Century* (1999). More recently, Miller has published articles on a variety of topics from the usefulness of mushrooms in environmental health to the commercial space race. He also keeps and regularly posts on a blog at his website. Frequent guest appearances on *CNN*, *Larry King Live*, and *The Today Show* have made him a well-known media figure. His advice to students using *The Prose Reader* is to find inspiration by "shining a light on people who might ordinarily be unnoticed, people who are generally treated with contempt, people who are stories waiting to be hatched, because they have a great deal in common with the rest of us."

Preparing to Read

First published in *Reader's Digest* (November 2007), "Class Act" follows the inspiring story of Brenda Combs, formerly a homeless crack addict, who rose out of the gutter to become an award-winning teacher in Phoenix.

Exploring Experience: As you prepare to read this selection, take a few minutes to think about various experiences that have helped define your current personality: What are these experiences? Why are they significant to you? What other people were involved in these experiences? How do these people perceive you as a person?

LEARNINGⓊNLINE Go to www.npr.org, and search for "College Students Hide Hunger, Homelessness." Before reading Miller's essay, listen to the NPR story about how students already in college are struggling financially. According to these interviews, what sacrifices are college students making to complete their education?

Before reading this essay, you may want to consult the flowchart on page 99.

Just north of the airport in Phoenix, in one of America's most violent   1
neighborhoods, the crackle of gunfire often ricochets between shabby
stucco houses. Jacked-up cars blaring hip-hop cruise past the dirt yards,
and the clatter of police helicopters echoes through the desert air. But if
you listen closely, you can hear a chorus of small voices wafting from a
classroom in a white brick school building. Brenda Combs is leading her
students in song. "When we wake up in the morning," she belts out in a
soulful contralto, "we can brush our teeth . . . comb our hair . . . eat some
food . . . and get ready for a brand-new day."

The kids in this summer class range in age from 5 to 12 and, like most   2
pupils at StarShine Academy—a charter school serving kindergarten through
12th grade—come from Phoenix's poorest families.[1] Some of their parents
are drug addicts; others are homeless. The woman by the chalkboard, for her
part, has achieved a kind of success that once would have seemed well beyond
her grasp. Combs, who runs the summer program and teaches third and
fourth grades the rest of the year, was recently listed in *Who's Who Among
America's Teachers*. When she received her master's in education from Grand
Canyon University last spring, First Lady Laura Bush sent congratulations.
As Combs was being interviewed on CNN, the university's CEO showed
up with a surprise graduation present: a full scholarship toward a Ph.D.

"Brenda is incredibly gifted," says StarShine Academy's founder, Patricia   3
McCarty. "I often think of how many people used to walk by her and say,
'She's a throwaway.'" What makes Combs such an extraordinary educator of
at-risk children—the kind whose students drop by later to thank her—may
be the years she spent living on the streets as a desperate crack addict. She
slept under bridges and rummaged through dumpsters for breakfast. And
she seldom used a comb or a toothbrush.

Combs, 45, likes to show teenage students her "before" photos, which   4
portray a gaunt, disheveled derelict with zombie eyes. "I know what it's like
to want to get high," she says, "to be hungry and abused. They trust me
because I've been there."

When Combs was a girl in Flagstaff, 135 miles to the north, few would   5
have expected her to follow such a torturous path. Her father was a baker
by day and a janitor by night; her mother, a part-time restaurant cook. Both
believed in education and hard work. Brenda, the eldest of three, had an
ear for music; when she taught herself to play "What a Friend We Have in
Jesus" on the piano as a kindergartner, her mother wept with pride. For her
family, church came before all else.

Thinking Critically

1 What is a "charter school"? How is it different from other public schools?

"My parents were very religious," she recalls, "and they had a firm grip 6 on their kids." Drinking, smoking, and cursing were prohibited; so were dating and slang. Brenda felt like a misfit among her more worldly peers, especially after the family moved from the inner city to a mostly white suburb. By the time she got to college, she was determined to live by her own rules. She lasted a year at Northern Arizona University, then quit and found work as a bank teller.

She also started partying. First came margaritas and daiquiris, then pot 7 and acid. A boyfriend introduced her to cocaine. Combs now believes she has an addictive personality.[2] At the time, she knew only that getting high banished her insecurities and inhibitions. She began drifting from job to job, committing petty crimes. Arrested for forgery and shoplifting, she got off with probation. But Combs's real undoing proved to be crack—smokable cocaine—which hit Flagstaff in the mid-1980s. Suddenly nothing else mattered. Home became a cheap motel or an acquaintance's sofa.

When Combs failed a drug test, violating probation, an attorney helped 8 her avoid prison. She went through rehab, and the two wound up falling in love. Combs took a job as a hairdresser and began pursuing her dream of becoming a singer, playing nightclubs on weekends. But her relapses doomed the relationship, and she plummeted back into addiction.

In 1992 she drifted to Phoenix. One night, she was walking past a house 9 where a raucous card game was in progress. A car screeched to a halt. "I remember hearing a clicking sound," Combs says. "Then I saw guns come out of the window." The target was a man she'd just asked for a cigarette. He threw himself on top of her, but both were wounded in the fusillade.

Combs's left ankle was so thoroughly shattered that surgeons considered 10 amputation. After months in hospitals, she returned to the streets, still on crutches.

"For me," she says, "cocaine was the best medication." 11

At StarShine Academy, one of Brenda Combs's favorite motivational tools 12 is a snow cone machine. She bought it a few years ago for her son, Mycole, now seven, but decided to share its bounty. Every Friday afternoon, she makes cones for each of the school's 130 students. "They work hard all week," she says. "They need a little reward."

Combs labors tirelessly to help kids beat the odds. "Miss Brenda made 13 me see that wherever you come from, you can do something great," says Ricky Gomez, 14, who recently won a scholarship for gifted students to a

---

Thinking Critically

[2] What are you addicted to in life? Why are some addictions more difficult to overcome than others?

Catholic high school. Combs, he says, steered him away from drugs and toward his dream of becoming an architect.[3]

She makes regular home visits, even when the domicile is a dilapidated   14
trailer. When a parent is in jail, Combs has been known to put up an extra child or two in her own small house. "She doesn't expect any credit for it," says Beth Brantley, who gave Combs her first teaching job seven years ago.

Because the school operates on a slim budget, Combs scours yard sales,   15
spending part of her $35,000 salary on art supplies, educational games and AV equipment. She spends her evenings devising lesson plans—a math game involving pizza slices, an English unit in which students publish their own books. To make ends meet as a single mother, she holds down part-time jobs: choir director, online college instructor. And on Sundays, after church, she brings food, water and a bit of hope to those who live on the streets. "I want to go back and let them know, Hey, I made it," she says. "If I can do it, you can too."

It wasn't the bullets that got Combs to change her ways. Over the years, she   16
was beaten, stabbed, burned with cigarettes and raped. She survived multiple overdoses and a pipeful of crack laced with rat poison. Then, one morning in 1995, she awoke beneath a highway overpass to find that her shoes had been stolen.

The ground that day was hot enough to raise blisters. Combs was literally   17
stuck. But the thief had stolen more than her shoes; he took the last scrap of her dignity. "It all just hit me," she recalls, "I thought, This cannot be the life that God intended for me."

After a friend rustled up a pair of sneakers, Combs walked to the police   18
station and turned herself in. Her probation officer handed her a catalog of rehab programs and ordered her to find one she could stick with. Combs chose a halfway house and set about healing herself. The year she spent there, she says, was the hardest she had ever known. The slightest emotional upset, the flare of a cigarette lighter, even certain songs on the radio, would set off ferocious cravings. Most of the other residents eventually relapsed. But for Combs, this time, there was no turning back.

After getting clean, Combs surrounded herself with supportive mentors   19
but didn't always heed their counsel. Her most serious misstep was marrying an addict who was trying to stay sober, with far less success. While Combs worked to pay the rent, Jose would disappear on binges; he sometimes beat her when he returned. The abuse continued even after she discovered she was pregnant. She was 37 and hadn't used illegal drugs for five years. No one could explain why, hours after Mycole's birth in January 2000, the infant suffered a near-fatal stroke. He was left with brain damage, and doctors warned that he might never learn to walk, talk, or feed himself.

Thinking Critically

[3] Has a teacher ever changed your life? When? How did it happen?

Combs filed for divorce when her son was three months old, after Jose,   20
in a rage, trashed their house and took a swipe at Mycole. At the time, she
was working days at a collection agency and nights at a restaurant. That fall,
her day boss told her to decide between keeping her job or rushing to the
hospital every time her son had a seizure. Combs quit on the spot.

Beth Brantley, who ran the day care center where Mycole spent much of   21
his time, saw an opportunity. Having just started a charter school for older
kids, she made an offer: If Combs would come work for her, Mycole could
stay for free.

"I'd never thought about teaching before," Combs says. But after a week,   22
she knew she'd found her calling.⁴ To enhance her skills and credentials,
she began taking education courses at a community college. By 2005 she
had earned her bachelor's degree at the online University of Phoenix and
enrolled in the master's program at Grand Canyon University. After Brantley
closed her school, Combs applied for a position at StarShine.

During the job interview, Patricia McCarty asked her why she wanted   23
to work in a hardscrabble neighborhood when she could earn far more in
a comfortable suburb. "She said, 'These kids are me,'" McCarty recalls.
"'And we're here to change the world.'"

Today Combs and her son live in a two-bedroom bungalow she helped   24
build with a small army of Habitat for Humanity volunteers. She has reconciled with her parents, who love to take Mycole on fishing trips. He is in
second grade now, and after years of intensive therapy, he's an avid basketball
player, an eager student, and a voracious reader.

Combs's own horizons continue to expand. McCarty is grooming her to   25
become principal of a new StarShine school. Organizations are asking her
to give speeches. Publishers want her to write an autobiography, and pro-
ducers want to turn it into a movie.

All the attention is a little dizzying, but she has weathered tougher   26
challenges. "Many doors are opening to me," she marvels. Then she laughs.
"I guess I'm ready."

UNDERSTANDING DETAILS

1. Describe Combs in your own words.
2. How did she succumb to drugs?
3. When did Combs decide to get clean once and for all? What were the
   circumstances?
4. In what ways do Combs's "horizons continue to expand" (paragraph 25)?

Thinking Critically

⁴ How do most people find their "callings" in life? Have you found yours? If not, how and
when do you think it will happen?

READING CRITICALLY

5. What is the purpose of this essay?
6. What is the importance of Combs's listing in *Who's Who Among America's Teachers?*
7. What choices in Combs's life define her character?
8. Why is she a good example for others in impoverished situations? What can her triumph over adversity teach them?

DISCOVERING RHETORICAL STRATEGIES

9. The author takes five paragraphs to set up the scene for this narrative. Is this an effective beginning for his essay? Explain your answer.
10. The essay is divided by spacing into seven sections. Label the theme and purpose of each section. In other words, how does each piece of the essay further its general message?
11. Who is Miller's target audience? On what do you base your answer?
12. Is the organization of this narrative essay engaging for the typical reader? Explain your answer.

MAKING CONNECTIONS

13. Imagine that Brenda Combs, Maya Angelou ("New Directions"), Harold Krents ("Darkness at Noon"), and/or Michael Dorris ("The Broken Cord") are having a discussion about the value of determination in life. Which of them would argue most vigorously that we all need a little help from others to be successful in life? Who would feel that we can rely only on ourselves?
14. How is Miller's narrative style different from that of Sandra Cisneros ("Only Daughter") and/or Russell Baker ("The Saturday Evening Post")? Which author seems most logical and organized to you? Why?
15. What advice about teaching do you think Brenda Combs would give to Amy Chua ("Battle Hymn of the Tiger Mother") and/or Dana Gioia ("On the Importance of Reading")? With whom would you agree most?

IDEAS FOR DISCUSSION/WRITING

Preparing to Write

Write freely about various personal memories in your life or your family's life that have helped shape your character: What are these memories? What do they represent? Which of these memories are demeaning? Which are uplifting? Challenging? Which of these memories are positive? Negative? Why are such stories important in our lives? What have been the principal turning points in your life?

Choosing a Topic

1. **LEARNING⏻NLINE** Brenda Combs is an inspirational model for many. Compare her story to the NPR narrative about Diego Sepulveda from Preparing to Read. Combs hit bottom before she realized she needed to change, whereas Sepulveda had much to lose if he didn't succeed at UCLA. As a continuation of these stories of struggles, your college newspaper has asked you to share your own battles to make ends meet and stay in school. Write a narrative essay in response to their request.

2. Write a narrative essay introducing yourself to your English classmates by telling them about a special experience in your life. Explain and define your identity through some well-chosen events.

3. Write a narrative essay that relates how you met the person in your life who is most supportive of you. What were the highlights of this meeting? What is your relationship with this person now? How did/does this person support you?

4. Write an essay on a special object that best represents you as a student in college. What is this item? How does it represent you? Shape your answers to these questions into a narrative essay.

Before beginning your essay, you may want to consult the flowchart on page 102.

SANDRA CISNEROS   (1954–   )

Only Daughter

Born in Chicago, Sandra Cisneros was the only daughter raised in a family with six brothers. She moved frequently during her childhood, eventually earning a B.A. in English from Loyola University and an M.F.A. in Creative Writing from the University of Iowa, where she developed her unique voice of a strong and independent working-class, Mexican-American woman. Her first book, *The House on Mango Street* (1984), is a loosely structured series of vignettes focusing on the isolation and cultural conflicts endured by Latina women in America. Later publications include *My Wicked, Wicked Ways* (1987), *Woman Hollering Creek* (1991), *The Future Is Mestizo: Life Where Cultures Meet* (2000), *Caramelo* (2002), and *Have You Seen Marie?* (2012). Critics have described her works of fiction as "poetic": "nearly every sentence contains an explosive sensory image. She gives us unforgettable characters that we want to lift off the page and hang out with for a while." Asked to analyze her writing style, Cisneros explains, "I am a woman, and I am a Latina. Those are the things that make my writing distinctive. Those are the things that give my writing power. They are the things that give it *sabor* (flavor), that give it *picante* (spice)." She currently lives in central Mexico with her cats, dogs, and parrots.

Preparing to Read

"Only Daughter," an essay first published in *Glamour,* chronicles one of the author's most memorable experiences on a visit to her parents' home in Chicago. Full of family history, the story uses the reunion as a focus for Cisneros's memories and observations about life in a Mexican family.

Exploring Experience: As you prepare to read this essay, take a few moments to consider the many social and cultural influences that shape your life: What is your family like? What activities do you enjoy? Have you ever felt that your family didn't accept these activities? Have you ever been angry at the extent to which social or cultural pressures have governed your life? How did you react to these forces? Can you think of a specific situation in which you overcame social or cultural differences? What were the circumstances? What was the result?

LEARNING⟲NLINE For a dynamic look into the Latino culture, go to www.pbs.org, and click on "Programs." Then search American Family, and select "American Family—Journey of Dreams." While reading Cisneros's narrative, consider how her experience relates to the accounts on this website.

Before reading this essay, you may want to consult the flowchart on page 99.

Once, several years ago, when I was just starting out my writing 1
career, I was asked to write my own contributor's note for an
anthology. I wrote: "I am the only daughter in a family of six
sons. *That* explains everything."

Well, I've thought that ever since, and yes, it explains a lot to me, but for 2
the reader's sake I should have written: "I am the only daughter in a *Mexican*
family of six sons." Or even: "I am the only daughter of a Mexican father and
a Mexican-American mother." Or: "I am the only daughter of a working-
class family of nine." All of these had everything to do with who I am today.

I was/am the only daughter and *only* a daughter. Being an only daughter 3
in a family of six sons forced me by circumstance to spend a lot of time by
myself because my brothers felt it beneath them to play with a *girl* in public.
But that aloneness, that loneliness, was good for a would-be writer—it
allowed me time to think and think, to imagine, to read and prepare myself.

Being only a daughter for my father meant my destiny would lead me to 4
become someone's wife. That's what he believed. But when I was in the
fifth grade and shared my plans for college with him, I was sure he understood. I remember my father saying, "*Que bueno, mi'ja,* that's good." That
meant a lot to me, especially since my brothers thought the idea hilarious.
What I didn't realize was that my father thought college was good for girls—
good for finding a husband. After four years in college and two more in
graduate school, and still no husband, my father shakes his head even now
and says I wasted all that education. [1]

In retrospect, I'm lucky my father believed daughters were meant for 5
husbands. It meant it didn't matter if I majored in something silly like English. After all, I'd find a nice professional eventually, right? This allowed me
the liberty to putter about embroidering my little poems and stories without
my father interrupting with so much as a "What's that you're writing?"

But the truth is, I wanted him to interrupt. I wanted my father to under- 6
stand what it was I was scribbling, to introduce me as "My only daughter,
the writer." Not as "This is my only daughter. She teaches." *Es maestra*—
teacher. Not even *profesora.*

In a sense, everything I have ever written has been for him, to win his 7
approval even though I know my father can't read English words, even
though my father's only reading includes the brown-ink *Esto* sports magazines from Mexico City and the bloody *¡Alarma!* magazines that feature yet
another sighting of *La Virgen de Guadalupe* on a tortilla or a wife's revenge
on her philandering husband by bashing his skull in with a *molcajete* (a kitchen

---

Thinking Critically

[1] Which type of discrimination is worst: gender, ethnic, or religious? Why do you think so?

mortar made of volcanic rock). Or the *fotonovelas,* the little picture paperbacks with tragedy and trauma erupting from the characters' mouths in bubbles.

A father represents, then, the public majority. A public who is disinterested in reading, and yet one whom I am writing about and for, and privately trying to woo.   8

When we were growing up in Chicago, we moved a lot because of my father. He suffered bouts of nostalgia. Then we'd have to let go of our flat, store the furniture with mother's relatives, load the station wagon with baggage and bologna sandwiches and head south. To Mexico City.   9

We came back, of course. To yet another Chicago flat, another Chicago neighborhood, another Catholic school. Each time, my father would seek out the parish priest in order to get a tuition break, and complain or boast: "I have seven sons." ❷   10

He meant *siete hijos,* seven children, but he translated it as "sons." "I have seven sons." To anyone who would listen. The Sears Roebuck employee who sold us the washing machine. The short-order cook where my father ate his ham-and-eggs breakfasts. "I have seven sons." As if he deserved a medal from the state.   11

My papa. He didn't mean anything by the mistranslation, I'm sure. But somehow I could feel myself being erased. I'd tug my father's sleeve and whisper: "Not seven sons. Six! and one *daughter.*"   12

When my oldest brother graduated from medical school, he fulfilled my father's dream that we study hard and use this—our heads, instead of this—our hands. Even now my father's hands are thick and yellow, stubbed by a history of hammer and nails and twine and coils and springs. "Use this," my father said, tapping his head, "and not this," showing us those hands. He always looked tired when he said it.   13

Wasn't college an investment? And hadn't I spent all those years in college? And if I didn't marry, what was it all for? Why would anyone go to college and then choose to be poor? ❸ Especially someone who has always been poor.   14

Last year, after ten years of writing professionally, the financial rewards started to trickle in. My second National Endowment for the Arts Fellowship. A guest professorship at the University of California, Berkeley. My book, which sold to a major New York publishing house.   15

At Christmas, I flew home to Chicago. The house was throbbing, same as always; hot *tamales* and sweet *tamales* hissing in my mother's pressure   16

Thinking Critically

❷ What are the principal differences between Cisneros and her father? How does her status as the "only daughter" affect their love for each other?

❸ What do you believe is the relationship between attending college and the salary you will earn after graduation?

cooker, and everybody—my mother, six brothers, wives, babies, aunts, cousins—talking too loud and at the same time, like in a Fellini film, because that's just how we are.

I went upstairs to my father's room. One of my stories had just been trans-   17
lated into Spanish and published in an anthology of Chicano writing, and I wanted to show it to him. Ever since he recovered from a stroke two years ago, my father likes to spend his leisure hours horizontally. And that's how I found him, watching a Pedro Infante movie on Galavision and eating rice pudding.

There was a glass filmed with milk on the bedside table. There were   18
several vials of pills and balled Kleenex. And on the floor, one black sock and a plastic urinal that I didn't want to look at but looked at anyway. Pedro Infante was about to burst into song, and my father was laughing. [4]

I'm not sure if it was because my story was translated into Spanish, or   19
because it was published in Mexico, or perhaps because the story dealt with Tepeyac, the *colonia* my father was raised in and the house he grew up in, but at any rate, my father punched the mute button on his remote control and read my story.

I sat on the bed next to my father and waited. He read it very slowly. As   20
if he were reading each line over and over. He laughed at all the right places and read lines he liked out loud. He pointed and asked questions: "Is this So-and-so?" "Yes," I said. He kept reading.

When he was finally finished, after what seemed like hours, my father looked   21
up and asked: "Where can we get more copies of this for the relatives?"

Of all the wonderful things that happened to me last year, that was the   22
most wonderful.

UNDERSTANDING DETAILS

1. How many children are in Cisneros's family? How many are boys?
2. Why does Cisneros's father always say he has seven sons? Why is this detail significant?
3. Why did Cisneros's father let her go to college? Explain your answer.
4. What are the differences in the way the author's father views his sons and his daughter?

READING CRITICALLY

5. What does Cisneros mean when she says, "I am the only daughter and *only* a daughter" (paragraph 3)?
6. What does her cultural heritage have to do with the fact that she is the only daughter?

Thinking Critically

[4] What do TV viewing habits tell us about someone?

7. Why does Cisneros write for her father even though he can't read English?

8. Why was her father's reaction to her story published in Spanish "the most wonderful" (paragraph 22) thing that happened to her last year? Why is her father's opinion so important to her?

DISCOVERING RHETORICAL STRATEGIES

9. From what point of view does Cisneros write this narrative essay? How does this particular point of view help us understand her attitude toward the experience?

10. In writing this essay, Cisneros is making a comment about families in general and Mexican families in particular. What is her ultimate message? What details help you understand this message? Does the fact that she doesn't capitalize "daughter" in her title have anything to do with this message?

11. How does Cisneros organize the details of this narrative? Is this the most effective order for what she is trying to say?

12. Although Cisneros's essay is primarily narrative, what other rhetorical strategies does she use to make her point? Give examples of each.

MAKING CONNECTIONS

13. In "Only Daughter," Sandra Cisneros describes the importance of her father's support of and appreciation for her writing career. Compare and contrast the theme of family support described by Sandra Cisneros, Russell Baker ("The Saturday Evening Post"), Robert Ramirez ("The Barrio"), and/or Mary Pipher ("Beliefs about Families"). Which author would argue that support from one's family is most crucial to our development as a person? Why?

14. Both Sandra Cisneros and Amy Tan ("Mother Tongue") became extremely successful writers in English although they spoke another language at home as they grew up. Can you find any other common denominators in the experiences of these two authors that account for their current skill in using the English language?

15. Compare and contrast the use of examples in the essays by Sandra Cisneros, Harold Krents ("Darkness at Noon"), Brent Staples ("A Brother's Murder"), and/or Frank Furedi ("Our Unhealthy Obsession with Sickness"). Which essay is most densely packed with examples? Which uses example most effectively? Which least effectively? Why?

IDEAS FOR DISCUSSION/WRITING

Preparing to Write

Write freely about a time in your life when you did not fit in with your own family: What were the circumstances? How did you feel? What were your alternatives? Did you take any action? What were the motivating forces for this action? Were you satisfied with the outcome? How do you feel about this experience now?

Choosing a Topic

1. **LEARNINGⓊNLINE** Revisit the PBS "American Family" website, and consider a time when you attempted to receive recognition from a family member. Using Cisneros's narrative as a model, write an essay describing your experience for PBS's "American Family" online collection.

2. Write a narrative essay telling your classmates about a time you did not fit in. Make a special effort to communicate your feelings regarding this experience. Remember to choose your details and point of view with an overall purpose in mind.

3. What is America's system of social classes? Where do you fit into the structure? Does our system allow for much mobility between classes? Write a narrative essay for your classmates explaining your understanding of the American class system. Use yourself and/or a friend as an example.

4. Explain in a coherent essay written for the general public why you think we are all sometimes motivated by cultural or personal influences beyond our control. Refer to Cisneros's essay or to experiences of your own to support your explanation.

Before beginning your essay, you may want to consult the flowchart on page 102.

The Saturday Evening Post

Russell Baker is one of America's foremost satirists and humorists. Born in Virginia, he grew up in New Jersey and Maryland, graduated from Johns Hopkins University, and then served for two years as a pilot in the U.S. Navy. Following the service, he became a newspaper reporter for the *Baltimore Sun*, which sent him to England as its London correspondent. He subsequently joined the staff of *The New York Times* as a member of its Washington bureau. From 1962 to 1998, he wrote his widely syndicated "Observer" column in the *Times*, which blended wry humor, a keen interest in language, and biting social commentary about the Washington scene. His books include *An American in Washington* (1961), *No Cause for Panic* (1964), and *Poor Russell's Almanac* (1972), plus two collections of early essays, *So This Is Depravity* (1980) and *The Rescue of Miss Yaskell and Other Pipe Dreams* (1983). *Growing Up* (1982), a best seller vividly recounting his own childhood, earned him the 1983 Pulitzer Prize for biography. His other publications include *The Good Times* (1989), which continues his life story from approximately age twenty until he began working for the *New York Times* in the early 1960s; *There's a Country in My Cellar: The Best of Russell Baker* (1990), a collection of his newspaper columns; *Inventing the Truth: The Art and Craft of Memoir* (1995, with William Zinsser), and *Looking Back,* a compilation of some of his articles written for the *New York Review of Books* (2002). Despite having retired from column writing in 1998, Baker continues to contribute an occasional article and book review to *The New York Times*. His advice to student writers is to "turn off the TV and pick up a book. It will ease your blood pressure. It may even wake up your mind."

Preparing to Read

The following skillfully written essay is an excerpt from Baker's autobiography, *Growing Up*. In it, the author recalls enduring memories from his youth that clearly project the experiences and emotions of his coming of age in 1920s rural Virginia.

Exploring Experience: As you prepare to read this selection, think for a moment about some of your own childhood memories: What were your strengths as a child? Your weaknesses? Have these character traits changed as you've matured? How are you like or unlike various members of your family? How do you react to these similarities and/or differences? What are your main goals in life? How do your character traits affect these goals?

LEARNING◯NLINE Explore the Norman Rockwell Museum website (www.nrm.org) by clicking "Exhibitions" and then "Current Exhibitions" to see online pictures of *Saturday Evening Post* covers and other artistic representations of the 1930s and 1940s. These images represent the time period that Russell Baker describes. How do these pictures differ from your childhood images?

Before reading this essay, you may want to consult the flowchart on page 99.

I began working in journalism when I was eight years old. It was my   1
mother's idea. She wanted me to "make something" of myself and, after
a levelheaded appraisal of my strengths, decided I had better start young
if I was to have any chance of keeping up with the competition. [1]

The flaw in my character which she had already spotted was lack of "gump-   2
tion." My idea of a perfect afternoon was lying in front of the radio rereading
my favorite Big Little Book, *Dick Tracy Meets Stooge Viller.* My mother despised
inactivity. Seeing me having a good time in repose, she was powerless to hide
her disgust. "You've got no more gumption than a bump on a log," she said.
"Get out in the kitchen and help Doris do those dirty dishes."

My sister Doris, though two years younger than I, had enough gumption   3
for a dozen people. [2] She positively enjoyed washing dishes, making beds,
and cleaning the house. When she was only seven, she could carry a piece
of short-weighted cheese back to the A&P, threaten the manager with legal
action, and come back triumphantly with the full quarter-pound we'd paid
for and a few ounces extra thrown in for forgiveness. Doris could have made
something of herself if she hadn't been a girl. Because of this defect, however, the best she could hope for was a career as a nurse or schoolteacher,
the only work that capable females were considered up to in those days.

This must have saddened my mother, this twist of fate that had allocated   4
all the gumption to the daughter and left her with a son who was content
with Dick Tracy and Stooge Viller. If disappointed, though, she wasted no
energy on self-pity. She would make me make something of myself whether
I wanted to or not. "The Lord helps those who help themselves," she said.
That was the way her mind worked.

She was realistic about the difficulty. Having sized up the material the   5
Lord had given her to mold, she didn't overestimate what she could do with
it. She didn't insist that I grow up to be President of the United States.

Fifty years ago parents still asked boys if they wanted to grow up to be   6
President, and asked it not jokingly but seriously. Many parents who were
hardly more than paupers still believed their sons could do it. Abraham
Lincoln had done it. We were only sixty-five years from Lincoln. Many a
grandfather who walked among us could remember Lincoln's time. Men of
grandfatherly age were the worst for asking if you wanted to grow up to be
President. A surprising number of little boys said yes and meant it.

I was asked many times myself. No, I would say, I didn't want to grow up to   7
be President. My mother was present during one of these interrogations. An
elderly uncle, having posed the usual question and exposed my lack of interest
in the Presidency, asked, "Well, what *do* you want to be when you grow up?"

Thinking Critically

[1] What does the first paragraph of the essay imply about Baker's opinion of his mother?
How are their personalities different?

[2] What proof does the author offer that his sister Doris had "gumption"?

I loved to pick through trash piles and collect empty bottles, tin cans with   8
pretty labels, and discarded magazines. The most desirable job on earth
sprang instantly to mind. "I want to be a garbage man," I said.

My uncle smiled, but my mother had seen the first distressing evidence   9
of a bump budding on a log. "Have a little gumption, Russell," she said. Her
calling me Russell was a signal of unhappiness. When she approved of me,
I was always "Buddy."

When I turned eight years old she decided that the job of starting me on   10
the road toward making something of myself could no longer be safely
delayed. "Buddy," she said one day, "I want you to come home right after
school this afternoon. Somebody's coming, and I want you to meet him."

When I burst in that afternoon, she was in conference in the parlor with an   11
executive [3] of the Curtis Publishing Company. She introduced me. He bent
low from the waist and shook my hand. Was it true as my mother had told him,
he asked, that I longed for the opportunity to conquer the world of business?

My mother replied that I was blessed with a rare determination to make   12
something of myself.

"That's right," I whispered.   13

"But have you got the grit, the character, the never-say-quit spirit it takes   14
to succeed in business?"

My mother said I certainly did.   15

"That's right," I said.   16

He eyed me silently for a long pause, as though weighing whether I could   17
be trusted to keep his confidence, then spoke man-to-man. Before taking a
crucial step, he said, he wanted to advise me that working for the Curtis
Publishing Company placed enormous responsibility on a young man. It
was one of the great companies of America. Perhaps the greatest publishing
house in the world. I had heard, no doubt, of the *Saturday Evening Post*?

Heard of it? My mother said that everyone in our house had heard of the   18
Saturday Post and that I, in fact, read it with religious devotion. [4]

Then doubtless, he said, we were also familiar with those two monthly pil-   19
lars of the magazine world, the *Ladies Home Journal* and the *Country Gentleman*.

Indeed we were familiar with them, said my mother.   20

Representing the *Saturday Evening Post* was one of the weightiest honors   21
that could be bestowed in the world of business, he said. He was personally
proud of being a part of the great corporation.

Thinking Critically

[3] Do you think the man introduced to Russell is really an "executive" of the Curtis Publishing Company? How does this word betray his mother's manipulative nature?

[4] What does Baker's mother mean when she claims that her son reads the *Saturday Evening
Post* "with religious devotion"?

My mother said he had every right to be.   22

Again he studied me as though debating whether I was worthy of a   23
knighthood. Finally: "Are you trustworthy?"

My mother said I was the soul of honesty.   24

"That's right," I said.   25

The caller smiled for the first time. He told me I was a lucky young man.   26
He admired my spunk. Too many young men thought life was all play.
Those young men would not go far in this world. Only a young man willing
to work and save and keep his face washed and his hair neatly combed could
hope to come out on top in a world such as ours. [5] Did I truly and sincerely
believe that I was such a young man?

"He certainly does," said my mother.   27

"That's right," I said.   28

He said he had been so impressed by what he had seen of me that he was   29
going to make me a representative of the Curtis Publishing Company. On
the following Tuesday, he said, thirty freshly printed copies of the *Saturday
Evening Post* would be delivered at our door. I would place these magazines,
still damp with the ink of the presses, in a handsome canvas bag, sling it over
my shoulder, and set forth through the streets to bring the best in journalism, fiction, and cartoons to the American public.

He had brought the canvas bag with him. He presented it with reverence   30
fit for a chasuble. He showed me how to drape the sling over my left shoulder and across the chest so that the pouch lay easily accessible to my right
hand, allowing the best in journalism, fiction, and cartoons to be swiftly
extracted and sold to a citizenry whose happiness and security depended
upon us soldiers of the free press.

The following Tuesday I raced home from school, put the canvas bag over   31
my shoulder, dumped the magazines in, and, tilting to the left to balance
their weight on my right hip, embarked on the highway of journalism.

We lived in Belleville, New Jersey, a commuter town at the northern   32
fringe of Newark. It was 1932, the bleakest year of the Depression. [6] My
father had died two years before, leaving us with a few pieces of Sears, Roebuck furniture and not much else, and my mother had taken Doris and me
to live with one of her younger brothers. This was my Uncle Allen. Uncle
Allen had made something of himself by 1932. As salesman for a soft-drink
bottler in Newark, he had an income of $30 a week; wore pearl-gray spats,
detachable collars, and a three-piece suit; was happily married; and took in
threadbare relatives.

Thinking Critically

[5] Is this still good advice today? What is your advice for success?

[6] What signs of the Depression can you find in this essay?

With my load of magazines I headed toward Belleville Avenue. That's where   33
the people were. There were two filling stations at the intersection with Union
Avenue, as well as an A&P, a fruit stand, a bakery, a barber shop, Zuccarelli's
drugstore, and a diner shaped like a railroad car. For several hours I made myself
highly visible, shifting position now and then from corner to corner, from shop
window to shop window, to make sure everyone could see the heavy black
lettering on the canvas bag that said THE SATURDAY EVENING POST. When the
angle of the light indicated it was suppertime, I walked back to the house.

"How many did you sell, Buddy?" my mother asked.   34

"None."   35

"Where did you go?"   36

"The corner of Belleville and Union Avenues."   37

"What did you do?"   38

"Stood on the corner waiting for somebody to buy a *Saturday Evening Post.*"   39

"You just stood there?"   40

"Didn't sell a single one."   41

"For God's sake, Russell!"   42

Uncle Allen intervened. "I've been thinking about it for some time," he   43
said, "and I've about decided to take the *Post* regularly. Put me down as a
regular customer." I handed him a magazine, and he paid me a nickel. It was
the first nickel I earned.

Afterwards my mother instructed me in salesmanship. I would have to   44
ring doorbells, address adults with charming self-confidence, and break
down resistance with a sales talk pointing out that no one, no matter how
poor, could afford to be without the *Saturday Evening Post* in the home.

I told my mother I'd changed my mind about wanting to succeed in the   45
magazine business.

"If you think I'm going to raise a good-for-nothing," she replied, "you've   46
got another think coming." She told me to hit the streets with the canvas
bag and start ringing doorbells the instant school was out next day. When I
objected that I didn't feel any aptitude for salesmanship, she asked how I'd
like to lend her my leather belt so she could whack some sense into me. I
bowed to superior will [7] and entered journalism with a heavy heart.

My mother and I had fought this battle almost as long as I could remem-   47
ber. It probably started even before memory began, when I was a country
child in northern Virginia and my mother, dissatisfied with my father's plain
workman's life, determined that I would not grow up like him and his people,
with calluses on their hands, overalls on their backs, and fourth-grade

---

Thinking Critically

[7] When Baker admits that he "bowed to superior will," he is being ironic since his mother
has threatened to whack him with a belt if he doesn't begin selling the magazine. What
other examples of irony can you find in the essay?

educations in their heads. She had fancier ideas of life's possibilities. Introducing me to the *Saturday Evening Post,* she was trying to wean me as early as possible from my father's world where men left with their lunch pails at sunup, worked with their hands until the grime ate into the pores, and died with a few sticks of mail-order furniture as their legacy. In my mother's vision of the better life there were desks and white collars, well-pressed suits, evenings of reading and lively talk, and perhaps—if a man were very, very lucky and hit the jackpot, really made something important of himself—perhaps there might be a fantastic salary of $5,000 a year to support a big house and a Buick with a rumble seat and a vacation in Atlantic City.

And so I set forth with my sack of magazines. I was afraid of the dogs that   48
snarled behind the doors of potential buyers. I was timid about ringing the doorbells of strangers, relieved when no one came to the door, and scared when someone did. Despite my mother's instructions, I could not deliver an engaging sales pitch. When a door opened I simply asked, "Want to buy a *Saturday Evening Post?*" In Belleville few persons did. It was a town of 30,000 people, and most weeks I rang a fair majority of its doorbells. But I rarely sold my thirty copies. Some weeks I canvassed the entire town for six days and still had four or five unsold magazines on Monday evening; then I dreaded the coming of Tuesday morning, when a batch of thirty fresh *Saturday Evening Posts* was due at the front door. [8]

"Better get out there and sell the rest of those magazines tonight," my   49
mother would say.

I usually posted myself then at a busy intersection where a traffic light   50
controlled commuter flow from Newark. When the light turned red, I stood on the curb and shouted my sales pitch at the motorists.

"Want to buy a *Saturday Evening Post?*"   51

One rainy night when car windows were sealed against me, I came back   52
soaked and with not a single sale to report. My mother beckoned to Doris.

"Go back down there with Buddy and show him how to sell these maga-   53
zines," she said.

Brimming with zest, Doris, who was then seven years old, returned with   54
me to the corner. She took a magazine from the bag, and when the light turned red, she strode to the nearest car and banged her small fist against the closed window. The driver, probably startled at what he took to be a midget assaulting his car, [9] lowered the window to stare, and Doris thrust a *Saturday Evening Post* at him.

"You need this magazine," she piped, "and it only costs a nickel."   55

Thinking Critically

[8] In what ways do you think selling is like writing?

[9] The description of Doris assaulting the car like a "midget" is one among many examples of humor in this essay. Can you find two other humorous images?

Her salesmanship was irresistible. Before the light changed half a dozen   56
times, she disposed of the entire batch. I didn't feel humiliated. To the contrary. I was so happy I decided to give her a treat. Leading her to the vegetable store on Belleville Avenue, I bought three apples, which cost a nickel, and gave her one.

"You shouldn't waste money," she said.   57

"Eat your apple." I bit into mine.   58

"You shouldn't eat before supper," she said. "It'll spoil your appetite." [10]   59

Back at the house that evening, she dutifully reported me for wasting a nickel.   60
Instead of a scolding, I was rewarded with a pat on the back for having the good sense to buy fruit instead of candy. My mother reached into her bottomless supply of maxims and told Doris, "An apple a day keeps the doctor away."

By the time I was ten I had learned all my mother's maxims by heart.   61
Asking to stay up past normal bedtime, I knew that a refusal would be explained with, "Early to bed and early to rise, makes a man healthy, wealthy, and wise." If I whimpered about having to get up early in the morning, I could depend on her to say, "The early bird gets the worm."

The one I most despised was, "If at first you don't succeed, try, try again."   62
This was the battle cry with which she constantly sent me back into the hopeless struggle whenever I moaned that I had rung every doorbell in town and knew there wasn't a single potential buyer left in Belleville that week. After listening to my explanation, she handed me the canvas bag and said, "If at first you don't succeed . . ."

Three years in that job, which I would gladly have quit after the first day   63
except for her insistence, produced at least one valuable result. My mother finally concluded that I would never make something of myself by pursuing a life in business and started considering careers that demanded less competitive zeal.

One evening when I was eleven, I brought home a short "composition"   64
on my summer vacation which the teacher had graded with an A. Reading it with her own schoolteacher's eye, my mother agreed that it was top-drawer seventh grade prose and complimented me. Nothing more was said about it immediately, but a new idea had taken life in her mind. Halfway through supper she suddenly interrupted the conversation.

"Buddy," she said, "maybe you could be a writer."   65

I clasped the idea to my heart. I had never met a writer, had shown no   66
previous urge to write, and hadn't a notion how to become a writer, but I loved stories and thought that making up stories must surely be almost as much

---

Thinking Critically

[10] What examples can you find of Doris growing up to be a carbon copy of her mother?

fun as reading them. Best of all, though, and what really gladdened my heart, was the ease of the writer's life.[11] Writers did not have to trudge through the town peddling from canvas bags, defending themselves against angry dogs, being rejected by surly strangers. Writers did not have to ring doorbells. So far as I could make out, what writers did couldn't even be classified as work.

I was enchanted. Writers didn't have to have any gumption at all. I did 67 not dare tell anybody for fear of being laughed at in the schoolyard, but secretly I decided that what I'd like to be when I grew up was a writer.

UNDERSTANDING DETAILS

1. How does Baker's ideal day differ from that of his sister?
2. According to the author's mother, what is the main flaw in his character? How does this flaw eventually affect his choice of a career?
3. Why does Baker feel he has no "aptitude for salesmanship" (paragraph 46)? What has led him to this conclusion?
4. Which of his mother's maxims does the author dislike the most? Explain his reaction.

READING CRITICALLY

5. Why does Baker begin this selection with a comparison of his personality and his sister's? What does this comparison have to do with the rest of the essay?
6. Why does the author's mother insist that he work for the *Saturday Evening Post*? What does she think he will gain from the experience? What does he actually learn?
7. What "battle" (paragraph 47) have the author and his mother been fighting for as long as he can remember? Who finally wins this battle?
8. Why is Baker so delighted with the idea of becoming a writer when he grows up? How is this notion compatible with his personality?

DISCOVERING RHETORICAL STRATEGIES

9. How does Baker arrange the details in this excerpt? Why do you think he organizes them in this way? How would a different arrangement have changed the essay?
10. Who do you think is Baker's intended audience? Describe them in detail. How did you come to this conclusion?
11. What is the climax of Baker's narrative? How does he lead up to and develop this climactic moment? What stylistic traits tell us that this is the most exciting point in the story?
12. Besides narration, what other rhetorical strategies does Baker draw on to develop his thesis? Give examples of each of these strategies.

Thinking Critically

11 Do you think a writer's life is "easy"? Why or why not?

MAKING CONNECTIONS

13. Baker insists on the importance of dedicating oneself to a career. Compare and contrast his feelings on this subject with similar sentiments found in essays by Sandra Cisneros ("Only Daughter") and/or Gloria Steinem ("The Politics of Muscle"). How dedicated do you intend to be to your own future career?

14. How is young Russell Baker's naive conception of a writer's "easy" life different from the views on writing expressed by Sandra Cisneros ("Only Daughter") and/or Amy Tan ("Mother Tongue")? Which of these authors would argue most fervently that writing is "hard work"? How do you feel about the process of writing? Is it easy or difficult for you? Explain your answer.

15. Russell Baker's mother had a strong influence over him as he grew up. Imagine a conversation among Baker, Amy Chua ("Battle Hymn of the Tiger Mother"), and/or Mary Pipher ("Beliefs about Families") concerning the importance of proper parental guidance as a child matures. Which author would be most adamant about the importance of the role of parents in a child's upbringing? Explain your answer.

IDEAS FOR DISCUSSION/WRITING

Preparing to Write

Write freely about yourself in relation to your aspirations: What type of person are you? What do you think about? What are your ideals? Your hopes? Your dreams? Your fears? What do you enjoy doing in your spare time? How are you different from other members of your family? Is anyone in your family a model for you? How have members of your immediate family affected your daily life—past and present? Your career goals? How do you anticipate that your family will affect your future?

Choosing a Topic   MyWritingLab™

1. **LEARNING◯NLINE** Reflect on your worst memory of working at a particular job or chore. Write an email to Baker in which you explain how an experience that seemed horrible at the time actually had positive results. Following Baker's example, establish a strong sense of time and place in your narrative. Add a photo or drawing to your narrative that, like those on the Norman Rockwell Museum website, captures the memory and the time period.

2. Write a narrative essay introducing yourself to your English class. To explain and define your identity, include descriptions of family members whenever appropriate.

3. Write a narrative that helps explain to a friend how you got involved in a current interest. To expand on your narrative, refer whenever possible to your long-term goals and aspirations.

4. Ten years from now, your local newspaper decides to devote an entire section to people getting started in careers. You are asked to submit the story of how you got involved in your profession (whatever it may be). Write a narrative that might appear in your hometown newspaper ten years from now; be sure to give the article a catchy headline.

Before beginning your essay, you may want to consult the flowchart on page 102.

Chapter Writing Assignments

Practicing Narration

1. Think of a story that is often repeated by your family members because of its special significance or its humor. Retell the story to an audience who does not know your family, and explain to your readers the story's significance.
2. What has been the most challenging and life-changing event in your life? Remember this event as clearly as you can by noting special details on scratch paper. Write an essay that describes what led up to this event, what happened, and how you reacted to the event. Explain why this experience was so challenging and/or life changing.
3. Think of a time when you received a very special gift. Tell the story of how you received this gift, who gave it to you, and why it was memorable. For a more sophisticated approach, try to think of gifts that are not material or tangible objects but rather intangible qualities or concepts (such as love, life, and happiness).

Exploring Ideas

4. Write an essay that identifies the most important qualities in a friend. Explain how each quality is important to a meaningful and fulfilling friendship.
5. Cut an advertisement out of a magazine or newspaper. Examine its "story" and the way the advertiser is selling the product. Write an essay that discusses the effect of advertising on individuals and on American society. How honest or believable should advertising be? What are our expectations for advertising?
6. Describe a time when you quit a job or hobby that others thought you should continue. Discuss the principal features of this activity, your frustration with them, and the main aspects of the job or hobby that others valued. In retrospect, do you think you made a wise decision?

Analyzing Visual Images

7. Look at the photo on the next page, and think of a time when you went to the beach. Tell a story based on your trip. What was most memorable? What simple pleasures pleased you most? Why was this particular trip to the beach important or noteworthy?
8. Reflect on the picture at the beginning of this chapter (p. 98). Develop the story that might lead up to this picture as its conclusion.

Larry Mulvehill/The Image Works.

Composing in Different Genres

9. Multimedia: Create a cartoon or a comic strip for an original story. This could be based on an actual experience of yours or a completely fictional idea. Create the artwork so the story is as clear as possible to the reader. You can supplement your drawings with words.
10. Multigenre: Write a fairytale for a preschool child. Create the story with words; then add photos or drawings if you choose.

Writing from Sources

For detailed information on writing from sources, see Part III.

11. Many Americans can trace their ancestry to a relative who immigrated to this country. Research one ethnic group—either your own or another that interests you—known for their immigration to the United States. Then, narrate a historical account, including factual information, from the perspective of an individual in that group.
12. Laws have become much more stringent regarding child labor in the United States, but are children across the world protected? What is your position on this issue? What are the causes leading to international abuse of child labor? What are some possible solutions? Research this issue, and write a documented essay comparing the systems and practices of child labor in two different cultures.

MyWritingLab™ Visit Ch. 5. Narration: Telling a Story in *MyWritingLab* to complete the writing assignments and test your understanding of the chapter learning objectives.

Chapter 6

EXAMPLE
Illustrating Ideas

LEARNING OBJECTIVES

After completing this chapter, you will be able to do the following:
- Define illustration
- Use examples to think critically
- Read example essays critically
- Write and revise effective example essays

Citing an example to help make a point is one of the most instinctive techniques we use in communication. If, for instance, you state that being an internationally ranked tennis player requires constant practice, a friend might challenge that assertion and ask what you mean by "constant practice." When you respond "at least three hours a day," your friend might ask for more specific proof. At this stage in the discussion, you could offer the following illustrations to support your statement: When not on tour, Andy Roddick practices three hours per day; Maria Sharapova, four hours; and Roger Federer, five hours. Your friend's doubt will have been answered through your use of examples.

DEFINING EXAMPLES

Well-chosen examples and illustrations are an essay's building blocks. They are drawn from your experience, your observations, and your reading. They help you *show* rather than *tell* what you mean, usually by supplying concrete details (references to what we can see, smell, taste, hear, or touch) to support abstract ideas (such as faith, hope, understanding, and love), by providing specifics ("I like chocolate") to explain generalizations ("I like sweets"), and by giving definite references ("Turn left at the second stoplight") to clarify vague statements ("Turn in a few blocks"). Though illustrations take many forms, writers often find themselves indebted to description or narration (or some combination of the two) to supply enough relevant examples to achieve their rhetorical intent.

As you might suspect, examples are important ingredients in producing exciting, vivid prose. Just as crucial is the fact that carefully chosen examples often encourage your readers to feel one way or another about an issue being discussed. If you tell your parents, for instance, that living in a college dormitory is not conducive to academic success, they may doubt your word, perhaps thinking that you are simply attempting to coerce money out of them for an apartment. You can help dispel this notion, however, by giving them specific examples of the chaotic nature of dorm life: the party down the hall that broke up at 2:00 A.M. when you had a chemistry exam that same morning at 8:00; the stereo next door that seems to be stuck on its highest decibel level at all hours of the day and night; and the new "friend" you recently acquired who thinks you are the best listener in the world—especially when everyone else has the good sense to be asleep. After such a detailed and well-documented explanation, your parents could hardly deny the strain of this difficult environment on your studies. Examples can be very persuasive.

The following paragraphs written by a student use examples to explain how the writer reacts to boredom in his life. As you read this excerpt, notice how the writer shows rather than tells the readers how he copes with boredom by providing exciting details that are concrete, specific, and definite.

We all deal with boredom in our own ways. Unfortunately, most of us have to deal with it far too often. Some people actually seek boredom. Being bored means that they are not required to do anything and that no one wants anything from them. In short, these people equate boredom with peace and relaxation. But for the rest of us, boredom is not peaceful. It produces anxiety.

Most people deal with boredom by trying to distract themselves from boring circumstances. I, for example, am a reader. At the breakfast table over a boring bowl of cereal, I read the cereal box, the milk carton, or the wrapper on the bread. (Have you ever noticed how many of those ingredients are unpronounceable?)

Waiting in a doctor's office, I will gladly read weekly news magazines from three years ago, a book for five-year-olds, advertisements for drugs, and even the physician's odd-looking diplomas on the walls. Have you ever been so bored you were reduced to reading through all the business cards in your wallet, searching for names similar to yours in the phone book, or browsing through

Example   145

the National Enquirer while waiting in the grocery line? I have. At any rate, that's my recipe for beating boredom. What's yours?

THINKING CRITICALLY THROUGH EXAMPLES

Working with examples gives you yet another powerful way of processing your immediate environment and the larger world around you. It involves a manner of thinking that is completely different from description and narration. Using examples to think critically means seeing a definite order in a series of specific, concrete illustrations related in some way that may or may not be immediately obvious to your readers.

Isolating this rhetorical mode involves playing with related details in such a way that they create various patterns that relay different messages to the reader. Often, the simple act of arranging examples helps both the reader and the writer make sense of an experience or idea. In fact, ordering examples and illustrations in a certain way may give one distinct impression, whereas ordering them in another way may send a completely different message. Each pattern creates a different meaning and, as a result, an entirely new effect.

With examples, more than with description and narration, patterns are discovered in the context of the topic, the writer's purpose, and the writer's ultimate message. Writers and readers of example essays must make a shift from chronological to logical thinking. A writer discussing variations in faces, for example, would be working with assorted memories of people, incidents, and age differences. All these details will eventually take shape in some sort of statement about faces, but these observations would probably not follow a strictly chronological sequence.

The exercises here will help you experience the mental differences among the rhetorical modes we have studied so far and will also prepare you to make sense of details and examples through careful arrangement and rearrangement of them in your essay. In addition, these exercises will continue to give you more information about your mind's abilities and range.

1. In the photograph on the following page, what kinds of examples do you see? Is this an example of simplicity or complexity? Good photography or bad photography? Make a list of at least five other ways this photograph could serve as an example.
2. For each of the following sentences, provide two to three examples that would illustrate the generalization:
   a. I really liked/disliked some of the movies released this year.
   b. Many career opportunities await a college graduate.
   c. Some companies make large sums of money by selling products with the names of professional sports teams on them.
3. Jot down five examples of a single problem on campus that bothers you. First, arrange these examples in an order that would convince the

Nando Azevedo/Fotolia.

president of your school that making some changes in this area would create a more positive learning environment. Second, organize your five examples in such a way that they would convince your parents that the learning environment at your current school cannot be salvaged and you should immediately transfer to another school.

READING AND WRITING EXAMPLE ESSAYS

A common criticism of college-level writers is that they often base their essays on unsupported generalizations, such as "All sports cars are unreliable." The guidelines discussed in this introduction will help you avoid this problem and use examples effectively to support your ideas.

As you read the essays in this chapter, take time to notice the degree of specificity the writers use to make various points. To a certain extent, the more examples you use in your essays, the clearer your ideas will be and the more your readers will understand and be interested in what you are saying.

Example   147

Notice also that these writers know when to stop—when "more" becomes too much and boredom sets in for the reader. Most college students err by using too few examples, however, so we suggest that, when in doubt about whether or not to include another illustration, you should go ahead and add one.

Reading Example Essays

Understanding how example essays work rhetorically will help you make decisions for your own writing. Here is a flowchart of questions that will guide your reading for this purpose.

Questions to Guide Your Reading

PREPARING TO READ Before you read the essays, answer the following questions:
- What assumptions can you make from the essay's **title**?
- What do you think the general **mood** of the essay will be?
- What is the essay's **purpose** and **audience**?
- What does the **synopsis** tell you about the essay?
- What can you learn from the author's **biography**?
- What do you predict the author's **point of view** toward the subject will be?

READING As you read the essays for the first time, answer the following questions:
- What is the writer's **main message**?
- What is the essay's **context**?
- How do **examples** communicate this message?

REREADING When you read the essays again, answer the following questions:
- What examples help the author **communicate** the essay's message?
- How are these examples **organized**?
- What other **rhetorical modes** does the author use?
- How does your understanding of the essay **change** with each rereading?

Preparing to Read.   Before you begin reading the essays in this chapter, take some time to think about each author's title: What can you infer about Christopher Nelson's attitude toward college from her title "Why We Are Looking At the 'Value' of College All Wrong"? What do you think is Richard Rodriguez's view of his past? In addition, try to discover the writer's audience and purpose at this point in the reading process; scanning the essay and surveying its synopsis in the Rhetorical Table of Contents will provide you with useful information for this task.

Also important as you prepare to read is information about the author and about how a particular essay was written. Most of this material is furnished for you in the biography preceding each essay. From it, you might learn why Harold Krents is qualified to write about blindness or why Brent Staples published "A Brother's Murder."

Finally, before you begin to read, take time to answer the Preparing to Read questions and to make some associations with the general subject of the essay: What do you know about your cultural and ethnic heritage (Richard Rodriguez)? What are some of your thoughts on the Internet (Roni Jacobson)?

Reading.   As you first read these essays, record any ideas that come to mind. Make associations freely with the content of each essay, its purpose, its audience, and the facts about its publication. For example, try to learn why Nelson writes about college or why Krents titles his essay "Darkness at Noon." At this point, you will probably be able to make some pretty accurate guesses about the audience each author is addressing. Creating a context for your reading—including the writer's qualifications; the essay's tone, purpose, and audience; and the publication data—is an important first step toward being able to analyze your reading material in any mode.

Each essay also contains questions at the bottom of the pages that guide you to think critically about the essay's subject and the claims the author is making about that topic. Answering these questions as you read will help you develop the skills to read critically and succeed in your other classes. Your responses will also help you generate ideas to build on as you continue to read. Ultimately, they help you build a bridge between your prereading thoughts and the exercises and writing assignments at the end of each essay.

Finally, after you have read an essay in this section once, preview the questions after the selection before you read it again. Let these questions focus your attention for your second reading.

Example   149

Rereading.   As you read the essays in this chapter for a second time, focus on the examples each writer uses to make his or her point: How relevant are these examples to the thesis and purpose of each essay? How many examples do the writers use? Do they vary the length of these examples to achieve different goals? Do the authors use examples their readers can easily identify with and understand? How are these examples organized in each case? Does this arrangement support each writer's purpose? For example, how relevant are Nelson's examples to her central idea? How many examples does Richard Rodriguez use to make each point? Does Krents vary the length of each of his examples to accomplish different purposes? How does Stein organize his examples? Does this arrangement help him accomplish his purpose? In what way? Does Staples use examples that everyone can identify with? How effective are his examples?

As you read, consider also how other rhetorical modes help each writer accomplish his or her purpose. What are these modes? How do they work along with examples to help create a coherent essay?

Last, answering the questions after each essay will help you check your grasp of its main points and will lead you from the literal to the analytical level in preparation for the discussion/writing assignments that follow.

For a thorough summary of reading tasks, you might want to consult the Reading Checklist at the end of Chapter 2.

Writing Example Essays

Now that you see how examples work in an essay, use the same features in your own writing. The flowchart on the next page provides some questions to guide you.

Preparing to Write.   Before you can use examples in an essay, you must first think of some. One good way to generate ideas is to use some of the prewriting techniques explained in Chapter 3 (pages 26–28) as you respond to the Preparing to Write questions that appear before the writing assignments for each essay. You should then consider these thoughts in conjunction with the purpose and audience specified in your chosen writing assignments. Out of these questions should come a number of good examples for your essay.

Writing.   In an example essay, a thesis statement or controlling idea will help you begin to organize your paper. (See pages 31–32 for more information on thesis statements.) Examples become the primary method of organizing an essay when they actually guide the readers from point to point in reference to the writer's thesis statement. The examples you use should always be relevant to the thesis and purpose of your essay. If, for

Questions to Guide Your Writing

PREPARING TO WRITE
Before you start writing, answer these questions:

- What is your **purpose**?
- Who is your **audience**?
- What **message** do you want to convey?

WRITING As you write your first draft consider these questions:

- What is your **thesis** or main message?
- Do the **examples** you are choosing support this thesis?
- Are these examples **arranged** as effectively as possible?
- What other **rhetorical modes** will support your thesis?

EDITING Be sure to proofread and edit your paper before turning it in.

- Are your **sentences** all complete?
- Do your words say exactly **what you mean**?
- Do you follow conventional **grammar and usage** rules?

REVISING After you write your first draft, use the following questions to revise your essay:

- Have you included enough **examples** to develop each of your topics adequately?
- Are the examples you have chosen **relevant** to your thesis?
- Have you arranged these examples in a **logical** manner?

instance, the person talking about tennis players cited the practice schedules of only unknown players, her friend certainly would not be convinced of the truth of her statement about how hard internationally ranked athletes work at their game. To develop a topic principally with examples, you can use one extended example or several shorter examples, depending on the nature and purpose of your assertion. If you are attempting to prove that Americans are more health conscious now than they were twenty years ago, citing a few examples from your own neighborhood will not provide enough evidence to be convincing. If, however, you are simply commenting on a neighborhood health trend, you can legitimately refer to these local cases. Furthermore, always try to find examples with which your audience

Example   151

can identify so that they can follow your line of reasoning. If you want your parents to help finance an apartment, citing instances from the lives of current rock stars will probably not prove your point because your parents may not sympathize with these particular role models.

The examples you choose must also be arranged as effectively as possible to encourage audience interest and identification. If you are using examples to explain the imaginative quality of Disneyland, for instance, the most logical approach would probably be to organize your essay by degrees (i.e., from least to most imaginative or from most to least original). But if your essay uses examples to help readers visualize your bedroom, a spatial arrangement of the details (moving from one item to the next) might be easiest for your readers to follow. If the subject is a series of important events, like graduation weekend, the illustrations might most effectively be organized chronologically. As you will learn from reading the selections that follow, the careful organization of examples leads quite easily to unity and coherence in your essays. *Unity* is a sense of wholeness and interrelatedness that writers achieve by making sure all their sentences are related to the essay's main idea; *coherence* refers to logical development in an essay, with special attention to how well ideas grow out of one another as the essay develops. Unity and coherence produce good writing—and that, of course, helps foster confidence and accomplishment in school and in your professional life.

Revising. As you reread your example essays, look closely at the choice and arrangement of details in relation to your purpose and audience:

For more detailed information on writing, see the Writing Checklist at the end of Chapter 3.

STUDENT ESSAY: EXAMPLES AT WORK

In the following essay, a student uses examples to explain and analyze her parents' behavior as they prepare for and enjoy their grandchildren during the Christmas holidays. As you read it, study the various examples the student writer uses to convince us that her parents truly undergo a transformation each winter.

Mom and Dad's Holiday Disappearing Act

General topic   Often during the winter holidays, people find surprises: Children discover the secret contents of brightly wrapped packages that have teased them for weeks; cooks are astonished by the wealth of smells and memories their busy kitchens can bring about; and workaholics stumble upon the true joy of a few days'

Details to capture holiday spirit

rest. My surprise over the past few winters has been the personality transformation my parents go through around mid-December as they change from Dad and Mom into Poppa and Granny. <u>They become grand-parents and are completely different from the people I know the other eleven and a half months of the year.</u>

<u>The first sign of my parents' metamorphosis is the delight they take in visiting toy and children's clothing stores.</u> These two people, who usually despise any-thing having to do with shopping malls, become crazed consumers. While they tell me to budget my money and shop wisely, they are buying every doll, dump truck, and velvet outfit in sight. However, this is only the beginning of the holidays!

<u>When my brother's children arrive</u>, Poppa and Granny come into full form. <u>First they throw out all ideas about a balanced diet for the grandkids.</u> While we were raised in a house where everyone had to take two bites of broccoli, beets, or liver (foods that appeared quite often on our table despite constant groaning), the grandchildren never have to eat any-thing that does not appeal to them. Granny carries marshmallows in her pockets to bribe the littlest ones into following her around the house while Poppa offers "surprises" of candy and cake to them all day long. Boxes of chocolate-covered cherries disappear while the bran muffins get hard and stale. The kids love all the sweets, and when the sugar revs up their energy levels, Granny and Poppa can always leave and do a bit more shopping or go to bed while my brother and sister-in-law try to deal with their supercharged, hyperactive kids.

<u>Once the grandchildren have arrived, Granny and Poppa also seem to forget all of the lectures on respon-sibility I so often hear in my daily life.</u> If little Tommy throws a fit at a friend's house, he is "overwhelmed by the number of adults"; if Mickey screams at his sister during dinner, he is "developing his own personality"; if Nancy breaks Granny's vanity mirror (after being told twice to put it down), she is "just a curious child." But if I track mud into the house while helping to

Example   153

unload groceries, I am being "careless," and if I scold one of the grandkids for tearing pages out of my calculus book, I am "impatient." If a grandchild talks back to her mother, Granny and Poppa chuckle at her spirit. If I mumble one word about all of this doting, Mom and Dad have a talk with me about petty jealousies.

Transition to conclusion   When my nieces and nephews first started appearing at our home for the holidays a few years ago, I was probably jealous, and I complained a lot. Now I spend more time simply sitting back and watching Mom and Dad change into what we call the "Incredible Huggers." They enjoy their time with these grandchildren so much that I easily forgive them their Granny and Poppa faults.   *Writer's attitude*

Writer's analysis of situation   I believe their personality change is due to the lack of responsibility they feel for their grandkids. In their role as grandparents, they don't have to worry about sugar causing cavities or temporary failures of self-discipline turning into lifetime faults. Those problems are up to my brother and sister-in-law to fix. All Granny and Poppa have to do is enjoy and love their grandchildren. They have all the fun of being parents without any of the obligations. And actually, I think they've earned the right to make this transformation—at least once a year.   *Specific reference to introduction*

Concluding remark

Student Writer's Comments

To begin this essay, I listed examples of my parents' antics during the Christmas holidays as parents and as grandparents and then tried to figure out how these examples illustrated patterns of behavior. Next, I scratched out an outline pairing my parents' actions with what I thought were the causes of those actions. However, once I sat down to write, I was completely stumped. I had lots of isolated ideas and saw a few patterns, but I had no notion of where this essay was going.

I thought I might put the theory that writing is discovery to the ultimate test and sit down to write out a very rough first draft. I wanted the introduction to be humorous, but I also wanted to maintain a dignified tone (so I wouldn't sound like a whiny kid!). I was really having trouble getting started. I decided to write down *anything* and then come back to the beginning later on. All of the examples and anecdotes were swimming around in my head wanting to be committed to paper. But I couldn't make sense of many of them, and I still couldn't see where I was headed. I found I needed my thesaurus and dictionary from the very beginning; they helped take the pressure off me to come up with the perfect word every time I was stuck. As I neared the middle of the paper, the introduction popped into my head, so I jotted down my thoughts and continued with the flow of ideas I needed for the body of my essay.

Writing my conclusion forced me to put my experiences with my parents into perspective and gave me an angle for revising the body of my essay. But my actual focus didn't come to me until I began to revise my entire paper. At that point, I realized I had never really tried to analyze how I felt toward my parents' actions or why they acted as they do during the Christmas holidays. I opened the conclusion with "I believe their [my parents'] personality change is due to" and sat in one place until I finished the statement with a reason that made sense out of all these years of frustration. It finally came to me: They act the way they do during the holidays because they don't have primary responsibility for their grandkids. It's a role they have never played before, and they are loving it. (Never mind how it is affecting me!) This basic realization led me to new insights about the major changes they go through during the holidays and ended up giving me a renewed appreciation of their behavior. I couldn't believe the sentence I wrote to close the essay: "I think they've earned the right to make this transformation—at least once a year." Writing this essay actually brought me to a new understanding of my parents.

Revising was a breeze. I felt as if I had just been through a completely draining therapy session, but I now knew what I thought of this topic and where my essay was headed. I dropped irrelevant examples, reorganized other details, and tightened up some of the explanations so they set up my conclusion more clearly. Both my parents and I were delighted with the results.

SOME FINAL THOUGHTS ON EXAMPLES

Although examples are often used to supplement and support other methods of development—such as cause/effect, comparison/contrast, and process analysis—the essays in this section focus principally on examples. A main idea is expressed in the introduction of each, and the rest of the essay provides examples to bolster that contention. As you read these essays, pay close attention to each author's choice and arrangement of examples; then try to determine which organizational techniques are most persuasive for each specific audience.

CHRISTOPHER NELSON   (1952–   )

Why We Are Looking at the "Value" of College All Wrong

Christopher B. Nelson received his B.A. from St. John's College in 1970 and graduated from the Utah University College of Law in 1973. After practicing law in Chicago for 18 years, he accepted his current post as President of St. John's at Annapolis, Maryland. An active voice in issues concerning higher education, Nelson serves on various boards and committees, among them the Board of Directors and the Accountability Committee of the National Association of Independent Colleges and Universities. He has served on the Board of Directors of the Maryland Independent Colleges and Universities Association and was past chair and a founding member of the Annapolis Group, a consortium of over 120 of the nation's leading liberal arts colleges. Nelson is considered a national spokesperson for the liberal arts and often contributes his ideas to the *Huffington Post* and the *Washington Post*. In addition to speaking on higher education issues, Nelson has lectured on Virgil, Plato, Homer, and John Henry Cardinal Newman. He is involved locally with the arts, the government, and various historical preservation efforts. He is currently an active contributor to a national conversation on the value of a college degree.

Preparing to Read

The following selection was first published in the *Washington Post* in Valerie Strauss's column on education. In this essay, Nelson takes a close look at the value of a liberal arts education and insists that we can't judge its success or failure by economic standards.

Exploring Experience: Before reading this piece, pause to consider the effect college is having on your life: How did you make the decision to attend college? What variables were involved in this decision? What have been some of the difficulties you have faced in college? Some of the joys? What goals do you have for yourself after college?

LEARNING◍NLINE Visit the U.S. Department of Education website at www.ed.gov, and select the "Data" tab on the top of the page. Read some of the articles and statistics on education. What types of examples do the writers use to support their claims? While reading "Why We Are Looking at the 'Value' of College All Wrong," consider how these examples are either similar to or different from the examples cited by Christopher Nelson.

Before reading this essay, you may want to consult the flowchart on page 147.

As college admission deadlines loom, new lists and rankings prolifer-   1
ate along with reports questioning the "value" of a college education. The obsession with quantification is rooted in a habit of
applying economic categories to everything. Yet education and economics
are essentially incompatible. The lens of economics distorts our judgment
about the true worth of higher education.

The incompatibility rests on a fundamental difference between econom-   2
ics and education. Begin with the idea of economics as the science of
scarcity.[1] The price of a commodity is largely dependent on its relative
scarcity. Economic value increases when a commodity becomes scarce, and
a commodity that is not scarce will become scarce if it is distributed widely
and used up indiscriminately. Scarcity is basic to the world view of
economics—so much so that the language of economics speaks as though
scarcity and value are inseparable.

The things that matter most in education, though, do not fit this para-   3
digm. They are not scarce, and yet they are extremely valuable—indeed they
are among the most valuable in human life. They do not become scarce by
being shared. Instead, they expand and grow the more they are shared.

One of these things is knowledge. Knowledge has never been exhausted   4
by spreading it to more and more people. Today, it is more abundant than
at any time in the past, and it reproduces more prolifically as it is shared.
Moreover, technology has made it possible to store knowledge efficiently
and to access it cheaply. No wonder that the economic paradigm is having
difficulty capturing and domesticating it into a well-behaved economic
commodity.

This is disconcerting for institutions that think of themselves primarily as   5
providers of information. If the knowledge is out there, freely accessible,
why then should anyone pay large sums of money to a knowledge gatekeeper[2]—let alone go into debt? Today, the confrontation between free
technological access and proprietary gatekeeping is leading to turmoil about
new models of delivery in higher education.

But the idea that a college or university is a purveyor of information is a   6
misplaced economic metaphor. Education is not information transfer. The
educated college graduate is not simply the same person who matriculated
four years earlier with more information or new skills. The educated graduate is a different person—one who has developed the innate human capacity
for learning, to the point of controlling it. The educated graduate is an

---

Thinking Critically

1. Explain the "science of scarcity" in your own words, and give an example of this principle
   from your experience.
2. What are some examples of a university serving as a "knowledge gatekeeper"?

independent learner,[3] able to seek out answers to whatever questions arise, and able to direct his or her own learning in accordance with the challenges that life presents in the circumstances of his or her own life.

The maturation of the student—not information transfer—is the real pur-   7
pose of colleges and universities. Of course, information transfer occurs during this process. One cannot become a master of one's own learning without learning something. But information transfer is a corollary of the maturation process, not its primary purpose. This is why assessment procedures that depend too much on quantitative measures of information transfer miss the mark. It is entirely possible for an institution to focus successfully on scoring high in rankings for information transfer while simultaneously failing to promote the maturation process that leads to independent learning.

It is, after all, relatively easy to measure the means used in getting an   8
education, to assess the learning of intermediate skills that prepare one for a higher purpose—things like mastering vocabulary and spelling, for instance, which help one to communicate. It is also easy to measure the handy, quantifiable by-products of a college education, like post-graduate earning, either in the short term or long term. But both of these kinds of measures fail to speak to education's proper end—the maturation of the student.

We need to move away from easy assessments that miss the point to more   9
difficult assessments that try to get at the maturation process. The Gallup-Purdue Index Report entitled "Great Jobs, Great Lives" found six crucial factors linking the college experience to success at work and overall well-being in the long term:

1. at least one teacher who made learning exciting
2. personal concern of teachers for students
3. finding a mentor
4. working on a long-term project for at least one semester
5. opportunities to put classroom learning into practice through internships or jobs
6. rich extracurricular activities

We should turn all our ingenuity toward measuring factors like these,   10
difficult as that task might be, and use these results to push back against easy assessments based on the categories of economics.

Unless we stop taking the easy way, unless we get past our habit of inter-   11
preting everything in economic terms, we will never grasp the true value of a college education.

Thinking Critically

[3] In what ways are you on your way to becoming an "independent learner"?

UNDERSTANDING DETAILS

1. According to Nelson, what is the "real purpose" (paragraph 7) of a college education?
2. What is the relationship of scarcity and value in economics?
3. What does Nelson mean when he says, "Education is not information transfer" (paragraph 6)?
4. List the six factors that the Gallup-Purdue Index found to be essential to success at work and in life in general. What do these factors have in common?

READING CRITICALLY

5. According to Nelson, why does the "lens of economics" (paragraph 1) prevent us from seeing the true value of higher education?
6. Explain Nelson's definition of "the educated graduate" (paragraph 6) in your own words. In what general ways will the college graduate be different from the same person who started college four years earlier?
7. In what ways are education and economics incompatible?
8. Why will easy methods of assessment not be an effective measure for higher education?

DISCOVERING RHETORICAL STRATEGIES

9. How does the first paragraph set the tone for the rest of the essay? What is the main message in this paragraph that Nelson explains in his essay?
10. What examples does Nelson use to prove his point?
11. What other rhetorical strategies does Nelson use to develop his essay? Give examples of each.
12. Do you think listing the factors for success from the Gallup-Purdue Index (paragraph 9) is an effective addition to this essay or not? Explain your answer in detail.

MAKING CONNECTIONS

13. Compare Christopher Nelson's comments about education with those made on being smart by Sara Gilbert ("The Different Ways of Being Smart"), Art Markman ("Can Video Games Make You Smart (Or At Least More Flexible)?"), and Nicholas Carr ("How the Internet Is Making Us Stupid"). To what extent would these authors agree on how to develop intelligence? To what extent would they disagree?
14. Based on Nelson's statement on the purpose of education, what do you think his opinions would be of Lincoln's and Darwin's contributions to the modern world ("How Lincoln and Darwin Shaped the Modern World" by Adam Gopnik)?
15. Compare and contrast the opinions of Nelson, Motoko Rich ("Literacy Debate: Online, R U Really Reading?"), and/or Dana Gioia ("On the Importance of Reading"). On what points do you think they would concur? On what would they not concur?

IDEAS FOR DISCUSSION/WRITING

Preparing to Write

Write freely about the value of an education: From your observations or experience, what are some of the principal benefits of going to college? What are the main challenges from your perspective? What pleasant or unpleasant experiences have you had in your college classes? What kind of student are you?

Choosing a Topic   MyWritingLab™

1. **LEARNING⏻NLINE** Select a topic related to education on which you feel you have some expertise. Return to the data section of the U.S. Department of Education website that you visited in Preparing to Read. Identify your own question about the topic, and write an essay that explores your question. In organizing your essay, be especially aware of the types of examples you decide to use. Find facts and/or statistics from the U.S. Department of Education website to develop your main point.

2. Write an essay for the general public explaining one particular advantage or disadvantage of going to college. In your essay, use several specific examples to make your point.

3. Write an editorial for your local newspaper on your own foolproof techniques for doing one of the following: (a) being a good student, (b) being a good student–athlete, or (c) working while going to college. Use specific examples to explain your main message.

4. Interview at least two relatives or friends who have attended or currently attend college; ask them about the type of student they are/were. Have them recall some particularly memorable details that characterized their behavior. Then write an essay explaining these two approaches to college. Use examples to support your observations.

Before beginning your essay, you may want to consult the flowchart on page 150.

RICHARD RODRIGUEZ   (1944–   )

Public and Private Language

Richard Rodriguez was raised in Sacramento, California, the son of industrious working-class Mexican immigrant parents. He attended parochial schools there and later continued his education at Stanford University, Columbia University, London's Warburg Institute, and, finally, the University of California at Berkeley, where he earned a Ph.D. in English Renaissance Literature. A writer and journalist, he is now Associate Editor of the Pacific News Service in San Francisco. "The Browning of America" is a phrase coined by Rodriguez to describe the cultural, racial, and ethnic blending of the population in the United States during the twentieth and twenty-first centuries. In 1982, he received wide critical acclaim for the publication of his autobiography, *Hunger of Memory: The Education of Richard Rodriguez*, which detailed his struggle to succeed in a totally alien culture. A regular contributor to the *Los Angeles Times*, he has also published essays in *New Republic, Time, Harper's, American Scholar, Columbia Forum*, and *College English*. Other books he has written are *Days of Obligation: An Argument with My Mexican Father* (1992), an autobiographical study of Mexican immigrants in America, and *Brown: The Last Discovery of America* (2002). More recently, Rodriguez has written *Darling: A Spiritual Autobiography* (2013), a collection of essays on religion, place, and sexuality in post-9/11 America. His current project is a book on Judaism, Islam, Christianity, and the desert. Asked to provide advice for students using *The Prose Reader*, Rodriguez explains, "There is no 'secret' to becoming a writer. Writing takes time—and patience, more than anything else. If you are willing to rewrite and rewrite and rewrite, you will become a good writer."

Preparing to Read

This essay was originally published in *Hunger of Memory*, an autobiography that Rodriguez wrote in 1982 about the experience of growing up in a culture alien to his cultural and ethnic heritage.

Exploring Experience: Before you actually read this essay, think about a time you tried to fit in somewhere: What were the circumstances? What did you do to fit in? Was your attempt successful? If you were unsuccessful, what went wrong? How important to you is "fitting in" or "assimilating" into a particular group? Why is assimilation important or unimportant to you? Explain your answer.

LEARNINGⓊNLINE Visit the Digital Dialects website (www.digitaldialects. com), and select a language you don't know. Then choose a game to play. See how even a simple game, such as a word search or hangman, can be difficult when you're using vocabulary you are not familiar with. Consider this challenge as you read about Rodriguez's struggles with English.

Before reading this essay, you may want to consult the flowchart on page 147.

S upporters of bilingual education today imply that students like me 1
miss a great deal by not being taught in their family's language. What
they seem not to recognize is that, as a socially disadvantaged child, I
considered Spanish to be a private language. What I needed to learn in
school was that I had the right—and the obligation—to speak the public
language of *los gringos.*[1] The odd truth is that my first-grade classmates
could have become bilingual, in the conventional sense of that word, more
easily than I. Had they been taught (as upper-middle-class children are often taught early) a second language like Spanish or French, they could have
regarded it simply as that: another public language. In my case such bilin-
gualism could not have been so quickly achieved. What I did not believe
was that I could speak a single public language.

Without question, it would have pleased me to hear my teachers address 2
me in Spanish when I entered the classroom. I would have felt much less
afraid. I would have trusted them and responded with ease. But I would have
delayed—for how long postponed?—having to learn the language of public
society. I would have evaded—and for how long could I have afforded to
delay?—learning the great lesson of school, that I had a public identity.

Fortunately, my teachers were unsentimental about their responsibility. 3
What they understood was that I needed to speak a public language. So their
voices would search me out, asking me questions. Each time I'd hear them,
I'd look up in surprise to see a nun's face frowning at me. I'd mumble, not
really meaning to answer. The nun would persist, "Richard, stand up. Don't
look at the floor. Speak up. Speak to the entire class, not just to me!" But I
couldn't believe that the English language was mine to use. (In part, I did
not want to believe it.) I continued to mumble. I resisted the teacher's
demands. (Did I somehow suspect that once I learned public language my
pleasing family life would be changed?) Silent, waiting for the bell to sound,
I remained dazed, diffident, afraid.

Because I wrongly imagined that English was intrinsically a public lan- 4
guage and Spanish an intrinsically private one, I easily noticed the difference
between classroom language and the language of home. At school, words
were directed to a general audience of listeners. ("Boys and girls.") Words
were meaningfully ordered. And the point was not self-expression alone but
to make oneself understood by many others. The teacher quizzed, "Boys
and girls, why do we use that word in this sentence? Could we think of a
better word to use there? Would the sentence change its meaning if the

---

Thinking Critically

[1] To what extent do you feel that immigrants to this country have a "right" and/or an
"obligation" to learn English?

words were differently arranged? And wasn't there a better way of saying much the same thing?" (I couldn't say. I wouldn't try to say.)

Three months. Five. Half a year passed. Unsmiling, ever watchful, my   5
teachers noted my silence. They began to connect my behavior with the difficult progress my older sister and brother were making. Until one Saturday morning three nuns arrived at the house to talk to our parents. Stiffly, they sat on the blue living room sofa. From the doorway of another room, spying the visitors, I noted the incongruity—the clash of two worlds, the faces and voices of school intruding upon the familiar setting of home. I overheard one voice gently wondering, "Do your children speak only Spanish at home, Mrs. Rodriguez?" While another voice added, "That Richard especially seems so timid and shy."

That Rich-heard!   6

With great tact the visitors continued, "Is it possible for you and your   7
husband to encourage your children to practice their English when they are home?" Of course, my parents complied. What would they not do for their children's well-being? And how could they have questioned the Church's authority, which those women represented?[2] In an instant, they agreed to give up the language (the sounds) that had revealed and accentuated our family's closeness. The moment after the visitors left, the change was observed. *"Ahora,* speak to us *en ingles,"* my father and mother united to tell us.

At first, it seemed a kind of game. After dinner each night, the family   8
gathered to practice "our" English. (It was still then *ingles,* a language foreign to us, so we felt drawn as strangers to it.) Laughing, we would try to define words we could not pronounce. We played with strange English sounds, often over-anglicizing our pronunciations. And we filled the smiling gaps of our sentences with familiar Spanish sounds. But that was cheating, somebody shouted. Everyone laughed. In school, meanwhile, like my brother and sister, I was required to attend a daily tutoring session. I needed a full year of special attention. I also needed my teachers to keep my attention from straying in class by calling out, *Rich-heard*—their English voices slowly prying loose my ties to my other name, its three notes. *Ri-car-do.*[3] Most of all I needed to hear my mother and father speak to me in a moment of seriousness in broken—suddenly heartbreaking—English. The scene was inevitable: One Saturday morning I entered the kitchen where my parents were talking in Spanish. I did not realize that they were talking in Spanish

---

Thinking Critically

[2] What is the relationship between the nuns' request and their religious authority?
[3] How do the English and Spanish pronunciations of the author's first name help reinforce his distinction between public and private language?

however until, at the moment they saw me, I heard their voices change to speak English. Those *gringo* sounds they uttered startled me. Pushed me away. In that moment of trivial misunderstanding and profound insight, I felt my throat twisted by unsounded grief. I turned quickly and left the room. But I had no place to escape to with Spanish. (The spell was broken.) My brother and sisters were speaking English in another part of the house.

Again and again in the days following, increasingly angry, I was obliged   9
to hear my mother and father: "Speak to us *en ingles.*" *(Speak)*. Only then did I determine to learn classroom English. Weeks after, it happened: One day in school I raised my hand to volunteer an answer. I spoke out in a loud voice. And I did not think it remarkable when the entire class understood. That day, I moved very far from the disadvantaged child I had been only days earlier. The belief, the calming assurance that I belonged in public, had at last taken hold.

Shortly after, I stopped hearing the high and loud sounds of *los gringos*.   10
A more and more confident speaker of English, I didn't trouble to listen to *how* strangers sounded, speaking to me. And there simply were too many English-speaking people in my day for me to hear American accents any-more. Conversations quickened. Listening to persons who sounded eccen-trically pitched voices, I usually noted their sounds for an initial few seconds before I concentrated on *what* they were saying. Conversations became content-full. Transparent. Hearing someone's *tone* of voice—angry or ques-tioning or sarcastic or happy or sad—I didn't distinguish it from the words it expressed. Sound and word were thus tightly wedded. At the end of a day, I was often bemused, always relieved, to realize how "silent," though crowded with words, my day in public had been. (This public silence mea-sured and quickened the change in my life.)

At last, seven years old, I came to believe what had been technically true   11
since my birth: I was an American citizen.

But the special feeling of closeness at home was diminished by then.   12
Gone was the desperate, urgent, intense feeling of being at home: rare was the experience of feeling myself individualized by family intimates. We remained a loving family, but one greatly changed. No longer so close; no longer bound tight by the pleasing and troubling knowledge of our public separateness. Neither my older brother nor sister rushed home after school anymore. Nor did I. When I arrived home there would often be neighbor-hood kids in the house. Or the house would be empty of sounds.

Following the dramatic Americanization of their children, even my par-   13
ents grew more publicly confident. Especially my mother. She learned the names of all the people on our block. And she decided we needed to have a telephone installed in the house. My father continued to use the word *gringo*. But it was no longer charged with the old bitterness or distrust. (Stripped of

any emotional content, the word simply became a name for those Americans not of Hispanic descent.) Hearing him, sometimes, I wasn't sure if he was pronouncing the Spanish word *gringo* or saying gringo in English.

Matching the silence I started hearing in public was a new quiet at home. [14] The family's quiet was partly due to the fact that, as we children learned more and more English, we shared fewer and fewer words with our parents. [4] Sentences needed to be spoken slowly when a child addressed his mother or father. (Often the parent wouldn't understand.) The child would need to repeat himself. (Still the parent misunderstood.) The young voice, frustrated, would end up saying, "Never mind"—the subject was closed. Dinners would be noisy with the clinking of knives and forks against dishes. My mother would smile softly between her remarks; my father at the other end of the table would chew and chew at his food, while he stared over the heads of his children.

My *mother!* My *father!* After English became my primary language, I no [15] longer knew what words to use in addressing my parents. The old Spanish words (those tender accents of sound) I had used earlier—*mama* and *papa*—I couldn't use anymore. They would have been too painful reminders of how much had changed in my life. On the other hand, the words I heard neighbor-hood kids call *their* parents seemed equally unsatisfactory. *Mother* and *Father; Ma, Papa, Pa, Dad, Pop* (how I hated the all-American sound of that last word especially)—all these terms I felt were unsuitable, not really terms of address for *my* parents. As a result, I never used them at home. Whenever I'd speak to my parents, I would try to get their attention with eye contact alone. In public conversations, I'd refer to "my parents" or "my mother and father."

My mother and father, for their part, responded differently, as their chil- [16] dren spoke to them less. She grew restless, seemed troubled and anxious at the scarcity of words exchanged in the house. It was she who would ques-tion me about my day when I came home from school. She smiled at small talk. She pried at the edges of my sentences to get me to say something more. (What?) She'd stopped her children's talking. By contrast, my father seemed reconciled to the new quiet. Though his English improved some-what, he retired into silence. At dinner he spoke very little. One night his children and even his wife helplessly giggled at his garbled English pronun-ciation of the Catholic Grace before Meals. Thereafter he made his wife recite the prayer at the start of each meal, even on formal occasions, when there were guests in the house. Hers became the public voice of the family. [5] On official business, it was she, not my father, one would usually hear on

---

Thinking Critically

[4] Why does the author's home life become quieter?
[5] Why did Rodriguez's mother become "the public voice" of the family?

the phone or in stores, talking to strangers. His children grew so accustomed to his silence that, years later, they would speak routinely of his shyness. (My mother would often try to explain: Both his parents died when he was eight. He was raised by an uncle who treated him like little more than a menial servant. He was never encouraged to speak. He grew up alone. A man of few words.) But my father was not shy, I realized, when I'd watch him speaking Spanish with relatives. Using Spanish, he was quickly effusive. Especially when talking with other men, his voice would spark, flicker, flare alive with sounds. In Spanish, he expressed ideas and feelings he rarely revealed in English. With firm Spanish sounds, he conveyed confidence and authority English would never allow him.

The silence at home, however, was finally more than a literal silence.   17
Fewer words passed between parent and child, but more profound was the silence that resulted from my inattention to sounds. At about the time I no longer bothered to listen with care to the sounds of English in public, I grew careless about listening to the sounds family members made when they spoke. Most of the time I heard someone speaking at home and didn't distinguish his sounds from the words people uttered in public. I didn't even pay much attention to my parents' accented and ungrammatical speech. At least not at home. Only when I was with them in public would I grow alert to their accents. Though, even then, their sounds caused me less and less concern. For I was increasingly confident of my own public identity.

I would have been happier about my public success had I not sometimes   18
recalled what it had been like earlier, when my family had conveyed its intimacy through a set of conveniently private sounds. Sometimes in public, hearing a stranger, I'd hark back to my past. A Mexican farm-worker approached me downtown to ask directions to somewhere. "Hijito . . . ?" he said. And his voice summoned deep longing. Another time, standing beside my mother in the visiting room of a Carmelite convent, before the dense screen which rendered the nuns' shadowy figures, I heard several Spanish-speaking nuns—their busy, singsong overlapping voices—assure us that yes, yes, we were remembered, all our family was remembered in their prayers. (Their voices echoed faraway family sounds.) Another day, a dark-faced old woman—her hand light on my shoulder—steadied herself against me as she boarded a bus. She murmured something I couldn't quite comprehend. Her Spanish voice came near, like the face of a never-before-seen relative in the instant before I was kissed. Her voice, like so many of the Spanish voices I'd hear in public, recalled the golden age of my youth. [6]

Thinking Critically

[6] How do the nuns' Spanish prayers remind the author of the "golden age" of his youth?

Hearing Spanish then, I continued to be a careful, if sad, listener to sounds. Hearing a Spanish-speaking family walking behind me, I turned to look. I smiled for an instant, before my glance found the Hispanic-looking faces of strangers in the crowd going by.

UNDERSTANDING DETAILS

1. In what ways was Spanish a private language for Rodriguez?
2. What happened when Rodriguez's two worlds met through the nuns who visited his home?
3. What "spell" is Rodriguez referring to in paragraph 8: "The spell was broken"? How was it broken?
4. How did the author finally assert his public self? What language was consistent with this identity?

READING CRITICALLY

5. How are language and identity connected for this author?
6. Why do you think Rodriguez didn't feel he had the right to use English as his language?
7. In the author's view, why was concentrating on "content-full" (paragraph 10) conversations good for him?
8. What does Rodriguez mean when he says, "This public silence measured and quickened the change in my life" (paragraph 10)?

DISCOVERING RHETORICAL STRATEGIES

9. Why do you think Rodriguez lets a single sentence stand as a paragraph in paragraph 11? What effect does this choice create in the essay?
10. Why did the family's mastery of English change the interaction of Rodriguez's family?
11. When in the essay does Rodriguez refer to the public confidence he and his family experience? What does he mean by this phrase? What is the context of each of the references to this notion?
12. Do you think the brief reference to the Spanish-speaking family is an effective conclusion to this essay? Why or why not?

MAKING CONNECTIONS

13. Compare and contrast Rodriguez's devotion to his own cultural heritage to that expressed by Lewis Sawaquat ("For My Indian Daughter"), Brent Staples ("A Brother's Murder"), Amy Tan ("Mother Tongue"), and/or Amy Chua ("The Battle of the Tiger Mother"). Which author is most intimately connected to his or her heritage? Why do you think this is so?
14. Which author is the best storyteller: Rodriguez, Kenneth Miller ("Class Act"), Russell Baker ("The Saturday Evening Post"), or Barbara Ehrenreich ("Nickel and Dimed")? Explain your answer.

15. How would Sandra Cisneros ("Only Daughter"), Amy Tan ("Mother Tongue"), and/or Mary Pipher ("Beliefs about Families") feel about Rodriguez's growing estrangement from his parents due to their difficulties with English?

IDEAS FOR DISCUSSION/WRITING

Preparing to Write

Write freely about the importance of "fitting in" or "assimilating" in your life. To what degree is assimilation important to you? Why is it important? What does assimilation into a particular group mean to you? What is more important than assimilation in your life today? What is less important? What does assimilation signify to you? Why do you think it carries this level of priority?

Choosing a Topic   MyWritingLab™

1. **LEARNING(¹)NLINE** Go to the Center for Digital Storytelling website (www .storycenter.org), and click "Stories." Then view the featured video under "At a Glance." Considering this video, choose one of your own family members, and describe in essay form a digital story you could create as a tribute to that person. What details of your relationship would be good examples of this person's significance in your life? Include as many specific details, such as events, photos, background music, as possible to convey your message to your audience.

2. The board of education for your high school district is thinking of offering classes in several different languages that are spoken in your area. This would allow students who speak a second language at home to do their schoolwork in that language as well. What would be the advantages of this approach? The disadvantages? Prepare a statement for a community meeting with the board arguing for or against this decision.

3. What specific actions create an intimacy in your family that matches the intimacy Rodriguez lost? Explain this intimacy to someone from another country, and discuss its value in your life.

4. You have been asked by a group of friends to attend a concert with them. You really want to go because you like the group of friends and the performers. So you decide to ask your parents to give you the money for the trip. Use your best reasoning on one or both of your parents or guardians to get them to fund this request.

Before beginning your essay, you may want to consult the flowchart on page 150.

Darkness at Noon

Raised in New York City, Harold Krents earned a B.A. and a law degree at Harvard, studied at Oxford University, worked as a partner in a Washington, D.C., law firm, was the subject of a long-running Broadway play, and wrote a popular television movie—all despite the fact that he was born blind. His "1-A" classification by a local draft board, which doubted the severity of his handicap, brought about the 1969 Broadway hit play *Butterflies Are Free* by Leonard Gershe. Krents once explained that he was merely the "prototype" for the central character: "I gave the story its inspiration—the play's plot is not my story; its spirit is." In 1972, Krents wrote *To Race the Wind,* which was made into a CBS-TV movie in 1980. During his career as a lawyer, Krents worked hard to expand legal protection for the handicapped and fought to secure their right to equal opportunity in the business world. He died in 1987 of a brain tumor.

Preparing to Read

In the following article, originally published in *The New York Times* in 1976, the author gives examples of different kinds of discrimination he has suffered because of his blindness.

Exploring Experience: As you prepare to read this essay, take a few minutes to think about disabilities or handicaps in general: Do you have a disability? If so, how are you treated by others? How do you feel others respond to your handicap? Do you know someone else who has a disability? How do you respond to that person? How do you think he or she wants to be treated? To what extent do you think disabilities should affect a person's job opportunities? What can be done to reduce societal prejudices against the disabled?

LEARNING◑NLINE In this essay, Harold Krents describes his frustrations with people's misconceptions about his disability. To gain a better understanding of his experience, go to www.nfb.org, the National Federation of the Blind's website for parents and teachers of blind children. Click "Publications"; then choose one of their magazines, open its most current issue, and scan its table of contents. Consider the issues mentioned in this magazine as you read Krents's account.

Before reading this essay, you may want to consult the flowchart on page 147.

Blind from birth, I have never had the opportunity to see myself and
have been completely dependent on the image I create in the eye of
the observer.[1] To date it has not been narcissistic.

There are those who assume that since I can't see, I obviously also cannot
hear. Very often people will converse with me at the top of their lungs,
enunciating each word very carefully. Conversely, people will also often
whisper, assuming that since my eyes don't work, my ears don't either.

For example, when I go to the airport and ask the ticket agent for assistance to the plane, he or she will invariably pick up the phone, call a ground
hostess and whisper: "Hi, Jane, we've got a 76 here." I have concluded that
the word "blind" is not used for one of two reasons: Either they fear that if
the dread word is spoken, the ticket agent's retina will immediately detach,
or they are reluctant to inform me of my condition of which I may not have
been previously aware.

On the other hand, others know that of course I can hear, but believe
that I can't talk. Often, therefore, when my wife and I go out to dinner, a
waiter or waitress will ask Kit if "*he* would like a drink" to which I respond
that "indeed *he* would."

This point was graphically driven home to me while we were in England.
I had been given a year's leave of absence from my Washington law firm to
study for a diploma in law degree at Oxford University. During the year I
became ill and was hospitalized. Immediately after admission, I was wheeled
down to the X-ray room. Just at the door sat an elderly woman—elderly I
would judge from the sound of her voice. "What is his name?" the woman
asked the orderly who had been wheeling me.

"What's your name?" the orderly repeated to me.

"Harold Krents," I replied.

"Harold Krents," he repeated.

"When was he born?"

"When were you born?"

"November 5, 1944," I responded.

"November 5, 1944," the orderly intoned.[2]

This procedure continued for approximately five minutes at which point
even my saint-like disposition deserted me. "Look," I finally blurted out,
"this is absolutely ridiculous. Okay, granted I can't see, but it's got to have
become pretty clear to both of you that I don't need an interpreter."

Thinking Critically

1 What "image" do you create "in the eye of the observer"? To what extent is this image
dependent on visual stimuli?

2 Why is the exchange between Krents and the hospital orderly so funny?

"He says he doesn't need an interpreter," the orderly reported to the   14
woman.

The toughest misconception of all is the view that because I can't see, I   15
can't work. I was turned down by over forty law firms because of my blindness, even though my qualifications included a cum laude degree from
Harvard College and a good ranking in my Harvard Law School class.

The attempt to find employment, the continuous frustration of being told   16
that it was impossible for a blind person to practice law, the rejection letters,
not based on my lack of ability but rather on my disability, will always remain
one of the most disillusioning experiences of my life.

I therefore look forward to the day, with the expectation that it is certain   17
to come, when employers will view their handicapped workers as a little
child did me years ago when my family still lived in Scarsdale.

I was playing basketball with my father in our backyard according to   18
procedures we had developed. My father would stand beneath the hoop,
shout, and I would shoot over his head at the basket attached to our
garage. Our next-door neighbor, aged five, wandered over into our yard
with a playmate. "He's blind," our neighbor whispered to her friend in a
voice that could be heard distinctly by Dad and me. Dad shot and missed;
I did the same. Dad hit the rim; I missed entirely; Dad shot and missed
the garage entirely. "Which one is blind?" [3] whispered back the little
friend.

I would hope that in the near future when a plant manager is touring the   19
factory with the foreman and comes upon a handicapped and nonhandi-
capped person working together, his comment after watching them work
will be, "Which one is disabled?"

UNDERSTANDING DETAILS

1. According to Krents, what are three common misconceptions about blind
   people?
2. What important details did you learn about Krents's life from this essay? How
   does he introduce this information?
3. In what ways was Krents frustrated in his search for employment? Was he qualified for the jobs he sought? Why or why not?
4. What attitude toward the handicapped does Krents look forward to in the
   future?

Thinking Critically

[3] How does the author use humor in this essay to humanize the situation and put his readers
at ease?

READING CRITICALLY

5. What does Krents mean when he says that his self-image gained through the eyes of others "has not been narcissistic" (paragraph 1)? Why do you think this is the case?

6. What is Krents's attitude toward his handicap? What parts of his essay reveal that attitude?

7. How do you account for the reactions to his blindness that Krents relates in this essay? Are you aware of such behavior in yourself? In others?

8. Do you think we will ever arrive at the point in the working world that Krents describes in the last paragraph? How can we get there? What advantages or disadvantages might accompany such a change?

DISCOVERING RHETORICAL STRATEGIES

9. How does Krents organize the three main points in his essay? Why does he put them in this order? What is the benefit of discussing employment last?

10. Krents often offers specific examples in the form of dialogue or spoken statements. Are these effective ways to develop his main points? Explain your answer.

11. Krents establishes a fairly fast pace in this essay as he discusses several related ideas in a small amount of space. How does he create this sense of speed? What effect does this pace have on his essay as a whole?

12. Although the author's dominant rhetorical mode in this essay is example, what other strategies does he use to develop his ideas? Give examples of each of these strategies.

MAKING CONNECTIONS

13. Compare the employment discrimination faced by Krents because of his blindness with the racial and social discrimination suffered by Lewis Sawaquat ("For My Indian Daughter") and/or Amy Tan ("Mother Tongue"). Which person has been treated most unfairly by society? Explain your answer.

14. How similar is Krents's use of humor to that of Russell Baker ("The Saturday Evening Post") and/or Nicholas Carr ("How the Internet is Making Us Stupid")? Which author do you find most amusing? Why?

15. How many examples does Krents use in his essay? Does he use more or fewer examples than Christopher Nelson ("Why We Are Looking at the 'Value' of College All Wrong") and/or Roni Jacobson ("A Digital Safety Net")? How does the number of examples affect the believability of each author's message?

IDEAS FOR DISCUSSION/WRITING

Preparing to Write

Write freely about disabilities: If you are disabled, what is your response to the world? Why do you respond the way you do? How does society respond to you? Are you pleased or not with your relationship to society in general? If you are not disabled, what do you think your attitude would be if you were disabled? How do you respond to disabled people? To what extent does your response depend on the disability? Are you satisfied with your reaction to other people's disabilities? Are you prejudiced in any way against people with disabilities? Do you think our society as a whole demonstrates any prejudices toward the disabled? If so, how can we correct these biases?

Choosing a Topic   MyWritingLab™

1. **LEARNING⏻NLINE** Select three of your favorite websites, and spend a few minutes visiting each one. Now return to them and consider how you would use the site if you were either blind or deaf. What accommodations, if any, have the websites made to assist differently abled users? Using Krents's article, the National Federation of the Blind's website (from Preparing to Read), and your experiences with these websites as examples, write an essay evaluating the accessibility of the Internet for those who are blind or deaf. Following Krents's writing as an example, consider the effect of different ways of organizing your examples.

2. As a reporter for your campus newspaper, you have been assigned to study and write about the status of services for the disabled on your campus. Is your school equipped with parking for the handicapped? A sufficient number of ramps for wheelchairs? Transportation for the handicapped? Other special services for the handicapped? Interview some disabled students to get their views on these services. Write an example essay for the newspaper, explaining the situation.

3. With your eyes closed, take a walk through a place that you know well. How does it feel to be nearly sightless? What senses begin to compensate for your loss of vision? Write an essay for your classmates detailing your reactions. Use specific examples to communicate your feelings.

4. Do you have any phobias or irrational fears that handicap you in any way? Write a letter to a friend explaining one of these "handicaps" and your method of coping with it.

Before beginning your essay, you may want to consult the flowchart on page 150.

RONI JACOBSON   (1989–   )

A Digital Safety Net

Roni Jacobson is a freelance journalist writing for a variety of journals and magazines on psychology and mental health. She earned her B.A. in Psychology and Arabic from Emery University and an M.A. in Science, Health, and Environmental Reporting from New York University. She had a job teaching Arabic in Minnesota before becoming a behavior therapist at the Marcus Autism Center. Her time at the Center gave her research experience and first-hand material for her stories. She worked as an intern at *The New York Times* and was a Graduate Fellow at *Scientific American*. Today, she contributes to *The Atlantic*, *New York Magazine*, *Scientific American*, *The New York Times*, *National Geographic*, *Salon*, *Newsweek*, and many other journals. She currently lives in Brooklyn, New York. You can read her most recent publications at her website, rsjacobson.com.

Preparing to Read

In the following essay, originally published in *Scientific American*, Roni Jacobson talks about the role of social media in reference to mental illness. She explains the ways social media can actually detect distress and intervene in different ways.

Exploring Experience: As you prepare to read this essay, take a few minutes to think about the cases of depression, anxiety, or other mental health issues you are aware of among your friends and family: Has social media made any differences in these situations? When has social media been a positive influence on a case? When has it been negative? What interventions are most effective with the particular stories you know of?

LEARNING⏻NLINE Visit the technological website Engadget (www.engadget.com). Scroll down, and look through the latest technological devices. Do you think all of them make communication easier? Are there any gadgets that try to improve communication but might make it less personal? While reading Jacobson's article, think about the impact of these devices on individuals and their mental health.

Before reading this essay, you may want to consult the flowchart on page 147.

People are increasingly broadcasting symptoms of mental illness on social media. We should listen. [1]

Peter's Facebook friends knew something was wrong months before he had a manic episode. He had been posting about expensive shopping trips and name-dropping celebrities he claimed to have partied with—seemingly out of character for the 26-year-old former dental student from Atlanta. When Peter (not his real name) ran away from home in April 2013, he unleashed a flurry of paranoid, all-caps status updates saying his family was out to get him. Meanwhile his sisters left messages on his Facebook wall begging him to come home.

What might have been a family affair a decade ago instead played out in front of hundreds of eyes, as friends and acquaintances watched the saga unfold on their news feeds. Some people sent him private messages. Others posted on his wall. Many commenters expressed support and concern, but a few were mocking and unhelpful. One person wrote "lol." Most people, however, only watched.

Mental health crises such as Peter's are being captured on social media with increasing regularity. Posts on Twitter by actors Charlie Sheen and Amanda Bynes, for example, chronicled their psychological unraveling before millions of followers, sparking intense debate among celebrity watchers about the appropriate reaction to their attention-grabbing tweets. [2]

People who witness such events among their own friends face a challenging question: Should they respond—and if so, how? "Mental illness is not like the flu," says computational social scientist Munmun De Choudhury of the Georgia Institute of Technology. Unlike other conditions, "people are often not comfortable discussing these things." The deep-rooted stigma of the topic discourages people from probing the emotional states of others. Yet silence compounds the problem because struggling individuals can come to believe they are suffering alone and avoid seeking help for fear of ridicule.

Social media could radically change this attitude. As people increasingly share very private experiences online, observers are gaining unparalleled insight into one another's mental lives. Digital interactions—through blog posts, social media updates, Instagram photos, and more—produce a wealth of data about a person's emotions and behaviors. Close family members and distant acquaintances alike can glimpse disturbing patterns in these outlets

1

2

3

4

5

Thinking Critically

[1] Do you know anyone personally who has asked for help with a mental illness on some form of social media? What were the circumstances?

[2] In what other ways has technology influenced how we relate to each other?

and offer simple forms of support. By breaking the silence, they can ease a colleague's or companion's pain—and they can chip away at the stigma that keeps many from seeking help in the first place.

Emotional Voyeurs

Social media might not seem like a panacea for mental illness at the out-   6
set. People often err on the side of silence when a typically private sentiment is expressed in a public manner. In a 2013 study, for example, Megan A. Moreno, an adolescent medicine specialist now at the University of Washington, and her colleagues asked college students whether they had ever seen a Facebook status update from a friend mentioning depression or anxiety. A majority said they had, but when the researchers asked students if they would respond to such a post, they were unsure. Most said they would if the post were written by a close friend or relative but not by a more distant acquaintance. In the latter case, they would expect someone closer to the person in distress to do the heavy lifting.

The students' aloofness may be partly explained by the bystander effect—   7
a psychological phenomenon first proposed in the 1960s, in which people become less likely to intervene in a crisis as the number of witnesses grows. A similar diffusion of responsibility occurs online. In multiple studies, researchers have posed as people requesting help by email and in chat rooms. The findings have been consistent: the bigger the online community, the less likely a recipient is to respond. On platforms such as Facebook and Twitter, where no one knows who has seen what, a sense of personal responsibility may be particularly elusive.

People might also hesitate because they cannot gauge whether a situation   8
is serious, suggests psychologist Jill Berger of the University of Maryland, who has surveyed college students' responses to online signs of suicidal thinking. Although they are concerned, she says, they do not want to "make a big deal" about something potentially mundane and risk an awkward interaction.

Even if a situation is not yet dire, Berger counsels that it warrants follow-   9
up. Social media acquaintances may be critically positioned to offer support. Writing a status update or tweeting about a problem can be easier than talking about it face-to-face, particularly for stigmatized issues such as mental illness. Evidence suggests that people feel less inhibited online. Furthermore, adolescents and young adults, who are at an age when mental disorders typically manifest, are more inclined to disclose sensitive information to peers than to adults.

Moreno believes that these posts are an important outlet for vulnerable   10
individuals. Often, she says, posters are looking for emotional support and

encouragement. On Facebook, "you don't have to wait in line for a therapy appointment—you can get that positive feedback within seconds." According to Moreno, posting frequently about mental health problems on social media could indicate that a person is not getting the help he or she needs offline. To a person in crisis, not getting a response may be "almost worse than getting a negative response," she adds, because it seems like "nobody is listening and nobody cares."

Unlocking Support

The work of scientists studying the reticence of onlookers makes it clear   11
that people do hear online cries for help—they just do not know how to reply. The good news is that people can be encouraged to take action. The bystander effect, for example, now appears to be more nuanced than was initially thought. Recent studies have found it to be less powerful than in early experiments, perhaps because people are more aware of it today.

And there may be ways to reduce or even reverse the effects. In a 2011   12
update on the bystander effect, Peter Fischer, a psychologist now at the University of Regensburg in Germany, and his colleagues analyzed data from all previous studies of the phenomenon and found that it diminishes significantly as the situation becomes more obviously dangerous. When faced with a sure emergency, the self-doubt that holds people back often disappears.

The key to unlocking support is therefore educating people about how   13
serious mental health crises can be, how to spot one and what witnesses can do to help. Mental health "first aid" programs, for example, can teach people how to recognize and respond to a mental health emergency in real life. Certain groups, such as college resident advisers (RAs), traditionally tasked with identifying distressed students, are learning to notice warning signs on social media as well. Moreno thinks that RAs and other youth leaders, such as team captains and church group organizers, are well positioned to detect crises unfolding online and either reach out themselves or pass the information along to a more qualified individual, such as a school counselor.

Meanwhile Facebook is encouraging its users to act when they see   14
troubling posts. In 2011 the company added a tool to anonymously report suicidal content. Once you submit a report, Facebook informs the person in distress that a contact has expressed concern and offers links to emergency hotlines and the opportunity to chat with a crisis worker.

Recipients are, of course, free to decline, but research indicates that most   15
people who post about their troubles do want help. In one of several recent studies, Moreno and her colleagues asked 60 college freshmen how they would like to be treated by someone who saw signs of their depression on Facebook. Almost every student said that they would be open to

communication from friends, professors and RAs. More than 30 percent said they would be okay with receiving a message from a stranger.

Most respondents, however, added that they preferred people to contact   16 them directly—either one-on-one, over the phone or via email—and with an open mind. "The emphasis was on this idea of being inquisitive: asking questions rather than making judgments," Moreno says.

In addition, some amount of automated support could help sufferers.   17 Researchers at Harvard University, Dartmouth College, and other institutions are now developing apps that monitor smartphone and social media activity to detect signs of distress. This data trail could allow clinicians to intervene before symptoms intensify or send users automated suggestions for how to improve their mood or get back in touch with reality. [3]

Learning to Listen

Beyond offering new lifelines for people under duress, social media may   18 now be lifting the veil of silence that has long shrouded mental disorders. Social scientists have found that throughout history, prejudice is best dismantled when people interact frequently with others unlike themselves. Indeed, a 2012 meta-analysis of approaches to reducing stigma concluded that simply having contact with people with mental health conditions trumps social activism and education in getting adults to abandon their preconceptions.

Social media onlookers might even experience a boost in empathy and   19 feel more willing to reach out after discovering a friend's struggles online. In a 2014 study led by health communication expert Nichole Egbert of Kent State University, students were also significantly more likely to support a depressed friend if they identified with his or her problem.

Along those lines, the New York City branch of the National Alliance   20 on Mental Illness launched a social media campaign called "I Will Listen" in October 2013. In a series of videos and Facebook posts, actress Mariel Hemingway, writer Andrew Solomon, and other public figures pledged to listen to those with mental illness "with an open mind and without judgment" and shared personal stories on these issues. Since the start of the campaign, dozens of people have followed suit, documenting their own experiences with mental illness on Twitter, Vimeo and Instagram with the hashtag #IWillListen. [4]

Thinking Critically

[3] What other ideas, besides apps, might help professionals intervene with people suffering mental distress?

[4] What do you know about the "I Will Listen" campaign?

As Moreno sees it, social media "offers us tools that we didn't have 10   21
years ago" when the same people were walking around with little social
support and few opportunities for others to witness their distress. Now that
we have the tools, it is just a matter of using them.

To a person in crisis, not getting a response may be "almost worse than   22
getting a negative response," Moreno says, because it seems like nobody
cares. Social technologies provide a lifeline for people with mental illness to
find help.

UNDERSTANDING DETAILS

1. What do you think Jacobson's main reason is for writing this essay?
2. What is the primary difference between our responses to mental illness a decade
   ago and today?
3. What does Jacobson mean by the term "bystander effect" (paragraph 7)?
4. How does Jacobson feel about the role of social media in any form of mental
   illness?

READING CRITICALLY

5. Why do you think people are less inhibited online?
6. In what ways might no response be "almost worse than getting a negative
   response" (paragraph 10), as Moreno claims?
7. Do you think the anonymous Facebook tool for reporting potential suicide
   cases is a good idea? Why or why not?
8. In what ways might social media be "lifting the veil of silence" (paragraph 18)
   that has covered mental illness for a long time?

DISCOVERING RHETORICAL STRATEGIES

9. Explain Jacobson's title for her essay. Is this title an effective way to capture the
   attention of her intended audience? Why or why not?
10. Why does Jacobson start her essay with Peter's story? How does this beginning
    prepare us for what she says?
11. What is the author illustrating with the references to Charlie Sheen and
    Amanda Bynes? Is this an effective way to make her point? Explain your answer.
12. Describe Jacobson's intended audience in as much detail as possible. Why do
    you think she aims her essay at this particular group?

MAKING CONNECTIONS

13. Compare and contrast Roni Jacobson's use of examples with those provided by
    Harold Krents ("Darkness at Noon") and Brent Staples ("A Brother's Murder").
    Which author's examples are most persuasive to you? Why?
14. Imagine that Jacobson was having a conversation about the impact of technol-
    ogy on our lives with Motoko Rich ("Literacy Debate: Online, R U Really
    Reading?"), Elizabeth Svoboda ("Virtual Assault"), Josh Rose ("How Social

Media is Having a Positive Impact on Our Culture"), and/or Susan Tardanico ("Is Social Media Sabotaging Real Communication?"). Which of these authors would argue most vehemently that modern technology is having predominantly positive effects on our culture? Who would say the negative effects of technology are more prevalent?

15. What would Jacobson think of Samantha Pugsley's comments about language and mental health in "How Language Impacts the Stigma Against Mental Health (And What We Must Do to Change It)"? What specific details led you to your conclusion?

IDEAS FOR DISCUSSION/WRITING

Preparing to Write

Write freely about your own relationship with social media: Do you take part in all forms of social media? What roles do these different forms of media play in your life? Which form of social media is most useful to you? Why is it useful? Which social media are most beneficial to human relationships in general? What forms of our electronic society have the potential of increasing our mental and physical health?

Choosing a Topic   MyWritingLab™

1. LEARNING⏻NLINE Keeping in mind the newest technological devices you saw online at www.engadget.com, think about how they might affect human relationships of all kinds. Do you believe that technology has improved or impaired your relationships? Using examples from your own life, write an essay for or against increased use of technology in our personal lives.

2. As a college student, you see people approach their personal problems in different ways every day. Some students address their problems directly; others avoid them and hope they disappear. Some let their problems interfere with their personal goals; others make sure they keep their goals in their sights. Write an essay for your school newspaper explaining your observations about the different ways people handle problems of all types. Use carefully chosen examples to illustrate your observations.

3. You have been asked to respond to a national survey on the role of the Internet in our lives. The organization conducting the survey wants to know the extent to which the Internet has helped or hindered you in your daily life. In a well-developed essay written for a general audience, explain the benefits and liabilities of the Internet in your life at present. Use specific examples to develop your essay.

4. Jacobson uses many examples and specific references throughout her essay. Discuss her choice of illustrations, her placements of them in her essay, and their ultimate effect on her primary message. Include their relationship to the rest of the essay and their implications for the audience in your discussion.

Before beginning your essay, you may want to consult the flowchart on page 150.

A Brother's Murder

Brent Staples was the first of nine children born to a truck driver and a housewife in Chester, Pennsylvania, a factory town fifteen miles south of Philadelphia. He was educated at the Philadelphia Military College and Penn Morton College, eventually graduating from Widener College with honors. A prestigious Danforth Fellowship took him to the University of Chicago, where he earned a Ph.D. in Psychology. His brilliant memoir, *Parallel Time: Growing Up in Black and White* (published by Pantheon Books in 1994), was a finalist for *The Los Angeles Times* Book Award and a winner of the Anisfield-Wolff Award, which was previously awarded to such luminaries as James Baldwin, Ralph Ellison, and Zora Neale Hurston. He also published *An American Love Story* in 1999 and is currently working on a book entitled *Neither White Nor Black: The Secret History of Mixed-Race*. A past editor of *The New York Times* Book Review section and an assistant metropolitan editor, Staples also has written on politics and culture for *The New York Times* editorial page. Recently, Staples has turned his talents to writing about current race issues and problems in the education system. He is an avid gardener and is especially fond of roses. When asked to give some advice to college writers, he explains that "ninety percent of writing is rewriting. The simple declarative sentence is your best friend in the world."

Preparing to Read

"A Brother's Murder" was first published in an anthology of African-American writing entitled *Bearing Witness*. In this emotional account of his brother's death, Staples realizes many important truths about the role of violence among African-American men.

Exploring Experience: Before reading this essay, think for a few moments about violence in general: From your observations, which kinds of people are most violent? Why do these people use violence? What do you think is the cause of most violent acts? In your opinion, why is the crime rate so high in American society today? Can we do anything to reduce this crime rate? What are some of your constructive suggestions for controlling violence today? Which are most realistic?

LEARNING⟨!⟩NLINE Brent Staples uses personal examples to explore the causes and effects of youth violence in his hometown. Visit the "Building Blocks for Youth" website located at www.cclp.org/building_blocks.php, and read some of the online articles listed on the homepage about violence in our communities. Consider the use of examples, such as statistics and dates, in the article as you read Brent Staples's essay.

Before reading this essay, you may want to consult the flowchart on page 147.

It has been more than two years since my telephone rang with the news
that my younger brother Blake—just 22 years old—had been murdered.
The young man who killed him was only 24. Wearing a ski mask, he
emerged from a car, fired six times at close range with a massive .44 Magnum, then fled. The two had once been inseparable friends. A senseless
rivalry—beginning, I think, with an argument over a girlfriend—escalated
from posturing, to threats, to violence, to murder. The way the two were
living, death could have come to either of them from anywhere. In fact, the
assailant had already survived multiple gunshot wounds from an incident
much like the one in which my brother lost his life.

As I wept for Blake, I felt wrenched backward into events and circumstances that had seemed light-years gone. Though a decade apart, we both
were raised in Chester, Pennsylvania, an angry, heavily black, heavily poor,
industrial city southwest of Philadelphia. There, in the 1960s, I was introduced
to mortality, not by the old and failing, but by beautiful young men who lay
wrecked after sudden explosions of violence. The first, I remember from my
14th year—Johnny, brash lover of fast cars, stabbed to death two doors from
my house in a fight over a pool game. The next year, my teen-age cousin,
Wesley, whom I loved very much, was shot dead. The summers blur. Milton,
an angry young neighbor, shot a crosstown rival, wounding him badly. William, another teen-age neighbor, took a shotgun blast to the shoulder in some
urban drama and displayed his bandages proudly. His brother, Leonard, severely
beaten, lost an eye and donned a black patch. It went on.

I recall not long before I left for college, two local Vietnam veterans—one
from the Marines, one from the Army—arguing fiercely, nearly at blows about
which outfit had done the most in the war. The most killing, they meant. Not
much later, I read in a magazine article that set that dispute in a context. In
the story, a noncommissioned officer—a sergeant, I believe—said he would
pass up any number of affluent, suburban-born recruits to get hard-core soldiers from the inner city. They jumped into the rice paddies with "their manhood on their sleeves," I believe he said. These two items—the veterans
arguing and the sergeant's words—still characterize for me the circumstances
under which black men in their teens and 20's kill one another with such
frequency. With a touchy paranoia born of living battered lives, they are desperate to be *real* men.[1] Killing is only *machismo* taken to the extreme. Incursions to be punished by death were many and minor, and they remain so: they
include stepping on the wrong toe, literally; cheating in a drug deal; simply
saying "I dare you" to someone holding a gun; crossing territorial lines in a

1

2

3

Thinking Critically

[1] What did wearing "their manhood on their sleeves" have to do with being "real" men
for Blake's group? What other actions or rituals might be more civilized and productive
in helping young people define themselves as "real"?

gang dispute. My brother grew up to wear his manhood on his sleeve. And when he died, he was in that group—black, male, and in its teens and early 20's—that is far and away the most likely to murder or be murdered.

I left the East Coast after college, spent the mid- and late-1970's in Chi-   4 cago as a graduate student, taught for a time, then became a journalist. Within 10 years of leaving my hometown, I was overeducated and "upwardly mobile," ensconced on a quiet, tree-lined street where voices raised in anger were scarcely ever heard. [2] The telephone, like some grim umbilical, [3] kept me connected to the old world with news of deaths, imprisonings, and misfortune. I felt emotionally beaten up. Perhaps to protect myself, I added a psychological dimension to the physical distance I had already achieved. I rarely visited my hometown. I shut it out.

As I fled the past, so Blake embraced it. On Christmas of 1983, I traveled   5 from Chicago to a black section of Roanoke, Virginia, where he then lived. The desolate public housing projects, the hopeless, idle young men crashing against one another—these reminded me of the embittered town we'd grown up in. It was a place where once I would have been comfortable, or at least sure of myself. Now, hearing of my brother's forays into crime, his scrapes with police and street thugs, I was scared, unsteady on foreign terrain.

I saw Blake's romance with the street life, and the hustler image had flow-   6 ered dangerously. One evening that late December, standing in some Roanoke dive among drug dealers and grim, hair-trigger losers, I told him I feared for his life. He had affected the image of the tough he wanted to be. But behind the dark glasses and the swagger, I glimpsed the baby-faced toddler I'd once watched over. I nearly wept. I wanted desperately for him to live. The young think themselves immortal, and a dangerous light shone in his eyes as he spoke laughingly of making fools of the policemen who had raided his apartment looking for drugs. He cried out as I took his right hand. A line of stitches lay between the thumb and index finger. Kickback from a shotgun, he explained, nothing serious. Gunplay had become part of his life.

I lacked the language simply to say: Thousands have lived this for you and   7 died. [4] I fought the urge to lift him bodily and shake him. This place and the way you are living smells of death to me, I said. Take some time away, I said. Let's go downtown tomorrow and buy a plane ticket anywhere, take a bus trip, anything to get away and cool things off. He took my alarm casually. We arranged to meet the following night—an appointment he would not keep. We embraced as though through glass. I drove away.

Thinking Critically

[2] How did Brent escape the claustrophobic environment of the ghetto, while his brother did not?

[3] How does the concept of mortality in paragraph 2 relate to the "grim umbilical" in paragraph 4?

[4] What does the author mean when he writes "Thousands have lived this for you and died"?

As I stood in my apartment in Chicago holding the receiver that evening   8
in February 1984, I felt as though part of my soul had been cut away. I
questioned myself then, and I still do. Did I not reach back soon or earnestly
enough for him? For weeks I awoke crying from a recurrent dream in which
I chased him, urgently trying to get him to read a document I had, as though
reading it would protect him from what had happened in waking life. His
eyes shining like black diamonds, he smiled and danced just out of my grasp.
When I reached for him, I caught only the space where he had been. ◈

UNDERSTANDING DETAILS

1. What does Staples mean when he refers to his brother's death by saying, "The
   way the two were living, death could have come to either of them from anywhere" (paragraph 1)?
2. What stages did Staples's brother and his murderer go through before Blake
   was killed?
3. Why do you think Staples wrote this essay? What is his main point?
4. What did Staples learn about African-American males by examining his
   brother's life?

READING CRITICALLY

5. In what ways does Brent Staples's brother represent an important segment of
   the African-American male population?
6. Why did Staples create a distance between his present life and his past?
7. What examples does Staples use to prove his theory that "killing is only
   machismo taken to the extreme" (paragraph 3)? Do you agree with this conclusion? Can you think of any examples that demonstrate the opposite position?
8. What was "Blake's romance with the street life" (paragraph 6)?

DISCOVERING RHETORICAL STRATEGIES

9. Describe in as much detail as possible Staples's intended audience. Why do you
   think he aims his essay at this particular group?
10. In what way does Staples's recurring dream (paragraph 8) symbolize the author's
    relationship with his brother? How does this final paragraph sum up Staples's
    feelings about the plight of African-American males in American society today?
11. In paragraph 7, Staples uses a simile (a special comparison between two unlike
    items, using *like* or *as*): "We embraced as though through glass." This image
    adds an extra dimension to Staples's description. Find another simile in this
    essay, and explain its effect on you.
12. This essay progresses most obviously through the use of examples. What other
    rhetorical strategies support this dominant mode? In what ways do they add
    to Staples's main point?

Thinking Critically

◈ How did the "spaces" these two men lived in help shape their lives? Which spaces best
define your life? To what extent do you become a different person when you move from
one space to another?

MAKING CONNECTIONS

13. Through hard work and a college education, Brent Staples was able to rise above the violent environment that contributed to his brother's death. Consider any of the following essays you have read, and explain how the central characters escaped their own difficult environments: Maya Angelou ("New Directions"), Kenneth Miller ("Class Act"), and/or Harold Krents ("Darkness at Noon.")

14. Examine Staples's essay through the lens of Sarah Toler's "Understanding the Birth Order Relationship." To what extent do Toler's observations about birth order help explain the relationship between Staples and his brother?

15. How do Brent Staples's insights about the community in which his brother lived differ from the sense of "community" in Robert Ramirez's "The Barrio" and Rose and Tardanico's essays on social media?

IDEAS FOR DISCUSSION/WRITING

Preparing to Write

Write freely about your view of violence in the United States today: What is the source of most of this violence? How can we control violence in American society? Why do you think violence is increasing? How else might we channel our innate violent reactions? What other suggestions do you have for reducing violent crimes today?

Choosing Your Topic   MyWritingLab™

1. **LEARNING⏻NLINE** Staples relates his painful experience to help explain the pervasiveness of youth violence. He selects personal examples rather than statistics or news stories to present his argument. Using www.cclp.org/building_blocks.php (from Preparing to Read) as a starting point, choose an issue about which you feel strongly, and write an essay in which you argue your position using carefully selected, relevant examples. Try to clarify general concepts by using specific details as Staples does. Use the Internet to find statistics or case studies, if necessary, to support your argument.

2. Write an essay for a college-educated audience based on one of the following statements: "Current pressure in contemporary society causes most of the violence today" or "People's natural instincts cause most of the violence in contemporary society."

3. Interview some people about how they manage their anger: What do they do when they get mad? How do they control their reactions? Have they ever become violent? Then write an essay for the students in your English class explaining your findings.

4. According to Staples, the military frame of mind—the urge to kill—is at the heart of "the circumstances under which black men in their teens and 20s kill one another with such frequency" (paragraph 3). Do you agree or disagree with this statement? Write a well-developed essay, using examples from your experience, to support your opinion.

Before beginning your essay, you may want to consult the flowchart on page 150.

Chapter Writing Assignments

Practicing Example

1. Think about some qualities that irritate you in other people's behavior (such as how someone drives, how someone talks on the phone, or how someone laughs). In an essay, use examples to explain a behavior that irritates you and the reason it bothers you so much.
2. Think about all the different roles people play, such as father, teacher, big brother, or sister. Who in your experience provides the best example of how one of these "roles" should be performed? Write an essay that explains why this person is the best example of this role.
3. What do you do best as a writer? Which parts of the writing process do you seem to deal with most successfully? Taking examples from your own writing, compose an essay that discusses your strengths as a writer.

Exploring Ideas

4. Should the United States as a country promote the use of a single national language, or should we instead acknowledge and encourage the use of multiple languages? Write an essay that explores the advantages and/or disadvantages of either single or multiple languages in American society. As you write, use specific examples to support your position.
5. In what ways do all forms of the media use stereotypes? Choose a specific "type" (such as liberal, conservative, radical, athlete), and, using as many specific examples as possible, explain how the media help or hinder our understanding of a certain personality or issue.
6. Discuss a time when someone embarrassed you publicly. Describe what happened and how it affected you. What, if anything, did you learn from the experience?

Analyzing Visual Images

7. The photo on the next page is entitled "Miracle on Ice" and reflects the moment when the United States, against all odds, defeated the Russians in the 1980 Olympic Games before going on to win the gold medal in ice hockey. This victory is an example of team members pulling together to accomplish a major goal and an improbable upset. Think of a time when you had to accomplish a difficult feat—against all odds—and needed others to help you overcome these obstacles. Write a narrative essay about this time, using specific examples to support your points.
8. Look at the picture at the beginning of this chapter (page 146). How does it make you feel? Think about other places in your own city that make you feel the same way, and explain your response in a narrative essay. Remember to use specific examples to help illustrate your point.

AP Images.

Composing in Different Genres

9. Multimedia: Using clip art, photographs, or pictures from magazines, create a collage that represents your view of college today. Use the pictures as examples that make a collective statement about higher education. Then see if someone in class can put your graphic statement into words.

10. Multigenre: Find a blog, website, wiki, or similar electronic source about finding one's identity. Read some of the conversations, and add your own comments to the strand; use examples to drive your points home. Print the conversation to bring to class after you have written enough to come to some substantive conclusions about your own identity.

Writing from Sources

For detailed information on writing from sources, see Part III.

11. Should governmental institutions and documents, such as schools, DMV agencies, and voting ballots, provide multilingual services? Research the issues surrounding this question, and find examples that support your position. Use your sources to argue for or against this practice in a documented essay.

12. Research the controversy surrounding privacy on networking website. Do you think that lack of privacy creates a safety threat? Do authorities have the right to use information you post against you? Take a position on this issue; then, citing examples from your research, write a documented essay arguing your case.

MyWritingLab™ Visit Ch. 6 Example: Illustrating Ideas in *MyWritingLab* to complete the writing assignments and test your understanding of the chapter learning objectives.

Chapter 7

PROCESS ANALYSIS
Explaining Step by Step

LEARNING OBJECTIVES

After completing this chapter, you will be able to do the following:
- Define process analysis
- Use process analysis to think critically
- Read process essays critically
- Write and revise effective process analysis essays

Human nature is characterized by the perpetual desire to understand and analyze the process of living well. The best-seller list is always crowded with books on how to know yourself better, how to be assertive, how to become famous, how to survive a natural disaster, or how to be rich and happy—all explained in three easy lessons. Open almost any popular magazine, and you will find numerous articles on how to lose weight, how elections are run in this country, how to dress for success, how a political movement evolved, how to gain power, or how to hit a successful topspin backhand. People naturally gravitate toward material that tells them how something is done, how something happened, or how something works, especially if they think the information will help them improve their lives in a significant way.

DEFINING PROCESS ANALYSIS

A *process* is a procedure that follows a series of steps or stages; *analysis* involves taking a subject apart and explaining its components to better understand the whole. Process analysis, then, explains an action, a mechanism, or an event from beginning to end. It concentrates on either a mental or a physical operation: how to solve a chemistry problem, how to tune up your car, how John F. Kennedy was shot, how the telephone system works. In fact, the explanation of the writing process beginning on page 25 of this book is a good case in point: It divides writing into three interrelated verbal activities and explains how they each work—separately and together.

A process analysis can take one of two forms: (1) It can give directions, thereby explaining how to do something (directive); or (2) it can give information about how something happened or how something works (informative). The first type of analysis gives directions for a task the reader may wish to attempt in the future. Examples include how to make jelly, how to lose weight, how to drive to Los Angeles, how to assemble stereo equipment, how to make money, how to use a microscope, how to knit, how to resuscitate a dying relationship, how to win friends, how to discipline your child, and how to backpack.

The second type of analysis furnishes information about what actually occurred in specific situations or how something works. Examples include how Hiroshima was bombed, how certain Hollywood stars live, how the tax system works, how the movie *Chicago* was filmed, how Babe Ruth earned a place in the Baseball Hall of Fame, how gold was first discovered in California, how computers work, how a kibbutz functions, and how the Gulf War began. These subjects and others like them respond to a certain fascination we all have with mastering some processes and understanding the intricate details of others. They all provide us with opportunities to raise our own standard of living, either by helping us directly apply certain processes to our own lives or by increasing our understanding of how our complex world functions.

The following student paragraph analyzes the process of constructing a garden compost pit. Written primarily for people who might wish to make such a pit, this piece is directive rather than informative. Notice in particular the amount of detail the student calls on to explain each stage of the process and the clear transitions she uses to guide us through her analysis.

No garden is complete without a functioning compost pit. Here's a simple, inexpensive way to make your garbage work for you! To begin with, make a pen out of hog wire or chicken wire, four feet long by eight feet wide by four feet high, splitting it down the middle with another piece of wire so that you end up with a structure that looks like a capital "E" on its side. This is a compost duplex. In the first pen, place a layer of soda ash, just sprinkled on the surface of the dirt. Then pile an inch or so of leaves, grass clippings, or sawdust on top of the soda ash. You're now ready for the exciting part. Start throwing in all the organic refuse from your kitchen (no meat, bones, or grease, please). After the food is a foot or so deep, throw in a shovelful of steer manure, and cover the entire mess with a thin layer of dirt. Then water it down. Continue this layering process until the pile is three to three-and-a-half feet high. Allow the pile to sit until it decomposes (from one month in warm climates to six months in colder weather). Next, take your pitchfork and start slinging the contents of pen one into pen two (which will land in reverse order, of course, with the top on the bottom and the bottom on the top). This ensures that everything will decompose evenly. Water this down and begin making a new pile in pen one. That's all there is to it! You now have a ready supply of fertilizer for your garden.

THINKING CRITICALLY THROUGH PROCESS ANALYSIS

Process analysis embodies clear, careful, step-by-step thinking that takes one of three different forms: chronological, simultaneous, or cyclical. The first follows a time sequence from "first this" to "then that." The second forces you to deal with activities or events that happen or happened at the same time, such as people quietly studying or just getting home from work when the major 1994 earthquake hit Los Angeles. The third form of process analysis requires you to process information that is continuous, like the rising and setting of the sun. No other thinking pattern will force you to slow down as much as process analysis because the process you are explaining probably won't make any sense if you leave out even the slightest detail.

Good process analysis can truly help your reader see an event in a totally new light. An observer looks at a product already assembled or at a completed event and has no way of knowing—without the help of a good process analysis—how it got to this final stage. Such an analysis gives the writer or speaker as well as the observer a completely new way of perceiving the subject in question. Separating process analysis from the other rhetorical modes lets you practice this method of thinking so that you will have a better understanding of the various mental procedures going on in your head. Exercising this possibility in isolation will help you feel its range and its intricacies so that you can become more adept at using it, fully developed, in combination with other modes of thought.

EpicStockMedia/Fotolia.

1. In this picture, the photographer manipulates our view by using a particular lens and by positioning the photo so that the man on the surfboard is almost in the middle of the scene. What are other ways we manipulate or influence people's views? Brainstorm about how you influence the views or ideas of people around you. What are your most effective techniques? Explain to someone else in class how you effectively influence people you know, or explain how to avoid unfairly manipulating or influencing others.

2. List as many examples of each type of process (chronological, simultaneous, and cyclical) as you can think of. Share your list with the class.

3. Write a paragraph telling how *not* to do something. Practice your use of humor as a technique for creating interest in the essay by emphasizing the "wrong" way, for example, to wash a car or feed a dog.

READING AND WRITING PROCESS ANALYSIS ESSAYS

Your approach to a process analysis essay should be fairly straightforward. As a reader, you should be sure you understand the author's statement of purpose and then try to visualize each step as you go along. As a writer, you need to adapt the mechanics of the way you normally write to the demands of a process analysis paper, beginning with an interesting topic and a number of clearly explained ideas or stages. As usual, the intended audience determines the choice of words and the degree of detail.

Reading Process Analysis Essays

Understanding how process analysis essays work rhetorically will help you make decisions for your own writing. Here is a flowchart of questions that will guide your reading for this purpose.

Questions to Guide Your Reading

PREPARING TO READ Before you read the essays, answer the following questions:

- What assumptions can you make from the essay's **title**?
- What do you think the general **mood** of the essay will be?
- What is the essay's **purpose** and **audience**?
- What does the **synopsis** tell you about the essay?
- What can you learn from the author's **biography**?
- What do you predict the author's **point of view** toward the subject will be?

READING As you read the essays for the first time, answer the following questions:

- What is the author's general **message**?
- Is the essay *directive* (explaining how to do something) or *informative* (giving information about how something happened)?
- Do the supporting **details** adequately explain the process or event?

REREADING When you read the essays again, answer the following questions:

- Does the author furnish an **overview** of the process?
- How is the essay **organized**—chronologically, cyclically, or simultaneously?
- What other **rhetorical modes** does the author use?
- How does your understanding of the essay **change** with each rereading?

Preparing To Read.   Preparing to read a process analysis essay is as uncomplicated as the essay itself. The title of Jay Walljasper's essay in this chapter, "Our Schedules, Our Selves," tells us exactly what we are going to learn about. Barbara Ehrenreich's title, "Nickel and Dimed," is a little more subtle, but gives us an idea about her topic. Scanning each selection to assess the author's audience will give you an even better idea of what to expect in these essays, and the synopsis of each in the Rhetorical Table of Contents will help focus your attention on its subject.

Also important as you prepare to read these essays are the qualifications of each author to write on the subject at hand: Has he or she performed the task, worked with the mechanism, or seen the event? Is the writer's experience firsthand? What is Jessica Mitford's experience with mortuaries? How does she know what goes on "Behind the Formaldehyde Curtain"? When Kanchier writes "Dare to Change Your Job and Your Life in 7 Steps," is she qualified to give advice on this topic? The biography preceding each essay will help you uncover this information and find out other publication details that will encourage you to focus on the material you are about to read.

Finally, before you begin reading, answer the prereading questions, and then do some brainstorming on the subject of the essay: How much do you understand about making changes in your life, and what do you think you can learn about the subject from Carole Kanchier? What do you want to know about making friends (Stephanie Vozza)?

Reading.   When you read the essays in this chapter for the first time, record your initial reactions to them. Consider the preliminary information you have been studying in order to create a context for each author's composition: What circumstances prompted Mitford's "Behind the Formaldehyde Curtain"? Who do you think is Ehrenreich's target audience in "Nickel and Dimed"? Why did Stephanie Vozza write "How to Make New Friends as an Adult"?

Included at the bottom of the pages of these essays are questions to help you think critically about the content and structure of each essay. These questions will provide ways for you to process the content and understand the structure of each essay so that you will be prepared to answer the questions and do the writing assignments at the end of the reading selections. They essentially help you build a mental bridge from the prereading activities that appear before each essay to those at the end of your reading assignments. Responding to these inquiries in writing will help you get the biggest benefit from this feature of the text because you will already have some thoughts on paper when you get your next writing task.

Also determine at this point whether the essay you are reading is *directive* (explaining how to do something) or *informative* (giving information about how something happened or how something works). This fundamental understanding of the author's intentions, along with a reading of the questions following the essay, will prepare you to approach the contents of each selection critically when you read it a second time.

Rereading.   As you reread these process analysis essays, look for an overview of the process at the beginning of the essay so you know where each writer is headed. The body of each essay, then, is generally a discussion of the stages of the process.

The central portion of an essay is often organized *chronologically* (as in Mitford's essay on current practices in mortuaries and Ehrenreich's essay on cleaning houses), with clear transitions so that readers can easily follow the writer's train of thought. Other methods of organization are *cyclical* (such as the essay by Walljasper on organizing one's time and Vozza's essay on making friends), describing a process that has no clear beginning or end, and *simultaneous* (such as Kanchier's essay on change,), in which many activities occur at the same time with a clear beginning and end. Most of these essays discuss the process as a whole at some point. During this second reading, you will also benefit from discovering what rhetorical modes each writer uses to support his or her process analysis and why these rhetorical modes work effectively. What does Walljasper's cause/effect reasoning add to his essay on time management? How do the descriptions in Mitford's essay on embalming heighten the horror of the American mortuary business? Do the examples that Vozza gives help explain how to make friends? How do all the rhetorical modes in each essay help create a coherent whole? After reading each essay for a second time, answer the questions that follow the selection to see if you are understanding your reading material on the literal, interpretive, and analytical levels before you take on the discussion/writing assignments.

For an overview of the entire reading process, you might consult the Reading Checklist at the end of Chapter 2.

Writing Process Analysis Essays

Now that you see how process analysis works in an essay, use the same features in your own writing. The flowchart on the next page provides some questions to guide you.

Prewriting.   As you begin a process analysis assignment, you first need to become as familiar as you can with the action, mechanism, or event you are going to describe. If possible, try to go through the process yourself at least once or twice. If you can't actually carry out the procedure, going through the process mentally and taking notes is a good alternative.

Questions to Guide Your Writing

PREPARING TO WRITE Before you start writing, answer these questions:

- What is your **purpose**?
- Who is your **audience**?

WRITING As you write your first draft, consider these questions:

- Do you provide an **overview** of the process at the beginning?
- Does your **first paragraph** introduce your subject, divide it into steps, describe the result of the process, and include a purpose statement as your thesis?
- Is your process analysis essay either *directive* or *informative*?
- Are the essay's details **organized** chronologically, simultaneously, or cyclically?
- Does the essay **end** with a description of the process or event as a whole?

EDITING Be sure to proofread and edit your paper before turning it in.

- Are your **sentences** all complete?
- Do your words say exactly **what you mean**?
- Do you follow conventional **grammar and usage** rules?

REVISING After you write your first draft, use the following questions to revise your essay:

- Is your **purpose statement** clear?
- Have you given your readers an **overview** of the process you are going to discuss?
- Do you go through the process **step by step**?
- At the **end** of the essay, do you help your readers see the process as a whole?

Then, try to read something about the process. After all this preparation (and careful consideration of your audience and purpose), you should be ready to brainstorm, freewrite, cluster, or use your favorite prewriting technique (see pages 26–28 of Chapter 3) in response to the prewriting questions before you start composing your paper.

Writing.   The essay should begin with an overview of the process or event to be analyzed. This initial section should introduce the subject, divide it into a number of recognizable steps, and describe the result once the process is complete. Your thesis in a process essay is usually a purpose statement that clearly and briefly explains your approach to the procedure you will discuss: "Building model airplanes can be divided into four basic steps" or "The American courts follow three stages in prosecuting a criminal case."

Next, a directive or informative essay should proceed logically through the various stages of the process, from beginning to end. The parts of a process usually fall nicely into chronological order, supported by such transitions as "at first," "in the beginning," "next," "then," "after that," and "finally." Some processes, however, are either simultaneous, forcing the writer to choose a more complex logical order for the essay (such as classification), or cyclical, requiring the writer to choose a starting point and then explain the cycle stage by stage. Playing the guitar, for example, involves two separate and simultaneous components that must work together: holding the strings against the frets with the fingers of one hand and strumming or plucking with the other hand. In analyzing this procedure, you would probably want to describe both parts of the process and then explain how the hands work together to produce music. An example of a cyclical process would be the changing of the seasons. To explain this concept to a reader, you would need to pick a starting point, such as spring, and describe the entire cycle, stage by stage, from that point onward.

In a process paper, you need to be especially sensitive to your intended audience, or they will not be able to follow your explanation. The amount of information, the number of examples and illustrations, and the terms to be defined all depend on the prior knowledge and background of your readers. A writer explaining to a group of amateur cooks how to prepare a soufflé would take an entirely different approach to the subject than he or she would if the audience were a group of bona fide chefs hoping to land jobs in elegant French restaurants. The professional chefs would need more sophisticated and precise explanations than their recreational counterparts, who would probably find such an approach tedious and complicated because of the extraneous details.

The last section of a process analysis paper should consider the process as a whole. If, for example, the writer is giving directions on how to build a model airplane, the essay might end with a good description or drawing of the plane. The informative essay on our legal system might offer a summary of the stages of judging and sentencing a criminal. And the essay on cooking a soufflé might finish with a photograph of the mouth-watering dish.

Revising.   To revise a process analysis essay, make sure your main purpose is apparent throughout your paper.

The Writing Checklist at the end of Chapter 3 will give you further guidelines for writing, revising, and proofreading.

STUDENT ESSAY: PROCESS ANALYSIS AT WORK

The student essay that follows analyzes the process of making a good first impression. Notice that once the student gives an overview of the process, she discusses the steps one at a time, being careful to follow a logical order (in this case, chronological) and to use clear transitions that guide her readers through her essay. Then, see how the end of the essay shows the process as a whole.

How to Make a Good First Impression

The pressure on today's young adults has reached unprecedented levels. From securing an internship to landing a dream job, any move at all can make the difference between success and failure. <u>For every opportunity you are given, a good first impression is crucial. Taking a few simple steps regarding your conversation, appearance, and demeanor can help you make the best first impression possible.</u>

Purpose statement for directive process analysis

Overview

<u>In order to make a good first impression</u>, you should <u>consider in advance what you will say.</u> Doing so will help you avoid rambling or stuttering when the time comes. If you need some information from a professor, form your questions before your meeting so that your thoughts come out smoothly and clearly. If you're getting ready for an interview, research the position and be ready to ask smart, thoughtful questions. Also, think about what an interviewer might ask you. You might even consider having a friend help you by asking questions the interviewer is likely to pose so you can practice answering.

Transition

First guideline (chronological organization)

<u>At the meeting itself</u>, the way you look is generally what people notice first about you, so <u>you should take some time with your appearance.</u> When you know you're about to meet someone for the first time,

Transition

Second guideline

especially in situations like a job interview or the first day of class, dress appropriately. If you're getting ready for a job interview, consider what kind of business you're applying for. If you want to intern at a law firm, you probably want to wear a suit, but if you hope to work at a movie theater, a collared shirt and nice jeans will suffice.

Transition   Also, <u>during your meeting</u>, you should <u>consider **Third** your body language</u>. To make a good impression, you **guideline** will need to walk, sit, and gesture in appropriate ways. In a formal interview, enter the room slowly, taking stock of the setting and the people present. Sit down gradually, and wait until someone addresses you before speaking. In a less formal scenario, you can move a little faster, and your overall demeanor can be slightly more relaxed. Ultimately, you want your first impression to be consistent with the situation you are in. Assess the circumstances, understand the setting, and fit yourself into its physical demands.

Transition   <u>In addition to your physical demeanor</u>, <u>be aware **Fourth** of your attitude and energy</u>. A confident, relaxed per- **guideline** son will always make a better first impression than a nervous, awkward one. If you feel nervous, breathe deeply and try to do whatever you can to relax. You will find that even if you can't change how you feel, you can change how you come across to other people by assuming a confident posture. Stand or sit straight and hold your head high; try not to fidget because this will make you seem nervous. Speak clearly, without talking too fast or too slowly, and try to project a confident, relaxed aura.

Final <u>Making a good first impression does not always **product** come naturally, but all of us can practice and improve our image</u>. You definitely want to showcase what is unique about you but only after you adapt to the situation at hand—in conversation, appearance, and manner. <u>If you remember these steps and practice **Concluding** them, you will be on your way to presenting the best **remark** version of yourself to the world</u>.

Student Writer's Comments

I wish I could say the beginning of this particular writing assignment was easy. When I was given this writing assignment, I was not immediately sure what I wanted to write about. I tested out two or three ideas before settling on "How to Make a Good First Impression." I had an experience in class where I found myself babbling on and on, and I had the thought, "Oh man, I just made a horrible impression." Thus, the idea for my essay was born.

First, I brainstormed some details and ideas on the topic. I thought through the steps I could follow to make a good first impression, and the essay evolved from there. I didn't worry about writing complete sentences at this point. I simply jotted down key points, like "physical appearance" and "think before you speak." Once I had gathered my ideas, I was able to organize them in an order that made sense to me. After going through this process of generating ideas, I was able to begin writing.

I knew I should be writing a directive essay for someone else who might want advice on how to make a good first impression. I found that the introduction was especially difficult; I didn't really know where to start. Just to get some momentum, I began with the body paragraphs. These flowed naturally, and by starting there, I believe I saved time I would have wasted if I had labored over the introduction first. By the time the rest of my essay was finished, I was able to go back and ask, "Why are first impressions important? Who should care about them?" Once I answered these questions, my introduction followed smoothly.

When I reread my draft, I realized that I had written a lot of my own personal experiences into the essay. This resulted in an informal essay. As I revised, I concentrated on removing myself from the essay and elevating my tone. Keeping my audience in mind helped me revise appropriately. I was eventually happy with the final product when I felt that I had reached a balance between offering good advice and wanting/needing the advice myself (because everyone, including me, will benefit from making good first impressions).

SOME FINAL THOUGHTS ON PROCESS ANALYSIS

In this chapter, a single process dictates the development and organization of each of the essays that follow. Both directional and informational methods are represented here. Notice in particular the clear purpose statements that set the focus of the essays in each case, as well as the other rhetorical modes (such as narration, comparison/contrast, and definition) that are used to help support the writers' explanations.

JAY WALLJASPER (1955–)

Our Schedules, Our Selves

An award-winning writer and speaker, Jay Walljasper is currently a senior fellow at the Project for Public Spaces, a nonprofit urban planning and design organization in New York City, and an editor of Onthecommons.org, a website devoted to drawing greater attention to all the important elements in society that everyone owns together. He is also an editor-at-large for *Ode Magazine*, a contributing writer for *National Geographic Traveler Magazine*, and a columnist for *Parks and Recreation* magazine. Specializing in urban, community, environmental, and travel issues, he has published articles in *Mother Jones*, *Preservation*, the *New Statesman*, *E Magazine*, the *Chicago Tribune Magazine*, and many other important journals and newspapers. Earlier in his career, he was the editor of the *Utne Reader* for fifteen years, a travel editor at *Better Homes and Gardens*, and a columnist for the British magazine *Resurgence*. He is also the author of three important books: *Visionaries: People and Ideas to Change Your Life* (2001), *The Great Neighborhood Book: A Do-It-Yourself Guide to Placemaking* (2007), and *All That We Share: A Field Guide to the Commons* (2011). In his spare time, he loves to explore cities, cross-country ski, and haunt used bookstores. Asked to give advice to students using *The Prose Reader*, he explained that the best place for a writer to look for material "is in the differences you see in the world around you and how that world is reflected back to us in the media."

Preparing to Read

The following essay, originally published in the *Utne Reader* (January/February 2003), chronicles the extent to which most of us are "slaves" to our schedules, allowing our responsibilities to control our lives, and offers some concrete ideas for taking control of our lives away from the clock.

Exploring Experience: Before reading this essay, take a few minutes to think about how you schedule your days: How tightly do you schedule your time? Do you make lists of things you want to do every day? Do you usually accomplish more or less than you want in a typical day? How large a part of your life is your education? Are you able to say *no* to events you don't want to participate in? Are your personal life and your job or school activities in a healthy balance? If not, what could you do to create a more balanced life for yourself?

LEARNING◑NLINE Conduct an Internet search for "time management advice," and notice how many websites are devoted to this topic. Explore one of the pertinent sites, and read the advice. Are these skills that you possess, or do you need help managing your time? Compare your life right now to your ideal schedule, and think about how you can improve your time management system.

Before reading this essay, you may want to consult the flowchart on page 191.

DAMN! You're 20 minutes—no, more like half an hour—late for your breakfast meeting, which you were hoping to scoot out of early to make an 8:30 seminar across town. And, somewhere in there, there's that conference call. Now, at the last minute, you have to be at a 9:40 meeting. No way you can miss it. Let's see, the afternoon is totally booked, but you can probably push back your 10:15 appointment and work through lunch. That would do it. Whew! The day has barely begun, and already you are counting the hours until evening, when you can finally go home and happily, gloriously, triumphantly, do nothing. You'll skip yoga class, blow off the neighborhood meeting, ignore the piles of laundry and just relax. Yes! . . . No! Tonight's the night of the concert. You promised Nathan and Mara weeks ago that you would go. *DAMN!*

Welcome to the daily grind—a grueling 24-7 competition against the clock that leaves even the winners wondering what happened to their lives.[1] Determined and sternly focused, we march through each day obeying the orders of our calendars. The idle moment, the reflective pause, serendipity of any sort have no place in our plans. Stopping to talk to someone or slowing down to appreciate a sunny afternoon will only make you late for your next round of activities. From the minute we rise in the morning, most of us have our day charted out. The only surprise is if we actually get everything done that we had planned before collapsing into bed at night.

On the job, in school, at home, increasing numbers of North Americans are virtual slaves to their schedules. Some of what fills our days are onerous obligations, some are wonderful opportunities, and most fall in between, but taken together they add up to too much. Too much to do, too many places to be, too many things happening too fast, all mapped out for us in precise quarter-hour allotments on our cell phones or day planners. We are not leading our lives, but merely following a dizzying timetable of duties, commitments, demands, and options. How did this happen? Where's the luxurious leisure that decades of technological progress was supposed to bestow upon us?

The acceleration of the globalized economy and the accompanying decline of people having any kind of a say over wages and working conditions is a chief culprit.[2] Folks at the bottom of the socio-economic ladder feel the pain most sharply. Holding down two or three jobs, struggling to pay the bills, working weekends, no vacation time, little social safety net, they often feel out of control about everything happening to them. But even

1

2

3

4

Thinking Critically

[1] To what extent are you a slave to your schedule? When do you have free time? What is your favorite leisure activity?

[2] What jobs are at the bottom of the "socio-economic ladder"? How do people move up and down this ladder?

successful professionals, people who seem fully in charge of their destinies, feel the pinch. Doctors, for example, working impossibly crowded schedules under the command of HMOs, feel overwhelmed. Many of them are now seeking union representation, traditionally the recourse of low-pay workers.

The onslaught of new technology, which promised to set us free, has   5 instead ratcheted up the rhythms of everyday life.[3] Cell phones, email, and laptop computers instill expectations of instantaneous action. While such direct communication can loosen our schedules in certain instances (it's easier to shift around an engagement on short notice), overall they fuel the trend that every minute must be accounted for. It's almost impossible to put duties behind you now, when the boss or committee chair can call you at a rap show or sushi restaurant, and documents can be emailed to you on vacation in Banff or Thailand. If you are never out of the loop, then are you ever not working?

Our own human desire for more choices and new experiences also plays   6 a role. Just like hungry diners gathering around a bountiful smorgasbord, it's hard not to pile too many activities on our plates. An expanding choice of cultural offerings over recent decades and the liberating sense that each of us can fully play a number of different social roles (worker, citizen, lover, parent, artist, etc.) has opened up enriching and exciting opportunities. Spanish lessons? Yes. Join a volleyball team? Why not. Cello and gymnastics classes for the kids? Absolutely. Tickets to a blues festival, food and wine expo, and political fundraiser? Sure. And we can't forget to make time for school events, therapy sessions, protest rallies, religious services, and dinner with friends.

Yes, these can all add to our lives. But with only 24 hours allotted to us   7 each day, something is lost too. You don't just run into a friend anymore and decide to get coffee. You can't happily savor an experience because your mind races toward the next one on the calendar. In a busy life, nothing happens if you don't plan it, often weeks in advance. Our "free" hours become just as programmed as the work day. What begins as an idea for fun frequently turns into an obligation obstacle course. Visit that new barbecue restaurant. *Done!* Go to tango lessons. *Done!* Fly to Montreal for a long weekend. *Done!*

We've booked ourselves so full of prescheduled activities there's no time   8 left for those magic, spontaneous moments that make us feel most alive.[4]

Thinking Critically

[3] In what ways has new technology "ratcheted up the rhythms of everyday life"? Does your use of technology save you time or take time away from you?

[4] Do you agree with the author that "magic, spontaneous moments" make us feel most alive? Why or why not?

We seldom stop to think of all the experiences we are eliminating from our lives when we load up our appointment book. Reserving tickets for a basketball game months away could mean you miss out on the first balmy evening of spring. Five p.m. skating lessons for your children fit so conveniently into your schedule that you never realize it's the time all the other kids in the neighborhood gather on the sidewalk to play.

A few years back, radical Brazilian educator Paulo Freire was attending a   9 conference of Midwestern political activists and heard over and over about how overwhelmed people felt about the duties they face each day. Finally, he stood up and, in slow, heavily accented English, declared, "We are bigger than our schedules." The audience roared with applause.

Yes, we are bigger than our schedules. So how do we make sure our lives   10 are not overpowered by an endless roster of responsibilities? Especially in an age where demanding jobs, two-worker households or single-parent families make the joyous details of everyday life—cooking supper from scratch or organizing a block party—seem like an impossible dream? There is no set of easy answers, despite what the marketers of new convenience products would have us believe. But that doesn't mean we can't make real steps to take back our lives.

Part of the answer is political. So long as Americans work longer hours   11 than any other people on Earth, we are going to feel hemmed in by our schedules.[5] Expanded vacation time for everyone, including part-time and minimum wage workers, is one obvious and overdue solution. Shortening the work week, something the labor movement and progressive politicians successfully accomplished in the early decades of the 20th century, is another logical objective. There's nothing preordained about 40 hours on the job; Italy, France, and other European nations have already cut back working hours. An opportunity for employees outside academia to take a sabbatical every decade or so is another idea whose time has come. And how about more vacation and paid holidays? Let's start with Martin Luther King's birthday, Susan B. Anthony's birthday, and your own! Any effort to give people more clout in their workplaces—from strengthened unions to employee ownership—could help us gain much-needed flexibility in our jobs, and our lives.

On another front, how you think about time can make a big difference   12 in how you feel about your life. Note how some of your most memorable

---

Thinking Critically

[5] Why do you think Americans work longer hours than people in other countries? Do you think work hours vary from state to state? From one region of the country to another?

moments occurred when something in your schedule fell through. The canceled lunch that allows you to spend an hour strolling around town. Friday night plans scrapped for a bowl of popcorn in front of the fireplace. Don't be shy about shucking your schedule whenever you can get away with it. And with some experimentation, you may find that you can get away with it a lot more than you imagined.

Setting aside some time on your calendar for life to just unfold in its own   13
surprising way can also nurture your soul. Carve out some nonscheduled hours (or days) once in a while and treat them as a firm commitment. And resist the temptation to turn every impulse or opportunity into another appointment. It's neither impolite nor inefficient to simply say, "let me get back to you on that tomorrow" or "let's check in that morning to see if it's still a good time." You cannot know how crammed that day may turn out to be, or how uninspired you might feel about another engagement, or how much you'll want to be rollerblading or playing chess or doing something else at that precise time.

In our industrialized, fast-paced society, we too often view time as just   14
another mechanical instrument to be programmed. But time possesses its own evershifting shape and rhythms and defies our best efforts to corral it within the tidy lines of our cell phones or datebooks. Stephan Rechtschaffen, author of *Time Shifting,* suggests you think back on a scary auto collision (or near miss) or spectacular night of lovemaking. Time seemed almost to stand still.[6] You can remember everything in vivid detail. Compare that to an overcrammed week that you recall now only as a rapid-fire blur. Keeping in mind that our days expand and contract according to their own patterns is perhaps the best way to help keep time on your side.

UNDERSTANDING DETAILS

1. Explain in your own words the problem of letting your schedule control your life from Walljasper's point of view.
2. Walljasper divides the solutions to the problem he identifies into two categories. What are those categories?
3. List the solutions that Walljasper offers in each category.
4. Explain the final sentence of Walljasper's essay: "Keeping in mind that our days expand and contract according to their own patterns is perhaps the best way to help keep time on your side" (paragraph 14).

Thinking Critically

[6] When does time seem to move slowly? When does it move rapidly? Do you think we are most productive when time moves fast or slow?

READING CRITICALLY

5. Name two major causes, according to Walljasper, of the time crunch we now live in.
6. Which of Walljasper's guidelines for managing your schedule could you benefit from most? How could it help you? Why do you have trouble in this area?
7. Why does Walljasper advise us to slow down? What are the benefits of following this suggestion?
8. According to the author, how can we balance our personal and professional lives? How realistic are these ideas?

DISCOVERING RHETORICAL STRATEGIES

9. The author starts this essay with a realistic example from a twenty-first-century life. Is this an effective beginning? Why or why not? What are some alternative ways to start this essay?
10. How does Walljasper organize his techniques for managing our schedules? Is this order successful? Explain your answer.
11. How would you characterize the tone or general attitude of this essay? Is this an effective approach to the subject? Explain your answer.
12. What other rhetorical modes does Walljasper use to support this process analysis essay? Give examples of each of these modes.

MAKING CONNECTIONS

13. Pretend that you are Jay Walljasper giving advice to young Russell Baker ("The Saturday Evening Post"), who wants to become a good salesperson. Which of Walljasper's suggestions should Baker follow most earnestly? Why? Which of these suggestions would be most helpful in your own life?
14. Walljasper's essay analyzing the process of managing our time and Jessica Mitford's essay ("Behind the Formaldehyde Curtain") analyzing funeral customs both try to persuade us to adopt a certain opinion as they describe a process. Which essay is more convincing to you? Explain your answer in detail.
15. Walljasper's contention that many of us are "enslaved" by our schedules invites us to consider other types of addiction throughout this book. Examine any of the following essays you have read, and explain which of them involves a process that would be particularly challenging to overcome: Stephanie Ericsson ("The Ways We Lie"), David Hanson ("Binge Drinking"), or Stephen King ("Why We Crave Horror Movies").

IDEAS FOR DISCUSSION/WRITING

Preparing to Write

Write freely about various aspects of your daily schedule: Do you make realistic schedules for yourself from day to day? What benefits can you receive from giving yourself more free time? Can you identify any disadvantages that could result from more free time for you? How can you avoid the problems that the author identifies? Do you schedule yourself too tightly, or do you build in time to pursue spontaneous activities and free thoughts? How does being a student fit into the advice Walljasper gives?

Choosing a Topic

MyWritingLab™

1. **LEARNING⏻NLINE** Think about the scheduling advice that you read in Preparing to Read and in Walljasper's article. Have you discovered any tips that would improve your daily routine? Write a process analysis essay about how you could incorporate this advice into your life. To what extent would you implement suggestions like taking longer vacations or spending more quality time with people you care about? Make sure you are specific about how you would apply this scheduling guidance to your everyday life.

2. You have been asked by the editor of your campus newspaper to adapt Walljasper's suggestions to the life of a student. Write a process analysis essay adjusting Walljasper's guidelines to a college environment.

3. Interview someone in your class about his or her ability to use time wisely. Use Walljasper's guidelines to establish whether the person schedules himself or herself well. Then, direct a process analysis essay to this person, briefly evaluating his or her time-management skills and then offering suggestions for improvement.

4. In the typical life of a student, sometimes course obligations (study as much as you can every day) seem to conflict with the fundamental tenets for leading a quality life (relax and enjoy yourself). Do you think these two aspects of life are incompatible, or are there ways to reconcile the two? Write an essay for your classmates detailing a solution to this dilemma.

Before beginning your essay, you may want to consult the flowchart on page 194.

Behind the Formaldehyde Curtain

Once called "Queen of the Muckrakers" in a *Time* magazine review, Jessica Mitford has written scathing exposés of the Famous Writers' School, American funeral directors, television executives, prisons, a "fat farm" for wealthy women, and many other venerable social institutions. She was born in England into the gentry, immigrated to the United States, and later became a naturalized American citizen. After working at a series of jobs, she achieved literary fame at age forty-six with the publication of *The American Way of Death* (1963), which relentlessly shatters the image of funeral directors as "compassionate, reverent family-friends-in-need." Her other major works include *Kind and Unusual Punishment: The Prison Business* (1973); *Poison Penmanship: The Gentle Art of Muckraking* (1979), an anthology of her articles in the *Atlantic, Harper's,* and other periodicals covering a twenty-two-year time span; two volumes of autobiography, *Daughters and Rebels* (1960) and *A Fine Old Madness* (1977); and *The American Way of Birth* (1992). Superbly skilled in the techniques of investigative reporting, satire, and black humor, Mitford was described in a *Washington Post* article as "an older, more even-tempered, better-read Jane Fonda who has maintained her activism long past middle age." Her advice to students planning to write in this genre? "You may not be able to change the world, but at least you can embarrass the guilty."

Preparing to Read

The following essay, taken from *The American Way of Death,* clearly illustrates the ruthless manner in which Mitford exposes the greed and hypocrisy of the American mortuary business.

Exploring Experience: As you prepare to read this article, think for a few minutes about funeral customs in our society: Have you attended a funeral service recently? Which rituals seemed particularly vivid to you? What purpose did these symbolic actions serve? What other interesting customs are you aware of in American society? What purpose do these customs serve? What public images do these customs have? Are these images accurate? Do you generally approve or disapprove of these customs?

LEARNING⏻NLINE In this controversial essay, Jessica Mitford graphically describes the embalming process. Before reading her article, familiarize yourself with some technical mortuary terms by searching for "Six Feet Under commercials" on YouTube to view some farcical ads that poke fun at the funeral industry.

Before reading this essay, you may want to consult the flowchart on page 191.

The drama begins to unfold with the arrival of the corpse at the   1
mortuary.

Alas, poor Yorick![1] How surprised he would be to see how his   2
counterpart of today is whisked off to a funeral parlor and is in short order
sprayed, sliced, pierced, pickled, trussed, trimmed, creamed, waxed, painted,
rouged, and neatly dressed—transformed from a common corpse into a
Beautiful Memory Picture. This process is known in the trade as embalming
and restorative art and is so universally employed in the United States and
Canada that the funeral director does it routinely, without consulting corpse
or kin. He regards as eccentric those few who are hardy enough to suggest
that it might be dispensed with. Yet no law requires embalming, no religious
doctrine commends it, nor is it dictated by considerations of health, sanitation, or even of personal daintiness. In no part of the world but in Northern
America is it widely used. The purpose of embalming is to make the corpse
presentable for viewing in a suitably costly container; and here too the
funeral director routinely, without first consulting the family, prepares the
body for public display.

Is all this legal? The processes to which a dead body may be subjected are   3
after all to some extent circumscribed by law. In most states, for instance,
the signature of next of kin must be obtained before an autopsy may be
performed, before the deceased may be cremated, before the body may be
turned over to a medical school for research purposes; or such provision
must be made in the decedent's will. In the case of embalming, no such
permission is required nor is it ever sought. A textbook, *The Principles and
Practices of Embalming,* comments on this: "There is some question regarding
the legality of much that is done within the preparation room." The author
points out that it would be most unusual for a responsible member of a
bereaved family to instruct the mortician, in so many words, to "*embalm*"
the body of a deceased relative. The very term "embalming" is so seldom
used that the mortician must rely upon custom in the matter. The author
concludes that unless the family specifies otherwise, the act of entrusting the
body to the care of a funeral establishment carries with it an implied permission to go ahead and embalm.

Embalming is indeed a most extraordinary procedure, and one must won-   4
der at the docility of Americans who each year pay hundreds of millions of
dollars for its perpetuation, blissfully ignorant of what it is all about, what is

---

Thinking Critically

[1] How do Mitford's description of the embalming process as a "drama" and her reference
to Shakespeare's *Hamlet* ("Alas, poor Yorick!") help set the tone for this essay?

done, how it is done. Not one in ten thousand has any idea of what actually takes place. Books on the subject are extremely hard to come by. They are not to be found in most libraries or bookshops.

In an era when huge television audiences watch surgical operations in   5 the comfort of their living rooms, when, thanks to the animated cartoon, the geography of the digestive system [2] has become familiar territory even to the nursery school set, in a land where the satisfaction of curiosity about almost all matters is a national pastime, the secrecy surrounding embalming can, surely, hardly be attributed to the inherent gruesomeness of the subject. Custom in this regard has within this century suffered a complete reversal. In the early days of American embalming, when it was performed in the home of the deceased, it was almost mandatory for some relative to stay by the embalmer's side and witness the procedure. Today, family members who might wish to be in attendance would certainly be dissuaded by the funeral director. All others, except apprentices, are excluded by law from the preparation room.

A close look at what does actually take place may explain in large measure   6 the undertaker's intractable reticence concerning a procedure that has become his major *raison d'être*. Is it possible he fears that public information about embalming might lead patrons to wonder if they really want this service? [3] If the funeral men are loath to discuss the subject outside the trade, the reader may, understandably, be equally loath to go on reading at this point. For those who have the stomach for it, let us part the formaldehyde curtain.

The body is first laid out in the undertaker's morgue—or rather, Mr. Jones   7 is reposing in the preparation room—to be readied to bid the world farewell.

The preparation room in any of the better funeral establishments has the   8 tiled and sterile look of a surgery, [4] and indeed the embalmer–restorative artist who does his chores there is beginning to adopt the term "dermasurgeon" (appropriately corrupted by some mortician-writers as "demisurgeon") to describe his calling. His equipment, consisting of scalpels, scissors, augers, forceps, clamps, needles, pumps, tubes, bowls, and basins, is crudely imitative of the surgeon's, as is his technique, acquired in a nine- or twelve-month post–high-school course in an embalming school. He is supplied by an advanced chemical industry with a bewildering array of fluids, sprays, pastes, oils, powders, creams, to fix or soften tissue, shrink or distend it as needed, dry it here, restore the moisture there. There are cosmetics, waxes and paints

---

Thinking Critically

[2] What does the author mean by the phrase "the geography of the digestive system"?

[3] Do you think this assertion is true? Why or why not?

[4] What does Mitford mean by the British term "surgery"? Find another example of British dialect in the essay.

to fill and cover features, even plaster of Paris to replace entire limbs. There are ingenious aids to prop and stabilize the cadaver: A Vari-Pose Head Rest, the Edwards Arm and Hand Positioner, the Repose Block (to support the shoulders during the embalming), and the Throop Foot Positioner, which resembles an old-fashioned stock.

Mr. John H. Eckels, president of the Eckels College of Mortuary Science, [9] thus describes the first part of the embalming procedure: "In the hands of a skilled practitioner, this work may be done in a comparatively short time and without mutilating the body other than by slight incision—so slight that it scarcely would cause serious inconvenience if made upon a living person. It is necessary to remove the blood, and doing this not only helps in the disinfecting, but removes the principal cause of disfigurements due to discoloration."

Another textbook discusses the all-important time element: "The earlier [10] this is done, the better, for every hour that elapses between death and embalming will add to the problems and complications encountered. . . ." Just how soon should one get going on the embalming? The author tells us, "On the basis of such scanty information made available to this profession through its rudimentary and haphazard system of technical research, we must conclude that the best results are to be obtained if the subject is embalmed before life is completely extinct—that is, before cellular death has occurred. In the average case, this would mean within an hour after somatic death." [5] For those who feel that there is something a little rudimentary, not to say haphazard, about this advice, a comforting thought is offered by another writer. Speaking of fears entertained in early days of premature burial, he points out, "One of the effects of embalming by chemical injection, how-ever, has been to dispel fears of live burial." How true; once the blood is removed, chances of live burial are indeed remote.

To return to Mr. Jones, the blood is drained out through the veins and [11] replaced by embalming fluid pumped in through the arteries. As noted in *The Principles and Practices of Embalming,* "every operator has a favorite injec-tion and drainage point—a fact which becomes a handicap only if he fails or refuses to forsake his favorites when conditions demand it." Typical favor-ites are the carotid artery, femoral artery, jugular vein, subclavian vein. There are various choices of embalming fluid. If Flextone is used, it will produce a "mild, flexible rigidity. [6] The skin retains a velvety softness, the tissues are rubbery and pliable. Ideal for women and children." It may be blended with

---

Thinking Critically

[5] What is the difference between "somatic death" and "cellular death"? Why is this distinc-tion important to the funeral profession?

[6] Why is the oxymoron "mild, flexible rigidity" humorous?

B. and G. Products Company's Lyf-Lyk tint, which is guaranteed to repro-
duce "nature's own skin texture . . . the velvety appearance of living tissue."
Suntone comes in three separate tints: Suntan; Special Cosmetic Tint, a pink
shade "especially indicated for young female subjects"; and Regular Cosmetic Tint, moderately pink.

About three to six gallons of a dyed and perfumed solution of formalde-   12
hyde, glycerin, borax, phenol, alcohol, and water is soon circulating through
Mr. Jones, whose mouth has been sewn together with a "needle directed
upward between the upper lip and gum and brought out through the left
nostril," with the corners raised slightly "for a more pleasant expression." If
he should be bucktoothed, his teeth are cleaned with Bon Ami and coated
with colorless nail polish. His eyes, meanwhile, are closed with flesh-tinted
eye caps and eye cement.

The next step is to have at Mr. Jones with a thing called a trocar. This is   13
a long, hollow needle attached to a tube. It is jabbed into the abdomen,
poked around the entrails and chest cavity, the contents of which are pumped
out and replaced with "cavity fluid." This done, and the hole in the abdomen sewn up, Mr. Jones's face is heavily creamed (to protect the skin from
burns which may be caused by leakage of the chemicals), and he is covered
with a sheet and left unmolested for a while.[7] But not for long—there is
more, much more, in store for him. He has been embalmed, but not yet
restored, and the best time to start the restorative work is eight to ten hours
after embalming, when the tissues have become firm and dry.

The object of all this attention to the corpse, it must be remembered,   14
is to make it presentable for viewing in an attitude of healthy repose.[8]
"Our customs require the presentation of our dead in the semblance of
normality . . . unmarred by the ravages of illness, disease, or mutilation,"
says Mr. J. Sheridan Mayer in his *Restorative Art*. This is rather a large order
since few people die in the full bloom of health, unravaged by illness and
unmarked by some disfigurement. The funeral industry is equal to the challenge: "In some cases the gruesome appearance of a mutilated or disease-
ridden subject may be quite discouraging. The task of restoration may seem
impossible and shake the confidence of the embalmer. This is the time for
intestinal fortitude and determination. Once the formative work is begun
and affected tissues are cleaned or removed, all doubts of success vanish. It
is surprising and gratifying to discover the results which may be obtained."

Thinking Critically

[7] How do such phrases as "have at Mr. Jones with a thing called a trocar" and "left
unmolested for a while" help Mitford satirize the embalming process?

[8] What is ironic about the phrase "in an attitude of healthy repose"? Find at least one other
example of irony.

The embalmer, having allowed an appropriate interval to elapse, returns   15
to the attack, but now he brings into play the skill and equipment of sculptor
and cosmetician. Is a hand missing? Casting one in plaster of Paris is a simple
matter. "For replacement purposes, only a cast of the back of the hand is
necessary; this is within the ability of the average operator and is quite
adequate." If a lip or two, a nose or an ear should be missing, the embalmer
has at hand a variety of restorative waxes with which to model replacements.
Pores and skin texture are simulated by stippling with a little brush, and over
this cosmetics are laid on. Head off? Decapitation cases are rather routinely
handled.[9] Ragged edges are trimmed, and head joined to torso with a series
of splints, wires, and sutures. It is a good idea to have a little something at
the neck—a scarf or a high collar—when time for viewing comes. Swollen
mouth: Cut out tissue as needed from inside the lips. If too much is removed,
the surface contour can easily be restored by padding with cotton. Swollen
necks and cheeks are reduced by removing tissue through vertical incisions
made down each side of the neck. "When the deceased is casketed, the pil-
low will hide the suture incisions. . . . As an extra precaution against leakage,
the suture may be painted with liquid sealer."

The opposite condition is more likely to present itself—that of emacia-   16
tion. His hypodermic syringe now loaded with massage cream, the embalmer
seeks out and fills the hollowed and sunken areas by injection. In this procedure the backs of the hands and fingers and the under-chin area should
not be neglected.

Positioning the lips is a problem that recurrently challenges the ingenuity   17
of the embalmer. Closed too tightly, they tend to give a stern, even disapproving expression. Ideally, embalmers feel, the lips should give the impression of being ever so slightly parted, the upper lip protruding slightly for a
more youthful appearance. This takes some engineering, however, as the
lips tend to drift apart. Lip drift[10] can sometimes be remedied by pushing
one or two straight pins through the inner margin of the lower lip and then
inserting them between the two front upper teeth. If Mr. Jones happens to
have no teeth, the pins can just as easily be anchored in his Armstrong Face
Former and Denture Replacer. Another method to maintain lip closure is
to dislocate the lower jaw, which is then held in its new position by a wire
run through holes which have been drilled through the upper and lower

---

Thinking Critically

9 How did you respond to the following statement: "Decapitation cases are rather routinely
handled"? Analyze your emotional reaction.

10 How can funeral directors solve the problem of "lip drift"? What is the effect of such
vivid details in the essay?

jaws at the midline. As the French are fond of saying, *il faut souffrir pour être belle.*

If Mr. Jones had died of jaundice, the embalming fluid will very likely   18
turn him green. Does this deter the embalmer? Not if he has intestinal fortitude. Masking pastes and cosmetics are heavily laid on, burial garments and
casket interiors are color-correlated with particular care, and Jones is displayed beneath rose-colored lights. Friends will say "How *well* he looks."
Death by carbon monoxide, on the other hand, can be rather a good thing
from the embalmer's viewpoint: "One advantage is the fact that this type of
discoloration is an exaggerated form of a natural pink coloration." This is nice
because the healthy glow is already present and needs but little attention.

The patching and filling completed, Mr. Jones is now shaved, washed,   19
and dressed. Cream-based cosmetic, available in pink, flesh, suntan, bru-
nette, and blond, is applied to his hands and face, his hair is shampooed and
combed (and, in the case of Mrs. Jones, set), his hands manicured. For the
horny-handed son of toil special care must be taken; cream should be applied
to remove ingrained grime, and the nails cleaned. "If he were not in the
habit of having them manicured in life, trimming and shaping is advised for
appearance—never questioned by kin."

Jones is now ready for casketing (this is the present participle of the verb   20
"to casket"). In this operation his right shoulder should be depressed slightly
"to turn the body a bit to the right and soften the appearance of lying flat
on the back." Positioning the hands is a matter of importance, and special
rubber positioning blocks may be used. The hands should be cupped slightly
for a more lifelike, relaxed appearance.[†] Proper placement of the body
requires a delicate sense of balance. It should lie as high as possible in the
casket, yet not so high that the lid, when lowered, will hit the nose. On the
other hand, we are cautioned, placing the body too low "creates the impression that the body is in a box."

Jones is next wheeled into the appointed slumber room where a few last   21
touches may be added—his favorite pipe placed in his hand or, if he was a
great reader, a book propped into position. (In the case of little Master Jones
a Teddy bear may be clutched.) Here he will hold open house for a few days,
visiting hours 10 A.M. to 9 P.M.

All now being in readiness, the funeral director calls a staff conference to   22
make sure that each assistant knows his precise duties. Mr. Wilber Kriege
writes, "This makes your staff feel that they are a part of the team, with a
definite assignment that must be properly carried out if the whole plan is to

---

Thinking Critically

[†] Why would a mortician want to create "a more lifelike, relaxed appearance" in a corpse?
How does this phrase fit into the author's overall purpose in the essay?

succeed. You never heard of a football coach who failed to talk to his entire team before they go on the field. They have drilled on the plays they are to execute for hours and days, and yet the successful coach knows the importance of making even the bench-warming third-string substitute feel that he is important if the game is to be won." The winning of *this* game is predicated upon glass-smooth handling of the logistics. The funeral director has notified the pallbearers whose names were furnished by the family, has arranged for the presence of clergyman, organist, and soloist, has provided transportation for everybody, has organized and listed the flowers sent by friends. In *Psychology of Funeral Service,* Mr. Edward A. Martin points out: "He may not always do as much as the family thinks he is doing, but it is his helpful guidance that they appreciate in knowing they are proceeding as they should. . . . The important thing is how well his services can be used to make the family believe they are giving unlimited expression to their own sentiment." [12]

The religious service may be held in a church or in the chapel of the funeral home; the funeral director vastly prefers the latter arrangement, for not only is it more convenient for him but it affords him the opportunity to show off his beautiful facilities to the gathered mourners. After the clergyman has had his say, the mourners queue up to file past the casket for a last look at the deceased. The family is *never* asked whether they want an open-casket ceremony; in the absence of their instruction to the contrary, this is taken for granted. Consequently, well over 90 percent of all American funerals feature the open casket—a custom unknown in other parts of the world. [13] Foreigners are astonished by it. An English woman living in San Francisco described her reaction in a letter to the writer: [23]

> I myself have attended only one funeral here—that of an elderly fellow worker of mine. After the service I could not understand why everyone was walking towards the coffin (sorry, I mean casket), but thought I had better follow the crowd. It shook me rigid to get there and find the casket open and poor old Oscar lying there in his brown tweed suit, wearing a suntan makeup and just the wrong shade of lipstick. If I had not been extremely fond of the old boy, I have a horrible feeling that I might have giggled. Then and there I decided that I could never face another American funeral—even dead.

The casket (which has been resting throughout the service on a Classic Beauty Ultra Metal Casket Bier) is now transferred by a hydraulically operated device called Porto-Lift to a balloon-tired, Glide Easy casket carriage which [24]

Thinking Critically

[12] What does the author mean by the phrase "giving unlimited expression to their own sentiment" when discussing the involvement of the deceased's family?

[13] How do you feel about "open casket" funeral ceremonies? Analyze your response to this custom.

will wheel it to yet another conveyance, the Cadillac Funeral Coach. This may be lavender, cream, light green—anything but black. Interiors, of course, are color-correlated, "for the man who cannot stop short of perfection."

At graveside, the casket is lowered into the earth. This office, once the   25 prerogative of friends of the deceased, is now performed by a patented mechanical lowering device. A "Life-time Green" artificial grass mat is at the ready to conceal the sere earth, and overhead, to conceal the sky, is a portable Steril Chapel Tent ("resists the intense heat and humidity of summer and the terrific storms of winter . . . available in Silver Grey, Rose, or Evergreen"). Now is the time for the ritual scattering of earth over the coffin, as the solemn words "earth to earth, ashes to ashes, dust to dust" are pronounced by the officiating cleric. This can today be accomplished "with a mere flick of the wrist with the Gordon Leak-Proof Earth Dispenser. No grasping of a handful of dirt, no soiled fingers. Simple, dignified, beautiful, reverent! The modern way!" The Golden Earth Dispenser (at $5) is of nickel-plated brass construction. It is not only "attractive to the eye and long wearing"; it is also "one of the 'tools' for building better public relations" if presented as "an appropriate non-commercial gift" to the clergyman. It is shaped something like a saltshaker.

Untouched by human hand, the coffin and the earth are now united.[14]   26

It is in the function of directing the participants through the maze of   27 gadgetry that the funeral director has assigned to himself his relatively new role of "grief therapist." He has relieved the family of every detail, he has revamped the corpse to look like a living doll, he has arranged for it to nap for a few days in a slumber room, he has put on a well-oiled performance in which the concept of *death* has played no part whatsoever—unless it was inconsiderately mentioned by the clergyman who conducted the religious service. He has done everything in his power to make the funeral a real pleasure for everybody concerned. He and his team have given their all to score an upset victory over death.

UNDERSTANDING DETAILS

1. List the major steps of the embalming process that the author reveals in this essay.
2. Why, according to Mitford, do funeral directors not want to make public the details of embalming? To what extent do you think their desire for secrecy is warranted?
3. Why isn't the permission of a family member needed for embalming? From Mitford's perspective, what does this custom reveal about Americans?
4. In what ways has embalming become the undertaker's *raison d'Être*? How do American funeral customs encourage this procedure?

Thinking Critically

[14] Why do you think it's important for the coffin and the earth to be united "Untouched by human hand"? In what way is this comment ironic?

READING CRITICALLY

5. What is Mitford's primary purpose in this essay? Why do you think she has analyzed this particular process in such detail?

6. Explain the title of this essay.

7. Do you think the author knows how gruesome her essay is? How can you tell? What makes the essay so horrifying? How does such close attention to macabre detail help Mitford accomplish her purpose?

8. What does Mitford mean when she argues that the funeral director and his team "have given their all to score an upset victory over death" (paragraph 27)? Who or what is "the team"? Why does Mitford believe death plays no part in American burial customs?

DISCOVERING RHETORICAL STRATEGIES

9. Why does Mitford begin her essay with a one-sentence paragraph? Is it effective? Why or why not?

10. A euphemism is a deceptively pleasant term used in place of a straightforward, less pleasant one. In what way is "Beautiful Memory Picture" (paragraph 2) a euphemism? How are we reminded of this phrase throughout the essay? What other euphemisms can you find in this selection?

11. What tone does Mitford establish in the essay? What is her reason for creating this particular tone? What is your reaction to it?

12. What other rhetorical strategies does Mitford use besides gruesome examples and illustrations to make her point? Give examples of each of these different strategies.

MAKING CONNECTIONS

13. Imagine that Stephen King ("Why We Crave Horror Movies") has just read Mitford's essay on funeral customs. According to King, what would be the source of our fascination with these macabre practices? Why do essays like Mitford's both intrigue and repulse us at the same time?

14. Compare and contrast Mitford's use of examples with those used by Harold Krents ("Darkness at Noon"), Roni Jacobson ("A Digital Safety Net"), and/or Amy Tan ("Mother Tongue"). How often does each author use examples? What is the relationship between the frequency of examples in each essay and the extent to which you are convinced by the author's argument?

15. In this essay, Mitford lifts the curtain on certain bizarre funeral practices in much the same way that Barbara Ehrenreich ("Nickel and Dimed") exposes the hardships of working in a minimum-wage job, Frank Furedi ("Our Unhealthy Obsession with Sickness") uncovers the abuses of the medical system, and Nicholas Carr ("How the Internet Is Making Us Stupid") reveals the problems resulting from our love affair with the Internet. Which of these "exposés" that you have read seems most devastating to you? Explain your answer.

IDEAS FOR DISCUSSION/WRITING

Preparing to Write

Write freely about a particularly interesting custom in America or in another country: Why does this custom exist? What role does it play in the society? What value does it have? What are the details of this custom? In what way is this custom a part of your life? Your family's life? What purpose does it serve for you? Is it worth continuing? Why or why not?

Choosing a Topic   MyWritingLab™

1. **LEARNING⏻ONLINE** Consider a task you find unpleasant, and write a farcical essay or commercial about it (like the Six Feet Under YouTube commercials you viewed in Preparing to Read). Make your piece as detailed as possible, offering stage directions and/or drawings for the essay or commercial if possible.

2. In a process analysis essay directed to your classmates, explain a custom you do not approve of. Decide on your tone and purpose before you begin to write.

3. In a process analysis essay directed to your classmates, explain a custom you approve of. Select a specific tone and purpose before you begin to write.

4. You have been asked to address a group of students at a college of mortuary science. In this role, you have an opportunity to influence the opinion of these students concerning the practice of embalming. Write a well-reasoned lecture to this group arguing either for or against the process of embalming.

Before beginning your essay, you may want to consult the flowchart on page 194.

CAROLE KANCHIER (1964–)

Dare to Change Your Job and Your Life in 7 Steps

Dr. Carole Kanchier, a registered psychologist, has counseled and coached over 40,000 adults in her professional life so far. Specializing in career counseling, she works with individuals from a variety of ages and backgrounds and with many different organizations, from Fortune 1000 companies to startups in finance, defense, education, and retail. She believes that change in the context of a career is an important aspect of life that helps us learn about ourselves and our own personal development. Kanchier regularly contributes articles to both digital and print publications on topics ranging from table manners to the importance of first impressions. Her book, *Dare to Change Your Job and Your Life* (2009), won the Book Award for Career Education Excellence and Innovation from the American Association for Career Education in the same year it was published. Respected both nationally and internationally, Kanchier has taught at many universities, including University of California, Berkeley, and the University of Alberta.

Preparing to Read

This excerpt was first published in *Psychology Today*. In it, the author offers seven specific suggestions for making desired changes in our careers and our lives. She bases her suggestions on interviews with many people who have actually made such changes.

Exploring Experience: As you prepare to read this essay, think about one activity that defines you and your current lifestyle: What is that activity? How does it define you? How has this activity enriched your life? What have you gained from this activity that would otherwise not have enriched your life?

LEARNINGⓊNLINE Visit the *Psychology Today* homepage at psychologytoday.com. Click the search engine icon in the top right-hand corner, and type in "Self-Help." Then, select the search result "Self-Help." Once you have arrived at the "Self-Help" page, choose any of the topics or articles that seem most relevant to your life. As you read your selected articles, try to identify the steps of the processes the authors are explaining.

Before reading this essay, you may want to consult the flowchart on page 191.

S mall, dark-haired, attractive, and warm, Melissa belies her 44 years. In   1
a sharp gray suit and becoming blouse, she projects a professional yet
approachable image. She is now director of training and development
for a large retail outlet—and loves it.

"I feel good about myself," she says, "and at the end of the day, I have lots   2
of energy left over." Melissa feels content because she believes she is doing
something worthwhile. Her new position gives her life meaning and purpose. But getting there wasn't easy. [1]

First a flight attendant, then a high school English teacher, then a man-   3
ager in a retail store, Melissa stumbled about from what was for her one
dead-end job to another. How did she finally find a meaningful, fulfilling,
well-paid career? And how did she do what so many of us fail to do—dare
to change? [2]

A career change can take months or even years of soul-searching—10 months   4
in Melissa's case. You need to know the steps, how to master the trouble-
some feelings that accompany change, where the possible dangers lie, and
how to maximize your gains while minimizing your losses. While creating
a life worth living isn't easy, Melissa and millions of others have shown that
anything is possible.

In interviews and surveys with more than 30,000 people over the past 25 years,   5
I have identified seven steps that are key to a successful career and life shift.

1. Become Aware of Negative Feelings

Your body and mind may be sending you messages about your job satis-   6
faction. The messages may be physical—lingering colds, flu, or headaches—
or verbal—"23 minutes till lunch!" or "One more day till Friday!"

Perhaps you've been working for several years in your job, and it appears   7
to be going well. You've had steady promotions, praise from superiors, and
admiration from colleagues. Then one day you get a queasy feeling that
something is lacking. But what? You run the film of your life in reverse but
you can't figure it out. These feelings may persist for months or even years,
depending on your ability to tolerate them, but, sooner or later, you have
to admit you have a problem.

2. Define the Problem

A good written definition of your problem can help to put you on the   8
road toward change.

Thinking Critically

[1] Do you feel good about where you are in life right now? What circumstances make you content?

[2] How do you feel about change? Why do you approach it the way you do?

First, ask yourself, "What's making me feel this way? What is it about my   9
situation that is unpleasant? Does this job help me reach my goals?" If not,
why?

Next, describe any barriers that may be blocking you from making a   10
move—perhaps fear of change; fear of losing a secure income, pension or
other benefits; fear that the change will interfere with your relationships; or
fear that you'll lose power or status.

Fear is the result of conditioning, and because it is learned, it can be   11
unlearned. Reprogram your old attitudes and beliefs with new ones by
learning and practicing specific ways to overcome the fears blocking your
path toward change. Think of FEAR as an acronym for "False Expectations
Appear Real." Don't spend time worrying about what might happen. Focus
on the now.

3. Listen to Ambivalence

Milton, a rehabilitation counselor, was approached by a prospective   12
partner to start an executive recruitment agency. For weeks before making
the move, he went straight to bed immediately after dinner and pulled the
sheets up over his head. He tried to make light of this behavior, but he had
undertaken many risks before and had never felt this way about them.

His underlying fears were prophetic. He later discovered that the hard-   13
sell, aggressive style required for executive recruiting was not for him. The
difference in basic values between Milton and his partner proved such a
handicap that, within five months, the two parted ways.

The decision to change can provoke mixed feelings. A certain amount of   14
ambivalence is natural. Inner emotional preparation—weighing losses as well
as gains, fears as well as hopes—is a necessary prerequisite for successful risk
taking.

But if the prospect of undertaking a change is so great that your stomach   15
is churning, you can't sleep, you have constant headaches, or you feel you're
developing an ulcer, your body, in its wisdom, is telling you to forgo the risk.

4. Prepare for Risk [3]

The key to avoiding potential potholes is to set tentative career goals [4]   16
before you explore new roads. Goals force you to focus on what you really
want. Years from now, as you review your life, what would you regret not
having done?

Thinking Critically
[3] why are most people afraid of taking risks?
[4] What are your major career goals?

Fantasize about the ultimate goal, your shining star. If you could do any-   17
thing in the world, what would it be? Write all of your ideas or fantasies in
a notebook. Include everything you want to do, be, and have. The sky is
the limit. Once you know what you want, you'll be more willing to take
the risks necessary to achieve it.

Choosing a satisfying career and lifestyle also requires a basic under-   18
standing of yourself. A variety of exercises can help. To identify your
strengths, for example, list some of the successes you've had—say, substitut-
ing for your son's soccer coach. Next to each success, identify what gave
you the positive feelings. Did you contribute to the team's first win of the
season?

Also list the skills and abilities you used to bring about that success. Were   19
you well organized and adept at working with parents? Finally, decide how
your interests, needs, accomplishments, and other personal strengths add up.
What pattern do they form?

Self-exploration is just part of the process. You also need to take a care-   20
ful look at your current situation, as well as the available alternatives. Some
popular reference tools, available at your local library, can help. Check out
the *Occupational Handbook,* the *Dictionary of Occupational Titles,* and the *Encyclopedia of Careers and Work Issues.* The Internet also offers excellent sites
for exploring general occupational fields, job descriptions, and educational
opportunities.

5. Narrow Your Options

Successful career management hinges on finding a position that's compat-   21
ible with your personal qualities and goals. Do you have the necessary intelligence and skills to do the work? Can you afford the training required for
the job? Might your shortcomings—health, vision, size, or strength, for
example—pose a problem?

To help narrow your options, draw a series of vertical and horizontal lines   22
so that your paper is divided into squares. Across the top of the page, list the
most important elements of your ideal job: income, responsibility, public
image, creativity, challenge, and so on (one in each square). Down the left
side of the page, list each occupational option you're considering.

Next, for each alternative, place a −1 in the appropriate box if that   23
job option doesn't satisfy the criterion listed at the top of the page. If
the criterion is met, but not as much as you'd like, record a 0. If the
criterion is well met, record a +1. Add the points for each job option
and place them in a column labeled "total" at the far right. The job with
the highest score meets the greatest number of criteria that you have
deemed important.

6. Take Action

Once you've determined your occupational goal, take steps to realize it.   24
You'll need a well-planned campaign to market yourself for the job, establish
your own business, or return to school.

Stay focused on your goals, and believe you will achieve them. View   25
failures along the way as learning experiences—detours that might offer an
unexpected dividend.

7. Evaluate the Decision

When you have worked hard at making a decision, take the time not just   26
to enjoy the outcome, but to evaluate it. Ask yourself

- Do I feel good about the move?
- What other gains did I derive from the move? What did I lose?
- What factors contributed to the success of my move?
- If I could do it all over again, what would I do differently?
- Who was most helpful in the process? Who let me down?

Evaluation is a continuous process. Assess your needs, goals, and job sat-   27
isfaction periodically to determine if your developing personality fits your
position and lifestyle. Don't wait for a crisis to clear your vision.

There really is no substitute for risk as a way to grow. Knowing you have   28
honestly faced the painful struggle and accepted the trade-offs, and yet proceeded in spite of them, is extremely gratifying.

Melissa learned that the tremendous investment of energy a successful job   29
search demands is exactly what enables people to look back and say, "Win,
lose, or draw, I gave it my everything." Being able to say with satisfaction
that you risked for a dream may be the biggest prize of all.

To remain fulfilled, however, you'll need to risk again and again until   30
you've created a life in which you feel comfortable being yourself, without
apology or pretense—a life in which you can continue to have choices.

UNDERSTANDING DETAILS

1. From Kanchier's perspective, what is the most important step on her list?
2. How can fear be learned and unlearned? Give an example from Kanchier's
   essay.
3. According to Kanchier, what role do goals play in the process of change?
4. According to the author, how is "a life in which you can continue to have
   choices" important (paragraph 30)?

READING CRITICALLY

5. Why does the author use the word "dare" with "change"? What is she implying?
6. In your opinion, which of the steps that Kanchier suggests would be most useful to you? Why would they be useful?
7. Would the bulleted list in paragraph 26 help you evaluate other situations besides jobs? Explain your answer.
8. What does Kanchier mean when she says, "Being able to say with satisfaction that you risked for a dream may be the biggest prize of all" (paragraph 29)?

DISCOVERING RHETORICAL STRATEGIES

9. Kanchier begins and ends this essay with details about Melissa. What effect does this approach have on you?
10. What type of process analysis essay is this: chronological, cyclical, or simultaneous? Explain your answer.
11. Kanchier uses several examples throughout this essay to support the items on her list. Is this an effective way to get her point across? What do all these examples demonstrate? What other way could the author have explained these items? Would this way have been more or less effective than offering examples?
12. What reasoning did Kanchier use to prioritize her list?

MAKING CONNECTIONS

13. Compare and contrast Carole Kanchier's approach to change with similar suggestions made by Maya Angelou ("New Directions"), Stephanie Vozza ("How to Make New Friends as an Adult"), and/or Samantha Pugsley ("How Language Impacts the Stigma Against Mental Health [And What We Must Do To Change It]"). Which author seems most devoted to his or her proposals? Why do you think this is so?
14. What could Russell Baker ("The Saturday Evening Post"), Amy Chua ("Excerpt from *Battle Hymn of the Tiger Mother*"), and/or Frank Furedi ("Our Unhealthy Obsession with Sickness") learn from Kanchier's guidelines in this essay? Which guidelines would each author embrace most enthusiastically?
15. If Kanchier, Josh Rose ("How Social Media Is Having a Positive Impact on Our Culture"), and Susan Tardanico ("Is Social Media Sabotaging Real Communication?") were discussing the Internet, what would they agree is the main role of social media in business? On what would they disagree in reference to the use of social media in the working world?

IDEAS FOR DISCUSSION/WRITING

Preparing to Write

Write freely about the activities that define you: Do they involve risks? How does your desire to be content affect your development as a person? What would you be like without these activities that define you?

Choosing a Topic

1. **LEARNING⏻NLINE** Think about the Self-Help topic you read about in Preparing to Read. Write your own essay about the process you would go through to achieve this change. Once you've finished writing, compare your process with the articles on the *Psychology Today* website.

2. What one activity represents you as a person? How does this activity characterize you? Write an essay explaining to your classmates how this activity defines your personality.

3. Kanchier is quite clear about how she came up with these steps to assist people with change as they move toward a state of contentment with their lives. Using Kanchier's process analysis as a model, write an essay explaining how to be a unique human being.

4. List five books, articles, essays, or comic books that you have read recently, and in a coherent essay, explain their effect on you and your view of the world.

Before beginning your essay, you may want to consult the flowchart on page 194.

BARBARA EHRENREICH   (1941–)

Nickel and Dimed

Barbara Ehrenreich is a respected author, lecturer, and social commentator with strong opinions on a wide range of topics. After earning a B.A. from Reed College in chemistry and physics and a Ph.D. from Rockefeller University in cell biology, she turned almost immediately to freelance writing, producing a succession of books and pamphlets on a dazzling array of subjects. Early publications examined student uprisings, healthcare in America, nurses and midwives, poverty, welfare, economic justice for women, and the sexual politics of disease. Among her twenty-one books are *Fear of Falling: The Inner Life of the Middle Class* (1989), *Blood Rites: Origins and History of the Passions of War* (1997), *Nickel and Dimed* (2001), *Bait and Switch: The (Futile) Pursuit of the American Dream* (2005), *This Land Is Their Land* (2008), and *Bright Sided: How the Relentless Promotion of Positive Thinking Has Undermined America* (2009). Ehrenreich is also well known as a frequent guest on television and radio programs, including *The Today Show*, *Good Morning America*, *Nightline*, and *Crossfire*. Her many articles and reviews have appeared in the *New York Times Magazine*, *Esquire*, the *Atlantic Monthly*, the *New Republic*, *Vogue*, *Harper's*, *Time*, and the *Wall Street Journal*. In recent years, she has focused her energies on the Economic Hardship Reporting Project, which promotes journalism on poverty. Her latest book is *Living with a Wild God: An Unbeliever's Search for the Truth about Everything* (2014), a memoir. Ehrenreich, whose favorite hobby is "voracious reading," lives in Syosset, New York.

Preparing to Read

The following excerpt from *Nickel and Dimed* relates some of Ehrenreich's adventures after she posed incognito as a domestic worker to find out whether or not surviving economically as a member of America's blue-collar underclass is possible.

Exploring Experience: As you prepare to read this essay, take a few minutes to think about work in general: Do you work? Do you enjoy your job? If you don't work, what marketable skills do you have? What jobs would you like in the future? Are you willing to start "at the bottom"? How flexible are you in your choice of employment?

LEARNING◖NLINE Before reading this essay, think about what you do to clean your house or how you would if you had to do it. Would you make a list of tasks you need to do? How much time would you devote to each chore? Would you take as much time as necessary to do the job well, or would you complete the work as fast as possible? Make some notes on your routine, and compare them with the "tricks" shown in the YouTube video "How to Fake a Clean House" (by Howcast) at www.youtube.com.

Before reading this essay, you may want to consult the flowchart on page 191.

A t last, after all the other employees have sped off in the company's eye-catching green-and-yellow cars, I am led into a tiny closet-sized room off the inner office to learn my trade via videotape. The manager at another maid service where I'd applied had told me she didn't like to hire people who had done cleaning before because they were resistant to learning the company's system, so I prepare to empty my mind of all prior housecleaning experience. There are four tapes—dusting, bathrooms, kitchen, and vacuuming—each starring an attractive, possibly Hispanic young woman who moves about serenely in obedience to the male voiceover. For vacuuming, begin in the master bedroom; when dusting, begin with the room directly off the kitchen. When you enter a room, mentally divide it into sections no wider than your reach. Begin in the section to your left, and, within each section, move from left to right and top to bottom. This way nothing is ever overlooked. 1

I like Dusting best, for its undeniable logic and a certain kind of austere 2 beauty. When you enter a house, you spray a white rag with Windex and place it in the left pocket of your green apron. Another rag, sprayed with disinfectant, goes into the middle pocket, and a yellow rag bearing wood polish in the right-hand pocket. A dry rag, for buffing surfaces, occupies the right-hand pocket of your slacks. Shiny surfaces get Windexed, wood gets wood polish, and everything else is wiped dust-free with disinfectant. Every now and then Ted pops in to watch with me, pausing the video to underscore a particularly dramatic moment: "See how she's working around the vase? That's an accident waiting to happen." If Ted himself were in a video, it would have to be a cartoon, because the only features sketched onto his pudgy face are brown button-like eyes and a tiny pug nose; his belly, encased in a polo shirt, overhangs the waistline of his shorts. "You know, all this was figured out with a stopwatch," he tells me with something like pride. When the video warns against oversoaking our rags with cleaning fluids, he pauses it to tell me there's a danger in undersoaking too, especially if it's going to slow me down. "Cleaning fluids are less expensive than your time." It's good to know that something is cheaper than my time or that in the hierarchy of the company's values I rank above Windex. 2

Vacuuming is the most disturbing video, actually a double feature begin- 3 ning with an introduction to the special backpack vacuum we are to use. Yes, the vacuum cleaner actually straps onto your back, a chubby fellow who introduces himself as its inventor explains. He suits up, pulling the straps

---

Thinking Critically

1 Have you ever thought much about the housekeepers who clean your hotel rooms? Have you ever left them a tip? Why or why not? How difficult do you think their job is? How much training does it require?

2 To what extent is the author using ironic humor in her description of these training videos?

tight across and under his chest and then says proudly into the camera: "See, I am the vacuum cleaner." It weighs only ten pounds, he claims, although, as I soon find out, with the attachments dangling from the strap around your waist, the total is probably more like fourteen. What about my petulant and much-pampered lower back? The inventor returns to the theme of human/ machine merger: when properly strapped in, we too will be vacuum cleaners, constrained only by the cord that attaches us to an electrical outlet, and vacuum cleaners don't have backaches. Somehow all this information exhausts me, and I watch the second video, which explains the actual procedures for vacuuming, with the detached interest of a cineast. Could the model maid be an actual maid and the model home someone's actual dwelling? And who are these people whose idea of decorating is matched pictures of mallard ducks in flight and whose house is perfectly characterless and pristine even before the model maid sets to work?

At first I find the videos on kitchens and bathrooms baffling, and it takes   4
me several minutes to realize why: there is no water, or almost no water, involved. I was taught to clean by my mother, a compulsive housekeeper who employed water so hot you needed rubber gloves to get into it and in such Niagara-like quantities that most microbes were probably crushed by the force of it before the soap suds had a chance to rupture their cell walls. But germs are never mentioned in the videos provided by The Maids. Our antagonists exist entirely in the visible world—soap scum, dust, counter crud, dog hair, stains, and smears—and are to be attacked by damp rag or, in hard-core cases, by Dobie (the brand of plastic scouring pad we use). We scrub only to remove impurities that might be detectable to a customer by hand or by eye; otherwise, our only job is to wipe. Nothing is said about the possibility of transporting bacteria, by rag or by hand, from bathroom to kitchen or even from one house to the next. It is the "cosmetic touches" that the videos emphasize and that Ted, when he wanders back into the room, continually directs my eye to. Fluff up all throw pillows and arrange them symmetrically. Brighten up stainless steel sinks with baby oil. Leave all spice jars, shampoos, etc., with their labels facing outward. [3] Comb out the fringes of Persian carpets with a pick. Use the vacuum cleaner to create a special, fernlike pattern in the carpets. The loose ends of toilet paper and paper towel rolls have to be given a special fold (the same one you'll find in hotel bathrooms). "Messes" of loose paper, clothing, or toys are to be stacked into "neat messes." Finally, the house is to be sprayed with the cleaning service's signature floral-scented air freshener, which will signal to the owners, the moment they return home, that, yes, their house has been "cleaned."

Thinking Critically

[3] How does Ehrenreich's use of specific details help enliven her essay?

UNDERSTANDING DETAILS

1. According to the training Ehrenreich received, what steps are involved in cleaning a room?
2. Who is Ted, and what does the author think of him?
3. Why does the author like the *Dusting* video best? How does this explain her approach to her job?
4. What does Ehrenreich mean when she writes, "It's good to know . . . that in the hierarchy of the company's values I rank above Windex" (paragraph 2)?

READING CRITICALLY

5. What is the general purpose of this selection?
6. Draw a graphic of the information on the three videos Ehrenreich was required to view. What does each video have in common? How are they different?
7. Which of Ehrenreich's comments about cleaning rang most true to you? Explain your answer.
8. Which of these three cleaning chores do you like best? What are the reasons for your preference?

DISCOVERING RHETORICAL STRATEGIES

9. What other rhetorical modes support Ehrenreich's process analysis?
10. Is this excerpt principally directive or informative?
11. List Ehrenreich's topics, and label her organization (chronological, simultaneous, or cyclical).
12. What do Ehrenreich's side comments add to the explanation of this process?

MAKING CONNECTIONS

13. Compare and contrast Ehrenreich's use of process analysis with that employed by Jessica Mitford ("Behind the Formaldehyde Curtain") and Stephanie Vozza ("How to Make New Friends as an Adult"). Which author's explanation seems most accessible and understandable to you? Why?
14. Both Ehrenreich and Russell Baker ("The Saturday Evening Post") discuss the frustrations of working. How would Ehrenreich respond to Baker's seemingly lazy approach to life? On what specific references in Ehrenreich's essay do you base your inferences?
15. Ehrenreich, Malcolm Cowley ("The View from 80"), Harold Krents ("Darkness at Noon"), and Michael Dorris ("The Broken Cord") all use examples masterfully to help make their essays believable and persuasive. Which author's use of examples seems most skillful to you? Why?

IDEAS FOR DISCUSSION/WRITING

Preparing to Write

Write freely about your response to new jobs: Do you enjoy learning new skills? Do you pick them up easily? Do you like to explore new talents in yourself?

Do you find you are generally open to change? How flexible are you in your life choices?

Choosing a Topic

1. **LEARNING◐NLINE** In this excerpt, Ehrenreich emphasizes that the maid service training videos do not mention cleaning for germs or bacteria. As you saw in the Preparing to Read YouTube video, there is a process for faking a clean house. Would you use any of these strategies in cleaning your own house, apartment, or dorm room? Write an essay outlining your process for cleaning your living area. Which tasks are absolutely necessary? Which might be optional?

2. Your campus newspaper is running a special series of articles focusing on "training" for being a successful college student. What is your main advice to college students? What exactly has helped you succeed in college? Write an essay offering your best advice to first-year college students.

3. Most people hope to find a job that fulfills and interests them as their lives progress. However, they generally don't start out with the job of their dreams. Write a letter to a high school student offering realistic advice on securing a good job during college.

4. Write your own process analysis essay explaining how to clean a certain object other than a house or apartment (like a car or a work area).

Before beginning your essay, you may want to consult the flowchart on page 194.

STEPHANIE VOZZA   (1973–   )

How to Make New Friends as an Adult

Stephanie Vozza earned a B.A. in Communications from Oakland University and Loras College. A very successful freelance writer and blogger, she has contributed to *Entrepreneur* and *Fast Company* as well as many custom and trade publications such as *Gift Shop Magazine, Specialty Retail Report, Independent Dealer,* and *Footwear News.* She has also written a successful book entitled *The Five-Minute Mom's Club: 105 Tips to Make a Mom's Life Easier* (2010) and has founded TheOrganizedParent.com. She lives in Michigan, where she chases her Jack Russell terriers and enjoys reading in her spare time. She subscribes to George Orwell's quote "Good writing is like a windowpane" and strives to give people a glimpse into each other's worlds.

Preparing to Read

This essay, originally published in *Fast Company* in 2014, talks frankly about how we can make friends as adults, which is an entirely different process than making friends when we are growing up. She divides her essay into two sections that provide clear guidelines.

Exploring Experience: As you prepare to read this article, pause for a moment to consider your own ability to make friends: Do you easily make friends? Do your close friends change from time to time? How important are friendships in your current lifestyle?

LEARNINGⓄNLINE Meetup.com is a website that allows social groups to advertise and list their profiles for new potential members. From book clubs to amateur sports groups to advocacy groups, members can create a profile on Meetup to help others find their group and join it. Visit Meetup. com, and type in your city name to find groups in your area. Explore two or three of the groups that sound most interesting to you. Why might such a website exist? Would you ever consider joining any of these groups after you graduate from college? Keep your response to this question in mind as you read Vozza's essay.

Before reading this essay, you may want to consult the flowchart on page 191.

When you're a kid, making new friends is fairly easy. There's 1 school, sports, and a slew of extracurricular activities where you meet other kids and form relationships. When you're an adult, however, the process isn't quite so effortless. Commitments such as work and family limit free time and—unlike during childhood—it can feel awkward to ask someone, "Do you want to hang out?"

"Professionals who accomplish amazing goals like starting companies 2 often admit that they have a hard time making friends," says Shasta Nelson (personal communication, October 30, 2014), author of *Friendships Don't Just Happen*. And the older you get, the fewer friends you probably have. While social circles increase through early adulthood, friendship networks peak and start to decrease as you move through your twenties, according to a 2013 study published in the *Psychological Bulletin* (Wrzus, Hänel, Wagner, & Neyer, 2013). Researchers found that the drop in friendships was often due to marriage, parenthood, and a desire to focus on closer relationships.

Unfortunately close relationships aren't guaranteed to last; a study by soci- 3 ologist Gerald Mollenhorst of Utrecht University in the Netherlands (Netherlands Organization for Scientific Research, 2009) found that we lose half our close friends every seven years and replace them with new relationships.[1]

"Life changes such as moves, career transitions, relationship changes, and 4 different life stages bring a shift in our friendships and frequently leave us drifting apart," says Nelson (personal communication, October 30, 2014), who launched the online friendship-building community GirlFriendCircles. com in 2008. "We all want the proverbial friend whose shoulder you can cry on, but that's an honor that is given with time."

And it's time we should find. According to researchers at Brigham Young 5 University (2010), having too few friends is the equivalent mortality risk to smoking 15 cigarettes a day and is riskier than obesity.

"When friendships themselves are healthy, they relieve stress, which is 6 extremely beneficial for health," says Robert Epstein (personal communication, November 12, 2014), senior research psychologist at the American Institute for Behavioral Research and Technology. "Most people find it hard to create a deep and meaningful friendship in adulthood,[2] but it's not so hard if you know what to do."

Make Friends Through Consistency

For friendships to form, you need consistency, says Nelson. "When we're 7 kids, this is automatic," says Nelson (personal communication,

---

Thinking Critically

[1] Have you lost any close friends in the past? What were the circumstances?

[2] Do you find making friends more difficult now than it was when you were a child?

October 30, 2014). "You go to school, summer camp and play outside with the other kids in the neighborhood until dinner is ready. As adults, we rarely have that kind of consistency outside of work."

Nelson suggests joining groups that meet on a regular basis, such as associations, networking groups, book clubs, classes, and workshops. "When you join a group, the consistency is built in; people are already showing up without you having to invite them," she says.◆3   8

The trick is that the friendship is limited to its "container"—the group— until someone initiates gathering outside of it, says Nelson. If friendships aren't practiced outside of the container, they will most likely die when the activity or class ends.   9

"People often take it personally when they leave a job and no one calls them," says Nelson. "But they forget to recognize that they stepped outside of the container. If you hadn't already initiated a friendship outside of the container, it most likely won't suddenly happen."   10

While Nelson recommends using friendship containers as long as possible, the goal is to move out of them. Start small. Invite work friends out for lunch, happy hour or over to watch the game. "The idea is to practice doing other stuff together, and glue more pieces of your lives to each other," she says. "It can take six to eight experiences with someone before you feel like you made a friend."   11

Be Willing to Be Vulnerable

To deepen relationships, Epstein says you must be willing to open yourself up: "Vulnerability is the key to emotional bonding, without which relationships tend to feel superficial and meaningless," says Epstein (personal communication, November 12, 2014).◆4   12

Children are naturally put into situations in which they feel vulnerable, such as school, and Epstein says adults should look for similar scenarios.   13

"Put yourself in situations in which you and potential friends will feel vulnerable, because such situations make people feel needy and provide occasions for other people to provide comfort or support," he says. Volunteer or get part-time work at a hospital. Sign up for courses on skiing or salsa dancing.   14

And while you can't plan for them, sometimes life circumstances lead to friendships: "A single experience—the bonding that took place between   15

Thinking Critically

◆3 What groups do you belong to? How have friendships developed in those groups?

◆4 Do you agree with this statement by Epstein? Give an example to support your response.

two strangers who were near the World Trade Center when it collapsed, for example—can produce a deep friendship that lasts a lifetime," Epstein says.

While you're building friendships, Nelson says it's important to work hard   16
to keep the communication upbeat (personal communication, October 30, 2014). "Be conscious about the value and joy you're adding to the other person," she says.

References

Brigham Young University. (2010). Stayin' alive: That's what friends are for. *Brigham Young University News*. Retrieved, from http://news.byu.edu/archive10-jul-relationships.aspx

Epstein, R. (2014, November 12). Personal Communication.

Nelson, S. (2014, October 30). Personal Communication.

Netherlands Organization for Scientific Research. (2009). Half of your friends lost in seven years. Retrieved from http://www.alphagalileo.org/ViewItem.aspx?ItemId=58115&CultureCode=en

Wrzus, C., Hänel, M., Wagner, J., & Neyer, F.J. (2013). Social network changes and life events across the life span: A meta-analysis. *Psychological Bulletin, 139(1)*, 53-80. doi: 10.1037/a0028601

UNDERSTANDING DETAILS

1. Why is making friends in adulthood more difficult than making friends in childhood?
2. According to sociologist Gerald Mollenhorst, how often do we lose and replace close friends?
3. According to Vozza, what are the two primary guidelines for making new friends as adults?
4. According to Vozza's sources, what are two of the benefits of friendships? What are two of the disadvantages of having too few friends?

READING CRITICALLY

5. Are friends important to you at this stage in your life? Why or why not?
6. Why do you think productive professionals have an especially difficult time making friends?
7. When you consider the friends that you have, did consistency and vulnerability play a role in their development?
8. Are you persuaded by this essay to find time to seek and develop healthy friendships in your life? What was most persuasive to you? Least persuasive?

DISCOVERING RHETORICAL STRATEGIES

9. How does Vozza start her essay? Is this an effective beginning? Why or why not?
10. Describe in detail Vozza's intended audience. How did you come to this conclusion?
11. What is the principal purpose of this essay? To what extent do you think it accomplishes its goals? Explain your answer.

12. How does Vozza introduce the experts she cites in this essay? Are they reliable sources for this topic? How does citing these sources affect your response to Vozza's message?

MAKING CONNECTIONS

13. According to Vozza, what is important about vulnerability to the process of making friends? Compare and contrast her definition of the word with the way other authors might define it: Kimberly Wozencraft ("Notes from the Country Club"), Maya Angelou ("New Directions"), Elizabeth Svoboda ("Virtual Assault"), and/or Dave Grossman ("We Are Training Our Kids to Kill").
14. Which of the following authors would most completely agree with Vozza's definition of friendship: Brent Staples ("A Brother's Murder"), Gloria Steinem ("The Politics of Muscle"), Michael Dorris ("The Broken Cord"), and/or John Tierney ("A Generation's Vanity, Heard Through Lyrics")?
15. What would Stephanie Vozza say to Karen Lachtanski ("Match the Right Communication to the Occasion") about communicating in relationships? Where would they agree and disagree on this issue?

IDEAS FOR DISCUSSION/WRITING

Preparing to Write

Write freely about the importance of friendship in society today: What makes someone a friend? What qualities must he or she have? When do you personally need or want friends? In your experience, do friends generally support or hinder your development as a person? Do they complement your commitments in college? Do they encourage or discourage productivity in you?

Choosing a Topic   MyWritingLab™

1. **LEARNING⏻ONLINE** Vozza uses process analysis to suggest ways an individual can make friends in adulthood. Using the Meetup.com website for inspiration, write a process analysis essay outlining the ways a working adult might meet people who share similar interests.
2. Take one of Vozza's suggestions for making new friends, and discuss its accuracy or inaccuracy in the context of your own experience. From your personal observations, will this guideline work to create friendships for most adults?
3. Over the years, the Internet has led to different types of friendships than the face-to-face friendships from the past. Using Vozza's essay as a model, write an essay explaining how to develop new friends online. Offer at least two guidelines, as she does.
4. One of your friends who is still in high school has asked you for information about social activities in college. Write to this friend, using process analysis to explain how to survive college while still having a life full of friends and extracurricular activities. Decide on a purpose and a point of view before you begin to write.

Before beginning your essay, you may want to consult the flowchart on page 194.

Chapter Writing Assignments

Practicing Process Analysis

1. Make a list of some of the activities you do well. Choose one activity, and think about exactly what you must do to perform this skill. Write an essay that describes to another person the process of doing this activity well. Be as specific and clear in your directions as you can.

2. Identify a task or responsibility that seems impossible for you to do well. What keeps you from performing this task with skill or efficiency? Write an essay that describes how to fail at this activity. Describe this method for failure in a humorous or sarcastic manner.

3. What is your best method for solving major life problems? Think of times in your life when you have had to solve a problem or make an important decision. Write an essay that explains to a person looking for problem-solving ideas the method you rely on when faced with important problems that must be solved.

Exploring Ideas

4. How do you think your ability to manage your time affects your daily life? Do you think this ability has mostly positive or negative effects on your lifestyle? Use specific examples to support your opinion.

5. Find a recent advertisement on television, in the newspaper, on the Internet, on a billboard, or on the radio that you think is especially successful. Examine this ad, and write an essay explaining why it succeeds. What makes it good? Whom does it reach? How effectively does it address its target population?

6. In your opinion, should students in college work or not? What are the advantages of working while in college? What are the disadvantages? Consider other important facets of our daily lives, such as time with friends, physical activities, social events, and the like, in your response.

Analyzing Visual Images

Blend/Superstock.

7. How do you achieve complete relaxation? Provide a step-by-step guide to accomplishing the kind of tranquility you see in this photograph.

8. Look at the picture on page 190 at the beginning of this chapter. Imagine having to explain the steps of surfing to someone who knows nothing about the sport. Think of a sport you know well, and try to explain the basic rules of that activity to someone who knows little or nothing about it.

Composing in Different Genres

9. Multimedia: Design a game for two players or more that offers guidelines on how students can succeed in college. Be creative in developing your game. Either describe it in a well-developed essay or make a version of the game itself.

10. Multigenre: Write a user's guide for being a good friend. As fully as possible, provide the details for this process through the format of a guide.

Writing from Sources

For detailed information on writing from sources, see Part III.

11. Choose a person in modern history who exhibited success in the face of adversity. Research his or her life. Is there anything notable about this person's early family life? What is characteristic of his or her professional life? From where does he or she draw motivation? How does this person handle hardship? Then, using examples from your research, write a documented essay explaining the qualities you believe foster and encourage success.

12. How do most people relax? What are the health benefits associated with relaxation? Consider the standard work week and vacation practices of the United States. How do they compare to those in other countries? Research this topic, and present your evidence in a documented essay discussing the advantages or disadvantages of relaxation on a person's physical and mental health.

MyWritingLab™ Visit Ch. 7 Process Analysis: Explaining Step by Step in *MyWritingLab* to complete the writing assignments and test your understanding of the chapter learning objectives.

Chapter 8

DIVISION/CLASSIFICATION
Finding Categories

OBJECTIVES

After completing this chapter, you will be able to do the following:
- Define division/classification
- Use division/classification to think critically
- Read division/classification essays critically
- Write and revise effective division/classification essays.

Both division and classification play important roles in our everyday lives: Bureau drawers separate one type of clothing from another; kitchen cabinets and drawers organize food, dishes, and utensils into groups; grocery stores shelve similar items together so shoppers can easily locate what they want to buy; school notebooks with tabs help students divide up their academic lives; newspapers classify local and national events to organize a great deal of daily information for the general public; and our own personal classification systems assist us in separating what we like from what we don't so that we can have access to our favorite foods, our favorite cars, our favorite entertainment, our favorite people. The two processes of division and classification are so natural to us, in fact, that we sometimes aren't even aware that we are using them.

DEFINING DIVISION/CLASSIFICATION

Division and classification are actually mirror images of each other. *Division* is the basic feature of process analysis, which we studied in Chapter 7; it moves from a general concept to subdivisions of that concept or from a single category to multiple subcategories. *Classification* works in the opposite direction, moving from specifics to a group with common traits or from multiple subgroups to a single, larger, and more inclusive category. These techniques work together in many ways: A college, for example, is *divided* into departments (single to multiple), whereas courses are *classified* by department (multiple to single); the medical field is *divided* into specialties, whereas doctors are *classified* by a single specialty; a cookbook is *divided* into chapters, whereas recipes are *classified* according to type; and athletics is *divided* into specific sports, whereas athletes are *classified* by the sport in which they participate. Division is the separation of an idea or an item into its basic parts, such as a home into rooms, a course into assignments, or a job into various duties or responsibilities; classification is the organization of items with similar features into a group or groups, such as finding all green-eyed people in a large group, omitting all carbohydrates from your diet, or watching only the track and field events during the Olympics.

Classification is an organizational system for presenting a large amount of material to a reader or listener. This process helps us make sense of the complex world we live in by letting us work with smaller, more understandable units of that world. Classification must be governed by some clear, logical purpose (such as focusing on all lower-division course requirements), which will then dictate the system of categories to be used. The plan of organization that results should be as flexible as possible, and it should illustrate the specific relationships of items in a group and of the groups themselves to one another.

As you already know, many different ways of classifying the same elements are possible. If you consider the examples at the outset of this chapter, you will realize that bureau drawers vary from house to house and even from person to person; that no one's kitchen is set up exactly the same way as someone else's; and that grocery stores have similar but not identical systems of classification. (Think, for instance, of the many different schemes for organizing dairy products, meats, foreign foods, etc.) In addition, your friends probably use a method different from yours to organize their school notebooks; different newspapers vary their presentation of the news; and two professors will probably teach the same course material in separate ways. We all have distinct and uniquely logical methods of classifying the elements in our own lives.

The following student paragraph about friends illustrates both division and classification. As you read it, notice how the student writer moves back and forth smoothly from general to specific and from multiple to single:

> *The word friend can refer to many different types of relationships. Close friends are "friends" at their very best: people for whom we feel respect, esteem, and, quite possibly, even love. We regard these people and their well-being with kindness, interest, and goodwill; we trust them and will go out of our way to help them. Needless to say, we could all use at least one close friend. Next come "casual friends," people with whom we share a particular interest or activity. The investment of a great amount of time and energy in developing this type of friendship is usually not required, though casual friends often become close friends with the passage of time. The last division of "friend" is most general and is composed of all those individuals whose acquaintance we have made and who feel no hostility toward us. When one is counting friends, this group should certainly be included, since such friendships often develop into "casual" or "close" relationships. Knowing people in all three groups is necessary, however, because all types of friends undoubtedly help us live healthier, happier lives.*

THINKING CRITICALLY THROUGH DIVISION/ CLASSIFICATION

The thinking strategies of division and classification are the flip sides of each other: Your textbook is *divided* into chapters (one item divided into many), but chapters are *classified* (grouped) into sections or units. Your brain performs these mental acrobatics constantly, but to be as proficient at this method of thinking as possible, you need to be aware of the cognitive activities you go through. Focusing on these two companion patterns of thought will develop your skill in dealing with these complex schemes as it simultaneously increases your overall mental capabilities.

You might think of division/classification as a driving pattern that goes forward and then doubles back on itself in reverse. Division is a movement from a single concept to multiple categories, whereas classification involves gathering multiple concepts into a single group. Dividing and/or classifying helps us make sense of our subject by using categories to highlight similarities and differences. In the case of division, you are trying to find what differences break the items into separate groups; with classification, you let the similarities among the items help you put the material into meaningful categories. Processing your material in this way helps your readers see your particular subject in a new way and often brings renewed insights to both reader and writer.

Experimenting with division and classification is important to your growth as a critical thinker. It will help you process complex information so you can more fully understand your options for dealing with material in all subject areas. Practicing division and classification separate from other rhetorical modes makes you concentrate on improving this particular pattern of thinking before adding it to your expanding arsenal of critical thinking skills.

Melanie Stetson Freeman/Christian Science Monitor/The Image Works.

1. List the items in the photograph. How could they be divided and classified into categories? What do you learn by looking at the photograph in this way?
2. Study the table of contents of a magazine that interests you. Into what sections is the magazine divided? What distinguishing features does each section have? Now study the various advertisements in the same magazine. What different categories would you use to classify these ads? List the ads in each category.
3. Make a chart classifying the English instructors at your school. Explain your classification system to the class.

READING AND WRITING DIVISION/CLASSIFICATION ESSAYS

Although writers of division/classification essays will probably use both division and classification in their essays, they should decide if they are primarily going to break down a topic into many separate parts or group together similar items into one coherent category; a writer's purpose will, of course, guide him or her in this decision. Readers must likewise recognize and understand which of these two parallel operations an author is using to structure an essay. Another important identifying feature of division/classification essays is an explanation (explicit or implicit) of the significance of a particular system of organization.

Reading Division/Classification Essays

Understanding how division/classification essays work rhetorically will help you make decisions for your own writing. Here is a flowchart of questions that will guide your reading for this purpose.

Questions to Guide Your Reading

PREPARING TO READ Before you read the essays, answer the following questions:

- What assumptions can you make from the essay's **title**?
- What do you think the general **mood** of the essay will be?
- What is the essay's **purpose** and **audience**?
- What does the **synopsis** tell you about the essay?
- What can you learn from the author's **biography**?
- What do you predict the author's **point of view** toward the subject will be?

READING As you read the essays for the first time, answer the following questions:

- What is the essay's **context**?
- Did the author **divide** and/or **classify**?
- What **details** support the essay's purpose?

REREADING When you read the essays again, answer the following questions:

- How is the essay **organized**?
- What other **rhetorical strategies** does the author use?
- How does the writer explain the **significance** of his or her approach?
- How does your understanding **change** with each rereading?

Preparing To Read.   As you approach the selections in this chapter, you should study all the material that precedes each essay so you can prepare yourself for your reading. First of all, what hints does the title give you about what you are going to read? How many different types of intelligence will Sara Gilbert introduce? Who do you think Sarah Toler's audience is in "Understanding the Birth Order Relationship"? Does Stephanie Ericsson's title give us any indication about her point of view in "The Ways We Lie"? Then see what you can learn from scanning each essay and reading its synopsis in the Rhetorical Table of Contents.

Also important as you prepare to read the essays in this chapter is your knowledge about each author and the conditions under which each essay was written: What does the biographical material tell you about Karen Lachtanski's "Match the Right Communication Type to the Occasion"? About Amy Tan's "Mother Tongue"? Knowing where these essays were first published will give you even more information about each author's purpose and audience.

Finally, before you begin to read, answer the Preparing to Read questions, and then think freely for a few minutes about the general topic: What do you want to know about birth order from Toler? What are some different types of lies you have told (Ericsson)?

Reading.   As you read each essay for the first time, write down your initial reactions to the topic itself, to the preliminary material, to the mood the writer sets, or to a specific incident in the essay. Make associations between the essay and your own experiences.

In addition, create a context for each essay by drawing on the preliminary material you just read about the essay: What is Tan implying about the relationship between language and culture, and why does she care about this relationship? What is significant about Tan's point of view in "Mother Tongue"? According to Ericsson, why are some lies necessary? Also in this first reading, notice when the writers divided (split up) or classified (gathered together) their material to make their point.

At the bottom of the pages of these essays are several questions that will help you think critically about the topics in this chapter. They prompt you to understand the writers' reasoning and the structure of each essay. Your responses to these questions will give you ideas to use in response to the exercises and writing assignments after each essay, providing a "bridge" from the activities before to the tasks after each essay. Writing out your responses is always the way to get the most benefit from these questions so that you have ideas to work with when you compose your own essays.

Finally, read the questions after each essay, and let them guide your second reading of the selection.

Rereading.   When you read these division/classification essays a second time, notice how the authors carefully match their dominant rhetorical approach (division or classification) to their purpose in a clear thesis. What, for example, is Lachtanski's thesis? Does it set up a clear division/classification essay? How does Gilbert approach division/classification with her subject? How does this approach further her purpose? What other rhetorical strategies support her thesis? Then see how these writers logically present their division or classification systems to their readers, defining new categories as their essays progress. Finally, notice how each writer either implicitly or explicitly explains the significance or value of his or her division/classification system. How does Toler explain her system of organization? And how does Ericsson give her organizing principle significance? Now answer the questions after each essay to check your understanding and to help you analyze your reading in preparation for the discussion/writing topics that follow.

For a more complete survey of reading guidelines, you may want to consult the Reading Checklist at the end of Chapter 2.

Writing Division/Classification Essays

Now that you see how division/classification works in an essay, use the same features in your own writing. The flowchart on the next page provides some questions to guide you.

Preparing To Write.   You should approach a division/classification essay in the same way you have begun all your other writing assignments—with some kind of prewriting activity that will help you generate ideas, such as the Preparing to Write questions featured in this chapter. The prewriting techniques outlined in Chapter 3 on pages 26–28 can help you approach these questions imaginatively. Before you even consider the selection and arrangement of details, you need to explore your subject, choose a topic, and decide on a specific purpose and audience. The best way to explore your subject is to think about it, read about it, and then write about it. Look at it from all possible angles, and see what patterns and relationships emerge. To choose a specific topic, you might begin by listing any groups, patterns, or combinations you discover within your subject matter. Your purpose should take shape as you form your thesis, and your audience is probably dictated by the assignment. Making these decisions before you write will make the rest of your task much easier.

Questions to Guide Your Writing

PREPARING TO WRITE Before you start writing, answer these questions:

- What is your **purpose**?
- Who is your **audience**?
- What is the essay's **context**?
- Will you primarily **divide** or **classify**?

WRITING As you write your first draft, consider these questions:

- Do you include your overall purpose in your **thesis**?
- What **details** support your essay's purpose?
- Do you divide your subject into distinct **categories**?
- Do you arrange the categories into a **logical** sequence?
- Do you **define and/or explain** each category?
- Do you explain the **significance** of your approach?

EDITING Be sure to proofread and edit your paper before turning it in.

- Are your **sentences** all complete?
- Do your words say exactly **what you mean**?
- Do you follow conventional **grammar and usage** rules?

REVISING After you write your first draft, use the following questions to revise your essay:

- Does your thesis **communicate** your purpose clearly?
- Have you divided your topic into separate **categories**?
- Are these categories **arranged** logically?
- Do you explain the **significance** of your classification system?

Writing. As you begin to write, certain guidelines will help you structure your ideas for a division/classification essay:

1. First, declare an overall purpose for your division/classification.
2. Then divide the item or concept you are dealing with into categories.
3. Arrange these categories into a logical sequence.

4. Define each category, explaining the differences among your categories and demonstrating those differences through examples.

5. Explain the significance of your classification system (Why is it worth reading? What will your audience learn from it?).

All discussion in such an essay should reinforce the purpose stated at the beginning of your paper. Other rhetorical modes—such as narration, example, and comparison/contrast—will naturally be used to supplement your classification.

To make your division/classification as workable as possible, take special care that your categories do not overlap and that all topics fall into their proper places. If, for example, you were dividing/classifying all the jobs performed by students in your writing class, the categories of (1) indoor work and (2) outdoor work would probably be inadequate because some jobs fit into both categories. At a pizza parlor, a florist, or a gift shop, for example, a delivery person's time would be split between indoor and outdoor work. So you would need to alter the classification system to avoid this problem. The categories of (1) indoor work, (2) outdoor work, and (3) a combination of indoor and outdoor work would be much more useful for this task. Making sure your categories don't overlap will help make your classification essays more readable and more accurate.

Revising.   As you rewrite your division/classification essays, consider carefully the probable reactions of your readers to the form and content of your paper:

More guidelines for writing and revising are available in the Writing Checklist at the end of Chapter 3.

STUDENT ESSAY: DIVISION/CLASSIFICATION AT WORK

The following student essay divides skiers into interesting categories based on their physical abilities. As you read it, notice how the student writer weaves the significance of his study into his opening statement of purpose. Also, pay particular attention to his logical method of organization and clear explanation of categories as he moves with ease from multiple to single and back to multiple again throughout the essay.

People on the Slopes

Subject   When I first learned to ski, I was amazed by the shapes who whizzed by me and slipped down trails marked only by a black diamond signifying "most difficult," while others careened awkwardly down the "bunny slopes." <u>These skiers, I discovered, could be</u> Thesis <u>divided into distinct categories—for my own enter-</u> statement <u>tainment and for the purpose of finding appropriate</u> Overall <u>skiing partners.</u> purpose

First   First are the "<u>poetic skiers</u>." They glide down the category mountainside silently with what seems like no effort Definition at all. They float from side to side on the intermediate slopes, their knees bent perfectly above parallel skis, while their sharp skills allow them to bypass slower Supporting skiers with safely executed turns at remarkable speeds. details

Second   The "<u>crazy skiers</u>" also get down the mountain category quickly, but with a lot more noise attending their Definition descent. At every hill, they yell a loud "Yahoo!" and slam their skis into the snow. These go-for-broke ath- letes always whiz by faster than everyone else, and they especially seem to love the crowded runs where they Supporting can slide over the backs of other people's skis. I often details (with find crazy skiers in mangled messes at the bottoms of humor) steep hills, where they are yelling loudly, but not the famous "Yahoo!"

        <u>After being overwhelmed by the crazy skiers</u>, I am Transition Third always glad to find other skiers like myself: "<u>the aver-</u> category <u>age ones</u>." We are polite on the slopes, concentrate on improving our technique with every run, and ski the Definition beginner slopes only at the beginning of the day to warm up. We go over the moguls (small hills) much Supporting more cautiously than the crazy or poetic skiers, but we details (com- still seek adventure with a little jump or two each day. parative) We remain a silent majority on the mountain.

Transition   <u>Below us in talent, but much more evident on the</u> <u>mountainside</u>, are what I call the "<u>eternal beginners</u>." Fourth These skiers stick to the same beginner slope almost category Definition every run of every day during their vacation. Should they venture onto an intermediate slope, they quickly assume the snowplow position (a pigeon-toed stance) Supporting and never leave it. Eternal beginners weave from one details side of the run to the other and hardly ever fall, because they proceed so slowly; however, they do yell quite a bit at the crazies who like to run over the backs of their skis.

Transition   <u>Having always enjoyed people-watching, I have fun each time I am on the slopes observing the myriad of skiers around me.</u> <u>I use these observations to pick out</u> Significance <u>possible ski partners for myself and others.</u> Since my of classifi- mother is an eternal beginner, she has more fun skiing cation system with someone who shares her interests than with my dad, who is a poetic skier with solitude on his mind. After taking care of Mom, I am free to find a partner I'll enjoy. My sister, the crazy skier of the family, just heads for the rowdiest group she can find! <u>As the years</u> Concluding <u>go by and my talents grow, I am trusting my percep-</u> remarks <u>tions of skier types to help me find the right partner for life on and off the slopes.</u> <u>No doubt watching my fellow skiers will always remain an enjoyable pastime.</u>

Student Writer's Comments

To begin this paper—the topic of which occurred to me as I flew over snow-capped mountains on a trip—I brainstormed. I jotted down the general groups of skiers I believed existed on the slopes and recorded characteristics of each group as they came to me. The ideas flowed quite freely at this point, and I enjoyed imagining the people I was describing. This prewriting stage brought back some great memories from the slopes that cluttered my thinking at times, but in most cases one useless memory triggered two or three other details or skiing stories that helped me make sense of my division/classification system.

I then felt ready to write a first draft but was having a lot of trouble coming up with a sensible order for my categories. So I just began to write. My categories were now clear to me, even though I wanted to work a little more on their labels. And the definitions of each category came quite naturally as I wrote. In fact, the ease with which they surfaced made me believe that I really had discovered some ultimate truth about types of skiers. I also had tons of details and anecdotes to work with from my brainstorming session. When I finished the body of my first draft (it had no introduction or conclusion yet), I realized that every paragraph worked nicely by itself—four separate category paragraphs. But these paragraphs didn't work together yet at all.

As I reworked the essay, I knew my major job was to reorganize my categories in some logical way and then smooth out the prose with transitions that would make the essay work as a unified whole. To accomplish this,

I wrote more drafts of this single paper than I can remember writing for any other assignment. But I feel that the order and the transitions finally work now. The essay moves logically from type to type, and I think my transitions justify my arrangement along the way. My overall purpose came to me as I was reorganizing my categories, at which point I was able to write my introduction and conclusion. After I had put my purpose into words, the significance of my division/classification system became clear. I saved it, however, for the conclusion.

The most exciting part of this paper was realizing how often I had used these mental groupings in pairing my family and friends with other skiers. I had just never labeled, defined, or organized the categories I had created. Writing this paper helped me verbalize these categories and ended up being a lot of fun (especially when it was finished).

SOME FINAL THOUGHTS ON DIVISION/CLASSIFICATION

The essays collected in this chapter use division and/or classification as their primary organizing principle. All these essays show both techniques at work to varying degrees. As you read these essays, you might also want to be aware of the other rhetorical modes that support these division/classification essays, such as description and definition. Finally, pay special attention to how these authors bring significance to their systems of classification and, as a result, to their essays themselves.

KAREN LACHTANSKI   (1971–   )

Match the Right Communication Type to the Occasion

Karen Lachtanski graduated from San Jose State University and worked in communications at several different companies in the U.S. for 15 years. She has written several articles about communication, including *"How to Bridge the Communications Gender Gap—From Both Sides," "It's All About Nuance. How to Convey and Discern Email Tone,"* and *"Unleash the Full Power of the Email Auto-Reply."* She currently serves as the public relations director of My.com, a company based in Amsterdam that created the independent email app myMail and the email service @my.com, working out of the U.S. headquarters of the company in Mountain View, California. She lives in the San Francisco Bay Area.

Preparing to Read

The following essay, originally published in *Entrepreneur* online, discusses the advantages and disadvantages of six different types of communication in light of the demands of our contemporary workforce. The author claims that matching purpose and audience to method of communication is essential to ensuring good, effective conversation.

Exploring Experience: Prior to reading this essay, consider the general types of communication you participate in daily. What are these types? How "fluent" are you in each type? What type of communication do you prefer for your classes? In your social life? In your work environment? With your family? How do these preferences differ? Why do you think they differ?

LEARNING◑NLINE Search the Internet for a business's website (for example, Apple, Target, Nestle), and identify some of the ways it communicates to you, the consumer, through images and words. Think about the observations you make on the business's website as you read Lachtanski's essay.

Before reading this essay, you may want to consult the flowchart on page 241.

" " T here is a tool for every task and a task for every tool," declares 1
the character Tywin Lannister in the HBO series *Game of Thrones*. While Tywin is referring to swords, the same can be said of communications tools.

Picking the right communication tool requires considering the task at 2
hand, the recipient, a message's urgency, and how important it is to eliminate a possible misunderstanding. ◆

An exchange might begin as an email conversation, transition to a messaging 3
app, and end up as a phone call. Is that a bad thing? Not necessarily. Consider the following communication options and the benefits and pitfalls of each:

Phone Calls

A phone call is great when a businessperson needs to reach someone right 4
away. But it's an interruption and one that often occurs without knowledge of what a recipient is doing. Is that person having dinner, watching a movie, or reading a bedtime story to a child?

Consider where someone is before dialing and whether the message is 5
urgent or the conversation could be scheduled so the other party is prepared to take the call. Since there are other, less intrusive options available, phone calls should be used sparingly.

An exception is calling a business for information.   6

Emails

People's inboxes are overflowing with work and personal email as well as 7
promotional messages from companies, though an inbox can be managed so that important information is easily retrieved. Email seems to be the easiest way to communicate for business: Just about everyone uses it, and it's very reliable.

But people manage their inboxes in different ways, with some individuals 8
checking theirs only a couple of times a day. So if a message needs a more immediate reply, consider instant messaging.

Instant Messages

Instant messages and their cousins, text messages, lend themselves to 9
communiqués when a sender is seeking a more immediate reply than with email. These short often abbreviated messages do not require a lengthy response. Instant messages sent to a phone require the sender knowing the mobile number of the person being reached.

Thinking Critically

◆ What is important with each of these elements in reference to successful communication?

Instant messages and texts tend to be shared between people who know   10
each other and who are comfortable using that method to communicate. Short
messages without the context of a tone of voice can be misunderstood.

Consider the urgency of a communication and level of familiarity with   11
the other person. Is there a high risk that a message would be misunderstood
or misinterpreted? Could an innocent "Where are you?" message be misinterpreted as "Why aren't you here?" when the intention was "We're having
the cake now but will wait until you arrive if you're close."

Many options have evolved for instant messaging, beyond AOL's AIM   12
and Google Hangouts, meaning a person might download several apps to
accommodate friends and business contacts around the world. For mobile
devices and personal use, applications include myChat, WhatsApp, Line and
ICQ while apps such as Kik, WeChat, and KakaoTalk have large communities in specific countries.

Ultimately, instant messages and texts should be used when you can   13
engage in quick, but short, conversations with someone you know.

Postal Mail

Often referred to as snail mail due to the time it takes to transmit in   14
comparison to its digital counterparts, letters sent by a postal service can still
be a valid way to communicate when a more personal touch is desired. At
a time when people often find their physical mailboxes overflowing with
bills, catalogs, and other advertisements, a handwritten envelope still gets
attention.

Whether it's a Christmas card from friends across the country or a per-   15
sonal note of thanks to a business partner, a message sent by post is still a
fairly reliable and inexpensive way to communicate a wish to stay in touch
from afar.

Face-to-face Conversations

In contrast to the digital alternatives described above, face-to-face con-   16
versations can clarify misunderstandings, let people take in body language
and other visual cues, get to know each other better and form a stronger bond. But when co-workers, customers, or suppliers are spread out
geographically, the pace of business dictates a digital means.

Video Exchanges

Use of video conferencing can eliminate lengthy emails threads and let   17
groups of people work on projects simultaneously. Many collaboration
tools include chat and video options so that real-time sharing of ideas can
occur.

For work discussions with co-workers, partners, and other business con-   18
tacts, the video service Skype and Lync, used in large Microsoft Exchange
corporate environments, are popular tools.

This category of communication tools is growing but their use is affected   19
by recipients' access to reliable Internet bandwidth and the costs. Old habits
die hard, and many people begin trying to communicate by email since
scheduling a large group meeting can be a gruesome task.

Ultimately, the tool selected for a communication task should take into   20
consideration the recipient and how often he or she uses this device. Keep
in mind that email and instant messaging lack context. Certain types of news
may be received best in person, phone, or video. And an email invitation
for lunch today may not be viewed until well after dinner.❷

UNDERSTANDING DETAILS

1. What is Lachtanski classifying in this essay? Explain her six categories.
2. Why does the author say, "Email seems to be the easiest way to communicate
   for business" (paragraph 7)?
3. According to Lachtanski, what are some of the limitations of electronic media
   in business?
4. What makes communication effective in business, according to this author?

READING CRITICALLY

5. Which of these types of communication do you use most often for your academic work? Does this answer vary from subject to subject? Offer examples to
   explain your response.
6. Do you agree with Lachtanski when she says, "A message sent by post is still
   a fairly reliable and inexpensive way to communicate a wish to stay in touch
   from afar" (paragraph 15)?
7. Which of the categories of communication listed in this essay do you suppose
   will be least effective in business in ten years? Explain your choice.
8. What other types of communication might we find in business in the future?

DISCOVERING RHETORICAL STRATEGIES

9. How does Lachtanski give significance or value to her system of classification?
10. Lachtanski begins her essay with a quote from *Game of Thrones*. Is this an effec-
    tive beginning or not? Explain your answer.
11. Why do you think the author discusses these categories in this particular order?
12. What other rhetorical techniques does Lachtanski use to accomplish her
    purpose?

Thinking Critically

❷ Where do you think business communication will go in the next five years? How will
your predictions help business?

MAKING CONNECTIONS

13. Compare and contrast Lachtanski's approach to business with that expressed by Russell Baker ("The Saturday Evening Post") and Carole Kanchier ("Dare to Change Your Job and Your Life in 7 Steps"). Whose approach to business would be most like yours? Why?

14. How do Karen Lachtanski, Sarah Toler ("Understanding the Birth Order Relationship"), and/or Amy Tan ("Mother Tongue") use division and classification to help explain their topics? Which author's method is easiest to follow? Why?

15. Imagine that Lachtanski is having a round-table discussion with the following authors about communication in general: Richard Rodriguez ("Public and Private Language"), Roni Jacobson ("A Digital Safety Net"), Stephanie Vozza ("How to Make New Friends as an Adult"), and/or Stephanie Ericsson ("The Ways We Lie"). Which of these authors that you have read value communication the most? Why do you think this is so?

IDEAS FOR DISCUSSION/WRITING

Preparing to Write

Write freely about various forms of communication you use on a daily basis. How have your methods of communication changed since you were a child? From your frame of reference, what type of communication is most effective in different situations? What specific experiences bring you to this conclusion? How important is communication in your life?

Choosing a Topic

MyWritingLab™

1. **LEARNING⏻NLINE** Think about the business website that you examined in Preparing to Read. Now imagine that you run a successful business and you want to communicate as effectively as possible with your employees and consumers. Design a homepage for your business, using other business websites for inspiration. Explain the details of your homepage in an essay.

2. Your English instructor has asked about your heritage. Respond to this question by classifying for him or her all the different ethnicities in your background. You might start this project by doing an Internet search of your family history. You can go back as far as you want. Then classify the results that you find, and discuss the characteristics of each classification. Decide on a point of view before you begin to write.

3. Your college newspaper is doing a series of articles on students who have come to your college from different countries. Interview a student whose culture interests you, and explain the primary rituals the student pursues by classifying them in an essay for other students to read.

4. If the daily activities we perform say something important about us, analyze yourself by writing an essay that classifies these different activities you carry out in a typical week. Discuss your choices as you proceed.

Before beginning your essay, you may want to consult the flowchart on page 244.

SARA GILBERT   (1975–   )

The Different Ways of Being Smart

The author of over 30 nonfiction books intended to guide, help, and support audiences of all ages, Sara Dulaney Gilbert received a master's degree from the Graduate School of Education at New York University. She writes extensively on topics for both teens and adults, such as life management, careers, education, wellness, raising children, and recovery issues. Her books include *Teens' Guide to Living with Alcoholism and Addiction* (2009), *How to be a Successful Online Student* (2000), *Complete Idiots' Guide to Single Parenting* (1998), *How to Do Your Best on Tests* (1998), and *You Can Speak Up in Class* (1991). Currently, Gilbert resides in Cold Spring, New York, where she works for Wellsprings LLC.

Preparing to Read

First published in *Using Your Head: The Many Ways of Being Smart*, this essay catalogs the various types of intelligence we have and offers real-world applications for each type.

Exploring Experience: As you prepare to read this article, take a few moments to think about how you categorize people and their actions: Do you ever judge people? On what do you base your judgments? Do you divide or classify them in any ways? Do these subdivisions help you understand any aspects of daily life? Or do they hinder your understanding in any way?

LEARNINGⓊNLINE In the Google search bar, search "Multiple Intelligences Assessment," and select the search result "Multiple Intelligences—Assessment-Literacynet.org." Take the Multiple Intelligences test to find your top three intelligences. What do you think of the classifications of intelligences that the test identifies? Do you agree with your results?

Before reading this essay, you may want to consult the flowchart on page 241.

Book smarts, art smarts, body smarts, street smarts, and people smarts: 1
These labels describe the various forms of intelligence and their use.
As you might imagine, psychologists and other researchers into the
nature of intelligence have come up with more formal terms for the types
that they have isolated. One set of labels in common use is convergent,
divergent, assimilating, and accommodating. The converger and assimilator
are like our book-smart person; the diverger, like our art-smart; and the
accommodator, like our street-smart and people-smart.

Whatever categorization we use, we will find some overlap within any 2
individual. In fact, there are probably as many answers to the question
"What are the different ways of being smart?" as there are people in the
universe, because each of us is unique. We can't be typecast; we each have
a wide spectrum of special talents.

Still, you probably know well at least one person whose talents generally 3
fall into each of our categories. Keep those people in mind as you read
through the detailed descriptions of them.

At first, it might seem that each of those types must call on very different 4
sorts of abilities to be smart in his or her own ways. But in fact, each of the
categories of intelligence on our list must use the same ingredients: learning
ability, memory, speed, judgment, problem-solving skill, good use of language and other symbols, and creativity. Also, the thought processes that go
on inside the heads of people with those varying kinds of smarts include the
same steps: planning, perceiving, imaging, remembering, feeling, and
acting.

Intelligence expresses itself in different forms, in part because of the dif- 5
fering physical qualities born and built into each person's body and brain,
and in part because of the values and motivations that each person has
learned.

However, the fact that each kind of smarts makes use of the same steps 6
means that anyone can learn or develop skills in any or all of the categories.
Let's take a closer look at the many ways of being smart.

A *book-smart* person is one who tends to do well in school, to score high 7
on tests, including intelligence tests. He or she is likely to be well organized,
to go about solving problems in a logical, step-by-step fashion, and to have
a highly developed language ability. Another label for a book-smart person
is "intellectual," meaning someone who uses the mind more to know than
to feel or to control, and a book-smart person is especially proud of having
knowledge. That knowledge may range from literature through science to
math, but it is probable that it is concentrated in one area. Research shows
that different knowledge areas occupy different clusters in the brain, so that
someone whose connections for complicated calculations are highly

developed may have less development in the areas controlling speech and writing.

Although, as we've said, current brain research indicates that learning   8
centers may be scattered throughout both hemispheres of the brain, the activities of the "logical" left side are probably most important in the lives of book-smart people. Book-smart people may also be quite creative: Many mathematical or scientific problems could not be solved, for instance, without creative insights, but the primary focus of a book-smart person is the increase of knowledge.[1]

Art-smart people, on the other hand, rely primarily on creativity. They   9
create music, paintings, sculpture, plays, photographs, or other forms of art often without being able to explain why or how they chose a particular form or design. They are said to be "right-brained" people, because it appears that the control centers for such skills as touch perception and intuition—the formation of ideas without the use of words—lie in the right hemisphere. Artistic people tend to take in knowledge more often by seeing, hearing, and feeling than by conscientious reading and memorizing.

An art-smart person may not do too well in school, not because he or   10
she is not bright, but because of an approach to problem solving that does not fit in well with the formats usually used by teachers and tests. A book-smart person might approach a problem on a math test logically, working step-by-step toward the right answer, while an art-smart person may simply "know" the answer without being able to demonstrate the calculations involved. On a social studies exam, the book-smart person will carefully recount all the facts while the more artistic one may weave stories and fantasies using the facts only as a base. In both cases, it's a good bet that the book-smart student will get the higher grade.[2]

People who are serious about becoming artists, of course, may need to   11
absorb a great deal of "book knowledge" in order to develop a solid background for their skills. There are other overlaps, as well: People with great musical ability, for instance, also tend to be skilled at mathematics, perhaps because of brain-cell interactions that are common to both processes. And in order to make use of any talent, art-smart people must have good body control as well.

The people we're calling *body-smart* have a lot of that kind of body con-   12
trol. Most of them start out with bodies that are well put together for some

---

Thinking Critically

[1] Do you know anyone who falls mostly into this category?

[2] Do you know any predominantly art-smart people? How are their personalities different from those who are mainly book-smart?

kind of athletics—they may have inherited good muscular development for a sport like football, or loose and limber joints for gymnastic-style athletics. Or they may be people whose hands are naturally well coordinated for performing intricate tasks.

But although the physical basis for their talent may come from their genes   13
and from especially sensitive brain centers for motor control, to make use of their "natural" skills they must bring higher levels of brain function into action. They must be able to observe accurately—to figure out how a move is made or an object is constructed—and they must think about how to do it themselves. This thinking involves a complex use of symbols that enables the brain to "tell" another part of itself what to do. In other situations, such as school, a body-smart person is probably best able to learn through some physical technique: In studying for an exam, for instance, he or she will retain information by saying it out loud, acting out the facts, or counting them off with finger taps. Although athletes or the manually talented are often teased as being "dumb" in schoolwork, that is not necessarily an accurate picture. To be good in using physical talents, a person must put in a lot of practice, be able to concentrate intently, and be stubbornly persistent in achieving a goal. And those qualities of will and self-control can also be put to good use in more "intellectual" achievements. [3]

Persistence is also an important quality of *street-smart* people. They are   14
the ones who are able to see difficulties as challenges, to turn almost any situation to advantage for themselves. As young people, they are the ones who are able to make the most money doing odd jobs, or who can get free tickets to a concert that others believe is completely sold out. As adults, they are the business tycoons, for instance, or the personalities who shoot to stardom no matter how much or little talent they have. A street-smart student may do well in the school subjects that he or she knows count for the most and will all but ignore the rest. When taking exams, street-smart people are likely to get better grades than their knowledge merits because they can "psych out" the test and because, when facing a problem or question they can't answer, they are skilled at putting on the paper something that looks good.

To be street-smart in these ways—to be able to achieve highly individu-   15
alistic goals and to be able to get around obstacles that totally stump others—a person must draw on a wide scope of mental powers. It takes excellent problem-solving ability, creative thought, good planning and goal setting,

---

Thinking Critically

[3] Do the athletes you know fit this description of body-smart? What is unique about their personalities?

accurate perception, persistent effort, skill with language, quick thinking, and a strong sense of intuition.[4]

Intuition plays a major role in *people smarts* as well. This kind of intelli-   16
gence allows a person to sense what others are thinking, feeling, wanting, and planning. Although we might tend to put this sort of skill down as basic "instinct," it actually relies on higher activities of the brain. People smarts rely on very accurate and quick perceptions of clues and relationships that escape the notice of many, and they include the ability to analyze the information taken in. A people-smart student can do well in school simply by dealing with individual teachers in the most productive way: Some can be charmed, some respond well to special requests for help, some reward hard work no matter what the results, and so forth. The people-smart student figures out easily what is the best approach to take. People with these talents also achieve well in other activities, of course—they become the leaders in clubs and organizations, and they are able to win important individuals, like potential employers, over to their side. They would probably be typed as right-brained people, like artists, but their skill with language, both spoken and unspoken, is one that draws heavily on the left side.[5]

Have you been able to compare these types with people you know in   17
your class, family, or neighborhood? Of course, no individual is actually a type: People with any one of the kinds of smarts that we've described also have some of the others. Skill in using one part of the brain does not mean that the other parts stay lazy.

Rather, some people are able to develop one set of brain-powered skills   18
to a higher degree than others who are able to strengthen other talents.

One person's choice of which skills to develop results from the rewards   19
that he or she receives from the family and the larger environment.

UNDERSTANDING DETAILS

1. Explain Gilbert's five categories of "smarts" in your own words.
2. What does the author mean in paragraph 2 when she says, "We can't be typecast"?
3. What are the "ingredients" (paragraph 4) the author uses to place each person in a dominant category?
4. According to Gilbert, why does intelligence express itself in different forms?

Thinking Critically

[4] Who among your family and friends comes to mind as street-smart? How are their personalities different from those who fall more completely in the other three categories?

[5] Can you think of anyone you know who is especially people-smart? How is he or she different in personality from your friends and family in the other categories?

READING CRITICALLY

5. Using the author's descriptions, with which intelligence do you identify most strongly?

6. What does Gilbert mean in paragraph 10 by "overlaps"? Explain some of the overlaps in your own development.

7. In what ways can an athlete's talents help him or her in academic work?

8. If the choices we make in developing particular skills are the result of rewards, what stimuli were most significant in developing your intelligences?

DISCOVERING RHETORICAL STRATEGIES

9. What is the general purpose of this selection?

10. What other rhetorical modes besides support Gilbert's division/classification essay?

11. How does Gilbert organize the categories in her essay? Is this an effective order? Explain your answer.

12. In the beginning of this essay, Gilbert invites the readers to think of people who might fit into each category and then at the end asks if the reader has "been able to compare these types with people you know in your class, family, or neighborhood" (paragraph 17). What effect do these two direct references to the reader have on you?

MAKING CONNECTIONS

13. If Sara Gilbert, Adam Gopnik ("How Lincoln and Darwin Shaped the Modern World"), Art Markman ("Can Video Games Make You Smart (Or at Least More Flexible)?"), and/or Nicholas Carr ("How the Internet Is Making Us Stupid") were having a conversation about how we develop and foster intelligence, which topics would the authors you have read agree on? How would each say intelligence is determined?

14. Whose method of dividing and classifying his/her subject seems most clearly organized to you: Sara Gilbert, Karen Lachtanski ("Match the Right Communication Type to the Occasion"), or Stephanie Ericsson ("The Ways We Lie")? What are the reasons for your choice?

15. Do you think Nicholas Carr ("How the Internet Is Making Us Stupid") would vary his comments about the Internet in reference to the different types of intelligence that Gilbert outlines? Which type of intelligence do you think would be most negatively affected by the Internet? Which type of intelligence would respond to the Internet most positively?

IDEAS FOR DISCUSSION/WRITING

Preparing to Write

Write freely about the ways you classify people and/or their actions: Do you think of people or actions in clear categories? If so, what characterizes each of these groups? How do these categories overlap? Have your general categories changed over the years? In what ways does your classification system assist you in your daily life? What are the advantages and disadvantages of dividing and classifying people or actions as you do?

Choosing a Topic

1. **LEARNING⏻NLINE** Gilbert and the multiple intelligence test both highlight the fact that different people have different intelligences. Although the names of their categories are different, many of them overlap. Using both classification systems for inspiration, choose either a friend or family member, and describe the differences between the ways you are smart and the ways he or she is smart.

2. Use division/classification to explain the types of people you deal with in your life. Divide the people you face into categories, and then discuss those categories in an essay written for your English class. Make sure you decide on a purpose and a point of view before you begin to write.

3. What criteria do you use in making decisions? Use division/classification to explain how you approach a decision and make up your mind. Decide on a purpose and point of view before you begin to write.

4. Write an essay for your classmates in which you convince them to try a specific activity. This might be anything from riding a roller coaster to filling out a job application. Be creative in your approach to this topic.

Before beginning your essay, you may want to consult the flowchart on page 244.

SARAH TOLER   (1982–   )

Understanding the Birth Order Relationship

Born and raised in Texarkana, Texas, Sarah Toler earned her B.A. in Writing and Cultural Studies at the University of Technology in Sydney, Australia, where she became interested in the emerging field of digital anthropology. Previously a copywriter at JC Penney, a senior editor at Red Bandana Publishing, and an editor at McGraw-Hill, she is currently Creative Director at Pocketstop, a small marketing and advertising agency in Dallas, Texas, where she specializes in digital advertising through television, radio, mobile phones, social media, and the Internet for such prominent clients as Marriott, Nikon, TGI Friday's, Sony Ericsson, Sunkist Soda, and others. She is also the founder of an advertising organization called SheSays, which offers support and education for her female colleagues in the profession. Currently, Toler is a freelance writer focusing on healthcare and community health. She also spends time volunteering at Promise House, an agency in Dallas County that serves the needs of unaccompanied homeless, runaway, and at-risk youth. Toler used to compete in roller derbies but has since given up that dangerous pastime for the more sedate pleasures of traveling across the globe. Her advice to students using *The Prose Reader* is to "read a lot so you can learn by osmosis." She claims that she "was born a writer the way that people are born with blue eyes or brown hair; I have an insatiable desire to study people." She also suggests joining a network of other writers who will critique your work. The author lives in a suburb of Dallas with her two dogs, whom she pampers shamelessly.

Preparing to Read

This essay was originally published in *Lifescript Magazine* on October 18, 2007. In it, Toler argues that birth order has played an important role in our lives since the day we are born.

Exploring Experience: As you prepare to read this article, take a few minutes to think about the personality differences between you and someone you know: Do you classify people automatically when you meet them? What types of people do you get along with best? Why do you think this is the case? What types of people annoy you the most? How do you explain your reaction to them? What traits in your personality are received most positively? Which of your traits are you trying to improve? Why are you attempting to make these changes?

LEARNING⏻NLINE Birth order can have a significant effect not only on your family dynamics, but also on friendships, professional and educational endeavors, and romantic relationships. Go to www.parents.com, and search "Sibling Rivalry." Scroll down, and click on the "Quiz," and select "Quiz: What's Your Birth Order Personality?" After you take this quiz, read the analysis of your personality. Is it accurate? Compare your results with those of others in the class.

Before reading this essay, you may want to consult the flowchart on page 241.

A t some point in your life, you have probably gone through a period 1
of self-discovery in which you took time to survey your strengths
and weaknesses.[1] But did you ever stop to think that those qualities
could be attributed to your birth order in your family? Have you heard time
and time again that you are bossy? If so, it is likely that you are an only child.
Are you a people pleaser? Then you would find it no surprise to know that
most middle children wedged in between an older and younger sibling strive
to keep the peace. Not convinced birth order and personality are connected?
Use this birth order article to find out how many of these characteristics
apply to you.

Unraveling the Meaning of Birth Order

Your birth order has played an important role in your life since the day 2
you were born. More than defining how you relate to your family, your
birth sequence has developed characteristics in your personality which have
affected your romantic relationships, friendships, and even your career. More
important than your actual birth order is the role you played in your family
structure. If you were the youngest child, but your older siblings were off to
college before you reached kindergarten, you probably identify more with
an only child and may exhibit qualities of both birth orders. An oldest child
whose parents showed favoritism toward his younger sister may have felt
neglected and display characteristics of a middle child.

The Only Child

As a kid, the only child often has a bad reputation, but it is one she has 3
likely earned. Known for being spoiled, only-borns receive the full attention
of parents and come to expect that attention as the norm from adults.

Coddled and overprotected, she enjoys being the center of attention, 4
whether in her school play or at the dinner table. Sharing a toy with a classmate or a parent's attention with an adult can seem devastating to her in
childhood.

In adulthood, she flourishes in her career and often becomes the kind 5
of innovative leader who makes changes in major processes. Dependable,
detail-oriented, focused, and organized, she will succeed at her ambitions
and surpass expectations.

Thinking Critically

[1] Write down your three most prominent strengths and your three most glaring weaknesses. After you have finished reading this essay, return to your lists, and see how many
of the traits you mentioned might have been a result of birth order.

The only child can be problematic in romantic relationships. Always right   6
and last to say "I'm sorry," her sensitivity combined with constant demanding can make her seem impossible to her frustrated partner.

Big dreams and timely plans make an only child an excellent friend. She   7
may have sibling-like bonds with her friends and can be financially generous
with those she values. However, do not expect her to be generous with her
personal belongings.

The First-Born Child

The oldest child is often the captain of the kickball team on the play-   8
ground or the math genius who requests extra credit assignments.[2] He has
a close group of friends who respect him and look to him for leadership,
whether the task is building a new fort or avoiding the class bully. His parents
focus more of their energies on his younger siblings, so he is independent
but may be a little misguided.

Always an over-achiever, he succeeds at a career in politics or manage-   9
ment. No matter what his career pursuits, he focuses on his specialty with
great detail. He may have a superiority complex that leaves colleagues unim-
pressed, but he will win their respect with his abilities. Failure becomes a
risk only because he does not trust anyone to do a job as well as he would,
so he takes on more than one person can handle.

His perfectionism overflows into his love life as well; he wants to provide   10
and care for his romantic relationship and partner. Friends envy his "perfect"
relationships, and he intends to keep it that way. He knows what he wants
in a mate and will be picky about every detail until he finds "Miss Right."

Controlling tendencies make his friendships rocky, but once he holds on   11
to a friend long enough to respect his shortcomings, he is a complete ally.
He loves to make everyone happy and nurtures his friendships by putting
in extra effort. He can be a worrier, but he is also one to stay in touch with
old buddies.

The Middle Child

Rolling with the punches is the key to survival for the sibling stuck in   12
the middle. Whether she is the second-, third-, or fourth-born, having both
an older and younger sibling means she gets less attention from parents and
even other adults. Because of this, she has a rational outlook and gets along
well in groups, even if people in the groups are very different from her.

Thinking Critically

[2] What factors, in addition to birth order, might account for personality traits in children?

She loves parties and social gatherings but thrives when given one-on-one time with parents or friends.

A slight sense of competition is instilled in her, but she is not an over-achiever at school or sports. She likes to stay in the middle because average performance keeps her under the radar.   13

A strong need to be liked by everyone around her makes her career pur-suits well-intentioned but rarely successful. The middle child does not enjoy making decisions and, as a result, may find the most suiting profession is one of service like social work or foster parenting.   14

Always a pleaser, she can easily get caught in a co-dependent relationship that spells disaster. Her nurturing nature should not be discouraged, though. The middle child will flourish in a romantic relationship with another co-dependent so that the two can depend on each other. She also makes an attentive, supportive parent or role model.   15

She will go to any length to show her friends she values them, and because of this, she will pick up some ill-intentioned friends along the way. People will take advantage of her, but only as long as she allows. Her skills of adaptation are incredible, so she will flourish no matter what the social situation. [3]   16

The Youngest Child

The youngest child is a born entertainer and very often the class clown. He loves attention, laughter, and playfulness and does not take much of anything seriously. Hobbies come and go in the childhood of "the baby" because he is having so much fun he cannot focus his energy on just one thing. He is the class favorite, and his birthday parties are the event of the year.   17

The baby rarely grows up. He picks up where he left off as a child and quickly becomes the office clown as an adult. Colleagues know him as the prankster, but he also appeals to them as a confidant. Not one to take criti-cism, he will bail out of a professional situation if he feels rejection approaching. He might have a few different careers in his lifetime because he gets bored easily. The youngest child can have great success if he finds a passion and sticks with it because he is an innovator who challenges the system.   18

Boredom leads to frustration in committed romantic relationships, and his need for fun can cause the baby some trouble. Self-centered and   19

Thinking Critically

[3] How many different roles did you play in your family when you were growing up? How did each of these roles help form your personality?

oblivious, maintaining communication in an adult relationship will take him some time and effort to master.

Friendships are rich and numerous for the youngest child. He is the social 20 butterfly of all the siblings and probably all of his friends. His inability to mature can become an issue if his friends outgrow his fun-loving nature.

What Does the Birth Order Relationship Mean to You?

If your quest is to further develop your career, love life, and friendships, 21 utilize this birth order article and continue to investigate the birth order relationship to identify your strengths and weaknesses.

Did you find a list of qualities with which you identify? It is likely you 22 can identify with some characteristics of each birth order, but one set is more dominant. If your dominant set does not match your actual birth order within your family, it is likely you had to fill many roles in your family and your personality is reflective of that. Look carefully. Each set of birth order traits has both negative and positive aspects that you can mold to better yourself.

UNDERSTANDING DETAILS

1. What are the four birth orders Toler analyzes? List the main qualities of each category.
2. According to Toler, what role does birth order play in our development?
3. What does Toler mean when she says, "Each set of birth order traits has both negative and positive aspects that you can mold to better yourself" (paragraph 22)?
4. How does birth order affect our roles in our families?

READING CRITICALLY

5. Which qualities described in this essay apply to you? Into which category do your dominant traits fall?
6. Which qualities that Toler describes contradict your preconceived ideas about birth order? Which confirm your preconceived notions? Explain your answer.
7. Are you convinced that birth order affects the formation of our personalities? Explain your answer.
8. According to Toler, what else can affect the way we behave?

DISCOVERING RHETORICAL STRATEGIES

9. Do you think the direct address to the reader in the first paragraph is effective? Explain your answer.
10. What is the general purpose of this essay?
11. What is the author's attitude toward birth order?
12. What other rhetorical modes, besides division/classification, does Toler use in this essay?

MAKING CONNECTIONS

13. Compare and contrast the way Toler divides her topic with the approach of Karen Lachtanski ("Match the Right Communication Type to the Occasion"), Amy Tan ("Mother Tongue"), and/or Stephanie Ericsson ("The Ways We Lie"). Which author's organizational system is most effective in achieving the essay's purpose? Explain your answer.

14. Imagine that Toler, Russell Baker ("The Saturday Evening Post"), Brent Staples ("A Brother's Murder"), and/or Mary Pipher ("Beliefs about Families") are having a conversation about how children develop their basic personalities. Which authors would argue most strongly that our personalities are already encoded in our DNA at birth? Which would stress the impact of the family environment in which we are raised? Where do you stand on this issue?

15. To what extent would Toler, Sandra Cisneros ("Only Daughter"), and/or Amy Chua ("Excerpt from *Battle Hymn of the Tiger Mother*") agree that parents should treat children differently based on each child's birth order?

IDEAS FOR DISCUSSION/WRITING

Preparing to Write

Write freely about the different personality types you deal with on a daily basis: Can you classify each type of person? What do these types of people have in common? Do you treat these various types in different ways? Do they make different demands on you? How do they behave as friends? As colleagues? As romantic partners? What problems does each group have?

Choosing a Topic   MyWritingLab™

1. **LEARNING⏻NLINE** Using the birth order quiz from www.parents.com as an interview tool and Toler's article for research, write an essay classifying the members of your family in reference to birth order. Do they fit Toler's classification system? Do any members of your family not fit into Toler's categories? How do you explain these discrepancies?

2. Assume that you are an expert on the variety and scope of college relationships. In an essay written for your classmates, divide and classify into categories your observations on relationships that will show students the full range of these associations in a college setting.

3. In an essay written for the general public, speculate about the reasons for the serious problem our nation has with bullying. Do you think bullying has anything to do with birth order? Use your own experience, interview others, or consult other reliable sources to investigate the reasons for this societal problem. Suggest how we could solve it in the United States.

4. Because you have been involved with many different forms of social networking, you have been asked to submit to your college newspaper an editorial classifying the various ways in which different types of people develop electronic friendships, paying particular attention to the reactions of college freshmen who are new to college.

Before beginning your essay, you may want to consult the flowchart on page 244.

AMY TAN (1952–   )

Mother Tongue

In a very short time, Amy Tan has established herself as one of the foremost Chinese-American writers. Her first novel, *The Joy Luck Club* (1989), which was praised as "brilliant . . . a jewel of a book" by the *New York Times* Book Review, focuses on the lives of four Chinese women in pre-1949 China and their American-born daughters in modern-day California. Through a series of vignettes, Tan weaves together the dreams and sorrows of these mothers and daughters as they confront oppression in China and equally difficult cultural challenges in the new world of the United States. Like the protagonists in *The Joy Luck Club,* Tan's parents, a Baptist minister and a licensed vocational nurse, emigrated to America shortly before Tan's birth. She showed an early talent for writing when, at age eight, she won an essay contest (and a transistor radio) with a paper entitled "Why I Love the Library." Following the tremendous success of her first novel, Tan apparently had great difficulty writing her second book, *The Kitchen God's Wife* (1991). As she was working on it, she began grinding her teeth, which resulted in two broken molars and a sizable dental bill. "I am glad that I shall never again have to write a second book," the author has confessed. "Actually, I cannot recall any writer—with or without a splashy debut—who said the second book came easily." Successful film and stage adaptations of *The Joy Luck Club* in 1993 were followed by *The Chinese Siamese Cat* (1994), *The Hundred Secret Senses* (1995), *The Year of No Flood* (1996), *The Bonesetter's Daughter* (2001), *The Opposite of Fate: A Book of Musings* (2003), *Saving Fish from Drowning* (2005), *Rules for Virgins* (2011), and *The Valley of Amazement* (2012).

Preparing to Read

In the following essay, originally published in *The Threepenny Review,* Amy Tan classifies the different "Englishes" she learned to use in her youth. These had a significant effect on her as she grew up to be a successful writer.

Exploring Experience: As you prepare to read this essay, take a few minutes to think about the different types of English that you use: How do you change your use of English when you relay the same message to different people? Why do you make these changes? Do you feel as if you do well in English class? On English tests? How could you become an even better writer and speaker of English than you already are?

LEARNING◯NLINE To better understand Tan's cultural context, go to www.youtube.com, and search "Becoming American: The Chinese Experience," starting with the video "Becoming American No Turning Back Part I" (Jackie Sutton). Follow this video with Becoming American Part II through Part IX. As you watch these videos, come up with at least four adjectives that describe the Chinese-American experience captured in these stories.

Before reading this essay, you may want to consult the flowchart on page 241.

I am not a scholar of English or literature. I cannot give you much more   1
than personal opinions on the English language and its variations in this
country or others.

I am a writer. And by that definition, I am someone who has always loved   2
language. I am fascinated by language in daily life. I spend a great deal of my
time thinking about the power of language—the way it can evoke an emotion, a visual image, a complex idea, or a simple truth. Language is the tool
of my trade. And I use them all—all the Englishes I grew up with.[1]

Recently, I was made keenly aware of the different Englishes I do use. I   3
was giving a talk to a large group of people, the same talk I had already given
to half a dozen other groups. The nature of the talk was about my writing,
my life, and my book, *The Joy Luck Club*. The talk was going along well
enough, until I remembered one major difference that made the whole talk
sound wrong. My mother was in the room. And it was perhaps the first time
she had heard me give a lengthy speech, using the kind of English I have
never used with her. I was saying things like, "The intersection of memory
upon imagination" and "There is an aspect of my fiction that relates to thus-
and-thus"—a speech filled with carefully wrought grammatical phrases,
burdened, it suddenly seemed to me, with nominalized forms, past perfect
tenses, conditional phrases, all the forms of standard English that I had
learned in school and through books, the forms of English I did not use at
home with my mother.

Just last week, I was walking down the street with my mother, and I again   4
found myself conscious of the English I was using, the English I do use with
her. We were talking about the price of new and used furniture and I heard
myself saying this: "Not waste money that way." My husband was with us as
well, and he didn't notice any switch in my English. And then I realized
why. It's because over the twenty years we've been together I've often used
the same kind of English with him, and sometimes he even uses it with me.
It has become our language of intimacy,[2] a different sort of English that
relates to family talk, the language I grew up with.

So you'll have some idea of what this family talk I heard sounds like, I'll   5
quote what my mother said during a recent conversation which I videotaped
and then transcribed. During this conversation, my mother was talking
about a political gangster in Shanghai who had the same last name as her
family's, Du, and how the gangster in his early years wanted to be adopted

---

Thinking Critically

1. Why does Tan use the word "Englishes"? What is she referring to?
2. What does the author mean by the phrase "our language of intimacy"? How many
different forms of your primary language do you use in your life?

by her family, which was rich by comparison. Later, the gangster became more powerful, far richer than my mother's family, and one day showed up at my mother's wedding to pay his respects. Here's what she said in part:

"Du Yusong having business like fruit stand. Like of the street kind. He [6] is Du like Du Zong—but not Tsung-ming Island people. The local people call *putong,* the river east side, he belong to that side local people. That man want to ask Du Zong father take him in like become own family. Du Zong father wasn't look down on him, but didn't take seriously, until that man big like become a mafia. Now important person, very hard to inviting him. Chinese way, came only to show respect, don't stay for dinner. Respect for making big celebration, he shows up. Mean gives lots of respect. Chinese custom. Chinese social life that way. If too important won't have to stay too long. He come to my wedding. I didn't see, I heard it. I gone to boy's side, they have YMCA dinner, Chinese age I was nineteen." [3]

You should know that my mother's expressive command of English belies [7] how much she actually understands. She reads the *Forbes* report, listens to *Wall Street Week,* converses daily with her stockbroker, reads all of Shirley MacLaine's books with ease—all kinds of things I can't begin to understand. Yet some of my friends tell me they understand 50 percent of what my mother says. Some say they understand 80 to 90 percent. Some say they understand none of it, as if she were speaking pure Chinese. But to me, my mother's English is perfectly clear, perfectly natural. It's my mother tongue. Her language, as I hear it, is vivid, direct full of observation and imagery. That was the language that helped shape the way I saw things, expressed things, made sense of the world.

Lately, I've been giving more thought to the kind of English my mother [8] speaks. Like others, I have described it to people as "broken" or "fractured" English. But I wince when I say that. It has always bothered me that I can think of no way to describe it other than "broken," as if it were damaged and needed to be fixed, as if it lacked a certain wholeness and soundness. I've heard other terms used, "limited English," for example. But they seem just as bad, as if everything is limited, including people's perceptions of the limited English speaker.

I know this for a fact, because when I was growing up, my mother's [9] "limited" English limited *my* perception of her. [4] I was ashamed of her English. I believed that her English reflected the quality of what she had to

---

Thinking Critically

[3] What is the author's main point here? Why did the gangster come to Tan's mother's wedding?

[4] How true is this in your life? To what extent do you judge others by their use of English?

say. That is, because she expressed them imperfectly, her thoughts were imperfect. And I had plenty of empirical evidence to support me: the fact that people in department stores, at banks, and at restaurants did not take her seriously, did not give her good advice, pretended not to understand her, or even acted as if they did not hear her.

My mother has long realized the limitations of her English as well. When   10
I was fifteen, she used to have me call people on the phone and pretend I was she. In this guise, I was forced to ask for information or even to complain and yell at people who had been rude to her. One time it was a call to her stockbroker in New York. She had cashed out her small portfolio, and it just so happened we were going to go to New York the next week, our very first trip outside California. I had to get on the phone and say in an adolescent voice that was not very convincing, "This is Mrs. Tan."

And my mother was standing in the back whispering loudly, "Why he   11
don't send me check, already two weeks late. So mad he lie to me, losing my money."

And then I said in perfect English, "Yes, I'm getting rather concerned.   12
You had agreed to send the check two weeks ago, but it hasn't arrived."

Then she began to talk more loudly. "What he want, I come to New   13
York tell him front of his boss, you cheating me?" And I was trying to calm her down, make her be quiet, while telling the stockbroker, "I can't tolerate any more excuses. If I don't receive the check immediately, I am going to have to speak to your manager when I'm in New York next week." And sure enough, the following week there we were in front of this astonished stockbroker, and I was sitting there red-faced and quiet, and my mother, the real Mrs. Tan, was shouting at his boss in her impeccable broken English. [5]

We used a similar routine just five days ago, for a situation that was far   14
less humorous. My mother had gone to the hospital for an appointment, to find out about a benign brain tumor a CAT scan had revealed a month ago. She said she had spoken very good English, her best English, no mistakes. Still, she said, the hospital did not apologize when they said they had lost the CAT scan and she had come for nothing. She said they did not seem to have any sympathy when she told them she was anxious to know the exact diagnosis, since her husband and son had both died of brain tumors. She said they would not give her any more information until the next time and she would have to make another appointment for that. So she said she would

---

Thinking Critically

[5] Why does Tan use the oxymoron "impeccable broken English" here? What does the phrase mean?

not leave until the doctor called her daughter. She wouldn't budge. And when the doctor finally called her daughter, me, who spoke in perfect English—lo and behold—we had assurances the CAT scan would be found, promises that a conference call on Monday would be held, and apologies for any suffering my mother had gone through for a most regrettable mistake.

I think my mother's English almost had an effect on limiting my possibili- 15 ties in life as well. Sociologists and linguists probably will tell you that a person's developing language skills are more influenced by peers. But I do think that the language spoken in the family, especially in immigrant families which are more insular, plays a large role in shaping the language of the child. [6] And I believe that it affected my results on achievement tests, IQ tests, and the SAT. While my English skills were never judged as poor, compared to math, English could not be considered my strong suit. In grade school I did moderately well, getting perhaps B's, sometimes B-pluses, in English and scoring perhaps in the sixtieth or seventieth percentile on achievement tests. But those scores were not good enough to override the opinion that my true abilities lay in math and science, because in those areas I achieved A's and scored in the ninetieth percentile or higher.

This was understandable. Math is precise; there is only one correct 16 answer. [7] Whereas, for me at least, the answers on English tests were always a judgment call, a matter of opinion and personal experience. Those tests were constructed around items like fill-in-the-blank sentence completion, such as "Even though Tom was _____, Mary thought he was _____." And the correct answer always seemed to be the most bland combinations of thoughts, for example, "Even though Tom was shy, Mary thought he was charming," with the grammatical structure "even though" limiting the correct answer to some sort of semantic opposites, so you wouldn't get answers like, "Even though Tom was foolish, Mary thought he was ridiculous." Well, according to my mother, there were very few limitations as to what Tom could have been and what Mary might have thought of him. So I never did well on tests like that.

The same was true with word analogies, pairs of words in which you were 17 supposed to find some sort of logical, semantic relationship—for example, "Sunset is to nightfall as _____ is to _____." And here you would be presented with a list of four possible pairs, one of which showed the same

---

Thinking Critically

6 Do you think this is true? How has the English you heard as a child influenced your use of language today?

7 Which subject do you like better—math or English? Which is more difficult for you? Why?

kind of relationship: *red* is to *stoplight, bus* is to *arrival, chills* is to *fever, yawn* is to *boring*. Well, I could never think that way. I knew what the tests were asking, but I could not block out of my mind the images already created by the first pair, *"sunset is to nightfall"*—and I would see a burst of colors against a darkening sky, the moon rising, the lowering of a curtain of stars. And all the other pairs of words—red, bus, stoplight, boring—just threw up a mass of confusing images, making it impossible for me to sort out something as logical as saying: "A sunset precedes nightfall" is the same as "a chill precedes a fever." The only way I would have gotten that answer right would have been to imagine an associative situation, for example, my being disobedient and staying out past sunset, catching a chill at night, which turns into feverish pneumonia as punishment, which indeed did happen to me.

I have been thinking about all this lately, about my mother's English, about achievement tests. Because lately I've been asked, as a writer, why there are not more Asian Americans represented in American literature. Why are there few Asian Americans enrolled in creative writing programs? Why do so many Chinese students go into engineering? Well, these are broad sociological questions I can't begin to answer. But I have noticed in surveys—in fact, just last week—that Asian students, as a whole, always do significantly better on math achievement tests than in English. And this makes me think that there are other Asian-American students whose English spoken in the home might also be described as "broken" or "limited." And perhaps they also have teachers who are steering them away from writing and into math and science, which is what happened to me.[8]

Fortunately, I happen to be rebellious in nature and enjoy the challenge of disproving assumptions made about me. I became an English major my first year in college, after being enrolled as pre-med. I started writing nonfiction as a freelancer the week after I was told by my former boss that writing was my worst skill and I should hone my talents toward account management.

But it wasn't until 1985 that I finally began to write fiction. And at first I wrote using what I thought to be wittily crafted sentences, sentences that would prove I had mastery over the English language. Here's an example from the first draft of a story that later made its way into *The Joy Luck Club*, but without this line: "That was my mental quandary in its nascent state." A terrible line, which I can barely pronounce.

Thinking Critically

[8] To what extent do you think ethnic bias exists in the career advice students receive in high school and college?

Fortunately, for reasons I won't get into today, I later decided I should   21
envision a reader for the stories I would write. And the reader I decided
upon was my mother, because these were stories about mothers. So with
this reader in mind—and in fact she did read my early drafts—I began to
write stories using all the Englishes I grew up with: the English I spoke to
my mother, which for lack of a better term might be described as "simple";
the English she used with me, which for lack of a better term might be
described as "broken"; my translation of her Chinese, which could certainly
be described as "watered down"; and what I imagined to be her translation
of her Chinese if she could speak in perfect English, her internal language, [9]
and for that I sought to preserve the essence, but neither an English nor a
Chinese structure. I wanted to capture what language ability tests can never
reveal: her intent, her passion, her imagery, the rhythms of her speech, and
the nature of her thoughts.

Apart from what any critic had to say about my writing, I knew I had   22
succeeded where it counted when my mother finished reading my book
and gave me her verdict: "So easy to read."

UNDERSTANDING DETAILS

1. What do you think is Tan's main reason for writing this essay?
2. What are the four "Englishes" that Tan grew up with? Explain each in your
   own words.
3. What is Tan referring to when she uses the term "mother tongue"?
4. How did Tan feel about her mother's "limited English" in the past?

READING CRITICALLY

5. How did Amy Tan become a writer? In what way did her rebellious nature
   help her make this decision?
6. How do all the Englishes Tan grew up with help her as a writer? Explain your
   answer.
7. What relationship does Tan see between achievement test scores and actual
   abilities?
8. Why did Tan choose her mother as the audience she envisions when she writes?

DISCOVERING RHETORICAL STRATEGIES

9. Why does Tan actually quote some of her mother's language early in her essay?
   What effect does this example have on you as a reader?
10. Tan discusses these types of English in a specific order. Explain this progression,
    and discuss whether it is effective in achieving her overall purpose.

Thinking Critically

[9] What does Tan mean when she refers to her mother's "internal language"?

11. Describe Tan's intended audience in as much detail as possible. Why do you think she aims her essay at this particular group?

12. What other rhetorical strategies does Tan use to help make her point? Give examples of each of these strategies.

MAKING CONNECTIONS

13. Compare and contrast Amy Tan's relationship with her mother and the parent–child relationships examined in any or all of the following essays: Lewis Sawaquat's "For My Indian Daughter," Russell Baker's "The Saturday Evening Post," and/or Amy Chua's "Excerpt from *Battle Hymn of the Tiger Mother*."

14. In her essay, Tan describes her love of English and her avocation as a writer despite her relatively weak performance on English achievement tests as a child. Examine the manner in which other people exceeded the expectations placed on them as expressed in Maya Angelou's "New Directions," Russell Baker's "The Saturday Evening Post," Harold Krents's "Darkness at Noon," and/or Adam Gopnik's "How Lincoln and Darwin Shaped the Modern World."

15. Discuss the theme of "the limitations of language" as it appears in any of the following essays you have read: Amy Tan's "Mother Tongue," Stephanie Ericsson's "The Ways We Lie," and/or Joe Keohane's "How Facts Backfire."

IDEAS FOR DISCUSSION/WRITING

Preparing to Write

Write freely about your own abilities in English: Do you feel you use more than one version of English? How does your oral English differ from your written English? Is English your first language? What do you think of yourself as a writer? As a reader? How well do you perform on English achievement tests?

Choosing a Topic   MyWritingLab™

1. **LEARNING⏻NLINE** Tan refers to the ways in which family, culture, and education affect how she speaks and writes. Using recent emails you have written, examine the "different Englishes" and other languages you use when communicating with diverse audiences. For example, what words do you use when writing to your friends, your family, or your professors? How do your language choices differ in each instance? What social pressures affect your use of "different Englishes"? Write an essay that examines your different uses of English and/or other languages. Consider your reasons varying your language when communicating with different people. Use specific examples from your emails to support and develop your essay.

2. As a college student, you see different people approaching their writing assignments in different ways every day. Some students get right down to work. Others procrastinate until the last minute. Some write in spurts until they have finished the task. Write an essay for your school newspaper explaining your observations about the different ways people write. Use carefully chosen

examples to illustrate your observations. You might even want to interview some of your peers about their writing rituals.

3. Pretend that your college newspaper is running a special issue distinguishing among different generations of students. In a coherent essay written for the readers of this newspaper, classify the students of your generation in some logical, interesting fashion. Remember that classification is a rhetorical movement from "many" to "one." Group the members of your generation by some meaningful guidelines or general characteristics that you establish. Be sure to decide on a purpose and a point of view before you begin to write.

4. In her essay, Tan refers to the fact that her teachers steered her "away from writing and into math and science" (paragraph 18) primarily because of her test scores. But she believes her test scores were not an accurate measurement of her ability in English because of her background in the language. Do you think test scores are ever used inappropriately to advise students? Do you think these scores are the best way we currently have to measure ability and aptitude? Direct your comments to the general public, and use several specific examples to support your opinion.

Before beginning your essay, you may want to consult the flowchart on page 244.

STEPHANIE ERICSSON   (1953–   )

The Ways We Lie

Born in Dallas, Stephanie Ericsson grew up in San Francisco and lived in London, Spain, New York, and Los Angeles before settling in Minneapolis, Minnesota, where she currently lives. After earning a filmmaking degree in college, she worked in advertising and then became a screenwriter's assistant and later a writer of situation comedies. She successfully overcame substance abuse and published *Shamefaced: The Road to Recovery* (1985) and *Women of AA: Recovering Together* (1985). When she was 32 years old, her husband died suddenly of a heart attack while she was two and a half months pregnant, thereby inspiring a number of journal entries and two frank and wrenching books on grief: *Companion Through the Darkness: Inner Dialogues on Grief* (1993) and *Companion into the Dawn: Inner Dialogues on Loving* (1994). Defining grief as "the constant reawakening that things are now different," she argues that it "shears away the masks of normal life and forces brutal honesty out of your mouth before propriety can stop you. It shoves away friends and scares away so-called friends and rewrites your address book for you." Her unique prose style is a very effective combination of her own journal entries mixed with brief essays that vividly chronicle wrenching emotions. A frequent speaker on the subject of loss, Ericsson has written extensively on human psychology and the mental and physical repercussions of addiction and deceit.

Preparing to Read

In this essay, first published in the *Utne Reader,* Stephanie Ericsson categorizes the different types of lies we all tell in an attempt to portray the reality we live in and clarify how lying affects our social morality.

Exploring Experience: As you prepare to read this selection, consider how often you lie or stretch the truth in a typical day: Do you find that you don't tell the truth in every situation? When do you stretch the truth? Why do you do it? What are the consequences of these lies? Do you feel guilty when you don't tell the whole truth? Why do you think you feel this way?

LEARNING⏻NLINE Visit the Blifaloo website (www.blifaloo.com), and click "Lie Detection" on the left bar under "Popular Features." Scroll down the page, and select "How to Detect Lies (part 1)." According to the article, what are some of the physical gestures, facial expressions, and verbal indicators that people display when they are lying? Have you ever been aware of these indicators in yourself or someone else?

Before reading this essay, you may want to consult the flowchart on page 241.

The bank called today and I told them my deposit was in the mail, even though I hadn't written a check yet. It'd been a rough day. The baby I'm pregnant with decided to do aerobics on my lungs for two hours, our three-year-old daughter painted the living-room couch with lipstick, the IRS put me on hold for an hour, and I was late to a business meeting because I was tired.

I told my client that traffic had been bad. When my partner came home, his haggard face told me his day hadn't gone any better than mine, so when he asked, "How was your day?" I said, "Oh, fine," knowing that one more straw might break his back. A friend called and wanted to take me to lunch. I said I was busy. Four lies in the course of a day, none of which I felt the least bit guilty about.

We lie. We all do. We exaggerate, we minimize, we avoid confrontation, we spare people's feelings, we conveniently forget, we keep secrets, we justify lying to the big-guy institutions. Like most people, I indulge in small falsehoods and still think of myself as an honest person. Sure I lie, but it doesn't hurt anything. Or does it? [1]

I once tried going a whole week without telling a lie, and it was paralyzing. I discovered that telling the truth all the time is nearly impossible. It means living with some serious consequences: The bank charges me $60 in overdraft fees, my partner keels over when I tell him about my travails, my client fires me for telling her I didn't feel like being on time, and my friend takes it personally when I say I'm not hungry. There must be some merit to lying.

But if I justify lying, what makes me any different from slick politicians or the corporate robbers who raided the S&L industry? Saying it's okay to lie one way and not another is hedging. I cannot seem to escape the voice deep inside me that tells me: When someone lies, someone loses.

What far-reaching consequences will I, or others, pay as a result of my lie? [2] Will someone's trust be destroyed? Will someone else pay my penance because I ducked out? We must consider the *meaning of our actions*. Deception, lies, capital crimes, and misdemeanors all carry meanings. *Webster's* definition of *lie* is specific:

1. a false statement or action especially made with the intent to deceive;
2. anything that gives or is meant to give a false impression.

A definition like this implies that there are many, many ways to tell a lie. Here are just a few.

Thinking Critically

[1] Do you think lying "doesn't hurt anything"? Have you ever been harmed by a lie?
[2] Have your lies ever hurt another person? How did the situation make you feel?

The White Lie

A man who won't lie to a woman has very little consideration for her feelings.

—*Bergen Evans*

The white lie assumes that the truth will cause more damage than a [8] simple, harmless untruth. Telling a friend he looks great when he looks like hell can be based on a decision that the friend needs a compliment more than a frank opinion. But, in effect, it is the liar deciding what is best for the lied to. Ultimately, it is a vote of no confidence. It is an act of subtle arrogance for anyone to decide what is best for someone else.

Yet not all circumstances are quite so cut and dried. Take, for instance, [9] the sergeant in Vietnam who knew one of his men was killed in action but listed him as missing so that the man's family would receive indefinite compensation instead of the lump sum pittance the military gives widows and children. His intent was honorable. Yet for twenty years this family kept their hopes alive, unable to move on to a new life. [3]

Façades

Et tu, Brute?

—*Caesar*

We all put up façades to one degree or another. When I put on a suit to [10] go to see a client, I feel as though I am putting on another face, obeying the expectation that serious businesspeople wear suits rather than sweatpants. But I'm a writer: Normally, I get up, get the kid off to school, and sit at my computer in my pajamas until four in the afternoon. When I answer the phone, the caller thinks I'm wearing a suit (though the UPS man knows better).

But façades can be destructive because they are used to seduce others into [11] an illusion. For instance, I recently realized that a former friend was a liar. He presented himself with all the right looks and the right words and offered lots of new consciousness theories, fabulous books to read, and fascinating insights. Then I did some business with him, and the time came for him to pay me. He turned out to be all talk and no walk. I heard a plethora of reasonable excuses, including in-depth descriptions of the big break around the corner. In six months of work, I saw less than a hundred bucks. When I confronted him, he raised both eyebrows and tried to convince me that I'd heard him wrong, that he'd made no commitment to me. A simple investigation into his past revealed a crowded graveyard of disenchanted former friends. [4]

Thinking Critically

[3] Do you approve of the sergeant's lie? Why or why not?

[4] What does the metaphor "a crowded graveyard of disenchanted former friends" mean to you? Where else does the author use metaphors?

Ignoring the Plain Facts

Well, you must understand that Father Porter is only human.

—A Massachusetts Priest

In the '60s, the Catholic Church in Massachusetts began hearing complaints that Father James Porter was sexually molesting children. Rather than relieving him of his duties, the ecclesiastical authorities moved him from one parish to another between 1960 and 1967, actually providing him with a fresh supply of unsuspecting families and innocent children to abuse. After treatment in 1967 for pedophilia, he went back to work, this time in Minnesota. The new diocese was aware of Father Porter's obsession with children, but they needed priests and recklessly believed treatment had cured him. More children were abused until he was relieved of his duties a year later. By his own admission, Porter may have abused as many as a hundred children.   12

Ignoring the facts may not in and of itself be a form of lying, but consider the context of this situation. If a lie is a false action done with the intent to deceive, then the Catholic Church's conscious covering for Porter created irreparable consequences. The church became a co-perpetrator with Porter.   13

Deflecting

When you have no basis for an argument, abuse the plaintiff.

—Cicero

I've discovered that I can keep anyone from seeing the true me by being selectively blatant. I set a precedent of being up-front about intimate issues, but I never bring up the things I truly want to hide; I just let people assume I'm revealing everything. It's an effective way of hiding.[5]   14

Any good liar knows that the way to perpetuate an untruth is to deflect attention from it. When Clarence Thomas exploded with accusations that the Senate hearings were a "high-tech lynching," he simply switched the focus from a highly charged subject to a radioactive subject. Rather than defending himself, he took the offensive and accused the country of racism. It was a brilliant maneuver. Racism is now politically incorrect in official circles—unlike sexual harassment, which still rewards those who can get away with it.   15

Some of the most skilled deflectors are passive-aggressive people who, when accused of inappropriate behavior, refuse to respond to the accusations. This you-don't-exist stance infuriates the accuser, who, understandably,   16

Thinking Critically

[5] Look up the term "deflecting." How does it differ from the white lie?

screams something obscene out of frustration. The trap is sprung and the act of deflection successful, because now the passive-aggressive person can indignantly say, "Who can talk to someone as unreasonable as you?" The real issue is forgotten and the sins of the original victim become the focus. Feeling guilty of name-calling, the victim is fully tamed and crawls into a hole, ashamed. I have watched this fighting technique work thousands of times in disputes between men and women, and what I've learned is that the real culprit is not necessarily the one who swears the loudest.

Omission

The cruelest lies are often told in silence.

—*R. L. Stevenson*

Omission involves telling most of the truth minus one or two key facts   17
whose absence changes the story completely. You break a pair of glasses that are guaranteed under normal use and get a new pair, without mentioning that the first pair broke during a rowdy game of basketball. Who hasn't tried something like that? But what about omission of information that could make a difference in how a person lives his or her life?

For instance, one day I found out that rabbinical legends tell of another   18
woman in the Garden of Eden before Eve. I was stunned. The omission of the Sumerian goddess Lilith from Genesis—as well as her demoniza-tion by ancient misogynists as an embodiment of female evil—felt like spiritual robbery. I felt like I'd just found out my mother was really my stepmother. To take seriously the tradition that Adam was created out of the same mud as his equal counterpart, Lilith, redefines all of Judeo-Christian history.

Some renegade Catholic feminists introduced me to a view of Lilith that   19
had been suppressed during the many centuries when this strong goddess was seen only as a spirit of evil. Lilith was a proud goddess who defied Adam's need to control her, attempted negotiations, and when this failed, said adios and left the Garden of Eden.

This omission of Lilith from the Bible was a patriarchal strategy to keep   20
women weak. Omitting the strong-woman archetype of Lilith from West-ern religions and starting the story with Eve the Rib has helped keep Christian and Jewish women believing they were the lesser sex for thou-sands of years.

Stereotypes and Clichés

Where opinion does not exist, the status quo becomes stereotyped and all original-ity is discouraged.

—*Bertrand Russell*

Stereotype and cliché serve a purpose as a form of shorthand.[6] Our need   21
for vast amounts of information in nanoseconds has made the stereotype
vital to modern communication. Unfortunately, it often shuts down original
thinking, giving those hungry for the truth a candy bar of misinformation
instead of a balanced meal. The stereotype explains a situation with just
enough truth to seem unquestionable.

All the "isms"—racism, sexism, ageism, et al.—are founded on and fueled   22
by the stereotype and the cliché, which are lies of exaggeration, omission,
and ignorance. They are always dangerous. They take a single tree and make
it a landscape. They destroy curiosity. They close minds and separate people.
The single mother on welfare is assumed to be cheating. Any black male
could tell you how much of his identity is obliterated daily by stereotypes.
Fat people, ugly people; beautiful people, old people, large-breasted women,
short men, the mentally ill, and the homeless man could tell you how much
more they are like us than we want to think. I once admitted to a group of
people that I had a mouth like a truck driver. Much to my surprise, a man
stood up and said, "I'm a truck driver, and I never cuss." Needless to say, I
was humbled.

Groupthink

Who is more foolish, the child afraid of the dark, or the man afraid of the light?
—Maurice Freehill

Irving Janis, in *Victims of Group Think,* defines this sort of lie as a   23
psychological phenomenon within decision-making groups in which loyalty
to the group has become more important than any other value, with the
result that dissent and the appraisal of alternatives are suppressed. If you've
ever worked on a committee or in a corporation, you've encountered
groupthink.[7] It requires a combination of other forms of lying—ignoring
facts, selective memory, omission, and denial, to name a few.

The textbook example of groupthink came on December 7, 1941. From   24
as early as the fall of 1941, the warnings came in, one after another, that
Japan was preparing for a massive military operation. The navy command in
Hawaii assumed Pearl Harbor was invulnerable—the Japanese weren't stupid
enough to attack the United States' most important base. On the other hand,
racist stereotypes said the Japanese weren't smart enough to invent a torpedo
effective in less than 60 feet of water (the fleet was docked in 30 feet); after
all, US technology hadn't been able to do it.

Thinking Critically

[6] In what way are stereotype and cliché a "form of shorthand"?

[7] What is "groupthink"? What are some examples of it? Have you ever been involved in it?

On Friday, December 5, normal weekend leave was granted to all the   25
commanders at Pearl Harbor even though the Japanese consulate in Hawaii
was busy burning papers. Within the tight, good-ole-boy cohesiveness of
the US command in Hawaii, the myth of invulnerability stayed well
entrenched. No one in the group considered the alternatives. The rest is
history.[8]

Out-and-Out Lies

The only form of lying that is beyond reproach is lying for its own sake.
                                                        —*Oscar Wilde*

Of all the ways to lie, I like this one the best, probably because I get tired   26
of trying to figure out the real meanings behind things. At least I can trust the
bald-faced lie. I once asked my five-year-old nephew, "Who broke the fence?"
(I had seen him do it.) He answered, "The murderers." Who could argue?

At least when this sort of lie is told it can be easily confronted. As the   27
person who is lied to, I know where I stand. The bald-faced lie doesn't toy
with my perceptions—it argues with them. It doesn't try to refashion reality, it tries to refute it. *Read my lips.* . . . No sleight of hand. No guessing. If
this were the only form of lying, there would be no such things as floating
anxiety or the adult-children-of-alcoholics movement.

Dismissal

Pay no attention to that man behind the curtain! I am the Great Oz!
                                                        —*The Wizard of Oz*

Dismissal is perhaps the slipperiest of all lies. Dismissing feelings, percep-   28
tions, or even the raw facts of a situation ranks as a kind of lie that can do
as much damage to a person as any other kind of lie.

The roots of many mental disorders can be linked back to the dismissal   29
of reality. Imagine that a person is told from the time she is a tot that her
perceptions are inaccurate. *"Mommy, I'm scared."* "No you're not, darling."
"I don't like that man next door, he makes me feel icky." "Johnny, that's a terrible
thing to say, of course you like him. You go over there right now and be
nice to him."

I've often mused over the idea that madness is actually a sane reaction to   30
an insane world.[9] Psychologist R. D. Laing supports this hypothesis in
Sanity, Madness and the Family, an account of his investigation into the families of schizophrenics. The common thread that ran through all of the

---

Thinking Critically

[8] What does "history" mean in this context?

[9] Do you agree that "madness is actually a sane reaction to an insane world"? Why or why not?

families he studied was a deliberate, staunch dismissal of the patient's perceptions from a very early age. Each of the patients started out with an accurate grasp of reality, which, through meticulous and methodical dismissal, was demolished until the only reality the patient could trust was catatonia.

Dismissal runs the gamut. Mild dismissal can be quite handy for forgiving 31 the foibles of others in our day-to-day lives. Toddlers who have just learned to manipulate their parents' attention sometimes are dismissed out of necessity. Absolute attention from the parents would require so much energy that no one would get to eat dinner. But we must be careful and attentive about how far we take our "necessary" dismissals. Dismissal is a dangerous tool, because it's nothing less than a lie.

Delusion

We lie loudest when we lie to ourselves.

—Eric Hoffer

I could write the book on this one. Delusion, a cousin of dismissal, is the 32 tendency to see excuses as facts. It's a powerful lying tool because it filters out information that contradicts what we want to believe. Alcoholics who believe that the problems in their lives are legitimate reasons for drinking rather than results of the drinking offer the classic example of deluded thinking. Delusion uses the mind's ability to see things in myriad ways to support what it wants to be the truth.

But delusion is also a survival mechanism we all use. If we were to fully 33 contemplate the consequences of our stockpiles of nuclear weapons or global warming, we could hardly function on a day-to-day level. We don't want to incorporate that much reality into our lives because to do so would be paralyzing.

Delusion acts as an adhesive to keep the status quo intact. It shamelessly 34 employs dismissal, omission, and amnesia, among other sorts of lies. Its most cunning defense is that it cannot see itself.

The liar's punishment [. . .] is that he cannot believe anyone else.

—George Bernard Shaw

These are only a few of the ways we lie. Or are lied to. As I said earlier, 35 it's not easy to entirely eliminate lies from our lives. No matter how pious we may try to be, we will still embellish, hedge, and omit to lubricate the daily machinery of living.[10] But there is a world of difference between telling functional lies and living a lie. Martin Buber once said, "The lie is the

---

Thinking Critically

10 In what way do lies "lubricate the daily machinery of living"?

spirit committing treason against itself." Our acceptance of lies becomes a cultural cancer that eventually shrouds and reorders reality until moral garbage becomes as invisible to us as water is to a fish.

How much do we tolerate before we become sick and tired of being sick   36
and tired? When will we stand up and declare our *right* to trust? When do we stop accepting that the real truth is in the fine print? Whose lips do we read this year when we vote for president? When will we stop being so reticent about making judgments? When do we stop turning over our personal power and responsibility to liars?

Maybe if I don't tell the bank the check's in the mail I'll be less tolerant   37
of the lies told to me every day. A country song I once heard said it all for me: "You've got to stand for something or you'll fall for anything."

UNDERSTANDING DETAILS

1. According to Ericsson, why do we all lie?
2. What are the ten types of lies the author delineates?
3. How do we justify lying in our lives?
4. Why does Ericsson claim that telling the truth all the time is "nearly impossible" (paragraph 4)?

READING CRITICALLY

5. What are some of the consequences Ericsson is referring to at the beginning of this essay?
6. Which of these types of lies do you tell most often? Why do you resort to them?
7. Which of these types of lies would you say is most damaging? Why is this so?
8. What is the difference between "telling functional lies and living a lie" (paragraph 35)?

DISCOVERING RHETORICAL STRATEGIES

9. What do the quotes that the author uses to introduce each type of lie add to the explanations of each category?
10. Why does Ericsson end her essay with lyrics from a song? What do they mean? What significance do they have in this essay?
11. What does the definition from *Webster's* dictionary add to Ericsson's essay?
12. What other rhetorical strategies does the author use besides division/classification?

MAKING CONNECTIONS

13. To what extent would Ericsson and/or Jessica Mitford ("Behind the Formaldehyde Curtain") agree on the need for "façades" in life?
14. Read Ericsson's section on "Stereotypes and Clichés," and then analyze Malcolm Cowley's "The View from 80," Sandra Cisneros's "Only Daughter,"

Amy Chua's "Excerpt from *Battle Hymn of the Tiger Mother*," and/or Gloria Steinem's "The Politics of Muscle" in terms of how much each of these authors has suffered from being a member of a group that society sometimes stereotypes.

15. Contrast the ways in which Ericsson, Sara Gilbert ("The Different Ways of Being Smart"), and/or Sarah Toler ("Understanding the Birth Order Relationship") divide and classify their various topics.

IDEAS FOR DISCUSSION/WRITING

Preparing to Write

Write freely about the role of lies in your life: What types of lies do you tell most often? Why do you tell these lies? How are these lies necessary to your life? How do you justify these lies? Would telling the truth all the time have any negative consequences for you? If so, what would these consequences be?

Choosing a Topic   MyWritingLab™

1. **LEARNING⏻NLINE** At the bottom of the Blifaloo article "How to Detect Lies" (from Preparing to Read) is a section inviting readers to post comments. Read the comments that others have posted, and then write a response that you would like to post in response to this information.

2. A friend found out you lied to him or her and demands an explanation. Instead of talking to your friend, you decide to write an explanation of the history of the lie, your justification for this lie, and an apology (if appropriate).

3. Write an essay explaining and analyzing our behavior when we lie. Use information you learned from Ericsson and your own experience when appropriate.

4. John Webster once said, "There is nothing so powerful as truth—and often nothing so strange." What does this statement mean to you? Write an essay to Ericsson explaining this concept.

Before beginning your essay, you may want to consult the flowchart on page 244.

Chapter Writing Assignments

Practicing Division/Classification

1. Do you think public schools should teach students ethics and personal values? If so, which values should schools teach to produce "good citizens"? Classify these values in an essay, and explain how these categories would have fit into your high school curriculum.

2. What problems are most destructive to a healthy relationship? Choose a specific type of relationship (friend, spouse, parent–child), and write an essay discussing various categories of problems that can cause the most trouble in these relationships. Explain why the qualities you identify would be destructive in the kind of relationship you describe.

3. Think about the ideal job for you. List the features that job must have. What categories do these features fall into? Why are these features ideal? Write an essay explaining the categories you have developed for the job you chose.

Exploring Ideas

4. We all have bad habits, but few people know how to break them. What advice do you have for people who want to change their behavior in some important way or break a bad habit? How do you know your method works?

5. Explain a tradition we are in danger of losing in society today. Discuss the value of the tradition itself and the ways this tradition is changing, along with the value and effects of this change. Make sure you discuss this topic in an unbiased way.

6. How do a person's cultural views and beliefs affect the educational process? In what ways does our current system of education acknowledge, hinder, or ignore our diverse cultural backgrounds? In a well-developed essay, discuss how our educational system successfully or unsuccessfully deals with our various cultural differences. Are the categories in your essay distinct from one another? What rhetorical strategies support your essay?

Analyzing Visual Images

Jeff Greenberg/The Image Works.

7. This photo classifies the food available at this restaurant. Choose a common topic like food, houses, or clothing (or another subject that interests you), and discuss in essay form how someone might classify the items in that category. For example, someone could discuss types of cars according to the characteristics of the people who are likely to buy them.

8. Look at the picture on page 240 at the beginning of this chapter. What do you think these people are doing? Why are they here? Consider the various reasons people might be in this particular place, and write an essay classifying them according to your assumptions.

Composing in Different Genres

9. Multimedia: Conduct a brief survey on a topic that interests you related to the Internet. Draft three or four questions relevant to your interest, and ask at least ten people to respond. Then divide the responses you receive into logical categories, and summarize your findings in a graph.

10. Multigenre: Create a graphic organizer, or drawing, of one of the essays in this chapter. Don't add words to the graphic. Swap graphics with someone in class who chose the same reading selection, and fill in each other's visual with words. Write an essay testifying to the value of combining graphic and verbal approaches to learning.

Writing from Sources

For detailed information on writing from sources, see Part III.

11. What are the differences among public, private, and international adoption? Classify these types of adoption based on their requirements. Consider the advantages and disadvantages of each type—for example, the financial commitment involved and the psychological obstacles that adoptive parents should be prepared to face. Find one or two credible sources that discuss circumstances surrounding adoption and use them in a research-based essay.

12. Environmental awareness has become very important in recent years. Research environmentalism to find different ways that people and businesses are responding to the crisis of climate change. Write a documented essay that recommends the best ways to be "green" in the twenty-first century.

MyWritingLab™ Visit Ch. 8 Division/Classification: Finding Categories in *MyWritingLab* to complete the writing assignments and test your understanding of the chapter learning objectives.

Chapter 9

COMPARISON/CONTRAST
Discovering Similarities and Differences

LEARNING OBJECTIVES

After completing this chapter, you will be able to do the following:
- Define comparison/contrast
- Use comparison/contrast to think critically
- Read comparison/contrast essays critically
- Write and revise effective comparison/contrast essays

Making comparisons is such a natural and necessary part of our everyday lives that we often do so without conscious effort. When we were children, we compared our toys with those of our friends, we contrasted our height and physical development to other children's, and we constantly evaluated our happiness in comparison with that of our parents and childhood companions. As we grew older, we habitually compared our dates, teachers, parents, friends, cars, and physical attributes. In college, we learn about anthropology by writing essays on the similarities and differences between two African tribes, about political science by contrasting the Republican and Democratic platforms, about business by comparing annual production rates, and about literature by comparing Shakespeare with Marlowe or Browning with Tennyson. Comparing and contrasting various elements in our lives helps us make decisions, such as which course to take or which house to buy, and it justifies preferences that we already hold, such as liking one city more than another or loving one person more than the next. In these ways and in many others, the skillful use of comparison and contrast is clearly essential to our social and professional lives.

DEFINING COMPARISON/CONTRAST

Comparison and contrast allow us to understand one subject by putting it next to another. Comparing involves discovering likenesses or similarities, whereas contrasting is based on finding differences. Like division and classification, comparison and contrast are generally considered part of the same process because we usually have no reason for comparing unless some contrast is also involved. Each technique implies the existence of the other. For this reason, the word *compare* is often used for both techniques.

Comparison and contrast are most profitably applied to two items that have something in common, such as cats and dogs or cars and motorcycles. A discussion of cats and motorcycles, for example, would probably not be very rewarding or stimulating because they do not have much in common. If more than two items are compared in an essay, they are still most profitably discussed in pairs: for instance, motorcycles and cars, cars and bicycles, or bicycles and motorcycles.

An *analogy* is an extended, sustained comparison. Often used to explain unfamiliar, abstract, or complicated thoughts, this rhetorical technique adds energy and vividness to a wide variety of college-level writing. The process of analogy differs slightly from comparison/contrast in three important ways: Comparison/contrast begins with subjects from the same class and places equal weight on both of them. In addition, it addresses both the similarities and the differences of these subjects. Analogy, conversely, seldom explores subjects from the same class and focuses principally on one familiar subject in an attempt to explain another, more complex one. Furthermore, it deals only with similarities, not with contrasts. A comparison/contrast essay, for example, might study two veterans' ways of coping with the trauma of the war in Iraq by pointing out the differences in their methods as well as the similarities. An analogy essay might use the familiar notion of a fireworks display to reveal the chilling horror of the lonely hours after dark during this war: "Nights in Baghdad were similar to a loud, unending fireworks display. We had no idea when the next blast was coming, how loud it would be, or how close. We cringed in terror after dark, hoping the next surprise would not be our own death." In this example, rather than simply hearing about an event, we participate in it through this highly refined form of comparison.

The following student paragraph compares and contrasts married and single life. As you read it, notice how the author compares similar social states and, in the process, justifies her current lifestyle:

> Recently I saw a bumper sticker that read, "It used to be wine, women, and song, and now it's beer, the old lady, and TV." Much truth may be found in this comparison of single and married lifestyles. When my husband and I used to date, for example, we'd go out for dinner and drinks and then maybe see a play or concert. Our discussions were intelligent, often ranging over global politics, science, literature, and other lofty topics. He would open doors for me, buy me flowers, and make sure I was comfortable and happy. Now, three years later, after marriage and a child, the baby bottle has replaced the wine bottle, the smell of diapers wipes out the scent of roses, and our nights on the town are infrequent, cherished events. But that's all right. A little bit of the excitement and mystery may be gone, but these intangible qualities have given way to a sturdy, dependable trust in each other and a quiet confidence about our future together.

THINKING CRITICALLY THROUGH COMPARISON/CONTRAST

Comparison and contrast are basic to a number of different thought processes. We compare and contrast quite naturally on a daily basis, but all of us would benefit greatly from being more aware of these companion strategies in our own writing. They help us not only in perceiving our environment but also in understanding and organizing large amounts of information.

The basic skill of finding similarities and differences will enhance your ability to create accurate descriptions, to cite appropriate examples, to present a full process analysis, and, of course, to classify and label subjects. It is a pattern of thought that is essential to more complex thinking strategies, so perfecting the ability to use it is an important step in your efforts to improve your critical thinking.

Once again, we are going to practice this strategy in isolation to get a strong sense of its mechanics before we combine it with other rhetorical modes. Isolating this mode will make your reading and writing even stronger than they are now because the individual parts of the thinking process will be more vigorous and effective, thus making your academic performance more powerful than ever.

1. Make a list of the similarities and differences in the photograph on the next page. What messages or ideas do you think the photographer is communicating through this photograph?

Zach Gold/Corbis.

2. Find magazine ads that use comparison/contrast to make a point or sell
   a product. What is the basis of each comparison? How effective or inef-
   fective is each comparison?
3. Have you ever been to the same place twice? Think for a moment about
   how the first and second visits to this place differed. How were they similar? What were the primary reasons for the similarities and differences in
   your perceptions of these visits?

READING AND WRITING COMPARISON/CONTRAST ESSAYS

Many established guidelines regulate the development of a comparison/
contrast essay and should be taken into account from both the reading and the
writing perspectives. All good comparative studies serve a specific purpose.
They attempt either to examine their subjects separately or to demonstrate
the superiority of one over the other. In evaluating two different types of
cars, for example, a writer might point out the amazing gas mileage of one
model and the smooth handling qualities of the other or the superiority of
one car's gas mileage over that of another. Whatever the intent, comparison/
contrast essays must be clear and logical and have a precise purpose.

Reading Comparison/Contrast Essays

Understanding how comparison/contrast essays work rhetorically will help you make decisions for your own writing. Here is a flowchart of questions that will guide your reading for this purpose.

Questions to Guide Your Reading

PREPARING TO READ Before you read the essays, answer the following questions:

- What assumptions can you make from the essay's **title**?
- What do you think the general **mood** of the essay will be?
- What is the essay's **purpose** and **audience**?
- What does the **synopsis** tell you about the essay?
- What can you learn from the author's **biography**?
- What do you predict the author's **point of view** toward the subject will be?

READING As you read the essays for the first time, answer the following questions:

- What is the writer **comparing**?
- What is the essay's **thesis**?
- How is the essay **organized**?
- What **details** support the essay's purpose?

REREADING When you read the essays again, answer the following questions:

- Is the writer's method of **organization** effective?
- Is the comparison fully **developed**?
- What other **rhetorical strategies** does the author use?
- How does your understanding of the essay **change** with each rereading?

Preparing to Read.   As you begin reading this chapter, pull together as much preliminary material as possible for each essay so you can focus your attention and have the benefit of prior knowledge before you start to read. In particular, you should try to discover what is being compared or contrasted and why. From the title of her essay, can you tell what Amy Chua is comparing in "Excerpt from *Battle Hymn of the Tiger Mother*"? What does Motoko Rich's title "Literacy Debate" suggest to you? From glancing at the essay itself and reading the synopsis in the Rhetorical Table of Contents, what do you think John Tierney's essay will try to accomplish?

Also, before you begin to read these essays, try to discover information about the author and about the conditions under which each essay was written. Why is Rich qualified to write about literacy? How does she reveal her background in her essay? What is Gloria Steinem's stand on women's bodybuilding? To what extent do you expect her opinions on this topic to color her comparison of women's past and present physical strength?

Finally, just before you begin to read, answer the Preparing to Read questions, and then make some free associations with the general topic of each essay: For example, what do you think might be some of the comparisons and contrasts between Lincoln and Darwin in "How Lincoln and Darwin Shaped the Modern World" (Adam Gopnik)? What is your general view on women's bodybuilding (Steinem)?

Reading.   As you read each comparison/contrast essay for the first time, be sure to record your own feelings and opinions. Some of the issues presented in this chapter are highly controversial. You will often have strong reactions to them, which you should try to write down as soon as possible.

In addition, you may want to comment on the relationships among the preliminary essay material, the author's stance in the essay, and the content of the essay itself. For example, what motivated Gopnik to write "How Lincoln and Darwin Shaped the Modern World"? Who is his primary audience? What is Tierney's tone in "A Generation's Vanity, Heard Through Lyrics," and how does it advance his purpose? Answers to questions such as these will provide you with a context for your first reading of these essays and will assist you in preparing to analyze the essays in more depth on your second reading.

Critical thinking questions are provided with each essay at the bottom of the pages in this chapter. If you dig in and try to answer each one, they will lead you to higher levels of thinking on these particular issues. They are designed to bridge the gap in understanding between the prereading and postreading activities surrounding each essay. Writing your responses to these questions will provide you with the best opportunity to learn how to think analytically about these topics.

At this point in the reading, you should make certain you understand each author's thesis and then take a close look at his or her principal method of organization: Is the essay arranged (1) point by point, (2) subject by subject, (3) as a combination of these two, or (4) as separate discussions of similarities and differences between two subjects? (See the chart on page 298 for an illustration of these options.) Last, preview the questions that follow the essay before you read it again.

Rereading.   When you read these essays a second time, you should look at the comparison or contrast much more closely than you have up to now. First, look again at the writer's method of organization (as outlined on page 298). How effective is it in advancing the writer's thesis?

Next, you should consider whether each essay is fully developed and balanced: Does Chua compare similar items? Does Gopnik discuss the same elements of his subjects? Does Rich deal with the main aspects of literacy? Is Steinem's treatment of her subjects well balanced? And does Tierney give his audience enough specific details to clarify the extent of his comparison? Do all the writers in this chapter use well-chosen transitions so you can move smoothly from one point to the next? Also, what other rhetorical modes support each comparison/contrast in this chapter?

Finally, the answers to the questions after each selection will let you evaluate your understanding of the essay and help you analyze its contents in preparation for the discussion/writing topics that follow.

For a more thorough inventory of the reading process, refer to the Reading Checklist at the end of Chapter 2.

Writing Comparison/Contrast Essays

Now that you see how comparison/contrast works in an essay, use the same features in your own writing. The flowchart on the next page provides some questions to guide you.

Preparing to Write.   As you consider various topics for a comparison/contrast essay, you should answer the Preparing to Write questions that precede the assignments and then use the prewriting techniques explained in Chapter 3 to generate even more ideas on these topics.

As you focus your attention on a particular topic, keep the following suggestions in mind:

1. Always compare/contrast items in the same category (e.g., compare two professors, but not a professor and a swimming pool).
2. Have a specific purpose or reason for writing your essay.
3. Discuss the same qualities of each subject (if you evaluate the teaching techniques of one professor, do so for the other professor as well).
4. Use as many pertinent details as possible to expand your comparison/contrast and to accomplish your stated purpose.

Questions to Guide Your Writing

PREPARING TO WRITE
Before you start writing, answer these questions:

- What is your **purpose**?
- Who is your **audience**?

WRITING
As you write your first draft, consider these questions:

- Does your **thesis** capture your purpose and the boundaries of your comparison?
- Are you comparing items in the **same general category**?
- What **details** will support your thesis?
- Does your **introduction** (1) identify your subjects, (2) explain the basis of your comparison, and (3) state the purpose and limits of your study?
- Is your paper **organized** point by point, subject by subject, as a combination of the two, or as a discussion of similarities and differences?
- Do you **balance** the treatment of your subjects?

EDITING
Be sure to proofread and edit your paper before turning it in.

- Are your **sentences** all complete?
- Do your words say exactly **what you mean**?
- Do you follow conventional **grammar and usage** rules?

REVISING
After you write your first draft, use the following questions to revise your essay:

- Does your **thesis** state the purpose and limits of your study?
- Do you compare/contrast items from the **same general category**?
- Do you discuss the **same qualities** of each subject?
- Do you **organize** your essay as effectively as possible?
- Do you **balance** the treatment of your topics?
- Does your **conclusion** summarize and analyze your main points?

5. Deal with all aspects of the comparison that are relevant to the purpose.
6. Balance the treatment of the different subjects of your comparison (i.e., don't spend more time on one than on another).
7. Determine your audience's background and knowledge so that you will know how much of your comparison should be explained in detail and how much can be skimmed over.

Next, in preparation for a comparison/contrast project, you might list all the elements of both subjects that you want to compare. This list can help you give your essay structure as well as substance. At this stage in the writing process, the task may seem similar to pure description, but a discussion of two subjects in relation to one another rapidly changes the assignment from description to comparison.

Writing.   The introduction of your comparison/contrast essay should (1) clearly identify your subjects, (2) explain the basis of your comparison/contrast, and (3) state your purpose and the overall limits of your particular study. Identifying your subject is, of course, a necessary and important task in any essay. Similarly, justifying the elements you will be comparing and contrasting creates interest and gives your audience some specifics to look for in the essay. Finally, your statement of purpose, or thesis (for example, to prove that one professor is superior to another), should include the boundaries of your discussion. You cannot cover all the reasons for your preference in one short essay, so you must limit your consideration to three or four basic categories (perhaps teaching techniques, the clarity of the assignments given, classroom attitude, and grading standards). The introduction is the place to make all these limits known.

You can organize the body of your paper in one of four ways: (1) a point-by-point, or alternating, comparison; (2) a subject-by-subject, or divided, comparison; (3) a combination of these two methods; or (4) a division between the similarities and differences.

The point-by-point comparison evaluates both subjects in terms of each category. If the issue, for example, is which of two cars to buy, you might discuss both models' gasoline mileage first; then, their horsepower; next, their ease in handling; and, finally, their standard equipment. Following the second method of organization, subject by subject, you would discuss the gasoline mileage, horsepower, ease in handling, and standard equipment of car A first and then follow the same format for car B. The third option would allow you to introduce, say, the standard equipment of each car point by point (or car by car) and then to explain the other features in your comparison (miles per gallon, horsepower, and ease in handling) subject by subject. To use the last method of organization, you might discuss the similarities between the two models first and the differences second (or vice versa). If the cars you are comparing have similar miles-per-gallon (MPG) ratings but completely different horsepower, steering systems, and optional equipment, you could discuss the gasoline mileage and then emphasize the differences by mentioning them later in the essay. If, instead, you are trying to emphasize the fact that the MPG ratings of these models remain consistent despite their differences, then reverse the order of your essay.

Point by Point	**Subject by Subject**
MPG, car A MPG, car B Horsepower, car A Horsepower, car B Handling, car A Handling, car B Equipment, car A Equipment, car B	MPG, car A Horsepower, car A Handling, car A Equipment, car A MPG, car B Horsepower, car B Handling, car B Equipment, car B

Combination	**Similarities/Differences**

Equipment, car A
Equipment, car B
 	
————
 	
MPG, car A
Horsepower, car A
Handling, car A
 	
MPG, car B
Horsepower, car B
Handling, car B
	Similarities:
	   MPG, cars A & B
	
	Differences:
	   Horsepower, cars A & B
	   Handling, cars A & B
	   Equipment, cars A & B

When confronted with the task of choosing a method of organization for a comparison/contrast essay, you need to find the pattern that best suits your purpose. If you want single items to stand out in a discussion, for instance, the best choice will be the point-by-point system; it is especially appropriate for long essays but has a tendency to turn into an exercise in listing if you don't pay careful attention to your transitions. If, however, the subjects themselves (rather than the itemized points) are the most interesting feature of your essay, you should use the subject-by-subject comparison; this system is particularly good for short essays in which the readers can retain what was said about one subject while they read about a second subject. Through this second method of organization, each subject becomes a unified whole, an approach to an essay that is generally effective unless the theme becomes awkwardly divided into two separate parts. You must also remember, if you choose this second method of organization, that the second (or last) subject is in the most emphatic position because that is what your readers will have seen most recently. The final two options for organizing a comparison/contrast essay give you some built-in flexibility so that you can create emphasis and attempt to manipulate reader opinion simply by the structure of your essay.

Using logical transitions in your comparison/contrast essays will establish clear relationships between the items in your comparisons and will also move your readers smoothly from one topic to the next. If you wish to indicate comparisons, use such words as *like, as, also, in like manner, similarly,* and *in addition;* to signal contrasts, try *but, in contrast to, unlike, whereas,* and *on the one hand/on the other hand.*

The conclusion of a comparison/contrast essay summarizes the main points and states the deductions drawn from those points. As you choose your method of organization, remember not to get locked into a formulaic approach to your subjects, which will adversely affect the readability of your essay. To avoid making your reader feel like a spectator at a verbal table-tennis match, be straightforward, honest, and patient as you discover and recount the details of your comparison.

Revising.   When you review the draft of your comparison/contrast essay, you once again need to make sure that you communicate your purpose as effectively as possible to your intended audience.

For further information on writing and revising your comparison/contrast essays, consult the Writing Checklist at the end of Chapter 3.

STUDENT ESSAY: COMPARISON/CONTRAST AT WORK

The following student essay compares the advantages and disadvantages of macaroni and cheese versus tacos in the life of a harried college freshman. As you read it, notice that the writer states his intention in the first paragraph and then expands his discussion with appropriate details to produce a balanced essay. Also, try to determine what effect he creates by using two methods of organization: first subject by subject, then point by point.

Dormitory Chef

To this day, I will not eat either macaroni and cheese or tacos. No, it's not because of any allergy; it's because during my freshman year at college, I prepared one or the other of these scrumptious dishes more times than I care to remember. However, my choice of which culinary delight to cook on any given night was not as simple a decision as one might imagine.

Topics

Basis of comparison

Thesis statement: Purpose and limits of comparison

Macaroni and cheese has numerous advantages for the dormitory chef. First of all, it is inexpensive. No matter how poor one may be, there's probably

Paragraph on Subject A: Macaroni and cheese

Point 1 (Price)

enough change under the couch cushion to buy a box at the market. All that starch for just a few dollars. What a bargain! *Second, it can be prepared in just one pan.* This is especially important given the meager resources of the average dorm kitchen. *Third, and perhaps most important, macaroni and cheese is odorless.* By odorless, I mean that no one else can smell it. It is a well-known fact that dorm residents hate to cook and that they love nothing better than to wander dejectedly around the kitchen with big, sad eyes after someone else has been cooking. But with macaroni and cheese, no enticing aromas are going to find their way into the nose of any would-be mooch.

Point 2 (Preparation)
Point 3 (Odor)

Tacos, *on the other hand*, are a different matter altogether. For the dorm cook, *the most significant difference is obviously the price*. To enjoy tacos for dinner, the adventurous dorm gourmet must purchase no fewer than five ingredients from the market: corn tortillas, beef, lettuce, tomatoes, and cheese. Needless to say, this is a major expenditure. *Second, the chef must adroitly shuffle these ingredients back and forth among his or her very limited supply of pans and bowls. Finally, tacos smell great.* That wouldn't be a problem if the tacos didn't also smell great to about twenty of the cook's newest—if not closest—friends, who appear with those same pathetic, starving eyes mentioned earlier. When this happens, the cook will be lucky to get more than two of his own creations.

Paragraph on Subject B: Tacos
Transition
Point 1 (Price)
Point 2 (Preparation)
Point 3 (Odor)

Tacos, then, wouldn't stand much of a chance if they didn't outdo *macaroni and cheese* in one area: taste. Taste is almost—but not quite—an optional requirement in the opinion of a frugal dormitory hash-slinger. Taste is just important enough so that tacos are occasionally prepared, despite their disadvantages.

Subject B
Transition
Subject A
Paragraph on Point 4: Taste

But tacos have other advantages besides their taste. With their enticing, colorful ingredients, they also look good. The only thing that can be said about the color of *macaroni and cheese* is that it's a color not found in nature.

Transition
Paragraph on Point 5: Color
Subject B
Subject A

On the other hand, macaroni and cheese is quick. It can be prepared in about ten minutes while

Transition
Subject A

Paragraph on Point 6: Time   <u>tacos</u> take more than twice as long. Admittedly, there are occasions—such as final exam week—when time is a scarce and precious resource.   Subject B

Transition   <u>As you can see</u>, quite a bit of thinking went into my daily choice of food in my younger years. These two   Summary

Analysis   dishes essentially got me through my freshman year and indirectly taught me how to make important decisions (such as what to eat). <u>However, I still feel a</u>   Concluding statement

<u>certain revulsion when I hear their names today.</u>

Student Writer's Comments

I compare and contrast so many times during a typical day that I took this rhetorical technique for granted. In fact, I had overlooked it completely. The most difficult part of writing this essay was finding two appropriate subjects to compare. Ideally, I knew they should be united by a similarity. So I brainstormed to come up with some possible topics. Then, working from this list of potential subjects, I began to freewrite to see if I could come up with two topics in the same category on which I could write a balanced comparison. Out of my freewriting came this reasoning: Macaroni and cheese and tacos, in reality, are two very different kinds of food from the same category. Proving this fact is easy and might even result in an interesting essay. Their similar property of being popular dorm foods unites the two despite their differences and also gives me two important reasons for writing the comparison: to discover why they are both popular dorm delicacies and to determine which one has more advantages for my particular purposes. In proportion to writing and revising, I spent most of my time choosing my topic, brainstorming, freewriting, and re-brainstorming to make sure I could develop every aspect of my comparison adequately. Most of my prewriting work took the form of two columns in which I recorded my opinions on the choice between macaroni and cheese versus tacos.

Sitting down to mold my lists into an essay posed an entirely new set of problems. From the copious notes I had taken, I easily wrote the introductory paragraph, identifying my topics, explaining the basis of my comparison/contrast, and stating the purpose and limits of my study (my thesis statement). But when I faced the body of the essay, I needed to find the best way to organize my opinions on these two dorm foods: point by point, subject by subject, a combination of these two, or a discussion of similarities and differences?

I wrote my first draft discussing my topics point by point. Even with an occasional joke and a few snide comments interjected, the essay reminded me of a boring game of Ping-Pong with only a few attempts at changing the pace. I started over completely with my second draft and worked through my topics subject by subject. I felt this approach was better, but not quite right for my particular purpose and audience. I set out to do some heavy-handed revising.

Discussing my first three points (price, preparation, and odor) subject by subject seemed to work quite well. I was actually satisfied with the first half of my discussion of these two subjects. But the essay really started to get sluggish when I brought up the fourth point: taste. As a result, I broke off my discussion there and rewrote the second half of my essay point by point, dealing with taste, color, and time each in its own paragraph. This change gave my essay the new direction it needed to keep the readers' attention and also offered me some new insights into my comparison. Then I returned to the beginning of my essay and revised it for readability, adding transitions and making sure the paper now moved smoothly from one point or subject to the next. Finally, I added my final paragraph including a brief summary of my main points and an explanation of the deductions I had made. My con-cluding remark ("However, I still feel a certain revulsion when I hear their names today.") came to me as I was putting the final touches on this draft.

What I learned from writing this particular essay is that comparison/ contrast thinking, more than thinking in other rhetorical modes, is much like a puzzle. I really had to spend an enormous amount of time thinking through, mapping out, and rethinking my comparison before I could start to put my thoughts in essay form. The results are rewarding, but I sure wore out a piece of linoleum on the den floor on the way to my final draft.

SOME FINAL THOUGHTS ON COMPARISON/CONTRAST

The essays in this section demonstrate various methods of organization as well as a number of distinct stylistic approaches to writing a comparison/ contrast essay. As you read these selections, pay particular attention to the clear, well-focused introductions; the different logical methods of organiza-tion; and the smooth transitions between sentences and paragraphs.

AMY CHUA   (1962–   )

Excerpt from Battle Hymn of the Tiger Mother

Born to immigrant Chinese parents in Champaign, Illinois, Amy Chua earned both her B.A. in Economics and her law degree from Harvard University. She is currently the John M. Duff Professor of Law at the Yale Law School specializing in international business transactions, ethnic conflict, and globalization. Her first book, *World on Fire: How Exporting Free Market Democracy Breeds Ethnic Hatred and Global Instability* (2003), explores the conflict caused in many societies by the unequal distribution of economic and political influence. Her second, *Day of Empire: How Hyperpowers Rise to Global Dominance—and Why They Fall* (2007), is a study of the successes and failures of seven major civilizations. With her third book, *Battle Hymn of the Tiger Mother* (2011), Chua ignited a firestorm of controversy by implying that traditional Chinese parents do a much better job of preparing their children for the rigors of life than their Western counterparts. Described by Chua as a "parenting memoir," the book defends the fact that her two daughters, Sophia and Louisa, were never allowed to attend sleepovers, never got grades below an A, never acted in a school play, never watched television or played computer games, and were forced to practice the piano or violin for hours at a time. Reacting to predictable criticism of such "extreme parenting," the author points to her two beautiful, talented, and well-adjusted daughters as proof that her child-rearing philosophy is above reproach. Chua currently lives with her husband, daughters, and Samoyeds in New Haven, Connecticut.

Preparing to Read

The following essay, excerpted from Chua's incendiary *Battle Hymn of the Tiger Mother* compares and contrasts the parenting styles of Chinese versus Western mothers.

Exploring Experience: As you prepare to read this essay, take a few moments to consider your own upbringing: What values did your parents or guardians instill in you? How did they help you learn these values? Who made decisions for you as you were growing up? How did these decisions affect the development of your personality? How did they affect your performance in school? Will you raise your children in the same way you were raised? Why or why not?

LEARNING◯NLINE To get an idea of how different cultures rear children, go to www.babble.com, and search "How They Do It: An Overview of Child Rearing Around the World." Read the various stories about raising children in different countries. As you read Chua's essay, reflect on how you were raised.

Before reading this essay, you may want to consult the flowchart on page 293.

A lot of people wonder how Chinese parents raise such stereotypically   1
successful kids. They wonder what these parents do to produce so
many math whizzes and music prodigies, what it's like inside the
family, and whether they could do it too.[1] Well, I can tell them, because
I've done it. Here are some things my daughters, Sophia and Louisa, were
never allowed to do:

- attend a sleepover
- have a playdate
- be in a school play
- complain about not being in a school play
- watch TV or play computer games
- choose their own extracurricular activities
- get any grade less than an A
- not be the No. 1 student in every subject except gym and drama
- play any instrument other than the piano or violin
- not play the piano or violin.

I'm using the term "Chinese mother" loosely. I know some Korean,   2
Indian, Jamaican, Irish, and Ghanaian parents who qualify too. Conversely,
I know some mothers of Chinese heritage, almost always born in the West,
who are not Chinese mothers, by choice or otherwise. I'm also using the
term "Western parents" loosely. Western parents come in all varieties.

All the same, even when Western parents think they're being strict, they   3
usually don't come close to being Chinese mothers. For example, my Western friends who consider themselves strict make their children practice their
instruments 30 minutes every day. An hour at most. For a Chinese mother,
the first hour is the easy part. It's hours two and three that get tough.

Despite our squeamishness about cultural stereotypes, there are tons of   4
studies out there showing marked and quantifiable differences between Chinese and Westerners when it comes to parenting. In one study of 50 Western
American mothers and 48 Chinese immigrant mothers, almost 70% of the
Western mothers said either that "stressing academic success is not good for
children" or that "parents need to foster the idea that learning is fun." By
contrast, roughly 0% of the Chinese mothers felt the same way. Instead, the
vast majority of the Chinese mothers said that they believe their children
can be "the best" students, that "academic achievement reflects successful
parenting," and that if children did not excel at school then there was "a

---

Thinking Critically

[1] Have you ever wondered why parents in certain ethnic groups seem to raise very
successful, overachieving children?

problem" and parents "were not doing their job." Other studies indicate that compared to Western parents, Chinese parents spend approximately 10 times as long every day drilling academic activities with their children. By contrast, Western kids are more likely to participate in sports teams.[2]

What Chinese parents understand is that nothing is fun until you're good   5 at it. To get good at anything you have to work, and children on their own never want to work, which is why it is crucial to override their preferences. This often requires fortitude on the part of the parents because the child will resist; things are always hardest at the beginning, which is where Western parents tend to give up. But if done properly, the Chinese strategy produces a virtuous circle. Tenacious practice, practice, practice is crucial for excellence; rote repetition is underrated in America. Once a child starts to excel at something—whether it's math, piano, pitching, or ballet—he or she gets praise, admiration, and satisfaction. This builds confidence and makes the once not-fun activity fun. This in turn makes it easier for the parent to get the child to work even more.

Chinese parents can get away with things that Western parents can't.   6 Once when I was young—maybe more than once—when I was extremely disrespectful to my mother, my father angrily called me "garbage" in our native Hokkien dialect. It worked really well. I felt terrible and deeply ashamed of what I had done. But it didn't damage my self-esteem or anything like that. I knew exactly how highly he thought of me. I didn't actually think I was worthless or feel like a piece of garbage.

As an adult, I once did the same thing to Sophia, calling her garbage in   7 English when she acted extremely disrespectfully toward me. When I mentioned that I had done this at a dinner party, I was immediately ostracized. One guest named Marcy got so upset she broke down in tears and had to leave early. My friend Susan, the host, tried to rehabilitate me with the remaining guests.

The fact is that Chinese parents can do things that would seem   8 unimaginable—even legally actionable—to Westerners. Chinese mothers can say to their daughters, "Hey fatty—lose some weight." By contrast, Western parents have to tiptoe around the issue, talking in terms of "health" and never ever mentioning the f-word, and their kids still end up in therapy for eating disorders and negative self-image.[3] (I also once heard a Western

---

Thinking Critically

[2] How does Chua's use of statistics help support her main points? Which do you find more convincing: her personal involvement in the subject matter or her references to outside studies? Why?

[3] What do you think is the best way for parents to help their overweight children? Whose approach would be best: Chinese or Western?

father toast his adult daughter by calling her "beautiful and incredibly competent." She later told me that made her feel like garbage.)

Chinese parents can order their kids to get straight As. Western parents   9
can only ask their kids to try their best. Chinese parents can say, "You're lazy. All your classmates are getting ahead of you." By contrast, Western parents have to struggle with their own conflicted feelings about achievement and try to persuade themselves that they're not disappointed about how their kids turned out.

I've thought long and hard about how Chinese parents can get away with   10
what they do. I think there are three big differences between the Chinese and Western parental mind-sets.

First, I've noticed that Western parents are extremely anxious about their   11
children's self-esteem. They worry about how their children will feel if they fail at something, and they constantly try to reassure their children about how good they are notwithstanding a mediocre performance on a test or at a recital. In other words, Western parents are concerned about their children's psyches. Chinese parents aren't. They assume strength, not fragility, and as a result they behave very differently.

For example, if a child comes home with an A-minus on a test, a Western   12
parent will most likely praise the child. The Chinese mother will gasp in horror and ask what went wrong. If the child comes home with a B on the test, some Western parents will still praise the child. Other Western parents will sit their child down and express disapproval, but they will be careful not to make their child feel inadequate or insecure, and they will not call their child "stupid," "worthless," or "a disgrace." Privately, the Western parents may worry that their child does not test well or have aptitude in the subject or that there is something wrong with the curriculum and possibly the whole school. If the child's grades do not improve, they may eventually schedule a meeting with the school principal to challenge the way the subject is being taught or to call into question the teacher's credentials.

If a Chinese child gets a B—which would never happen—there would   13
first be a screaming, hair-tearing explosion. The devastated Chinese mother would then get dozens, maybe hundreds of practice tests and work through them with her child for as long as it takes to get the grade up to an A.

Chinese parents demand perfect grades because they believe that their   14
child can get them.[4] If their child doesn't get them, the Chinese parent assumes it's because the child didn't work hard enough. That's why the

---

Thinking Critically

[4] Does Chua imply here that Western parents don't have as much faith in their children's potential as Chinese parents do? Do you think this is true? Why or why not?

solution to substandard performance is always to excoriate, punish, and shame the child. The Chinese parent believes that their child will be strong enough to take the shaming and to improve from it. (And when Chinese kids do excel, there is plenty of ego-inflating parental praise lavished in the privacy of the home.)

Second, Chinese parents believe that their kids owe them everything. The reason for this is a little unclear, but it's probably a combination of Confucian filial piety and the fact that the parents have sacrificed and done so much for their children. (And it's true that Chinese mothers get in the trenches, putting in long grueling hours personally tutoring, training, interrogating, and spying on their kids.) Anyway, the understanding is that Chinese children must spend their lives repaying their parents by obeying them and making them proud.   15

By contrast, I don't think most Westerners have the same view of children being permanently indebted to their parents. My husband, Jed, actually has the opposite view. "Children don't choose their parents," he once said to me. "They don't even choose to be born. It's parents who foist life on their kids, so it's the parents' responsibility to provide for them. Kids don't owe their parents anything. Their duty will be to their own kids." This strikes me as a terrible deal for the Western parent.[5]   16

Third, Chinese parents believe that they know what is best for their children and therefore override all of their children's own desires and preferences. That's why Chinese daughters can't have boyfriends in high school and why Chinese kids can't go to sleepaway camp. It's also why no Chinese kids would ever dare say to their mother, "I got a part in the school play! I'm Villager Number Six. I'll have to stay after school for rehearsal every day from 3:00 to 7:00, and I'll also need a ride on weekends." God help any Chinese kid who tried that one.   17

Don't get me wrong: It's not that Chinese parents don't care about their children. Just the opposite. They would give up anything for their children. It's just an entirely different parenting model.   18

Here's a story in favor of coercion, Chinese-style. Lulu was about 7, still playing two instruments and working on a piano piece called "The Little White Donkey" by the French composer Jacques Ibert. The piece is really cute—you can just imagine a little donkey ambling along a country road with its master—but it's also incredibly difficult for young players because the two hands have to keep schizophrenically different rhythms.   19

Thinking Critically

[5] How indebted do you think most Western children are to their parents? Would you say that you love and honor your parents? Why or why not?

Lulu couldn't do it. We worked on it nonstop for a week, drilling each   20
of her hands separately, over and over. But whenever we tried putting the
hands together, one always morphed into the other, and everything fell
apart. Finally, the day before her lesson, Lulu announced in exasperation
that she was giving up and stomped off.

"Get back to the piano now," I ordered.   21

"You can't make me."   22

"Oh yes, I can."   23

Back at the piano, Lulu made me pay. She punched, thrashed, and kicked.   24
She grabbed the music score and tore it to shreds. I taped the score back
together and encased it in a plastic shield so that it could never be destroyed
again. Then I hauled Lulu's dollhouse to the car and told her I'd donate it
to the Salvation Army piece by piece if she didn't have "The Little White
Donkey" perfect by the next day. When Lulu said, "I thought you were
going to the Salvation Army, why are you still here?" I threatened her with
no lunch, no dinner, no Christmas or Hanukkah presents, no birthday parties for two, three, four years. When she still kept playing it wrong, I told
her she was purposely working herself into a frenzy because she was secretly
afraid she couldn't do it. I told her to stop being lazy, cowardly, self-
indulgent, and pathetic.

Jed took me aside. He told me to stop insulting Lulu—which I wasn't   25
even doing, I was just motivating her—and that he didn't think threatening
Lulu was helpful.[6] Also, he said, maybe Lulu really just couldn't do the
technique—perhaps she didn't have the coordination yet—had I considered
that possibility?

"You just don't believe in her," I accused.   26

"That's ridiculous," Jed said scornfully. "Of course I do."   27

"Sophia could play the piece when she was this age."   28

"But Lulu and Sophia are different people," Jed pointed out.   29

"Oh no, not this," I said, rolling my eyes. "Everyone is special in their   30
special own way," I mimicked sarcastically. "Even losers are special in their
own special way. Well don't worry; you don't have to lift a finger. I'm willing to put in as long as it takes, and I'm happy to be the one hated. And you
can be the one they adore because you make them pancakes and take them
to Yankees games."

I rolled up my sleeves and went back to Lulu. I used every weapon and   31
tactic I could think of. We worked right through dinner into the night, and

---

Thinking Critically

[6] What do you think Chua sees as the distinction between "motivating" and "insulting"?
Why does her husband question her treatment of her daughter? Who was being a better
parent at this moment? Who was being more helpful to Lulu?

I wouldn't let Lulu get up, not for water, not even to go to the bathroom. The house became a war zone, and I lost my voice yelling, but still there seemed to be only negative progress, and even I began to have doubts.

Then, out of the blue, Lulu did it. Her hands suddenly came together—her right and left hands each doing their own imperturbable thing—just like that.   32

Lulu realized it the same time I did. I held my breath. She tried it tentatively again. Then she played it more confidently and faster, and still the rhythm held. A moment later, she was beaming.   33

"Mommy, look—it's easy!" After that, she wanted to play the piece over and over and wouldn't leave the piano. That night, she came to sleep in my bed, and we snuggled and hugged, cracking each other up. When she performed "The Little White Donkey" at a recital a few weeks later, parents came up to me and said, "What a perfect piece for Lulu—it's so spunky and so *her*."   34

Even Jed gave me credit for that one. Western parents worry a lot about their children's self-esteem. But as a parent, one of the worst things you can do for your child's self-esteem is to let them give up. On the flip side, there's nothing better for building confidence than learning you can do something you thought you couldn't. [7]   35

There are all these new books out there portraying Asian mothers as scheming, callous, overdriven people indifferent to their kids' true interests. For their part, many Chinese secretly believe that they care more about their children and are willing to sacrifice much more for them than Westerners, who seem perfectly content to let their children turn out badly. I think it's a misunderstanding on both sides. All decent parents want to do what's best for their children. The Chinese just have a totally different idea of how to do that.   36

Western parents try to respect their children's individuality, encouraging them to pursue their true passions, supporting their choices, and providing positive reinforcement and a nurturing environment. By contrast, the Chinese believe that the best way to protect their children is by preparing them for the future, letting them see what they're capable of, and arming them with skills, work habits, and inner confidence that no one can ever take away.   37

UNDERSTANDING DETAILS

1. According to the author, what are the main characteristics of "Chinese mothers"?
2. Explain in your own words the three primary differences between Chinese and Western mothers.

Thinking Critically

[7] According to Chua, what is the relationship between success and self-esteem? Do you agree with her? Why or why not?

3. What role does Jed play in this essay?
4. How important is self-esteem in both the Chinese home and the Western home?

READING CRITICALLY

5. What is your general reaction to Chua's parenting strategies? Explain your answer in detail.
6. What major philosophical differences separate Chinese parents from Western parents?
7. How does your upbringing compare to the Chinese approach? Give at least two examples to demonstrate the similarities or differences.
8. Does Chua's story of Lulu and "The Little White Donkey" persuade you that coercion works in raising children? Explain your answer.

DISCOVERING RHETORICAL STRATEGIES

9. What is Chua's general purpose in this essay?
10. Do you think starting this essay with a list of "things my daughters, Sophia and Louisa, were never allowed to do" (paragraph 1) is effective or not? Explain your answer.
11. Who is Chua's primary audience?
12. What rhetorical strategies besides comparison and contrast does Chua use to get her message across?

MAKING CONNECTIONS

13. Chua, Sandra Cisneros ("Only Daughter"), Amy Tan ("Mother Tongue"), and Michael Dorris ("The Broken Cord") all discuss the relationship between parents and children. How do any of these authors that you have read differ in their prescriptions for raising children?
14. Chua's battle with her daughter over learning to play "The Little White Donkey" on the piano (paragraphs 19–34) echoes examples of determination displayed in Lewis Sawaquat's "For My Indian Daughter," Maya Angelou's "New Directions," and Kenneth Miller's "Class Act." Which author of those that you have read overcame the most difficult challenge? Why do you believe this?
15. Analyze the principal differences between the manner in which Chua employs comparison/contrast to structure her essay and the way the following authors use the same technique: Motoko Rich ("Literacy Debate"), Gloria Steinem ("The Politics of Muscle"), and/or John Tierney ("A Generation's Vanity, Heard Through Lyrics"). Who uses this rhetorical mode most effectively? Explain your reasoning with examples from these essays.

IDEAS FOR DISCUSSION/WRITING

Preparing to Write

Write freely about your upbringing: List some activities your parents would not allow you to do. How important were these activities to you? What choices did your parents make for you in high school? What choices did they let you make for yourself? To what extent do you think these choices affected your performance in school? Were you motivated to study in high school? How do you account for your degree of motivation?

Choosing a Topic   MyWritingLab™

1. **LEARNING⏻NLINE** After reading Chua's essay, what do you think of her parenting style? Write an essay comparing and contrasting the way you were raised with methods of parenting in other cultures, drawing in particular on the overview from Preparing to Read and Chua's essay. Ask your parents for details and clarification about your own upbringing. If you have one or more children of your own, compare and contrast your parenting style with that of others.

2. Compare and/or contrast the upbringing of two of your friends. Interview your friends and their parents to gain insight into the values they hold and the choices they made.

3. Analyze your relationship with two different people based on how they were raised. How influential was their upbringing on their relationships with you? What parts of your upbringing most dramatically affected your ability to make and maintain friendships with them?

4. In response to Chua's essay, choose one of her parenting guidelines, and launch an argument for or against it based on your personal experience. Support your argument with elements from this article and/or other sources as appropriate.

Before beginning your essay, you may want to consult the flowchart on page 296.

ADAM GOPNIK   (1956–   )

How Lincoln and Darwin Shaped the Modern World

Adam Gopnik was born in Philadelphia, Pennsylvania, to Irwin and Myrna Gopnik, both professors at McGill University. After growing up in Montreal, Canada, where he and his family lived in Habitat 67, a world-famous model community experiment, Gopnik received his BA from McGill University and completed graduate work at the New York University of Fine Arts. He began writing for *The New Yorker* in 1986, contributing fiction, humor, book reviews, essays, and art criticism. In 1995, he became the magazine's Paris correspondent. His "Paris Journals," essays describing life in Paris, were later collected and published in a book entitled *Paris to the Moon* (2000), which eventually became a *New York Times* best seller. Gopnik's other books include *Through the Children's Gate* (2006), a comedy on parenting; *The King in the Window* (2005) and *The Steps Across the Water* (2010), both children's novels; *Angels and Ages* (2010); and *Winter: Five Windows on the Season* (2011). His most recent book is *The Table Comes First* (2011), which is about food, cooking, and restaurants. He has also worked with the BBC, has been awarded three National Magazine Awards for Essay and Criticism, as well as the George Polk Award for Magazine Reporting. Gopnik is currently a staff writer for *The New Yorker* and lives in New York with his wife, Martha Parker, and their two children.

Preparing to Read

Adapted by the author from his book *Angels and Ages,* "How Lincoln and Darwin Shaped the Modern World" explains how two unassuming individuals, born on the same day in two different countries, came to develop into major historical figures as they naturally took the lead in different aspects of the modern world.

Exploring Experience: As you prepare to read this essay, consider your natural inclination to take the lead in certain circumstances: When are you comfortable stepping into the lead? What are you passionate about? What do you want to change in society? Why do you want to make changes in this area? Do you think you will leave any legacies behind from your life?

LEARNING◯NLINE To get a sense of the historical figures discussed in this essay, visit Biography.com, and search both Abraham Lincoln and Charles Darwin. Peruse the links associated with the two men, and take a few notes on the impact they made on the world. Then use your notes as a context for the following essay.

Before reading this essay, you may want to consult the flowchart on page 293.

We are all pebbles dropped in the sea of history, where the splash strikes one way and the big tides run another, and though what we *feel* is the splash, the splash takes place only within those tides.[1] In almost every case, the incoming current drowns the splash; once in a while the drop of the pebble changes the way the ocean runs. On February 12, 1809, two boys were born within a few hours of each other on either side of the Atlantic. One entered life in a comfortable family home, nicely called the Mount, that still stands in the leafy English countryside of Shrewsbury, Shropshire; the other opened his eyes for the first time in a nameless, long-lost log cabin in the Kentucky woods. Charles Darwin was the fifth of six children, born into comfort but to a family that was far from "safe," with a long history of free-thinking and radical beliefs. He came into a world of learning and money—one grandfather, Josiah Wedgwood, had made a fortune in ceramic plates. Abraham Lincoln was the second of three, born to a dirt-poor farmer, Thomas Lincoln, who, when he wrote his name at all, wrote it (his son recalled) "bunglingly."

The two boys born on the same day into such different lives had become, as they remain, improbable public figures of that alteration of minds—they had become what are now called in cliché "icons," secular saints. They hadn't made the change, but they had helped to midwife the birth. With the usual compression of popular history, their reputations have been reduced to single words, mottoes to put beneath a profile on a commemorative coin or medal: "Evolution!" for one and "Emancipation!" for the other.[2] Though, with the usual irony of history, the mottoes betray the men. Lincoln came late—in the eyes of Frederick Douglass, maddeningly late—and reluctantly to emancipation, while perhaps the least original thing in Darwin's amazingly original work was the idea of evolution. (He figured out how it ran; he took a fancy poetic figure that his granddad, Erasmus Darwin, had favored and put an engine and a fan belt in it.) We're not wrong to work these beautiful words onto their coins, though: they were the engineers of the alterations. They found a way to make those words live. Darwin and Lincoln did not make the modern world. But, by becoming "icons" of free human government and slow natural change, they helped to make our moral modernity.

The shared date of their birth is, obviously, "merely" a coincidence— what historians like to call an "intriguing coincidence." But coincidence is

---

Thinking Critically

[1] Explain the metaphor of the pebbles in the sea of history in your own words. How does this set up your expectations for this essay?

[2] What other single words, besides "Evolution" and Emancipation," describe the accomplishments of these two men?

the vernacular of history, the slang of memory—the first strong pattern where we begin to search for more subtle ones. Like the simultaneous deaths of Thomas Jefferson and John Adams on July 4, 1826, the accidental patterns of birth and death point to other patterns of coincidence in bigger things. Lincoln and Darwin can be seen as symbols of the two pillars of the society we live in: one representing liberal democracy and a faith in armed republicanism and government of the people; the other the human sciences, a belief that objective knowledge about human history and the human condition, who we are and how we got here, exists. This makes them, plausibly, "heroes." But they are also amazing men, something more than heroes, defined by their private struggles as much as by their public acts. [3]

Both men are our contemporaries still, [4] because they were among the   4
first big men in history who belonged to what is sometimes called "the bourgeois ascendancy." They were family men. They loved their wives uxoriously, lived for their children and were proud of their houses. Darwin was born to money, and though he kept some gentry tastes and snobberies, like the royal family of Albert and Victoria, who superintended most of his life, he chose to live not in imitation of the old aristocracy but in the manner of the new bourgeoisie—involving his children in every element of his life, having them help with his experiments, writing an autobiography for them and very nearly sacrificing his chance at history for the love of his religious wife. Lincoln's rise in history was to the presidency— but his first and perhaps even harder rise was to the big middle-class house and expensive wife he adored. What we wonder at is that a simple Springfield lawyer could become president; from his point of view, what probably was really amazing was that a cabin-born bumpkin had become a Springfield lawyer.

Both men were shaped in crucial ways by the worst of still-present   5
19th-century woes, the death of children at the height of their charm and wisdom. They both even had what one might call the symptomatic diseases of middle-class modernity, the kind that we pick out among the great roll call of human ills to name and obsess over. Lincoln was a depressive; Darwin subject to anxiety so severe that he wrote down one of the most formidable definitions of a panic attack that exists. Though the source of these ailments—in nature or genes, bugs or traumas—remains mysterious, their presence, the way they manifested themselves, is part of the familiarity the

---

Thinking Critically

[3] Do you know anyone in your immediate environment who has become a hero because of his or her accomplishments?

[4] How can both men still be our contemporaries when they are no longer alive?

two men have for all the distance between us. They had the same domestic pleasures, and the same domestic demons, as we do.

We must be realistic about what they were like: not saints nor heroes nor Gods but people.[5] Darwin and Lincoln are admirable and in their way even lovable men. But Lincoln, we have always to remember, was a war commander who had men shot and boy deserters hanged. We would, I think, be taken aback at a meeting. Lincoln summed up in one word was *shrewd*, a backwoods lawyer with a keen sense of human weakness and a knack for clever argument, colder than we would think, and more of a pol and more of a wiseguy than we would like him to be: someone more concerned with winning—elections, cases and arguments—than with looking noble. Lincoln was smart, shrewd and ambitious before he was, as he became, wise, far-seeing and self-sacrificing. If we were around to watch him walk across a room, instead of stride through history, what we would see is the normal feet that left the noble prints.

Darwin we would likely find far more frumpy and tedious than we would like our heroes to be—one of those naturalists who run on and on narrowly on their pet subjects. He would have frowned and furrowed his brow and made helpless discomfited harrumphs if any of today's fervent admirers arrived and asked him what he thought of man's innate tendencies to relish Tchaikovsky. One can easily imagine him brought back to earth and forced onto a television studio platform with eager admirers (like this one) pressing him for his views on sexual equality or the origins of the love of melody in the ancient savanna, and his becoming more and more unhappy and inarticulate, and at last swallowed up in a vast, sad, melancholy, embarrassed English moan.

Not that Lincoln didn't care about morality, but he cared more about winning wars and arguments than about appearing to be a paragon. Not that Darwin wasn't interested in speculative consequences of his theory, he was—but the habit of pontification was completely alien to him, unless it was reassuringly tied with a bow of inductive observation.

Fifty years ago, not many would have chosen Darwin and Lincoln as central figures of the modern imagination. Freud and Marx would perhaps have been the minds that we saw as the princes of our disorder. But with the moral (and lesser intellectual) failure of Marxism, and the intellectual (and lesser moral) failure of Freud, their ideas have retreated back into the history of modernity, of the vast systematic ideas that proposed to explain it

---

Thinking Critically

5 Why is the point about these men being "not saints nor heroes nor Gods but people" important to Gopnik's main message?

all to you. Lincoln and Darwin, by contrast, have never been more present: Lincoln is the subject of what seems to be the largest biographical literature outside those of Jesus and Napoleon, while Darwin continues not only to cause daily fights but to inspire whole new sciences—or is it pseudosciences? For the irony is that the most radical thing around, at the birth of the new millennium, turned out to be liberal civilization—both the parliamentary, "procedural" liberalism of which Lincoln, for all his inspirational gifts, was an adherent, and the scientific liberalism, the tradition of cautious pragmatic free thought, that engaged Darwin, who was skeptical of grand systems even as he created one. Science and democracy still look like the hope of the world (even as we recognize that their intersection gave us the means to burn alive every living thing on the planet at will).

The deepest common stuff the two men share, though, is in what they said and wrote—their mastery of a new kind of liberal language. They matter most because they wrote so well. Lincoln got to be president essentially because he made a couple of terrific speeches, and we remember him most of all because he gave a few more as president. Darwin was a writer who published his big ideas in popular books. A commercial publishing house published *The Origin of Species* in the same year that it published novels and memoirs, and Darwin's work remains probably the only book that changed science in ways that an amateur can still sit down now and read right through. It's so well written that we don't think of it as well written, just as Lincoln's speeches are so well made that they seem to us as obvious and natural as smooth stones on the beach. (We don't think, "Well said!" we just think, "That's right!")   10

Darwin and Lincoln helped remake our language and forge a new kind of rhetoric that we still respond to in politics and popular science alike. They *particularized* in everything, and their general vision rises from the details and the nuance, their big ideas from small sightings. They shared logic as a form of eloquence, argument as a style of virtue, close reasoning as a form of uplift. Each, using a kind of technical language—the fine, detailed language of naturalist science for Darwin; the tedious language of legal reasoning for the American—arrived at a new ideal of liberal speech. The way that Darwin uses insanely detailed technical arguments about the stamen of an orchid to pay off, many pages later, in a vast cosmic point about the nature of survival and change on a planetary time scale, and the way that Lincoln uses lawyerly arguments about who signed what and when among the Founders to make the case for war, if necessary, to end slavery—these things have in common their hope, their faith, in plain English, that people's minds and hearts can be altered by the slow crawl of fact as much as by the long reach of revelation. Their phrases still ring because they were struck on bells cast of solid bronze, not chimes set blowing in the breeze.   11

In all these ways—their love of family, their shrewdness and sensitivity, their invention of a new kind of plain speaking—these two men are worth looking at together precisely because they *aren't* particularly remarkable. The things that they loved and pursued, the things that intrigued and worried them, were the same things that most other intelligent people in their day worried about and that worry and intrigue us still. Even mountains are made of pebbles, built up over time, and an entire mountain range of minds has risen slowly between them and us. Most of the rest have been submerged by time, but Darwin and Lincoln remain high peaks within those mountains of modernity, and they look out toward each other. From the top of one you can see the other, and what you see is what we are.

12

UNDERSTANDING DETAILS

1. What is Gopnik's primary message in this essay?
2. According to Gopnik, what are the major differences in the families of these two famous men?
3. Explain "the bourgeois ascendancy" (paragraph 4) in your own words.
4. In what ways are Lincoln and Darwin both heroes?

READING CRITICALLY

5. What clues in the first paragraph help you predict what this essay will be about?
6. Why were both Lincoln and Darwin "improbable public figures" (paragraph 2)?
7. Why does Gopnik call Darwin and Lincoln "central figures of the modern imagination" (paragraph 9)? What characteristics do they share that qualifies them for this label?
8. In what ways did their writing contribute to our definition of society today?

DISCOVERING RHETORICAL STRATEGIES

9. What does the title convey to you?
10. Who do you think is Gopnik's intended audience?
11. List Gopnik's main points, and explain how his essay is organized.
12. Gopnik begins and ends his essay with a metaphor that compares us to pebbles in the first paragraph and Lincoln and Darwin to high peaks on a mountain range in the last paragraph. Is this an effective beginning and end for this essay? Why or why not? How do these metaphor provide a frame for the essay?

MAKING CONNECTIONS

13. Imagine that Gopnik is discussing the concept of heroism with NASA ("What Is Mars?"), Barbara Ehrenreich ("Nickel and Dimed"), Amy Tan ("Mother Tongue"), and/or Dave Grossman ("We Are Training Our Kids to Kill"). How differently would any of these authors you have read see heroism? What qualities would they say make a hero?
14. Compare and contrast Gopnik's comments about accomplishments with similar acknowledgments offered by Sandra Cisneros ("Only Daughter"), Gloria

Steinem ("The Politics of Muscle"), and/or Wayne Norman ("When Is a Sport Not a Sport?"). Which of these authors would you agree with most about what makes a noteworthy accomplishment? Why would you agree with that author?

15. How does Gopnik use the rhetorical technique of comparison/contrast differently than Motoko Rich ("Literacy Debate: Online, R U Really Reading") and/or John Tierney ("A Generation's Vanity, Heard Through Lyrics")? Which author's essay were you able to follow most easily? Explain your answer.

IDEAS FOR DISCUSSION/WRITING

Preparing to Write

Write freely about your desire (or lack of desire) to make a change in society today: What would you like to change? Why do you want to make a change in this area? On what do you base this decision? Would you be willing to take on a leadership role in this area? Why would you take on this role? How would you carry it out? What would be your primary goal in this role?

Choosing a Topic

MyWritingLab™

1. **LEARNING⏻NLINE** After visiting Biography.com from Preparing to Read and reading Gopnik's article, what are some of the differences between our historical perception of Lincoln and Darwin and the more mundane details of their real lives? Imagine that, in 50 years, someone has written a Biography.com article about you. What would be the highlights? How would those details be different from what you actually accomplish in your life?

2. Compare and/or contrast the roles you expect to achieve in your life with the roles your parents or guardians had in theirs. Will you be more or less involved in leadership than your parents/guardians were? Why will you choose these particular roles in your lives?

3. A classmate of yours is considering running for president of the student body. In preparation for talking to her, record your thoughts in essay form about whether or not running for office is a good idea. What are the pros and cons of this decision? What do you recommend?

4. Are you more committed to school, work, or family at this point in your life? What are your reasons for this commitment? Does the commitment fluctuate during the year? Explain your response in an essay written for your classmates.

Before beginning your essay, you may want to consult the flowchart on pages 296.

MOTOKO RICH (1971–)

Literacy Debate: Online, R U Really Reading?

An economics writer for *The New York Times* since May 2010, Motoko Rich was born in Los Angeles and raised biculturally in Japan and California. After earning a history degree *summa cum laude* from Yale and an English degree from Cambridge University, she began her journalism career at the *Financial Times* in London and then worked as a staff reporter for *The Wall Street Journal* for six years. She joined *The New York Times* in 2003, reporting for the House and Home section, then moved to the Style section, where she covered real estate trends. In 2008, she began writing a series of articles about how the Internet and other technological advances are changing the way people read. In her current role as a writer on economic issues, Rich has published articles on a wide range of topics, including optimism and the American dream, job losses during the financial crisis, the United States Mortgage Relief Program, economic insecurity, the gap in STEM field achievement between native-born and foreign-born college graduates, sex-abuse scandals, foreign retailers in India, the economic lessons in children's books, and minimum wage jobs. Rich, who lives in Brooklyn with her husband, Mark Topping, and their two children, advises students to spend time reading books rather than surfing the Web: "Hours spent prowling the Internet are the enemy of reading—diminishing literacy [and] wrecking attention spans." More recently, Rich has been writing for *The New York Times,* where she focuses on the U.S. economy, using employment data, consumer spending, manufacturing, and finances to humanize statistics and find trends.

Preparing to Read

First published in *The New York Times* (July 27, 2008), "Literacy Debate: Online, R U Really Reading?" examines whether reading "in the digital age" is making our society more or less literate.

Exploring Experience: As you prepare to read this essay, think about your own reading habits: What types of reading do you do in a typical week? Do you read both printed and online material? Do you enjoy both types? Which do you think is most important for your academic success? Which do you think is most important for becoming a well-rounded, literate human being? How might reading all kinds of material prepare you for life beyond college?

LEARNING⏻NLINE Before reading Rich's essay, spend at least 15 minutes online, reading some of your favorite websites. What do you like to read when you are online? Are there different types of online reading? How is reading online different from reading offline? Do you prefer one over the other? Explain your answer.

Before reading this essay, you may want to consult the flowchart on page 293.

Books are not Nadia Konyk's thing. Her mother, hoping to entice   1
her, brings them home from the library, but Nadia rarely shows an
interest. Instead, like so many other teenagers, Nadia, 15, is addicted
to the Internet. She regularly spends at least six hours a day in front of the
computer here in this suburb southwest of Cleveland.

A slender, chatty blonde who wears black-framed plastic glasses, Nadia   2
checks her e-mail and peruses myyearbook.com, a social networking site, reading messages or posting updates on her mood. She searches for music videos
on YouTube and logs onto Gaia Online, a role-playing site where members
fashion alternate identities as cutesy cartoon characters. But she spends most of
her time on quizilla.com or fanfiction.net, reading and commenting on stories
written by other users and based on books, television shows or movies.❶

Her mother, Deborah Konyk, would prefer that Nadia, who gets A's and   3
B's at school, read books for a change. But at this point, Ms. Konyk said,
"I'm just pleased that she reads something anymore."

Children like Nadia lie at the heart of a passionate debate about just what   4
it means to read in the digital age. The discussion is playing out among
educational policy makers and reading experts around the world, and within
groups like the National Council of Teachers of English and the International Reading Association.

As teenagers' scores on standardized reading tests have declined or stag-   5
nated, some argue that the hours spent prowling the Internet are the enemy
of reading—diminishing literacy, wrecking attention spans, and destroying
a precious common culture that exists only through the reading of books.

But others say the Internet has created a new kind of reading, one that   6
schools and society should not discount. The Web inspires a teenager like
Nadia, who might otherwise spend most of her leisure time watching television, to read and write.

Even accomplished book readers like Zachary Sims, 18, of Old Green-   7
wich, Connecticut, crave the ability to quickly find different points of view
on a subject and converse with others online. Some children with dyslexia
or other learning difficulties, like Hunter Gaudet, 16, of Somers, Connecticut, have found it far more comfortable to search and read online.

At least since the invention of television, critics have warned that elec-   8
tronic media would destroy reading. What is different now, some literacy
experts say, is that spending time on the Web, whether it is looking up
something on Google or even britneyspears.org, entails some engagement
with text.

Thinking Critically

❶ How effective is it for Rich to begin her essay with personal details about a specific
teenager? To what extent did this opening grab your attention?

Setting Expectations

Few who believe in the potential of the Web deny the value of books. But   9
they argue that it is unrealistic to expect all children to read *To Kill a Mocking-
bird* or *Pride and Prejudice* for fun. [2] And those who prefer staring at a television
or mashing buttons on a game console, they say, can still benefit from reading
on the Internet. In fact, some literacy experts say that online reading skills will
help children fare better when they begin looking for digital-age jobs.

Some Web evangelists say children should be evaluated for their proficiency   10
on the Internet just as they are tested on their print reading comprehension.
Starting next year, some countries will participate in new international assessment of digital literacy, but the United States, for now, will not.

Clearly, reading in print and on the Internet are different. On paper, text   11
has a predetermined beginning, middle, and end, where readers focus for a
sustained period on one author's vision. On the Internet, readers skate
through cyberspace at will and, in effect, compose their own beginnings,
middles, and ends.

Young people "aren't as troubled as some of us older folks are by reading   12
that doesn't go in a line," said Rand J. Spiro, a professor of educational psychology at Michigan State University who is studying reading practices on
the Internet. "That's a good thing because the world doesn't go in a line
and the world isn't organized into separate compartments or chapters."

Some traditionalists warn that digital reading is the intellectual equivalent   13
of empty calories. [3] Often, they argue, writers on the Internet employ a
cryptic argot that vexes teachers and parents. Zigzagging through a cornu-
copia of words, pictures, video, and sounds, they say, distracts more than
strengthens readers. And many youths spend most of their time on the
Internet playing games or sending instant messages, activities that involve
minimal reading at best. . . .

"Whatever the benefits of newer electronic media," Dana Gioia, the   14
chairman of the N.E.A., wrote in the report's introduction, "they provide
no measurable substitute for the intellectual and personal development initiated and sustained by frequent reading."

The question of how to value different kinds of reading is complicated   15
because people read for many reasons. There is the level required of daily
life—to follow the instructions in a manual or to analyze a mortgage

---

Thinking Critically

[2] Have you read any books "for fun" recently? Which ones? Did you enjoy them? Why
or why not?

[3] How is "digital reading" equivalent to "empty calories"? What other metaphors does the
author use in the same paragraph (13)?

contract. Then there is a more sophisticated level that opens the doors to elite education and professions. And, of course, people read for entertainment, as well as for intellectual or emotional rewards. It is perhaps that final purpose that book champions emphasize the most.

"Learning is not to be found on a printout," David McCullough, the   16
Pulitzer Prize-winning biographer, said in a commencement address at Boston College in May. "It's not on call at the touch of the finger. Learning is acquired mainly from books and most readily from great books."

What's Best for Nadia?

Deborah Konyk always believed it was essential for Nadia and her 8-year-   17
old sister, Yashca, to read books. She regularly read aloud to the girls and took them to library story hours. "Reading opens up doors to places that you probably will never get to visit in your lifetime, to cultures, to worlds, to people," Ms. Konyk said.

Ms. Konyk, who took a part-time job at a dollar store chain a year and a   18
half ago, said she did not have much time to read books herself. There are few books in the house. But after Yashca was born, Ms. Konyk spent the baby's nap time reading the Harry Potter novels to Nadia, and she regularly brought home new titles from the library.

Despite these efforts, Nadia never became a big reader. Instead, she   19
became obsessed with Japanese anime cartoons on television and comics like "Sailor Moon." Then, when she was in the sixth grade, the family bought its first computer. When a friend introduced Nadia to fanfiction.net, she turned off the television and started reading online. Now she regularly reads stories that run as long as 45 Web pages. Many of them have elliptical plots and are sprinkled with spelling and grammatical errors. One of her recent favorites was "My absolutely perfect normal life . . . ARE YOU CRAZY? NOT!," a story based on the anime series "Beyblade." In one scene, the narrator, Aries, hitches a ride with some masked men and one of them pulls a knife on her. "Just then I notice (Like finally) something sharp right in front of me," Aries writes. "I gladly took it just like that until something terrible happened. . . ."

Nadia said she preferred reading stories online because "you could add   20
your own character and twist it the way you want it to be." "So like in the book somebody could die," she continued, "but you could make it so that person doesn't die or make it so like somebody else dies who you don't like."

Nadia also writes her own stories. She posted "Dieing Isn't Always Bad,"   21
about a girl who comes back to life as half cat, half human, on both fanfiction.net and quizilla.com.

Nadia said she wanted to major in English at college and someday hopes   22
to be published. She does not see a problem with reading few books. "No
one's ever said you should read more books to get into college," she said. [4]

The simplest argument for why children should read in their leisure time   23
is that it makes them better readers. According to federal statistics, students
who say they read for fun once a day score significantly higher on reading
tests than those who say they never do.

Reading skills are also valued by employers. A 2006 survey by the Conference   24
Board, which conducts research for business leaders, found that nearly 90 percent of employers rated "reading comprehension" as "very important" for
workers with bachelor's degrees. Department of Education statistics also show
that those who score higher on reading tests tend to earn higher incomes.

Critics of reading on the Internet say they see no evidence that increased   25
Web activity improves reading achievement. "What we are losing in this country and presumably around the world is the sustained, focused, linear attention
developed by reading," said Mr. Gioia of the N.E.A. "I would believe people
who tell me that the Internet develops reading if I did not see such a universal
decline in reading ability and reading comprehension on virtually all tests."

Nicholas Carr sounded a similar note in "Is Google Making Us Stupid?"   26
in the *Atlantic* magazine. Warning that the Web was changing the way he—
and others—think, he suggested that the effects of Internet reading extended
beyond the falling test scores of adolescence. [5] "What the Net seems to be
doing is chipping away my capacity for concentration and contemplation,"
he wrote, confessing that he now found it difficult to read long books.

Literacy specialists are just beginning to investigate how reading on the   27
Internet affects reading skills. A recent study of more than 700 low-income,
mostly Hispanic and black sixth through 10th graders in Detroit found that
those students read more on the Web than in any other medium, though
they also read books. The only kind of reading that related to higher academic performance was frequent novel reading, which predicted better
grades in English class and higher overall grade point averages.

Elizabeth Birr Moje, a professor at the University of Michigan who led   28
the study, said novel reading was similar to what schools demand already.
But on the Internet, she said, students are developing new reading skills that
are neither taught nor evaluated in school.

One early study showed that giving home Internet access to low-income   29
students appeared to improve standardized reading test scores and school
grades. "These were kids who would typically not be reading in their free

---

Thinking Critically

[4] Do you think reading books makes people smarter? If so, how?

[5] Do you believe using the Internet has changed the way you think? Why or why not?

time," said Linda A. Jackson, a psychology professor at Michigan State who led the research. "Once they're on the Internet, they're reading."

Neurological studies show that learning to read changes the brain's cir-   30
cuitry. Scientists speculate that reading on the Internet may also affect the brain's hard wiring in a way that is different from book reading.

"The question is, does it change your brain in some beneficial way?" said   31
Guinevere F. Eden, director of the Center for the Study of Learning at Georgetown University. "The brain is malleable and adapts to its environment. Whatever the pressures are on us to succeed, our brain will try and deal with it." [6]

Some scientists worry that the fractured experience typical of the Internet   32
could rob developing readers of crucial skills. "Reading a book, and taking the time to ruminate and make inferences and engage the imaginational processing, is more cognitively enriching, without doubt, than the short little bits that you might get if you're into the 30-second digital mode," said Ken Pugh, a cognitive neuroscientist at Yale who has studied brain scans of children reading.

But This Is Reading Too

Web proponents believe that strong readers on the Web may eventually   33
surpass those who rely on books. Reading five websites, an op-ed article, and a blog post or two, experts say, can be more enriching than reading one book. "It takes a long time to read a 400-page book," said Mr. Spiro of Michigan State. "In a tenth of the time," he said, the Internet allows a reader to "cover a lot more of the topic from different points of view."

Zachary Sims, the Old Greenwich, Connecticut, teenager, often stays   34
awake until 2 or 3 in the morning reading articles about technology or politics—his current passions—on up to 100 websites. "On the Internet, you can hear from a bunch of people," said Zachary, who will attend Columbia University this fall. "They may not be pedigreed academics. They may be someone in their shed with a conspiracy theory. But you would weigh that."

Though he also likes to read books (earlier this year he finished and loved   35
"The Fountainhead" by Ayn Rand), Zachary craves interaction with fellow readers on the Internet. "The Web is more about a conversation," he said. "Books are more one-way."

The kinds of skills Zachary has developed—locating information quickly   36
and accurately, corroborating findings on multiple sites—may seem obvious to heavy Web users. But the skills can be cognitively demanding. Web

---

Thinking Critically

6 In what ways do these references to other scholars and authors establish Rich's credibility?

readers are persistently weak at judging whether information is trustworthy. In one study, Donald J. Leu, who researches literacy and technology at the University of Connecticut, asked 48 students to look at a spoof web-site (http://zapatopi.net/treeoctopus/) about a mythical species known as the "Pacific Northwest tree octopus." Nearly 90 percent of them missed the joke and deemed the site a reliable source.

Some literacy experts say that reading itself should be redefined. Inter-   37
preting videos or pictures, they say, may be as important a skill as analyz-ing a novel or a poem.⑦ "Kids are using sound and images so they have a world of ideas to put together that aren't necessarily language oriented," said Donna E. Alvermann, a professor of language and literacy education at the University of Georgia. "Books aren't out of the picture, but they're only one way of experiencing information in the world today."

A Lifelong Struggle

In the case of Hunter Gaudet, the Internet has helped him feel more   38
comfortable with a new kind of reading. A varsity lacrosse player in Somers, Connecticut, Hunter has struggled most of his life to read. After learning he was dyslexic in the second grade, he was placed in special education classes, and a tutor came to his home three hours a week. When he entered high school, he dropped the special education classes, but he still reads books only when forced, he said. In a book, "they go through a lot of details that aren't really needed," Hunter said. "Online just gives you what you need, nothing more or less." When researching the 19th-century Chief Justice Roger B. Taney for one class, he typed Taney's name into Google and scanned the Wikipedia entry and other biographical sites. Instead of reading an entire page, he would type in a search word like "college" to find Taney's alma mater, assembling his information nugget by nugget.

Experts on reading difficulties suggest that for struggling readers, the Web   39
may be a better way to glean information. "When you read online there are always graphics," said Sally Shaywitz, the author of "Overcoming Dyslexia" and a Yale professor. "I think it's just more comfortable and—I hate to say easier—but it more meets the needs of somebody who might not be a fluent reader."

Karen Gaudet, Hunter's mother, a regional manager for a retail chain   40
who said she read two or three business books a week, hopes Hunter will eventually discover a love for books. But she is confident that he has the reading skills he needs to succeed. "Based on where technology is going and the world is going," she said, "he's going to be able to leverage it."

Thinking Critically

⑦ Do you think this assertion about interpretation of images is true?

When he was in seventh grade, Hunter was one of 89 students who par-   41
ticipated in a study comparing performance on traditional state reading tests
with a specially designed Internet reading test. Hunter, who scored in the
lowest 10 percent on the traditional test, spent 12 weeks learning how to
use the Web for a science class before taking the Internet test. It was composed of three sets of directions asking the students to search for information
online, determine which sites were reliable, and explain their reasoning.
Hunter scored in the top quartile. In fact, about a third of the students in
the study, led by Professor Leu, scored below average on traditional reading
tests but did well on the Internet assessment.

The Testing Debate

To date, there have been few large-scale appraisals of Web skills. The   42
Educational Testing Service, which administers the SAT, has developed a
digital literacy test known as iSkills that requires students to solve informational problems by searching for answers on the Web. About 80 colleges and
a handful of high schools have administered the test so far.

But according to Stephen Denis, product manager at ETS, of the more   43
than 20,000 students who have taken the iSkills test since 2006, only 39
percent of four-year college freshmen achieved a score that represented
"core functional levels" in Internet literacy. Now some literacy experts want
the federal tests known as the nation's report card to include a digital reading
component. . . . Mary Crovo of the National Assessment Governing Board,
which creates policies for the national tests, said several members of a committee that sets guidelines for the reading tests believed large numbers of
low-income and rural students might not have regular Internet access, ren-
dering measurements of their online skills unfair.

Some simply argue that reading on the Internet is not something that   44
needs to be tested—or taught. "Nobody has taught a single kid to text
message," said Carol Jago of the National Council of Teachers of English
and a member of the testing guidelines committee. "Kids are smart. When
they want to do something, schools don't have to get involved." Michael
L. Kamil, a professor of education at Stanford who lobbied for an Internet
component as chairman of the reading test guidelines committee, disagreed.
Students "are going to grow up having to be highly competent on the Internet," he said. "There's no reason to make them discover how to be highly
competent if we can teach them." [8]

Thinking Critically

[8] What is your position on this issue? Should students be taught how to read on the Internet? If so, who should teach them? Their parents? Friends? Schools?

The United States is diverging from the policies of some other countries.   45
Next year, for the first time, the Organization for Economic Cooperation
and Development, which administers reading, math, and science tests to a
sample of 15-year-old students in more than 50 countries, will add an electronic reading component. The United States, among other countries, will
not participate. A spokeswoman for the Institute of Education Sciences, the
research arm of the Department of Education, said an additional test would
overburden schools.

Even those who are most concerned about the preservation of books   46
acknowledge that children need a range of reading experiences. "Some of
it is the informal reading they get in e-mails or on websites," said Gay Ivey,
a professor at James Madison University who focuses on adolescent literacy.
"I think they need it all."

Web junkies can occasionally be swept up in a book. After Nadia read   47
Elie Wiesel's Holocaust memoir "Night" in her freshman English class,
Ms. Konyk brought home another Holocaust memoir, "I Have Lived a
Thousand Years," by Livia Bitton-Jackson. Nadia was riveted by heartbreak-
ing details of life in the concentration camps. "I was trying to imagine this
and I was like, I can't do this," she said. "It was just so—wow."

Hoping to keep up the momentum, Ms. Konyk brought home another   48
book, "Silverboy," a fantasy novel. Nadia made it through one chapter before
she got engrossed in the Internet fan fiction again.

UNDERSTANDING DETAILS

1. What is Rich comparing in this essay?
2. Explain in your own words the two opposing opinions on literacy that Rich
   presents.
3. What are "Web evangelists" (paragraph 10)?
4. According to literacy specialists, what does frequent novel reading predict?

READING CRITICALLY

5. What are the main differences between reading in print and reading on the
   Internet?
6. Based on information in this article, define "reading" in your own words.
7. Do you think fan fiction was a good outlet for Nadia? Explain your answer.
8. Do you agree with Nicholas Carr that the Web changes the way we think?

DISCOVERING RHETORICAL STRATEGIES

9. How does Rich organize this essay? Is it an effective approach to her topic?
10. Why does the author identify specific children by name throughout the essay?
    Explain your answer.
11. Who do you think is the author's intended audience?

12. What other rhetorical strategies besides comparison and contrast does Rich use to achieve her purpose in this essay? Give examples of each strategy.

MAKING CONNECTIONS

13. Imagine a roundtable discussion featuring Rich, Russell Baker ("The Saturday Evening Post"), Christopher Nelson ("Why We are Looking at the 'Value' of College All Wrong"), Dana Gioia ("On the Importance of Reading"), and/or Nicholas Carr ("How the Internet Is Making Us Stupid") on the importance of reading in life. Which author would most likely appreciate the value of reading on the Internet? Who would be against it? What is your own opinion?

14. Compare and contrast the way Rich uses scholarly quotations with how John Tierney ("A Generation's Vanity, Heard Through Lyrics") uses them. Which author's approach is more convincing to you? Why?

15. If Rich were having a discussion with Nicholas Carr ("How the Internet Is Making Us Stupid"), which author do you think would be more supportive of increasing the amount of time America's high school students spend on the Internet in their classrooms? What is your opinion on this important issue?

IDEAS FOR DISCUSSION/WRITING

Preparing to Write

Write freely about the role reading plays in your life: How many different types of material do you read? Make a complete list of them. What kind of reading do you like best? Why do you like it? How often do you "read" online? How are reading in print and reading online different for you? Do you notice your mind responding in different ways to these two tasks?

Choosing a Topic

MyWritingLab™

1. **LEARNINGⓄNLINE** Reflect on the way you read online: What do you read? Do you stay in one location, or do you jump around? Do you find the time reading online rewarding? How is your online reading different from your offline reading? Do you think students' ability to do both types of reading should be evaluated? Write an essay arguing that online literacy should or should not be taught and/or assessed in our schools.

2. Do you agree or disagree with the literacy experts who say that reading itself should be redefined? Take a stand, and write your own argument, with carefully chosen evidence, in response to this notion.

3. Using the information presented in this article, write an essay persuading a group of high school students to read more novels before they get to college. Why would this be good to do?

4. *Scholastic* magazine has asked you to compare textbook reading and leisure reading from a college student's point of view. Consider the advantages and disadvantages of each. Be sure to decide on a purpose before you begin to write your comparison.

Before beginning your essay, you may want to consult the flowchart on pages 296.

The Politics of Muscle

Once described as a writer with "unpretentious clarity and forceful expression," Gloria Steinem is one of the foremost organizers and champions of the modern women's movement. She was born in Toledo, Ohio, earned a B.A. at Smith College, and pursued graduate work in political science at the universities of Delhi and Calcutta in India before returning to the United States to begin a freelance career in journalism. One of her earliest and best-known articles, "I Was a Playboy Bunny," was a witty exposé of the entire Playboy operation, written in 1963 after she had worked undercover for two weeks in the New York City Playboy Club. In 1968, she and Clay Felker founded *New York* magazine; then, in 1972, they started *Ms.* magazine, which sold out its entire 300,000-copy run in eight days. Steinem's subsequent publications have included *Outrageous Acts and Everyday Rebellions* (1983), *Marilyn: Norma Jean* (1986), *Bedside Book of Self-Esteem* (1989), *Moving Beyond Words* (1994), and *Doing Sixty and Seventy* (2006). Her latest project is a book entitled *Road to the Heart: America as If Everyone Mattered*. An articulate and passionate spokesperson for feminist causes, Steinem has been honored nine times by the *World Almanac* as one of the twenty-five most influential women in the United States.

Preparing to Read

Taken from the author's newest book, *Moving Beyond Words*, "The Politics of Muscle" is actually an introduction to a longer essay entitled "The Strongest Woman in the World," which celebrates the virtues of women's bodybuilding champion Bev Francis.

Exploring Experience: As you prepare to read this essay, examine for a few minutes your own thoughts about the associations Americans make with weakness and strength in both men and women: Which sex do you think of as stronger? In the United States, what does strength have to do with success? With failure? Do these associations vary for men and women? What does weakness suggest in American culture? Do these suggestions vary for men and women? What are the positive values Americans associate with muscles and strength? With helplessness and weakness? What are the negative values Americans associate with muscles and strength? With helplessness and weakness? What connections have you made from your experience between physical strength and gender roles?

LEARNING◯NLINE Read expert opinions about Gloria Steinem by conducting an Internet search for "Perspectives of Gloria Steinem." As you read these perspectives, consider the ways Steinem uses her writing for social and political activism.

Before reading this essay, you may want to consult the flowchart on page 293.

I come from a generation of women who didn't do sports. Being a   1
cheerleader or a drum majorette was as far as our imaginations or role
models could take us. Oh yes, there was also being a strutter—one of a
group of girls (and we were girls then) who marched and danced and turned
cartwheels in front of the high school band at football games. Did you
know that big football universities actually gave strutting scholarships? That
shouldn't sound any more bizarre than football scholarships, yet somehow
it does. Gender politics strikes again.

But even winning one of those rare positions, the stuff that dreams were   2
made of, was more about body display than about the considerable skill they
required.[1] You could forget about trying out for them if you didn't have the
right face and figure, and my high school was full of girls who had learned
to do back flips and twirl flaming batons, all to no avail. Winning wasn't
about being the best in an objective competition or achieving a personal best,
or even about becoming healthy or fit. It was about *being chosen*.

That's one of many reasons why I and other women of my generation   3
grew up believing—as many girls still do—that the most important thing
about a female body is not what it does but how it looks. The power lies
not within us but in the gaze of the observer. In retrospect, I feel sorry for
the protofeminist gym teachers who tried so hard to interest us in half-court
basketball and other team sports thought suitable for girls in my high school,
while we worried about the hairdo we'd slept on rollers all night to achieve.
Gym was just a stupid requirement you tried to get out of, with ugly gym
suits whose very freedom felt odd on bodies accustomed to being constricted for viewing.[2] My blue-collar neighborhood didn't help much
either, for it convinced me that sports like tennis or golf were as remote as
the country clubs where they were played—mostly by men anyway. That
left tap dancing and ballet as my only exercise, and though my dancing
school farmed us out to supermarket openings and local nightclubs, where
we danced our hearts out in homemade costumes, those events were about
display too, about smiling and pleasing and, even during the rigors of ballet,
about looking ethereal and hiding any muscles or strength.

My sports avoidance continued into college, where I went through shock   4
about class and wrongly assumed athletics were only for well-to-do prep
school girls like those who brought their own lacrosse sticks and riding
horses to school. With no sports training to carry over from childhood—and
no place to become childlike, as we must when we belatedly learn basic

---

Thinking Critically

[1] What does Steinem mean by the term "body display"?

[2] To what extent are women's bodies still "constricted for viewing" today?

skills—I clung to my familiar limits. Even at the casual softball games where *Ms.* played the staffs of other magazines, I confined myself to cheering. As the *Ms.* No Stars, we prided ourselves on keeping the same lineup, win or lose, and otherwise disobeying the rules of the jockocracy, so I contented myself with upsetting the men on the opposing team by cheering for their female team members.[3] It's amazing how upset those accustomed to conventional divisions can become when others refuse to be divided by them.

In my case, an interest in the politics of strength had come not from my own   5
experience but from observing the mysterious changes in many women around me. Several of my unathletic friends had deserted me by joining gyms, becoming joggers, or discovering the pleasure of learning to yell and kick in self-defense class. Others who had young daughters described the unexpected thrill of seeing them learn to throw a ball or run with a freedom that hadn't been part of our lives in conscious memory. On campuses, I listened to formerly anorexic young women who said their obsession with dieting had diminished when they discovered strength as a third alternative to the usual fat-versus-thin dichotomy.[4] Suddenly, a skinny, androgynous, "boyish" body was no longer the only way to escape the soft, female, "victim" bodies they associated with their mothers' fates. Added together, these examples of before-and-after-strength changes were so dramatic that the only male analogues I could find were Vietnam amputees whose confidence was bolstered when they entered marathons in wheelchairs or on artificial legs, or paralyzed accident survivors whose sense of themselves was changed when they learned to play wheelchair basketball. Compared to their handicapped female counterparts, however, even those men seemed to be less transformed. Within each category, women had been less encouraged to develop whatever muscle and skills we had.

Since my old habits of ignoring my body and living inside my head weren't   6
that easy to break, it was difficult to change my nonathletic ways. Instead, I continued to learn secondhand from watching my friends, from reading about female strength in other cultures, and from asking questions wherever I traveled.

Though cultural differences were many, there were political similarities   7
in the way women's bodies were treated that went as deep as patriarchy itself. Whether achieved through law and social policy, as in this and other industrialized countries, or by way of tribal practice and religious ritual, as in older cultures, an individual woman's body was far more subject to other people's rules than was that of her male counterpart. Women always seemed to be owned to some degree as the means of reproduction. And as

---

Thinking Critically

[3] What do you think the author means by a "jockocracy"? What are some of its "rules"?

[4] In what way is "strength" a "third alternative to the usual fat-versus-thin dichotomy"?

possessions, women's bodies then became symbols of men's status,[5] with a value that was often determined by what was rare. Thus, rich cultures valued thin women, and poor cultures valued fat women. Yet all patriarchal cultures valued weakness in women. How else could male dominance survive? In my own country, for example, women who "belong" to rich white men are often thinner (as in "You can never be too rich or too thin") than those who "belong" to poor men of color; yet those very different groups of males tend to come together in their belief that women are supposed to be weaker than men; that muscles and strength aren't "feminine."

If I had any doubts about the psychological importance of cultural empha-   8
sis on male/female strength difference, listening to arguments about equality put them to rest. Sooner or later, even the most intellectual discussion came down to men's supposedly superior strength as a justification for inequality, whether the person arguing regretted or celebrated it. What no one seemed to explore, however, was the inadequacy of physical strength as a way of explaining oppression in other cases. Men of European origin hadn't ruled in South Africa because they were stronger than African men, and blacks hadn't been kept in slavery or bad jobs in the United States because whites had more muscles. On the contrary, males of the "wrong" class or color were often confined to laboring positions precisely because of their supposedly greater strength, just as the lower pay females received was often rationalized by their supposedly lesser strength.[6] Oppression has no logic—just a self-fulfilling prophecy, justified by a self-perpetuating system.

The more I learned, the more I realized that belief in great strength dif-   9
ferences between women and men was itself part of the gender mind-game. In fact, we can't really know what those differences might be, because they are so enshrined, perpetuated, and exaggerated by culture. They seem to be greatest during the childbearing years (when men as a group have more speed and upper-body strength, and women have better balance, endurance, and flexibility) but only marginal during early childhood and old age (when females and males seem to have about the same degree of physical strength). Even during those middle years, the range of difference *among* men and *among* women is far greater than the generalized difference *between* males and females as groups. In multiracial societies like ours, where males of some races are smaller than females of others, judgments based on sex make even less sense. Yet we go right on assuming and praising female weakness and male strength.

But there is a problem about keeping women weak, even in a patriarchy.   10
Women are workers, as well as the means of reproduction. Lower-class

---

Thinking Critically

[5] In what ways are women's bodies "symbols of men's status"?

[6] According to the author, what is the relationship between muscles and social class? Do you agree with this assertion? Why or why not?

women are especially likely to do hard physical labor. So the problem becomes: How to make sure female strength is used for work but not for rebellion? The answer is: Make women ashamed of it. Though hard work requires lower-class women to be stronger than their upper-class sisters, for example, those strong women are made to envy and imitate the weakness of women who "belong" to, and are the means of reproduction for, upper-class men—and so must be kept even *more* physically restricted if the lines of race and inheritance are to be kept "pure." That's why restrictive dress, from the chadors, or full-body veils, of the Middle East to metal ankle and neck rings in Africa, from nineteenth-century hoop skirts in Europe to corsets and high heels here, started among upper-class women and then sifted downward as poor women were encouraged to envy or imitate them. So did such bodily restrictions as bound feet in China, or clitoridectomies and infibulations in much of the Middle East and Africa, both of which practices began with women whose bodies were the means of reproduction for the powerful, and gradually became generalized symbols of femininity.[7] In this country, the self-starvation known as anorexia nervosa is mostly a white, upper-middle-class, young-female phenomenon, but all women are encouraged to envy a white and impossibly thin ideal.

Sexual politics are also reflected through differing emphases on the repro-   11 ductive parts of women's bodies. Whenever a patriarchy wants females to populate a new territory or replenish an old one, big breasts and hips become admirable. Think of the bosomy ideal of this country's frontier days, or the *zaftig,* Marilyn Monroe-type figure that became popular after the population losses of World War II. As soon as increased population wasn't desirable or necessary, hips and breasts were deemphasized. Think of the Twiggy look that arrived in the 1960s.

But whether bosomy or flat, *zaftig* or thin, the female ideal remains   12 weak, and it stays that way unless women ourselves organize to change it. Suffragists shed the unhealthy corsets that produced such a tiny-waisted, big-breasted look that fainting and smelling salts became routine. Instead, they brought in bloomers and bicycling. Feminists of today are struggling against social pressures that exalt siliconed breasts but otherwise stick-thin silhouettes. Introducing health and fitness has already led to a fashion industry effort to reintroduce weakness with the waif look, but at least it's being protested. The point is: Only when women rebel against patriarchal standards does female muscle become more accepted.[8]

Thinking Critically

7 How are "bound feet" and "clitoridectomies" in other cultures symbols of femininity? Name some symbols of femininity in American culture today.

8 Why will female muscle become more accepted when women rebel against patriarchal standards? Do you agree with this assertion? Why or why not?

For these very political reasons, I've gradually come to believe that   13
society's acceptance of muscular women may be one of the most intimate,
visceral measures of change. Yes, we need progress everywhere, but an
increase in our physical strength could have more impact on the everyday
lives of most women than the occasional role model in the boardroom or in
the White House.

UNDERSTANDING DETAILS

1. According to Steinem, what is "gender politics" (paragraph 1)?
2. In what ways does Steinem equate "winning" with "being chosen" (paragraph 2)?
   Why is this an important premise for her essay?
3. What does Steinem mean when she says, "Oppression has no logic" (paragraph 8)?
   Explain your answer in detail.
4. In what ways does "power" lie with the observer rather than within the female?

READING CRITICALLY

5. Why does Steinem call the female body a "victim" body (paragraph 5)? What
   did girls' mothers have to do with this association?
6. Do you agree with the author that a woman's body is "far more subject to
   other people's rules than . . . that of her male counterpart" (paragraph 7)?
   Explain your answer, giving examples from your own experience.
7. What is Steinem implying about the political overtones connected with female
   weakness and male strength? According to Steinem, why are these judgments
   so ingrained in American social and cultural mores?
8. What are Steinem's reasons for saying that "society's acceptance of muscular
   women may be one of the most intimate, visceral measures of change" (paragraph 13)? Do you agree with this statement? Explain your reaction in detail.

DISCOVERING RHETORICAL STRATEGIES

9. Who do you think is Steinem's intended audience for this essay? On what do
   you base your answer?
10. In your opinion, what is Steinem's primary purpose in this essay? Explain your
    answer in detail.
11. How appropriate is the title of this essay? What would be some possible
    alternate titles?
12. What rhetorical modes support the author's comparison/contrast? Give exam-
    ples of each.

MAKING CONNECTIONS

13. To what extent would Sandra Cisneros ("Only Daughter"), Barbara Ehren-
    reich ("Nickel and Dimed"), and/or Mary Pipher ("Beliefs about Families")
    agree with Gloria Steinem's assertions about the differences between men
    and women? Do you agree or disagree with her assertions? Give at least three
    reasons for your opinion.

14. If Steinem is correct that American women have not traditionally found power in their muscles, where have they found it? If you were able to ask Elizabeth Svoboda ("Virtual Assault") this same question, what do you think her response would be? With whom would you agree more? Explain your answer.

15. How would Wayne Norman ("When Is a Sport Not a Sport?") feel about the revolution in women's bodybuilding Steinem describes? To what extent might he see this trend as a positive force in sports?

IDEAS FOR DISCUSSION/WRITING

Preparing to Write

Write freely about the definition and role of strength and weakness in American society: What does strength generally mean in American society? What does weakness mean? What associations do you have with both modes of behavior? Where do these associations come from? What are the political implications of these associations? The social implications? In what ways are strength and weakness basic to the value system in American culture?

Choosing a Topic

MyWritingLab™

1. **LEARNINGⓊNLINE** Gloria Steinem organizes her comparison of males and females around the issue of "muscle." What other comparisons can be made between men and women? Visit both an online men's magazine and an online women's magazine, and examine the headings. Find an issue that is explored in both magazines, and write an essay that analyzes their similarities and differences. Following Steinem's example, organize your analysis around a single issue, and include your own perspective where appropriate.

2. Compare two different approaches to the process of succeeding in a specific job or activity. Develop your own guidelines for making the comparison; then, write an essay for your fellow students about the similarities and differences you have observed between these two different approaches. Be sure to decide on a purpose and a point of view before you begin to write.

3. Interview your mother and your father about their views on physical strength in their separate family backgrounds. If you have grandparents or stepparents, interview them as well. Then compare and contrast these various influences in your life. Which of them are alike? Which are different? How have you personally dealt with these similarities and differences? Be sure to decide on a purpose and a point of view before you begin to write.

4. In her essay, Steinem argues that "an increase in our [women's] physical strength could have more impact on the everyday lives of most women than the occasional role model in the boardroom or in the White House" (paragraph 13). Do you agree with the author? Write an essay to be published in your hometown newspaper explaining your views on this issue.

Before beginning your essay, you may want to consult the flowchart on page 296.

JOHN TIERNEY   (1953–   )

A Generation's Vanity, Heard Through Lyrics

Born outside of Chicago and raised in the Midwest, Pittsburgh, and South America, John Tierney, an American journalist educated at Yale, began his career as coeditor of *Yale Daily News Magazine* and went on to write for the *Bergen Record*, the *Washington Star*, and *Science* magazine, as well as contributing to *Health, Discover, Atlantic Monthly, Esquire, National Geographic Traveler, Newsweek, Outside, Rolling Stone, Vogue, The Wall Street Journal, The Washington Post*, and the *Washington Monthly*. Tierney has worked for *The New York Times* since 1990, where he previously wrote the *TierneyLab* blog and currently writes a science column, *Findings*. He has also been a columnist for the *Times* Op-Ed page and wrote "The Big City," a column about New York, from 1994 to 2002. Identifying himself as a libertarian, he has written on topics ranging from rent stabilization to recycling, from Amtrak to the war on drugs. His article "Recycling Is Garbage" (1996) holds the hate mail record at the *New York Times Magazine*. Tierney has written and coauthored numerous books, including *God Is My Broker: A Monk Tycoon Reveals the 7 ½ Laws of Spiritual and Financial Growth* (1999) and *The Best-Case Scenario Handbook* (2002). His most recent book, coauthored with Roy Baumeister, was a *New York Times* best seller entitled *Willpower: Rediscovering the Greatest Human Strength* (2011). Tierney's reporting has taken him around the world and has won him awards from American Association for the Advancement of Science, the American Institute of Physics, and the New York Publishers Association. He currently lives in New York with his wife, Dana, and son, Luke.

Preparing to Read

Originally published in 2011 in *The New York Times*, this article by John Tierney catalogs various ways in which music can characterize a generation. In it, he suggests that the lyrics of songs reveal the collective character and values of the people who wrote them, as well as of those who enjoy them.

Exploring Experience: As you prepare to read this essay, consider for a few minutes your preferences in music: What type of music do you like most? What do you think this preference says about you as a person? What do you think it says about your generation as a whole? Do you like more than one type of music?

LEARNING◍NLINE In the following essay, Tierney suggests that contemporary music has created a culture of narcissism that represents this generation. Visit youtube.com to watch videos by some contemporary artists. Pay special attention to any patterns or trends that you see in the videos. What do these trends communicate to you?

Before reading this essay, you may want to consult the flowchart on page 293.

A couple of years ago, as his fellow psychologists debated whether   1
narcissism was increasing, Nathan DeWall heard Rivers Cuomo
singing to a familiar 19th-century melody. Mr. Cuomo, the lead
singer and guitarist for the rock band Weezer, billed the song as "Variations
on a Shaker Hymn."

Where 19th-century Shakers had sung "'Tis the gift to be simple, 'tis the   2
gift to be free," Mr. Cuomo offered his own lyrics: "I'm the meanest in the
place; step up; I'll mess with your face." Instead of the Shaker message of
love and humility, Mr. Cuomo sang over and over, "I'm the greatest man
that ever lived."

The refrain got Dr. DeWall wondering: "Who would actually sing that   3
aloud?" Mr. Cuomo may have been parodying the grandiosity of other
singers—but then, why was there so much grandiosity to parody? Did the
change from "Simple Gifts" to "Greatest Man That Ever Lived" exemplify
a broader trend? [1]

Now, after a computer analysis of three decades of hit songs, Dr. DeWall   4
and other psychologists report finding what they were looking for: a statistically significant trend toward narcissism and hostility in popular music. As
they hypothesized, the words "I" and "me" appear more frequently along
with anger-related words, while there's been a corresponding decline in
"we" and "us" and the expression of positive emotions.

"Late adolescents and college students love themselves more today than   5
ever before," Dr. DeWall, a psychologist at the University of Kentucky, says.
His study covered song lyrics from 1980 to 2007 and controlled for genre
to prevent the results from being skewed by the growing popularity of, say,
rap and hip-hop.

Defining the personality of a generation with song lyrics may seem a bit   6
of a reach, but Dr. DeWall points to research done by his co-authors that
showed people of the same age scoring higher in measures of narcissism on
some personality tests. [2] The extent and meaning of this trend have been
hotly debated by psychologists, some of whom question the tests' usefulness
and say that young people today aren't any more self-centered than those of
earlier generations. The new study of song lyrics certainly won't end the
debate, but it does offer another way to gauge self-absorption: the Billboard
Hot 100 chart. The researchers find that hit songs in the 1980s were more
likely to emphasize happy togetherness, like the racial harmony sought by
Paul McCartney and Stevie Wonder in "Ebony and Ivory" and the group

---

Thinking Critically

[1] What do you think this shift represents?

[2] Do you think song lyrics can actually represent the essence of a generation? Explain your
answer.

exuberance promoted by Kool & the Gang: "Let's all celebrate and have a good time." Diana Ross and Lionel Richie sang of "two hearts that beat as one," and John Lennon's "(Just Like) Starting Over" emphasized the preciousness of "our life together."

Today's songs, according to the researchers' linguistic analysis, are more likely to be about one very special person: the singer. "I'm bringing sexy back," Justin Timberlake proclaimed in 2006. The year before, Beyoncé exulted in how hot she looked while dancing—"It's blazin', you watch me in amazement." And Fergie, who boasted about her "humps" while singing with the Black Eyed Peas, subsequently released a solo album in which she told her lover that she needed quality time alone: "It's personal, myself and I." 7

Two of Dr. DeWall's co-authors, W. Keith Campbell and Jean M. Twenge, published a book in 2009 titled *The Narcissism Epidemic*, which argued that narcissism is increasingly prevalent among young people—and possibly middle-aged people too, although it's hard for anyone to know because most of the available data comes from college students. 8

For several decades, students have filled out a questionnaire called the Narcissism Personality Inventory, in which they've had to choose between two statements like "I try not to be a show-off" and "I will usually show off if I get the chance." The level of narcissism measured by these questionnaires has been rising since the early 1980s, according to an analysis of campus data by Dr. Twenge and Dr. Campbell. 9

That trend has been questioned by other researchers who published fresh data from additional students. But in the latest round of the debate, the critics' data has been reanalyzed by Dr. Twenge, who says that it actually supports her argument. In a meta-analysis published last year in *Social Psychological and Personality Science*, Dr. Twenge and Joshua D. Foster looked at data from nearly 50,000 students—including the new data from critics—and concluded that narcissism has increased significantly in the past three decades. 10

During this period, there have also been reports of higher levels of loneliness and depression—which may be no coincidence, according to the authors of the song-lyrics study. These researchers, who include Richard S. Pond of the University of Kentucky, note that narcissism has been linked to heightened anger and problems maintaining relationships.[3] Their song-lyrics analysis shows a decline in words related to social connections and positive emotions (like "love" or "sweet") and an increase in words related to anger and antisocial behavior (like "hate" or "kill"). 11

Thinking Critically
[3] In what ways do you think anger and problems with relationships might be related? In what ways might they influence one another?

"In the early '80s lyrics, love was easy and positive, and about two peo-   12
ple," says Dr. Twenge, a psychologist at San Diego State University. "The
recent songs are about what the individual wants, and how she or he has
been disappointed or wronged."

Of course, in an amateur nonscientific way, you can find anything you want   13
in song lyrics from any era. Never let it be said that the Rolling Stones were
soft and cuddly. In "Sympathy for the Devil" the devil gets his due, and he gets
to sing in the first person. In 1989, Bobby Brown bragged that "no one can
tell me what to do" in his hit song about his awesomeness, "My Prerogative."

Country singers have always had their moments of self-absorption and   14
self-pity. But the classic somebody-done-somebody-wrong songs aren't necessarily angry. When Hank Williams sang "Your Cheatin' Heart" he didn't
mention trashing his sweetheart's car, as in "Before He Cheats" by Carrie
Underwood: "I took a Louisville slugger to both headlights."

Some psychologists are skeptical that basic personality traits can change   15
so much from one generation to the next (or from one culture to another).
Even if students are scoring higher on the narcissism questionnaire, these
skeptics say, it may just be because today's students are more willing to admit
to feelings that were always there.

Dr. Twenge acknowledges that students today may feel more free to admit   16
that they agree with statements on the questionnaire like "I am going to be
a great person" and "I like to look at myself in the mirror." But self-report
bias probably isn't the only reason for the changing answers, she says, and in
any case this new willingness to brag is in itself an important cultural change.

The song-lyrics analysis, published in the journal *Psychology of Aesthetics,*   17
Creativity and the Arts, goes up to 2007, which makes it fairly up-to-date by
scientific standards. But by popular music standards, 2007 is an eon ago.
Could narcissism have declined since then?

It would take a computerized linguistic analysis to be sure, but there are   18
reasons to doubt it. In 2008, the same year as Weezer's "Greatest Man That
Ever Lived," Little Jackie had a popular song titled "The World Should
Revolve Around Me."

The current Billboard chart includes the Cee-Lo Green comic ode to   19
hostility with its unprintable refrain (for the Grammy television audience,
he changed it to "Forget you") as well as Keri Hilson's paean to her own
beauty: "All eyes on me when I walk in, no question that this girl's a 10."
Regardless of whether the singers really mean it, there's obviously a market
for these sentiments. 4

Thinking Critically

4 Do you think there is "market" for narcissism and egotism? If so, how does it manifest
itself?

"The culture isn't going to change wholesale overnight, and neither are   20
song lyrics," Dr. Twenge says. But she has some time-honored common-
sense advice for people who want to change themselves and their
relationships.

"As much as possible, take your ego out of the situation," Dr. Twenge   21
says. "This is very difficult to do, but the perspective you gain is amazing.
Ask yourself, 'How would I look at this situation if it wasn't about me?' Stop
thinking about winning all the time. A sure sign something might not be
the best value: Charlie Sheen talks about it a lot."

UNDERSTANDING DETAILS

1. What inspired Tierney to study song lyrics?
2. According to Tierney, what do song lyrics tell us about people?
3. How did Tierney obtain the statistics for the songs he analyzed?
4. What characterized the songs of the 1980s? What characterized the songs after
   the '80s?

READING CRITICALLY

5. Why does DeWall say, "Late adolescents and college students love themselves
   more today than ever before" (paragraph 5)? Do you agree with this statement
   from your observations?
6. Offer another explanation for the increased use of "I" in songs during the
   1980s.
7. Do the personality inventories that the researchers gave support the linguistic
   analysis of the lyrics in each decade? Explain your answer.
8. What did Twenge and Foster discover from their data on students?

DISCOVERING RHETORICAL STRATEGIES

9. What effect does the inclusion of actual names of researchers have on the essay?
10. Who do you think is Tierney's intended audience? On what do you base your
    answer?
11. Which rhetorical modes does Wood use to support his comparison? How
    effective are these choices in fulfilling his purpose?
12. How effective is the reference in the last line to Charlie Sheen? What does the
    author want us to think at the end?

MAKING CONNECTIONS

13. To what degree do Tierney, Christopher Nelson ("Why We are Looking at the
    'Value' of College All Wrong"), Sarah Toler ("Understanding the Birth Order
    Relationship"), and/or Stephanie Vozza ("How to Make New Friends as an
    Adult") understand people? In your opinion, which one is most knowledgeable
    about human nature?

14. How does Tierney's method of comparison/contrast differ from that used by Motoko Rich ("Literacy Debate")? Which do you find easier to follow? Why?

15. Compare the tone of Tierney's essay with that of Jessica Mitford ("Behind the Formaldehyde Curtain") and/or Frank Furedi ("Our Unhealthy Obsession with Sickness"). Who is most serious? Who is most lighthearted? Is each of their tones or moods appropriate for their purpose?

IDEAS FOR DISCUSSION/WRITING

Preparing to Write

Write freely about your thoughts on our current culture: What are our most significant cultural characteristics? Are these features to be proud of? What is the contemporary mood in America at present? What are the main factors that affect this mood? Do you think the mood of the younger generation is different from that of their parents and grandparents?

Choosing a Topic

MyWritingLab™

1. **LEARNINGⓊNLINE** Return to youtube.com, and watch the music videos "Ebony and Ivory" by Paul McCartney and Stevie Wonder and "Celebration" by Kool and the Gang. How do these videos compare with Hank Williams's "Your Cheatin' Heart" and Carrie Underwood's "Before He Cheats"? Choose two songs from two different decades, and write an essay describing their tone, purpose, and lyrics. What is the difference in their messages and the way they deliver them?

2. As if you are writing for a magazine popular with your peers, explain what an ideal cultural identification would be for our country today. Are we close to the features you outline? What are some of the threats to this identify?

3. Does your college or university have an identity? Discuss the concept of its social identity by comparing it to some other aspect of our culture. Give examples to support your main point.

4. Compare and contrast your own identity with that of one of your friends. How do you each fit into the larger society? Do you want to change your identity? If so, in what ways?

Before beginning your essay, you may want to consult the flowchart on pages 296.

Chapter Writing Assignments

Practicing Comparison/Contrast

1. Compare one feature of your culture to the same aspect of someone else's culture. Make sure you are not making random or biased judgments but are exploring similarities, differences, and their significance.
2. Compare the styles of two different writers in *The Prose Reader*. First, identify the major features of each writer's style. Then narrow your ideas to a few points of comparison. For example, perhaps one writer is serious and another funny; one writer may write long, complex sentences, while another writes mostly simple sentences. Discuss the effects each essay has on its readers based on these specific differences in style.
3. Discuss the major differences between two views of a political issue or between two political candidates. Identify the main sources of the differences, and then defend the point of view you believe is most reasonable.

Exploring a Theme

4. What does being "an individual" mean? How important is individualism to you personally? When might being an individual clash with the needs of society? Identify and discuss a situation in which individualism and the needs of society might conflict. If such a conflict occurs, which needs should prevail, and why?
5. Identify a disturbing trend that you see in American society. Describe this trend in an essay, providing examples from your observations and experiences.
6. Think about a business or organization that is not what it appears to be. Then write an essay explaining the differences between the image this business or organization projects and the way it actually functions. Include specific examples to illustrate the differences between its image and the reality experienced by its customers or clients.

Analyzing Visual Images

David Beckerman Photography.

7. Based on this photo, we can see that couples behave very differently. Compare a relationship you have had with a relationship you've seen, such as your parents' relationship or marriage, a previous relationship in which you were involved, or the relationship of someone else you know that seems very different from your own.

8. Look at the picture on page 292 at the beginning of the chapter. Do you think the woman in the photograph is holding up a picture of herself or someone else, possibly a daughter or sister? Explain your answer by discussing the different comparisons/contrasts you considered in order to reach your conclusion.

Composing in Different Genres

9. Multimedia: Create a Venn diagram that compares the most salient features of two different public figures. Record each individual's unique characteristics outside the overlapping circles and the features that they share in the center of the diagram. Then write an essay explaining your diagram. (Look up a Venn diagram on the Internet to get you started if necessary.)

10. Multigenre: Choose one of your favorite products (food, clothing, hair product, electronic device), and write a product analysis of it for a catalog, comparing and contrasting it to other similar products. Be thorough and factual in your explanation, but make your support for the product clear through your choice of details and descriptors.

Writing from Sources

For detailed information on writing from sources, see Part III.

11. Compare the typical family dynamics of today with those of another era. How is today's family different from one in another period? What does research say about the family life of another century or another decade in this century? After consulting a few sources, compare and contrast the characteristics of families from two different eras.

12. In the past century, the United States saw radical changes in societal norms, such as the civil rights movement, women's suffrage, and equal rights for persons with disabilities. Did these groups gain recognition through legislative means or civil disobedience? Research two of these movements, and write a documented essay comparing and contrasting the tactics behind their success.

MyWritingLab™ Visit Ch. 9 Comparison/Contrast: Discovering Similarities and Differences in *MyWritingLab* to complete the writing assignments and test your understanding of the chapter learning objectives.

Chapter 10

DEFINITION
Limiting the Frame of Reference

LEARNING OBJECTIVES

After completing this chapter, you will be able to do the following:
- Define definition
- Use definition to think critically
- Read definition essays critically
- Write and revise effective definition essays

Definitions help us function smoothly in a complex world. All effective communication, in fact, is continuously dependent on our unique human ability to understand and employ accurate definitions of a wide range of words, phrases, and abstract ideas. If we did not work from a set of shared definitions, we would not be able to carry on coherent conversations, write comprehensible letters, or respond to even the simplest radio and television programs. Definitions help us understand basic concrete terms (such as *automobiles, laser beams*, and *gross national product*), discuss various events in our lives (such as snowboarding, legal proceedings, and a Cinco de Mayo celebration), and grasp difficult abstract ideas (such as democracy, ambition, and resentment). The ability to comprehend definitions and use them effectively helps us keep our oral and written level of communication accurate and accessible to a wide variety of people.

DEFINING DEFINITION

Definition is the process of explaining a word, object, or idea in such a way that the reader (or listener) knows as precisely as possible what we mean. A good definition sets up intellectual boundaries by focusing on the special qualities of a word or phrase that set it apart from other, similar words or phrases. Clear definitions always give the writer and the reader a mutual starting point on the sometimes bumpy road to successful communication.

Definitions vary from short, dictionary-length summaries to longer, "extended" accounts that determine the form of an entire essay. Words or ideas that require expanded definitions are usually abstract, complex, or unavoidably controversial; they generally bear many related meanings or many shades of meaning. Definitions can be *objective* (technically precise and generally dry) or *subjective* (colored with personal opinion), and they can be used to instruct, to entertain, or to accomplish a combination of these two fundamental rhetorical goals.

In the following paragraph, a student defines *childhood* by putting it into perspective with other important stages of life. Though mostly entertaining, the paragraph is also instructive as the student objectively captures the essence of this phase of human development:

> *Childhood is a stage of growth somewhere between infancy and adolescence. Just as each developmental period in our lives brings new changes and concerns, childhood serves as the threshold to puberty—the time we learn to discriminate between good and bad, right and wrong, love and lust. Childhood is neither a time of irresponsible infancy nor responsible adulthood. Rather, it is marked by duties that we don't really want, challenges that excite us, feelings that puzzle and frighten us, and limitless opportunities that help us explore the world around us. Childhood is a time when we solidify our personalities in spite of pressures to be someone else.*

THINKING CRITICALLY THROUGH DEFINITION

Definitions are building blocks in communication that help us make certain we are functioning from the same understanding of terms and ideas. They give us a foundation to work from in both reading and writing. Definitions force us to think about meanings and word associations that make other logical strategies stronger and easier to work with.

The process of thinking through our definitions forces us to come to some understanding about a particular term or concept we are mentally wrestling with. Articulating that definition helps us move to other modes of thought and higher levels of understanding. Practicing definitions in isolation to get a feel for them is much like separating the skill of pedaling from the process of riding a bike. The better you get at pedaling, the more natural the rest of the cycling process becomes. The following exercises ask you to practice definitions in a number of different ways. Being more conscious of what definition entails will make it more useful to you in both your reading and your writing.

Tetra Images/Getty Images.

1. What does the ring in this photograph mean? Identify at least three ways in which people could define this ring. Write your definitions as precisely as possible, and share one with your class.
2. Define in one or two sentences one of the concrete words and one of the abstract words listed here.
   Concrete: *cattle, book, ranch, water, gum*
   Abstract: *freedom, progress, equality, fairness, boredom*
   What were some of the differences between the processes you went through to explain the concrete word and the abstract word? What can you conclude from this brief exercise about the differences in defining abstract and concrete words?
3. Define the word *grammar*. Consult a dictionary, several handbooks, and maybe even some friends to get their views on the word's meaning. Then write a humorous definition of *grammar* that consolidates all these views into a single definition.

READING AND WRITING DEFINITION ESSAYS

Extended definitions, which may range from two or three paragraphs to an entire essay, seldom follow a set pattern of development or organization. Instead, as you will see from the examples in this chapter, they draw on a number of different techniques to help explain a word, object, term, concept, or phenomenon.

Reading Definition Essays

Understanding how definition essays work rhetorically will help you make decisions for your own writing. Here is a flowchart of questions that will guide your reading for this purpose.

Questions to Guide Your Reading

PREPARING TO READ Before you read the essays, answer the following questions:

- What assumptions can you make from the essay's **title**?
- What do you think the general **mood** of the essay will be?
- What is the essay's **purpose** and **audience**?
- What does the **synopsis** tell you about the essay?
- What can you learn from the author's **biography**?
- What do you predict the author's **point of view** toward the subject will be?

READING As you read the essays for the first time, answer the following questions:

- What is the essay's **context**?
- Is the essay **objective** or **subjective**?
- How is the definition **introduced**?

REREADING When you read the essays again, answer the following questions:

- How does the author **develop** the definition?
- What other **rhetorical strategies** does the author use?
- How does your understanding of the essay **change** with each rereading?

Preparing To Read.   As you begin to read each of the definition essays in this chapter, take some time to consider the author's title and the synopsis of the essay in the Rhetorical Table of Contents: How much can you learn about Wayne Norman's topic from his title, "When Is a Sport Not a Sport?" What do you sense is the general mood of Mary Pipher's "Beliefs about Families"? What do you know about "Binge Drinking" (David Hanson)?

Equally important as you prepare to read is scanning an essay and finding information from its prefatory material about the author and the circumstances surrounding the composition of the essay. What do you think is Robert Ramirez's purpose in his definition of the barrio? And what can you learn from Elizabeth Svoboda about "Virtual Assault"?

Last, as you prepare to read these essays, answer the prereading questions before each essay, and then spend a few minutes thinking freely about the general subject of the essay at hand: What interests you about sports (Norman)? What do you want to know from Pipher about families?

Reading.   As you read a definition essay, as with all essays, be sure to record your initial reactions to your reading material. What are some of your thoughts or associations in relation to each essay?

As you get more involved in the essay, reconsider the preliminary material so you can create a context within which to analyze what the writer is saying: What is Norman's purpose in writing "When Is a Sport Not a Sport?" Does his tone effectively support that purpose? Who do you think is Ramirez's primary audience? Do you think his essay will effectively reach that group of people? In what ways is Svoboda qualified to write about schools?

Throughout each essay in this chapter are provocative questions at the bottom of the pages meant to guide you to analysis and critical thinking. These questions ask you to consider the authors' ideas as they relate to one another and to your own experience. Your responses to these questions will then give you thoughtful material to work with on the tasks after each essay. These questions essentially bridge the gap between the prereading questions and the activities after each essay. Writing down your thoughts will be especially beneficial to you as you gather your own ideas together in response to a writing assignment.

Finally, determine at this point whether the author's treatment of his or her subject is predominantly objective or subjective. Then, make sure you understand the main points of the essay on the literal, interpretive, and analytical levels by reading the questions that follow.

Rereading.   When you read these definition essays for a second time, check to see how each writer actually sets forth his or her definition: Does the writer put each item in a specific category with clear boundaries? Do you understand how the item being defined is different from other items in the same category? Did the author name the various components of the item, explain its etymology (linguistic origin and history), discuss what it is not, or perform a combination of these tasks?

To evaluate the effectiveness of a definition essay, you need to reconsider the essay's primary purpose and audience. If Norman is trying to get the general reader to consider what a sport is, how effective is he? In like manner, is Pipher successful in communicating to the same audience the value of the family unit?

Especially applicable is the question of what other rhetorical strategies help the author communicate this purpose. What other modes does Ramirez use to help him define the barrio? Through what other modes does Hanson define binge drinking?

For an inventory of the reading process, you can review the Reading Checklist at the end of Chapter 2.

Writing Definition Essays

Now that you see how definition works in an essay, use the same features in your own writing. The flowchart on the next page provides some questions to guide you.

Preparing to Write.   As with other essays, you should begin the task of writing a definition essay by answering the prewriting questions featured in this text and then exploring your subject and generating other ideas. (See the explanation of various prewriting techniques on pages 26–28 of Chapter 3.) Be sure you know what you are going to define and how you will approach your definition. You should then focus on a specific audience and purpose as you approach your writing assignment.

Writing.   The next step toward developing a definition essay is usually to describe the general category to which the word belongs and then to contrast the word with all other words in that group. To define *exposition*, for example, you might say that it is a type of writing. Then, to differentiate it from other types of writing, you could go on to say that its main purpose is to "expose," or present, information, as opposed to rhetorical modes such as description and narration, which describe and tell stories. In addition, you might want to cite some expository methods such as example, process analysis, division/classification, and comparison/contrast.

Questions to Guide Your Writing

PREPARING TO WRITE
Before you start writing, answer these questions:

- What is the **purpose** of your definition?
- How will you **approach** your topic?
- Who is your **audience**?

WRITING As you write your first draft, consider these questions:

- What is your **thesis statement**?
- What is your essay's **context**?
- Does the **beginning** of your essay suit your purpose?
- What is your **point of view** (objective or subjective)?
- What **rhetorical strategies** do you use to expand your essay?

EDITING Be sure to proofread and edit your paper before turning it in.

- Are your **sentences** all complete?
- Do your words say exactly **what you mean**?
- Do you follow conventional **grammar and usage** rules?

REVISING After you write your first draft, use the following questions to revise your essay:

- Have you chosen an effective **beginning** for your paper?
- Did you create a reasonable **context** for your definition?
- What other **rhetorical strategies** did you use to develop your ideas?
- Have you achieved your overall **purpose** as effectively as possible?

Yet another way to begin a definition essay is to provide a term's etymology. Tracing a word's origin often illuminates its current meaning and usage as well. *Exposition,* for example, comes from the Latin *exponere,* meaning "to put forth, set forth, display, declare, or publish" (*ex* = out; *ponere* = to put or place). This information can generally be found in any good dictionary or encyclopedia.

Another approach to defining a term is to explain what it does *not* mean. For example, *exposition* is not creative writing. By limiting the readers' frame of reference in these various ways, you are helping to establish a working definition for the term under consideration.

Finally, rhetorical methods that we have already studied, such as description, narration, example, process analysis, division/classification, and comparison/ contrast, are particularly useful to writers in expanding their definitions. To clarify the term *exposition,* you might *describe* the details of an expository theme, **narrate** a story about the wide use of the term in today's classroom, or **give examples** of assignments that would produce good expository writing. In other situations, you could **analyze** various writing assignments and discuss the **process** of producing an expository essay, **classify** exposition apart from creative writing, and then **divide** it into categories similar to the headings of this book, or **compare** and **contrast** it with creative writing. Writers also use definition quite often to support other rhetorical modes.

Revising.   Reviewing and revising a definition essay is a relatively straightforward task. Guidelines to direct your writing and revising appear in the Writing Checklist at the end of Chapter 3.

STUDENT ESSAY: DEFINITION AT WORK

In the following essay, a student defines *Dungeons and Dragons* by rethinking "game night" for this generation. Notice how the writer puts this game in a category and then explains the limits of that category and the uniqueness of this game within the category. To further inform her audience about the features of *Dungeons and Dragons,* the student itemizes the game's basic characteristics, offers a number of examples that explain those characteristics, provides several comparisons, and, finally, conducts a brief discussion of the causes and effects that exemplify this particular game.

A Game of Epic Proportions

I am on a <u>mission</u>. My mission may be challenging, but it is not impossible. I am a Dungeon Master, the fearless leader of a party of warriors facing matchless battles on a weekly basis. However, the mission I face now is greater and more challenging than any that I have ever faced before. <u>This mission is to redefine</u> *Dungeons and Dragons* <u>for the broader level of partici-</u> <u>pation that it deserves and, by doing so, defend the</u> <u>game against its reputation for drawing nerdy loners to</u> <u>basements to play make believe.</u> *Dungeons and Dragons* is a game that many more people would enjoy if they put aside their biases, and <u>as the Dungeon Master,</u>

General subject

Introduction of term to be defined

Reason for definition

General category of word to be defined

Writer's credibility

I am prepared to take you on the journey of discovery to redefine this polarizing and vastly misunderstood game.

Limitations set

In simplest terms, *Dungeons and Dragons* is a role-playing game in which players in groups each take on individual characters with particular strengths and weaknesses. Taking on a role in a game might seem strange, but that is not very different from the way a football player puts on a tough-guy act to intimidate his opponent. In *D&D* (the widespread abbreviation for *Dungeons and Dragons*), if someone is playing a Paladin, he or she must act nobly; if someone is playing a Dwarf, he or she will have a much tougher persona; and so on. As children, we all played games like this. We pretended we were soldiers or superheroes and ran around with our friends in makeshift capes wielding makeshift weapons. *Dungeons and Dragons* is fun because we all have the innate desire to imagine and play. In *D&D*, we get to carry out this natural inclination with complexity and sophistication.

General characteristic 1

Comparison

Examples

As a form of entertainment, *D&D is a combination of many other types of games.* It depends on the luck of the dice, as many board games do. It involves acting out situations and completing specific tasks, like party games such as *Charades*. In addition, *D&D* is a game of strategy, like *Settlers of Catan*. *Dungeons and Dragons* is similar to these games in many ways, but it must be played cooperatively in groups.

General characteristic 2

Division/ Classification

Comparison

D&D is, at its core, a social game. Players must rely on their fellow adventurers if they hope to do well. Most sessions of playing the game are funny, exciting, tense, and full of conversation. There are occasional moments of anxious silence as players await their fate together, but the reputation of *D&D* as a game of anti-social loners is completely inaccurate because players have to talk and work with other people throughout the whole process. Like most games, *D&D* requires communication and teamwork, the elements of all positive social activities.

General characteristic 3

What it is not

When people play *Dungeons and Dragons,* they embark on an adventure, which is essentially a story.

General characteristic 4

Definition

Examples   For example, let's say a group of frost giants lives in the mountains outside of a city and a group of adventurers must investigate and take care of the problem. If players have a group of people who play often enough, they can form a "campaign," <u>which is a series of connected</u>   Definition
<u>and increasingly intense adventures</u>. The end of one
Examples   adventure leads to the next adventure. For example, players might have investigated the frost giants and discovered, while in their cave, a journal describing an ancient artifact of unrivaled power. Thus begins the next adventure, which officially starts a campaign.

Cause/   Finally, we come to <u>the ingredient of *Dungeons and*</u>
Effect   <u>*Dragons* that holds it all together and promotes creativ-</u>   General
<u>ity. The Dungeon Master for each game is the inventor</u>   charac-
<u>and writer of the story.</u> He or she guides the party and,   teristic 5
in some ways, decides their fate. The Dungeon Master helps determine whether the adventure is a thrill or a flop, depending on how creative he or she is. Of
Definition   course, for a beginning Dungeon Master, books can help guide the story, but the really skilled Dungeon Master makes the stories up as he or she goes along, leading to an infinite number of adventures.

Dungeons and Dragons is fun—<u>perhaps nerdy but</u>   Summary
<u>just a different way of socializing</u>. This game draws a wide variety of players that would surprise people; my group consists of a range of people from a guitar player in a hardcore band to a graduate student in English. The key to *Dungeons and Dragons* is to dive in and commit to it. If people give it a chance, they will
Process   most likely enjoy using their imaginations and explor-
Analysis   ing a world straight out of *The Lord of the Rings* or *The*
Hobbit. <u>Dungeons and Dragons</u> gives people the oppor-   Concluding
<u>tunity to temporarily escape from their daily routine</u>   statement
<u>by adding fun and adventure to their lives through a</u>
<u>creative gaming experience.</u>

Student Writer's Comments

The most difficult part of writing this definition essay was choosing a topic. I wanted it to be a word or phrase with different shades of meaning, but it also had to be either something I knew more about than the average person or something I saw in an unusual way. I went through a variety of options before I realized that I didn't need to define an abstract concept; I could define something concrete—and fun. *Dungeons and Dragons* is something I know more about than the average person, and it is often grossly misunderstood. I knew it would also be a lot of fun to write about, which I believe should always be a major consideration in choosing a subject for an essay.

I first made a list of the main components of the game *Dungeons and Dragons*. This list included many more topics than I ended up using in my actual essay. I combined some items into a single body paragraph, and I didn't include others that were irrelevant. I actually wrote an entire body paragraph about the members of my current group before realizing I didn't need the entire paragraph to make my point; I used only one sentence of that paragraph in my conclusion.

Other than the initial list that I generated, I didn't need to do much pre-writing. I started writing the essay from the beginning although I did have some serious problems with the introduction. I wanted to connect the essay to my audience, so I approached it by addressing in a humorous fashion their predictable biases against the game. I also related *Dungeons and Dragons* to other games that I was pretty sure the readers would know.

The most interesting part of composing this particular essay was realizing that in defining the game *Dungeons and Dragons*, I also had to explain various terms that are part of the game. I had to explain *campaign* and *Dungeon Master* and *role-playing* in order to define the game itself. I arranged the essay topics in order of importance, beginning with what I felt was most essential to understanding the game. I tried to imagine that I was my own audience, asking successive questions and organizing the essay by answering those questions.

As I reworked my essay before handing it in, I tried to add more humor from my own experience with the game and made sure I used other rhetorical modes to support my definition. I revised my paper to make some of the connections I had in mind clearer by either adding transitions or explaining the relationships in other words.

I spent so much time revising the content of the essay during the writing stage that by the time I completed a draft, the essay needed very little actual revising. So I read it through for typos and grammatical errors and corrected the errors that I found. I also had a friend look it over; he identified a few more errors I hadn't seen. I felt confident and happy with the final product I turned in.

SOME FINAL THOUGHTS ON DEFINITION

The following selections feature extended definitions whose main purpose is to explain a specific term or idea to their readers. Each essay in its own way helps its audience identify with various parts of the definitions, and each successfully communicates the unique qualities of the term or idea in question. Notice what approaches to definition each writer takes and how these approaches limit the readers' frame of reference in the process of effective communication.

WAYNE NORMAN   (1961–   )

When Is a Sport Not a Sport?

Wayne Norman received his BA from Trent University and his doctorate from the London School of Economics. Currently serving as the Mike and Ruth Mackowski Professor of Ethics in the Kenan Institute for Ethics and the Department of Philosophy at Duke University, he has also served as Chair in Business Ethics at the Université de Montréal and the University of British Columbia. In addition, Norman has taught at the University of Ottawa and the University of Western Ontario. Norman is also Associate Editor of *Business Ethics Quarterly*. Having published (as author, coauthor, and editor) 5 books and over 75 articles, Norman's research can be split into two categories: Business Ethics, where he focuses on responsible company practices, and Political Philosophy, where he focuses on citizenship, nationalism, and multiculturalism. In 2001, he won, with a five-person MBA Core Team, the Allen Blizzard Award for Best Collaborative Teaching in Higher Education. Norman is currently working on an idea of business ethics in relation to the economic and legal theory of the firm and keeps a blog, "The Sporting Life," in which he uses sports as a platform from which to discuss philosophy, politics, sociology, and politics. He also plays blues guitar and harp in the band Mona Lisa's Highway Blues.

Preparing to Read

The following essay, originally published as a blog post, attempts to define the term *sport*. Norman supports his definition with examples, quotations from sources, and a comparison of the characteristics of different sports.

Exploring Experience: As you prepare to read this essay, pause a few moments to think about the basic features that make an activity a sport: What are its characteristics? Are all competitions sports? When does a competition become a sport? What qualifies a sport as an Olympic sport?

LEARNING(!)NLINE In preparing to read this essay, go online to Olympic .org, the homepage for the Olympic Games. Scroll over the "Sports" tab to see all the sports that are represented in the Olympics. Are there any sports pictured on the site that you believe should not be in the Olympics or any sports that are missing but should be represented?

Before reading this essay, you may want to consult the flowchart on page 348.

I magine you and I have different definitions of what a sport is.[1] How do we test or prove which one is best? If we have different theories about whether it is raining or not, we can just look out the window to see who's right. But if we have different definitions we usually end up having to hold these up against the way ordinary people speak. And it turns out that for lots of everyday words or concepts like "sports," people speak in pretty loose ways. We talk about two dudes trying to pick up chicks in a bar a sport. Some loner standing knee-deep in a swamp shooting at ducks might be called a sport hunter. Some of the nerdiest kids in high school are mathletes: competitive puzzle solvers.

Of course, one brash alternative is to say, "Ordinary language be damned: here is my definition of sport, and according to this definition lots of things people think are sports—like golf, and bowling, and luge, and the 100m dash—are not real sports!" The problem is, what argument can you give for your unique new definition if somebody doesn't buy it?

As I have hinted and argued throughout this blog, hidden in that attempt to define not-so-great sports out of existence (as sports, at any rate) are important intuitions about what makes some sports great. But these intuitions are best articulated and explained not by arguing about definitions, but by making a normative case for why the quality of that sporting or spectator experience is better or richer. Again, we don't have a good name for this kind of normative argument.[2] When we're arguing for why some action or rule is better in life, we call it ethics. When arguing about why some work of art is better, we call it aesthetics. But we don't have a respectable term for the kinds of topics in this blog, though they bear resemblance to both ethics and aesthetics. "Sportsthetics" sounds too much like protective equipment.

But I digress. In fact, I'm about to back track. We usually can't settle deep disputes about definitions, but we can eliminate some bad definitions, especially if these are being used for other purposes[3] (e.g., if someone's definition of "sport" is used to show why competitive cheerleading isn't a sport and when this is done in order to deny school resources to this activity).

Consider how our concept of sport is related to, and distinguished from, other concepts like game, competition, physical skill, and ability.

We notice that the classic sports, from fencing and tennis to curling and all varieties of football, contain all these elements. But we can also easily

---

Thinking Critically

1. To what extent do you think people disagree about the definition of a sport?
2. What do you think Norman means by *normative argument*?
3. Why do people need to agree on definitions of terms like *sports*? How does eliminating "bad definitions" help this process?

identify activities involving just one or two of these that are clearly not sports. Chess and charades are competitive games but we would never call them sports. Piano playing and ballet require advanced physical skills and abilities, but we never think of describing them as sports either—not even in the context of competitions to see who is the best pianist or ballerina.

Now I would contend that many of the least interesting sports—as sports,   7
they might be interesting in other ways—are those that involve a particular physical skill that preceded its being considered a sport; and we start thinking of it as a sport merely because we have staged a competition between different people practicing this activity. Many of the classic racing/throwing/shooting sports have this form. Indeed, most Olympic sports are like that. We ran, swam, threw projectiles, lifted heavy stuff, rode horses, skied, shot arrows and fired weapons, rowed boats, and so on, long before we decided it would be cool to see who could do these things the best.

As sports, most of these things are no more or less compelling than com-   8
petitions between pianists, ballroom dancers, amateur singers, child spellers, or people with heads full of trivial knowledge, ◆ which is not to say these kinds of things aren't compelling. They can all provide tremendous drama and test the limits of the human spirit in its quest to achieve difficult goals and to conquer the human frailty that keeps many of us from ever achieving as much as we want. We can identify with participants of contests and be inspired by them. And some of what they do, whether it is sprinting gracefully or singing like angels, can be beautiful to behold.

But it's not really sport, is it? For one thing, most of those simple racing,   9
throwing, lifting, etc. competitions don't even really involve anything that we could rightly call a game. My favorite sports columnist, *Salon*'s King Kaufman, called these kinds of sports "indirect competitions."

> "It's athlete vs. clock or athlete vs. competitor's score. The competitors take their turns, sequentially. They never face each other—I mean literally, face each other, the way a hockey forward and defenseman do, or the way two boxers or wrestlers or even tennis players do. That facing each other, that me trying to stop you and you trying to stop me, is what makes the great sports great."

When each athlete is simply trying to perform the demanding skill as best   10
he or she can, blocking out if at all possible how the competitors are performing, there is a lot less to engage with or admire, apart from their courage and determination. As Kaufman put it in that column from the 2002 Winter

---

Thinking Critically

◆4▸ How are sports similar to the activities listed here?

Olympics, "The Winter Olympics are filled with sports like that. All of the racing sports, the skiing and bobsled and speed skating and luge, are exercises in déjà vu. One guy flying down a mountain on skis looks pretty much like another guy flying down a mountain on skis, and doing it in one minute, 39.13 seconds looks a heck of a lot like doing it in one minute, 41.25 seconds, which is a range that on Monday encompassed 20 skiers."

I might add that there is a further category of "indirect competitions"   11
that are especially dubious as a full-blown sports—namely, those in which we can't even objectively measure the winner by time, distance, height, or weight, but instead need a panel of judges to evaluate more subjectively the form. Feel free to call these sports, but if we do, we really have almost no compelling argument against thinking that any physically demanding activity—from yoga, to dozens of forms of dance and acrobatics to, yes, competitive cheerleading—can't be considered a sport worthy of the Olympics if enough people start doing it and a governing body can invent some criteria for good form. And how often, really, do most people want to watch these competitions. In most cases, no more than an hour or two every 4 years.

Does this seem right? Great sports are the ones that involve games, not   12
just contests—games where defense matters as much as offense and, as I tried to argue in a series of posts on soccer, defense that involves tactics, along with physical and mental play, that are as admirable as those on offense.

But what, exactly, is a "game"?   13

UNDERSTANDING DETAILS

1. Explain Norman's definition of a sport. What is its main characteristic?
2. How is the author using the term *normative* in paragraph 3?
3. According to Norman, what is the difference between a classic sport and a competition?
4. What does the author mean when he says, "All of the racing sports . . . are exercises in déjà vu" (paragraph 10)? Do you agree with this description? Explain your answer.

READING CRITICALLY

5. Do you agree with Norman's definition of a sport?
6. How do you think so many forms of competition have become Olympic sports?
7. How are happiness and goodness related in the American culture? In your life?
8. Why is defining the concept of a sport important?

DISCOVERING RHETORICAL STRATEGIES

9. Why do you think Norman poses a question in his title? Do you feel this is an effective start to his essay?
10. What approaches to definition does Norman use in this essay? Give an example of each.
11. Do the sources Norman cites help him make his point effectively or not? Explain your answer.
12. What rhetorical strategies, besides definition, does the author use in this essay? Give examples of each strategy.

MAKING CONNECTIONS

13. Compare and contrast the ways in which any of the following authors you have read limit the frame of reference in their definition essays: Wayne Norman, Robert Ramirez ("The Barrio"), and/or Mary Pipher ("Beliefs about Families").
14. Imagine that Wayne Norman is having a discussion about competition with the following authors: NASA ("What Is Mars?"), Sandra Cisneros ("Only Daughter"), Sara Gilbert ("The Different Ways of Being Smart"), and/or Amy Chua ("Excerpt from *Battle Hymn of the Tiger Mother*"). How would definitions of competition differ among any of these authors that you have read? Whose definition of *competition* would be closest to your own? Why?
15. How would the following authors answer Norman's final question—What, exactly, is a "game"?: David Hanson ("Binge Drinking") and/or Art Markman ("Can Video Games Make You Smart [Or At Least More Flexible]?"). They might also answer by saying what is not a game.

IDEAS FOR DISCUSSION/WRITING

Preparing to Write

Write freely about the different relationships in your family: What special qualities characterize each of these family members? Whom do you like the best? How many different roles do you play in your family (e.g., father/mother, son/daughter, brother/sister, husband/wife)? Which of these roles do you like best? Why? What makes some of your relationships with family members better than others? To what extent are you able to control these relationships?

Choosing a Topic   MyWritingLab™

1. **LEARNING⏻NLINE** Revisit the Olympics website, Olympic.org. Now that you have read the essay, how has your definition of "sports" changed? Reevaluate your answer to the Learning Online question in Preparing to Read. Has your answer changed? Are there any sports that you now think should be included in the Olympic Games? Are there any sports included that you now believe should not be considered a sport?

2. In an essay written for your classmates, explain the role of defining in our writing. Why is being able to define an important ability? What general role does defining play in writing?
3. Using the process of definition, explain an important quality of American culture in relation to society in general.
4. Choose one of the definitional techniques explained in the introduction to this chapter, and, in an essay written for the general public, define the word *spectator* in the context of a well-developed, logically organized society. Introduce your main topic at the beginning of your essay; then explain and illustrate it clearly as your essay progresses. You may use other definition techniques in addition to your main choice.

Before beginning your essay, you may want to consult the flowchart on page 351.

ROBERT RAMIREZ   (1949–   )

The Barrio

Robert Ramirez was born and raised in Edinburg, a southern Texas town near the Mexican border in an area that has been home to his family for almost two hundred years. After graduating from the University of Texas–Pan American, he taught Freshman Composition and worked for a while as a photographer. For the next several years, he was a salesman, reporter, and announcer/anchor for the CBS affiliate station KGBT-TV in Harlingen, Texas. His current job has brought him full circle, back to the University of Texas–Pan American, where he serves as a development officer responsible for alumni fundraising. He loves baseball and once considered a professional career, but he now contents himself with bike riding, swimming, and playing tennis. A conversion to the Baha'i faith in the 1970s has brought him much spiritual happiness. When asked to give advice to students using *The Prose Reader,* Ramirez responded, "The best writing, like anything else of value, requires a great deal of effort. Rewriting is 90 percent of the process. Sometimes, if you are fortunate, your work can take on a life of its own, and you end up writing something important that astounds and humbles you. This is what happened with 'The Barrio,' which is much better than the essay I originally intended. There's an element of the divine in it, as there is in all good writing."

Preparing to Read

First titled "The Woolen Sarape," Ramirez's essay was written while he was a student at the University of Texas–Pan American. His professor, Edward Simmens, published it in an anthology entitled *Pain and Promise: The Chicano Today* (1972). In it, the author defines the exciting, colorful, and close-knit atmosphere typical of many Hispanic *barrios*, or communities.

Exploring Experience: As you prepare to read this essay, take a few moments to think about a place that is very special to you: What are its physical characteristics? What memories are connected to this place for you? What kinds of people live there? What is the relationship of these people to each other? To people in other places? Why is this place so special to you? Is it special to anyone else?

LEARNING(')NLINE Gain a clearer understanding of Robert Ramirez's definition of home by viewing "Cisco's Journal" on the PBS website: Go to www.pbs.org; click on "Programs"; select "American Family-Journey of Dreams": select "About the Series"; click on "Cisco's Journal" on the left side bar. Click on the links for "Cisco's Journal" to see an artistic interpretation of life in the barrio.

Before reading this essay, you may want to consult the flowchart on page 348.

The train, its metal wheels squealing as they spin along the silvery tracks, rolls slower now. Through the gaps between the cars blinks a streetlamp, and this pulsing light on a barrio street corner beats slower, like a weary heartbeat, until the train shudders to a halt, the light goes out, and the barrio is deep asleep.

Throughout Aztlán (the Nahuatl term meaning "land to the north"), trains grumble along the edges of a sleeping people. From Lower California, through the blistering Southwest, down the Rio Grande to the muddy Gulf, the darkness and mystery of dreams[1] engulf communities fenced off by railroads, canals, and expressways. Paradoxical communities, isolated from the rest of the town by concrete columned monuments of progress, and yet stranded in the past. They are surrounded by change. It eludes their reach, in their own backyards, and the people, unable and unwilling to see the future, or even touch the present, perpetuate the past.

Leaning from the expressway or jolting across the tracks, one enters a different physical world permeated by a different attitude. The physical dimensions are impressive. It is a large section of town which extends for fifteen blocks north and south along the tracks, and then advances eastward, thinning into nothingness beyond the city limits. Within the invisible (yet sensible) walls of the barrio are many, many people living in too few houses. The homes, however, are much more numerous than on the outside.

Members of the barrio describe the entire area as their home. It is a home, but it is more than this. The barrio is a refuge from the harshness and the coldness of the Anglo world.[2] It is a forced refuge. The leprous people are isolated from the rest of the community and contained in their section of town. The stoical pariahs of the barrio accept their fate, and from the angry seeds of rejection grow the flowers of closeness between outcasts, not the thorns of bitterness and the mad desire to flee. There is no want to escape, for the feeling of the barrio is known only to its inhabitants, and the material needs of life can also be found here.

The *tortillería* fires up its machinery three times a day, producing steaming, round, flat slices of barrio bread. In the winter, the warmth of the tortilla factory is a wool serape in the chilly morning hours, but in the summer, it unbearably toasts every noontime customer.

The *panadería* sends its sweet messenger aroma down the dimly lit street, announcing the arrival of fresh, hot, sugary *pan dulce*.

Thinking Critically

[1] What does Ramirez mean by the "mystery of dreams"? What is mysterious about dreams?

[2] In what ways might the "Anglo world" be harsh and cold to Ramirez? Give examples from your own experience.

The small corner grocery serves the meal-to-meal needs of customers, 7 and the owner, a part of the neighborhood, willingly gives credit to people unable to pay cash for foodstuffs.

The barbershop is a living room with hydraulic chairs, radio, and televi- 8 sion, where old friends meet and speak of life as their salted hair falls aimlessly about them.

The pool hall is a junior level country club where 'chucos, strangers in 9 their own land, get together to shoot pool and rap, while veterans, unaware of the cracking, popping balls on the green felt, complacently play dominoes beneath rudely hung *Playboy* foldouts.

The *cantina* is the night spot of the barrio. It is the country club and the 10 den where the rites of puberty are enacted. Here the young become men. [3] It is in the taverns that a young dude shows his *machismo* through the quantity of beer he can hold, the stories of *rucas* he has had, and his willingness and ability to defend his image against hardened and scarred old lions.

No, there is no frantic wish to flee. It would be absurd to leave the famil- 11 iar and nervously step into the strange and cold Anglo community when the needs of the Chicano can be met in the barrio.

The barrio is closeness. From the family living unit, familial relationships 12 stretch out to immediate neighbors, down the block, around the corner, and to all parts of the barrio. The feeling of family, a rare and treasurable sentiment, pervades and accounts for the inability of the people to leave. The barrio is this attitude manifested on the countenances of the people, on the faces of their homes, and in the gaiety of their gardens.

The color-splashed homes arrest your eyes, arouse your curiosity, and 13 make you wonder what life scenes are being played out in them. The flimsy, brightly colored, wood-frame houses ignore no neon-brilliant color. Houses trimmed in orange, chartreuse, lime green, yellow, and mixtures of these and other hues beckon the beholder to reflect on the peculiarity of each home. Passing through this land is refreshing like Brubeck, not narcoticizing like revolting rows of similar houses, which neither offend nor please.

In the evenings, the porches and front yards are occupied with men 14 calmly talking over the noise of children playing baseball in the unpaved extension of the living room, while the women cook supper or gossip with female neighbors as they water the *jardines.* The gardens mutely echo the expressive verses of the colorful houses. The denseness of multicolored plants and trees gives the house the appearance of an oasis or a tropical island hideaway, sheltered from the rest of the world.

Thinking Critically

[3] What relationship does the author imply between drinking and maturity?

Fences are common in the barrio, but they are fences and not the walls   15
of the Anglo community.[4] On the western side of town, the high wooden
fences between houses are thick, impenetrable walls, built to keep the neighbors at bay. In the barrio, the fences may be rusty, wire contraptions or thick
green shrubs. In either case you can see through them and feel no sense of
intrusion when you cross them.

Many lower-income families of the barrio manage to maintain a com-   16
fortable standard of living through the communal action of family members
who contribute their wages to the head of the family. Economic need creates interdependence and closeness. Small barefooted boys sell papers on
cool, dark Sunday mornings, deny themselves pleasantries, and give their
earnings to *mamá*. The older the child, the greater the responsibility to help
the head of the household provide for the rest of the family.

There are those, too, who for a number of reasons have not achieved a   17
relative sense of financial security. Perhaps it results from too many children
too soon, but it is the homes of these people and their situation that numbs
rather than charms. Their houses, aged and bent, oozing children, are fis-
sures in the horn of plenty. Their wooden homes may have brick-pattern
asbestos tile on the outer walls, but the tile is not convincing.

Unable to pay city taxes or incapable of influencing the city to live up to   18
its duty to serve all the citizens, the poorer barrio families remain trapped
in the nineteenth century and survive as best they can. The backyards have
well-worn paths to the outhouses, which sit near the alley. Running water
is considered a luxury in some parts of the barrio. Decent drainage is usually
unknown, and when it rains, the water stands for days, an incubator of
health hazards and an avoidable nuisance. Streets, costly to pave, remain
rough, rocky trails. Tires do not last long, and the constant rattling and shak-
ing grind away a car's life and spread dust through screen windows.

The houses and their *jardines,* the jollity of the people in an adverse world,   19
the brightly feathered alarm clock pecking away at supper and cautiously
eyeing the children playing nearby, produce a mystifying sensation at finding
the noble savage alive in the twentieth century.[5] It is easy to look at the
positive qualities of life in the barrio and look at them with a distantly envious feeling. One wishes to experience the feelings of the barrio and not the
hardships. Remembering the illness, the hunger, the feeling of time running
out on you, the walls, both real and imagined, reflecting on living in the past,
one finds his envy becoming more elusive, until it has vanished altogether.

Thinking Critically

4 According to Ramirez, how are "fences" different from "walls"?

5 What is a "noble savage"? How does the author use the term in this context?

Back now beyond the tracks, the train creaks and groans, the cars jostle 20
each other down the track, and as the light begins its pulsing, the barrio, with
all its meanings, greets a new dawn with yawns and restless stretchings.

UNDERSTANDING DETAILS

1. Define the barrio in your own words.
2. What is the difference between fences in the barrio and in the Anglo community?
3. In Ramirez's view, what creates "interdependence and closeness" (paragraph 16)? How does this phenomenon work in the barrio?
4. According to Ramirez, why are the houses in the barrio so colorful? What do you think is the relationship between color and happiness in the barrio?

READING CRITICALLY

5. Why does Ramirez call the people in the barrio "leprous" (paragraph 4)?
6. What does the author mean when he says, "The barrio is closeness" (paragraph 12)? How does this statement compare with the way you feel about your neighborhood? Why can't people leave the barrio?
7. Why might people look at the barrio with "a distantly envious feeling" (paragraph 19)? What other feelings may alter or even erase this sense of envy?
8. In what ways does the barrio resemble the communal living of various social groups in the 1960s?

DISCOVERING RHETORICAL STRATEGIES

9. How does Ramirez use the train to help him define the barrio? In what ways would the essay be different without the references to the train?
10. Ramirez uses metaphors masterfully throughout this essay to help us understand the internal workings of the barrio. He relies on this technique especially in paragraphs 4 through 10. For example, a metaphor that explains how relationships develop in the barrio is "The stoical pariahs of the barrio accept their fate, and from the angry seeds of rejection grow the flowers of closeness between outcasts, not the thorns of bitterness and the mad desire to flee" (paragraph 4). In this garden metaphor, "rejection" is likened to "angry seeds," "closeness between outcasts" to "flowers," and "bitterness" to "thorns." Find four other metaphors in these paragraphs, and explain how the comparisons work. What are the familiar and less familiar items in each comparison?
11. What tone does Ramirez establish in this essay? How does he create this tone?
12. The dominant method the author uses to organize his essay is definition. What other rhetorical strategies does Ramirez use to support his definition?

MAKING CONNECTIONS

13. Compare and contrast the "feeling of family" described by Ramirez with that depicted by Ray Bradbury ("Summer Rituals"), Sandra Cisneros ("Only Daughter"), and/or Mary Pipher ("Beliefs about Families").

14. Ramirez does a wonderful job of creating a sensual experience in his essay as he chronicles the vivid sights, sounds, smells, tastes, and textures of life in the barrio. In the same way, Ray Bradbury ("Summer Rituals") and Garrison Keillor ("Hoppers") appeal to our senses in their descriptive essays. Which author's prose style (from these essays you have read) do you find most sensual? Explain your answer.

15. Whereas Ramirez defines the "barrio" through description, Elizabeth Svoboda ("Virtual Assault") defines her topic in another fashion. How do the two authors differ in constructing their definitions? Which technique do you find most persuasive? Explain your answer.

IDEAS FOR DISCUSSION/WRITING

Preparing to Write

Write freely about a place that is special to you: Describe this place from your perspective. Is this place special to anyone else? Describe this place from someone else's perspective. How do these descriptions differ? What characteristics differentiate this place from other places? What makes this place special to you? Use some metaphors to relay to your readers your feelings about certain features of this place. Do you think this place will always be special to you? Why or why not?

Choosing a Topic

MyWritingLab™

1. **LEARNING⏻NLINE** What does the term *home* mean to you? Using "Cisco's Journal" (from Preparing to Read), create a virtual tour of a place you have lived. Describe each room, the neighborhood, and/or the region. Develop your definition of *home* so that the readers can walk with you through each element.

2. Ramirez's definition of the barrio demonstrates a difference between an insider's view and an outsider's view of the same location. In an essay for your classmates, define your special place from both the inside and the outside. Then discuss the similarities and differences between these two points of view.

3. In essay form, define the relationships among the people who are your extended family. These could be people from your neighborhood, your school, your job, or a combination of places. How did these relationships come about? Why are you close to these people? Why are these people close to you? To each other?

4. What primary cultural or social traditions have made you what you are today? In an essay written to a close friend, define the two or three most important traditions you practiced as a child, and explain what effects they had on you.

Before beginning your essay, you may want to consult the flowchart on page 351.

ELIZABETH SVOBODA   (1990–   )

Virtual Assault

Elizabeth Svoboda grew up in the suburbs of Western New York and received her BA from Yale. She makes her living as a freelance writer, penning articles ranging in topic from dinosaurs and creationist biology classes to the science of motivation. She has contributed to publications such as *Discover, Popular Science, Psychology Today,* and *The New York Times,* to name a few. Her book, *What Makes a Hero?: The Surprising Science of Selflessness* (2013), looks at how people come to act in heroic and altruistic ways. Svoboda has also been awarded the Evert Clark/ Seth Payne Award from the National Association of Science Writers. She currently lives in San Jose with her husband, Eric, and their son, Nate.

Preparing to Read

This essay first appeared in *Scientific American Mind* in 2014. In it, Elizabeth Svoboda defines what she believes are the key elements of cyberbullying, along with some suggestions for stopping them.

Exploring Experience: As you prepare to read this essay, think about your immediate environment: Are you or your friends threatened by anything or anyone on a regular basis? How is this threat provoked? What can you do to control this threat? How does this threat make you feel? Are the threats virtual or in person? Which approach is easier for you to control? Why do you think that is so?

LEARNING◯NLINE Before you read the following essay, type "cyberbullying" into Google, and then click the "News" tab to see current cyberbullying issues and cases. Read through at least one of these news articles. Freewrite your first reactions to this article and to cyberbullying in general.

Before reading this essay, you may want to consult the flowchart on page 348.

When 25-year-old Caitlin Seida dressed up as Lara Croft from the movie *Tomb Raider* one Halloween, she posted a picture of herself enjoying the night's festivities on Facebook. At most, she figured a few friends might see the photograph and comment.

The picture remained in Seida's social circle for more than three years. Then one day in 2013 a friend sent Seida a link with a cryptic note: "You're Internet famous." Clicking the link took her to a site called the International Association of Haters, where her Halloween photo—which she had posted publicly by mistake—bore the oversized caption "Fridge Raider." Hundreds of commenters dragged Seida through the mud for wearing a skimpy costume while being overweight. "Heifers like her should be put down," one commenter wrote. "What a waste of space," another piped in.

Horrified, Seida did some more quick searches and realized her photo had gone viral, racking up poisonous comments on dozens of sites. Reading the messages was like absorbing a series of body blows. "I felt like shit," Seida says. "I cried and cried and cried some more." With a paralegal friend's help, she contacted Web site owners to get the offending images and posts taken down, but she knew her efforts would likely fall short. "I can herd cats more easily than I can control what's posted online." [1]

Despite the publicity devoted to teenage cyberbullies, online aggression is hardly confined to the high school set. About one in four adults has been cyberbullied or knows someone who has, according to a recent poll by the online design firm Rad Campaign, along with Lincoln Park Strategies and Craigslist founder Craig Newmark. [2] The abuse can come in the form of insulting e-mails, tag team-style pile-ons in Internet forums or personal attacks in news article comment sections. Victims are often so profoundly affected that they descend into depression or even contemplate suicide. Yet the problem has largely gone unaddressed because so few observers take it seriously and because it can be unclear which comments qualify as bullying. [3] "People are reluctant to report it," says Chris Piotrowski, a cyberbullying expert and research consultant at the University of West Florida. "A lot of them feel like, '[If] I go to the police, what are they going to do?'"

Researchers are uncovering the psychological forces behind such poisonous verbiage and the harm it causes, and their work points to ways of preventing vicious avalanches of verbal aggression—or at least minimizing

---

Thinking Critically

1. Why do you think the author begins her essay with a story? How does this story about Caitlin Seida help set the tone for the rest of the article?
2. Have you been or do you know someone who has been cyberbullied?
3. Has your high school addressed bullying in any way? Was it successful?

the damage. An important part of the solution involves all of us. As members of the Internet democracy, we each have the power to re-direct negative group tendencies in ways that promote online civility. "Don't wait for the other two or 300 [people] to do something," says Mary Aiken, director of the CyberPsychology Research Center at the Royal College of Surgeons in Ireland. "It's up to users to create a better environment."

"They got the better of me, and they won" [4]

The trope of the swaggering bully is almost as old as human history.   6
Whether children or adults, bullies blast their targets with scathing words and profane put-downs—and they do not let up, even when the victim begs for mercy. Bullying behavior probably has evolutionary roots, argues social anthropologist Christopher Boehm of the University of Southern California. Early humans who were good at lording it over others enjoyed a boost in their social standing, and as a result, they produced more offspring.

Contrary to popular wisdom, bullies are not merely compensating for   7
their own low self-esteem. In a 2013 study of thousands of middle school students, psychologist Jaana Juvonen of the University of California, Los Angeles, and her colleagues found that bullies are often perched at the *top* of the social hierarchy and demean others to cement their position. Upbringing also plays a key role: according to social learning theory, we learn how to interact with others by observing those close to us. Aggressive parents and other role models, then, may produce aggressive kids. The fallout can be devastating: Bullying victims suffer significant distress, sometimes for decades. The U.S. Secret Service reports that in most school shooting incidents, shooters felt persecuted or bullied before launching their attacks.

Now that people are socializing in virtual realms, an age-old dynamic has   8
taken hold in a new environment. Cyberbullying is usually defined as intimidation, hurt or harassment conducted using cell phones, the Internet or other electronic devices, but as Piotrowski points out, the contours of this definition are somewhat blurry. "What defines cyberabuse? [5] To one person, it's someone who's being rude. To another person, it's an offensive statement. Another person might say it's [an attack that's] escalating."

At its most obvious, cyberbullying is extremely brutal. Women's-rights   9
activist Caroline Criado-Perez endured dozens of unhinged online trolling attacks from woman haters after she convinced the Bank of England to feature Jane Austen on its 10-pound note. "I remember the man who told

---

Thinking Critically

[4] Why is this statement in quotation marks? What does it refer to?
[5] What is "cyberabuse" to you?

me a group of them would mutilate my genitals with scissors and set my house on fire while I begged to die," Criado-Perez told the *New Statesman* in January. "I remember the fear, the horror, the despair. I remember not being able to sleep. I remember thinking it would never end." (Although Criado-Perez did contact the police, she felt they did not take her complaints seriously.)

As Criado-Perez's experience suggests, online persecution can take an   10
outsize toll on mental health. Victims of cyberabuse often show symptoms consistent with post-traumatic stress disorder, including flashbacks, runaway anxiety, guilt or depression. They report low self-esteem and feelings of helplessness. "It's a serious problem that has serious psychological consequences," says social psychologist S. Alexander Haslam of the University of Queensland in Australia. Even people used to the public eye may reach a breaking point when tormentors go too far. Australian journalist Charlotte Dawson—herself an antibullying activist—broke down earlier this year after absorbing a relentless barrage of Twitter messages mocking her depression and encouraging her to kill herself. She was found dead in her Sydney apartment, where she had hanged herself. "It just triggered that feeling of helplessness when the trolls got to me," Dawson said in a 2012 interview on Australia's *60 Minutes* after a previous round of Twitter attacks. "They got the better of me, and they won."

Mob Mentality

Just like real-world bullies, the worst online gangsters often display anti-   11
social personality traits. Some may show characteristics of psychopathy such as aggression and disregard for fellow human beings; others are sadistic. In a 2014 study, psychologist Erin E. Buckels of the University of Manitoba and her colleagues surveyed more than 1,200 Internet users and found that those who agreed with statements such as "I enjoy making jokes at the expense of others" and "I enjoy playing the villain in games and torturing other characters" were more likely to show traits associated with personality disorders. It stands to reason that people who have real-life antisocial tendencies might show similar contempt for others in the online realm.

Still, plenty of psychologically balanced adults take online potshots at   12
others, says psychologist John Suler of Rider University, partially because cyberspace lets them create a virtual persona that is separate from their everyday identity. They know that when they retreat behind the cloak of anonymity, they probably will not have to answer for their actions.[6]

Thinking Critically

[6] How does anonymity escalate bullying?

The phenomenon of the faceless, nameless online bully is a familiar one; surveys suggest only about one in four online bullying victims know their attackers in real life. "From the abuser's point of view, [online bullying] is low risk, high reward," Piotrowski says. "They're thinking, 'I won't get caught because it's online,'" and they get the buzz of feeling elevated because they are pushing someone else down. In a 2012 study, psychologists Noam Lapidot-Lefler, now at the Max Stern Academic College of Emek Yezreel, and Azy Barak of the University of Haifa instructed participants to debate a contentious topic in pairs over online chat; they noted that people were more likely to threaten their debate partners when posting under an alias than when using their real names.

But the most noxious and prevalent instances of online bullying emerge   13 from a combination of anonymity and group forces. In 2001 social psychologist Tom Postmes, now at the University of Groningen in the Netherlands, and his colleagues reported that when online participants were anonymous, they were more likely to conform to the behavior of the groups they belonged to—a tendency that is problematic when the group's members are rude or aggressive. Similarly, in a 2012 study, psychology researcher Adam Zimmerman of the University of North Florida studied 126 online participants in a word-unscrambling game and found that those who did not use their real names were more likely than identified participants to write aggressive blog posts about their fellow players, especially when they observed other participants acting aggressively. "We get permission [to bully] from the people around us," Zimmerman says. "It gives us the idea that we could also do that if we want to."

When nameless, faceless online participants assume the identity of the   14 group that surrounds them, a virtual mod mentality takes hold. People are impulsive and aggressive and tend to copy one another, often leading to tag-team attacks like those hurled at Seida. "When people engage in online bullying, they are often doing it in front of a particular audience they imagine is approving," Haslam says. If a chat forum's terms of engagement—stated or unstated—allow people to be bullied without consequence, new participants are probably going to conform to the norms set by the bullies. Even people with good intentions can succumb. "If others are piling on someone, you might join in even if you weren't setting out to hurt anyone," adds psychologist Scott O. Lilienfeld of Emory University.

Once insult-slinging gets under way in a chat room or e-mail thread, it   15 can escalate quickly, perhaps because empathy is more elusive in a virtual environment. Cyberaggressors cannot see their victims' tears or the fear in their eyes. Their targets are abstractions. In addition, the bullying persists in ways that would have been unthinkable in the era before Google and Facebook. Victims relive that punch-in-the-gut feeling every time humiliating photos of them appear on a new Web site or insults appear in search results for their name. Also, as Seida learned, erasing the attacks or even getting bullies to admit to the harm they have caused is fiendishly difficult. When Seida and a friend tracked down some of her tormentors and sent them personal notes, they were rebuffed. "We sent them messages and a little certificate that said, 'Why don't you be a human being and take down the comments you made?' Nobody apologized."

Bullying can affect bystanders, too. In a study published in 2013 Colorado State University communications specialist Ashley Anderson and her colleagues recruited more than 1,000 people to read an online article about the risks and benefits of nanotechnology. Readers who were exposed to "flame wars" in which commenters slammed nanotech or insulted its defenders tended to see nanotechnology's risks as more pronounced than did readers who had *not* seen such verbal attacks, regardless of whether the arguments held water. If, as these results suggest, bullies' comments are often persuasive, passive observers might start to buy into some of the attackers' claims ("Theresa is a slutbag ho"). 16

Setting New Norms

The toxic fallout from online attacks has led some respected news outlets to kill off virtual discussion communities. "We are as committed to fostering lively, intellectual debate as we are to spreading the word of science far and wide," wrote *Popular Science's* then digital editor Suzanne LaBarre last fall, announcing that the magazine planned to eliminate its Web site's comment section. "The problem is when trolls overwhelm the former, diminishing our ability to do the latter." 17

The decision by *Popular Science* to nix online comments provoked outcry. Efforts to curb online bullying and flame wars often err in the direction of limiting open discussion. Part of the reason is practical. Policing individual online interactions—by, say, enforcing language restrictions on discussion boards or cleaning up news comment sections—can be a time-consuming task for Web site managers. What is more, few victims report bullying to site administrators because they think nothing will be done about the problem or because they fear retribution from attackers. 18

So far legislative solutions to the online aggression problem do not seem all that effective, even though 48 states have laws against electronic harassment. California's legal code, for instance, gives administrators grounds to suspend or expel students for participating in online bullying, and Louisiana's legal code reads, "Whoever commits the crime of cyberbullying shall be fined not more than five hundred dollars, imprisoned for not more than six months, or both." Such laws, however, are seldom enforced, in part because cyberbullying victims do not always report being abused—and when victims 19 *do* complain, administrators and discussion board owners do not always notify state authorities.

In the absence of systematic policing by Web site managers or the govern-   20 ment, some administrators have begun testing automated antibullying tools. A system produced by the video game company Riot Games, for instance, detects patterns of negative behavior from particular online players and sends them a quick message, gently letting them know they have crossed a line. "For neutral and positive players," Jeffrey Lin, a lead designer at Riot, told *GamesIndustry* magazine, "this subtle nudge is often enough to get them back on track."

Yet some hard-core bullies are unfazed by automated warnings and keep   21 right on unloading their venom. In such cases, community members should step in—whether by writing a response to the aggressor on the forum or reporting bullying comments as abuse. When members of an online forum, discussion group or e-mail thread consistently refuse to tolerate bullying, new participants will probably conform to that established norm, turning the group into a force for good.

All online participants determine what a community's norms are. "If trolls   22 show up, if the community as a whole can say, 'This is not something we want here,' it can convince that person to move on," Suler says. Taking a stand not only helps the victim but is also good for you: When people see others being bullied and fail to speak up, their own psychological health often suffers.

Concerned onlookers can also help curb bullying's spread by reaching out   23 to victims individually via e-mail or direct message. Aggression often begets aggression—cyberbullying victims may turn around and bully others, according to San Diego State University psychologist Jean M. Twenge. But you can mitigate this effect by offering the abused your support and condemning the attacks. In a 2007 study, Twenge and her colleagues found that when people made a short, friendly connection with someone else following an episode of social exclusion, the victim was less likely to show aggression afterward. "Having even one person accept you seemed to mitigate the [aggression] effect," says Twenge, author of *Generation Me*. "Reach out and say, 'I'm sorry this happened.'"

Such outreach is especially crucial because even antibullying education   24 may not deter determined trolls. According to a 2013 study by University of Texas at Arlington criminologist Seokjin Jeong and Byung Hyun Lee of Michigan State University, students were *more* likely to be bullied at schools that had installed antibullying programs, perhaps because the programs inadvertently gave bullies ideas for tormenting their victims.[7]

Thinking Critically

[7] What suggestions for curbing or stopping cyberbullying can you add to Svoboda's list?

Rallying Friends

Many months after enduring online ridicule, Seida decided she was not 25 going to let the bullies' vile comments define her. To give her detractors the middle finger, she did a boudoir photo shoot while wearing the now infamous Lara Croft costume. "If they're going to talk, I might as well give them something to talk about!" she says.

Seida's brush with cyberbullies inspired her to reach out to others on the 26 receiving end of vicious online attacks. Along with a photographer friend, she created ifeeldelicious.com, a site designed to help victims of online bullying repair the damage to their dignity and psyche. She and other members ran a successful campaign against a notorious bully they called "the King of Mean," rallying others to boycott and speak out against his insult-ridden Web site and social media sites. She advises people who face relentless online jibes to gather a group of friends who appreciate them. Indeed, knowing someone else has your back goes a long way toward softening the impact of drive-by online attacks. "Talk to somebody—find a support system," Seida says. "If you keep it inside, it's just going to eat you alive."

UNDERSTANDING DETAILS

1. Explain cyberbullying in your own words.
2. What is the connection between school shootings and bullying?
3. What are the main characteristics of bullies?
4. What does mob mentality have to do with cyberbullying?

READING CRITICALLY

5. Read the article again, and underline the author's thesis in one color and her topic sentences in another color. What is the relationship of these sentences?
6. Which of Svoboda's examples in your opinion was most effective in driving her point home? Why was it effective?
7. Why is the virtual environment "low risk, high reward" (paragraph 12) for bullies?
8. Which of Svoboda's suggestions for controlling cyberbullying do you think could produce the best results? Explain your answer.

DISCOVERING RHETORICAL STRATEGIES

9. What is the main purpose of this essay? Does it achieve this purpose, in your opinion?
10. Who is the audience for this essay? How did you come to that conclusion?
11. Svoboda starts her essay with an actual story about cyberbullying. Is this an effective opening for her definition? Why or why not? How does she use the same incident to bring her essay to a close?
12. What rhetorical modes does Svoboda draw on to develop her definition? Do these choices help her achieve her purpose? Explain your answer.

MAKING CONNECTIONS

13. Which of the following authors would agree most enthusiastically with Svoboda that "rallying friends" is a productive solution for cyberbullying: Roni Jackson ("A Digital Safety Net"), Stephanie Vozza ("How to Make New Friends as an Adult"), and/or Samantha Pugsley ("How Language Impacts the Stigma Against Mental Health [And What We Must Do to Change It]")? How could friends help control cyberbullying from each of these perspectives?

14. To what extent would any of the following authors you have read claim with Svoboda that we need to be conscious of our level of civility: Garrison Keillor ("Hoppers"), Christopher Nelson ("Why We are Looking at the 'Value' of College All Wrong"), and/or Samantha Pugsley ("How Language Impacts the Stigma Against Mental Health [And What We Must Do to Change It]")? Explain your conclusions.

15. How would the definition of "abuse" in this article be qualified by Sandra Cisneros ("Only Daughter"), Russell Baker ("The Saturday Evening Post"), Jessica Mitford ("Behind the Formaldehyde Curtain"), and/or Michael Dorris ("The Broken Cord")? Would any of these authors agree with each other about the main details of this definition?

IDEAS FOR DISCUSSION/WRITING

Preparing to Write

Write freely about the importance of civility in society: Why is civility important? How can we achieve civility? How does bullying work against civility? How does the level of civility in our society affect our culture? How does it affect us as individuals?

Choosing a Topic   MyWritingLab™

1. **LEARNING⏻NLINE** In the light of Seida's personal story of cyberbullying, return to the news article you read in Preparing to Read. Compare the article to the essay, and discuss the definition of cyberbullying as it relates to both the news article and Svoboda's essay.

2. As a graduate of your high school, you have been asked by the Board of Education to define civility for your school. The board has asked you to include in your prepared statement an explanation of the characteristics students should possess when they leave high school so that they will be positive, productive citizens in our society.

3. Do you agree with Svoboda's suggestions for stopping cyberbullying? Write an essay responding to her suggestions by analyzing each suggestion and predicting how it will succeed or fail.

4. How do you think we will be managing all types of bullying in ten years? Will it still be a threat to all of us? What will be the consequences of bullying? What needs to happen for us to gain control of this threat to our civility?

Before beginning your essay, you may want to consult the flowchart on page 351.

MARY PIPHER   (1947–   )

Beliefs About Families

The oldest of seven children, Mary Pipher was born in Springfield, Missouri. She earned her B.A. in Cultural Anthropology at the University of California, Berkeley, and her Ph.D. in Clinical Psychology at the University of Nebraska. Currently a professor in the graduate clinical training program at the University of Nebraska, she became a writer only after her children had been raised, declaring that "Writing has been the great gift of my middle years. It is my reason to wake up in the morning." Her first book, *Hunger Pains: The Modern Woman's Tragic Quest for Thinness* (1987), was followed by *Reviving Ophelia: Saving the Selves of Adolescent Girls* (1994), an enormously influential study of the world of teenage girls. Other books she has written are *The Shelter of Each Other: Rebuilding Our Families* (1996), which examines family relationships in America today; *Another Country: Navigating the Emotional Terrain of Our Elders* (1999), an analysis of how the United States isolates and misunderstands its senior citizens; *The Middle of Everywhere: The World's Refugees Come to Our Town* (2002); *Letters to a Young Therapist: The Art of Mentoring* (2003); *Writing to Change the World* (2006); *Seeking Peace: Chronicles of the Worst Buddhist in the World* (2009), and *The Green Boat: Reviving Ourselves in Our Capsized Culture* (2013). An avid outdoorswoman who loves hiking, backpacking, and watching sunsets, Pipher has the following words for students using *The Prose Reader:* "What all good writers have in common is a yearning to communicate."

Preparing to Read

The following essay from *The Shelter of Each Other: Rebuilding Our Families* attempts to define the notion of "family" in contemporary society.

Exploring Experience: As you prepare to read this essay, take a few moments to think about the role family plays in your life: Are you close to your biological family? Are you a part of any other groups that function like a family? How do they work? Are you aware of your roles in these various groups? What is the relationship between your role in your immediate family and your personal goals?

LEARNING◯NLINE To gain a perspective on the varied media representations of "family," go to www.youtube.com, search "Leave It to Beaver," and watch any of the top search results. Contrast this family with the one portrayed in *American Beauty* at the Internet Movie Database website (www.imdb.com). (Enter "American Beauty" into the search field, and view the 1999 movie trailer.) Consider how these "families" relate to Pipher's definition as you read her essay.

Before reading this essay, you may want to consult the flowchart on page 348.

When I speak of families, I usually mean biological families. 1
There is a power in blood ties that cannot be denied.[1] But in
our fragmented, chaotic culture, many people don't have biological families nearby. For many people, friends become family. Family is
a collection of people who pool resources and help each other over the long
haul. Families love one another even when that requires sacrifice. Family
means that if you disagree, you still stay together.

Families are the people for whom it matters if you have a cold, are feud- 2
ing with your mate or training a new puppy. Family members use magnets
to fasten the newspaper clippings about your bowling team on the refrigera-
tor door. They save your drawings and homemade pottery. They like to hear
stories about when you were young. They'll help you can tomatoes or
change the oil in your car. They're the people who will come visit you in
the hospital, will talk to you when you call with "a dark night of the soul"
and will loan you money to pay the rent if you lose your job. Whether or
not they are biologically related to each other, the people who do these
things are family.[2]

If you are very lucky, family is the group you were born into. But some 3
are not that lucky. When Janet was in college, her parents were killed in a
car wreck. In her early twenties she married, but three years later she lost
her husband to leukemia. She has one sister, who calls mainly when she's
suicidal or needs money. Janet is a congresswoman in a western state, a hard
worker and an idealist. Her family consists of the men, women, and children
she's grown to depend on in the twenty-five years she's lived in her community. Except for her beloved dog, nobody lives with her. But she brings
the cinnamon rolls to one family's Thanksgiving dinner and has a Mexican
fiesta for families at her house on New Year's Eve. She attends Bar Mitzvahs,
weddings, school concerts, and soccer matches. She told me with great
pride, "When I sprained my ankle skiing last year, three families brought
me meals."

I think of Morgan, a jazz musician who long ago left his small town and 4
rigid, judgmental family. He had many memories of his father whipping
him with a belt or making him sleep in the cold. Once he said to me, "I
was eighteen years old before anyone ever told me I had something to
offer." Indeed he does. He plays the violin beautifully. He teaches impro-
visation and jazz violin and organizes jazz events for his town. His family

---

Thinking Critically

[1] What does Pipher mean when she says, "There is a power in blood ties that cannot be
denied"?

[2] What is your definition of "family"? How is it different from Pipher's?

is the family of musicians and music lovers that he has built around him over the years.

If you are very unlucky, you come from a nuclear family that didn't care [3] for you. Curtis, who as a boy was regularly beaten by his father, lied about his age so that he could join the Navy at sixteen. Years later he wrote his parents and asked if he could return home for Christmas. They didn't answer his letter. When I saw him in therapy, I encouraged him to look for a new family, among his cousins and friends from the Navy. Sometimes cutoffs, tragic as they are, are unavoidable.

I think of Anita, who never knew her father and whose mother aban- [6] doned her when she was seven. Anita was raised by an aunt and uncle, whom she loved very much. As an adult she tracked down her mother and tried to establish a relationship, but her mother wasn't interested. At least Anita was able to find other family members to love her. She had a family in her aunt and uncle.

Family need not be traditional or biological. But what family offers is not [7] easily replicated. Let me share a Sioux word, *tiospaye,* which means the people with whom one lives. The *tiospaye* is probably closer to a kibbutz than to any other Western institution. The *tiospaye* gives children multiple parents, aunts, uncles and grandparents. It offers children a corrective factor for problems in their nuclear families. If parents are difficult, there are other adults around to soften and diffuse the situation. Until the 1930s, when the *tiospaye* began to fall apart with sale of land, migration and alcoholism, there was not much mental illness among the Sioux. When all adults were respon- sible for all children, people grew up healthy.

What *tiospaye* offers and what biological family offers is a place that all [8] members can belong to regardless of merit. Everyone is included regardless of health, likability or prestige. What's most valuable about such institutions is that people are in by virtue of being born into the group. People are in even if they've committed a crime, been a difficult person, become physi- cally or mentally disabled or are unemployed and broke. That ascribed status was what Robert Frost valued when he wrote that home "was something you somehow hadn't to deserve." [4]

Many people do not have access to either a supportive biological family [9] or a *tiospaye.* They make do with a "formed family." Others simply prefer a

---

Thinking Critically

[3] Why does the author think that people who come from families that don't care for them are "unlucky"?

[4] Why does the author quote from the poet Robert Frost? What special insight does this quotation bring to Pipher's essay?

community of friends to their biological families. The problem with formed families is they often have less staying power. They might not take you in, give you money if you lose a job or visit you in a rest home if you are paralyzed in a car crash. My father had a stroke and lost most of his sight and speech. Family members were the people who invited him to visit and helped him through the long tough years after his stroke. Of course, there are formed families who do this. With the AIDS crisis, many gays have supported their friends through terrible times. Often immigrants will help each other in this new country. And there are families who don't stick together in crisis. But generally blood is thicker than water. Families come through when they must.

Another problem with formed families is that not everyone has the skills   10
to be included in that kind of family. Friendship isn't a product that can be obtained for cash. People need friends today more than ever, but friends are harder to make in a world where people are busy, moving, and isolated. Some people don't have the skills. They are shy, abrasive, or dull. Crack babies have a hard time making friends, as do people with Alzheimer's. Formed families can leave many people out.

From my point of view the issue isn't biology. Rather the issues are   11
commitment and inclusiveness. I don't think for most of us it has to be either/or. A person can have both a strong network of friends and a strong family. [5] It is important to define family broadly so that all kinds of families, such as single-parent families, multigenerational families, foster families and the families of gays are included. But I agree with David Blankenberg's conclusion in his book *Rebuilding the Nest:* "Even with all the problems of nuclear families, I will support it as an institution until something better comes along."

Americans hold two parallel versions of the family—the idealized version   12
and the dysfunctional version. The idealized version portrays families as wellsprings of love and happiness, loyal, wholesome, and true. This is the version we see in *Leave It to Beaver* or *Father Knows Best.* The dysfunctional version depicts families as disturbed and disturbing, and suggests that salvation lies in extricating oneself from all the ties that bind. Both versions have had their eras. In the 1950s the idealized version was at its zenith. Extolling family was in response to the Depression and war, which separated families. People who had been wrenched away from home missed their families and

---

Thinking Critically

[5] Which is more important to you now: "a strong network of friends" or "a strong family"? Which group do you think will be more important to you twenty years from now? Explain your answer.

thought of them with great longing. They idealized how close and warm they had been.

In the 1990s the dysfunctional version of family seems the most influen- 13 tial. This belief system goes along with the culture of narcissism, which sells people the idea that families get in the way of individual fulfillment. Currently, many Americans are deeply mistrustful of their own and other people's families. Pop psychology presents families as pathology-producing. Talk shows make families look like hotbeds of sin and sickness. Day after day people testify about the diverse forms of emotional abuse that they suffered in their families. Movies and television often portray families as useless impediments.

In our culture, after a certain age, children no longer have permission to 14 love their parents. We define adulthood as breaking away, disagreeing and making up new rules.[6] Just when teenagers most need their parents, they are encouraged to distance themselves from them. A friend told me of walking with her son in a shopping mall. They passed some of his friends, and she noticed that suddenly he was ten feet behind, trying hard not to be seen with her. She said, "I felt like I was drooling and wearing purple plaid polyester." Later her son told her that he enjoyed being with her, but that his friends all hated their parents and he would be teased if anyone knew he loved her. He said, "I'm confused about this. Am I supposed to hate you?"

This socialized antipathy toward families is unusual. Most cultures revere 15 and respect family. In Vietnam, for example, the tender word for lover is "sibling." In the Kuma tribe of Papua New Guinea, family members are valued above all others. Siblings are seen as alter egos[,][7] essential parts of the self. The Kuma believe that mates can be replaced, but not family members. Many Native American tribes regard family members as connected to the self. To be without family is to be dead.

From the Greeks, to Descartes, to Freud and Ayn Rand, Westerners have 16 valued the independent ego. But Americans are the most extreme. Our founders were rebels who couldn't tolerate oppression. When they formed a new government they emphasized rights and freedoms.

American values concerning independence may have worked better 17 when we lived in small communities surrounded by endless space. But we have run out of space and our outlaws live among us. At one time the outlaw

---

Thinking Critically

6 Do you agree with Pipher that adulthood in our culture means "breaking away, disagreeing and making up new rules"? Why or why not?

7 Do you have a sibling? In what sense is he or she an "alter ego"?

mentality was mitigated by a strong sense of community. Now the values of community have been superseded by other values.

We have pushed the concept of individual rights to the limits. Our laws   18
let adults sell children harmful products. But laws are not our main problem. People have always been governed more by community values than by laws.[8] Ethics, rather than laws, determine most of our behavior. Unwritten rules of civility—for taking turns, not cutting in lines, holding doors open for others and lowering our voices in theaters—organize civic life. Unfortunately, those rules of civility seem to be crumbling in America. We are becoming a nation of people who get angry when anyone gets in our way.

Rudeness is everywhere in our culture. Howard Stern, G. Gordon Liddy,   19
and Newt Gingrich are rude. It's not surprising our children copy them. Phil Donahue and Jay Leno interrupt, and children learn to interrupt. A young man I know was recently injured on a volleyball court. The player who hurt him didn't apologize or offer to help him get to an emergency room. An official told him to get off the floor because he was messing it up with his blood and holding up the game. I recently saw an old man hesitate at a busy intersection. Behind him drivers swore and honked. He looked scared and confused as he turned into traffic and almost wrecked his car. At a festival a man stood in front of the stage, refusing to sit down when people yelled out that they couldn't see. Finally another man wrestled him to the ground. All around were the omnipresent calls of "Fuck You." Over coffee a local politician told me she would no longer attend town meetings. She said, "People get out of control and insult me and each other. There's no dialogue, it's all insults and accusations."

We have a crisis in meaning in our culture. The crisis comes from our   20
isolation from each other, from the values we learn in a culture of consumption and from the fuzzy, self-help message that the only commitment is to the self and the only important question is—Am I happy? We learn that we are number one and that our own immediate needs are the most important ones. The crisis comes from the message that products satisfy and that happiness can be purchased.

We live in a money-driven culture.[9] But the bottom line is not the only   21
line, or even the best line for us to hold. A culture organized around profits instead of people is not user friendly to families. We all suffer from existential

---

Thinking Critically

8 What is the difference between "community values" and "laws"? Give an example of each.

9 Do you agree that we live in a "money-driven culture"? Explain your answer.

flu, as we search for meaning in a culture that values money, not meaning. Everyone I know wants to do good work. But right now we have an enormous gap between doing what's meaningful and doing what is reimbursed.

UNDERSTANDING DETAILS

1. How does Pipher define *families?* What particular activities characterize a "family" member?
2. What do "commitment and inclusiveness" (paragraph 11) have to do with being in a family?
3. According to Pipher, what are the two parallel versions of the family, and when were they dominant?
4. According to Pipher, what poses the biggest problem to the integrity of the family as a unit?

READING CRITICALLY

5. In what way does the Sioux word *tiospaye* (paragraph 7) describe the traits of a family?
6. According to Pipher, why do "people need friends today more than ever" (paragraph 10)?
7. What is difficult about "formed families" (paragraph 10)?
8. Do you agree with Pipher that we have "a crisis of meaning in our culture" (paragraph 20)? Explain your answer in detail.

DISCOVERING RHETORICAL STRATEGIES

9. Why does the author introduce the stories of Janet, Morgan, Curtis, and Anita?
10. What do you think Pipher's purpose is in this essay?
11. Pipher approaches her definition from many different angles before suggesting that American culture is facing a crisis in understanding and agreeing on what a family is. How do her various definitions support her statement about a crisis? Explain your answer.
12. What rhetorical modes support the author's definition? Give examples of each.

MAKING CONNECTIONS

13. Which parts of Mary Pipher's definition of "family" would Ray Bradbury ("Summer Rituals") and/or Robert Ramirez ("The Barrio") most agree with? Explain your answer.
14. Imagine that Russell Baker ("The Saturday Evening Post"), Amy Chua ("Excerpt from *Battle Hymn of the Tiger Mother*"), and/or Mary Pipher are discussing the extent to which people in a family have to compromise. Which author would you probably agree with, and why?
15. Compare and contrast the ways in which Mary Pipher, Robert Ramirez ("The Barrio"), and/or David Hanson ("Binge Drinking") begin their definition essays.

IDEAS FOR DISCUSSION/WRITING

Preparing to Write

Write freely about the qualities that constitute a good family member: How do you recognize a good family member? What characterizes him or her? Do you personally appreciate your biological family? Are you a part of other families? If so, what are the characteristics of these families? Why is some type of family important to our well-being? What role does the notion of family play in your self-definition?

Choosing a Topic

MyWritingLab™

1. **LEARNING⏻NLINE** Conduct an Internet search on international representations of "family." Start with the United Nations Children's Fund (UNICEF) website (www.unicef.org). Use terms such as "family practices" to begin your search. Write an essay in which you expand Pipher's definition of *family* to include at least three detailed examples of global family practices. Use Pipher's developed example of Sioux customs as a model for your expanded descriptions.

2. Write an essay for your classmates defining "a family" that you belong to.

3. In a well-organized essay, use examples to define the dysfunctional family as it exists today. Be as specific as possible.

4. The relationship between family and individual has changed since your parents were in school. Explain to them the current relationship between you and your family. What are the connections between your personal goals and your role in your immediate family?

Before beginning your essay, you may want to consult the flowchart on pages 351.

DAVID HANSON   (1941–   )

Binge Drinking

Having received his Ph.D. in Sociology from Syracuse University in 1972, David J. Hanson has dedicated his professional life to researching alcohol use and abuse. He is currently the Professor Emeritus of Sociology at the State University of New York at Potsdam, an Advisory Board member for the American Association for the Advancement of Science, and a member of the Board of Advisors for the National Youth Rights Association. Hanson has also served as the President of New York State Sociological Association and given expert testimony at two state assemblies on Capitol Hill on the marketing and selling of alcohol. His over 300 publications on the subject have been cited in textbooks from 15 different fields of study, and he has appeared on numerous television programs, including the "Dr. Laura" program, the Fox News Channel, BBC, NPR, and over 60 radio programs in the United States. Hanson maintains two websites, Alcohol: Problems and Solutions and Alcoholfacts.org. Most recently, his article "Historical Evolution of Alcohol Consumption in Society" was included in *Alcohol: Science, Policy and Public Health* (2013), published by Oxford University Press.

Preparing to Read

This essay was first published on one of David Hanson's websites, "Alcohol: Problems and Solutions." On this site, Hanson analyzes the causes and effects of alcohol use in society today.

Exploring Experience: As you prepare to read this essay, consider how our society currently deals with alcohol and our youth: Do you think that drinking among students is increasing or decreasing? What role does binge drinking play in the lives of students? Do you think binge drinking is a threat to our society? To our colleges?

LEARNING⏻NLINE Peruse the website Drinkaware.co.uk, and analyze your opinions on drinking. How much alcohol is too much in a given setting? Is drinking worth the effects it has on your body? What factors most often affect the choices you make about drinking?

Before reading this essay, you may want to consult the flowchart on page 348.

To most people, binge drinking brings to mind a self-destructive and unrestrained drinking bout lasting for at least a couple of days during which time the heavily intoxicated drinker "drops out" by not working, ignoring responsibilities, squandering money, and engaging in other harmful behaviors such as fighting or risky sex. This view is consistent with that portrayed traditionally in dictionary definitions, in literature, in art, and in plays or films such as *Come Back, Little Sheba*, *Lost Weekend*, and *Leaving Las Vegas*. 1

It is also consistent with the usage of physicians, psychologists, and other clinicians. As the editor of the *Journal of Studies on Alcohol* emphasized, binge describes an extended period of time (typically at least two days) during which a person repeatedly becomes intoxicated and gives up his or her usual activities and obligations in order to become intoxicated. It is the combination of prolonged use and the giving up of usual activities that forms the core of the clinical definition of binge (Schuckit). 2

A Swedish study, for example, defined a binge as the consumption of half a bottle of spirits or two bottles of wine on the same occasion (Hansagi et al.). A study in Italy found that people considered consuming an average of eight drinks a day to be normal drinking—clearly not bingeing (Farchi et al.). 3

But in the United States, some researchers began defining bingeing as consuming five or more drinks on an occasion (an "occasion" can refer to an entire day and evening). They soon modified their new definition by considering the consumption of four or more drinks by a woman on an occasion to be bingeing. 4

Consider a woman who has two glasses of wine with her leisurely dinner and then sips two more drinks over the course of a four or five hour evening. In the view of most people, such a woman would be acting responsibly. Indeed her blood alcohol content would remain low. It's difficult to imagine that she would even be able to feel the effects of the alcohol. However, the new definition categorized her as a binger! 5

The effect of this new definition was to suddenly "create" widespread binge drinking on college campuses across the United States.[1] That, in turn, created the perceived need to fund researchers to document, study, and make recommendations concerning this "new and dangerous epidemic." Alcohol researchers and activists were suddenly in demand as highly paid speakers, consultants, and investigators of this threat to our children and the future of the country. 6

Other researchers explained that it is counter-productive to brand as pathological the consumption of four or five drinks over the course of an 7

Thinking Critically

[1] How did the new definition of binge drinking in the U.S. affect college campuses?

evening of eating and socializing. It is clearly inappropriate to equate it with a binge (Dimeff et al.).[2]

How useful is such an unrealistic definition? It is very useful if the intent   8
is to inflate the extent of a social problem. And it would please members of the Prohibition Party and the Women's Christian Temperance Union (both of which still exist). But it is not very useful if the intent is to accurately describe reality to the average person.

It is highly unrealistic and inappropriate to apply a prohibitionist defini-   9
tion[3] to describe drinking in the United States today. Perhaps we should define binge drinking as any intoxicated drinking that leads to certain harmful or destructive behaviors. Perhaps we should specify the period of time during which a person is intoxicated. Perhaps we could even require that a person be significantly intoxicated before being labeled a "binger."

Serious criticisms of the inadequacies of the new definition led to various   10
revisions. For example, The National Institute on Alcohol Abuse and Alcoholism (NIAAA) now defines binge drinking as drinking that brings blood alcohol concentration (BAC) to 0.08.5 No conduct problems are necessary and the "binger" could easily be quietly enjoying an evening with friends.

The Substance Abuse and Mental Health Services Administration (SAM-   11
HSA), which conducts the annual National Survey on Drug Use and Health, defines binge drinking for the purposes of its surveys as drinking five or more drinks on the same occasion on at least one day in the past 30 days ("Drinking"). The length of an occasion is not defined and could be an entire day and evening. Indeed, college parties typically last at least seven hours.

Different researchers, organizations, and agencies now define *binge* in   12
different ways, but they are all far different from the medical and clinical definition as well as the implicit understanding generally held by the public. These unrealistic definitions share one thing in common: they are misleading at best.[4]

The conclusion is clear: Be very skeptical the next time you hear or read a   13
report about "binge" drinking. Were the people in question really bingeing? By any reasonable definition, most almost certainly were not.

The Extent of "Binge" Drinking

While a continuing barrage of newspaper articles, TV shows, and reports   14
by special interest groups claim that binge drinking among young people is

---

Thinking Critically

[2] Do you consider four or five drinks in an evening binge drinking? Why or why not?
[3] Why does Hanson call the new definition of binge drinking a "prohibitionist definition"?
[4] What does Hanson find misleading about all the new versions of binge drinking?

a growing epidemic, the actual fact is quite to the contrary. So-called binge drinking among young people is clearly declining, and it has been doing so for many years.

As seen in this graphic, "binge" drinking among high school seniors has declined from 41.2% to 22.1% between 1980 and 2013. That's a drop of almost one-half. Surveys of eighth and tenth graders began in 1991. Since that time, the proportion of eighth graders who "binge" has fallen about one-half, from 10.1% down to 5.1%. Among tenth graders it has fallen from 21.0% down to 13.7% (Johnston et al., *Overview* 68). 15

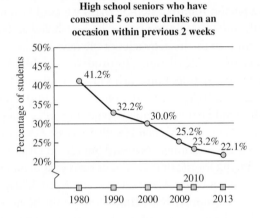

High school seniors who have consumed 5 or more drinks on an occasion within previous 2 weeks

Similarly, the proportions of "binge" drinking college students and other young adults who are one to four years beyond high school have both dropped significantly since 1980 (Johnston et al., *Volume 2* 396–97). 16

The proportion of adolescents in the U.S. who engaged in so-called binge drinking during the previous month fell by 30.3% between 2008 and 2013 (*Behavioral Health Barometer* 5). The incidence of such drinking has been below the federal government's Healthy People 2020 target since 2010. 17

The facts are clear. "Binge" drinking is down and alcohol abstinence is up among school and college students in the U.S. Yet the false impression persists that we're suffering from an epidemic of "bingeing." 18

So What's the Harm?

This misperception is dangerous because when young people go to school or college falsely thinking that "everybody" is drinking and bingeing, they are more likely to drink and to "binge" in order to conform. Correcting 19 this misperception is important because it can empower young people and break the vicious self-fulfilling prophesy that helps perpetuate collegiate alcohol abuse.[5]

Individual students almost always believe that most others on campus   20
drink more often and more heavily than they do and the disparity between the perceived and the actual behaviors tends to be quite large. By conducting surveys of actual student behavior and publicizing the results, the extent of heavy drinking can be quickly and significantly reduced (Turner et al.; Moreira et al.; Scribner et al.).

Too many college students still abuse alcohol. But those who exaggerate   21
the problem and distort its magnitude are actually making the problem worse. If we are to further reduce alcohol abuse and the problems it causes, we have to publicize the actual facts and correct damaging misperceptions. Doing so will empower students to do what they as individuals generally want to do: Drink less or not drink at all.

The challenge of correcting dangerous misperceptions about college stu-   22
dent drinking is enormous. Many researchers, reporters, writers, bureau-crats, and others have a vested interest in inflating the extent of "binge" drinking. But scare tactics are actually counter-productive, and it turns out that the most effective way to reduce alcohol abuse is simply to tell the truth and make sure that young people understand the facts.

Works Cited

Behavioral Health Barometer: United States, 2014. Substance Abuse and Mental Health Services Administration, 2015. HHS Publication No. SMA–15–4895.

Dimeff, Linda A., et al. "Binge Drinking in College." *Journal of the American Medical Association*, vol. 273, no. 24, June 1995, pp. 1903-04. Letter to the Editor.

"Drinking Levels Defined." *National Institute on Alcohol Abuse and Alcohol-ism*, www.niaaa.nih.gov/alcohol-health/overview-alcohol-consumption/moderate-binge-drinking. Accessed 28 Jan. 2015.

Farchi, Gino, et al. "Alcohol and Mortality in the Italian Rural Cohorts of the Seven Countries Study." *International Journal of Epidemiology*, vol. 28, no. 4, 2000, pp. 667-71.

Thinking Critically

[5] Do you agree that clearing up misperceptions about bingeing is important? What is your reasoning?

Hansagi, Helen, et al. "Alcohol Consumption and Stroke Mortality: 20-Year Follow-Up of 15,077 Men and Women." *Stroke*, vol. 26, no. 10, 1995, pp. 1768-73.

Johnston, Lloyd D., et al. *Monitoring the Future: National Survey Results on Drug Use, 1975–2013: Volume 2, College Students and Adults Ages 19–55.* Institute for Social Research, U of Michigan, 2014.

Johnston, Lloyd D., et al. *Monitoring the Future: National Results on Drug Use, 1975–2013: Overview, Key Findings on Adolescent Drug Use.* Institute for Social Research, U of Michigan, 2014.

Moreira, Maria Teresa, et al. "Social Norms Interventions to Reduce Alcohol Misuse in University or College Students." *Cochrane Database of Systematic Reviews*, no. 3, July 2009, doi:10.1002/14651858.CD006748.pub2.

Schuckit, Marc A. "The Editor Responds." *The Journal of Studies on Alcohol*, vol. 59, no. 1, Jan. 1998, pp. 123-24.

Scribner, Richard A., et al. "Alcohol Prevention on College Campuses: The Moderating Effect of the Alcohol Environment on the Effectiveness of Social Norms Marketing Campaigns." *Journal of Studies on Alcohol and Drugs*, vol. 72, no. 2, 2011, pp. 232-39.

Turner, James, H., et al. "Declining Negative Consequences Related to Alcohol Misuse Among Students Exposed to a Social Norms Marketing Intervention on a College Campus." *Journal of American College Health*, vol. 57, no. 1, July-Aug. 2008, pp. 85-94.

UNDERSTANDING DETAILS

1. Explain the basic problem that Hanson uncovers in this essay.
2. What is the new definition of binge drinking in the United States? In what ways is this definition misleading?
3. How would Hanson like to alter this definition?
4. What are the facts about binge drinking among students? What trends does Hanson uncover?

READING CRITICALLY

5. Why would this new definition of binge drinking please members of the Prohibition Party and the Women's Christian Temperance Union?
6. What consequences does the new definition of binge drinking have for colleges?
7. In what ways does this new definition "inflate the extent of a social problem" (paragraph 8)? What are some of the dangers of this "inflation"?
8. Why are the misperceptions of binge drinking dangerous—especially for college students?

DISCOVERING RHETORICAL STRATEGIES

9. List the main points Hanson makes about binge drinking. Why does he address these points in this particular order?
10. Who do you think is the intended audience of this essay?
11. What rhetorical modes does the author draw on to produce this essay? Give an example of each strategy.
12. How would you characterize the tone of this essay?

MAKING CONNECTIONS

13. To what extent would Malcolm Cowley ("The View from 80"), Christopher Nelson ("Why We Are Looking at the 'Value' of College All Wrong"), and Jessica Mitford ("Behind the Formaldehyde Curtain") agree with David Hanson about the importance of full disclosure? Which of these exposés is most important to the integrity of American values. What is the reasoning behind your response?
14. Compare and contrast Hanson's use of examples with those employed by Brent Staples ("A Brother's Murder"), Jay Walljasper ("Our Schedules, Our Selves"), and/or Amy Tan ("Mother Tongue"). Who uses examples most skillfully? Why do you think this is so?
15. What would Stephanie Ericsson ("The Ways We Lie") say to Hanson about the way the researchers on alcohol and drinking have mislead the public about binge drinking?

IDEAS FOR DISCUSSION/WRITING

Preparing to Write

Write freely about the use of alcohol in the U.S. society: What is the extent of drinking in our society? What is the extent of drinking among students? How can misinformation and misperceptions affect the drinking patterns of our youth? Why are students and young people especially susceptible to definitions and trends?

Choosing a Topic   MyWritingLab™

1. **LEARNINGⓊNLINE** After reading Hanson's essay, your opinions about binge drinking might have changed. Using the information on Drinkaware.co.uk for extra support, write an essay including a definition of what you consider unacceptable drinking behavior and a statement explaining your definition of "binge drinking." Be as specific as possible.
2. Imagine that you are the head counselor at your high school and you have noticed a healthy decline in the use of drugs and alcohol among seniors at your school. You call an assembly to discuss this issue and highlight this trend as a model for the younger students at your school. Because you have very little time with them, you write your speech out in the form of an essay before you deliver it. What could you say to compliment the students on this pattern and make sure they maintain sensible drinking habits?

3. *Psychology Today* has asked you, as an adolescent psychologist, to write an essay analyzing the differences and similarities between girls' and boys' social behavior in high school, especially as it relates to drinking. What are some of the similarities and differences? The editor needs you to summarize your observations for their journal.

4. Having survived high school, you are in a position of being able to advise younger students. In a well-developed essay, give a high school student whom you know some advice about drinking during his or her high school years.

Before beginning your essay, you may want to consult the flowchart on page 351.

Chapter Writing Assignments
Practicing Definition

1. Identify a term people use to describe you (for example, *trustworthy, sloppy,* or *athletic*). In a well-developed essay, define this term as clearly as you can, and discuss whether or not it accurately represents you. Support your claim with carefully chosen details.
2. In what ways do our families define us? How do our families shape who we are and who we have become? In an essay, define the concept of family by explaining how your family members relate to each other.
3. Think of an object you value greatly. For example, a ring might represent a special relationship. Then, in essay form, explain what this object says about you. Why is it your favorite? What does it mean to you?

Exploring Ideas

4. Have you ever felt jealous? What do you think are the most common sources of jealousy? Do you think that jealousy is mostly a productive or unproductive emotion? Write an essay discussing the main qualities of jealousy. What do most people need to know about this feeling?
5. Think of all the "communities" to which you belong (for example, school, church, neighborhood, friends). Choose one that is really important to you, and, in an essay, identify the major features of this community. What makes this community so important in your life?
6. In essay form, describe an ugly part of your campus or city, and explore some important ways this place could be improved or changed. What effects do you think these changes might have on your community or campus? How did you come to this conclusion?

Analyzing Visual Images

Anthony Correia/Reuters/Landov.

7. The preceding photo was taken shortly after 9/11. Looking at this picture carefully, how would you characterize the scene in words—confusion, rescue efforts, heroes, terrorism? Explore the associations you have with this photograph, and then write an essay in which you clearly define one of these terms. Use examples to clarify your definition.

8. Look at the picture on page 347 at the beginning of this chapter. Why do you think the man is holding this ring? Based on your answer, what do you think this ring signifies—love, honor, deceit, betrayal? Write an essay that explains how this picture captures the word you associate with it.

Composing in Different Genres

9. Multimedia: Create a website that (subjectively) defines the term *education*. You can approach your definition through pictures, words, videos, quotations, collages, clip art. What does education mean to you? Capture its essence in an original homepage that you design.

10. Multigenre: What is your favorite possession? Write catalog copy describing this product for a manual that prides itself on objective definitions that are accurate and well developed.

Writing from Sources

For detailed information on writing from sources, see Part III.

11. Choose a modern technological device that you rely on, such as a computer, cell phone, or automobile. Research its evolution from inception to the product you know and use today. Write an essay, citing two to three sources, that outlines the origin, stages of development, and obstacles surrounding the device you have chosen.

12. Different cultures throughout history have had many divergent ideals. Choose a culture other than your own, and research the defining characteristics of happiness. Is happiness connected to spiritual, moral, or physical contentment? You may want to look at how the definition of happiness has evolved within one culture over time. Write an essay supported by your research that defines the elements required for happiness.

MyWritingLab™ Visit Ch. 10. Definition: Limiting the Frame of Reference in *MyWritingLab* to complete the writing assignments and test your understanding of the chapter learning objectives.

Chapter 11

CAUSE/EFFECT
Tracing Reasons and Results

LEARNING OBJECTIVES

After completing this chapter, you will be able to do the following:
- Define cause and effect
- Use cause and effect to think critically
- Read cause/effect essays critically
- Write and revise effective cause/effect essays

Wanting to know why things happen is one of our earliest, most basic instincts: Why can't I go out, Mommy? Why are you laughing? Why won't the dog stop barking? Why can't I swim faster than my big brother? These questions, and many more like them, reflect the innately inquisitive nature that dwells within each of us. Closely related to this desire to understand *why* is our corresponding interest in *what* will happen in the future as a result of some particular action: What will I feel like tomorrow if I stay up late tonight? How will I perform in the track meet Saturday if I practice all week? What will be the result if I mix together these two potent chemicals? What will happen if I turn in my next English assignment two days early?

A daily awareness of this intimate relationship between causes and effects allows us to begin to understand the complex and interrelated series of events that make up our lives and the lives of others. For example, trying to understand the various causes of the conflict between Palestine and Israel teaches us about international relations; knowing our biological reactions to certain foods helps us make decisions about what to eat; understanding the interrelated reasons for the outbreak of World War II offers us insight into historical trends and human nature; knowing the effects of sunshine on various parts of our bodies helps us make decisions about how much ultraviolet exposure we can tolerate and what suntan lotion to use; and understanding the causes of the United States' most recent recession will help us respond appropriately to the next economic crisis we encounter. More than anything else, tracing causes and effects teaches us how to think clearly and react intelligently to our multifaceted environment.

In college, you will often be asked to use this natural interest in causes and effects to analyze particular situations and to discern general principles. For example, you might be asked some of the following questions on essay exams in different courses:

Anthropology: Why did the Mayan culture disintegrate?

Psychology: Why do humans respond to fear in different ways?

Biology: How do lab rats react to caffeine?

History: What were the positive effects of the Spanish–American War?

Business: Why did so many computer manufacturing companies go bankrupt in the early 1980s?

Your ability to answer such questions will depend in large part on your skill at understanding cause/effect relationships.

DEFINING CAUSE/EFFECT

Cause/effect analysis requires the ability to look for connections between different elements and to analyze the reasons for those connections. As the name implies, this rhetorical mode has two separate components: cause and effect. A particular essay might concentrate on cause (Why do you live in a dorm?), on effect (What are the resulting advantages and disadvantages of living in a dorm?), or on some combination of the two. In working with causes, we are searching for any circumstances from the past that may have caused a single event; in looking for effects, we seek occurrences that took place after a particular event and resulted from that event. Like process analysis, cause/effect makes use of our intellectual ability to analyze. Process analysis addresses *how* something happens, whereas causal analysis discusses *why* it happened and *what* the result was. A process analysis paper, for example, might explain how to advertise more effectively to increase sales, whereas a cause/effect study would discover that three specific elements contributed to an increase in sales: effective advertising, personal service, and selective discounts. The study of causes and effects, therefore, provides many different and helpful ways for humans to make sense of and clarify their views of the world.

Looking for causes and effects requires an advanced form of thinking. It is more complex than most rhetorical strategies we have studied because it can exist on a number of different and progressively more difficult levels. The most accurate and effective causal analysis accrues from digging for the real or ultimate causes or effects, as opposed to those that are merely superficial or immediate. Detectives Alex Eames and Robert Goren would be out of work on *Law and Order: Criminal Intent,* for example, if they stopped their investigation at the immediate cause of death (slipping in the bathtub) rather than searching diligently for the *real* cause (an overdose of cocaine administered by an angry companion, which resulted in the slip in the tub). Similarly, voters would be easy to manipulate if they considered only the immediate effects of a tax increase (a slightly higher tax bill) rather than the ultimate benefits that would result (the many years of improved education their children would receive because of the specialized programs allowed by such an increase). Only the discovery of the actual reasons for an event or an idea will lead to the logical and accurate analysis of causes and effects important to a basic understanding of various aspects of our lives.

Faulty reasoning assigns causes to a sequence of actions without adequate justification. One such logical fallacy is called *post hoc, ergo propter hoc* ("after this, therefore because of this"): The fact that someone lost a job after walking under a ladder does not mean that the two events are causally related; by the same token, if we get up every morning at 5:30 A.M., just before the sun rises, we cannot therefore conclude that the sun rises *because* we get up (no matter how self-centered we are!). Faulty reasoning also occurs when we oversimplify a particular situation. Most events are connected to a multitude of causes and effects. Sometimes one effect has many causes: A student may fail a history exam because she's been working two part-time jobs, she was sick, she didn't study hard enough, and she found the instructor very boring. One cause may also have many effects. If a house burns down, the people who lived in it will be out of a home. If we look at such a tragic scene more closely, however, we may also note that the fire traumatized a child who lived there, helped the family learn what good friends they had, encouraged the family to double their future fire insurance, and provided the stimulus they needed to make a long-dreamed-of move to another city. One event has thus resulted in many interrelated effects. Building an argument on insecure foundations or oversimplifying the causes or effects connected with an event will seriously hinder the construction of a rational essay. No matter what the nature of the cause/effect analysis, it must always be based on clear observation, accurate facts, and rigorous logic.

In the following paragraph, a student writer analyzes some of the causes and effects connected with the controversial issue of euthanasia. Notice how he makes connections and then analyzes those connections as he consistently explores the immediate and ultimate effects of being able to stretch life beyond its normal limits through new medical technology:

> *Along with the many recent startling advancements in medical technology have come a number of complex moral, ethical, and spiritual questions that beg to be answered. We now have the ability to prolong the life of the human body for a very long time. But what rights do patients and their families have to curtail cruel and unusual medical treatment that stretches life beyond its normal limits? This dilemma has produced a ripple effect in society. Is the extension of life an unquestionable goal in itself, regardless of the quality of that life? Modern scientific technology has forced doctors to reevaluate the exact meaning and purpose of their profession. For example, many medical schools and undergraduate university programs now routinely offer classes on medical ethics—an esoteric and infrequently taught subject only a few years ago. Doctors and scholars alike are realizing that medical personnel alone cannot be expected to decide on the exact parameters of life. In like manner, the judicial process must now evaluate the legal complexities of mercy killings and the rights of patients to die with dignity and without unnecessary medical intervention. The insurance business, too, wrestles with the catastrophic effects of new technology on the costs of today's hospital care. In short, medical progress entails more than microscopes, chemicals, and high-tech instruments. If we are to develop as a thoughtful, just, and merciful society, we must consider not only the physical well-being of our nation's patients, but their emotional, spiritual, and financial status as well.*

THINKING CRITICALLY THROUGH CAUSE/EFFECT

Thinking about causes and effects is one of the most advanced mental activities we perform. It involves complex operations that we must think through carefully, making sure all connections are reasonable and accurate. Unlike other rhetorical patterns, cause/effect thinking requires us to see specific relationships between two or more items. To practice this strategy, we need to look for items or events that are causally related—that is, one that has caused the other. Then, we can focus on either the causes (the initial stimuli), the effects (the results), or a combination of the two.

Searching for causes and effects requires a great deal of digging that is not necessary for most of the other writing modes. Cause/effect necessitates the ultimate in investigative work. The mental exertion associated with this thinking strategy is sometimes exhausting, but it is always worth going through when you discover relationships that you never saw before or when you uncover links in your reasoning that were previously unknown or obscure to you.

If you've ever had the secret desire to be a private eye or an investigator of any sort, practicing cause/effect reasoning can be lots of fun. It forces you to see relationships among multiple items and then to make sense of those connections. Completing exercises in this skill by itself will once again help you perfect the logistics of cause/effect thinking before you mix and match it with other thinking strategies.

Bettman/Corbis.

1. In Sam Shere's famous 1937 photo of the *Hindenburg* bursting into flames, we can see that this voyage of the Zeppelin from Germany to the United States ended in disaster. Ninety-seven people were aboard when the *Hindenburg* went down, and none of them expected to die. Think of other examples of technological inventions or changes that resulted in an outcome different from what people expected. Identify the expectations, the actual results, and what can be learned from these results.

2. Choose a major problem you see in our society, and list what you think are the main causes of this problem on one side of a piece of paper and the effects on the other side. Compare the two lists to see how they differ. Then, compare and contrast your list with those written by other students.

3. What "caused" you to become a student? What influences led you to this choice at this point in your life? How has being a student affected your life? List several overall effects.

READING AND WRITING CAUSE/EFFECT ESSAYS

Causal analysis is usually employed for one of three main purposes: (1) to prove a specific point (such as the necessity for stricter gun control), in which case the writer generally deals totally with facts and with conclusions drawn from those facts; (2) to argue against a widely accepted belief (for example, the assertion that cocaine is addictive), in which case the writer relies principally on facts, with perhaps some pertinent opinions; or (3) to speculate on a theory (for instance, why the crime rate is higher in most major cities than it is in rural areas), in which case the writer probably presents hypotheses and opinions along with facts. This section explores these purposes in cause/effect essays from the standpoint of both reading and writing.

Reading Cause/Effect Essays

Understanding how cause/effect essays work rhetorically will help you make decisions for your own writing. On the next page is a flowchart of questions that will guide your reading for this purpose.

Preparing to Read.   As you set out to read the essays in this chapter, begin by focusing your attention on the title and the synopsis of the essay you are about to read and by scanning the essay itself: What do you think Stephen King is going to talk about in "Why We Crave Horror Movies"? What does the synopsis in the Rhetorical Table of Contents tell you about Michael Dorris's "The Broken Cord" or about Dana Gioia's "On the Importance of Reading"?

Also, at this stage in the reading process, you should try to learn as much as you can about the author of the essay and the reasons he or she wrote it. Ask yourself questions like the following: What is King's intention in "Why We Crave Horror Movies"? Who is Joe Keohane's intended audience in "How Facts Backfire"? And what is Art Markman's point of view in "Can Video Games Make You Smart (Or At Least more Flexible)?"

Questions to Guide Your Reading

PREPARING TO READ Before you read the essays, answer the following questions:
- What assumptions can you make from the essay's **title**?
- What do you think the general **mood** of the essay will be?
- What is the essay's **purpose** and **audience**?
- What does the **synopsis** tell you about the essay?
- What can you learn from the author's **biography**?
- What do you predict the author's **point of view** toward the subject will be?

READING As you read the essays for the first time, answer the following questions:
- What is the essay's **purpose**?
- What are the **real causes and/or effects**?
- What **assertions** does the author make?

REREADING When you read the essays again, answer the following questions:
- How does the writer narrow and **focus** the essay?
- What concrete **evidence** supports the author's conclusions?
- Does the writer make clear and logical **connections** between ideas?
- What **conclusions** does the author draw?
- How does your understanding of the essay **change** with each rereading?

Finally, before you begin to read, answer the prereading questions for each essay, and then consider the proposed essay topic from a variety of perspectives: For example, concerning Gioia's topic, how important to you is reading and/or writing? Which segments of American society are most aware of the value of these skills? Which the least? What do you want to know from Keohane about facts? Do you completely understand the difference between facts and opinions?

Reading.   As you read each essay in this chapter for the first time, record your spontaneous reactions to it, drawing as often as possible on the preliminary material you already know: What do you think of horror movies (King)? What is Dorris suggesting about babies with fetal alcohol syndrome? Have you experienced an addiction of any kind? Why did Keohane choose the title he did?

Whenever you can, try to create a context for your reading: What is the tone of Gioia's comments about reading and writing? How does this tone help him communicate with his audience? What do you think Markman's purpose is in his essay concerning video games? How clearly does he get this purpose across to you?

Also, during this reading, note the essay's thesis, and check to see if the writer thoroughly explores all possibilities before settling on the primary causes and/or effects of a particular situation; in addition, determine whether the writer clearly states the assertions that naturally evolve from a discussion of the topic.

At the bottom of the essays' pages in this chapter are some questions that will help you process this reading material critically or analytically. These questions are designed to provide a bridge that will connect your thoughts before you read the essay with your tasks at the end of your reading by helping you see relationships among ideas that will lead you to higher levels of thinking. Recording your answers in writing is the best way to approach these questions, but your instructor might have some other guidelines for you.

Finally, read the questions following each essay to get a sense of the main issues and strategies in the selection.

Rereading.   When you reread these essays, you should focus mainly on the writer's craft. Notice how the authors narrow and focus their material, how they make clear and logical connections between ideas in their essays, how they support their conclusions with concrete examples, how they use other rhetorical modes to accomplish their cause/effect analysis, and how they employ logical transitions to move us smoothly from one point to another. Most important, however, ask yourself if the writer actually discusses the real causes and/or effects of a particular circumstance: What does King say are the primary reasons people crave horror movies? According to Keohane, why are people unwilling to change their opinions? What are the primary causes and effects outlined in Markman's essay?

For a thorough outline of the reading process, consult the Reading Checklist at the end of Chapter 2.

Writing Cause/Effect Essays

Now that you see how cause and effect work in an essay, use the same features in your own writing. Here is a flowchart of questions that will guide you.

Questions to Guide Your Writing

PREPARING TO WRITE
Before you start writing, answer these questions:
- What is your **purpose**?
- Who is your **audience**?

WRITING As you write your first draft, consider these questions:
- Do you state your purpose in your **thesis**?
- What are the **real causes and effects**?
- How are your ideas **connected**?
- Do you use concrete **evidence** to support your thesis?
- Do you **summarize** and draw conclusions?

EDITING Be sure to proofread and edit your paper before turning it in.
- Are your **sentences** all complete?
- Do your words say exactly **what you mean**?
- Do you follow conventional **grammar and usage** rules?

REVISING After you write your first draft, use the following questions to revise your essay:
- Is your **thesis** stated clearly at the outset of your paper?
- Does it include your **subject** and your **purpose**?
- Do you explore all **relevant** causes and/or effects?
- Do you accomplish your **purpose** as effectively as possible?
- Do you use **logical** reasoning throughout the essay?

Preparing To Write.   Beginning a cause/effect essay requires—as does any other essay—exploring and limiting your subject, specifying a purpose, and identifying an audience. The Preparing to Write questions before the essay assignments, coupled with the prewriting techniques outlined on pages 26–28, encourage you to consider specific issues related to your reading. The assignments themselves will then help you limit your topic and determine a particular purpose and audience for your message. For cause/effect essays, determining a purpose is even more important than usual because your readers can get hopelessly lost unless your analysis is clearly focused.

Writing.   For all its conceptual complexity, a cause/effect essay can be organized quite simply. The introduction generally presents the subject(s) and states the purpose of the analysis in a clear thesis. The body of the paper then explores all relevant causes and/or effects, typically progressing either from least to most influential or from most to least influential. Finally, the concluding section summarizes the various cause/effect relationships established in the body of the paper and clearly states the conclusions that can be drawn from those relationships.

The following additional guidelines should assist you in producing an effective cause/effect essay in all academic disciplines:

1. Narrow and focus your material as much as possible.
2. Consider all possibilities before assigning real or ultimate causes or effects.
3. Show connections between ideas by using transitions and key words—such as *because, reasons, results, effects,* and *consequences*—to guide your readers smoothly through your essay.
4. Support all inferences with concrete evidence.
5. Be as objective as possible in your analysis so that you don't distort logic with personal biases.
6. Understand your audience's opinions and convictions so that you know what to emphasize in your essay.
7. Qualify your assertions to avoid overstatement and oversimplification.

These suggestions apply to both cause/effect essay assignments and exam questions.

Revising.   As you revise your cause/effect essays, you should ask yourself some specific questions that are featured in the graphics in this introduction.

Other guidelines for writing and revising your essays appear in the Writing Checklist at the end of Chapter 3.

STUDENT ESSAY: CAUSE/EFFECT AT WORK

In the following essay, the student writer analyzes the plague of all college students: procrastination. Notice that she states her subject and purpose at the beginning of the essay and then presents a combination of facts and opinions in her exploration of the topic. Notice also that, in her analysis, the writer is careful to draw clear connections between her perceptions of the issue and various objective details in an attempt to trace the effects of this medium in our society today. At the end of her essay, look at her summary of the logical relationships she establishes in the body of the essay and her statements about the conclusions she draws from these relationships.

Driven to Distraction

Background   <u>Anyone who attends college has the desire to succeed, yet we as college students face many distractions from our goals.</u> To begin with, a large number of us find working necessary in order to live comfortably while attending college. In addition, since a sharp mind abhors a dull life, many of us tend to fill every spare moment with activities, both technological and social. Working, keeping up with technology, and maintaining a social life are the main elements that compete with our time for schoolwork. <u>All of these "distractions," which can lead to procrastination, make focusing on academic success a challenge.</u>   Thesis statement

Transition   <u>Attending college sets students up for excellent career opportunities in the future,</u> but <u>many of us cannot afford college tuition without having some sort of job.</u> College students do all sorts of paid labor, from flipping burgers to heavy lifting. Some of us Concrete work part time; others work double shifts. Despite examples the differences in these work situations, they all have one element in common: they take time away from schoolwork.   First cause

Transition   <u>After work,</u> nobody really wants to study right away; <u>grabbing a computer, smartphone, or game controller and relaxing for a while is much more desirable.</u> Escapists might play their favorite video game and lose track of time while training monsters or schooling noobs. After they watch a few (or a few too Concrete many) videos on YouTube, dinner is on the schedule. examples Once the before and after pictures of the day's activities have gone out via Instagram, it's finally time to get some homework done. But the temptation to check Facebook and Twitter is simply too great. Modern computers and smartphones are convenient and   Second cause extremely helpful in many situations, but, if we allow them to, they can seriously hinder our study habits.

Transition   Throughout college, interactions with technology *Third cause* often lead to personal meetings. After all, friendships require time to cultivate. Parties and other events are commonplace in college, and such gatherings often last late into the night, which once again postpones *Concrete* our homework. But how can we be expected to *examples* nurture and maintain any relationships unless we attend an occasional party? Balancing friends and studying can be close to impossible.

   Perhaps the most distracting type of personal rela- *Third cause* tionship is the romantic kind since it can occupy *(continued)* young lovers' minds every minute of the day. Falling in love is by far the most all-consuming distraction from focused studying. When in love, people often lose track of their priorities and sometimes can't even *Concrete* concentrate on simple tasks, like what to do next. *examples* The feeling of drifting in outer space, common to those newly in love, is not conducive to studying. Whatever the reasons, most social encounters gener- ally pose some sort of serious interference with col- lege obligations.

Ultimate   The demands of working and having a social life, *effect* along with the need for an occasional anti-stress break, leave very little time for studying, which is why many students wait until the very last minute to start writing papers and doing other assignments. Unfortunately, by the time we sit down, we may not be sure how to begin; the pressure of having to synthesize a large amount of material in a short amount of time can be completely overwhelming. But most students can at least claim that the distractions keeping them from their studies brought some degree of pleasure to their lives. Paychecks from their jobs are always pleasant to receive—even when the job is not ideal. Time spent playing video games or exploring the Internet can make the day seem brighter as well. And both friendly and romantic relationships can make life much more enjoyable. Though these distractions sometimes lead to procrastination, if they are carefully balanced with *Proposed* well-planned study periods, neither students nor their *solution* academic performance should suffer.

Student Writer's Comments

In general, I think my writing process made this essay easier to write than I had anticipated. However, if I hadn't done the prewriting activities I did, I think this assignment would have been much more challenging.

I began by doing a freewrite to get my thoughts out about the topic. I set a timer for myself and wrote without stopping for five minutes. I allowed myself not to think too hard about anything; I just let the ideas flow. This was somewhat experimental; I had never done this for a paper before. The freewrite revealed that I really did have something to say. It gave me confidence that transforming my ideas into an essay would not be too much of a stretch.

I went through my freewrite and highlighted the main points I wanted to communicate. I also numbered the points to help me organize. My most interesting discovery was that the last sentence of my freewrite felt really natural to use for my introduction. I didn't expect that!

After organizing my freewrite, I crafted an informal outline—more of a plan—for my essay. My outline—like my freewrite—was completely in my own conversational voice. I figured I would make it more formal later when I revise.

With such extensive prewriting, the actual drafting process was fairly painless. I rephrased as I typed and tried to consider sentence arrangement and word choice, but the structure flowed naturally. As I typed, I also realized my essay was missing an important element—a conclusion. I wrote the last paragraph in the drafting phase, even though it hadn't been a part of my prewriting. It must have been forming in my head as I wrote because it came out on the page right on schedule.

My official editing consisted mostly of focusing on grammar, typos, sentence structure, etc. I felt confident about my content; I just wanted to make sure I didn't have any minor mistakes that would detract from my message.

SOME FINAL THOUGHTS ON CAUSE/EFFECT

The essays in this chapter deal with both causes and effects in a variety of ways. As you read each essay, try to discover its primary purpose and the ultimate causes and/or effects of the issue under discussion. Note also the clear causal relationships that each author sets forth on solid foundations supported by logical reasoning. Although the subjects of these essays vary dramatically, each essay exhibits the basic elements of effective causal analysis.

STEPHEN KING   (1947–   )

Why We Crave Horror Movies

"People's appetites for terror seem insatiable," Stephen King once remarked, an insight that may help justify his phenomenal success as a writer of horror fiction since the mid-1970s. His books have sold more than 100 million copies, and the movies made from them have generated more income than the gross domestic product of several small countries. After early jobs as a janitor, a laundry worker, and a high school English teacher in Portland, Maine, King turned to writing full time following the spectacular sales of his first novel, *Carrie* (1974), which focuses on a shy, socially ostracized young girl who takes revenge on her cruel classmates through newly developed telekinetic powers. King's subsequent books have included *The Shining* (1976), *Firestarter* (1980), *Cujo* (1981), *Christine* (1983), *Pet Sematary* (1983), *Misery* (1987), *The Stand* (1990), *The Waste Lands* (1992), *Delores Claiborne* (1993), *Desperation* (1996), *Bag of Bones* (1999), *Dreamcatcher* (2001), *The Dark Tower V: Wolves of the Calla* (2003), *11/22/63* (2011), and *Mile 81* (2012). He is currently writing the *Mr. Mercedes* trilogy, of which the first installment was published in 2014. Asked to explain why readers and moviegoers are so attracted to his tales of horror, King explained that most people's lives "are full of fears—that their marriage isn't working, that they aren't going to make it on the job, that society is crumbling all around them. But we're really not supposed to talk about things like that, and so they don't have any outlets for all those scary feelings. But the horror writer can give them a place to put their fears." A cheerful though somewhat superstitious person, King, who now lives in Bangor, Maine, admits to doing most of his best writing during the morning hours. "You think I want to write this stuff at night?" he once asked a reviewer.

Preparing to Read

This essay, originally published in *Playboy* magazine, attempts to explain why horror movies satisfy our most basic instincts.

Exploring Experience: As you prepare to read this article, consider your thoughts on the emotional condition of people in the United States: How emotionally healthy are Americans? Were they more emotionally healthy 20 years ago? A century ago? What makes a society emotionally healthy? Emotionally unhealthy? How can a society maintain good health? What is the relationship between emotional health and a civilized society?

LEARNING ONLINE Conduct an Internet search on two recently released horror movies. Use the title of the film as well as the phrase "movie trailer" as your search terms. Find links that allow you to watch each film's preview trailer. How do you feel after watching the trailers? Do you like or dislike this type of film?

Before reading this essay, you may want to consult the flowchart on page 402.

I think that we're all mentally ill; those of us outside the asylums only hide   1
it a little better—and maybe not all that much better, after all. We've all
known people who talk to themselves, people who sometimes squinch
their faces into horrible grimaces when they believe no one is watching,
people who have some hysterical fear—of snakes, the dark, the tight place,
the long drop . . . and, of course, those final worms and grubs that are waiting so patiently underground. [1]

When we pay our four or five bucks and seat ourselves at tenth-row   2
center in a theater showing a horror movie, we are daring the nightmare.

Why? Some of the reasons are simple and obvious. To show that we can,   3
that we are not afraid, that we can ride this roller coaster. [2] Which is not to
say that a really good horror movie may not surprise a scream out of us at
some point, the way we may scream when the roller coaster twists through
a complete 360 or plows through a lake at the bottom of the drop. And
horror movies, like roller coasters, have always been the special province of
the young; by the time one turns 40 or 50, one's appetite for double twists
or 360-degree loops may be considerably depleted.

We also go to reestablish our feelings of essential normality; the horror   4
movie is innately conservative, even reactionary. Freda Jackson as the horrible melting woman in *Die, Monster, Die!* confirms for us that no matter
how far we may be removed from the beauty of a Robert Redford or a
Diana Ross, we are still light-years from true ugliness.

And we go to have fun.   5

Ah, but this is where the ground starts to slope away, isn't it? Because this   6
is a very peculiar sort of fun, indeed. The fun comes from seeing others
menaced—sometimes killed. One critic has suggested that if pro football has
become the voyeur's version of combat, then the horror film has become
the modern version of the public lynching.

It is true that the mythic, "fairy-tale" horror film intends to take away the   7
shades of gray. . . . It urges us to put away our more civilized and adult
penchant for analysis and to become children again, seeing things in pure
blacks and whites. It may be that horror movies provide psychic relief on
this level because this invitation to lapse into simplicity, irrationality, and
even outright madness is extended so rarely. We are told we may allow our
emotions a free rein . . . or no rein at all.

If we are all insane, then sanity becomes a matter of degree. If your insan-   8
ity leads you to carve up women, like Jack the Ripper or the Cleveland

---

Thinking Critically

[1] What are the worms and grubs waiting for? What tone does this detail help create in the essay?

[2] How does King use the image of a roller coaster as a metaphor here? What does the roller coaster represent?

Torso Murderer, we clap you away in the funny farm (but neither of those two amateur-night surgeons was ever caught, heh-heh-heh); if, on the other hand, your insanity leads you only to talk to yourself when you're under stress or to pick your nose on your morning bus, then you are left alone to go about your business . . . though it is doubtful that you will ever be invited to the best parties.

The potential lyncher is in almost all of us[3] (excluding saints, past and present; but then, most saints have been crazy in their own ways), and every now and then, he has to be let loose to scream and roll around in the grass. Our emotions and our fears form their own body, and we recognize that it demands its own exercise to maintain proper muscle tone. Certain of these emotional muscles are accepted—even exalted—in civilized society; they are, of course, the emotions that tend to maintain the status quo of civilization itself. Love, friendship, loyalty, kindness—these are all the emotions that we applaud, emotions that have been immortalized in the couplets of Hallmark cards and in the verses (I don't dare call it poetry) of Leonard Nimoy. 9

When we exhibit these emotions, society showers us with positive reinforcement; we learn this even before we get out of diapers. When, as children, we hug our rotten little puke of a sister and give her a kiss, all the aunts and uncles smile and twit and cry, "Isn't he the sweetest little thing?" Such coveted treats as chocolate-covered graham crackers often follow. But if we deliberately slam the rotten little puke of a sister's fingers in the door, sanctions follow—angry remonstrance from parents, aunts, and uncles; instead of a chocolate-covered graham cracker, a spanking. 10

But anticivilization emotions[4] don't go away, and they demand periodic exercise. We have such "sick" jokes as, "What's the difference between a truckload of bowling balls and a truckload of dead babies?" (You can't unload a truckload of bowling balls with a pitchfork . . . a joke, by the way, that I heard originally from a ten-year-old.) Such a joke may surprise a laugh or a grin out of us even as we recoil, a possibility that confirms the thesis: If we share a brotherhood of man, then we also share an insanity of man. None of which is intended as a defense of either the sick joke or insanity but merely as an explanation of why the best horror films, like the best fairy tales, manage to be reactionary, anarchistic, and revolutionary all at the same time. 11

Thinking Critically

[3] Do you agree with the author that a "potential lyncher" lurks inside all of us? Why or why not?

[4] What are "anticivilization emotions"? Give an example, and explain how it fits into this category.

The mythic horror movie, like the sick joke, has a dirty job to do. 12 It deliberately appeals to all that is worst in us. It is morbidity unchained, our most base instincts let free, our nastiest fantasies realized . . . , and it all happens, fittingly enough, in the dark. For those reasons, good liberals often shy away from horror films. For myself, I like to see the most aggressive of them—*Dawn of the Dead,* for instance—as lifting a trap door in the civilized forebrain and throwing a basket of raw meat to the hungry alligators swimming around in that subterranean river beneath.

Why bother? Because it keeps them from getting out, man. It keeps them 13 down there and me up here. It was Lennon and McCartney who said that all you need is love, and I would agree with that.

As long as you keep the gators fed.   14

UNDERSTANDING DETAILS

1. Why, in King's opinion, do civilized people enjoy horror movies?
2. According to King, in what ways are horror movies like roller coasters?
3. According to King, how are horror films like public lynchings?
4. What is the difference between "emotions that tend to maintain the status quo of civilization" (paragraph 9) and "anticivilization emotions" (paragraph 11)?

READING CRITICALLY

5. How can horror movies "reestablish our feelings of essential normality" (paragraph 4)?
6. What is "reactionary, anarchistic, and revolutionary" (paragraph 11) about fairy tales? About horror films?
7. Why does the author think we need to exercise our anticivilization emotions? What are some other ways we might confront these emotions?
8. Explain the last line of King's essay: "As long as you keep the gators fed" (paragraph 14).

DISCOVERING RHETORICAL STRATEGIES

9. What is the cause/effect relationship that King notes in society between horror movies and sanity?
10. Why does King begin his essay with such a dramatic statement as "I think that we're all mentally ill" (paragraph 1)?
11. Who do you think is the author's intended audience for this essay? Describe them in detail. How did you come to this conclusion?
12. What different rhetorical strategies does King use to support his cause/effect analysis? Give examples of each.

MAKING CONNECTIONS

13. Apply Stephen King's definition of *horror* to such frightening experiences as the preparation of a dead body for its funeral (Jessica Mitford, "Behind the

Formaldehyde Curtain") and/or caring for a child with fetal alcohol syndrome (Michael Dorris, "The Broken Cord"). In what way is each of these events "horrible"? What are the principal differences between watching a horror movie and living through a real-life horror?

14. In this essay, King gives us important insights into his own writing process, especially into how horror novels and movies affect their audiences. Compare and contrast his revelations about writing with those advanced by Sandra Cisneros ("Only Daughter"), Amy Tan ("Mother Tongue"), and/or Adam Gopnik ("How Lincoln and Darwin Shaped the Modern World"), all of whom discuss the importance of writing in various scenarios. Whose comments about writing speak most directly to you? Explain your answer.

15. Compare King's remarks about "fear" with related insights on the topic by such other authors as Elizabeth Svoboda ("Virtual Assault"), and/or Dave Grossman ("We Are Training Our Kids to Kill"). How would each of these writers define the term differently? With which author's definition would you most likely agree? Explain your answer.

IDEAS FOR DISCUSSION/WRITING

Preparing to Write

Write freely about how most people maintain a healthy emotional attitude: How would you define emotional well-being? When are people most emotionally healthy? Most emotionally unhealthy? What do your friends and relatives do to maintain a healthy emotional life? What do you do to maintain emotional health? What is the connection between our individual emotional health and the extent to which our society is civilized?

Choosing a Topic   MyWritingLab™

1. **LEARNING⟨ᴗ⟩NLINE** King's essay focuses on the benefits of watching horror films. What are other practices we have that on the surface may seem inconsequential but actually serve an important purpose? Select one such practice, and write an essay in which you identify its causes and effects. Conduct an Internet search on your topic, and use credible references to support your theories. Try to use relevant, vivid imagery, as King does, to engage your audience.

2. Think of a release other than horror films for our most violent emotions. Is it an acceptable release? Write an essay for the general public explaining the relationship between this particular release and our "civilized" society.

3. If you accept King's analysis of horror movies, what role in society do you think other types of movies play (e.g., love stories, science-fiction movies, and comedies)? Choose one type, and explain its role to your college composition class.

4. Your psychology instructor has asked you to explain your opinions on the degree of sanity or insanity in the United States at present. In what ways are we sane? In what ways are we insane? Write an essay for your psychology instructor explaining in detail your observations along these lines.

Before beginning your essay, you may want to consult the flowchart on page 404.

MICHAEL DORRIS   (1945–1997)

The Broken Cord

Michael Dorris, a descendant of Modoc Native Americans and Irish and French settlers, grew up in Kentucky and Montana. He earned his B.A. at Georgetown University and his M.A. at Yale and was for many years a professor of Anthropology and Native-American Studies at Dartmouth, where he was also head of the Native-American Studies Program. His training was quite eclectic. "I came to cultural anthropology," he has explained, "by way of an undergraduate program in English and classics and a Master's Degree in history of the theater." During his distinguished academic career, he was also a Guggenheim Fellow (1978), a Rockefeller Fellow (1985), a member of the Smithsonian Institution Council, a National Endowment for the Humanities consultant, a National Public Radio commentator, and a member of the editorial board of the *American Indian Culture and Research Journal*. His many publications include *Native Americans: Five Hundred Years After* (1975); a best-selling novel, *A Yellow Raft in Blue Water* (1987); *The Broken Cord* (1989), a work of nonfiction that won the Heartland Prize, the Christopher Medal, and the National Book Critics Circle Award; *Morning Girl* (1992), a book of short stories; and two more novels, *Working Men* (1993) and *Rooms in the House of Stone* (1993). Dorris also coauthored several books with his wife, Louise Erdrich, including *Route Two and Back* (1991), a collection of travel essays. Prior to his death, he advised student writers to "work at as many kinds of jobs as possible while you are young and keep daily journals of their experiences and impressions."

Preparing to Read

The following excerpt from *The Broken Cord* details some of Dorris's frustrations in raising his adopted son, Adam, who suffered from fetal alcohol syndrome until his death in 1991.

Exploring Experience: As you prepare to read this article, take a few moments to think about your own physical and mental growth: What do you know about your birth? How did you develop as a child? Are you reaching your physical and mental potential? How do you know? Are there any barriers between you and this potential? What are they? How can you surmount them? How will you maintain your potential?

LEARNING⏻NLINE Go to the national website for Fetal Alcohol Syndrome (www.nofas.org), and find facts and photos about this condition described in Dorris's essay. Consider the information you learn as you read the following article.

Before reading this essay, you may want to consult the flowchart on page 402.

A dam's birthdays are, I think, the hardest anniversaries, even though   1
as an adoptive father I was not present to hear Adam's first cry, to
feel the aspirated warmth of his body meeting air for the first time.
I was not present to count his fingers, to exclaim at the surprise of gender,
to be comforted by the hope at the heart of his new existence.

From what I've learned, from the sum of gathered profiles divided by the   2
tragedy of each case, the delivery of my premature son was unlikely to have
been a joyous occasion. Most fetal alcohol babies emerge not in a tide, the
facsimile of saline, primordial, life-granting sea, but instead enter this world
tainted with stale wine. Their amniotic fluid literally reeks of Thunderbird
or Ripple, and the whole operating theater stinks like the scene of a three-
day party. Delivery room staff who have been witness time and again tell of
undernourished babies thrown into delirium tremens when the cord that
brought sustenance and poison is severed.◆ Nurses close their eyes at the
memory. An infant with the shakes, as cold turkey as a raving derelict
deprived of the next fix, is hard to forget.

Compared to the ideal, Adam started far in the hole, differently from the   3
child who began a march through the years without the scars of fetters on
his ankles, with eyes and ears that worked, with nothing to carry except
what he or she collected along the path.

Adam's birthdays are reminders for me. For each celebration commemo-   4
rating that he was born, there is the pang, the rage, that he was not born
whole. I grieve for what he might have, what he should have been. I magnify and sustain those looks of understanding or compassion or curiosity that
fleet across his face, fast as a breeze, unexpected as the voice of God—the
time he said to me in the car, the words arising from no context I could see,
"Kansas is between Oklahoma and Texas." But when I turned in amazement,
agreeing loudly, still ready after all these years to discover a buried talent or
passion for geography, for anything, that possible person had disappeared.

"What made you say that?" I asked.   5

"Say what?" he answered. "I didn't say anything."   6

The sixteenth birthday, the eighteenth. The milestones. The driver's   7
license, voting, the adult boundary-marker birthdays. The days I envisioned
while watching the mail for the response to my first adoption application, the
days that set forth like distant skyscrapers as I projected ahead through my
years of fatherhood. I had given little specific consideration to what might
come between, but of those outstanding days I had been sure. They were the
pillars I followed, the oases of certainty. Alone in the cabin in Alaska or in the

---

Thinking Critically

◆ Why is it ironic that the umbilical cord brings both "sustenance and poison"?

basement apartment near Franconia while I waited for the definition of the rest of my life to commence, I planned the elaborate cake decorations for those big birthdays, the significant presents I would save to buy. Odd as it may seem, the anticipation of the acts of letting Adam go began before I even knew his name.[2] I looked forward to the proud days on which the world would recognize my son as progressively more his own man. Those were among the strongest hooks that bonded me to him in my imagination.

As each of these anniversaries finally came and went, nothing like I expected them to be, I doubly mourned. First, selfishly, for me, and second for Adam, because he didn't know what he was missing, what he had already missed, what he would miss. I wanted to burst through those birthdays like a speeding train blasts a weak gate, to get past them and back into the anonymous years for which I had made no models, where there were no obvious measurements, no cakes with candles that would never be lit.   8

It was a coincidence that Adam turned twenty-one as this book neared   9 completion, but it seemed appropriate. On the morning of his birthday, I rose early and baked him a lemon cake, his favorite, and left the layers to cool while I drove to Hanover to pick him up. His gifts were wrapped and on the kitchen table—an electric shaver, clothes, a Garfield calendar.[3] For his special dinner he had requested tacos, and as always I had reserved a magic candle—the kind that keeps reigniting no matter how often it is blown out—for the center of his cake.

I was greeted at Adam's house by the news that he had just had a seizure,   10 a small one this time, but it had left him groggy. I helped him on with his coat, bent to tie his shoelace, all the while talking about the fun we would have during the day. He looked out the window. Only the week before he had been laid off from his dishwashing job. December had been a bad month for seizures, some due to his body's adjustment to a change in dosage and some occurring because Adam had skipped taking medicine altogether. The bowling alley's insurance carrier was concerned and that, combined with an after-Christmas slump in business, decided the issue. Now he was back at Hartford for a few weeks while Ken Krambert and his associates sought a new work placement. I thought perhaps Adam was depressed about this turn of events, so I tried to cheer him up as we drove south on the familiar road to Cornish.

"So, Adam," I said, making conversation, summoning the conventional   11 words, "do you feel any older? What's good about being twenty-one?"

Thinking Critically

[2] Why does Dorris anticipate "letting Adam go" before he even knows his name?

[3] How does the odd combination of an electric shaver and a Garfield calendar help us understand Adam's condition?

He turned to me and grinned. There *was* something good.   12

"Well," he answered, "now the guys at work say I'm old enough to   13
drink."

His unexpected words kicked me in the stomach. They crowded every   14
thought from my brain.

"Adam, you can't," I protested. "I've told you about your birth-mother,   15
about your other father. Do you remember what happened to them?" I
knew he did. I had told him the story several times, and we had gone over
it together as he read, or I read to him, parts of this book.

Adam thought for a moment. "They were sick?" he offered finally.   16
"That's why I have seizures?"

"No, they weren't sick. They died, Adam. They died from drinking. If   17
you drank, it could happen to you." My memory played back all the statistics
about sons of alcoholic fathers and their particular susceptibility to substance
abuse. "It would not mix well with your medicine."

Adam sniffed, turned away, but not before I recognized the amused dis-   18
belief in his expression. He did not take death seriously, never had. It was
an abstract concept out of his reach and therefore of no interest to him.
Death was less real than Santa Claus—after all, Adam had in his album a
photograph of himself seated on Santa Claus's lap. Death was no threat, no
good reason to refuse his first drink.

My son will forever travel through a moonless night with only the roar   19
of wind for company.[4] Don't talk to him of mountains, of tropical beaches.
Don't ask him to swoon at sunrises or marvel at the filter of light through
leaves. He's never had time for such things, and he does not believe in them.
He may pass by them close enough to touch on either side, but his hands
are stretched forward, grasping for balance instead of pleasure. He doesn't
wonder where he came from, where he's going. He doesn't ask who he is,
or why. Questions are a luxury, the province of those at a distance from the
periodic shock of rain. Gravity presses Adam so hard against reality that he
doesn't feel the points at which he touches it. A drowning man is not separated from the lust for air by a bridge of thought—he is one with it—and
my son, conceived and grown in an ethanol bath, lives each day in the act
of drowning. For him there is no shore.

UNDERSTANDING DETAILS

1. Why are Adam's birthdays difficult for Dorris?
2. What are some of the problems Adam was born with?

Thinking Critically

[4] Explain this metaphor in your own words: "My son will forever travel through a moonless night with only the roar of wind for company."

3. Why will Adam never reach his full potential?

4. In what ways did Dorris feel Adam's birthdays would be "oases of certainty" (paragraph 7)? How did the actual celebrations differ from these expectations?

READING CRITICALLY

5. Why does Dorris "doubly" mourn (paragraph 8) his son's birthdays? Explain your answer.

6. In what way was "the definition of the rest of [Dorris's] life" (paragraph 7) connected with his son's birthdays?

7. In what way is death like Santa Claus for Adam? Explain your answer.

8. What does Dorris mean when he says "Questions are a luxury" for his son (paragraph 19)?

DISCOVERING RHETORICAL STRATEGIES

9. At what points in this essay does Dorris either directly or indirectly analyze the causes of Adam's behavior? When does he study its effects (on either himself or his son)? Divide a piece of paper in half. List the causes of Adam's behavior on one side and the effects on the other. Record the paragraph references in each case. Then, discuss the pattern that emerges from your two lists. Does Dorris give more attention to the causes or the effects of Adam's behavior? Why do you think the author develops his essay around this particular emphasis?

10. Dorris uses several comparisons to help his readers understand what raising a child with fetal alcohol syndrome is like. Look, for example, at paragraph 19, in which he compares Adam's life to "a moonless night" and to "the act of drowning." Find two other vivid comparisons in this essay. What do all these comparisons add to the essay? What effect do they have on the essay as a whole?

11. What tone does Dorris establish in his essay? Describe it in three or four well-chosen words. How does he create this tone? What effect does this particular tone have on you as a reader?

12. What rhetorical strategies does Dorris use to support his cause/effect analysis? Give examples of each.

MAKING CONNECTIONS

13. Contrast Dorris's definition of "addiction" with the definitions in any of the following essays that discuss other addictive topics: Kimberly Wozencraft's "Notes from the Country Club," Jay Walljasper's "Our Schedules, Our Selves," and/or Stephen King's "Why We Crave Horror Movies." What specific substance is addictive in these essays? Which addiction do you think would be most difficult to recover from? Explain your answer.

14. Love and concern for a child is the principal topic of Dorris's essay, as it is in Lewis Sawaquat's "For My Indian Daughter," Russell Baker's "The Saturday Evening Post," and Amy Chua's "Excerpt from *Battle Hymn of the Tiger Mother*." If these authors were to come together to discuss parent–child relationships, do

you think they would agree on any of the main issues? If so, what would these areas of agreement be for the essays you have read?

15. Birthdays are milestones in Dorris's essay, just as they are for Malcolm Cowley in "The View from 80." What are the principal differences in the ways each author celebrates these milestones? Why do these differences exist?

IDEAS FOR DISCUSSION/WRITING

Preparing to Write

Write freely about the process of growing up and reaching your potential: What special problems did you experience while growing up? How did you deal with these problems? How did your parents deal with these problems? Do you feel you are heading toward your full potential, or have you already reached it? How do you plan to reach or maintain your potential? What experiences or people have disappointed you mainly because they were not what you expected? What were their shortcomings? Can these shortcomings be remedied? What effects do such shortcomings have on society as a whole?

Choosing a Topic

MyWritingLab™

1. **LEARNING⏻NLINE** In his article, Dorris personalizes the effects of alcoholism on unborn children. Conduct an Internet search on other threats to infant and child health. To begin your search, you may want to visit the website for the Centers for Disease Control and Prevention (www.cdc.gov). Choose a topic that interests you, and write an article for the student health column of your campus's newspaper. Describe the causes and effects of your chosen topic. Find a way to personalize your essay so that it will strike a nerve with your intended audience.

2. In a conversation with your mother, father, or another close relative, explain what problems you found most difficult as you were growing up, and speculate about the causes of those problems. In dialogue form, record the conversation as accurately as possible. Add an introduction, a conclusion, and an explanation of your discussion to mold the conversation into an essay.

3. In the last paragraph of his essay, Dorris implies that his son is slowly drowning in his birth-mother's alcohol abuse. This essay is Dorris's process of grieving about "what [his son] was missing, what he had already missed, what he would miss" (paragraph 8). In an essay of your own, explain something (a process, a person, an event, a relationship, or an activity) that disappointed you mainly because your expectations weren't met. What were the principal reasons for your disappointment? What were the effects of your disappointment? What could have changed the situation?

4. Many forms of addiction and abuse plague our society at present. In an essay written for your composition class, choose one of these problems, and speculate on its primary causes and effects in society today. As often as possible, give specific examples to support your observations.

Before beginning your essay, you may want to consult the flowchart on page 404.

DANA GIOIA   (1950–   )

On the Importance of Reading

American author, teacher, and administrator Dana Gioia is a fascinating study in contrasts. Born to a Mexican-American mother and an Italian immigrant father, he grew up in Gardena, California, then earned his B.A. from Stanford, his M.A. from Harvard, and his M.B.A. from the Stanford Business School. From 1977–1992, he worked at General Foods Corporation, where he was Vice President of Marketing, and helped develop a variety of products, including "Jell-O Jigglers." His secret passion, however, was reading and writing poetry, which he pursued whenever possible. Two critically acclaimed books of poetry—*Daily Horoscope* (1986) and *The Gods of Winter* (1991)—were published during this time, the success of which encouraged him to quit his job and concentrate solely on his writing. A third book, *Interrogations at Noon* (2001), won the American Book Award. In 2002, President George W. Bush named Gioia chair of the National Endowment of the Arts. Infusing the agency with new vitality, Gioia created such innovative programs as "Shakespeare in American Communities," "NEA Jazz Masters," and the widely acclaimed "Big Read Program." In 2007, he gave a controversial commencement address at his alma mater, Stanford University, in which he claimed, "When virtually all of a culture's celebrated figures are in sports or entertainment, how few possible role models we offer the young." Currently the Judge Widney Professor of Poetry and Public Culture at the University of Southern California, Gioia has also written a number of college textbooks, including *The Art of the Short Story* (2005), *Introduction to Fiction* (2009), and *Literature for Life* (2012).

Preparing to Read

Originally delivered as an Osher Foundation talk, "On the Importance of Reading" was later published in *Commonwealth Magazine* (June 2006). In it, Gioia decries the rapid decline in reading and the consequences of this "failure of collective imagination" in our country today.

Exploring Experience: As you prepare to read this essay, think about how important reading is in your life: What types of books do you read? What percentage of your reading is for school? For pleasure? Do you enjoy reading? How are reading and writing related for you? Are you a good writer? How do you account for your writing ability?

LEARNING(ONLINE Dana Gioia's enthusiasm for reading and writing has lead him to become a very passionate spokesperson for education and the arts. To get a better sense of his contributions to these aspects of our culture, go to www.danagioia.net, and scan some of his recent interviews. Then read one of his interviews closely, and note the pattern of his responses. Do his responses form a specific philosophy? What is his primary message?

Before reading this essay, you may want to consult the flowchart on page 402.

Every 10 years the National Endowment for the Arts (NEA) does a survey among American households. It's the largest of its kind in the world. We take 17,000 households, which the U.S. Census Bureau matches to reflect the total American population as of the previous year's census. We interview those people in their homes—a very extensive interview about their participation in arts and civic activities—and we follow up with other phone interviews. This allows us to judge in an objective way (the error rate is about two-tenths of 1 percent—about 20 times the size of your normal national poll) how the arts are doing. We did this a few years ago. Never in my wildest dreams did I expect to find what we found. To summarize, reading has declined among every group of adult Americans: every age group, educational group, income group, region, and race—although Asian reading is flat (the *single* number of several *thousand* in this report that is actually directionally positive). In some cases the declines have been precipitous. This has been going on for 20 years, but the trends are getting worse, and the worst declines are among younger American adults. In the last 20 years, younger American adults have gone from being the people in our society who read the most to the people who read the least. [1]

Reading proficiency has fallen among all Americans, and it has fallen the worst among adults aged 18 to 24, 25 to 34. It has fallen the worst among men, and, indeed, if you look at our study and other studies, only about one-third of adult males are doing what we call "literary reading." Know that literary reading sounds much better than it is. We define literary reading as any imaginative text—essentially any novel, short story, poem or dramatic work in a book, magazine, newspaper, or online. If you carry a poem in your wallet and you look at it once a year, we count you. If you have just finished Thomas Mann's *Buddenbrooks* in German for the third time, or you've read one page of a Harlequin Romance and given up because it's too hard, we count you as equals. We are very egalitarian!

What you see for the first time in American history is that less than half of the U.S. adult American population is reading literature. I'm going to talk about what the causes of the problem are, and then I'll talk about the consequences and the solutions.

To go into the data a little bit further, we see that we're producing the first generation of educated people, in some cases college graduates, who no longer become lifelong readers. This is disturbing for reasons above and beyond those that a poet might be expected to bring to the podium.

Thinking Critically

[1] Why do you think reading among young adults has declined so drastically? Are you reading as much now as you were five years ago. Why or why not?

Literature awakens, enlarges, enhances, and refines our humanity in a way that almost nothing else can.

Franz Kafka once said that the book is the axe by which we break open the frozen seas within us. That metaphor is very true. We tend, by our very nature, to be encased in our own egos. What literature does—nowhere more powerfully than in fiction (the novel and the short story)—is put us in the inner lives of other people in the dailyness of their psychological, social, economic, and imaginative existence. This makes us feel, more intensely probably than anything else, the reality of other points of view, of other lives. [2] That is obviously in jeopardy if we now have a society in which the majority of adults are no longer reading. But there are other things that we can actually measure. Something seems to happen with readers that does not happen with non-readers. I cannot scientifically prove that it's causal, but I can scientifically prove with a wearisome amount of data that it is at the very least correlative.

If you are a reader, you are overwhelmingly more likely to engage in positive social and civic behavior versus non-readers. If you read, you're 300 percent more likely to go to the theater and museums, 200 percent more likely to go to the movies, and over twice—in some measures three times—as likely to do volunteer work or charity work. And the argument that this is a function of income—because the more education you have, the more likely you are to read; the more education you have, the higher your income is—isn't true. The poorest group of American readers does volunteer work and charity work at twice the level of the richest non-readers. You see other things that are rather surprising. If you are a reader, you're more likely to exercise, more likely to go to sports games, more likely to play amateur sports—bowling or softball—and much more likely to be aware of and involved in your own community. There is a deep and arguably statistical connection between readers and civic involvement. The kind of communities that we want to live in are, by definition, communities of readers. The kinds of citizens a democracy needs are readers.

The interesting thing about people who read versus people who don't read, is that they do exactly the same things—except that one group reads and the other one doesn't. Readers play video games, watch television; they do these things, but they do them in a balanced way, versus people who are, increasingly, simply passive consumers of electronic entertainment.

If you look at our data and the data of other studies, you are almost compelled to believe that there is now a bifurcation in the American population between one group, which takes an active stance towards managing their own

---

Thinking Critically

[2] Have Americans gotten more or less in touch with other people's points of view during the last decade? Why do you think this is so?

lives, and another group, which is increasingly passive. The passive people come home, watch TV, play video games, go onto the Internet, talk on the phone, go back to the TV, put a DVD in—and then it's time to go to bed. ❸

I believe that there is something fundamentally intellectual and spiritual   9
that happens to readers through the combination of the sustained focused attention that you bring to reading, the use of your imagination to create pictures of the scenes, characters and situations, and also your use of memory to draw those pictures out, versus being passive and having the images, pacing, tone and everything given to you.

This is a disturbing situation, and it's not likely to get better. Why isn't it   10
likely to get better? This is rather scary. If you see what's happening with pre-adults, you see the same kinds of declines among high school students and eighth graders. You see this decline in the amount of reading, the command of reading, and the ability to read at any complex level. As a Californian, I'm particularly ashamed. If you look at eighth graders, California ranks 49th out of 50 states. If you look at fourth graders, we rank 48th. I know all the excuses—immigration and things like this—but as a Mexican-American Californian, I am ashamed. Our public education system is not doing its job—especially in this state, which once enjoyed one of the greatest public school systems in the world.

The problem is now at a tipping point. In the last 20 years, the number   11
of adult readers in the United States has stayed the same. The number of non-readers has increased by 40 million. There are now a few more non-readers than readers. If we allow the problem to get much worse, the better part of this cultural capacity for reading, imagination, civic engagement, and human enlargement will be irrecoverable.

Why did it happen? First, something isn't happening in schools. Somehow,   12
we are not connecting reading with the expectation of pleasure and the sense that reading is a necessary component of a life of self-realization, of exploration of who you are and what your individual potential is. ❹ That used to be the goal of high school and college education in some ways—maybe quite modestly in high school, but ambitiously in college. Now it seems we are increasingly trying to focus on producing entry-level workers for a service economy. That is not the same as producing free citizens for a democracy.

Second, and this isn't arguable, we are now surrounded by a great welter   13
of electronic alternatives to reading. About 20 years ago, the average American household had one TV, one record player, one radio and maybe one

---

Thinking Critically

❸ Are you more "active" or "passive"? Do you sometimes wish you had a better balance in your life between the two extremes? Why?

❹ How could our schools do a better job of getting students excited about reading?

phone. Now we've got two to three TVs, two video games, two computers, countless phones (if you count both wired and cell phones), DVDs, VCRs, the Internet, etc. Even when you leave the house, you have your iPod, so there's now an opportunity or a risk—depending on how you want to define it—of never cutting off this predetermined flow of electronic entertainment, of which you are largely a passive consumer.

Third, and this is why it's such a pleasure to be speaking at The Commonwealth Club, is that the media in our culture do not seriously discuss or present reading or the rest of the arts. The talk shows of 30, 40 years ago actually were talk shows; now they are opportunities for product placements of new consumer goods.   14

I was raised in an immigrant household where the adults did not speak English. I would see Robert Frost and Carl Sandburg on television—inconceivable nowadays for a network show. This vision that the media gives us of ourselves is narrower and more commercial than ever before. That is a reflection of the culture at large, which does not honor reading, literature, the arts, and the imagination in a way designed to capture and develop someone's attention.   15

If you went into a classroom of high school seniors or college freshmen and asked them how many NBA players they could name, you might get the whole league. How many baseball players? You'd get hundreds. How many hip-hop artists? You'd get dozens, maybe over 100. How many movie stars? You'd get countless names. Then ask them to name one living American painter, sculptor, poet, dramatist, architect, philosopher, historian, theologian, biologist, physicist or mathematician. You'd get nothing. These professions are not life roles that we honor in our society, even by the simple act of paying attention and acknowledging.[5] Consequently, if you think of the role models for a young person in this society, they are terribly, terribly limited to sports and entertainment (which are really both forms of entertainment), and maybe a few public figures. That is a failure of collective imagination. It is a frightening situation for our society to find itself in. This diminishment of the possibilities of life through a diminishment of public culture is leading to a diminishment of the very intellectual, imaginative, cultural capacity of our citizenry on a broader level. This is a crisis. This is a problem of the gravest nature for a democracy to face, because if we do not have a majority of adult citizens who can actively manage their own lives and engage with their own communities and the people and institutions around them, we are a passive society.   16

Thinking Critically

[5] Do you agree with Gioia that most Americans do not respect or care about painters, poets, architects, or historians? If so, why do you think this is true? If you don't agree, explain your answer.

UNDERSTANDING DETAILS

1. What is the purpose of the survey the NEA conducts every 10 years?
2. What was the most surprising discovery uncovered by this survey?
3. How does the NEA define "literary reading"?
4. According to Gioia, what are some of the causes of the decline in reading proficiency?

READING CRITICALLY

5. How does Kafka's metaphor comparing books to "the axe by which we break open the frozen seas within us" (paragraph 5) apply to the main point Gioia is making in this essay?
6. Why do you think readers are more likely to exercise, to go to athletic events, to play sports, and to be more involved in their own community than nonreaders?
7. According to Gioia, what happens to readers intellectually and spiritually?
8. What are the main reasons Americans are not able to read at complex levels?

DISCOVERING RHETORICAL STRATEGIES

9. This essay builds to a dramatic climax, like a good short story. Where is this climax in the essay? What is its focus?
10. List the main points Gioia is making about reading. Does he present these in an effective order? Explain your answer.
11. Do you think the information Gioia cites about Americans being able to name entertainers but not live artists is accurate? In what ways does this claim support Gioia's main points?
12. The author ends this essay with a statement about the "failure of collective imagination" (paragraph 16). Is this an effective ending? Explain your answer.

MAKING CONNECTIONS

13. Imagine that Dana Gioia ("On the Importance of Reading"), Motoko Rich ("Literacy Debate: Online, R U Really Reading?"), and Nicholas Carr ("How the Internet is Making Us Stupid") were having a conversation about the value of reading in our society. To what extent would they agree about the reasons people should read more? Where would they disagree?
14. Dana Gioia, Stephen King ("Why We Crave Horror Movies"), and Joe Keohane ("How Facts Backfire"), all discuss the relationship between causes and effects. Which of these authors does the best job of distinguishing between "superficial" and "real or ultimate" causes? Which of these essays did you find most convincing? Why?
15. Do you think Gioia would agree with Amy Chua ("Excerpt from *Battle Hymn of the Tiger Mother*") that children should be forced to work hard in school? How would Chua feel about Gioia's contention that children should be encouraged to read literature for pleasure? How would each author define the term "education"?

IDEAS FOR DISCUSSION/WRITING

Preparing to Write

Write freely about the role of reading and writing in your life: How do they help you? Do they hinder you in any way? How are they related for you? Which one do you enjoy more? Which one is your stronger suit? Why do you think this is the case? In your opinion, can someone be a good writer, but not a good reader? Can someone be a good reader, but not a good writer? Explain your reasoning.

Choosing a Topic

MyWritingLab™

1. **LEARNING⏻NLINE** From the interviews you found at www.danagioia.net in Preparing to Read, create an interview of your own about the reading habits of college students. You might ask questions like the following: Do you read your textbooks? Do you read for fun outside your classes? Do you enjoy reading? Did you read as you were growing up? What types of books do you enjoy for leisure reading? Survey at least 10 students. Then compile your results in an essay for your classmates.

2. Compose an autobiography of your memories about reading, starting with your earliest recollections. Retrace your experiences with reading up to the present, including the kinds of books you have read, the circumstances surrounding your reading experiences, the people who read to you, the places where you read, your feelings about reading, and your current reading habits.

3. Compose a writing autobiography of your memories about writing, starting with your earliest recollections about writing. Retrace your experiences with writing up to the present, including the types of writing you do, the circumstances surrounding your writing experiences, the people or companies you write to, the places where you write, your feelings about writing, and your current writing habits.

4. Analyze the relationship between reading and writing, using your experience and the stories of others to support your main points.

Before beginning your essay, you may want to consult the flowchart on page 404.

How Facts Backfire

Born and raised in Quincy, Massachusetts, and educated at Villanova University, Joe Keohane began his journalistic career writing political columns for a Boston-based weekly alternative newspaper called the *Dig*, where he was eventually promoted to editor-in-chief. He was then hired as a city columnist and later a staff writer for *Boston Magazine*, after which he spent some time in South America and then moved to New York City. He currently lives in Brooklyn, where he is pursuing a successful career as a freelance writer and editor, with publications in such well-known newspapers and magazines as *The New York Times*, *GQ*, Condé Nast's *Portfolio*, *The Washington Post*, *Slate*, *The Boston Globe*, *The Dallas News*, and *The Utne Reader*. Along with his freelance work, he was the editor-in-chief at *Hemisphere* magazine from 2011–2013. His articles and columns have covered a wide range of topics, including mass transit, local politics, alcohol, smut, Scientology, gerrymandering electoral districts, coin shortages in Buenos Aires, and hamburger chains. Currently articles editor of *Esquire* magazine, he spends much of his free time playing bass in what he has described as "a ferocious honky-tonk band" called The Steamboat Disasters. Asked to give advice to students using *The Prose Reader*, Keohane urged them to "read everything, all the time. You have to be a great reader before you can be a great writer."

Preparing to Read

Originally published in *The Boston Globe* (July 11, 2010), the following essay makes the unsettling assertion that people who have already made their minds up about a topic will seldom let facts change their incorrect opinions.

Exploring Experience: Before you read this essay, think about how important having fair, well-informed opinions is to you: On what sources do you base most of your opinions? How readily do you form opinions? Do you find you can alter your opinions easily if you have good reasons? What would cause you to change your mind on an issue? Are your opinions flexible or rigid? Why do you think this is the case?

LEARNING♦NLINE Before reading Keohane's essay, visit the website urbanlegends.about.com, and read some of the articles about urban legends. Is there anything that you believe strongly in, despite lacking hard facts? Why do you think people tend to believe urban legends?

Before reading this essay, you may want to consult the flowchart on page 402.

I t's one of the great assumptions underlying modern democracy that an   1
informed citizenry is preferable to an uninformed one. "Whenever the
people are well-informed, they can be trusted with their own government," Thomas Jefferson wrote in 1789. This notion, carried down through
the years, underlies everything from humble political pamphlets to
presidential debates to the very notion of a free press. Mankind may be
crooked timber, as Kant put it, uniquely susceptible to ignorance and misinformation, but it's an article of faith that knowledge is the best remedy. If
people are furnished with the facts, they will be clearer thinkers and better
citizens. If they are ignorant, facts will enlighten them. If they are mistaken,
facts will set them straight. [1]

In the end, truth will out. Won't it?   2

Maybe not. Recently, a few political scientists have begun to discover a   3
human tendency deeply discouraging to anyone with faith in the power of
information. It's this: Facts don't necessarily have the power to change our
minds. In fact, quite the opposite. In a series of studies in 2005 and 2006,
researchers at the University of Michigan found that when misinformed
people, particularly political partisans, were exposed to corrected facts in
news stories, they rarely changed their minds. In fact, they often became
even more strongly set in their beliefs. Facts, they found, were not curing
misinformation. Like an underpowered antibiotic, facts could actually make
misinformation even *stronger*.

This bodes ill for a democracy, because most voters—the people making   4
decisions about how the country runs—aren't blank slates. They already
have beliefs and a set of facts lodged in their minds. The problem is that
sometimes the things they think they know are, objectively, probably false.
And in the presence of the correct information, such people react very, very
differently than the merely uninformed. Instead of changing their minds to
reflect the correct information, they can entrench themselves even deeper.

"The general idea is that it's absolutely threatening to admit you're   5
wrong," says political scientist Brendan Nyhan, the lead researcher on the
Michigan study. The phenomenon—known as "backfire"—is "a natural
defense mechanism to avoid that cognitive dissonance." [2]

These findings open a long-running argument about the political igno-   6
rance of American citizens to broader questions about the interplay between

---

Thinking Critically

1. Are you well enough informed to be a good citizen? Why or why not? Where do you
get most of your news: television, newspapers, magazines, the Internet? Which of these
sources do you think is most credible?

2. How often do you admit that you have been wrong? Why is this simple admission so
difficult for most people?

the nature of human intelligence and our democratic ideals. Most of us like to believe that our opinions have been formed over time by careful, rational consideration of facts and ideas and that the decisions based on those opinions, therefore, have the ring of soundness and intelligence. In reality, we often base our opinions on our *beliefs*, which can have an uneasy relationship with facts. And rather than facts driving beliefs, our beliefs can dictate the facts we choose to accept. They can cause us to twist facts so they fit better with our preconceived notions. Worst of all, they can lead us to uncritically accept bad information just because it reinforces our beliefs.[3] This reinforcement makes us more confident we're right and even less likely to listen to any new information. And then we vote.

This effect is only heightened by the information glut, which offers—   7 alongside an unprecedented amount of good information—endless rumors, misinformation, and questionable variations on the truth. In other words, it's never been easier for people to be wrong and at the same time feel more certain that they're right.

"Area Man Passionate Defender of What He Imagines Constitution To   8 Be" read a recent *Onion* headline. Like the best satire, this nasty little gem elicits a laugh, which is then promptly muffled by the queasy feeling of recognition. The last five decades of political science have definitively established that most modern-day Americans lack even a basic understanding of how their country works. In 1996, Princeton University's Larry M. Bartels argued, "the political ignorance of the American voter is one of the best documented data in political science."

On its own, this might not be a problem: People ignorant of the facts   9 could simply choose not to vote. But instead, it appears that misinformed people often have some of the strongest political opinions. A striking recent example was a study done in the year 2000, led by James Kuklinski of the University of Illinois at Urbana-Champaign. He led an influential experiment in which more than 1,000 Illinois residents were asked questions about welfare—the percentage of the federal budget spent on welfare, the number of people enrolled in the program, the percentage of enrollees who are black, and the average payout. More than half indicated that they were confident that their answers were correct—but in fact only 3 percent of the people got more than half of the questions right. Perhaps more disturbingly, the ones who were the *most* confident they were right were by and large the ones who knew the least about the topic. (Most of these participants expressed views that suggested a strong anti-welfare bias.)

Thinking Critically

[3] Do you base your opinions more on "beliefs" or "facts"? Which provide stronger evidence?

Studies by other researchers have observed similar phenomena when   10
addressing education, health care reform, immigration, affirmative action,
gun control, and other issues that tend to attract strong partisan opinion.
Kuklinski calls this sort of response the "I know I'm right" syndrome and
considers it a "potentially formidable problem" in a democratic system. "It
implies not only that most people will resist correcting their factual beliefs,"
he wrote, "but also that the very people who most need to correct them
will be least likely to do so."[4]

What's going on? How can we have things so wrong and be so sure that   11
we're right? Part of the answer lies in the way our brains are wired. Generally, people tend to seek consistency. There is a substantial body of psychological research showing that people tend to interpret information with an
eye toward reinforcing their preexisting views. If we believe something
about the world, we are more likely to passively accept as truth any information that confirms our beliefs and actively dismiss information that doesn't.
This is known as "motivated reasoning." Whether or not the consistent
information is accurate, we might accept it as fact, as confirmation of our
beliefs. This makes us more confident in said beliefs and even less likely to
entertain facts that contradict them.

New research, published in the journal *Political Behavior* last month, sug-   12
gests that once those facts—or "facts"—are internalized, they are very difficult to budge. In 2005, amid the strident calls for better media fact-checking
in the wake of the Iraq war, Michigan's Nyhan and a colleague devised an
experiment in which participants were given mock news stories, each of
which contained a provably false, though nonetheless widespread, claim
made by a political figure: that there were WMDs found in Iraq (there
weren't), that the Bush tax cuts increased government revenues (revenues
actually fell), and that the Bush administration imposed a total ban on stem
cell research (only certain federal funding was restricted). Nyhan inserted a
clear, direct correction after each piece of misinformation, and then mea-
sured the study participants to see if the correction took.

For the most part, it didn't. The participants who self-identified as con-   13
servative believed the misinformation on WMD and taxes even *more* strongly
after being given the correction.[5] With those two issues, the more strongly
the participant cared about the topic—a factor known as salience—the

---

Thinking Critically

4 When was the last time you experienced the "I know I'm right" syndrome? Were you
   right or wrong when you had this feeling? Do you agree with Keohane's major premise
   in this article, or do you think you're right and he's wrong?

5 Do you find the results of this study ironic or counterintuitive? What would you expect
   the participants to do after their erroneous beliefs had been corrected by facts?

stronger the backfire. The effect was slightly different on self-identified liberals: When they read corrected stories about stem cells, the corrections didn't backfire, but the readers did still ignore the inconvenient fact that the Bush administration's restrictions weren't total.

It's unclear what is driving the behavior—it could range from simple defensiveness to people working harder to defend their initial beliefs—but as Nyhan dryly put it, "It's hard to be optimistic about the effectiveness of fact-checking." 14

It would be reassuring to think that political scientists and psychologists have come up with a way to counter this problem, but that would be getting ahead of ourselves. The persistence of political misperceptions remains a young field of inquiry. "It's very much up in the air," says Nyhan. 15

But researchers are working on it. One avenue may involve self-esteem. Nyhan worked on one study in which he showed that people who were given a self-affirmation exercise were more likely to consider new information than people who had not. In other words, if you feel good about yourself, you'll listen—and if you feel insecure or threatened, you won't. This would also explain why demagogues benefit from keeping people agitated. The more threatened people feel, the less likely they are to listen to dissenting opinions, and the more easily controlled they are. 16

There are also some cases where directness works. Kuklinski's welfare study suggested that people will actually update their beliefs if you hit them "between the eyes" with bluntly presented, objective facts that contradict their preconceived ideas. He asked one group of participants what percentage of its budget they believed the federal government spent on welfare and what percentage they believed the government should spend. Another group was given the same questions, but the second group was immediately told the correct percentage the government spends on welfare (1 percent). They were then asked, with that in mind, what the government should spend. Regardless of how wrong they had been before receiving the information, the second group indeed adjusted their answer to reflect the correct fact.[6] 17

Kuklinski's study, however, involved people getting information directly from researchers in a highly interactive way. When Nyhan attempted to deliver the correction in a more real-world fashion, via a news article, it backfired. Even if people do accept the new information, it might not stick over the long term, or it may just have no effect on their opinions. In 2007, 18

Thinking Critically

[6] How did Kuklinski's study attempt to correct the results of previous studies? Did his procedure work? Why?

John Sides of George Washington University and Jack Citrin of the University of California at Berkeley studied whether providing misled people with correct information about the proportion of immigrants in the US population would affect their views on immigration. It did not.

And if you harbor the notion—popular on both sides of the aisle—that   19
the solution is more education and a higher level of political sophistication in voters overall, well, that's a start, but not the solution. A 2006 study by Charles Taber and Milton Lodge at Stony Brook University showed that politically sophisticated thinkers were even less open to new information than less sophisticated types. These people may be factually right about 90 percent of things, but their confidence makes it nearly impossible to correct the 10 percent on which they're totally wrong. Taber and Lodge found this alarming, because engaged, sophisticated thinkers are "the very folks on whom democratic theory relies most heavily."

In an ideal world, citizens would be able to maintain constant vigilance,   20
monitoring both the information they receive and the way their brains are processing it. But keeping atop the news takes time and effort. And relentless self-questioning, as centuries of philosophers have shown, can be exhausting. Our brains are designed to create cognitive shortcuts—inference, intuition, and so forth—to avoid precisely that sort of discomfort while coping with the rush of information we receive on a daily basis.[7] Without those shortcuts, few things would ever get done. Unfortunately, with them, we're easily suckered by political falsehoods.

Nyhan ultimately recommends a supply-side approach. Instead of focus-   21
ing on citizens and consumers of misinformation, he suggests looking at the sources. If you increase the "reputational costs" of peddling bad info, he suggests, you might discourage people from doing it so often. "So if you go on 'Meet the Press' and you get hammered for saying something misleading," he says, "you'd think twice before you go and do it again."

Unfortunately, this shame-based solution may be as implausible as it   22
is sensible. Fast-talking political pundits have ascended to the realm of highly lucrative popular entertainment, while professional fact-checking operations languish in the dungeons of wonkery. Getting a politician or pundit to argue straight-faced that George W. Bush ordered 9/11 or that Barack Obama is the culmination of a five-decade plot by the government of Kenya to destroy the United States—that's easy. Getting him to register shame? That isn't.

Thinking Critically

[7] Have you ever realized that your brain was taking one of these "cognitive shortcuts" (paragraph 20)? Why do you think our minds naturally do this?

UNDERSTANDING DETAILS

1. What do you think Thomas Jefferson meant in 1789 when he said, "Whenever the people are well-informed, they can be trusted with their own government" (paragraph 1)?
2. In what ways is the concept of "backfire" a "natural defense mechanism" (paragraph 5)?
3. How are "beliefs" different from "facts"?
4. According to Kuklinski, how does directness change people's minds?

READING CRITICALLY

5. Are you surprised at the University of Michigan researchers' finding that facts often don't change our minds?
6. How is the process of "backfire" a threat to democracy?
7. Do you agree with Keohane that "it's never been easier for people to be wrong and at the same time feel more certain that they're right" (paragraph 7)?
8. What does the brain's function have to do with our ability to accept or reject new information? Why do our brains take "cognitive shortcuts" (paragraph 20)?

DISCOVERING RHETORICAL STRATEGIES

9. List the causes and effects this essay studies. How are they organized here?
10. What is the general mood of Keohane's essay?
11. What other rhetorical strategies support this cause/effect essay? Give examples of each.
12. Is it effective to end the essay with a reference to the way we might process information in an ideal world?

MAKING CONNECTIONS

13. Imagine that Keohane, Brian Denis Egan ("The Role of Critical Thinking in Effective Decision Making"), and/or Motoko Rich ("Literacy Debate") were having a discussion about the importance of teaching facts rather than beliefs in our educational system. What specific suggestions would they have for improving the way high school and college students are taught?
14. Many of the essays in *The Prose Reader* attempt to alter public beliefs by countering them with facts. How successfully do each of the following authors use factual evidence to change opinions that you have previously held: Jessica Mitford ("Behind the Formaldehyde Curtain") on American mortuaries, David Hanson ("Binge Drinking") on drinking in college, and/or Dave Grossman ("We Are Training Our Kids to Kill") on violent video games? Which author is most persuasive with his or her use of facts? Why?
15. Contrast the ways in which Keohane, Stephen King ("Why We Crave Horror Movies"), and/or Michael Dorris ("The Broken Cord") reveal the relationships between causes and effects in their essays. Which author's use of this rhetorical technique seems most logical and convincing to you? Explain your answer.

IDEAS FOR DISCUSSION/WRITING

Preparing to Write

Write freely on your views about forming opinions and changing your mind: How quickly do you form most of your opinions? On what do you base these opinions? If you encounter facts that conflict with your own views, do you generally change your mind? How readily do you change your opinions on an issue? What types of information are most convincing to you?

Choosing a Topic

MyWritingLab™

1. **LEARNING⏻NLINE** Now that you know about the "backfire effect," revisit the website urbanlegends.about.com from Preparing to Read. Pick one urban legend, and write a short essay examining why you think this urban legend could be taken seriously. Alternatively, you may write a short essay examining a different myth or suspicion with which you have personal experience, arguing why you or someone you know takes this suspicion seriously.

2. Your college newspaper is doing a story on people's basic value systems. Write an essay for the newspaper explaining in detail the origin of your most passionate values, as well as the ways they are revealed in your life. In other words, cover both the causes and effects of these values.

3. Your college counselor/advisor wants to know if you see yourself as intellectually healthy. Do you consider facts before you form your own opinions? In a detailed essay written for this counselor, who is writing a letter of recommendation for you, explain why you are or are not in good intellectual health. What events, attitudes, or activities have played a part in developing your ability to evaluate information responsibly?

4. Americans seem to be obsessed with their rights to their own opinions these days. Why do you think this is so? How and when did this obsession begin? Explain your reasoning in an essay written for your peers.

Before beginning your essay, you may want to consult the flowchart on page 404.

ART MARKMAN   (1962–   )

Can Video Games Make You Smart (Or At Least More Flexible)?

Art Markman is the Annabel Irion Worsham Centennial Professor of Psychology and Marketing at the University of Texas at Austin. He received his B.S. in Cognitive Science from Brown University in 1988 and then went on to receive his Ph.D. from the University of Illinois in 1992. Before teaching at the University of Texas, Markman taught at Northwestern University and Columbia University. His research focuses on four main areas: the ways people see things to be similar and how they process similarity; category learning; decision making; and the ways motivational factors affect learning, decision making, and cognition in general. Markman's passion is bringing his research to the public. He blogs for many sites, including *Psychology Today* and *Fast Company*. He is also on the scientific advisory board for the *Dr. Phil Show* and the *Dr. Oz Show*, and he co-hosts a radio show called *Two Guys on Your Head*. For relaxation, he enjoys spending quality time with his family and playing saxophone in a blues band.

Preparing to Read

The following essay, from *Psychology Today,* focuses on one of the positive results of playing video games and suggests that it might even affect learning in constructive ways.

Exploring Experience: As you begin to read this essay, take a few minutes to consider the effect of some of your extracurricular activities on your academic performance: What are some of your activities outside of school? How do they affect your performance as a student? Which ones help your focus and concentration? Which ones work against your academic responsibilities? Which activities do you like the best? Why do you like them?

LEARNING⏻NLINE In his essay, Markman describes the skills one can build by playing certain video games. Visit miniclip.com, scroll down to "Puzzle Games," and play a few of the Top Games. After you have played, write your thoughts about what skills are required to complete these tasks.

Before reading this essay, you may want to consult the flowchart on page 402.

T he potential ills of video game play have been broadcast all over the   1
media.[1] Playing violent video games can prime aggressive behavior.
Kids who get video game systems perform worse in school after
they get the system than they did before.

Not all effects of video games are bad, though. There is evidence that   2
playing video games can make people faster at processing visual information
like searching for an object among a set of other distracters.

One hallmark of smart thinking is flexibility.[2] People who are able to   3
see the same object in different ways and can keep lots of possibilities in
mind at the same time are often able to develop novel and creative solutions
to problems. A paper by Brian Glass, Todd Maddox, and Brad Love in the
August 2013 issue of *PLoS One* suggests that some kinds of video games can
help to teach this skill.

They compared the effects of playing real-time strategy games to playing   4
games that require no particular strategic thinking. The participants in this
study were all women, because the experimenters had trouble finding
enough men who do not play video games regularly. The women were
assigned to one of three groups.

One group played a simple version of the game StarCraft. In this game,   5
participants have to create, organize, and deploy armies to attack an enemy.
In the simple version of the game, the player had one base and the enemy
had one base. In the more complex version of the game, the player had two
bases and the enemy had two bases. The overall difficulty of the game was
then set up so that the simple and complex versions of the game were about
equally hard to win. This way, the games differed primarily in how much
information players needed to keep in mind while playing. The control
condition had people play a life simulation (the SIMS), which does not
require much strategy or memory. Participants played their assigned game
for 40 hours.

As a test, participants were given a pre-test and post-test of a series of tasks   6
that tap cognitive abilities. Some of the tests require cognitive flexibility. For
example, in the classic Stroop task, people name the color of a font for words
that name colors. The typical finding is that people are slow to name the
color when the word names a different color than the font.

In task switching procedures, people flip back and forth between the   7
responses they make. For example, in one task, people are shown a letter
and a number (say e4). On some trials, they are prompted to identify

---

Thinking Critically

1 What are some negative consequences from playing video games that come to your mind?

2 What does flexibility in thinking mean? Give an example from your experience.

whether the letter is a vowel or consonant, while on other trials, they are prompted to identify whether the number is odd or even. People generally slow down when asked to switch from one task (say identifying letters) on one trial to the other task (identifying numbers) on the next. The faster you are able to switch between tasks, though, the more flexibly you are thinking.

Other tasks did not require flexibility. For example, a visual search task requires finding a particular object among a set of distracters. That task requires perceptual speed, but not flexibility. [3]   8

The results of the study were striking. Participants who played StarCraft showed significant improvement on the cognitive flexibility tasks, but not the other tasks compared to those who played the SIMS. The improvement was largest for those who played the complex version of the game, and smaller for those who played the simple version.   9

Additional analyses found that the people who played the complex version of the game had to keep more information in mind while playing than those who played the simple version. Practice using all of this information may have been the root of the improvement on the flexibility tasks.   10

These results are intriguing. It is hard to get people to work on difficult tasks for long in school settings, but much easier to get them to work for long hours while playing video games. If games can be structured to promote skills that improve flexible thinking, then they can be a valuable tool in helping people to get smarter. [4]   11

That said, flexible thinking is only a part of being smarter. In order to really do smart things, you also need to know a lot of information in order to be able to use that knowledge to solve problems. As much fun as video games may be, they will not substitute for the hours you need to put in to become an expert in at least one domain.   12

UNDERSTANDING DETAILS

1. What are some "potential ills" (paragraph 1) of playing video games?
2. In your own words, explain the experiment that Glass, Maddox, and Love conducted.
3. What is "task switching" (paragraph 7)?
4. What does Markman mean when he says video games "will not substitute for the hours you need to put in to become an expert in at least one domain" (paragraph 12)?

Thinking Critically

[3] What is the difference between "perceptual speed" and "flexibility"?

[4] How could video games be used in schools to improve students' performance?

READING CRITICALLY

5. How do some video games promote flexibility in thinking?
6. Why did the researchers choose the game StarCraft for their experiment?
7. How can games be "a valuable tool in helping people to get smarter" (paragraph 11)?
8. What does being smart have to do with solving problems, as the author implies in the last paragraph of this essay?

DISCOVERING RHETORICAL STRATEGIES

9. Why do you think Markman wrote this essay? What was he trying to accomplish by writing it?
10. Who do you think is Markman's primary audience for this essay?
11. Why do you think Markman starts with some of the negative consequences of playing video games? Is this an effective beginning for what he is trying to prove? Why or why not?
12. Does the study that Markman cites prove his point? Are you convinced that some video games promote flexible thinking? What details from the study are most persuasive to you?

MAKING CONNECTIONS

13. Markman, Sara Gilbert ("The Different Ways of Being Smart"), and Nicholas Carr ("How the Internet is Making Us Stupid") all comment either directly or indirectly on human intelligence. In reference to their main points, which ideas would these authors agree on? On what would they disagree?
14. Markman openly discusses various effects of video games on those who play them in much the same way that Roni Jacobson ("A Digital Safety Net"), Nicolas Carr ("How the Internet Is Making Us Stupid"), Josh Rose ("How Social Media Is Having a Positive Impact on Our Culture"), and Susan Tardanico ("Is Social Media Sabotaging Real Communication?") discuss different aspects of the Internet. Which would agree on the advantages of the Internet? Which would agree on the disadvantages?
15. The relationship Markman discusses between video games and flexible thinking demonstrates a positive cause/effect connection. Find an essay in this chapter of the book that implies a negative connection between a cause and its effect. How are the two essays different? How are they the same?

IDEAS FOR DISCUSSION/WRITING

Preparing to Write

Write freely about your basic abilities as a college student: How important are good study skills to you? What affects your grades most dramatically? Are you aware of ways to improve your thinking? What specific activities affect your academic performance the most? Do they help or hinder your thinking? What elements affect the thinking of other students you know? What effects have you observed in college students that result from poor thinking skills? How do you improve your thinking? Do you recommend this method to others?

Choosing a Topic   MyWritingLab™

1. **LEARNING(⏻)NLINE** Thinking back to the games you played in Preparing to Read (and perhaps are playing now), do you agree with the findings that Markman discusses in his essay? Do you feel that playing video games benefits, rather than harms, your intelligence or not? Explain your answer.

2. Poor study skills can cause a number of problems in college students' lives. Conduct a survey of the causes and effects of good academic performance in the lives of several students at your school. Write an essay for the college community explaining these causes and effects.

3. Your campus newspaper is printing a special issue highlighting the psychological health of different generations of college students. Interview some people who represent a generation other than your own. Then characterize for the newspaper the students in the generation you selected. In essay form, introduce the features you have discovered, and then discuss their causes and effects.

4. Some people believe self-esteem is a result of peer groups; others say that it is a result of one's family environment. What do you think? *Time* magazine is soliciting student reactions on this issue and has asked for your opinion. Where do you stand on this question? Give specific examples that support your opinion. Respond in essay form.

Before beginning your essay, you may want to consult the flowchart on page 404.

Chapter Writing Assignments

Practicing Cause/Effect

1. Think about a time in your life when you had definite, clear expectations of an event or experience. Where did these expectations come from? Were they high or low? Were they fulfilled or not? If not, what went wrong? Explain the situation surrounding this experience in a coherent essay.

2. Brainstorm about some challenges or difficult times you have faced. Then describe the most important challenge you have overcome. Explain why this experience was so difficult and what helped you face and conquer it.

3. What do you believe are the major causes of violence in American society? Write an essay that explains why the causes you cite are real or valid. Can you propose any possible solutions to the predicament you describe?

Exploring Ideas

4. How does our reading help us perceive the world? Do you think short stories, plays, and poems help us understand people's behavior and feelings? Write an essay responding to these questions.

5. Compare your memory of a particular childhood experience with that of another family member. How accurately do you both seem to remember this same event? What do you think accounts for the differences in what we remember about various events? What do these differences say about us? Write an essay exploring these questions, using the event from your childhood to support your discussion.

6. Television has been blamed for causing violent behavior, shortening attention spans, and exposing young people to sexually explicit images. Should we as a society monitor what appears on television more closely, or should parents be responsible for censoring what their children watch? Write an essay that takes a stand on this issue.

Analyzing Visual Images

Jim West/Alamy.

7. Examine the preceding photo, and think about the paths that we take in our lives. Discuss a time when you decided to explore a new path, and explain the effect this change had on your life.

8. Look at the picture on page 400 at the beginning of this chapter, which depicts the famous Zeppelin *Hindenburg* (one of the largest airships ever) bursting into flames in 1937. You might be interested in researching the causes and effects of this disaster. Consider other similar disasters that changed the way people think about traveling, and write an essay explaining all the causes and effects that were connected with this change.

Composing in Different Genres

9. Multimedia: Create a photo essay that details the role of reading in your life. What types of sources do you read? Do you read mainly paper or electronic works? Do you read both prose and graphic documents? Do you read mostly fiction, nonfiction, poetry, or drama? Do you consider videos and movies forms of reading?

10. Multigenre: Write an episode (complete with dialogue and stage directions) for your favorite detective show. Think through the main plot that you want to develop, and then create a script to communicate your ideas. (If you feel particularly creative, you can video your episode with the help of your friends or classmates.)

Writing from Sources

For detailed information on writing from sources, see Part III.

11. Substance abuse can materialize in several ways. Choose one form of substance abuse to research, and examine the ways it can affect individuals in their personal lives, their workplace, and their relationships. Then write an essay citing two or three sources that discuss the effects that you researched.

12. How does the way the media portray body image affect the average American? What types of people are most susceptible to negative reaction? Can you think of any positive portrayals in the media? While thinking about these questions, research the connection between the media's portrayal of body image and eating and psychological disorders that men and women face today. Write an essay discussing the cause/effect relationship between the media and body image using evidence from your research.

MyWritingLab™ Visit Ch. 11. Cause/Effect: Tracing Reasons and Results in *MyWritingLab* to complete the writing assignments and test your understanding of the chapter learning objectives.

Chapter 12

ARGUMENT AND PERSUASION
Inciting People to Thought or Action

LEARNING OBJECTIVES

After completing this chapter, you will be able to do the following:
- Define argument
- Use argument to think critically
- Read argument essays critically
- Write and revise effective argument essays

Almost everything we do or say is an attempt to persuade. Whether we dress up to impress a potential employer or argue openly with a friend about an upcoming election, we are trying to convince various people to see the world our way. However, some aspects of life are particularly dependent on persuasion. Think, for example, of all the television, magazine, and billboard ads we see urging us to buy certain products or of the many impassioned appeals we read and hear on such controversial issues as school prayer, abortion, gun control, and nuclear energy. Religious leaders devote their professional lives to convincing people to live a certain way and believe in certain religious truths, whereas scientists and mathematicians use rigorous logic and natural law to convince us of other hypotheses. Politicians make their living persuading voters to elect them and then support them throughout their terms in office. In fact, anyone who wants something from another person or agency, ranging from federal money for a research project to a new bicycle for Christmas, must use some form of persuasion to get what he or she desires. The success or failure of this type of communication is easily determined: If the people being addressed change their actions or attitudes in favor of the writer or speaker, the attempt at persuasion has been successful.

DEFINING ARGUMENT AND PERSUASION

The terms *argument* and *persuasion* are often used interchangeably, but one is actually a subdivision of the other. Persuasion names a purpose for writing. To persuade your readers is to convince them to think, act, or feel a certain way. Much of the writing you have been doing in this book has persuasion as one of its goals: A description of an African tribe might have a "dominant impression" you want your readers to accept; in an essay comparing various ways of celebrating Thanksgiving, you might try to convince your readers to believe that these similarities and differences actually exist; and in writing an essay exam on the causes of the Vietnam War, you are trying to convince your instructor that your reasoning is clear and your conclusions sound. In a sense, some degree of persuasion propels all writing.

More specifically, however, the process of persuasion involves appealing to one or more of the following: reason, emotion, or a sense of ethics. An *argument* is an appeal predominantly to your readers' reason and intellect. You are working in the realm of argument when you deal with complex issues that are debatable; opposing views (either explicit or implicit) are a basic requirement of argumentation. But argument and persuasion are taught together because good writers are constantly blending these three appeals and adjusting them to the purpose and audience of a particular writing task. Although reason and logic are the focus of this chapter, you need to learn to use all three methods of persuasion as skillfully as possible to write effective essays.

An appeal to reason relies on logic and intellect and is usually most effective when you are expecting your readers to disagree with you in some way. This type of appeal can help you change your readers' opinions or influence their future actions through the sheer strength of logical validity. If you want to argue, for example, that pregnant women should refrain from smoking cigarettes, you could cite abundant statistical evidence that babies born to mothers who smoke have lower birth weights, more respiratory problems, and a higher incidence of sudden infant death syndrome than the children of nonsmoking mothers. Because smoking clearly endangers the health of the unborn child, reason dictates that mothers who wish to give birth to the healthiest possible babies should avoid smoking during pregnancy.

Emotional appeals, however, attempt to arouse your readers' feelings, instincts, senses, and biases. Used most profitably when your readers already agree with you, this type of essay generally validates, reinforces, and/or incites in an effort to get your readers to share your feelings or ideas. To urge our lawmakers to impose stricter jail sentences for alcohol abuse, for example, you might describe a recent tragic accident involving a local 12-year-old girl who was killed by a drunk driver as she rode her bicycle to school one morning. By focusing on such poignant visual details as the condition of her mangled bike, the bright red blood stains on her white dress, and the anguish on the faces of parents and friends, you could build a powerfully persuasive essay that would be much more effective than a dull recitation of impersonal facts and nationwide statistics.

An appeal to ethics, the third technique writers often use to encourage readers to agree with them, involves cultivating a sincere, honest tone that will establish your reputation as a reliable, qualified, experienced, well-informed, and knowledgeable person whose opinions on the topic under discussion are believable because they are ethically sound. Such an approach is often used in conjunction with logical or emotional appeals to foster a verbal environment that will result in minimal resistance from its readers. Premier model Cindy Crawford is a master at creating this ethical, trustworthy persona as she tries to persuade television viewers to buy beauty products. In fact, the old gag question "Would you buy a used car from this man?" is our instinctive response to all forms of attempted persuasion, whether the salesperson is trying to sell us Puppy Chow or gun control, hair spray or school prayer. The more believable we are as human beings, the better chance we will have of convincing our audience.

The following student paragraph is directed primarily toward the audience's logical reasoning ability. Notice that the writer states her assertion and then gives reasons to convince her readers to change their ways. The student writer also brings both emotion and ethics into the argument by choosing her words and examples with great precision.

> *Have you ever watched a pair of chunky thighs, a jiggling posterior, and an extra-large sweatshirt straining to cover a beer belly and thought, "Thank God I don't look like that! I'm in pretty good shape . . . for someone my age." Well, before you become too smug and self-righteous, consider what kind of shape you're really in. Just because you don't look like Shamu the whale doesn't mean you're in good condition. What's missing, you ask? Exercise. You can diet all day, wear the latest slim-cut designer jeans, and still be in worse shape than someone twice your age if you don't get a strong physical workout at least three times a week. Exercise is not only good for you, but it can also be fun—especially if you find a sport that makes you happy while you sweat. Your activity need not be expensive: Jogging, walking, basketball, tennis, and*

handball are not costly, unless you're seduced by the glossy sheen of the latest sporting fashions and accessories. Most of all, however, regular exercise is important for your health. You can just as easily drop dead from a sudden heart attack in the middle of a restaurant when you're slim and trim as when you're a slob. Your heart and lungs need regular workouts to stay healthy. So do yourself a favor, and add some form of exercise to your schedule. You'll feel better and live longer, and your looks will improve too!

THINKING CRITICALLY THROUGH ARGUMENT AND PERSUASION

Argument and persuasion require you to present your views on an issue through logic, emotion, and good character in such a way that you convince an audience of your point of view. This rhetorical mode comes at the end of this book because it is an extremely complex and sophisticated method of reasoning. The more proficient you become with this strategy of thinking and presenting your views, the more you will get what you want out of life (and out of school). Winning arguments means getting the pay raises you need, the refund you deserve, and the grades you've worked so hard for.

In a successful argument, your logic must be flawless. Your conclusions should be based on clear evidence, which must be organized in such a way that it builds to an effective, convincing conclusion. You should constantly have your purpose and audience in mind as you build your case; at the same time, issues of emotion and good character should support the flow of your logic.

Exercising your best logical skills is extremely important to all phases of your daily survival—in and out of the classroom. Following a logical argument in your reading and presenting a logical response to your course work are the hallmarks of a good student. Right now, put your best logic forward, and work on your reasoning and persuasive abilities in the following series of exercises. Isolate argument/persuasion from the other rhetorical strategies so that you can practice it and strengthen your ability to argue before you combine it with other methods.

1. Charles Moore uses the photograph on the next page to document how the police in Birmingham, Alabama, used a dog to harass a peaceful protester in a 1963 civil rights struggle. Identify another social struggle or protest that you believe is important. Brainstorm about the many views people might hold about this issue. Choose one, and identify the types of evidence you would need to support this view, the resolutions you might offer, and the concessions you would be willing to make to resolve the issue. Make a five- to ten-minute presentation arguing your point to your class or to a small group in your class.

Charles Moore/Black Star.

2. Bring to class two magazine ads: one that tries to sell a product and another that tries to convince the reader that a particular action or product is wrong or bad (unhealthy, misinterpreted, politically incorrect, etc.). How does each ad appeal to the reader's logic? How does the advertiser use emotion and character in his or her appeal?
3. Fill in the following blanks: The best way to _____ is to _____. (For example, "The best way to lose weight is to exercise.") Then list ways you might use to persuade a reader to see your point of view in this statement.

READING AND WRITING ARGUMENT/PERSUASION ESSAYS

Although persuasive writing can be approached essentially in three different ways—logically, emotionally, and/or ethically—our stress in this chapter is on logic and reason because they are at the heart of most college writing. As a reader, you will see how various forms of reasoning and different methods of organization affect your reaction to an essay. Your stand on a particular issue will control the way you process information in argument and persuasion essays. As you read the essays in this chapter, you will also learn to recognize emotional and ethical appeals and the different effects they create. In your role as a writer, you need to be fully aware of the options available to you as you compose. Although the basis of your writing will be logical argument, you will see that you can learn to control your readers' responses to your essays by choosing your evidence carefully, organizing it wisely, and seasoning it with the right amount of emotion and ethics—depending on your purpose and audience.

Reading Argument/Persuasion Essays

Understanding how argument/persuasion essays work rhetorically will help you make decisions for your own writing. Here is a flowchart of questions that will guide your reading for this purpose.

Questions to Guide Your Reading

PREPARING TO READ Before you read the essays, answer the following questions:

- What assumptions can you make from the essay's **title**?
- What do you think the general **mood** of the essay will be?
- What is the essay's **purpose** and **audience**?
- What does the **synopsis** tell you about the essay?
- What can you learn from the author's **biography**?
- What do you predict the author's **point of view** toward the subject will be?

READING As you read the essays for the first time, answer the following questions:

- What is the essay's main **claim** or **assertion**?
- What **evidence** does the author put forward?
- What ideas do you **agree with**?
- What ideas do you **disagree with**?
- What **appeals** does the author use?

REREADING When you read the essays again, answer the following questions:

- How does the writer integrate the **appeals** in the essay?
- What is the **tone** of the essay? How does the author establish this tone?
- What other **rhetorical strategies** does the author use?
- How does your understanding of the essay **change** with each rereading?

Preparing To Read.   As you prepare to read the essays in this chapter, spend a few minutes browsing through the preliminary material for each selection: What does Frank Furedi's title, "Our Unhealthy Obsession with Sickness," prepare you for? What can you learn from scanning Nicholas Carr's essay, "How the Internet Is Making Us Stupid," and reading the synopsis of Dave Grossman's essay ("We Are Training Our Kids to Kill") in the Rhetorical Table of Contents?

Also, you should bring to your reading as much information as you can from the authors' biographies: Why do you think Dave Grossman writes about violence and the media? Does he have the proper qualifications to teach us about how "We Are Training Our Kids to Kill"? What is the source of Samantha Pugsley's interest in language and mental health ("How Language Impacts the Stigma Against Mental Health (And What We Must Do to Change It)")? For the essays in this chapter that present several viewpoints on an argument (on social media and DNA testing), what biographical details prepare us for each writer's stand on the issue? Who were the original audiences for these opposing viewpoints?

Last, before you read these essays, try to generate some ideas on each topic so that you can take the role of an active reader. In this text, the Preparing to Read questions will help you get ready for this task. Then, you should speculate further on the general subject of the essay: How do you think the Internet is affecting human nature? What are the main arguments related to the effects of language on mental health? What side do you think Pugsley is on?

Reading.   Be sure to record your spontaneous reactions to the persuasive essays in this chapter as you read them for the first time: What are your opinions on each subject? Why do you hold these opinions? Be especially aware of your responses to the essays representing opposing viewpoints at the end of the chapter; know where you stand in relation to each side of the issues here.

Use the preliminary material before an essay to help you create a framework for your responses to it: What motivated Furedi to publish his arguments on illness? What makes Grossman so knowledgeable about children and TV violence? Which argument on social media do you find most convincing? On postconviction DNA testing?

Throughout each essay in the chapter are questions at the bottom of the pages that further critical thinking. They essentially bridge the gap between the inquiries before each essay and the exercises after the essays. If you answer these questions as they appear in the text, you will be building a framework of understanding that you can draw on when you finally get to the writing assignments at the end of each reading. Putting your responses in writing is the most beneficial way to make the material your own in a way that just thinking about the questions can't accomplish.

Your main job at this stage of reading is to determine each author's primary claim or proposition (thesis statement) and to create an inquisitive environment for thinking critically about the essay's ideas. In addition, take a look at the questions after each selection to make sure you are picking up the major points of the essay.

Rereading.   As you reread these persuasive essays, notice how the writers integrate their appeals to logic, to emotion, and to ethics. Also, pay attention to the emphasis the writers place on one or more appeals at certain strategic points in the essays: What combination of appeals does Dave Grossman use in "We Are Training Our Kids to Kill"? In what way does the tone of his writing support what he is saying? How does he establish this tone? Which appeal is most prominent in the Pugsley essay? What questions do you have in reference to the three essays on DNA testing? What questions do the authors leave unanswered?

In addition, determine what other rhetorical strategies help these writers make their primary points. How do these strategies enable each writer to establish a unified essay with a beginning, a middle, and an end?

Then answer the questions after each reading selection to make certain you understand the essay on the literal, interpretive, and analytical levels in preparation for the discussion/writing assignments that follow.

For a list of guidelines for the entire reading process, see the Reading Checklist at the end of Chapter 2.

Writing Argument/Persuasion Essays

Now that you see how argument and persuasion work in an essay, use the same features in your own writing. The flowchart on the next page provides some questions to guide you.

Preparing To Write.   The first stage of writing an essay of this sort involves, as usual, exploring and then limiting your topic. As you prepare to write your persuasive paper, first try to generate as many ideas as possible—regardless of whether they appeal to logic, emotion, or ethics. To do this, review the prewriting techniques on pages 26–28, and answer the Preparing to Write questions. Then choose a topic. Next, focus on a purpose and a specific audience before you begin to write.

Writing.   Most persuasive essays should begin with an assertion or a proposition stating what you believe about a certain issue. This thesis should generally be phrased as a debatable statement, such as, "If individual states reinstituted the death penalty, Americans would notice an immediate drop in violent crimes." At this point in your essay, you should also justify the significance of the issue you will be discussing: "Such a decline in the crime

Questions to Guide Your Writing

PREPARING TO WRITE
Before you start writing, answer these questions:

- Do you narrow and **focus** your material as much as possible?
- What is your **purpose**?
- What is your **audience's background**?

WRITING As you write your first draft, consider these questions:

- Did you state your claim in a **debatable thesis**?
- Do you justify the **significance** of your topic?
- Did you choose **evidence** that supports your thesis?
- Do you use a combination of logical, ethical, and emotional **appeals**?
- Is your essay **organized** effectively for what you are trying to accomplish?
- Do you conclude with a **summary** and **recommendations**?

EDITING Be sure to proofread and edit your paper before turning it in.

- Are your **sentences** all complete?
- Do your words say exactly **what you mean**?
- Do you follow conventional **grammar and usage** rules?

REVISING After you write your first draft, use the following questions to revise your essay:

- Is your **thesis statement** clear?
- Is the main thrust of your essay an **appeal to reason**?
- Have you chosen **examples** carefully to support your thesis?
- Does your **conclusion** restate your argument, make a recommendation, and bring your essay to a close?

rate would affect all our lives and make this country a safer place in which to live."

The essay should then support your thesis in a variety of ways. This support may take the form of facts, figures, examples, opinions by recognized authorities, case histories, narratives/anecdotes, comparisons, contrasts, or cause/effect studies. This evidence is most effectively organized from least to most important when you are confronted with a hostile audience (so that you can lead your readers through your reasoning step by step) and from most to least important when you are facing a supportive audience (so that you can build on their loyalty and enthusiasm as you advance your thesis). In fact, you will be able to engineer your best support if you know your audience's opinions, feelings, and background before you write your essay, so that your intended "target" is as clear as possible. The body of your essay will undoubtedly consist of a combination of logical, emotional, and ethical appeals—all leading to some final summation or recommendation.

The concluding paragraph of a persuasive essay should restate your main assertion (in terms slightly different from your original statement) and should offer some constructive recommendations about the problem you have been discussing (if you haven't already done so). This section of your paper should clearly bring your argument to a close in one final attempt to move your audience to accept or act on the viewpoint you present. Let's look more closely now at each of the three types of appeals used in such essays: logical, emotional, and ethical.

To construct a *logical* argument, you have two principal patterns available to you: inductive reasoning or deductive reasoning. The first encourages an audience to make what is called an "inductive leap" from several particular examples to a single, useful generalization. In the case of the death penalty, for instance, you might cite a number of examples, figures, facts, and case studies illustrating the effectiveness of capital punishment in various states, thereby leading up to your firm belief that the death penalty should be reinstituted. Used most often by detectives, scientists, and lawyers, the process of inductive reasoning addresses the audience's ability to think logically by moving them systematically from an assortment of selected evidence to a rational and ordered conclusion.

In contrast, deductive reasoning moves its audience from a broad, general statement to particular examples supporting that statement. In writing such an essay, you would present your thesis statement about capital punishment first and then offer clear, orderly evidence to support that belief. Although the mental process we go through in creating a deductive argument is quite sophisticated, it is based on a three-step form of reasoning called the *syllogism,* which most logicians believe is the foundation of logical thinking. The traditional syllogism has

A major premise: All humans fear death.

A minor premise: Criminals are humans.

A conclusion: Therefore, criminals fear death.

As you might suspect, this type of reasoning is only as accurate as its original premises, so you need to be sure your premises are true so that your argument will be valid.

In constructing a logical argument, you should take great care to avoid several types of fallacies in reasoning found most frequently in lower-division college papers. Fallacies occur when you use faulty evidence, when you misrepresent your evidence, or when you use evidence that is irrelevant to your argument. Avoiding fallacies is important because readers who discover a fallacy or problem in logic are likely to question the writer's credibility and perhaps even the writer's interpretation of other evidence. Although the following is not an exhaustive list, these fallacies illustrate why most writers purposely try to avoid using fallacious or faulty reasoning:

Hasty Generalization: When we present a claim that is based on too few examples, we are making a hasty generalization. For example, if we state that students never get enough sleep, we are committing this fallacy. To avoid these kinds of blanket statements, writers need to qualify their claims so they are accurate: Many students don't get enough sleep.

Non Sequitur: A *non sequitur* occurs when we make a statement that does not logically follow the previous statement. Some people say, for example, "That car she just bought is very expensive. She must be rich." This second sentence is not a conclusion we can draw from the first sentence.

Either/Or Fallacy: Writers commit the either/or fallacy when they present an argument as if only two views exist, but actually other views are possible as well. For example, someone might argue that a person could not protest the war in Iraq and still be a patriotic American. A citizen can express a negative view about one policy and still be patriotic, so the explanation of two sides only (supporting the war or being unpatriotic) is an example of the either/or fallacy.

False Cause and Effect: This logical flaw involves making a causal argument based solely on chronology. To avoid this fallacy, the cause must be proved: "First, the group of politicians criticized the war; then the terrorists bombed a building in Baghdad. See what happens when we criticize the war!"

False Authority: An appeal to a false authority occurs when a writer cites an example or opinion of someone who is not an expert in the field. Having an actor advertise a product unrelated to his or her career is an example of this fallacy. When writers choose an expert, they must make sure the person can actually offer a relevant and meaningful testimonial or perspective.

Begging the Question: This is circular logic. For example, skydiving is dangerous because it is not safe. To avoid this fallacy, bring new information into the explanation: Skydiving is dangerous because a lot can go wrong on the way down to the ground.

Bandwagon: This fallacy is based on the false logic that some action is preferable because it is supported by many people. Examples often occur in advertising when companies claim that their product is the best because so many people are using it.

If you build your argument on true statements and abundant, accurate evidence, your essay will be effective, and your argument is likely to be persuasive. Avoiding fallacies is also easier when you thoroughly examine your evidence and carefully present supporting ideas and information to your reader. As a writer, you have the ultimate responsibility to find credible evidence and to present it in a well-reasoned and clear essay.

Persuading through *emotion* necessitates controlling your readers' instinctive reactions to what you are saying. You can accomplish this goal in two different ways: (1) by choosing your words with even greater care than usual and (2) by using figurative language whenever appropriate. In the first case, you must be especially conscious of using words that have the same general denotative (or dictionary) meaning but bear decidedly favorable or unfavorable connotative (or implicit) meanings. For example, notice the difference between *slender* and *scrawny, patriotic* and *chauvinistic,* or *compliment* and *flattery.* Your careful attention to the choice of such words can help readers form visual images with certain positive or negative associations that subtly encourage them to follow your argument and adopt your opinions. Second, the effective use of figurative language—especially similes and metaphors—makes your writing more vivid, thus triggering your readers' senses and encouraging them to accept your views. Both of these techniques will help you manipulate your readers into the position of agreeing with your ideas.

Ethical appeals, which establish you as a reliable, well-informed person, are accomplished through (1) the tone of your essay and (2) the number and type of examples you cite. Tone is created through deliberate word choice: Careful attention to the mood implied in the words you use can convince your readers that you are serious, friendly, authoritative, jovial, or methodical—depending on your intended purpose. In like manner, the examples you supply to support your assertions can encourage readers to see you as experienced, insightful, relaxed, or intense. In both of these cases, winning favor for yourself will usually also gain approval for your opinions.

Revising.   To rework your persuasive essays, you should play the role of your readers and impartially evaluate the different appeals you have used to accomplish your purpose.

Any additional guidance you may need as you write and revise your persuasive essays is furnished in the Writing Checklist at the end of Chapter 3.

STUDENT ESSAY: ARGUMENT AND PERSUASION AT WORK

The following student essay uses all three appeals to make its point about the injustice of police brutality. First, the writer sets forth her character references (ethical appeal) in the first paragraph, after which she presents her thesis and its significance. The support for her thesis is a combination of logical and emotional appeals in the body paragraphs, heavy on the logical, as the writer moves her paragraphs from general to particular in an effort to convince her readers to adopt her point of view and adjust their language use accordingly.

The Injustice of Police Brutality

Growing up, I received two different impressions of law enforcement. The music I listened to denounced the police as oppressors while movies presented stories about cops as heroes. <u>I have never been personally</u> **[Ethical appeal]** <u>mistreated by any officer of the law, but I have more than one acquaintance who has been, and that has made me realize that such treatment is more common than it should be.</u> Those whose job is to uphold the law do not always perform it justly. **[Logical appeal]** <u>The duty of the police is to "protect and serve."</u> However, some overzealous police officers do not serve justice and, instead, do a disservice to the community by turning to violence. <u>Rather than preventing crime, these offi-</u> **[Significance of assertion]** <u>cers commit it, and instead of saving lives, they take them. Though law enforcement agents are themselves</u> **[Assertion or thesis statement]** <u>in danger, that fact does not justify the unnecessary, counterproductive acts of brutality that they sometimes commit.</u>

<u>The primary purpose of any police force is crime</u> **[Logical appeal]** <u>prevention.</u> Squad cars patrol the streets and armed officers walk their beats to protect law-abiding citizens from those who would do them harm. When a crime **[Examples organized deductively]** occurs, police officers are supposed to stop it. In those instances where prevention of a crime proves impossible, the job of the police is to capture the criminal to forestall further offenses. In short, the function

of any police force (the universal symbol for which is a shield) is to guard the people of its community against harm.

Emotional appeal

<u>Since police officers often face personal danger in the line of duty, their attention may shift over time from performing acts of heroism to ensuring self-preservation.</u> Forced to choose between the life of a stranger and his or her own, a police officer would naturally choose to live, just as anyone else would. But this choice should not include taking the life of another person except in extreme circumstances.

Examples organized deductively

Explanation

<u>When police officers commit unjustified acts of brutality in the performance of their duties, they are committing a crime.</u> The fact that they enforce the law does not render them above it. Granted, police officers should be allowed the same right to defend themselves that private citizens have. Also, since law enforcement officers find themselves in dangerous situations more often than other citizens do, they should be armed with the means to defend themselves. But some officers too quickly resort to the use of firearms. In many cases, officers outnumber the criminals they face and, therefore, should be able to take those offenders into custody without the use of violent means. In instances in which handcuffs won't suffice, pepper spray, night sticks, and Tasers may be used to subdue a suspect without resorting to deadly force. However, those tools should be used only to quell the threat posed by a violent suspect, not to cause him pain or injury. Whatever the nature of a suspect's apparent crime, the job of the police is not to punish that offense; due process must be followed. The amount of force used should not exceed what is necessary to perform an arrest. Officers should use violence only to prevent harm to themselves or to other law-abiding citizens.

Logical appeal

Examples organized deductively

Emotional appeal

<u>More often than not, the victims of police brutality are members of minority groups.</u> The case has been made that this is because minorities are more likely to live in dangerous neighborhoods, but there is another side to this argument. If African Americans and Latinos face more danger than other groups do, they are

Examples organized deductively

the ones the police should strive hardest to protect. Currently, it seems as though many police departments target citizens of color both as suspects and as potential candidates for police brutality.

<u>Police action has been shown to be excessive in many high-profile cases.</u> Even after thirty years of progress in civil rights, the brutal beating of Rodney King was broadcast nationwide for all to see. <u>Mr. King, unarmed and lying defenseless on the ground, was struck repeatedly by several officers.</u> Despite this obvious abuse of power, the LAPD defended the attack as lawful. More recently, following a questionable police shooting in Ferguson, Missouri, city officials were criticized by the U.S. Justice Department for allowing—or in some cases encouraging—the abuse of police power. Both of these injustices led to protests by citizens who had lost confidence in their local police departments. Even worse, the police response in each situation only exacerbated the problem and perpetuated a cycle of violence and mistrust.

<u>The damage resulting from police brutality is not limited to bodily or psychological harm.</u> Victims of police brutality—and the families of the victims of these acts—are due financial compensation for their pain, suffering, and loss, which are funded by our tax dollars. Furthermore, when abuses of police power lead to civil unrest, the results can include large-scale property damage as well as further injury or even death.

<u>Ultimately, when they commit acts of brutality, the police become complicit in the crime they are tasked with preventing, and no amount of personal danger can justify that. The job of the police officer is to save his or her fellow citizens from harm. We need to return to the time when all communities are able to trust their police officers to use good judgment and make the right choices in executing their responsibilities.</u>

Logical appeal (margin note)

Emotional appeal (margin note)

Examples organized deductively (margin note)

Emotional appeal (margin note)

Explanation (margin note)

Restatement/ Conclusion (margin note)

Student Writer's Comments

When I was assigned to write an argumentative essay, I thought of this topic almost immediately. Police brutality had been in the news recently, and I had received second-hand knowledge of the topic through some of my friends and other sources. Nonetheless, I decided to do a little bit of research before I started writing because I wanted to see the issue from as many angles as possible. Once I did that, I was ready to start writing.

I began by jotting down a few general ideas that would later become the topic sentences for the paragraphs in my first draft. After elaborating on each idea with a few more sentences, I moved the paragraphs around, trying different arrangements to see which sequence would be most effective for my main points. Then I made sure I had examples in each paragraph to support my claims. I could see in this essay in particular how these examples were serving as the actual building blocks of the essay.

I decided to begin my essay with some personal information in order to establish credibility and to set the tone for the overall composition. As I continued writing, I was careful not to let my feelings on the subject overpower the logic of my argument. I found it helpful to imagine that I was delivering a speech to a crowd of people who were undecided regarding this issue.

Once the paragraphs were fully developed and in their proper order, I began working on my coherence and readability. I added transitions between my ideas so I could guide the readers through my reasoning step by step. This task came quite naturally to me because I imagined I was explaining each of my paragraphs to someone in my crowd of listeners.

Finally, I went through the essay one last time to check for errors. I read just for the mistakes I continue to make: pronoun agreement, fragments, and run-together sentences. I corrected my errors and was ready to turn it in. After all of my hard work, I was quite pleased with the way the essay turned out.

SOME FINAL THOUGHTS ON ARGUMENT AND PERSUASION

As you can tell from the selections that follow, the three different types of persuasive appeals usually complement one another in practice. Most good argumentative essays use a combination of these methods to achieve their purposes. Good persuasive essays also rely on various rhetorical modes we have already studied—such as example, process analysis, division/classification, comparison/contrast, definition, and cause/effect—to advance their arguments. In the following essays, you will see a combination of appeals and a number of different rhetorical modes at work.

FRANK FUREDI   (1947–   )

Our Unhealthy Obsession with Sickness

An extremely prolific author, Frank Furedi was born in Hungary, immigrated to England, and earned both his master's degree and doctorate at the School of Oriental and African Studies of London University. In the 1970s, under the pseudonym "Frank Richards," he was the cofounder and chair of the Revolutionary Communist Party in Britain. Formerly a professor of Sociology at the University of Kent, he has written fourteen books, including *The Soviet Union Demystified* (1986), *The Mau Mau War in Perspective* (1989), *Mythical Past, Elusive Future: History and Society in an Anxious Age* (1991), *Culture of Fear: Risk Taking and the Morality of Low Expectation* (1997), *Paranoid Parenting* (2001), and *The Politics of Fear: Beyond Left and Right* (2005). His most recent publications include *On Tolerance: A Defence of Moral Independence* (2011) and *Authority: A Sociological History* (2013), which examines how the modern world is more comfortable with challenging authority than with accepting it. He also writes for a variety of publications, including *The Guardian, The Daily Mail, The Wall Street Journal,* and the *Times* and does frequent media interviews, in which he often decries what he describes as the "dumbing down" of society. He advises student writers "not to obsess about the actual act of writing. Spend most of your time working on what it is you are trying to say."

Preparing to Read

This selection, written by Frank Furedi, was first delivered as a speech at a health conference and then published in *Spiked Online* (March 23, 2005). In it, Furedi explains the problems with our new concentration in society today on illness rather than wellness. (This essay contains British spellings.)

Exploring Experience: Before you read this essay, think about your approach to your health and the health of others: Do you focus unnecessarily on your health problems? Are health issues a part of your daily conversation? Does your health play a major part in your definition as a person? What do you make of the new focus on "wellness" in our daily affairs?

LEARNING❂NLINE Visit and explore the U.S. Department of Health and Human Services website at www.healthfinder.gov. Do you think the government should be responsible for providing this type of information? Is it beneficial or not to have information like this readily available to the public?

Before reading this essay, you may want to consult the flowchart on page 448.

We live in a world where illnesses are on the increase. The distinguishing feature of the twenty-first century is that health has become a dominant issue, both in our personal lives and in public life. It has become a highly politicised issue too and an increasingly important site of government intervention and policymaking. With every year that passes, we seem to spend more and more time and resources thinking about health and sickness. I think there are four possible reasons for this.

First, there is the imperative of **medicalisation**. When the concept of medicalisation was first formulated, in the late 1960s and early 1970s, it referred to a far narrower range of phenomena than is the case today, and it was linked to the actions of a small number of professionals rather than having the all-pervasive character that it does now.

Essentially, the term medicalisation means that problems we encounter in everyday life are reinterpreted as medical ones. So problems that might traditionally have been defined as existential—that is, the problems of existence—have a medical label attached to them. Today, it is difficult to think of any kind of human experience that doesn't come with a health warning or some kind of medical explanation.

It is not only the experience of pain or distress or disappointment or engagement with adversity that is medicalised and seen as potentially traumatic and stress-inducing; even human characteristics are medicalised now. Consider shyness. It is quite normal to be shy; there are many circumstances where many of us feel shy and awkward. Yet shyness is now referred to as "social phobia." And, of course, when a medical label is attached to shyness, it is only a matter of time before a pharmaceutical company comes up with a "shyness pill." Pop these pills, and you too can become the life and soul of the party! [1]

One of my hobbies is to read press releases informing us of the existence of a new illness, the "illness of the week," if you like. Recently I received one that said, "Psychologists say that love sickness is a genuine disease and needs more awareness and diagnoses. Those little actions that are normally seen as the symptoms of the first flush of love—buying presents, waiting by the phone, or making an effort before a date—may actually be signs of a deep-rooted problem to come. Many people who suffer from love sickness cannot cope with the intensity of love and have been destabilised by falling in love or suffer on account of their love being unrequited. . . . "

Thinking Critically

[1] Why do you think we medicate personality traits?

Of course, an intense passion can and does have an impact upon our 6
bodies. But when even love can be seen as the harbinger of illness, what
aspect of our lives can be said to be illness-free? What can we possibly do
that will not apparently induce some sickness or syndrome? Medicalisation
no longer knows any limits. It is so intrusive that it can impact on virtually
any of our experiences, creating a situation where illness is increasingly
perceived as normal.

This leads to my second point—there is now a **presupposition that** 7
illness is as normal as health. Earlier theories of medicalisation still considered illness to be the exception; now, being ill is seen as a normal state,
possibly even more normal than being healthy. We are all now seen as being
potentially ill; that is the default state we live in today.

This can be glimpsed in the increasing use of the term "wellness," with 8
well men's clinics and well women's clinics. "Wellness," another relatively
recent concept, is a peculiar term. It presupposes that being well is not a
natural or normal state. After all, there are no such things as "sunshine clinics" or "evening clinics"; such normal things do not normally need an
institution attached to them. And why would you have to visit a wellness
clinic if you were well anyway? It makes little sense.

Wellness has become something you have to work on, something to 9
aspire to and achieve. [2] This reinforces the presupposition that not being
well—or being ill—is the normal state. That is what our culture says to us
now: you are not okay; you are not fine; you are potentially ill. The message
seems to be that if you do not subscribe to this project of keeping well, you
will revert to being ill.

In supermarkets, especially in middle-class neighbourhoods, buying food 10
has become like conducting a scientific experiment. Individuals spend hours
looking at how many carbohydrates there are, whether it's organic, natural,
holistic. Spending time reading labels is one way of doing your bit to keep well.

Being potentially ill is now so prevalent that we have reached a situation 11
where illness becomes a part of our identity, part of the human condition.
Some of us might not flaunt it, walking around saying, "I've got a gum
disease" or "I've got a bad case of athlete's foot." That doesn't sound very
sexy and is unlikely to go down well at the dinner table. But it has become
acceptable to talk openly about other illnesses—to declare that you are a
cancer survivor or to flaunt a disability. As we normalise illness, our identity
becomes inextricably linked to illness. So it is normal to be ill, and to be
ill is normal.

Thinking Critically

[2] How can we achieve "wellness" in our lives? Name three specific actions that can make
us or keep us "well."

The nature of illness changes when it becomes part of our identity. [3]   12
When we invest so much emotion in an illness, when it becomes such a
large aspect of our lives through the illness metaphor, we start to embrace
it, and it can be very difficult to let go of that part of our identity. This is
why illness tends to become more durable and last longer. Sickness is no
longer a temporary episode: it is something that, increasingly, afflicts one for
life. You are scarred for life, with an indelible stamp on your personality.
This can be seen in the idea of being a cancer survivor or some other kind
of survivor; we are always, it seems, in remission. The illness remains part
of us and shapes our personality.

As this happens, illnesses start to acquire features that are no longer nega-   13
tive. In the past, illness was seen as a bad thing. Today you can read illness
diaries in the *Guardian* and other newspapers and magazines. We often hear
the phrase: "I've learned so much about myself through my illness." It
becomes a pedagogic experience: "I may have lost a leg and half my brain
cells, but I'm learning so much from this extremely unique experience." It's
almost like going to university, something positive, to be embraced, with
hundreds of books telling us how to make the most of the experience of
sickness.

We are not simply making a virtue out of a necessity; rather we are con-   14
sciously *valuing* illness. From a theoretical standpoint, we might view illness
as the first order concept and wellness as the second order concept. Wellness
is subordinate, methodologically, to the state of being ill.

The third influence is today's cultural script, the cultural narrative that   15
impacts on our lives, which increasingly **uses health to make sense of
the human experience**. The more uncertainty we face, the more difficult
we find it to make statements of moral purpose, the more ambiguous we
feel about what is right and wrong, then the more comfortable we feel using
the language of health to make sense of our lives. At a time of moral and
existential uncertainty, health has become an important idiom through
which to provide guidance to individuals.

This is now so prevalent that we no longer even notice when we are   16
doing it. For example, we no longer tell teenagers that pre-marital sex is
good or bad or sinful. Instead we say that pre-marital sex is a health risk.
Sex education programmes teach that you will be emotionally traumatised if
pressured into having sex and will be generally healthier if you stay at home
and watch TV instead.

Thinking Critically

[3] Do you have an illness that has become part of your identity? If so, how does it affect
your daily life?

There are few clear moral guidelines that can direct our behaviour today,   17
but we have become very good at using health to regulate people's lives in
an intrusive and systematic fashion. Even medicine and food have acquired
moral connotations. So some drugs are said to be bad for the environment,
while others, especially those made with a natural herb, are seen as being
morally superior. Organic food is seen as "good," not only in nutritional
terms, but in moral terms. Junk food, on the other hand, is seen as evil.

If you look at the language that is used to discuss health and medicine or   18
obese people and their body shapes, it isn't just about health: we are making
moral statements. A fat person is considered to have a serious moral problem, rather than simply a health one.[4] As we become morally illiterate, we
turn to health to save us from circumstances where we face a degree of moral
or spiritual disorientation.

The fourth influence is **the politicisation of health**. Health has become   19
a focus of incessant political activity. Politicians who have little by way of
beliefs or passions, and don't know what to say to the public, are guaranteed
a response if they say something health-related. Some also make a lot of
money from the health issue, from pharmaceutical companies to alternative
health shops to individual quacks selling their wares. All are in the business,
essentially, of living off today's health-obsessed cultural sentiment.

Governments today do two things that I object to in particular. First they   20
encourage introspection, telling us that unless men examine their testicles,
unless we keep a check on our cholesterol level, then we are not being
responsible citizens. You are letting down yourself, your wife, your kids,
everybody. We are encouraged continually to worry about our health. As a
consequence, public health initiatives have become, as far as I can tell, a
threat to public health.[5] Secondly, governments promote the value of *health
seeking*. We are meant always to be seeking health for this or that condition.
The primary effect of this, I believe, is to make us all feel more ill.

Here's a prediction—Western societies are not going to overcome the   21
crisis of healthcare; it is beyond the realms of possibility. No matter what
policies government pursue or how much money they throw at the problem, even if they increase health expenditure fourfold, the problem will
not go away. As long as the normalisation of illness[6] remains culturally
affirmed, more and more of us are likely to identify ourselves as sick and

---

Thinking Critically

[4] Do you consider obesity to be a "moral" problem? Explain your reasoning.

[5] Why does the author say that public health initiatives have become "a threat to public
health"? What are some other ironies in the health profession?

[6] What does Furedi mean by "the normalisation of illness"? Which illnesses seem most
"normal" to you?

will identify ourselves as sick for a growing period of time. The solution to this problem lies not in the area of policymaking, or even medicine, but in the cultural sphere.

UNDERSTANDING DETAILS

1. What does Furedi see as the reasons for our obsession with health today?
2. What are "illness diaries"? How might they affect our approach to health issues?
3. What are the consequences of society's new state of mind that illness is normal?
4. According to Furedi, what is the solution to this new focus on illness?

READING CRITICALLY

5. Read the essay again, and draw lines in the body of the essay to separate his four main points. Then give examples from your own experience for each of his categories.
6. Why do you think health has become a dominant issue in American society today?
7. Do you agree with Furedi that we are "seen as being *potentially* ill" (paragraph 7) today? Explain your answer.
8. From your own experience, give some examples of wellness being subordinate to illness.

DISCOVERING RHETORICAL STRATEGIES

9. In what order does Furedi introduce the reasons in his argument? Is this an effective order? Explain your answer in detail.
10. Who do you think was Furedi's original audience? Explain your answer.
11. What rhetorical strategies does the author use to advance his argument? Give an example of each one you find.
12. What is the tone of this essay?

MAKING CONNECTIONS

13. Examine Furedi's essay in light of Jessica Mitford's "Behind the Formaldehyde Curtain." To what extent do current funeral practices attempt to erase the "illnesses" we suffer in life?
14. Imagine that Furedi was having a round-table discussion about "sickness" with the following authors: Malcolm Cowley ("The View from 80"), Harold Krents ("Darkness at Noon"), and/or Michael Dorris ("The Broken Cord"). Which of these people could most successfully argue that his or her infirmity should be treated as an "illness"? Would you agree? Why or why not?
15. Compare and contrast the use of argument in any of the essays by the following authors that you have read: Furedi, Dave Grossman ("We Are Training our Kids to Kill"), and Samantha Pugsley ("How Language Impacts the Stigma Against Mental Health [And What We Must Do to Change It]"). Who uses this rhetorical technique most skillfully? Explain your answer.

IDEAS FOR DISCUSSION/WRITING

Preparing to Write

Write freely about our approach to health in the United States: Where is your focus in reference to Furedi's argument—on illness or wellness? Why do you think that is your focus? Is your focus different from that of other members of your family? From that of your friends?

Choosing a Topic

MyWritingLab™

1. **LEARNING⏻NLINE** Do you agree with Furedi's argument about our preoccupation with disease? Revisit the U.S. Department Health and Human Services website at www.healthfinder.gov to review how involved the U.S. government is in our health care. Do you think that the government should be involved in health education and care, or should it be considered a personal matter? Write an essay arguing for or against government involvement in the healthcare industry.

2. You have been asked to speak to a group of high school students about your perception of health in the United States. What do you want to tell them? What will be your dominant message? Write out a draft of your speech.

3. We are especially consumed today with psychological disorders, like depression, stress, anxiety, and the like, conditions that Furedi called "existential" (paragraph 3). Do you think these are conditions that should be treated like diseases or everyday emotional problems? Gather your thoughts on this question, and present them in the form of a well-reasoned argumentative essay.

4. Do you agree with Furedi's main point that we are obsessed with illness? Write a response to this selection in the form of an essay of your own.

Before beginning your essay, you may want to consult the flowchart on page 451.

How the Internet Is Making Us Stupid

Nicholas Carr received his B.A. from Dartmouth College and his M.A. in English and American Literature and Language from Harvard University. He is now a writer, focusing on technology and culture. His books, which have been translated into more than twenty-five languages, include *Does IT Matter?* (2004), *The Big Switch: Rewiring the World, from Edison to Google* (2008), and *The Shallows: What the Internet Is Doing to Our Brains* (2011), which was a Pulitzer Prize Award finalist and *New York Times* bestseller. His newest book, *The Glass Cage: Automation and Us* (2014), explores the ramifications of our culture's dependence on technology. He has been published in the *Atlantic*, *The Wall Street Journal*, *The New York Times*, *Wired*, and *Nature*, among others. A former member of the *Encyclopedia Britannica's* editorial board of advisors and writer-in-residence at the University of California at Berkley's school of journalism, he currently writes the popular blog *Rough Type*, where he continues to write about technology, economics, and culture.

Preparing to Read

Many of Carr's articles provide insight into how our brains work in reference to various aspects of the Internet. In this particular article, Carr argues that the Internet is affecting the way we think to the point of making us stupid.

Exploring Experience: Before you read this essay, consider what you know about the effect of the Internet on our thinking: Are you aware of how you think when you are using the Internet? How is your thinking different when you are off the Internet? What are some positive aspects of the Internet in your life as a student? What are its negative aspects? When is the Internet most useful to you as a student? Does it ever hinder your work on college assignments?

LEARNINGONLINE Think about a typical day in your life without the Internet. To reinforce this message, visit Calmsound.com, sit quietly, and listen to the sounds provided for five minutes without doing anything else. At the end of this exercise, write a reflection of your feelings and thoughts as you were listening to the sounds.

Before reading this essay, you may want to consult the flowchart on page 448.

Although the World Wide Web has been around for just 20 years, it is hard to imagine life without it. It has given us instant access to vast amounts of information, and we're able to stay in touch with friends and colleagues more or less continuously.

But our dependence on the Internet has a dark side. A growing body of scientific evidence suggests that the net, with its constant distractions and interruptions, is turning us into scattered and superficial thinkers. [1]

I've been studying this research for the past three years, in the course of writing my new book *The Shallows: How the Internet Is Changing the Way We Think, Read and Remember*. But my interest in the subject is not just academic. It's personal. I was inspired to write the book after I realised that I was losing my own capacity for concentration and contemplation. Even when I was away from my computer, my mind seemed hungry for constant stimulation, for quick hits of information. I felt perpetually distracted.

Could my loss of focus be a result of all the time I've spent online? In search of an answer to that question, I began to dig into the many psychological, behavioural, and neurological studies that examine how the tools we use to think with—our information technologies—shape our habits of mind.

The picture that emerges is troubling, at least to anyone who values the subtlety, rather than just the speed, of human thought. People who read text studded with links, the studies show, comprehend less than those who read words printed on pages. People who watch busy multimedia presentations remember less than those who take in information in a more sedate and focused manner. People who are continually distracted by emails, updates and other messages understand less than those who are able to concentrate. And people who juggle many tasks are often less creative and less productive than those who do one thing at a time. [2]

The common thread in these disabilities is the division of attention. The richness of our thoughts, our memories, and even our personalities hinges on our ability to focus the mind and sustain concentration. Only when we pay close attention to a new piece of information are we able to associate it "meaningfully and systematically with knowledge already well established in memory," writes the Nobel Prize-winning neuroscientist Eric Kandel. Such associations are essential to mastering complex concepts and thinking critically.

Thinking Critically

[1] Do you feel your thinking is "scattered and superficial" from the Internet?

[2] Try reading something with distractions and something else with no distractions at all. Is your understanding of the material different in these two situations?

When we're constantly distracted and interrupted, as we tend to be when   7
looking at the screens of our computers and mobile phones, our brains can't
forge the strong and expansive neural connections that give distinctiveness
and depth to our thinking. Our thoughts become disjointed, our memories
weak. The Roman philosopher Seneca may have put it best 2,000 years ago:
"To be everywhere is to be nowhere."

In an article in *Science* last year, Patricia Greenfield, a developmental psy-   8
chologist who runs UCLA's Children's Digital Media Center, reviewed
dozens of studies on how different media technologies influence our cognitive abilities. Some of the studies indicated that certain computer tasks, like
playing video games, increase the speed at which people can shift their focus
among icons and other images on screens. Other studies, however, found
that such rapid shifts in focus, even if performed adeptly, result in less rigorous and "more automatic" thinking.

In one experiment at a U.S. university, half a class of students was allowed   9
to use internet-connected laptops during a lecture, while the other had to
keep their computers shut. Those who browsed the web performed much
worse on a subsequent test of how well they retained the lecture's content.
Earlier experiments revealed that as the number of links in an online document goes up, reading comprehension falls, and as more types of information are placed on a screen, we remember less of what we see.

Greenfield concluded that "every medium develops some cognitive skills   10
at the expense of others". Our growing use of screen-based media, she said,
has strengthened visual-spatial intelligence, which can strengthen the ability
to do jobs that involve keeping track of lots of rapidly changing signals, like
piloting a plane or monitoring a patient during surgery. But that has been
accompanied by "new weaknesses in higher-order cognitive processes," including "abstract vocabulary, mindfulness, reflection, inductive problem solving,
critical thinking, and imagination." We're becoming, in a word, shallower.[3]

Studies of our behaviour online support this conclusion. German   11
researchers found that web browsers usually spend less than 10 seconds looking at a page. Even people doing academic research online tend to "bounce"
rapidly between different documents, rarely reading more than a page or
two, according to a University College London study.

Such mental juggling takes a big toll. In a recent experiment at Stanford   12
University, researchers gave various cognitive tests to 49 people who do a
lot of media multitasking and 52 people who multitask much less frequently.
The heavy multitaskers performed poorly on all the tests. They were more

---

Thinking Critically

[3] Are you aware of becoming "shallower" in your thinking? What are the circumstances?

easily distracted, had less control over their attention, and were much less able to distinguish important information from trivia.

The researchers were surprised by the results. They expected the intensive multitaskers to have gained some mental advantages. But that wasn't the case. In fact, the multitaskers weren't even good at multitasking. "Everything distracts them," said Clifford Nass, one of the researchers. [4]   13

It would be one thing if the ill effects went away as soon as we turned off our computers and mobiles. But they don't. The cellular structure of the human brain, scientists have discovered, adapts readily to the tools we use to find, store and share information. By changing our habits of mind, each new technology strengthens certain neural pathways and weakens others. The alterations shape the way we think even when we're not using the technology.   14

The pioneering neuroscientist Michael Merzenich believes our brains are being "massively remodelled" by our ever-intensifying use of the web and related media. In the 1970s and 1980s, Mr Merzenich, now a professor emeritus at the University of California in San Francisco, conducted a famous series of experiments that revealed how extensively and quickly neural circuits change in response to experience. In a conversation late last year, he said that he was profoundly worried about the cognitive consequences of the constant distractions and interruptions the internet bombards us with. The long-term effect on the quality of our intellectual lives, he said, could be "deadly".   15

Not all distractions are bad. As most of us know, if we concentrate too intensively on a tough problem, we can get stuck in a mental rut. But if we let the problem sit unattended for a time, we often return to it with a fresh perspective and a burst of creativity. Research by the Dutch psychologist Ap Dijksterhuis indicates that such breaks in our attention give our unconscious mind time to grapple with a problem, bringing to bear information and cognitive processes unavailable to conscious deliberation. We usually make better decisions, his experiments reveal, if we shift our attention away from a mental challenge for a time.   16

But Dijksterhuis's work also shows that our unconscious thought processes don't engage with a problem until we've clearly and consciously defined the problem. If we don't have a particular goal in mind, he writes, "unconscious thought does not occur."   17

The constant distractedness that the net encourages—the state of being, to borrow a phrase from T S Eliot, "distracted from distraction by distraction" [5]—is very different from the kind of temporary, purposeful   18

Thinking Critically

[4] Are you surprised by the results of this Stanford University experiment? Why or why not?

[5] How does T. S. Eliot's quotation about distraction apply to Carr's research?

diversion of our mind that refreshes our thinking. The cacophony of stimuli short-circuits both conscious and unconscious thought, preventing our minds from thinking either deeply or creatively. Our brains turn into simple signal-processing units, shepherding information into consciousness and then back out again.

What we seem to be sacrificing in our surfing and searching is our capac-   19
ity to engage in the quieter, attentive modes of thought that underpin contemplation, reflection and introspection. The web never encourages us to slow down. It keeps us in a state of perpetual mental locomotion. The rise of social networks like Facebook and Twitter, which pump out streams of brief messages, has only exacerbated the problem.

There's nothing wrong with absorbing information quickly and in bits   20
and pieces. We've always skimmed newspapers more than we've read them, and we routinely run our eyes over books and magazines to get the gist of a piece of writing and decide whether it warrants more thorough reading. The ability to scan and browse is as important as the ability to read deeply and think attentively. What's disturbing is that skimming is becoming our dominant mode of thought. [6] Once a means to an end, a way to identify information for further study, it's becoming an end in itself—our preferred method of both learning and analysis. Dazzled by the net's treasures, we have been blind to the damage we may be doing to our intellectual lives and even our culture.

UNDERSTANDING DETAILS

1. According to Carr, how do our current information technologies affect our general thinking processes?
2. In what ways does the "division of attention" (paragraph 6) encouraged by the Internet limit our concentration?
3. What examples does Carr give to support his argument?
4. What is the main claim neuroscientist Michael Merzenich made about our brains?

READING CRITICALLY

5. How are the distractions of the Internet most likely to affect student performance? Could the results vary from subject to subject? In what ways?
6. Why is deep, reflective thinking important? Where might it be most productive?
7. What does Carr mean by "perpetual mental locomotion" (paragraph 19)? How do social networks affect this tendency?

Thinking Critically

[6] Based on the main points Carr makes in this essay, has skimming become your "dominant mode of thought"?

8. Explain Carr's concluding statement: "Dazzled by the net's treasures, we have been blind to the damage we may be doing to our intellectual lives and even our culture" (paragraph 20).

DISCOVERING RHETORICAL STRATEGIES

9. Carr starts his essay with an acknowledgment of some of the positive results of the Internet. Is this an effective beginning? Why or why not?
10. What is the thesis of this essay? Where does this thesis statement appear?
11. How do the specific references to experts in the field further Carr's argument? Are these citations effective in your opinion? Why or why not?
12. List Carr's main claims. Does he cover the most important ideas on this subject?

MAKING CONNECTIONS

13. Imagine that Carr, Michael Dorris ("The Broken Cord"), and/or Dave Grossman ("We Are Training Our Kids to Kill") are discussing how difficult it is to break an addiction. Which of these addictions do you think would be most difficult to stop? Why?
14. Compare and contrast Carr's use of examples with those employed by Brent Staples ("A Brother's Murder"), Jessica Mitford ("Behind the Formaldehyde Curtain"), and/or Amy Tan ("Mother Tongue"). Who uses examples most skillfully? Why do you think this is so?
15. Do you think Sara Gilbert ("The Different Ways of Being Smart") would agree with Carr that the Internet is making us stupid? Whose side would you be on? Why?

IDEAS FOR DISCUSSION/WRITING

Preparing to Write

Write freely about your habits of mind: What supports the type of thinking you need to do your college assignments? What are the most common distractions in your life? How do you handle these distractions when you are studying? Do you find they hinder your thinking in any way? What are the circumstances surrounding your best work in college? How can you create these circumstances? What is the relationship between the quality of your thinking and your ability to learn?

Choosing a Topic   MyWritingLab™

1. **LEARNING⏻NLINE** Think back to the exercise in Preparing to Read. What do you think about the fact that you can access a part of nature through technology? Does this change your thinking about Carr's essay?
2. Your old high school has noticed a serious decrease in student performance and grades in the past year. Because you used to hold a seat in the student government, your high school has asked you to come back to your school and talk to the seniors about study habits. What will you say? This is such a sensitive issue that the school officials have asked to see a copy of your speech before you deliver it. Prepare your talk, being aware that you need to win the students' trust as you also give them realistic suggestions.

3. From what you have observed in college so far, analyze the behavior of your peers. How do they generally manage their time during the week? How does that change on the weekend? Explain your observations in an essay to your English instructor with a focus on ways to improve the general time management of your fellow students.

4. How much time do you spend online every day? How do you spend the majority of your time online? How does the Internet support your college work? How does it hinder your college work? Now that you have read Carr's essay, what changes do you want to make in your use of the Internet? Write an essay in response to Carr's research, outlining various changes in your own use of the Internet.

Before beginning your essay, you may want to consult the flowchart on page 451.

DAVE GROSSMAN   (1956–   )

We Are Training Our Kids to Kill

Lieutenant Colonel Dave Grossman is a retired professor of Psychology and Military Science and a former U.S. Army Ranger who founded a new field of scientific study he calls "killology," which investigates how and why people kill each other during wartime, the psychological costs of battle, the root causes of violent crime, and the process of healing that victims of violence must go through (see www.killology.com). Following a B.S. at Columbus College in Georgia (where he was elected to Phi Beta Kappa) and an M.Ed. at the University of Texas, Grossman joined the army, where he rose quickly through the ranks to Lieutenant Colonel and served as a professor at both the U.S. Military Academy at West Point and as Chair of the Department of Military Science at Arkansas State University. The author of three books— *On Killing: The Psychological Cost of Learning to Kill in War and Society* (1995), *Stop Teaching Our Kids to Kill: A Call to Action Against TV, Movie, and Video Game Violence* (with Gloria DeGaetano, 1999), and *On Combat* (2004)—he spends nearly three hundred days on the road each year consulting and giving workshops about combat and violence. He also writes military science fiction and will soon publish a new book entitled *The Two-Space War*. His advice to students using *The Prose Reader* is to avoid a steady diet of violent visual images, which "will lobotomize the brain and make thinking and writing more difficult. If you cleanse your mind (particularly the frontal cortex) with periods of contemplation and reading, you will become a much better writer."

Preparing to Read

The following controversial essay, originally published in *The Saturday Evening Post* in July/August 1999, contains a clear, well-reasoned analysis of the dangers connected with violence on TV and in video games. The author, Dave Grossman, is especially concerned with the way in which these media sources actually train our children to kill.

Exploring Experience: Before you read this essay, think about your views on violence in the media: Do you think watching violence on television and in the movies or playing video games can lead to violent acts? How useful are movie ratings for violence and sex? At what age do you think children should be able to see violence without adult supervision or censorship? Who do you think should control the violence children are exposed to? To what extent should we censor violence in the media? What specific types of violent behavior should be regulated in the media? What should not be censored?

LEARNING⊕NLINE Go to your favorite online news source. How many of the headlines describe violent acts? Consider this information while reading Grossman's argument.

Before reading this essay, you may want to consult the flowchart on page 448.

I am from Jonesboro, Arkansas. I travel the world training medical, law 1
enforcement, and U.S. military personnel about the realities of warfare.
I try to make those who carry deadly force keenly aware of the magnitude of killing. Too many law enforcement and military personnel act like
"cowboys," never stopping to think about who they are and what they are
called to do. I hope I am able to give them a reality check.

So here I am, a world traveler and an expert in the field of "killology," [1] 2
when the (then) largest school massacre in American history happens in my
hometown of Jonesboro, Arkansas. That was the March 24, 1998, schoolyard shooting deaths of four girls and a teacher. Ten others were injured, and
two boys, ages 11 and 13, were jailed, charged with murder.

Virus of Violence

To understand the why behind Littleton, Jonesboro, Springfield, Pearl, 3
and Paducah, and all the other outbreaks of this "virus of violence," [2] we
need to first understand the magnitude of the problem. The per capita murder rate doubled in this country between 1957—when the FBI started
keeping track of the data—and 1992. A fuller picture of the problem, however, is indicated by the rate at which people are attempting to kill one
another—the aggravated assault rate. That rate in America has gone from
around 60 per 100,000 in 1957 to over 440 per 100,000 in 2002. As bad as
this is, it would be much worse were it not for two major factors.

The first is the increased imprisonment of violent offenders. The prison 4
population in America nearly quintupled between 1975 and 2002. According to criminologist John A. DiIulio, "dozens of credible empirical analyses . . . leave no doubt that the increased use of prisons averted millions of
serious crimes." [3] If it were not for our tremendous imprisonment rate (the
highest of any industrialized nation), the aggravated assault rate and the
murder rate would undoubtedly be even higher.

The second factor keeping the murder rate from being even worse is 5
medical technology. According to the U.S. Army Medical Service Corps, a
wound that would have killed nine out of ten soldiers in World War II, nine
out of ten could have survived in Vietnam. Thus, by a very conservative
estimate, if we still had a 1940-level medical technology today, our murder

---

Thinking Critically

[1] What do you think the term "killology" means?

[2] What does Grossman mean by the "virus of violence" in our country? In what ways is
this problem like a disease?

[3] Do you agree with the assertion that "the increased use of prisons averted millions of
serious crimes"? Explain your reasoning.

rate would be ten times higher than it is. The murder rate has been held down by the development of sophisticated lifesaving skills and techniques, such as helicopter medevacs, 911 operators, paramedics, CPR, trauma centers, and medicines.

Today, both our assault rate and murder rate are at phenomenally high levels. Both are increasing worldwide. In Canada, according to their Center for Justice, per capita assaults increased almost fivefold between 1964 and 2002, attempted murder increased nearly sevenfold, and murders doubled. Similar trends can be seen in other countries in the per capita violent crime rates reported to Interpol between 1977 and 2002. In Australia and New Zealand, the assault rate increased approximately four-fold, and the murder rate nearly doubled in both nations. The assault rate tripled in Sweden and approximately doubled in Belgium, Denmark, England and Wales, France, Hungary, the Netherlands, and Scotland. Meanwhile, all these nations had an associated (but smaller) increase in murder.

This virus of violence is occurring worldwide. The explanation for it has to be some new factor that is occurring in all of these countries. There are many factors involved, and none should be discounted: for example, the prevalence of guns in our society. But violence is rising in many nations with Draconian gun laws. And though we should never downplay child abuse, poverty, or racism, there is only one new variable present in each of these countries that bears the exact same fruit: media violence presented as entertainment for children. ◆ 4

Killing Is Unnatural

Before retiring from the military, I spent almost a quarter of a century as an army infantry officer and a psychologist, learning and studying how to enable people to kill. Believe me, we are very good at it. But it does not come naturally; you have to be taught to kill. And just as the army is conditioning people to kill, we are indiscriminately doing the same thing to our children, but without the safeguards.

After the Jonesboro killings, the head of the American Academy of Pediatrics Task Force on Juvenile Violence came to town and said that children don't naturally kill. It is a learned skill. And they learn it from abuse and violence in the home and, most pervasively, from violence as entertainment in television, the movies, and interactive video games.

Thinking Critically

◆ 4 How much violence do you think the average six-year-old child sees on television each day? What do you think is the cumulative effect of watching it for many years?

Killing requires training because there is a built-in aversion to killing one's   10
own kind. [5] I can best illustrate this fact by drawing on my own military
research into the act of killing.

We all know how hard it is to have a discussion with a frightened or angry   11
human being. Vasoconstriction, the narrowing of the blood vessels, has literally closed down the forebrain—that great gob of gray matter that makes
one a human being and distinguishes one from a dog. When those neurons
close down, the midbrain takes over and your thought processes and reflexes
are indistinguishable from your dog's. If you've worked with animals, you
have some understanding of what happens to frightened human beings on
the battlefield. The battlefield and violent crime are in the realm of midbrain
responses.

Within the midbrain, there is a powerful, God-given resistance to killing   12
your own kind. Every species, with a few exceptions, has a hardwired resistance to killing its own kind [6] in territorial and mating battles. When
animals with antlers and horns fight one another, they head-butt in a non-
fatal fashion. But when they fight any other species, they go to the side to
gut and gore. Piranhas will turn their fangs on anything, but they fight one
another with flicks of the tail. Rattlesnakes will bite anything, but they
wrestle one another. Almost every species has this hardwired resistance to
killing its own kind.

When we human beings are overwhelmed with anger and fear, we slam   13
head-on into that midbrain resistance that generally prevents us from killing.
Only sociopaths—who by definition don't have that resistance—lack this
innate violence immune system.

Throughout all human history, when humans have fought each other,   14
there has been a lot of posturing. Adversaries make loud noises and puff
themselves up, trying to daunt the enemy. There is a lot of fleeing and sub-
mission. Ancient battles were nothing more than great shoving matches. It
was not until one side turned and ran that most of the killing happened, and
most of that was stabbing people in the back. All of the ancient military
historians report that the vast majority of killing happened in pursuit when
one side was fleeing.

In more modern times, the average firing rate was incredibly low in Civil   15
War battles. British author Paddy Griffith demonstrates in his book *The
Battle Tactics of the Civil War* that the killing potential of the average Civil

---

Thinking Critically

[5] Do you think this is true? Do most people have an innate aversion to killing other human
beings? Explain your reasoning.

[6] What does the phrase "hardwired resistance" mean in this context?

War regiment was anywhere from five hundred to a thousand men per minute. The actual killing rate was only one or two men per minute per regiment. At the Battle of Gettysburg, of the 27,000 muskets picked up from the dead and dying after the battle, 90 percent were loaded. This is an anomaly, because it took 90 percent of their time to load muskets and only 5 percent to fire. But even more amazing, of the thousands of loaded muskets, over half had multiple loads in the barrel—one had 23 loads in the barrel. [7]

In reality, the average man would load his musket and bring it to his shoulder, but he could not bring himself to kill. He would be brave, he would stand shoulder to shoulder, he would do what he was trained to do; but at the moment of truth, he could not bring himself to pull the trigger. And so he lowered the weapon and loaded it again. Of those who did fire, only a tiny percentage fired to hit. The vast majority fired over the enemy's head.   16

During World War II, U.S. Army Brig. Gen. S. L. A. Marshall had a team of researchers study what soldiers did in battle. For the first time in history, they asked individual soldiers what they did in battle. They discovered that only 15 to 20 percent of the individual riflemen could bring themselves to fire at an exposed enemy soldier.   17

That is the reality of the battlefield. Only a small percentage of soldiers are able and willing to participate. Men are willing to die. They are willing to sacrifice themselves for their nation; but they are not willing to kill. It is a phenomenal insight into human nature; but when the military became aware of that, they systematically went about the process of trying to fix this "problem." From the military perspective, a 15 percent firing rate among riflemen is like a 15 percent literacy rate among librarians. And fix it the military did. By the Korean War, around 55 percent of the soldiers were willing to fire to kill. And by Vietnam, the rate rose to over 90 percent.   18

The method in this madness: desensitization.   19

How the military increases the killing rate of soldiers in combat is instructive because our culture today is doing the same thing to our children. The training methods militaries use are brutalization, classical conditioning, operant conditioning, and role modeling. I will explain each of these in the military context and show how these same factors are contributing to the phenomenal increase of violence in our culture.   20

Brutalization and desensitization are what happens at boot camp. From the moment you step off the bus, you are physically and verbally abused: 21

Thinking Critically

[7] What do all these statistics imply about the willingness of Civil War soldiers to fire their muskets?

countless push-ups, endless hours at attention or running with heavy loads, while carefully trained professionals take turns screaming at you. [8] Your head is shaved; you are herded together naked and dressed alike, losing all individuality. This brutalization is designed to break down your existing mores and norms and force you to accept a new set of values that embraces destruction, violence, and death as a way of life. In the end, you are desensitized to violence and accept it as a normal and essential survival skill in your brutal new world.

Something very similar to this desensitization toward violence is happen-   22
ing to our children through violence in the media—but instead of 18-year-olds, it begins at the age of 18 months when a child is first able to discern what is happening on television. At that age, a child can watch something happening on television and mimic that action. But it isn't until children are six or seven years old that the part of the brain kicks in that lets them understand where information comes from. Even though young children have some understanding of what it means to pretend, they are developmentally unable to distinguish clearly between fantasy and reality. [9]

When young children see somebody shot, stabbed, raped, brutalized,   23
degraded, or murdered on TV, to them it is as though it were actually happening. To have a child of three, four, or five watch a "splatter" movie, learning to relate to a character for the first 90 minutes and then in the last 30 minutes watch helplessly as that new friend is hunted and brutally murdered, is the moral and psychological equivalent of introducing your child to a friend, letting her play with that friend, and then butchering that friend in front of your child's eyes. And this happens to our children hundreds upon hundreds of times.

Sure, they are told, "Hey, it's all for fun. Look, this isn't real; it's just TV."   24
And they nod their little heads and say OK. But they can't tell the difference. Can you remember a point in your life or in your children's lives when dreams, reality, and television were all jumbled together? That's what it is like to be at that level of psychological development. That's what the media are doing to them.

The *Journal of the American Medical Association* published the definitive epi-   25
demiological study on the impact of TV violence. The research demonstrated what happened in numerous nations after television made its appearance as

---

Thinking Critically

[8] What do you think is the relationship between brutalization and desensitization in armed forces training?

[9] According to the author, at what age are children able to understand the difference between fantasy and reality? How does this affect their reaction to televised violence?

compared to nations and regions without TV. The two nations or regions being compared are demographically and ethnically identical; only one variable is different: the presence of television. In every nation, region, or city with television, there is an immediate explosion of violence on the playground, and within 15 years there is a doubling of the murder rate. Why 15 years? That is how long it takes for the brutalization of a three- to five-year-old to reach the "prime crime age." That is how long it takes for you to reap what you have sown when you brutalize and desensitize a three-year-old. [10]

Today the data linking violence in the media to violence in society are superior to those linking cancer and tobacco. Hundreds of sound scientific studies demonstrate the social impact of brutalization by the media. The *Journal of the American Medical Association* concluded that "the introduction of television in the 1950s caused a subsequent doubling of the homicide rate, i.e., long-term childhood exposure to television is a causal factor behind approximately one half of the homicides committed in the United States, or approximately 10,000 homicides annually." The article went on to say that "if, hypothetically, television technology had never been developed, there would today be 10,000 fewer homicides each year in the United States, 70,000 fewer rapes, and 700,000 fewer injurious assaults" (June 10, 1992).

Classical Conditioning

Classical conditioning is like the famous case of Pavlov's dogs they teach in Psychology 101. The dogs learned to associate the ringing of the bell with food, and once conditioned, the dogs could not hear the bell without salivating.

The Japanese were masters at using classical conditioning with their soldiers. Early in World War II, Chinese prisoners were placed in a ditch on their knees with their hands bound behind them. And one by one, a select few Japanese soldiers would go into the ditch and bayonet "their" prisoner to death. This is a horrific way to kill another human being. Up on the bank, countless other young soldiers would cheer them on in their violence. Comparatively few soldiers actually killed in these situations, but by making the others watch and cheer, the Japanese were able to use these kinds of atrocities to classically condition a very large audience to associate pleasure with human death and suffering. [11] Immediately afterwards, the soldiers

---

Thinking Critically

[10] How is the brutalization and desensitization of soldiers in training different from the indoctrination of a three-year-old through televised violence?

[11] How and why did the World War II Japanese army teach its soldiers to "associate pleasure with human death and suffering"?

who had been spectators were treated to sake, the best meal they had in months, and to so-called comfort girls. The result? They learned to associate committing violent acts with pleasure.

The Japanese found these kinds of techniques to be extraordinarily effec-   29
tive at quickly enabling very large numbers of soldiers to commit atrocities in the years to come. Operant conditioning (which we will look at shortly) teaches you to kill, but classical conditioning is a subtle but powerful mechanism that teaches you to like it.[12]

This technique is so morally reprehensible that there are very few exam-   30
ples of it in modern U.S. military training, but there are some clear-cut examples of it being done by the media to our children. What is happening to our children is the reverse of the aversion therapy portrayed in the movie *A Clockwork Orange*. In *A Clockwork Orange,* a brutal sociopath, a mass murderer, is strapped to a chair and forced to watch violent movies while he is injected with a drug that nauseates him. So he sits and gags and retches as he watches the movies. After hundreds of repetitions of this, he associates violence with nausea. And it limits his ability to be violent.

We are doing the exact opposite: Our children watch vivid pictures of   31
human suffering and death, and they learn to associate it with their favorite soft drink and candy bar, or their girlfriend's perfume.

After the Jonesboro shootings, one of the high-school teachers told me   32
how her students reacted when she told them about the shootings at the middle school. "They laughed," she told me with dismay. A similar reaction happens all the time in movie theaters when there is bloody violence. The young people laugh and cheer and keep right on eating popcorn and drinking pop. We have raised a generation of barbarians who have learned to associate violence with pleasure, like the Romans cheering and snacking as the Christians were slaughtered in the Colosseum.[13]

The result is a phenomenon that functions much like AIDS, a phenom-   33
enon I call AVIDS—Acquired Violence Immune Deficiency Syndrome. AIDS has never killed anybody. It destroys your immune system, and then other diseases that shouldn't kill you become fatal. Television violence by itself does not kill you. It destroys your violence immune system and conditions you to derive pleasure from violence. And once you are at close range with another human being and it's time for you to pull that trigger,

---

Thinking Critically

[12] What is the difference between "operant conditioning" and "classical conditioning"? Which do you think is more sinister? Which is more powerful?

[13] Do you agree with the author when he says "we have raised a generation of barbarians who have learned to associate violence with pleasure"? Why or why not?

Acquired Violence Immune Deficiency Syndrome can destroy your mid-brain resistance.

Operant Conditioning

The third method the military uses is operant conditioning, a very pow- 34 erful repetitive procedure of stimulus-response, stimulus-response. A benign example is the use of flight simulators to train pilots. An airline pilot in training sits in front of a flight simulator for endless hours; when a particular warning light goes on, he is taught to react in a certain way. When another warning light goes on, a different reaction is required. Stimulus-response, stimulus-response, stimulus-response. One day the pilot is actually flying a jumbo jet; the plane is going down, and 300 people are screaming behind him. He is wetting his seat cushion, and he is scared out of his wits; but he does the right thing. Why? Because he has been conditioned to respond reflexively to this particular crisis.

When people are frightened or angry, they will do what they have been 35 conditioned to do. In fire drills, children learn to file out of the school in orderly fashion. One day there is a real fire, and they are frightened out of their wits; but they do exactly what they have been conditioned to do, and it saves their lives.[14]

The military and law enforcement community have made killing a con- 36 ditioned response. This has substantially raised the firing rate on the modern battlefield. Whereas infantry training in World War II used bull's-eye targets, now soldiers learn to fire at realistic, man-shaped silhouettes that pop into their field of view. That is the stimulus. The trainees have only a split second to engage the target. The conditioned response is to shoot the target, and then it drops. Stimulus-response, stimulus-response, stimulus-response— soldiers or police officers experience hundreds of repetitions. Later, when soldiers are on the battlefield or a police officer is walking a beat and some- body pops up with a gun, they will shoot reflexively and shoot to kill. We know that 75 to 80 percent of the shooting on the modern battlefield is the result of this kind of stimulus-response training.

Now, if you're a little troubled by that, how much more should we be 37 troubled by the fact that every time a child plays an interactive point-and- shoot video game, he is learning the exact same conditioned reflex and motor skills?

I was an expert witness in a murder case in South Carolina offering 38 mitigation for a kid who was facing the death penalty. I tried to explain

---

Thinking Critically

[14] What are some other positive results of "operant conditioning"?

to the jury that interactive video games had conditioned him to shoot a gun to kill. He had spent hundreds of dollars on video games learning to point and shoot, point and shoot. One day he and his buddy decided it would be fun to rob the local convenience store. They walked in, and he pointed a snub-nosed .38 pistol at the clerk's head. The clerk turned to look at him, and the defendant shot reflexively from about six feet. The bullet hit the clerk right between the eyes—which is a pretty remarkable shot with that weapon at that range—and killed this father of two. Afterward, we asked the boy what happened and why he did it. It clearly was not part of the plan to kill the guy—it was being videotaped from six different directions. He said, "I don't know. It was a mistake. It wasn't supposed to happen."

In the military and law-enforcement worlds, the right option is often not   39
to shoot. But you never, ever put your money in that video machine with the intention of not shooting. There is always some stimulus that sets you off. And when he was excited, and his heart rate went up, and vasoconstriction closed his forebrain down, this young man did exactly what he was conditioned to do: he reflexively pulled the trigger, shooting accurately just like all those times he played video games.

This process is extraordinarily powerful and frightening. The result is ever   40
more "homemade" sociopaths who kill reflexively. Our children are learning how to kill and learning to like the idea of killing; and then we have the audacity to say, "Oh my goodness, what's wrong?" [15]

One of the boys involved in the Jonesboro shootings (and they are just   41
boys) had a fair amount of experience shooting real guns. The other one, to the best of our knowledge, had almost no experience shooting. Between them, those two boys fired 27 shots from a range of over 100 yards, and they hit 15 people. That's pretty remarkable shooting. We run into these situations often—kids who have never picked up a gun in their lives pick up a real gun and are incredibly accurate. Why? Video games.

UNDERSTANDING DETAILS

1. According to Grossman, what is the "virus of violence" (paragraph 3)?
2. What evidence does the author use to argue that "killing is unnatural"?
3. What three methods does the military use to train its soldiers to kill?
4. How does Grossman claim we are training our children to kill?

Thinking Critically

[15] In what ways does the author indict all of us in the creation of "homemade sociopaths"?

READING CRITICALLY

5. What two factors does the author believe control the murder rate in the United States? How do these factors affect this rate?
6. How are the techniques used in video games similar to those taught in military training?
7. How did the U.S. military train more soldiers to actually fire their guns?
8. How can we control this epidemic of violence that Grossman outlines?

DISCOVERING RHETORICAL STRATEGIES

9. What do you think Grossman's purpose is in this essay?
10. Who do you think would be most interested in this essay?
11. What effect do you think this essay will have on parents?
12. Describe the writer's point of view in a complete sentence.

MAKING CONNECTIONS

13. To what extent would Grossman, Brent Staples ("A Brother's Murder") and/ or Elizabeth Svoboda ("Virtual Assault") agree that violence is encoded in our human DNA? What outside influences, according to any of these authors, make us a violent culture? Which of these three authors makes the most convincing case for his or her point of view? Explain your answer.
14. Imagine a conversation among Grossman, Kimberly Wozencraft ("Notes from the Country Club"), and/or Samantha Pugsley ("How Language Impacts the Stigma Against Mental Health [And What We Must Do to Change It]") about social stigma connected with their various messages. What preconceptions do people have in this country about their topics? Why do you think people have these reactions?
15. How do you think Robert Ramirez ("The Barrio"), Amy Chua ("Excerpt from *Battle Hymn of the Tiger Mother*"), and/or Mary Pipher ("Beliefs about Families") would each respond to Grossman's implication that parents need to be more vigilant in monitoring what their children watch on television? What is your own opinion on this issue?

IDEAS FOR DISCUSSION/WRITING

Preparing to Write

Write freely about your feelings concerning censorship: Should violence on TV be censored in any way? Why or why not? At what age can children safely watch violence in the media? Do you believe a relationship exists between watching violence and acting in a violent manner? Who is most responsible for restricting or editing the violence that children see?

Choosing a Topic   MyWritingLab™

1. **LEARNING⏻NLINE** Do you believe that video games, movies, television shows, or popular music influence youth violence? In a Google search, type

"violence and media" into the search box, and read some of the opinions on this subject. Write an argument in which you take a position regarding this controversial issue. Following Grossman's style, use several different types of examples to support your claims.

2. *Time* magazine has asked you to respond directly to Grossman's article. Do you think his argument about the relationship between children and video games is reasonable? Give specific examples to support your contention.

3. As an apprentice at a TV station, you have been asked to represent your age group by giving your opinion on the network's inclusion of violence in its programming. What is your opinion concerning TV violence? In what ways do you think your opinion represents the consensus of U.S. society as a whole?

4. Research and describe the censorship practices of another country. Explain specifically how that country's views on censorship are carried out in practice. Give as many examples as possible to support your explanation.

Before beginning your essay, you may want to consult the flowchart on page 451.

SAMANTHA PUGSLEY   (1990–   )

How Language Impacts the Stigma Against Mental Health (And What We Must Do to Change It)

Samantha Pugsley is a writer and photographer based in Charlotte, North Carolina. She is both a commercial and fine art photographer, whose art has been featured in *The New York Times, The Huffington Post, Golden Age Magazine,* and the *Photographer Blogger.* As a freelance writer, she most often writes for *Thought Catalog* and *XOJane,* where her areas of interest center around gender equality, marriage, female sexuality and reproductive rights, and mental health reform. She is a self-proclaimed "super nerd" who spends her days enjoying video games, exploring the Marvel universe, and writing fan fiction.

Preparing to Read

Originally published in *Thought Catalog* in 2014, "How Language Impacts the Stigma Against Mental Health (And What We Must Do to Change It)" is an indictment of how irresponsibly we misuse references to mental illness in our everyday language.

Exploring Experience: As you prepare to read this essay, consider your views on various mental health issues: Have you or someone you know suffered from depression, anxiety, or any other mental disorders? Have you ever mis-used any of these terms to refer to situations that are not really mental health problems? Why do you think we refer to these disorders in relatively loose ways?

LEARNINGⒸNLINE Visit MentalHealth.gov, and click on the "Talk About Mental Health" tab. Peruse the various areas of the website to locate a topic that interests you. Read the quotes, note the advice, and watch the videos associated with your choice to establish a context for reading Pugsley's essay.

Before reading this essay, you may want to consult the flowchart on page 448.

L anguage is powerful.   1
Even dead languages are still taught and revered today. (Anyone   2
else take Latin in high school?) The rate at which language changes
is fascinating. And now, it evolves faster than ever before in an effort to stay
relevant to the current generation. Dictionaries are updated every year to
include brand new words and new definitions of old words that are being
used differently. For the most part, these shifts are great. A growing language
is one way to measure societal success.[1] It means there are new inventions
and new ideas that mark continued growth.

Not every change is positive. The mental health field has been especially   3
susceptible to the negative ones. Over the past decade or so, it's become
commonplace to use mental disorder terminology to describe common,
often trivial situations or problems. It seems harmless. They've been used so
often they've become integrated into and accepted as part of our everyday
language. The truth is that by using these phrases to describe everyday problems, we're trivializing mental illness.[2] Thanks to this trivialization, those
who suffer now have the added hardship of having to prove they really need
help and aren't just being dramatic or asking for attention. They can't simply
say "I have OCD" or "I'm depressed" because these have become common
ways to describe all sorts of things.

I'm not preaching to you from atop a high horse. I'm guilty. Not long   4
ago I was talking to an acquaintance about music. I said, "I'm so OCD
about volume. I like it to be an even number." She proceeded to nicely
explain to me that she suffered from Obsessive-Compulsive Disorder. She
told me that when she changes the volume, she has to touch the knob
exactly six times before actually moving it. And she had to do it every single
time. There was a list of other things, some so debilitating I wondered how
she was able to even get out of bed in the morning. I realized that my particularity with volume was nothing like what she dealt with every single
day. But after years of hearing other people refer to their specific preferences
as "OCD," I had internalized that as acceptable language. In using "OCD"
so glibly, I had diminished her struggle with the disorder, and that is
completely unfair to her.

You probably don't even realize you're doing it. I didn't. I'm grateful she   5
took the time to explain it to me instead of just shrugging it off and letting
me continue to do it. It's my hope that by pointing out some of the main

---

Thinking Critically

[1] In what ways does "a growing language . . . measure societal success"?

[2] How does the trivialization of the mental health phrases cause additional hardships for
those who actually suffer from these diseases?

offenders I can help you all to do the same. Here are five common phrases we use that trivialize mental illness:

1) "I'm *so* OCD."

The term "OCD" is often used to show a particularity or preference, like   6
how I find satisfaction in keeping my volume at an even number. In reality, Obsessive-Compulsive Disorder is a crippling condition that often traps the person suffering in debilitating cycles of recurrent thoughts and behaviors that he or she can't control. These obsessions often lead to rituals or compulsions that have to be performed in an effort to alleviate the anxiety. That's a far cry from wanting the volume to be an even number, isn't it?

2) "That was ADD of me."

ADD is often used as a synonym for distraction. You might be talking   7
to a friend and zone out. If they call you out, you might laugh and say you had an ADD moment. Attention-Deficit Disorder is so much more than just an issue of distraction. Especially in adults, it can cause anxiety, depression, and mood swings. Often, adults with untreated ADD have emotional imbalances, can find it hard to obtain employment, and struggle with meaningful relationships. By all means, if you struggle with ADD and find that joking ("I had an ADD moment") helps you cope with your disorder, please do so. But if you aren't struggling, there are better ways to describe your fleeting moments of distraction.

3) "This is so stressful. I'm about to have a panic attack."

This one hits close to home for me. As someone who suffers from a panic   8
disorder, the overuse of the phrase "panic attack" makes it difficult for me to be taken seriously when I'm actually having one. One time in college I felt very anxious after a test. I was walking out with a classmate and said, "I think I'm having a panic attack." He laughed and said, "I know, right? I probably failed." Not long after, I was holed up in the bathroom trying to console myself. If he had taken me seriously instead of thinking I was being dramatic about the test, he might have taken time to help. Anxiety often gets misinterpreted as regular stress. People throw the terms around interchangeably. While most everyone experiences moments of anxiety, it's a disorder when it becomes frequent, happens for no reason, or starts impacting your everyday life. Panic attacks are serious business. They come in all shapes and sizes but the really bad ones can make the person suffering feel like they're going to die: racing heart, shortness of breath, chest pains, passing out and other serious symptoms. So the next time you're stressed, take a moment to consider those who really do have panic attacks before you use it.

4) "I'm *so* depressed."

This one is tough because "sad" and "depressed" have basically become   9
synonyms in our language. When you look up the symptoms of depression,
sadness is even listed there. Those who have never experienced depression
can't understand how debilitating it is. It's a disorder that controls your
entire life. It's a sadness that consumes you to the point where you might
feel no point in living. When you equate your sadness to depression, you
diminish the severity of the actual disorder. People get used to hearing the
word to describe everyday lows, the ones that eventually go away. This
flippant usage has birthed responses like "It's okay. Things will work out,"
or even worse, "Just get over it." And yeah, no one wants to hear these,
but when someone is depressed, saying stuff like this can actually be deadly.
When someone's struggling with depression, responses like this fuel the
disorder by creating guilt, shame, and feelings of worthlessness. If we stop
using "depressed" to mean "sad," those who have depression might have
an easier time asking for help. They'll be taken seriously and not mistaken
for "just being sad."

5) "I would just kill myself."

If you take one thing away from this piece, please let it be this: **Do not**   10
trivialize suicide. I've heard people say, "If I looked like that, I would
just kill myself," and "If I fail, I'll just kill myself." People sometimes look
at others' misfortune and say, "If that happened to me, I would kill myself."
It's become a way to emphasize a bad situation. It's also used to indicate
boredom or annoyance like when people make a gun shape with their
fingers, put it to their head, and make a gunshot noise. Those who struggle
with suicidal thoughts often never reach out for help until it's too late. I
believe societal attitudes about suicide are largely to blame. Changing our
language is one step we can take towards changing those attitudes. We
need to stop using suicide to illustrate negativity. It makes those who are
struggling feel worse about themselves and less likely to reach out for
support.

As a side note: It's a myth that talking to someone about suicide will make   11
them more likely to follow through. If you know someone who is struggling, talk to them about it. Be direct. Ask them if they are contemplating
suicide. If they say yes, help them find help and be a support through the
process. Sometimes all people need is a reminder that there is someone out
there who cares.

There are so many others—far more than the length of this article can   12
allow. Everything from using the term "bipolar" to describe everyday mood
swings to calling someone "schizophrenic" if they do something out of

character.[3] If you've used any of these phrases (I have), you aren't a bad person. It isn't your fault that you've internalized language that's become widely accepted and used regularly. But, if you choose to, you can make a conscious effort to stop. The best part about language is that it can change and we can be the catalyst. We can stop trivializing these very serious disorders and create a safer, more constructive place for those who are struggling. There's already so much stigma surrounding mental illness. If we change the way we talk about it, bringing these phrases up in meaningful conversation instead of using them as a way to dramatize our everyday lives, we can take steps towards removing stigma.

UNDERSTANDING DETAILS

1. According to Pugsley, what is the relationship between language and mental health?
2. What are some positive aspects of a changing language?
3. How have mental health issues been affected by recent shifts in our language use?
4. What are the five phrases from mental health that we often misuse? How do the misuses trivialize these mental illnesses?

READING CRITICALLY

5. Why does Pugsley believe that "language is powerful" (paragraph 1)?
6. Have you ever misused one of the terms that Pugsley mentions in this essay? What were the circumstances?
7. Why does the author highlight "do not trivialize suicide" (paragraph 10)?
8. Do you agree with Pugsley that "if you choose to, you can make a conscious effort to stop" (paragraph 12)? How will stopping the misuse of references to mental health issues help those actually suffering from mental illnesses?

DISCOVERING RHETORICAL STRATEGIES

9. Explain the essay's title.
10. List Pugsley's topics, and explain how this essay is organized.
11. Who do you think is Pugsley's audience?
12. Is the final sentence an effective ending to this essay? Explain your answer.

MAKING CONNECTIONS

13. What would Pugsley and Carole Kanchier ("Dare to Change Your Job and Your Life in 7 Steps") agree on if they were discussing the topic of

---

Thinking Critically

[3] What other mental health references are commonly misused in our everyday language?

change? Would either of them put any limitations on the prospect of making changes?

14. Compare and contrast Pugsley's tone with that displayed by Stephen King ("Why We Crave Horror Movies"), Frank Furedi ("Our Unhealthy Obsession with Sickness"), and/or Dave Grossman ("We Are Training Our Kids to Kill"). Which author seems most intense? Which author uses humor? Are the moods the authors used to convey their messages the most effective choices?

15. Which of the following authors' arguments did you find most persuasive:, Pugsley, Frank Furedi ("Our Unhealthy Obsession with Sickness"), or Nicholas Carr ("How the Internet is Making Us Stupid")? Which were least convincing? Explain your answer with examples from the essays.

IDEAS FOR DISCUSSION/WRITING

Preparing to Write

Write freely on the role of language in our society: How powerful is it in your estimation? Can we control our thinking by our language use? What other terms, besides mental illness references, do we misuse? What is the effect of these inaccuracies? Why should we be more accurate in all of our language use?

Choosing a Topic   MyWritingLab™

1. **LEARNING⏻NLINE** Return to the MentalHealth.gov homepage from Preparing to Read. Imagine you have a friend that is struggling with a mental health disorder. Using the website, convince your friend to get help by explaining what is available and how you can assist him or her.

2. Write an argument either for or against the conscientious use of language in all aspects of life. How serious should we be about accurate language use? Does it really make a difference in how we think and act? Or should we relax and not take ourselves too seriously? What is your reasoning? Support your position with well-chosen evidence.

3. How does discipline of any sort make us stronger? What elements of discipline transfer to other activities in our lives? Choose an activity or event that required you to use some real discipline, and write an essay arguing for or against its general importance as a life skill.

4. Key U.S. cities are forming advisory committees to recommend some action in response to the insensitive use of language that leads to all kinds of aggressive behavior, including bullying, fighting, and suicide. You have been asked by your local city council to represent the college population on this committee. First, identify the dominant language problems in our country. Then write an essay introducing these problems and offering realistic solutions to them.

Before beginning your essay, you may want to consult the flowchart on page 451.

OPPOSING VIEWPOINTS

Social Media

The following essays take differing positions on the impact of social media on our culture today.

The first essay, by Josh Rose, argues that social media have a positive influence on society. Starting in 1995, Rose created some of the first episodic web shows on the Internet and, for the following five years, was part of the creative impetus behind some of the most popular online industries, ranging from entertainment to automotive. Currently, Rose is the Chief Creative Officer of Multi-Platform Campaigns at Weber Shandwick, an award-winning marketing firm, where he helps generate cross-media ideas for company brands. He has won several awards for his work. He currently lives in Los Angeles, where he is also a photographer.

Susan Tardanico, who argues that social media are "sabotaging real communication," began her professional life as a reporter, weekend anchor, and assistant assignment editor in the greater Boston area. In 1988, Tardanico began a 20-year tenure with Textron, where she became the first female and youngest executive to report to a division president. More recently, she is executive in residence at the Center for Creative Leadership, as well as founding partner and CEO of the Authentic Leadership LLC. Tardanico contributes regularly to *Forbes* magazine and is an adjunct faculty member of Georgetown and New York universities. She also works as a motivational speaker.

Preparing to Read

The following essays were first published in *Mashable* and *Forbes* magazine, respectively. They take opposing viewpoints on the many complex issues associated with social media. See where you stand in reference to these two viewpoints as you read their arguments.

Exploring Experience: Before you begin to read these essays, think about various social media and their effect on society: When is social media constructive? When is it destructive? How often do you consult social media in a typical day? What has social media added to our lives? What has it taken away?

LEARNING(ↄ)NLINE Go to whatever social media you use most often (Facebook, Twitter, Instagram, Snapchat, etc.), and reflect on the effects of these sources in your personal life. Do these forms of media make you feel more connected to or disconnected from the people around you?

Before reading these essays, you may want to consult the flowchart on page 448.

JOSH ROSE   (1971–   )

How Social Media Is Having a Positive Impact on Our Culture

Two events today, although worlds apart, seem inextricably tied   1
together. And the bond between them is as human as it is
electronic.

First, on my way to go sit down and read the newspaper at my coffee   2
shop, I got a message from my 10-year-old son, just saying good morning
and letting me know he was going to a birthday party today. I don't get to
see him all the time. He's growing up in two houses, as I did. But recently,
I handed down my old iPhone 3G to him to use basically as an iPod Touch.
We both installed an app called <u>Yak</u>, so we could communicate with each
other when we're apart.

The amount of calming satisfaction it gives me to be able to communicate   3
with him through technology is undeniably palpable and human. It's the
other side of the "I don't care what you ate for breakfast this morning" argument against the mundane broadcasting of social media. In this case, I absolutely care about this. I'd listen to him describe a piece of bacon and hang
on every word. Is it better than a conversation with "real words"? No. But
is it better than waiting two more days, when the mundane moment that I
long to hear about so much is gone? Yes. I guess one man's TMI is another
man's treasure. [1]

Moments later, I sat down and opened the paper. A headline immedi-   4
ately stood out: "In China, microblogs finding abducted kids" with the
subhead, "A 6-year-old who was snatched when he was 3 is discovered with
a family 800 miles away." Apparently, the occurrence of reclaimed children
through the use of China's version of <u>Twitter</u>—and other online forums—
has become triumphant news over there. I'm reading about the father's tears,
the boy's own confusing set of emotions, the rapt attention of the town and
country, and I'm again marveling at the human side of the Internet.

The Paradox of Online Closeness

I recently asked the question to my Facebook friends: "Twitter, Face-   5
book, Foursquare . . . is all this making you feel closer to people or farther

---

Thinking Critically

[1] What exactly does this sentence mean?

away?" It sparked a lot of responses and seemed to touch one of our generation's exposed nerves. What is the effect of the Internet and social media on
our humanity?

From the outside view, digital interactions appear to be cold and inhu-   6
man. There's no denying that. And without doubt, given the choice between
hugging someone and "poking" someone, I think we can all agree which
one feels better. The theme of the responses to my Facebook question
seemed to be summed up by my friend Jason, who wrote, "Closer to people
I'm far away from." Then, a minute later, he wrote, "but maybe farther from
the people I'm close enough to." And then he added, "I just got
confused." [2]

It *is* confusing. We live in this paradox now, where two seemingly con-   7
flicting realities exist side-by-side. Social media simultaneously draws us
nearer and distances us. But I think very often, we lament what we miss
and forget to admire what we've become. [3] And it's human nature to want
to reject the machine at the moment we feel it becoming ubiquitous. We've
seen it with the printing press, moving pictures, television, video games, and
just about any other advanced technology that captures our attention. What
romantic rituals of relationship and social interaction will die in the process?
Our hearts want to know.

In the *New Yorker* this week, Adam Gopnik's article "How the Internet   8
Gets Inside Us" explores this cultural truism in depth. It's a fantastic read
and should be mandatory for anyone in an online industry. He breaks down
a whole slew of new books on the subject and categorizes it all into three
viewpoints: "the Never-Betters, the Better-Nevers, and the Ever-Wasers." [4]
In short, those who see the current movement as good, bad, or normal. I
think we all know people from each camp. But ultimately, the last group is
the one best equipped to handle it all.

Filling in the Space with Connections

Another observation from the coffee shop: In my immediate vicinity, four   9
people are looking at screens, and four people are reading something on
paper. And I'm doing both. I see Facebook open on two screens, but I'm
sure at some point, it's been open on all of them. The dynamic in this coffee

---

Thinking Critically

[2] Why does the author's friend Jason say, "I just got confused"?

[3] What does Rose mean when he says, "We lament what we miss and forget to admire
what we've become"?

[4] Explain in your own words Gopnik's three categories that describe the current online
industry.

shop is quite a bit more revealing than any article or book. Think about the varied juxtapositions of physical and digital going on. People aren't giving up long-form reading, considered thinking, or social interactions. They are just filling all the space between. And even that's not entirely true as I watch the occasional stare out the window or long glance around the room.

The way people engage with the Internet and social media isn't like any kind of interaction we've ever seen before. It's like an intertwining sine wave [5] that touches in and out continuously. And the Internet itself is more complex and interesting than we often give it credit for. Consider peer-to-peer networking as just one example, where the tasks are distributed among the group to form a whole. It's practically a metaphor for the human mind. Or a township. Or a government. Or a family.   10

The Internet doesn't steal our humanity; it reflects it. The Internet doesn't get inside us; it shows what's inside us. And social media isn't cold; it's just complex and hard to define. I've always thought that you really see something's value when you try to destroy it. As we have now laid witness to in recent news, the Internet has quickly become the atom of cultural media, intertwined with our familial and cultural bonds, and destroyed only at great risk. I think if we search our own souls and consider our own personal way of navigating, we know this is as true personally as it is globally. The machine does not control us. It is a tool. As advanced today as a sharpened stick was a couple million years ago. Looked at through this lens, perhaps we should re-frame our discussions about technology from how it is changing us to how we are using it.   11

Thinking Critically

[5] in what ways is our interaction with the Internet "like an intertwining sine wave"?

SUSAN TARDANICO   (1970–   )

Is Social Media Sabotaging Real Communication?

On a crisp Friday afternoon last October, Sharon Seline exchanged   1
text messages with her daughter who was in college. They "chat-
ted" back and forth, mom asking how things were going and
daughter answering with positive statements followed by emoticons showing
smiles, b–i–g smiles and hearts. Happiness.

Later that night, her daughter attempted suicide.   2

In the days that followed, it came to light that she'd been holed up in   3
her dorm room, crying and showing signs of depression—a completely
different reality from the one that she conveyed in texts, Facebook posts,
and tweets.

As human beings, our only real method of connection is through authen-   4
tic communication. [1] Studies show that only 7% of communication is based
on the written or verbal word. A whopping 93% is based on nonverbal body
language. Indeed, it's only when we can hear a tone of voice or look into
someone's eyes that we're able to know when "I'm fine" doesn't mean
they're fine at all or when "I'm in" doesn't mean they're bought in at all.

This is where social media gets dicey. [2] Awash in technology, anyone can   5
hide behind the text, the e-mail, the Facebook post or the tweet, projecting
any image they want and creating an illusion of their choosing. They can
be whoever they want to be. And without the ability to receive nonverbal
cues, their audiences are none the wiser.

This presents an unprecedented paradox. [3] With all the powerful social   6
technologies at our fingertips, we are more connected—and potentially
more *disconnected*—than ever before.

Every relevant metric shows that we are interacting at breakneck speed   7
and frequency through social media. But are we *really* communicating? With
93% of our communication context stripped away, we are now attempting
to forge relationships and make decisions based on phrases. Abbreviations.
Snippets. Emoticons. Which may or may not be accurate representations
of the truth.

Thinking Critically

[1] What is "authentic communication" for Tardanico?
[2] When does social media "get dicey"?
[3] What is this paradox that Tardanico is referring to?

A New Set of Communication Barriers

Social technologies have broken the barriers of space and time, enabling   8
us to interact 24/7 with more people than ever before. But like any revolutionary concept, it has spawned a set of new barriers and threats. Is the focus
now on communication *quantity* versus quality? *Superficiality* versus authen-
ticity? In an ironic twist, social media has the potential to make us *less* social,
a surrogate for the real thing. For it to be a truly effective communication
vehicle, all parties bear a responsibility to be genuine, accurate, and not allow
it to replace human contact altogether.

In the workplace, the use of electronic communication has overtaken   9
face-to-face and voice-to-voice communication by a wide margin. This
major shift has been driven by two major forces: the speed/geographic dis-
persion of business and the lack of comfort with traditional interpersonal
communication among a growing segment of our employee population—
Gen Y and Millennials. Studies show that these generations—which will
comprise more than 50% of the workforce by 2020—would prefer to use
instant messaging or other social media than stop by an office and talk with
someone. This new communication preference is one of the "generational
gaps" plaguing organizations [4] as Boomers try to manage to a new set of
expectations and norms in their younger employees, and vice versa.

With these two trends at play, leaders must consider the impact on busi-   10
ness relationships and the ability to effectively collaborate, build trust, and
create employee engagement and loyalty.

Further, because most business communication is now done via e-mails,   11
texts, instant messaging, intranets, blogs, websites and other technology-
enabled media—*sans* body language—the potential for misinterpretation is
growing. Rushed and stressed, people often do not take the time to consider
the nuances of their writing. Conflicts explode over a tone of an e-mail, or
that all-important cc: list. When someone writes a text in all capital letters,
does it mean they're yelling? Are one- or two-word responses a sign that the
person doesn't want to engage? On the flip side, does a smiley face or an
acknowledgement of agreement really mean they're bought in and aligned?
Conclusions are drawn on frighteningly little information.

We Need a New Golf Course

The idea of doing business on the golf course seems anachronistic these   12
days, but the reason why the concept became so iconic is because it proved

---

Thinking Critically

[4] What is the "generational gap" that Tardanico is talking about here?

that when colleagues spend personal time together—*face to face*—more progress can be made, deals can get done and relationships can deepen, allowing the colleagues to function more effectively off the course.

This concept has been proven over and over again with correlations 13 between face-to-face relationship-building and employee engagement and loyalty. And years ago, we learned about the power of "Management By Walking Around" in Tom Peters' groundbreaking book *In Search of Excellence.*

So in this wired world, what's our new golf course? How do we com- 14 municate effectively and build deeper, more authentic relationships when we have only words (truncated at best) instead of voice, face and body expression to get all the important and powerful nuances that often belie the words?

UNDERSTANDING DETAILS

1. According to Josh Rose, what characterizes "the human side of the Internet" (paragraph 5? How can it be a positive force in our lives?
2. Why is social media so valuable to Rose?
3. What does Tardanico say is "one of the generational gaps" (paragraph 9) in communication?
4. According to Tardanico, how is "the potential for misinterpretation" (paragraph 11) growing?

READING CRITICALLY

5. What does Rose mean by "The Internet doesn't steal our humanity; it reflects it" (paragraph 11)?
6. Both authors refer to a similar paradox in social media. Explain this paradox from each of their perspectives.
7. Why do you think body language plays such a large part in communication?
8. What does Tardanico mean when she says, "All parties bear a responsibility to be genuine, accurate, and not allow it to replace human contact altogether" (paragraph 4)?

DISCOVERING RHETORICAL STRATEGIES

9. Do both authors use enough examples to prove their points? Cite instances from each essay to support your answer.
10. These two authors make their points in very similar writing voices. Describe the tone or mood of each essay, and explain whether you think that particular voice is effective or not for the author's purpose.
11. Rose compares the interaction on the Internet to "an intertwining sine wave" (paragraph 10); Tardanico claims we need "a new golf course" in our "wired world" (paragraph 14). How do these two metaphors further each of these arguments? Are they effective choices for their messages?

12. What other rhetorical strategies does each essay use to make its point? Give examples of each strategy.

MAKING CONNECTIONS

13. Briefly summarize the arguments advanced by Rose and Tardanico about social media. Which point of view comes closest to your own? Explain your reasoning.
14. If Rose and Tardanico were having a conversation with Nicholas Carr ("The Internet is Making Us Stupid") about the Internet, on which topics would they agree? On which would they disagree?
15. Imagine that Rose and Tardanico are having a round-table discussion about communication in college with Sandra Cisneros ("Only Daughter"), Richard Rodriguez ("Public and Private Language"), Leigh Richards ("What Are the Types of Communication in Business"), and/or Stephanie Ericsson ("The Ways We Lie"). Which of these authors would speak most vigorously about the importance of communication in reference to success in college? Who would claim that communication is secondary to raw productivity in college? Where do you fall on this continuum?

IDEAS FOR DISCUSSION/WRITING

Preparing to Write

Write freely about your views on the role of social media in society today: What do social media sources offer us? In what ways do these media weaken human communication? In what ways do they strengthen it? What does social media allow us to do in our civilization that would not be possible without it?

Choosing a Topic   MyWritingLab™

1. **LEARNING⏻NLINE** Return to the Learning Online question in Preparing to Read—whether or not social media make you feel more connected or disconnected from the people around you. After reading both of these essays, has your opinion changed? Locate posts on your favorite form of social media that make you feel particularly connected to a friend or family member. Then, find posts that make you feel disconnected from the world around you. Write an essay that answers the following question: Does social media connect or alienate us from the world around us? Provide ample evidence to support your claim.
2. When to start using social media and how long to use social media each day are boundaries that parents must establish for their children. What is your opinion on this issue? Use facts and statistics from these two essays to support your point of view.
3. Using information furnished by Rose and Tardanico, write an essay that explains what you think the effect of the Internet is on our humanity. In addressing this issue, argue for a specific balance of social networking and live interaction with people to ensure our ability to be decent, caring, sensitive members of the human race.

4. Cyberbullying is a real danger in the world of social networking today. Your local library is sponsoring a writing contest on this topic with a first-place prize of $1,000. All contestants must write an essay on the following topic: "How can we convince high school students to use social media responsibly and never to resort to cyberbullying?" Write an essay on this topic that would win the first-place award.

Before beginning your essay, you may want to consult the flowchart on page 451.

Postconviction DNA Testing

The following three essays each offer a different viewpoint on the controversial question of whether DNA testing, also called "genetic fingerprinting," should be used consistently in legal cases.

Tim O'Brien, who argues that the use of DNA should be encouraged, is an attorney and award-winning journalist who covered the Supreme Court for more than twenty-two years. He also served as the principal Washington correspondent for CNN's *Moneyline News Hour*. He is now serving as distinguished visiting professor of law at Hofstra University.

James Dao, who suggests in his article that DNA testing is helpful in some cases and not in others, has been a writer for *The New York Times* since 1992. Currently, Dao is deputy editor on the National Desk and oversees the coverage of a variety of political and social topics, ranging from health care and marijuana legalization to prisons and state finances.

Peter Roff, who argues against the widespread use of DNA testing, has over 30 years experience in Washington, D.C. as a writer, blogger, editor, and speech writer. He is a contributing editor for *U.S. News and World Report* and is a founder and Senior Fellow at Frontiers of Freedom, an organization that promotes reform in the U.S. educational system.

Preparing to Read

Each of the next three essays takes a different stand on DNA: One talks about using DNA to prove someone's innocence; the second tells us how DNA testing cleared one convict and implicated another; and the third argues for limiting DNA testing on previously convicted prisoners.

Exploring Experience: As you prepare to read these essays, share with the rest of your class what you know about DNA: What is DNA? What are the benefits and drawbacks of DNA testing? What is the source of your information? Why is DNA testing such an interesting feature of most investigations?

LEARNING◑NLINE Before you read the following essays, visit the Death Penalty Information Center website at www.deathpenaltyinfo.org. Search "Fact Sheet," and choose deathpenaltyinfo.org/FactSheet.pdf. Scroll through the statistics regarding the number of death penalty executions that have taken place over the past several years. Note the number of people currently on death row in each state. What are your thoughts about this information? What does public opinion say about the death penalty in the final chart?

Before reading these essays, you may want to consult the flowchart on page 448.

TIM O'BRIEN   (1946–   )

Postconviction DNA Testing Should Be Encouraged

M y editors and I thought it was a good story: the black, one-eyed, 1
homosexual rapist who claimed it was a case of mistaken identity.
P.S.: He also walked with a limp. [1]

The U.S. Supreme Court had agreed to review the case in its 1988 term, 2
because it had raised an important constitutional question: Do the police
have any obligation to preserve potentially exculpatory evidence?

The Case of Larry Youngblood

The defendant, Larry Youngblood, had been convicted of abducting a 3
10-year-old boy from a church carnival and repeatedly sodomizing him.
Youngblood had argued that if the police had preserved semen samples taken
from the boy's clothing, DNA tests would have shown they had arrested the
wrong man.

Never mind that the tests in question weren't ordinarily available at the 4
time of the trial (although they are now routine). Never mind that Youngblood fit the description provided by the victim or that the traumatized child
also identified Youngblood in court as the perpetrator. Never mind that the
evidence appeared so overwhelming that it took the jury only 40 minutes
to convict Youngblood and send him on his way to a 10-year prison term.

The legal issue the case raised was significant; it was to resonate years later 5
in the O.J. Simpson case[1] and doubtless many other lesser cases. In my heart,
I questioned the judgment of the public defenders who would bring such
an important issue to the Supreme Court with such an obviously guilty
defendant. If, as Oliver Wendell Holmes put it, hard cases make bad law,
then what do bad cases make? [2]

But public defenders Dan Davis and Carol Witteis seemed less concerned 6
with the precedent the court might set than with winning freedom for their
client. Could they possibly believe he was really innocent? Yes, without a
doubt, they both said. Defense lawyers can believe, or appear to believe,
anything.

Thinking Critically

[1] Do you think this is a good beginning to the essay? Why or why not?

[2] What does this Oliver Wendell Holmes maxim mean to you? Paraphrase it in your own
words.

Supreme Court justices are supposed to decide cases on the basis of the   7
law, but like all humans, they too can be influenced by the facts. And the
facts in this case couldn't have been worse for Youngblood. Moreover, he
lived alone, had a history of mental illness and had had previous run-ins with
the law.

As expected, the Supreme Court upheld Youngblood's conviction, decid-   8
ing his fate with exceptional speed, just as the jury had two years earlier.
Only three justices dissented, with the late Harry Blackmun writing that
"the Constitution requires a fair trial, not merely a 'good faith' try at a fair
trial."

Mistaken Identity

A good story? We didn't know the half of it. [In August 2000] Young-   9
blood's conviction was vacated—thrown out by the Pima County Superior
Court in Tucson. While the small amount of semen that was preserved was
insufficient for reliable testing at the time of the appeal, new testing procedures that only recently became available were conducted by the Tucson
police. They showed conclusively what attorneys Witteis and Davis knew
all along: The police really did have the wrong man. It was a case of mistaken identity. ❸

Youngblood may have been less a victim of bad facts than of societal   10
biases that can seep into and poison the criminal justice process. Could his
race have been a factor? His multiple disabilities, mental and physical? His
perceived sexual orientation? The fact that he had been accused of a hor-
rendous crime that cried out for retribution?

There is no scientific way to quantify the effects of these illicit consider-   11
ations in Youngblood's case, nor anyone else's for that matter. And the
Supreme Court, in another case, has ruled that even a statistical probability
of bias is insufficient to set aside a conviction, even a death sentence. DNA
testing, by providing statistical proof of innocence (or guilt), may be the only
way to effectively offset invidious biases.

Yet at every turn prosecutors are resisting the use of DNA tests whenever   12
it might mean reopening an old case. There are now hundreds of inmates
on death row who claim DNA tests would show they were not guilty of the
crimes for which they were convicted. Most, perhaps even all, are mistaken.
But in light of what happened to Larry Youngblood, the complaints that
such tests are too expensive and time-consuming or that a jury's verdict must

---

Thinking Critically

❸ How did the newly analyzed DNA evidence save this particular defendant?

be accorded finality ring hollow indeed. The Tucson police have graciously conceded that it was "unfortunate" Youngblood spent so much time incarcerated for a crime he didn't commit, but they say they did what they thought was right at the time. Youngblood is angry to have been robbed of "the best part of my life," and he wants to sue the police. All agree it should not have happened.

To prevent it from happening again, courts must be receptive to any 13 credible claim that new tests might prove the actual innocence of one who has already been convicted. Had Larry Youngblood been charged with first degree murder, he'd probably be dead now. ◆⁴

Note

1. In 1995 former football star O.J. Simpson was found not guilty of murdering his ex-wife and her friend. Controversies over evidence had been a significant factor in the murder trial.

Thinking Critically

④ How convincing is this single example? Would you vote to require DNA testing for all such offenses based on this one case? Why or why not?

JAMES DAO   (1942–   )

In Same Case, DNA Clears Convict and Finds Suspect

I n his final years in prison, Kirk Bloodsworth had a passing acquaintance   1
with a fellow inmate, Kimberly Shay Ruffner. Mr. Bloodsworth, a
prison librarian, delivered books to Mr. Ruffner. Sometimes they lifted
weights together. But Mr. Bloodsworth said Mr. Ruffner seemed to behave
"kind of peculiar" when they were together.

Mr. Bloodsworth may now know the reason why. This morning, the   2
police in Baltimore County charged Mr. Ruffner in the murder and rape of
a 9-year-old in 1984, Dawn Hamilton, the very crime that Mr. Bloodsworth
was serving time for when he met Mr. Ruffner.

"I'm so happy," said Mr. Bloodsworth, 43, a fisherman from Cambridge,   3
Md. "This tells the world that I'm innocent."

The charges against Mr. Ruffner open a new chapter in a case that has   4
become a prime example of the two-edged nature of DNA testing: not only
as a means of clearing the wrongly accused, but also of identifying new
suspects in cold cases. 1

In 1993, Mr. Bloodsworth became the first person in the nation con-   5
victed in a death penalty case to be exonerated through DNA testing, which
eliminated him as a source of semen stains on the girl's underpants. He had
served nine years in prison, including two on death row, when he was
released by a judge and pardoned by the governor.

Last spring, a Baltimore County forensic biologist who was studying   6
evidence from the case found stains on a sheet that had not been analyzed,
a spokesman for the Police Department said. Investigators conducted DNA
tests on the stains and ran the results through a national database last month.
Mr. Ruffner's name popped up.

The police did not have to go far to charge Mr. Ruffner. He was still   7
serving time for attempted rape and attempted murder in the prison in
Baltimore where he had met Mr. Bloodsworth.

Defense lawyers say they hope the dual use of DNA evidence in the case   8
will reduce resistance among prosecutors to allow prisoners to challenge

---

Thinking Critically

1 What is the "two-edged nature" of DNA testing? In which of these two situations is
DNA testing more valuable? Explain your reasoning.

convictions with DNA tests. They say the case demonstrates that DNA can not only prove innocence, but also pinpoint culprits. ❷

"Maryland, and the nation, would be remiss if we did not learn from today's news," said Peter Loge, director of the Criminal Justice Reform Education Fund, which has championed Mr. Bloodsworth's case. 9

The new charges were filed at a crucial time in a debate in Florida over a law from 2001 that will soon bar prisoners from seeking DNA testing for old cases. The law set Oct. 1 as the deadline for such requests. It also allows the destruction of DNA evidence, except in death penalty cases. 10

Defense lawyers contend that the Hamilton case clearly shows how DNA can be used to reopen cold cases. If a law like Florida's had been in effect in Maryland 12 years ago, they say, Mr. Bloodsworth would still be behind bars. 11

"This should be a cautionary tale to those in Florida who are insisting on this deadline for destroying biological evidence," said Barry Scheck, codirector of the Innocence Project at the Benjamin L. Cardozo Law School in Manhattan. "It's a law enforcement calamity." 12

Many prosecutors contend that DNA testing, though reliable, is not a sure-fire way to prove innocence where there is other evidence of guilt. DNA testing, they say, should be seen as only one piece of a bigger evidentiary puzzle. ❸ 13

"I don't know of many people in my business who don't see the accuracy of DNA testing," George W. Clarke, deputy district attorney for San Diego County, said. "It's more the significance of those results. Those questions aren't about to go away." 14

For Mr. Bloodsworth, today's developments had a far more personal significance. Though he was pardoned a decade ago, he said some people had continued to view him as a child murderer. Worse, he feared that prosecutors remained convinced of his guilt and might try to bring new charges against him. 15

So after the assistant state's attorney who had prosecuted him, Ann Brobst, called him on Thursday night to ask for a meeting, Mr. Bloodsworth and his wife could not sleep. 16

"We were prepared for anything," Mr. Bloodsworth's lawyer, Deborah Crandall, said. 17

Instead, in a meeting this morning at a Burger King, Ms. Brobst told Mr. Bloodsworth of the DNA evidence against Mr. Ruffner and apologized 18

Thinking Critically

❷ In this particular case, how did DNA testing "prove innocence" and "pinpoint" a culprit?

❸ Do you agree that DNA testing should be seen "as only one piece of a bigger evidentiary puzzle," or should it be the most important evidence in a court case?

for wrongly prosecuting him. Mr. Bloodsworth, who has become an out-spoken advocate for reforming federal death penalty laws, said he cried and then hugged Ms. Brobst.

In an interview, the state's attorney for Baltimore County, Sandra A. O'Connor, said that the police and prosecutors had acted responsibly in the case, but that DNA technology did not exist at the time of Mr. Blood-sworth's trial. What did exist were the statements of five witnesses who said they saw him with the girl on the day she was killed.   19

"Obviously," Ms. O'Connor said, "the system failed in the case of Mr. Bloodsworth." ◆[4]   20

Thinking Critically

[4] How often do you think our judicial system fails? What are the most serious flaws of this system? What can we do about them?

PETER ROFF   (1966–   )

Postconviction DNA Testing Should Not Be Encouraged

T o deprive an individual of their liberty—even for a short time—is   1
be done with the utmost care. The Anglo-American system of
jurisprudence gives every benefit of every doubt to the accused. At trial, the
state must prove guilt beyond a reasonable doubt while the accused is pre-
sumed to be innocent.

What Justice Oliver Wendell Holmes said in defense of the Fourth   2
Amendment is generally true where the free exercise of liberty is at issue:
"It is less evil that some criminals should escape than that the government
should play an ignoble part (in gathering evidence)." [1]

This does not, however, require evidence be re-examined years after the   3
fact because the science changes.

Prisons Full of Innocent People?

Technology may have advanced to the point where certain types of evi-   4
dence may conclusively identify a guilty party. This is just part of the entire
equation, admittedly an important part. Yet the idea that many of the
inmates on death row or serving long sentences could be freed by new DNA
evidence has been ingrained in the American mind by Hollywood. While
dramatic, it is hardly true and runs counter to the argument, most often
heard from inmates and their lawyers that the prisons are full of innocent
people, wrongfully convicted.

While the presence of DNA at a crime scene can be used to establish   5
guilt in a court of law, the converse is not automatically true. The absence
of a particular individual's DNA at a crime scene is not alone proof of
their innocence. [2] Prosecutors and legislators arguing against the unlimited
opportunity for taxpayer-funded DNA tests in pursuit of the exoneration of
convicted felons are correct in their objections.

Thinking Critically

[1] What does "ignoble" mean? Paraphrase this quotation in your own words. Do you agree
with it? Why or why not?

[2] Can you think of a recent court case in which the absence of DNA was an important
piece of the evidence? How might the case have turned out if DNA had been available?

It is the entire body of evidence that must be considered, not just the   6
results of lab tests performed on old clothing.

Doubtful Evidence

The rights of the accused are protected in the courtroom, often at the   7
expense of the victims'. Physical evidence, eyewitness testimony and
evidence often circumstantial in nature but attesting to means, motive, and
opportunity are considered during trial under accepted rules of evidence.
Can that chain of evidence still be as reliable 10, 15, or 20 years after the
fact? It is doubtful. ❸

Can the state, fairly and years later, represent the interests of the victim   8
and society as a whole if the judicial system lets doubt—which increases over
time—adhere to the benefit of the accused, especially when DNA tests often
produce more doubt than proof?

In the same way repeated death penalty appeals slowed the wheels of   9
justice for many years, these DNA requests will tax the already overburdened
legal system, depriving the victims and the wrongfully accused of their day
in court in a timely manner.

The requests for these tests amount more to lawyerly shams rather [than   10
to] efforts to overcome justice denied. The state is right to limit them.

UNDERSTANDING DETAILS

1. According to Tim O'Brien, what facts worked against Youngblood in his trial?
2. How did "the system" fail in Bloodsworth's case (Dao, paragraph 20)?
3. What is Roff's main argument in his essay?
4. Explain Oliver Wendell Holmes's comment in paragraph 2 of the Roff essay:
   "It is less evil that some criminals should escape than that the government
   should play an ignoble part (in gathering evidence)."

READING CRITICALLY

5. Why does Tim O'Brien say that Youngblood would probably be dead if he had
   been charged with first-degree murder?
6. Why was the Hamilton case (Dao) a landmark in DNA testing?
7. Why would Bloodsworth still be behind bars if the Florida law about DNA
   testing were applied to Maryland?
8. In what ways are death penalty appeals and DNA requests similar?

Thinking Critically

❸ What point is the author making about the length of time from the original crime and
the reliability of the evidence?

DISCOVERING RHETORICAL STRATEGIES

9. In paragraph 4, O'Brien writes a series of sentences starting with "Never mind." What effect does this group of sentences have on the rest of the essay? How does this paragraph stand apart from the other paragraphs?
10. Is the opening paragraph of the Dao essay effective? Why or why not?
11. Roff includes two subheadings in his essay. In what ways do they help you move logically through his essay?
12. Why does Roff refer to Hollywood in his essay?

MAKING CONNECTIONS

13. Briefly summarize the arguments advanced by O'Brien, Dao, and Roff concerning the use of DNA testing. Which point of view comes closest to your own? Why?
14. Compare and contrast the ways in which all three authors use examples in their essays. Who do you think uses examples most skillfully? What brought you to this conclusion?
15. Imagine that Kimberly Wozencraft ("Notes from the Country Club") and/or Brent Staples ("A Brother's Murder") were having a discussion with O'Brien, Dao, and Roff about the necessity of presenting physical evidence in a court of law. Which authors would argue most forcefully that such evidence must be displayed before a conviction can be attained? Why?

IDEAS FOR DISCUSSION/WRITING

Preparing to Write

Write freely about your knowledge of DNA testing after reading these essays: What are its advantages? Its disadvantages? Its limitations? Why is the public so interested in its use? Do you think DNA testing will deter criminals in any way? Do all the detective shows on television represent DNA and its usefulness fairly?

Choosing a Topic

MyWritingLab™

1. **LEARNING◯NLINE** Return to the Death Penalty Information Center (www.deathpenaltyinfo.org), and search "Innocence Project." Scroll down the page to see various articles on people found innocent based on DNA results. Then read some of these stories about people who were wrongly convicted because DNA testing was not available at the time of their trials. Notice the appeals to logic (logos) in the overall statistics and the appeals to emotion and character (pathos and ethos) in the individual stories. Choose one of the personal stories to use for information, and write a letter to a defense attorney requesting that he or she reopen the case to consider new DNA evidence. Try to incorporate all three appeals—to logos, pathos, and ethos—in your letter.
2. DNA testing is sensationalized on *detective* television shows such as *CSI* and *Law and Order* to the point that real-life juries often expect such conclusive evidence

when they serve on a case. How might these expectations affect our judicial system? To what extent does Hollywood actually influence what goes on in our courtrooms? Argue for or against putting these unrealistic shows on the air.

3. You have been asked to write a response to Roff's essay for publication as a companion piece. Using his format, develop your own argument for or against limiting DNA testing. Research this issue on the Internet a bit before you begin to write.

4. Americans are currently fascinated with investigative TV shows. *CSI, Law and Order,* and *Forensic Files* are at the top of the Nielsen ratings. Do you see any connection between the increasing popularity of these shows and the violent crime rate in the United States today? Take a stand for or against the airing of this type of show as it relates to crime.

Before beginning your essay, you may want to consult the flowchart on page 451.

Chapter Writing Assignments

Practicing Argument/Persuasion

1. What are the primary issues surrounding the misuse of social networking? Why are these problems so prominent in our culture? How can we control these difficulties? Write an essay that presents an argument for taking a particular approach to the problems related to social media in our country.

2. Many people argue that the media actually run the elections in the United States. What is your opinion on this issue? What should be the role of the media in the political arena? How should we force them to limit themselves to this role? In what ways do the media help us understand certain important issues? In what ways do they hinder our understanding? Write an essay in which you argue for a specific relationship between the media and politics, including elections, referendums, and bond issues. Support your position with concrete details.

3. Look up the term *justice* in the dictionary. Ask a variety of people about their positive and negative responses to our judicial system. Write an essay in which you explain your position on justice, using your interviews as background and support.

Exploring Ideas

4. Do you think people are prone to violence because of inborn qualities or because of learned behavior? Why are some people violent while others are not? Where, in your opinion, does this difference come from—nature or nurture?

5. Do you think any limits should be put on free speech? If so, what should these limits be? If not, why not? What is the reasoning behind your opinion? Write an essay supporting your position with examples.

6. American society seems to be prone to obsessions—for example, sickness, obesity, anorexia, drugs, alcohol, and the like. Write an essay explaining why you think this is so. What suggestions do you have for curbing these tendencies? Be sure to include specific examples to support your argument.

Analyzing Visual Images

David Grossman/Alamy.

7. Choose a current issue, and design several slogans that would effectively argue your point of view. Discuss in essay form how effectively these slogans would persuade others.

8. Look at the picture on page 447 at the beginning of this chapter, which captures the Civil Rights movement and the struggle for equal rights. Many today would argue that racism is no longer an issue and that equal rights have, in fact, been granted to all races, genders, religious sects, etc. Argue for or against this statement, using examples from your own experience, including your reading and observations, to support your claim.

Composing in Different Genres

9. Multimedia: Create an advertisement for your favorite extracurricular activity (hobby, pastime, sport). You can use a combination of words and graphics, but make sure it strikes an effective balance among ethos, pathos, and logos for an audience of college students.

10. Multigenre: Write a realistic, well-argued letter inquiring about an available job you would like to have. Consult the campus newspaper, the local news, or an employment agency for possible listings. Gather

your thoughts about the qualifications for the position and your target audience before you begin to write.

Writing from Sources

For detailed information on writing from sources, see Part III.

11. Consider the different belief systems and practices associated with holistic and Western medicines. Which approach do you think is the healthiest? Citing research from two to three sources, write a well-documented essay arguing your position on this topic.

12. Bullying has become almost epidemic among today's teens and college students. Think of another problem that young people in the United States are battling, such as eating disorders or obesity. Research the topic, and then write a convincing essay that discusses the importance of this issue and the actions you feel are necessary to solve the problem.

MyWritingLab™ Visit Ch. 12. Argument and Persuasion: Inciting People to Thought or Action in *MyWritingLab* to complete the writing assignments and test your understanding of the chapter learning objectives.

Chapter 13

WRITING IN DIFFERENT GENRES
Combining Rhetorical Modes

OBJECTIVES

After completing this chapter, you will be able to do the following:
- Explore the relationships among thinking, reading, and writing;
- Read and appreciate different genres;
- Observe various rhetorical modes working together.

In each of the preceding chapters, although each essay demonstrated several rhetorical modes, we examined a single mode to discover how that pattern worked in both reading and writing. As the book progressed, the rhetorical strategies became more complex and more interdependent.

Our primary purpose in this text has been to demonstrate how thinking, reading, and writing work together as fine machinery to help all of us function as intelligent, productive human beings. Part I analyzes the relationships among thinking, reading, and writing, whereas Part II reveals the crucial interdependence of these skills and ends with this chapter, which features these skills at work in five different genres: autobiography, speech, poetry, fiction, and photography.

These final reading selections are offered here as a review of your work in this text, so let your mind run freely through this material as you recall in a leisurely way what you have learned in the previous chapters. These readings bring together the theoretical framework of this book as they illustrate how thinking, reading, and writing inform each other and work together to make meaning. They also integrate the rhetorical patterns in such a way that each reading selection is a complex blend of the various modes, thereby providing a summary of the strategies you have been studying in this text.

AUTOBIOGRAPHY

RICHARD WRIGHT   (1908–1960)

The Library Card

One morning I arrived early at work and went into the bank lobby where the Negro porter was mopping. I stood at a counter and picked up the Memphis *Commercial Appeal* and began my free reading of the press. I came finally to the editorial page and saw an article dealing with one H. L. Mencken. I knew by hearsay that he was the editor of the *American Mercury,* but aside from that I knew nothing about him. The article was a furious denunciation of Mencken, concluding with one, hot, short sentence: Mencken is a fool.

I wondered what on earth this Mencken had done to call down upon him the scorn of the South. The only people I had ever heard denounced in the South were Negroes, and this man was not a Negro. Then what ideas did Mencken hold that made a newspaper like the *Commercial Appeal* castigate him publicly? Undoubtedly he must be advocating ideas that the South did not like. Were there, then, people other than Negroes who criticized the South? I knew that during the Civil War the South had hated northern whites, but I had not encountered such hate during my life. Knowing no more of Mencken than I did at that moment, I felt a vague sympathy for him. Had not the South, which had assigned me the role of a nonman, cast at him its hardest words?

Now, how could I find out about this Mencken? There was a huge library near the riverfront, but I knew that Negroes were not allowed to patronize its shelves any more than they were the parks and playgrounds of the city. I had gone into the library several times to get books for the white men on the job. Which of them would now help me to get books? And how could I read them without causing concern to the white men with whom I worked? I had so far been successful in hiding my thoughts and feelings from them, but I knew that I would create hostility if I went about the business of reading in a clumsy way.

I weighed the personalities of the men on the job. There was Don, a Jew; but I distrusted him. His position was not much better than mine and I knew that he was uneasy and insecure; he had always treated me in an off-hand, bantering way that barely concealed his contempt. I was afraid to ask him to help me get books; his frantic desire to demonstrate a racial solidarity with the whites against Negroes might make him betray me.

Then how about the boss? No, he was a Baptist and I had the suspicion 5
that he would not be quite able to comprehend why a black boy would want
to read Mencken. There were other white men on the job whose attitudes
showed clearly that they were Kluxers or sympathizers, and they were out
of the question.

There remained only one man whose attitude did not fit into an anti- 6
Negro category, for I had heard the white men refer to him as a "Pope
lover." He was an Irish Catholic and was hated by the white Southerners.
I knew that he read books, because I had got him volumes from the library
several times. Since he, too, was an object of hatred, I felt that he might
refuse me but would hardly betray me. I hesitated, weighing and balancing
the imponderable realities.

One morning I paused before the Catholic fellow's desk.   7

"I want to ask you a favor," I whispered to him.   8

"What is it?"   9

"I want to read. I can't get books from the library. I wonder if you'd let 10
me use your card?"

He looked at me suspiciously.   11

"My card is full most of the time," he said.   12

"I see," I said and waited, posing my question silently.   13

"You're not trying to get me into trouble, are you, boy?" He asked, star- 14
ing at me.

"Oh, no sir."   15

"What book do you want?"   16

"A book by H. L. Mencken."   17

"Which one?"   18

"I don't know. Has he written more than one?"   19

"He has written several."   20

"I didn't know that."   21

"What makes you want to read Mencken?"   22

"Oh, I just saw his name in the newspaper," I said.   23

"It's good of you to want to read," he said. "But you ought to read the 24
right things."

I said nothing. Would he want to supervise my reading?   25

"Let me think," he said. "I'll figure out something."   26

I turned from him and he called me back. He stared at me quizzically.   27

"Richard, don't mention this to the other white men," he said.   28

"I understand," I said. "I won't say a word."   29

A few days later he called me to him.   30

"I've got a card in my wife's name," he said. "Here's mine."   31

"Thank you, sir."   32

"Do you think you can manage it?"   33

"I'll manage fine," I said.   34

"If they suspect you, you'll get in trouble," he said.   35

"I'll write the same kind of notes to the library that you wrote when you   36
sent me for books," I told him. "I'll sign your name."

He laughed.   37

"Go ahead. Let me see what you get," he said.   38

That afternoon I addressed myself to forging a note. Now, what were the   39
names of books written by H. L. Mencken? I did not know any of them. I
finally wrote what I thought would be a foolproof note: *Dear Madam: Will
you please let this nigger boy*—I used the word "nigger" to make the librarian
feel that I could not possibly be the author of the note—*have some books by
H. L. Mencken?* I forged the white man's name.

I entered the library as I had always done when on errands for whites,   40
but I felt that I would somehow slip up and betray myself. I doffed my hat,
stood a respectful distance from the desk, looked as unbookish as possible,
and waited for the white patrons to be taken care of. When the desk was
clear of people, I still waited. The white librarian looked at me.

"What do you want, boy?"   41

As though I did not possess the power of speech, I stepped forward and   42
simply handed her the forged note, not parting my lips.

"What books by Mencken does he want?" she asked.   43

"I don't know, ma'am," I said, avoiding her eyes.   44

"Who gave you this card?"   45

"Mr. Falk," I said.   46

"Where is he?"   47

"He's at work, at the M——— Optical Company," I said. "I've been in   48
here for him before."

"I remember," the woman said. "But he never wrote notes like this."   49

Oh, God, she's suspicious. Perhaps she would not let me have the books?   50
If she had turned her back at that moment, I would have ducked out the
door and never gone back. Then I thought of a bold idea.

"You can call him up, ma'am," I said, my heart pounding.   51

"You're not using these books, are you?" she asked pointedly.   52

"Oh, no, ma'am. I can't read," I said.   53

"I don't know what he wants by Mencken," she said under her breath.   54

I knew now that I had won; she was thinking of other things and the race   55
question had gone out of her mind. She went to the shelves. Once or twice
she looked over her shoulder at me, as though she was still doubtful. Finally
she came forward with two books in her hand.

"I'm sending him two books," she said. "But tell Mr. Falk to come in   56
next time, or send me the names of the books he wants. I don't know what
he wants to read."

I said nothing. She stamped the card and handed me the books. Not   57
daring to glance at them, I went out of the library, fearing that the woman
would call me back for further questioning. A block away from the library
I opened one of the books and read a title: *A Book of Prefaces.* I was nearing
my nineteenth birthday and I did not know how to pronounce the word
"preface." I thumbed the pages and saw strange words and strange names.
I shook my head, disappointed. I looked at the other book; it was called
Prejudices. I knew what that word meant; I had heard it all my life. And
right off I was on guard against Mencken's books. Why would a man want
to call a book *Prejudices?* The word was so stained with all my memories of
racial hate that I could not conceive of anybody using it for a title. Perhaps
I had made a mistake about Mencken? A man who had prejudices must
be wrong.

When I showed the books to Mr. Falk, he looked at me and frowned.   58

"That librarian might telephone you," I warned him.   59

"That's all right," he said. "But when you're through reading those books,   60
I want you to tell me what you get out of them."

That night in my rented room, while letting the hot water run over my   61
can of pork and beans in the sink, I opened *A Book of Prefaces* and began to
read. I was jarred and shocked by the style, the clear, clean, sweeping
sentences. Why did he write like that? And how did one write like that?
I pictured the man as a raging demon, slashing with his pen, consumed with
hate, denouncing everything American, extolling everything European or
German, laughing at the weaknesses of people, mocking God, authority.
What was this? I stood up, trying to realize what reality lay behind the meaning of the words. . . . Yes, this man was fighting, fighting with words. He
was using words as a weapon, using them as one would use a club. Could
words be weapons? Well, yes, for here they were. Then, maybe, perhaps, I
could use them as a weapon? No. It frightened me. I read on and what
amazed me was not what he said, but how on earth anybody had the courage to say it.

Occasionally I glanced up to reassure myself that I was alone in the room.   62
Who were these men about whom Mencken was talking so passionately?
Who was Anatole France? Joseph Conrad? Sinclair Lewis, Sherwood Ander-
son, Dostoevski, George Moore, Gustave Flaubert, Maupassant, Tolstoy,
Frank Harris, Mark Twain, Thomas Hardy, Arnold Bennett, Stephen Crane,
Zola, Norris, Gorky, Bergson, Ibsen, Balzac, Bernard Shaw, Dumas, Poe,
Thomas Mann, O. Henry, Dreiser, H. G. Wells, Gogol, T. S. Eliot, Gide,
Baudelaire, Edgar Lee Masters, Stendhal, Turgenev, Huneker, Nietzsche,
and scores of others? Were these men real? Did they exist or had they
existed? And how did one pronounce their names?

I ran across many words whose meanings I did not know, and I either   63
looked them up in a dictionary or, before I had a chance to do that,
encountered the word in a context that made its meaning clear. But what
strange world was this? I concluded the book with the conviction that I had
somehow overlooked something terribly important in life. I had once tried
to write, had once reveled in feeling, had let my crude imagination roam,
but the impulse to dream had been slowly beaten out of me by experience.
Now it surged up again and I hungered for books, new ways of looking and
seeing. It was not a matter of believing or disbelieving what I read, but of
feeling something new, of being affected by something that made the look
of the world different.

As dawn broke I ate my pork and beans, feeling dopey, sleepy. I went to   64
work, but the mood of the book would not die; it lingered, coloring everything I saw, heard, did. I now felt that I knew what the white men were
feeling. Merely because I had read a book that had spoken of how they lived
and thought, I identified myself with that book. I felt vaguely guilty. Would
I, filled with bookish notions, act in a manner that would make the whites
dislike me?

I forged more notes and my trips to the library became frequent. Reading   65
grew into a passion. My first serious novel was Sinclair Lewis's *Main Street*.
It made me see my boss, Mr. Gerald, and identify him as an American type.
I would smile when I saw him lugging his golf bags into the office. I had
always felt a vast distance separating me from the boss, and now I felt closer
to him, though still distant. I felt now that I knew him, that I could feel the
very limits of his narrow life. And this had happened because I had read a
novel about a mythical man called George F. Babbitt.

The plots and stories in the novels did not interest me so much as the   66
point of view revealed. I gave myself over to each novel without reserve,
without trying to criticize it; it was enough for me to see and feel something different. And for me, everything was something different. Reading
was like a drug, a dope. The novels created moods in which I lived for days.
But I could not conquer my sense of guilt, my feeling that the white men
around me knew that I was changing, that I had begun to regard them
differently.

Whenever I brought a book to the job, I wrapped it in newspaper—a   67
habit that was to persist for years in other cities and under other circumstances. But some of the white men pried into my packages when I was
absent and they questioned me.

"Boy, what are you reading those books for?"   68
"Oh, I don't know, sir."   69
"That's deep stuff you're reading, boy."   70
"I'm just killing time, sir."   71

"You'll addle your brains if you don't watch out."   72

I read Dreiser's *Jennie Gerhardt* and *Sister Carrie* and they revived in me a   73
vivid sense of my mother's suffering; I was overwhelmed. I grew silent,
wondering about the life around me. It would have been impossible for me
to have told anyone what I derived from these novels, for it was nothing less
than a sense of life itself. All my life had shaped me for the realism, the natu-
ralism of the modern novel, and I could not read enough of them.

Steeped in new moods and ideas, I bought a ream of paper and tried to   74
write; but nothing would come, or what did come was flat beyond telling.
I discovered that more than desire and feeling were necessary to write and
I dropped the idea. Yet I still wondered how it was possible to know people
sufficiently to write about them? Could I ever learn about life and people?
To me, with my vast ignorance, my Jim Crow station in life, it seemed a task
impossible of achievement. I now knew what being a Negro meant. I could
endure the hunger; I had learned to live with hate. But to feel that there
were feelings denied me, that the very breath of life itself was beyond my
reach, that more than anything else hurt, wounded me. I had a new
hunger.

In buoying me up, reading also cast me down, made me see what was   75
possible, what I had missed. My tension returned, new, terrible, bitter, surg-
ing, almost too great to be contained. I no longer *felt* that the world about
me was hostile, killing; I *knew* it. A million times I asked myself what I could
do to save myself, and there were no answers. I seemed forever condemned,
ringed by walls.

I did not discuss my reading with Mr. Falk, who had lent me his library   76
card; it would have meant talking about myself and that would have been
too painful. I smiled each day, fighting desperately to maintain my old
behavior, to keep my disposition seemingly sunny. But some of the white
men discerned that I had begun to brood.

"Wake up there, boy!" Mr. Olin said one day.   77

"Sir!" I answered for the lack of a better word.   78

"You act like you've stolen something," he said.   79

I laughed in the way I knew he expected me to laugh, but I resolved to   80
be more conscious of myself, to watch my every act, to guard and hide the
new knowledge that was dawning within me.

If I went north, would it be possible for me to build a new life then? But   81
how could a man build a life upon vague, unformed yearnings? I wanted
to write and I did not even know the English language. I bought English
grammars and found them dull. I felt that I was getting a better sense of the
language from novels than from grammars. I read hard, discarding a writer
as soon as I felt that I had grasped his point of view. At night the printed
page stood before my eyes in sleep.

Mrs. Moss, my landlady, asked me one Sunday morning: 82

"Son, what is this you keep on reading?"   83

"Oh, nothing. Just novels."   84

"What you get out of 'em?"   85

"I'm just killing time," I said.   86

"I hope you know your own mind," she said in a tone which implied that   87
she doubted if I had a mind.

I knew of no Negroes who read the books I liked and I wondered if any   88
Negroes ever thought of them. I knew that there were Negro doctors,
lawyers, newspapermen, but I never saw any of them. When I read a Negro
newspaper I never caught the faintest echo of my pre-occupation in its
pages. I felt trapped and occasionally, for a few days, I would stop reading.
But a vague hunger would come over me for books, books that opened up
new avenues of feeling and seeing, and again I would forge another note to
the white librarian. Again I would read and wonder as only the naïve and
unlettered can read and wonder, feeling that I carried a secret, criminal
burden about with me each day.

That winter my mother and brother came and we set up housekeeping,   89
buying furniture on the installment plan, being cheated and yet knowing no
way to avoid it. I began to eat warm food and to my surprise found that
regular meals enabled me to read faster. I may have lived through many illnesses and survived them, never suspecting that I was ill. My brother
obtained a job and we began to save toward the trip north, plotting our time,
setting tentative dates for departure. I told none of the white men on the
job that I was planning to go north; I knew that the moment they felt I was
thinking of the North they would change toward me. It would have made
them feel that I did not like the life I was living, and because my life was
completely conditioned by what they said or did, it would have been tan-
tamount to challenging them.

I could calculate my chances for life in the South as a Negro fairly clearly   90
now.

I could fight the southern whites by organizing with other Negroes, as   91
my grandfather had done. But I knew that I could never win that way; there
were many whites and there were but few blacks. They were strong and we
were weak. Outright black rebellion could never win. If I fought openly I
would die and I did not want to die. News of lynchings were frequent.

I could submit and live the life of a genial slave, but that was impossible.   92
All of my life had shaped me to live by my own feelings, and thoughts. I
could make up to Bess and marry her and inherit the house. But that, too,
would be the life of a slave; if I did that, I would crush to death something
within me, and I would hate myself as much as I knew the whites already

hated those who had submitted. Neither could I ever willingly present myself to be kicked, as Shorty had done. I would rather have died than do that.

I could drain off my restlessness by fighting with Shorty and Harrison.   93
I had seen many Negroes solve the problem of being black by transferring their hatred of themselves to others with a black skin and fighting them. I would have to be cold to do that, and I was not cold and I could never be.

I could, of course, forget what I had read, thrust the whites out of my   94
mind, forget them; and find release from anxiety and longing in sex and alcohol. But the memory of how my father had conducted himself made that course repugnant. If I did not want others to violate my life, how could I voluntarily violate it myself?

I had no hope whatever of being a professional man. Not only had I been   95
so conditioned that I did not desire it, but the fulfillment of such an ambition was beyond my capabilities. Well-to-do Negroes lived in a world that was almost as alien to me as the world inhabited by whites.

What, then, was there? I held my life in my mind, in my consciousness   96
each day, feeling at times that I would stumble and drop it, spill it forever. My reading had created a vast sense of distance between me and the world in which I lived and tried to make a living, and that sense of distance was increasing each day. My days and nights were one long, quiet, continuously contained dream of terror, tension, and anxiety. I wondered how long I could bear it.

SPEECH

EMMA WATSON   (1990–   )

Gender Equality Is Your Issue Too

Today we are launching a campaign called "HeForShe." 1
I am reaching out to you because I need your help. We want to 2
end gender inequality—and to do that we need everyone to be
involved.

This is the first campaign of its kind at the UN: we want to try and gal- 3
vanize as many men and boys as possible to be advocates for gender equality.
And we don't just want to talk about it, but make sure it is tangible.

I was appointed six months ago and the more I have spoken about femi- 4
nism the more I have realized that fighting for women's rights has too often
become synonymous with man-hating. If there is one thing I know for
certain, it is that this has to stop.

For the record, feminism by definition is: "The belief that men and 5
women should have equal rights and opportunities. It is the theory of the
political, economic and social equality of the sexes."

I started questioning gender-based assumptions when at eight I was con- 6
fused at being called "bossy," because I wanted to direct the plays we would
put on for our parents—but the boys were not.

When at 14 I started being sexualized by certain elements of the press. 7

When at 15 my girlfriends started dropping out of their sports teams 8
because they didn't want to appear "muscly."

When at 18 my male friends were unable to express their feelings. 9

I decided I was a feminist and this seemed uncomplicated to me. But my 10
recent research has shown me that feminism has become an unpopular word.

Apparently I am among the ranks of women whose expressions are seen 11
as too strong, too aggressive, isolating, anti-men and, unattractive.

Why is the word such an uncomfortable one? 12

I am from Britain and think it is right that as a woman I am paid the same 13
as my male counterparts. I think it is right that I should be able to make
decisions about my own body. I think it is right that women be involved
on my behalf in the policies and decision-making of my country. I think it
is right that socially I am afforded the same respect as men. But sadly I can
say that there is no one country in the world where all women can expect
to receive these rights.

No country in the world can yet say they have achieved gender 14
equality.

These rights I consider to be human rights but I am one of the lucky 15
ones. My life is a sheer privilege because my parents didn't love me less
because I was born a daughter. My school did not limit me because I was a
girl. My mentors didn't assume I would go less far because I might give birth
to a child one day. These influencers were the gender equality ambassadors
that made me who I am today. They may not know it, but they are the
inadvertent feminists who are changing the world today. And we need more
of those.

And if you still hate the word—it is not the word that is important but 16
the idea and the ambition behind it. Because not all women have been
afforded the same rights that I have. In fact, statistically, very few have been.

In 1995, Hillary Clinton made a famous speech in Beijing about women's 17
rights. Sadly many of the things she wanted to change are still a reality today.

But what stood out for me the most was that only 30 per cent of her 18
audience were male. How can we affect change in the world when only half
of it is invited or feel welcome to participate in the conversation?

Men—I would like to take this opportunity to extend your formal invita- 19
tion. Gender equality is your issue too.

Because to date, I've seen my father's role as a parent being valued less by 20
society despite my needing his presence as a child as much as my mother's.

I've seen young men suffering from mental illness unable to ask for help 21
for fear it would make them look less "macho"—in fact in the UK suicide
is the biggest killer of men between 20–49 years of age; eclipsing road accidents, cancer and coronary heart disease. I've seen men made fragile and
insecure by a distorted sense of what constitutes male success. Men don't
have the benefits of equality either.

We don't often talk about men being imprisoned by gender stereotypes 22
but I can see that that they are and that when they are free, things will
change for women as a natural consequence.

If men don't have to be aggressive in order to be accepted women won't 23
feel compelled to be submissive. If men don't have to control, women won't
have to be controlled.

Both men and women should feel free to be sensitive. Both men and 24
women should feel free to be strong. . . . It is time that we all perceive gender on a spectrum not as two opposing sets of ideals.

If we stop defining each other by what we are not and start defining 25
ourselves by what we are—we can all be freer and this is what HeForShe is
about. It's about freedom.

I want men to take up this mantle. So their daughters, sisters and mothers 26
can be free from prejudice but also so that their sons have permission to be
vulnerable and human too—reclaim those parts of themselves they abandoned and in doing so be a more true and complete version of
themselves.

You might be thinking who is this Harry Potter girl? And what is she 27
doing up on stage at the UN. It's a good question and trust me, I have been
asking myself the same thing. I don't know if I am qualified to be here. All
I know is that I care about this problem. And I want to make it better.

And having seen what I've seen—and given the chance—I feel it is my 28
duty to say something. English Statesman Edmund Burke said: "All that is
needed for the forces of evil to triumph is for enough good men and women
to do nothing."

In my nervousness for this speech and in my moments of doubt I've told 29
myself firmly—if not me, who, if not now, when. If you have similar doubts
when opportunities are presented to you I hope those words might be
helpful.

Because the reality is that if we do nothing it will take 75 years, or for me 30
to be nearly a hundred before women can expect to be paid the same as men
for the same work. 15.5 million girls will be married in the next 16 years as
children. And at current rates it won't be until 2086 before all rural African
girls will be able to receive a secondary education.

If you believe in equality, you might be one of those inadvertent feminists 31
I spoke of earlier.

And for this I applaud you. 32

We are struggling for a uniting word but the good news is we have a 33
uniting movement. It is called HeForShe. I am inviting you to step forward,
to be seen to speak up, to be the "he" for "she". And to ask yourself if not
me, who? If not now, when?

Thank you. 34

POETRY

BILLY COLLINS   (1941–   )

Marginalia

Sometimes the notes are ferocious,   1
skirmishes against the author
raging along the borders of every page
in tiny black script.
If I could just get my hands on you,   5
Kierkegaard, or Conor Cruise O'Brien,
they seem to say,
I would bolt the door and beat some logic into your head.
Other comments are more offhand, dismissive—
"Nonsense." "Please!" "HA!!"—   10
that kind of thing.
I remember once looking up from my reading,
my thumb as a bookmark,
trying to imagine what the person must look like
who wrote "Don't be a ninny"   15
alongside a paragraph in The Life of Emily Dickinson.
Students are more modest
needing to leave only their splayed footprints
along the shore of the page.
One scrawls "Metaphor" next to a stanza of Eliot's.   20
Another notes the presence of "Irony"
fifty times outside the paragraphs of A Modest Proposal.
Or they are fans who cheer from the empty bleachers,
Hands cupped around their mouths.
"Absolutely," they shout   25
to Duns Scotus and James Baldwin.
"Yes." "Bull's-eye." "My man!"
Check marks, asterisks, and exclamation points
rain down along the sidelines.
And if you have managed to graduate from college   30
without ever having written "Man vs. Nature"
in a margin, perhaps now
is the time to take one step forward.
We have all seized the white perimeter as our own
and reached for a pen if only to show   35

we did not just laze in an armchair turning pages;
we pressed a thought into the wayside,
planted an impression along the verge.
Even Irish monks in their cold scriptoria
jotted along the borders of the Gospels   40
brief asides about the pains of copying,
a bird singing near their window,
or the sunlight that illuminated their page—
anonymous men catching a ride into the future
on a vessel more lasting than themselves.   45
And you have not read Joshua Reynolds,
they say, until you have read him
enwreathed with Blake's furious scribbling.
Yet the one I think of most often,
the one that dangles from me like a locket,   50
was written in the copy of Catcher in the Rye
I borrowed from the local library
one slow, hot summer.
I was just beginning high school then,
reading books on a davenport in my parents' living room,   55
and I cannot tell you
how vastly my loneliness was deepened,
how poignant and amplified the world before me seemed,
when I found on one page
A few greasy looking smears   60
and next to them, written in soft pencil—
by a beautiful girl, I could tell,
whom I would never meet—
"Pardon the egg salad stains, but I'm in love."

WILLIAM STAFFORD   (1914–1993)

When I Met My Muse

I glanced at her and took my glasses   1
off—they were still singing. They buzzed
like a locust on the coffee table and then
ceased. Her voice belled forth, and the
sunlight bent. I felt the ceiling arch, and   5
knew that nails up there took a new grip
on whatever they touched. "I am your own
way of looking at things," she said. "When
you allow me to live with you, every
glance at the world around you will be   10
a sort of salvation." And I took her hand.

FICTION

JESSICA ANYA BLAU   (1963–   )

Red-Headed

I had no idea what I was going to do after college, no idea what I should 1
do in my life. I had been a French major and had thought of working
for Club Med on some French-speaking island somewhere. But I was
in love. My boyfriend, Ricardo, hadn't graduated yet, and I wasn't willing
to leave him behind.

That summer Ricardo got an internship at a hospital in Oakland, 2
California (he was pre-med and planned on becoming a cardiologist), so we
moved from Berkeley to Oakland where we lived in an art deco apartment
building near Lake Merritt, a man-made lake in the middle of the city. Our
side of the lake hadn't been gentrified yet. There was what we called a
Drug-in-the-Box across the street: at a sidewalk level window, people
walked by all times of day and night, stuck their hand in the window, then
walked away. The only thing we ever saw of the Drug-in-the-Box dealer
was his arm: lean, sinewy, quick as a biting snake. Next door were pay-by-
the-week apartments. Someone called 911 from that building at least three
or four times a week. At the little market on the first floor, a security man
with a gun in his holster stood day and night. We heard gunfire a few times,
and Ricardo once found himself down on the ground with two police guns
pointed at his head when he was in the market buying a soda and was mistaken for the guy who was hiding behind the canned goods aisle.

Late one fall night we heard screams and looked out our window to find 3
a man beating up a woman in the parking lot. Ricardo hid behind the slats
of the blinds, lowered his voice three octaves and yelled, "LEAVE HER
ALONE; I'M CALLING THE POLICE." The guy stopped what he was
doing. He and the woman straightened themselves up and looked in the
direction of our window, both of them squinting to find where the voice
had come from.

"MIND YOUR OWN BUSINESS," the woman finally yelled. "THIS 4
DON'T HAVE NOTHING TO DO WITH YOU!"

When the man shifted his shoulders and head a bit, like he was trying 5
to sniff out our scent, we shut the window and latched it, ran to the front
door to make sure it was locked, and secreted ourselves in the bedroom
with the door shut.

About a month after we moved in, the manager of our apartment build- 6
ing died—an old woman who, I had been told, marched out into the hallway each Christmas and plopped a small plastic decorated tree on top of the
radiator. The owner of the building asked if I wanted to be the new manager. Ricardo and I would get free rent, our utilities and phone bill paid,
and a small salary. I wouldn't have to do the maintenance work; there was a
man for that. I'd just have to direct the maintenance man, collect the rents,
and rent out vacant apartments. This is how I ended up with my first post-
college job.

What the building owner didn't tell me about was the old woman with 7
a beehive hairdo (apartment 3F) who wanted her place sprayed for roaches
so often that the hallway outside her door smelled like the chimney out-
pourings from a factory in Elizabeth, New Jersey. He didn't tell me about
the Viet Nam vet (2E) who had several calendars with pictures of naked
women on his walls. He asked to use my bathroom once when he was dropping off the rent check and peed a wreath of yellow urine on the seat. The
owner also failed to mention the alcoholic who rented a basement studio
(B1), vomited on his walls, and had cartoons playing on his TV all day. And
then there were the users and dealers. The stuttering crack addict, Frank
O'Malley (B6), once came to our door in his neon orange skivvy underpants. With a cigarette wagging in one hand, he repeated one phrase over
and over again, as if his brain were stuck like a car spinning its wheels to get
out of a muddy ditch: "I want my ccccc-cable television! I want my ccccc-
cable television!"

The Cherokee Indian man, Rex (1E), was as gentle and sweet as a llama, 8
but always paid his rent late because his crack-addicted girlfriend often stole
his social security checks, leaving him penniless. For a quarter you could eat
a great big meal at the church down the street, Rex told me. I gave him a
quarter every day, so even if he wasn't up on his rent, he was up on his meals.
Once, Ricardo and I went to dinner at the church with Rex. We wanted
to see if the meal was as great as he raved it was. Ricardo concurred. I found
it inedible.

Rikki (4D) was an androgynously thin man with black Shirley Temple 9
curls, who claimed he was living off savings. Rikki had three brand new cars
(a Mercedes, BMW, and SAAB) and the showroom furniture off the floor
of Emporium Capwells. He paid the rent in cash, and when I told him I
didn't want that much cash in the apartment he brought me a check every
month, written out in his hand, on a check book that had a name other
than his. One day a plain white truck pulled up, and four enormous men
carried out the contents of Rikki's apartment and drove away in the Mercedes and BMW. Rikki came to our door, sweat glossing his face like oil, as

he jangled his keys. He had to get out of town quick, that second in fact, and would Ricardo and I be interested in buying the SAAB for ten-thousand dollars—it was brand new, had all the extras. Ricardo told him we'd buy it for five hundred dollars. Rikki laughed, but came back ten hours later with the keys. This is how Ricardo and I got our first car. Until then we both took buses or the BART train to get around.

Ricardo liked everyone in the building—he was the kind of person who could see the good in anyone. He even liked the maintenance man, Ed, who called him Cubano, even though Ricardo wasn't Cuban. Ricardo explained to Ed one day that he was from Texas and his family was from Mexico. Ed slitted-up his baggy eyes, looked Ricardo up and down, and said, "I lived in Miami for ten years, Ricardo, and I know a Cuban when I see one." It's true Ricardo looked like a modern-day Ricky Ricardo—square head, hair as black as oil, and light brown eyes that reminded me of suede. But he'd never even met anyone from Cuba.

Ricardo and I would often lie in bed at night laughing as I told him about all my encounters with the tenants that day. He claimed that he couldn't fall asleep until he had heard at least one story about someone in the building.

The only person who could get Ricardo upset was the stumpy, grey-faced woman in apartment 4B. Like me, her name was Rachel. At least once a week, she called me on the phone and said in her wavering, operatic voice, "Hi Rachel, *this* is Rachel!" And then she would go on to chronicle all the Jews she had met in her life and how each one had betrayed her in some way. She always capped this rant by saying, "And the red-headed Jews are the *worst Jews!*"

I am red-headed. And I'm Jewish. But there is nothing on me that states that I am Jewish. In fact, people often think I'm Irish—I even have green eyes. But unlike Ricardo, who, with his beautiful brown skin and his name, *Ricardo Gonzales,* is clearly Hispanic, I am not clearly anything.

Rachel told me about the red-headed Jew who sold her a car in 1964. It never ran properly, and when she drove it off the lot it was immediately worth less than half what she paid for it. She told me about the red-headed Jew who sold her a mattress in 1985 that had springs that would carve circles into your back while you slept. She told me about the carpet, the couch, the encyclopedia set, and dishes she had bought from red-headed Jews. It seemed that everywhere Rachel went during her seven decades on this planet, there were red-headed Jews who were trying to rip her off. I wanted to say to her, "Rachel, if all the red-headed Jews in the world are liars and cheats, why do you keep buying things from them?" But I never did.

Ricardo wanted me to tell Rachel that I was Jewish. He wanted me to point out that perhaps some of these red-headed salesmen weren't Jews at all.

And he wanted me to ask her if she hadn't noticed that swindling salesmen come in every form, color, and size. Ricardo himself once got ripped off by an overweight albino Texan who sold him a color TV that made everything pink or green. "The guy was wearing a cross," Ricardo told me. "Tell Rachel that there was no way he was a red-headed Jew!" But I never said anything. I took Rachel's rent checks and listened to her talk about how much she hated the red-headed Jew who owned the building because he had raised the rent after he put a new laundry room in the basement. And I took Rachel's phone calls and listened patiently through the litany of the red-headed Jews. I knew all the characters and circumstances in each story she had created about her life. If I had been an artist, I could have drawn the scenes perfectly. And in the peaceful dark of our bedroom each night, I relayed it all to Ricardo with exacting detail.

Once, when I was telling Ricardo the story Rachel had told me earlier   16
in the day (a red-headed Jewish dentist had pulled out her good teeth, replaced them with caps, while letting her bad teeth lie rotting, bloody, and throbbing in her mouth), he threw up both his hands and stopped me.

"Rachel," he said. "You have to *do* something about this woman!"   17

"What am I going to do?" I said. "Even if I tell her I'm Jewish, I'll never   18
get her to see the world differently. She'll just make up some story about me, and I'll be another person on her list of evil red-headed Jews."

"But you have to *do* something!" That was Ricardo. He was always doing   19
things. He was on his way to medical school to learn things, to do things, to heal people, to save the world one heart at a time. But I wasn't like that. I wasn't doing things to people so much as I was watching them, listening to them, recording them in my mind and in my memory.

"Well write it down, at least," Ricardo said. I wrote all the time, in jour-   20
nals and diaries that I had kept up since the time I could form letters in cursive. And I wrote letters to friends, to my family, to Ricardo—each word in a messy slant on yellow blue-lined paper. No one wrote back, but I didn't mind. I understood that sitting down and writing a letter isn't as easy for everyone else as it is for me.

That week, I wrote a short story called, "Red-Headed," about a young   21
Jewish woman who was managing an apartment building where there was a wizened, old tenant named Rachel who hated all the Jews. I sent the story out to twelve different literary magazines. Each one rejected it. And when I sat down and rewrote the story over and over again in spite of the rejections, I realized that not only was I a red-headed Jew, I was also a writer.

PHOTOGRAPHY

JIM BRYANT   (1950–)

The Gate

Bryant, Jim: "The Gate." Used by permission.

Part III

Reference
Reading and Writing from Sources

R-1 Introducing the Documented Essay

We use sources every day in both formal and informal situations. For example, we might explain the source of a phone message or refer to an instructor's comments in class. We may use someone else's opinion in an essay or quote an expert to prove a point. We cite sources both in speaking and in writing through summary, paraphrase, and direct quotation. Most of your college instructors will ask you to write papers using sources so they can see how well you understand the course material. The use of sources in academic papers requires you to understand what you have read and to integrate this reading material with your own opinions and observations—a process that demands a high level of skill in thinking, reading, and writing.

R-1.1 DEFINING DOCUMENTED ESSAYS

Documented essays provide you with the opportunity to perform sophisticated and exciting exercises that draw on the thinking, reading, and writing abilities you have built up over the course of your academic career. They also require you to put all the rhetorical modes to work at their most analytical level. Documented essays demonstrate the process of analytical thinking at its best in different disciplines. In the academic world, documented essays are also called *research papers, library papers,* and *term papers.* They are generally written for one of three reasons: (1) to **report**, (2) to **interpret**, or (3) to **analyze**.

The most straightforward, uncomplicated type of documented essay *reports* information, as in a survey of problems that children have in preschool. The second type of documented essay both presents and *interprets* its findings. It examines a number of different views on a specific issue and weighs these views in drawing its own conclusions. A topic that might fall into this category would be whether children who have attended preschool are more sociable than those who have not. After considering evidence on both sides, the writer would draw his or her own conclusions on this topic. A documented essay that *analyzes* a particular topic presents a hypothesis, tests the hypothesis, and analyzes or evaluates its conclusions. This type of essay calls for the most advanced form of critical thinking. It might look, for example, at the reasons preschool children are more or less socially adaptable than nonpreschool children. At its most proficient, this type of writing requires a sophisticated degree of evaluation that encourages you to judge your reading, evaluate your sources, and ultimately scrutinize your own reasoning ability as the essay takes shape. Each of these types of research papers calls for a higher level of thinking, and each evolves from the previous category. In other words, interpreting requires reporting, and analyzing draws on both reporting and interpreting.

R-1.2 SAMPLE DOCUMENTED PARAGRAPH

In the following paragraph from a student essay, the writer uses sources to report on, interpret, and analyze the problem of solid waste disposal in the United States. Notice how the student writer draws his readers into the essay with a commonly used phrase about America and then questions the validity of its meaning. The student's opinions give shape to the paragraph while his use of sources helps identify the problem and support his contentions as he uses several rhetorical modes to prove his point.

"America the Beautiful" is a phrase used to describe the many wonders of nature found throughout our country. America's natural beauty will fade, however, if solutions to our solid waste problems are not discovered soon. America is a rich nation socially, economically, and politically. But these very elements may be the cause of America's wastefulness. Americans now generate approximately 160 million tons of solid waste a year—3½ pounds per person per day. We live in a consumer society where "convenience," "ready-to-use," and "throw-away" are terms that spark the consumer's attention (Cook 60). However, many of the products associated with these terms create a large part of our problem with solid waste (Grossman 39). We are running out of space for our garbage. The people of America are beginning to produce responses to this problem. Are we too late? A joint effort from individuals, businesses, industries, and local, state, and federal governments is necessary to establish policies and procedures to combat this war on waste. The problem requires not one solution, but a combination of solutions involving technologies and people working together to provide a safe and healthy environment for themselves and future generations.

R-1.3 DOCUMENTED ESSAY REFERENCE CHART

A **documented essay** is really just an essay with supporting material that comes from outside sources. The following chart compares a standard essay and a research paper.

Standard Essay		Research Paper
Introduction with thesis statement	←——→	*Introduction with thesis statement*
Body paragraphs with facts and personal experience to support the thesis statement	←——→	*Body paragraphs with documented evidence to support the thesis statement*
Concluding paragraph	←——→	*Concluding paragraph*

Keep this outline in mind as you read how to construct a good documented essay. Laying out clear guidelines is the best place to start.

R-2 Reading a Documented Essay

You should read a documented essay in much the same way that you read any essay. In all cases, you should prepare to read, read, and then reread several times—each time with a slightly different purpose. The main difference is that you are paying attention not only to what the writer concludes but also to how the writer's sources support that conclusion.

R-2.1 PREPARING TO READ A DOCUMENTED ESSAY

As you approach a documented essay, you should first take a few minutes to look at the preliminary material for that selection: What can you learn from scanning Goldstein's essay ("'Our Brains Are Evolving to Multitask,' Not! The Illusion of Multitasking") or from reading the synopsis in the Rhetorical Table of Contents? What does Goldstein's title prepare you to read?

Also, you should learn as much as you can from the author's biography: What is Goldstein's interest in multitasking? What biographical details prepare us for his approach to this topic? Does he have the proper qualifications to write about this subject?

Another important part of preparing to read a documented essay is surveying the sources the author cites. Turn to the end of the essay, and look at the sources. What publications does Goldstein draw from? Are these books and magazines well respected? Do you recognize any of the authorities he quotes?

Last, before you read these essays, try to generate some ideas on each topic so you can participate as fully as possible in your reading. The Preparing to Read questions will get you ready for this task. Then, try to speculate further on the topic of each essay: What is the connection for Goldstein between multitasking, efficiency, and evolution? What does this relationship tell us about human nature in general?

R-2.2 READING A DOCUMENTED ESSAY

As you read, respond to both the research and the writing. Record your responses as you read each essay for the first time: What are your reactions to the information you are reading? Are the sources appropriate? How well do they support the author's main points?

Use the preliminary material to help you create a framework for your responses to the essays: What motivated Goldstein to publish his essay on multitasking? Do you find his argument convincing? Who was his primary audience when the essay was first published? In what ways is the tone of his essay appropriate for that audience?

Your main jobs at this stage are to determine the essay's primary assertion (thesis statement), note the sources that support this thesis, and ask yourself questions about the essay so you can respond critically to your reading.

Annotate the essay with your personal reactions, and make sure you understand all the author's vocabulary.

> As in previous chapters, carefully crafted questions at the bottom of the pages of the essay will guide you from prereading predictions to higher levels of critical thinking in preparation for your writing assignments at the end of the selection. These questions will be especially helpful with more complex reading tasks like the ones in this chapter. The essay in this chapter is similar to the material you will read in your other courses throughout your college experience. The questions at the bottom of these pages will essentially teach you how to approach this type of reading and understand it in all its complexity. Read these questions, but don't answer them until your second reading.

After you have read the essay for the first time, summarize its main ideas in some fashion. You could outline the ideas to get an overview of the piece; draw a graph or map of the topics in the essay (in much the same way that you would draw a map of an area for someone unfamiliar with it); or write a traditional summary of the ideas to check your understanding of the main points of the selection. Any of these tasks can be completed from your original notes and underlining. Each will give you a slightly more thorough understanding of what you have read.

Finally, read the questions and assignments following the essay to help focus your thinking for the second reading. Don't answer the questions at this time; just read them to make sure you are picking up the main ideas from the selection and thinking about relevant connections among those ideas.

R-2.3 REREADING A DOCUMENTED ESSAY

As you reread a documented essay, take time to think about the difference between fact and opinion, to weigh and evaluate the evidence provided, to consider the sources the writer uses, to determine what information the writer omits, and to confirm your own views on the issues presented. During this stage, you will also need to examine the sources to determine whether or not their information is credible. All these skills demand the use of critical thinking strategies at their most sophisticated level.

Your second reading of a documented essay is a time to develop a deeper understanding of the author's main ideas and argument. Concentrate on reading "with the grain," as the rhetorician John Bean calls it, meaning you are essentially trying to adopt the author's reasoning in an attempt to learn how he or she thinks and came to certain conclusions. This reading will expand your reasoning capacity and stimulate new ideas.

Also during this reading, you should answer the questions at the bottom of the pages of the essay (the "bridge" questions), which are marked by numbers within diamonds. Then you might pose some additional questions of your own. As always, you will get the most out of this process if you respond in writing. Keeping a journal to collect these responses is especially effective.

During your third reading, you should consciously read "against the grain," actively doubting and challenging what the author is saying. Look closely at the assumptions on which the essay is based: How does the writer move from idea to idea? What hidden assertions lie behind these ideas? Do you agree or disagree with these assertions? Your assessment of these unspoken assumptions will often play a major role in your critical response to an essay. In Goldstein's essay, do you accept the unspoken connection he makes between multitasking and reduced productivity? What parts of the essay hinge upon your acceptance of this connection? What other assumptions are fundamental to Goldstein's reasoning? If you accept his thinking along the way, you are more likely to agree with the general flow of Goldstein's essay. If you discover a flaw in his premises or assumptions, your acceptance of his argument will begin to break down.

Next, answer the questions after the essay, which will help you understand and remember what you have read on the literal, interpretive, and analytical levels. Some of the questions ask you to restate important points the author makes (literal understanding) while others help you see relationships among the different ideas presented (interpretive understanding) and evaluate them (analytical). Also, be aware of your own thought processes as you sort facts from opinions. Know where you stand personally in relation to the issues.

You need to approach this final stage of reading with an inquiring mind, asking questions and looking for answers. Be especially conscious of the appeals (logical, emotional, and ethical) at work in the essay (see the section "Reading and Writing Argument/Persuasion Essays" in Chapter 12), and take note of other rhetorical strategies that support the author's main argument. Also, be aware of your own thought processes as you separate facts from opinions.

R-2.4 A CHECKLIST FOR READING DOCUMENTED ESSAYS

The following guidelines summarize the reading process for documented essays.

READING DOCUMENTED ESSAYS

Preparing to Read
√ What assumptions can you make from the essay's title?
√ Can you guess what the general mood of the essay is?
√ What are the essay's purpose and audience?
√ What does the synopsis tell you about the essay?
√ What can you learn from the author's biography?

Reading

√ What is the author's main assertion or thesis?
√ What are your personal associations with the essay?
√ What sources does the author cite to support the thesis?
√ What questions do you have about this topic?

Rereading

√ How does the author use facts and opinions in the essay?
√ Are the sources the writer cites valid and reliable?
√ Does the author interpret facts accurately?
√ What do you agree with in the essay?
√ What do you disagree with in the essay?
√ What are your own conclusions on this topic?

R-2.5 READING AN ANNOTATED ESSAY

Following is a documented essay written by Allan Goldstein on a subject that affects us all today: multitasking. The essay is annotated to highlight the features that make a documented essay successful and effective.

ALLAN GOLDSTEIN   (1952–)

"Our Brains Are Evolving to Multitask," Not! The Illusion of Multitasking

Born in Orange, New Jersey, Allan Goldstein has found success in life without a formal university degree. After studying string bass at the Berklee College of Music in Boston, he worked in sales positions and the insurance industry. In 1993, he experienced a program called Mindfulness-Based Stress Reduction (MBSR), originally developed by Jon Kabat-Zinn at the University of Massachusetts in 1979. Although its origins are in Buddhist teachings, MBSR has no particular religious affiliation. With more than 250 centers worldwide, it seeks to help people with chronic pain and other health problems via a combination of breath-based meditation and yoga through what its practitioners call "a moment-to-moment nonjudgmental awareness," which results in stress reduction, lower blood pressure, and other important medical benefits. Eventually moving to Oahu, Hawaii, Goldstein presented and promoted MBSR to the island community. Goldstein is currently associate director of the Center for Mindfulness at the University of California, San Diego, which has been in existence for the past ten years. In his spare time, the author is a licensed massage therapist who plays blues harmonica and enjoys living near the ocean. His advice to students using *The Prose Reader* is to "do multiple drafts of their essays, since writing is an organic process."

Preparing to Read

Originally published online on July 1, 2011, by the UCSD Center for Mindfulness, the essay argues that multitasking is the antithesis of "mindfulness" because "our ability to perform tasks suffers as we shift our attention from one task to another."

Exploring Experience: As you prepare to read this article, think about your approach to performing your daily chores: Do you ever try to complete several chores at the same time? Are you aware of changing your focus when you are doing several tasks at once? Do you listen to music or the TV when you study? What does this practice do to your concentration? Do you adjust your method of studying to different purposes, such as exams, class discussions, or oral reports?

LEARNING⟨Ư⟩NLINE Write down your definition of *multitasking*. Does the definition change in different situations: At home? At school? At work? Online? What do you think the relationship is between multitasking and learning? Do an Internet search for tips about multitasking. In what areas do sources offer advice? Do any sources suggest that multitasking is negative? Do some sources believe multitasking has positive effects? Explain your findings.

Before reading this essay, you may want to consult the checklist on pages 540–541.

Special Note: For the purpose of learning how to read documented essays and then preparing to write your own, the following essay is carefully annotated. Use these margin notes to capture the essence of Goldstein's documented essay as you also think about using his strategies to create your own essay.

I recently overheard a proclamation, which has become somewhat of a mantra, recited by today's college students. A student proudly making the following declaration regarding her ability to pay attention to multiple digital screens at once said, "Our brains are evolving to multitask!" That simple yet profound statement left me wondering if this could really be true. How in one or two computerized generations of human beings could our brains evolve so dramatically? Is there such a thing as multitasking, and how is our performance affected when we are concurrently attending to computers, smart phones, iPads, and our daily chores? [1]
Recent research in neuroscience has shown that our brains are capable of forming new neural connections, known as neuroplasticity, but this student's assertion seems to be pointing towards a rapid leap in evolution

Margin notes:
Introduction of subject

Research/ Discussion

Thinking Critically

[1] How many times each day do you multitask? Are you good at it, or does it leave you feeling somewhat frustrated and fragmented?

Credibility of author

that goes well beyond that. Through my work in the field of Mindfulness–Based Stress Reduction (MBSR), I have come to believe that what we commonly refer to as multitasking does not exist and that the level of our ability to perform tasks suffers as we shift our attention from one task to another. In fact, the empirical data from studies in the field of neuroscience is proving that there is no such thing as multitasking!

Thesis statement

2

The online version of the *Merriam-Webster Dictionary* defines multitasking as "the concurrent performance of several jobs by a computer" and "the performance of multiple tasks at the same time" ("Multitasking"). These two definitions divide multitasking into two distinct categories. The first definition refers to performing multiple tasks simultaneously, such as driving while talking on the phone or listening to the radio while at the same time trying to remember directions. The second definition is pointing towards moving from one task to another, such as text messaging, followed by shifting to doing homework on a computer, and shifting again to grab a hurried bite from a late dinner— over and over, again and again. Now consider that all of us, especially college students given their current digital, computer, screen-oriented lifestyles, are doing more and more of this all the time. If this is true, and I believe it is, we can see why it is good for our psyches to think we are evolving to do it.

Definition

Division/ Classification

3

So what exactly is the data derived from recent research in the field of multitasking showing?[2] In the PBS *Frontline* presentation "Digital Nation," by Douglas Rushkoff and Rachel Dretzin, Dr. Clifford Nass is interviewed about his studies at Stanford University on the performance levels of extreme multitaskers: "These are kids who are doing 5, 6, or more things at once all the time." Contrary to the fact that most multitaskers think they are extremely good at it, the results of Nass's first-of-its-kind studies are troubling: "It turns out multitaskers are terrible at every aspect of multi-tasking! They get distracted constantly. Their memory

Source of quotation

Research

Quotation

Findings

Thinking Critically

[2] How does the author add credibility to his argument by references to research in the field?

is very disorganized. Recent work we've done suggests that they're worse at analytic reasoning. We worry that

Cause/Effect it may be we're creating people who may not be able to think well and clearly" (qtd. in Dretzin). **In-text citation**

4 Taking a step back from the profound statement "our brains are evolving to multitask," let's look at the

Research question question, Are students developing new skills and competence that facilitates multitasking? In "What Else Do College Students 'Do' While Studying? An Investigation of Multitasking" by Charles Calderwood, Philip L. Ackerman, and Erin Marie Conklin, findings show a correlation among college students between multitasking and study skills: "Higher homework task

Quotation motivation and self-efficacy for concentrating on homework were associated with less frequent and shorter duration multitasking behaviors, while higher negative affect was linked to greater multitasking duration during the study session" (27). **Source of quotation**

Findings

First conclusion

In-text citation

5 In my experience, there is a fundamental common sense to all this. If you focus all your attention on one **Second conclusion** task at a time, it seems logical that the results would be better than if your attention is divided or distracted by other tasks. [3] Our children may argue they are evolving

Explanation to move beyond this, yet the data support what our mothers and generations before us always knew as they gave advice such as, "Finish what you are doing!"

Acknowledgment of opposition In our culture, there is certainly a perception that **6** people can successfully multitask and a belief that the more we do it the more efficient at it we become. After all, most of us would say we are multitasking many times during the day. So what are the motivations behind all our multitasking? In her blog article "Beyond **Source of paraphrase** Simple Multi-Tasking: Continuous Partial Attention," Linda Stone makes a distinction between simple multitasking and what cognitive scientists refer to as **Paraphrase** "complex multitasking" to explain her theory of Continuous Partial Attention (CPA). [4] In simple

---

Thinking Critically

3 Do you agree with Goldstein's assertion here? As an experiment, try focusing on only one task, and then do the same task while simultaneously watching TV or writing an e-mail to a friend. Do you notice any difference in your competence and/or level of concentration?

4 What does Linda Stone mean by the term "CPA"? How is it different from "simple multitasking"?

multitasking, each task is given the same priority. One task may even be routine, like stirring pasta while talking to our spouse. Stone claims the driving force in simple multitasking is to be more productive. In complex multitasking, the motivation is not to miss anything by maintaining a field of CPA. As Stone explains, "In the case of continuous partial attention, we're motivated by a desire not to miss anything. We're engaged in two activities that both demand cognition." One of these cognitive tasks may also seem more important than another, requiring our brains to be focused on it while remaining alert to the several other less important cognitive tasks requiring our attention. Stone continues, "When we do this, we may have the feeling that our brains process multiple activities in parallel. Researchers say that while we can rapidly shift between activities, our brains process serially."

Stone's theory of CPA is supported in the article "Cognitive Control in Media Multitaskers" by Eyal Ophir, Clifford Nass, and Anthony D. Wagner. The abstract of their study states the following surprising finding: "Heavy media multitaskers performed worse on a test of task-switching ability, likely due to reduced ability to filter out interference from the irrelevant task set." It is important to note Stone's CPA is not multitasking; rather, she is referring to the kind of attention we hold while we are complex multitasking. Maintaining our attention in this state of hyper-vigilance keeps our fight or flight response activated. According to Stone, some people will feel alive, on top of things, and connected. She concedes this can serve us well at times. However, Stone claims the shadow side of being on continuous, continuous partial attention (CCPA) is a constant activation of the fight or flight response. The complex multitasker is in a continuous state of overstimulation with a perpetual feeling of lack of fulfillment that can lead to stress-related diseases. This holds true with my own experiences hearing about and seeing the conditions that create stress in the lives of participants in MBSR programs.

Margin annotations:

- Division/ Classification
- Explanation
- Quotation
- Quotation
- Research
- Source of quotation
- Quotation
- Explanation
- Source of paraphrase
- Paraphrase
- Cause/ Effect
- Example

7

R-2

Summary   Indeed, neuroscientists are discovering that different   8
parts of the brain are switching on and off, resulting
in the serial processing that Stone references. This
switching happens so fast that it appears we are performing multiple tasks simultaneously. We can conclude that, contrary to the first definition of
multitasking, "the concurrent performance of several   In-text
Third   jobs by a computer" ("Multitasking," def. 1), that our   citation
conclusion   brains do not process tasks concurrently. Regarding
the second definition of multitasking, "the performance of multiple tasks at the same time" ("Multitask-   In-text
ing," def. 2), we see we are not really performing tasks   citation
Fourth   at the same time, but instead switching back and forth
conclusion   between them with some of us in an unfulfilled state
of continuous partial attention.

Research   In an interview for *The Atlantic* titled "Corporations'   9
Newest Productivity Hack: Meditation," Joe Pinsker
Source of   quotes David Gelles, the author of *Mindful Work*: "Mul-   Quotation
quotation   titasking is a myth. I think we rarely, if ever, can actually
do two things at the same time. I think what we're
doing is very rapid task-switching, which leads to
inherent inefficiencies." Many naysayers may try to
Explanation   claim this is simply a semantic argument, and to some
degree, I would agree. Words are divisive by nature and
often fall short in truly representing what they are
meant to describe. Perhaps it is time to throw out the   Fifth
word "multitasking," as the definitions no longer fit,   conclusion
and invent words that better represent our current scientific understanding of the way our brains function.
How about "serialtasking" or "taskswitching"? [5]   Explanation
Solution to   If we identify that our lives have sped up to a point   10
problem   that may be causing us physical harm and if we have
a desire to do something about it, there are several
antidotes to our cultural addiction of the illusion of
multitasking. This will require a change that most people may be resistant to make. In the article "Master-   Research
ing Multitasking," Urs Gasser and John Palfrey suggest,
"We have to embrace and master it while providing
limits from time to time to create contemplative space

Thinking Critically

[5] What are other possible labels for the way our brains function?

In-text citation for young people" (16). We can focus more on individual tasks by bringing a strong mindful awareness to our actions while performing them. By taking breaks and time outs, we can shift our attention back to our senses. In one sense, I'm hopeful as I see a cultural shift, perhaps as a backlash to all the stimulation, to embrace mindfulness. Alternatively letting go of even one aspect of multitasking, like text messaging, can be painful for some people, let alone shutting down and going offline.

Sixth conclusion

Summary   The empirical evidence supports the hypothesis that there is no such thing as multitasking. Multitasking is a misnomer. The word points to something that at best can be looked at as individual tasks being performed through a very rapid switching back and forth in the way our brains function or through performing tasks Explanation with continuous partial attention. Research, particularly in the field of neuroscience, is compiling data that show multitasking can negatively affect performance and lead to increased levels of stress. We are all part of one big current cultural experiment where we are the scientists, the laboratory, and the results, and it is not a trivial matter. The quality of our lives and our health may depend on our ability to truly understand and wisely manage the effects of our perceptions, beliefs, and actions surrounding our illusion of multitasking.

11

Final conclusion

Works Cited

Calderwood, Charles, et al. "What Else Do College Students 'Do' While Studying? An Investigation of Multitasking." *Computers and Education*, vol. 75, June 2014, pp. 19-29. *PsycINFO*, doi:10.1016/ j.compedu.2014.02.004.

Dretzin, Rachel, and Douglas Rushkoff, writers. "Digital Nation: Life on the Virtual Frontier." *Frontline*, season 28, episode 1, PBS, 2 Feb. 2010. *PBS*, www.pbs.org/wgbh/frontline/film/digitalnation/.

Gasser, Urs, and John Palfrey. "Mastering Multitasking." *Educational Leadership*, vol. 66, no. 6, Mar. 2009, pp. 14-19.

"Multitasking." *Merriam-Webster*, www.merriam-webster .com/dictionary/multitasking. Accessed 20 Apr. 2015.

Ophir, Eyal, et al. "Cognitive Control in Media Multitaskers." *Proceedings of the National Academy*

Sources organized in alphabetical order

of Sciences of the United States of America, vol. 106, no. 37, Sept. 2009, pp. 15583–87. *PubMed Central*, doi:10.1073/pnas.0903620106.

Pinsker, Joe. "Corporations' Newest Productivity Hack: Meditation." *The Atlantic*, 10 Mar. 2015, www.theatlantic.com/business/archive/2015/03/corporations-newest-productivity-hack-meditation/387286/.

Stone, Linda. "Beyond Simple Multi-Tasking: Continuous Partial Attention." *Lindastone.net*, 30 Nov. 2009, lindastone.net/2009/11/30/beyond-simple-multi-tasking-continuous-partial-attention/.

UNDERSTANDING DETAILS

1. What is Goldstein's main assertion in this essay?
2. What is MBSR? How is it related to multitasking?
3. According to Linda Stone, what is the difference between "simple" and "complex" multitasking (paragraph 6)?
4. What does Goldstein mean when he says, "In our culture, there is certainly a perception that people can successfully multitask and a belief that the more we do it the more efficient at it we become" (paragraph 6)?

READING CRITICALLY

5. According to this essay, what are our brains actually doing when we try to multitask?
6. What do the sources in this essay say the relationship is between multitasking and concentration?
7. What does Goldstein mean by the "illusion of multitasking" (paragraph 11)?
8. What data is most persuasive to you in this essay? What is least persuasive? Explain your answer.

DISCOVERING RHETORICAL STRATEGIES

9. What do you think is the author's main purpose in this essay?
10. Who do you think is the author's main audience? How did you come to this conclusion?
11. List the author's main points about multitasking in this essay. Are they presented in a logical, effective order? Explain your answer.
12. What does Goldstein's use of data in this essay add to his argument? Explain your answer in detail.

MAKING CONNECTIONS

13. If Goldstein, Amy Chua ("Excerpt from *Battle Hymn of the Tiger Mother*"), Motoko Rich ("Literacy Debate"), and/or Joe Keohane ("How Facts Backfire")

were having a conversation about the importance of focusing on one task at a time, who would be the strongest advocate for this point of view? Why?

14. Which of the author's references to other sources do you find most effective? Which were least effective? Compare and contrast Goldstein's frequent use of in-text citations with the complete lack of documentation in Sarah Toler's "Understanding the Birth Order Relationship." Did Goldstein's essay seem more credible because of his inclusion of scholarly citations? Why or why not?

15. Which other rhetorical modes featured in *The Prose Reader* does Goldstein use to advance his argument? Which ones does he rely on most often? Why do you think he does this?

IDEAS FOR DISCUSSION/WRITING

Preparing to Write

Write freely about your current impressions of multitasking: Do you move from task to task differently depending on the situation? What characterizes the shifts you make when studying? When watching television or socializing? Are you conscious of adjusting your concentration and focus to different scenarios? Does multitasking have positive consequences for you? Explain your answer.

Choosing a Topic   MyWritingLab™

1. **LEARNING⟲NLINE** Goldstein ultimately claims that attempting to multi-task has negative effects on learning and productivity for most people. Use the tips you discovered in your prereading Internet search to develop a documented essay that either supports or refutes Goldstein's main assertions about multitasking. Take care to support your own claims with relevant, reliable evidence.

2. In this essay, the author cites Stone's analysis that "we may have the feeling that our brains process multiple activities in parallel . . . [but] our brains process serially" (paragraph 6). Use Goldstein's article as one of your sources; then read further on the brain and multitasking. Next, write a well-documented essay expressing your understanding of how the brain works while trying to multi-task. Organize your paper clearly, and present your findings logically, using proper documentation (citations and bibliography) to support your discoveries.

3. In paragraph 11 of his essay, Goldstein refers to the "illusion of multitasking." Consult additional sources to learn more about the causes and effects of this "illusion." Then, referring to Goldstein's argument, write a well-documented essay explaining in depth your discoveries about this phenomenon.

4. In his last paragraph, Goldstein claims, "The quality of our lives and health may depend on our ability to truly understand and wisely manage the effects of our perceptions, beliefs, and actions surrounding our illusion of multitasking." Do you agree or disagree with this statement? Explain your reaction in a clearly reasoned argumentative essay. Cite Goldstein's selection whenever necessary.

Before beginning your essay, you may want to consult the checklist on pages 567–568.

R-3 Preparing to Write Your Own Documented Essay

As you consider various topics, you should ask yourself one important question before you begin planning your essay: Will you be able to find enough information to back up your thesis statement? To make sure you are able to locate enough material to use as persuasive evidence in the body paragraphs of your essay, you must do a good job of choosing a subject, narrowing it, and writing a provocative and interesting thesis statement. You will then prove this thesis statement with the information you find when you search for sources on your topic.

R-3.1 CHOOSING A TOPIC

Just as with any writing assignment, you begin the task of writing a documented essay by exploring and limiting your topic. In this case, however, you will draw on other sources to help. You should seek out both primary and secondary sources related to your topic. **Primary sources** are works of literature, historical documents, letters, diaries, speeches, eyewitness accounts, and your own experiments, observations, and conclusions; **secondary sources** explain and analyze information from other sources. Any librarian can help you search for both types of sources related to your topic.

After you have found a few sources on your general subject, you should review and evaluate what you have discovered so you can limit your topic further. Depending on the required length of your essay, you will want to find a topic broad enough to be researched, established enough to let you discover ample sources on it in the library, and significant enough to demonstrate your ability to grapple with important ideas and draw meaningful conclusions. The Preparing to Write questions can help you generate and focus your ideas.

Our student writer decided to write on topic #1 after reading and rereading Goldstein's essay. She narrowed her subject in the following way:

General Subject: Multitasking

    More Specific: Multitasking and computers

        More Specific: The effects of multitasking on the Internet

This limited topic would be perfect for a documented essay. You could search for books, catalogs, and periodicals on the relationships between multitasking, the Internet, and productivity. While you are looking, you should be thinking about how to narrow your subject even further.

R-3.2 WRITING A GOOD, CLEAR THESIS STATEMENT

Just as a thesis statement is the controlling idea of an essay, a thesis statement provides the controlling idea for your argument in a documented essay. This statement will guide the writing of your entire paper. Your assignments throughout college will usually be broad topics. To compose a good documented essay, you need to narrow a broad topic to an idea that you can prove within a limited number of pages. A working thesis statement will provide the direction for your essay, and the evidence you collect in your research is what proves that thesis statement. But you should keep in mind that your thesis is likely to be revised several times as the range of your knowledge changes and your paper takes different turns while you research and write.

Also as in a standard essay, the thesis statement in your documented essay is a contract between you and your readers. The thesis statement tells your readers what the main idea of your essay will be and sets guidelines for the paragraphs in the body of your essay. If you don't deliver what your thesis statement promises, your readers will be disappointed. The thesis statement is usually the last sentence in the introduction. It outlines your purpose and position on the essay's general topic and gives your readers an idea of the type of resources you will use to develop your essay.

Our student wrote this thesis statement for her essay after reading several sources:

The Internet has played a crucial role in promoting media multitasking and, contrary to many claims, is the perfect venue for multitaskers to increase their productivity and enhance their lives, causing the benefits of multitasking on the Internet to far outweigh its disadvantages.

Her entire essay responds to Goldstein's claim that multitasking has a purely negative effect on people's productivity and quality of life. Although our student writer presents some negative aspects of multitasking online, she believes, as her thesis states, that multitasking while using the Internet can also be advantageous when done judiciously. The paragraphs following this thesis statement supply evidence that proves her claim.

R-4 Finding Sources

No matter what you are studying in college, you need to know how to find sources and evaluate them. On the Internet, you can access an enormous amount of information that will help you generate paper topics, teach you new information, challenge your thinking, support and/or refute your opinions, and sometimes even make you smile. In today's electronic world, learning how to assess and use the resources available through the library's services is a basic academic survival skill.

Many of the sources you will use for your documented essays are available on the World Wide Web, often through subscribed databases that your library manages. In addition to online journals, magazines, and books, you might locate relevant information from electronic newsletters, message boards, or blogs. Remember, though, that not all sources are equally accurate and reliable. Based on your topic, you need to exercise your best judgment and get your instructor's help in assessing the most useful online sources for your purposes.

R-4.1 SOURCES THAT ARE RELEVANT, RELIABLE, AND RECENT

The evidence of a documented essay lies in the sources that you use to back up your thesis statement. The sources must always be **R**elevant, **R**eliable, and **R**ecent. This "3Rs" approach to supporting evidence in a documented essay will help you write a solid essay with convincing evidence.

Here are some questions that will help you evaluate sources:

The 3Rs: Relevant, Reliable, Recent

Relevant
- Does the source focus on your subject?
- Does the source deal with the topic in depth?

Reliable
- What is the origin of the source?
- Is the author an expert in the field?
- Is the author biased?
- Does the source represent all sides of an issue?
- Are the author's claims well supported?

Recent
- Is the source current enough for your subject and your purpose?

Our student writer's thesis suggests that multitasking while using the Internet has some positive effects on learning and productivity. To convince her readers that her thesis is correct, she consulted books, scientific and online journals, and general circulation publications. Here is a breakdown of some of the sources she read:

- **Book**: *The Organized Mind*
- **Scientific journal**: *American Scientist*
- **Online journal:** *The Wilson Quarterly*
- **General circulation publication:** *The Atlantic*

In these sources, our student writer found information she could use to support her thesis statement. Even though these are not highly technical scientific sources, the evidence in them fulfills our "3R" criteria: **R**elevant, **R**eliable, and **R**ecent.

R-4.2 CONSULTING ACADEMIC DATABASES

Most instructors would agree that students should use primarily scholarly Web sources that have been through rigorous academic screening. These include academic databases—such as WilsonWeb, EBSCOhost, ABI/INFORM, and LexisNexis—that you can access through your library. These sources are considered credible, whereas others that are not "peer-reviewed" can often be biased and inaccurate. As a result, they are less reliable.

The best places to begin searching for sources are interdisciplinary databases, full-text indexes, and electronic journal collections. You should have access to these services from home through your library's homepage or from a computer in your library. You may need a reference librarian to help you find these for the first time.

Academic databases can direct you to a large number of books and journals on a wide range of subjects; however, they may not always include links to complete articles. Some, such as Wilson's OmniFile or EBSCO's Academic Search, are general databases that provide access to full texts in a variety of subject areas. Others, such as LexisNexis and WilsonWeb, offer materials from subject-specific disciplines. The following are online indexes found in academic databases.

Index or Collection

Biological and Agriculture Index	*EBSCO host*
Business Full Text	*Expanded Academic ASAP*
Education Full Text	*HRAF*
General Science Full Text	*LexisNexis*
Humanities Full Text	*WilsonWeb*
OmniFile Full Text Mega	Academic Press's *IDEAL*
Readers' Guide Full Text	American Chemical
Social Sciences Full Text	Society's *Web Editions*
ABI Inform	American Mathematical Journals
Dow Jones	*JSTOR*
	Project Muse

Once you access an online database, index, or collection, you can easily find articles and books on your topic. You can do online searches by author, title, or subject, but because you will most likely be looking for articles on a specific topic, you should use the subject function most frequently. When you search for a title by subject, be aware of *Boolean connectors or operators,* which will allow you to narrow your search.

Using Boolean Connectors or Operators

The Boolean connectors or operators for requesting a search are *AND, OR,* and *NOT.* By using these words, you can limit the search and find information directly related to your topic. Most databases no longer require that you type in the Boolean operators manually. They provide multiple search boxes, normally separated by a default AND. You would type in each term (for example, *multitask* in the first box and *Internet* in the second). Then, you should separate your terms with the Boolean connector "AND" (for example, *multitask* AND *Internet*). This asks the computer to find all the records in which these two terms are combined. If you put "OR" between the key words (*multitask* OR *Internet*), you are separating the words and asking the computer to find articles and books for either one of them. If you add "NOT" (*multitask* NOT *Internet*), you limit the search by excluding a term from the search.

R-4.3 SEARCHING FOR WEBSITES

To find a website related to your topic, go to the Internet through your favorite browser (for example, Firefox, Google Chrome, Safari). When you access a search engine such as www.google.com or www.yahoo .com, you will search millions of websites. Using the advanced search option in a search engine will allow you to narrow or expand your search. Most search engines will then begin by helping you narrow your search and providing a list of other possible topics. Here are variations that our student writer explored while conducting her research.

Topic
Multitasking and Internet

Other Possible Topics
Multitasking online
Media multitasking
Multitasking and productivity
Multitasking and classroom
Internet and learning

When the search is complete, your search engine will list the websites in the order of most to least probable relevance to you. It will also briefly describe each website. After the description, you will usually find the website address.

Evaluating Websites

Because anyone can put material on the Internet, you need to make sure you are not using biased or unreliable information. To use websites intelligently, follow four guidelines:

1. *Understand the URL addresses you consult.* As you search for reliable Web sources, you should know that the endings of the URLs refer to different sources: *.com* stands for "commercial," *.edu* for "education," *.gov* for "government," and *.org* for "organization." As you consult these sources, first determine whether the sites are maintained and current.
2. *Pay attention to the argument a site makes.* Who is the author, and what is his or her purpose for entering information on the site? If you log on to a Martin Luther King, Jr. site and are inundated with racial slurs, chances are you've found a site that was created by a faction of the Ku Klux Klan or a similar group. If the information does not fit the site or if the author has an obvious agenda, avoid the site altogether.
3. *Make sure the site is providing fact and not opinion.* For academic purposes, facts and statistics are generally more useful than opinions. If you are looking for a site that deals with gun control, you'll want to avoid the site that tells you story after story about innocent children dying from playing with loaded guns but fails to give you any unbiased information. Instead, you'll want to find a site that gives you examples that can be verified and supported with statistics.
4. *Make sure the site provides information about the other sides of the argument.* If a site provides you only with details about its own viewpoint, you should wonder why it is omitting information. If you find a site on prayer in school and see opinions about why prayer should not be allowed in schools, you should be curious about why the site doesn't present other arguments. The best sites provide all sides of an argument so that they can show why one side is more valid than the others. When you find a website that does not offer balanced information, consider it biased, and avoid it altogether.

These four guidelines will help you determine whether you should use information you find on the Web. But if you want to be certain the information you are using will be acceptable to your instructor, you should rely principally on academic sources, such as published literature in the library databases. There are, however, a number of "open source" academic websites where you can access articles that have been peer-reviewed or refereed. This means the authors of the essays send them to the publication and the editors of the publication send the essays anonymously to readers for review. A reader will recommend an article for publication if it is well researched and worth reading. If you can, use only these sources. Note, however, that you still need to evaluate your peer-reviewed sources to ensure that their arguments are sound.

Sample "Hits"

The following are three "hits" or sources found by www.google.com for the topic *multitasking and the Internet*.

1 Effects of Online Multitasking on Reading Comprehension of Expository Text

Much of college students' computer use, including for academic reading, occurs under conditions of multitasking. In three experiments, we investigated their technology use and habitual multitasking and the learning effects of multitasking with online communication while reading expository text.
www.cyberpsychology.eu/view.php?cisloclanku=2013120901&article=2

2 Why the Modern World Is Bad for Your Brain

In an era of email, text messages, Facebook and Twitter, we're all required to do several things at once. But this constant multitasking is taking its toll. Here neuroscientist Daniel J. Levitin explains how our addiction to technology is making us less efficient.
www.theguardian.com/science/2015/jan/18/modern-world-bad-for-brain-daniel-j-levitin-organized-mind-information-overload

3 Multitasking, Social Media and Distraction: Research Review

Over the past decade, academic research has increasingly examined issues of multitasking and distraction as people try to squeeze more activities into their busy lives. Prior to the Internet age, some cognition science research focused on how behavior might be better understood, improved and made more efficient in business, hospital or other high-pressure settings. But as digital technology has become ubiquitous in many people's daily routines—and as multitasking has become a "lifestyle" of sorts for many younger people—researchers have tried to assess how humans are coping in this highly connected environment and how "chronic multitasking" may diminish our capacity to function effectively.
http://journalistsresource.org/studies/society/social-media/multitasking-social-media-distraction-what-does-research-say

R-4.4 USING THE LIBRARY

Once you have compiled a list of books and journals from databases and indexes or from websites, you should use your library to check out books or copy journal articles that were not available online. Publishers usually make their current content available online, but you may need to locate older articles in the library's periodical collection and copy them.

First, you need to access your library's online catalog to see if your library has the book. If you have difficulty locating a book using the catalog, ask a librarian for help. You might also inquire whether this information is available online. You can search for authors and subjects through your library's catalog in much the same way that you would search online databases or program search engines. Since you have already done the preliminary research, all you have to do is look for the books and journals you need. Find the "title" section of the catalog, and type in the title of the book or journal you need.

If you are searching for a chapter or an essay contained in a book, be sure to type in the main book title. For example, if you were to search for "Mind over Multitasking" (by Peg Oliveira), your library computer would tell you that the library does not carry it. You must type in the title of the book it came from, *The Culture of Efficiency,* to find the essay. Once you have located the titles of your books or journals in the library's catalog, you should write down the call numbers so you can find the sources in your library. Then it's just a matter of finding the book itself in the stacks. If you need help, don't hesitate to ask a librarian.

R-5 Avoiding Plagiarism

Plagiarism is using someone else's words or ideas as if they were your own. It comes from a Latin word meaning "kidnapper." Because it is dishonest, plagiarism is a serious offense in college and beyond. Among student writers, plagiarism usually takes one of three forms: (1) using words from another source without quotation marks; (2) using someone else's ideas in the form of a summary or paraphrase without citing the source; and (3) using someone else's essay as your own. When you work with sources, you must give credit to the authors who wrote them. In other words, if you quote, paraphrase, or summarize from another source, you must provide your reader with information about that source, such as the author's name, the title of the book or article, and specifics about when it was published. Whenever you use other people's words or ideas without giving them credit, you are plagiarizing.

If you don't cite your sources properly, your readers will think the words and ideas are yours when they actually came from someone else. When you steal material in this way in college, you can be dismissed from school. When you commit the same offense in the professional world, you can get fired or end up in court. So make sure you understand what plagiarism is as you move through this chapter.

R-5.1 TYPES OF MATERIAL

A documented paper usually blends three types of material:

1. *Common knowledge,* such as the places and dates of events (even if you have to look them up). When you refer to information such as historical events, dates of presidents' terms, and other well-known facts, like the effects of ultraviolet rays or smoking, you do not have to cite a source. This material is called *common knowledge* because it can be found in a

R-5

number of different sources. You can use this information freely because you are not borrowing anyone's original words or ideas.

Example: Computers, which gained widespread popularity in the 1980s and 1990s, offered people more opportunities to multitask using different forms of media.

2. *Someone else's thoughts and observations.* If, however, you want to use someone's original words or ideas, you must give that person credit by revealing where you found this information. This process is called *citing* or *documenting* your sources, and it involves noting in your paper where you found the idea. Because documented essays are developed around sources that support your position, citations are an essential ingredient in any documented essay.

Example: President Bill Clinton once said about the Internet, "Advances in computer technology and the Internet have changed the way America works, learns, and communicates. The Internet has become an integral part of America's economic, political, and social life."

3. *Your own thoughts and observations.* These are conclusions that you draw from the sources you are reading.

Example: While multitasking can often be distracting, it is a mandatory aspect of Internet use and cannot be avoided.

Of these three types of information, you must document or cite your exact source only for the second type. Negligence in citing your sources, whether purposeful or accidental, is *plagiarism*.

R-5.2 ACKNOWLEDGING YOUR SOURCES

Avoiding plagiarism is quite simple: Just make sure you acknowledge the sources of ideas or language that you are using to support your own contentions. Acknowledging your sources also gives you credit for the reading you have done and for the ability you have developed to synthesize and use sources to support your observations and conclusions. To give credit to your sources, you acknowledge them in two ways: (1) with in-text citations that provide your reader with the author, page or paragraph numbers, and sometimes dates for each summary, paraphrase, or direct quotation you use and (2) with a list of sources at the end of your paper that provides complete publication information on all the sources you have used in your essay. These two types of documentation work together to provide your readers with all the information they need to locate and assess the sources you read.

Two forms of documentation can sometimes cause problems. First, when you paraphrase (or put another writer's ideas into your own words), you cannot use the author's words or sentence structure. In addition, you must cite your source at the end of a paraphrase. Second, when you put an author's words in quotation marks, you must copy the words exactly as they are in the original source without making any changes.

In our student writer's paper, every source she uses is acknowledged at least twice: (1) in the paper directly after a quotation or idea and (2) at the end of the paper in a list. The first type of citation is known as an *in-text citation*, and the second is a list of *Works Cited* in the paper. At the note-taking stage, you should make sure that you have all the information on your sources you will need later to acknowledge them in proper form in your paper. Having to track down missing details when you prepare your lists of works cited can be frustrating and time consuming.

R-5.3 DIRECT QUOTATION, PARAPHRASE, AND SUMMARY

As you read your sources and take notes for your paper, your notes will probably fall into one of four categories: (1) *direct quotation from sources;* (2) *paraphrase*—a restatement in your own words of someone else's ideas or observations; (3) *summary*—a condensed statement of someone else's thoughts or observations; or (4) *a combination of these forms.* Be sure to make a distinction in your notes between actual quotes and paraphrases or summaries. Also, record the sources (including page and/or paragraph numbers) of all your notes—especially of quoted, summarized, and paraphrased material—which you may need to cite in your essay.

This section explains these three options to you. We begin with an original source and show you how to acknowledge material from this source in different ways.

The following quotation is from "Kids Really *Are* Different These Days" by Diana D. Coyl. It was published in the journal *Phi Delta Kappan* in 2009.

Original Source

"Some children communicate more through electronic devices and spend less face time with family members and peers. Text messaging and e-mails provide limited or no access to other people's emotions, and the rich language of non-verbal communication that occurs in real-time interactions is lost. In addition, the quality of family time may be compromised if parents or children are using technology. Consider how family dinner conversation might be affected if family members are watching television, listening to music, checking e-mail, answering the phone, or text-messaging" (Coyl 405).

Direct Quotation

If you use a direct quotation from another source, you must put the exact material you want to use in quotation marks:

Diana D. Coyl, in her article "Kids Really Are Different These Days," responds to people who dismiss the threat of multitasking:
Some children communicate more through electronic devices and spend less face time with family members and peers. Text messaging and emails provide limited or no access to other people's emotions, and the rich language of non-verbal communication that occurs in real-time interactions is lost. In addition, the quality of family time may be compromised if parents or children are using technology. Consider how family dinner conversation might be affected if family members are watching television, listening to music, checking e-mail, answering the phone, or text-messaging. (405)

Direct Quotation with Some Words Omitted

If you want to leave something out of the quotation, use three dots (with spaces before and after each dot); known as an *ellipsis*, this form of punctuation signals the omission of words. Also, make sure that you place brackets [ ] around any words that you alter in the quotation or add to it.

Diana D. Coyl, in her article "Kids Really Are Different These Days," states, "Text messaging and e-mails provide limited or no access to other people's emotions . . . [and] the quality of family time may be compromised if parents or children are using technology" (405).

Paraphrase

When you paraphrase, you are restating the main ideas of a quotation **in your own words.** *Paraphrase* means "similar phrasing," so it is usually about the same length as the original. Paraphrasing is a difficult skill to master, but one trick you can use is to read the material, put it aside, and write a sentence or two from memory. Then compare what you wrote with the original to make sure they are similar but not exactly the same. If you look at the source while you are trying to paraphrase it, you might inadvertently take words or phrases from the original, which would make you guilty of plagiarism.

Even though a paraphrase is in your own words, you still need to let your readers know where you found the information. A paraphrase of our original source might read like this:

Diana D. Coyl, in her article "Kids Really Are Different These Days," discusses how multitasking and Internet use can affect children. By communicating via electronic devices, many children miss out on physical interactions, making it difficult for them to learn social cues and nonverbal skills. Additionally, quality family time is compromised when children or parents are constantly using technology instead of bonding (405).

Summary

To summarize, state the author's main idea in your own words. A summary is much briefer than the original or a paraphrase. As with a paraphrase, you need to furnish the details of your original source. Here is a summary of our original source:

> In her article "Kids Really Are Different These Days," Diana D. Coyl contends that children who multitask with technology may be missing out on many other important aspects of life (405).

R-6 Staying Organized

As you gather information, consider keeping a "research journal" where you can record your own opinions, interpretations, and analyses in response to your reading. This journal should be separate from your notes on sources a place where you can make your own discoveries about your topic by jotting down thoughts and relationships among ideas you encounter, by keeping a record of sources you read and others you want to look at, by tracking and developing your own ideas and theories, and by clarifying your thinking.

R-6.1 TAKING NOTES ON SOURCES

As you read your sources, think about whether you might directly quote, paraphrase, or summarize the material. A general rule to follow is that you never want to have more than 10 percent of directly quoted information in your paper, which means 90 percent of the information you use from sources should be paraphrased or summarized. The best way to determine whether you should use a direct quotation is by asking yourself if this is the best possible way to relay this information. If you can't phrase it any better than the original or if the author of the quotation is famous enough to give your argument credibility, then you should use a direct quotation. In most cases, however, try to put your research into your own words. Only occasionally should you use the author's exact words. So when you are reading and taking notes on your sources, you should keep this in mind.

Paper or electronic notecards are an excellent tool for taking notes because you can move them around as your paper takes shape. Put only one idea on each notecard. Writing down ideas and quotations on notecards allows you to reorganize your cards and put thoughts into different paragraphs. Then rearrange your cards until you think the order will support your thesis.

The best way to start keeping track of the information for the citations in your paper is when you are taking notes. If you cannot find the original source for material you want to use in your paper and, therefore, cannot tell your reader where you found it, then you cannot use the material. Listed here is all the information you will need to cite a source in your paper:

For a book:
- Book title
- Author or authors
- Editor or editors (if applicable)
- Publisher
- Year of publication

For an article:
- Article title
- Author or authors
- Title of the magazine or journal
- Date of issue (for a magazine)
- Year and volume number (for a journal)
- Pages on which the article appeared (for a print article and for an article accessed via a database)
- The URL or DOI (digital object identifier) for an article accessed online
- The name of the database (if you accessed the article via a database)

If you put all this information on one card, you can record just the author's last name on all other cards from that same source. If you are using more than one book or article by the same author, add the source's date to the card. For both books and articles, you should also record the page where you found the information. That way you can easily find it again or cite it in your paper.

The format in which this information should be presented will depend on the field of study. A good handbook will help you with the formats of the various documentation styles, which include Modern Language Association (MLA) style for the humanities, American Psychological Association (APA) style for the social sciences, and *Chicago Manual of Style* (CMS) style for mathematics and science. Make sure you understand which documentation style your instructor wants you to use because they differ in important ways. These styles are all explained in detail in section R-8, Documenting.

Our student writer used the Modern Language Association citation style. Here is a citation for the Coyl essay in MLA format:

Coyl, Diana D. "Kids Really *Are* Different These Days." *Phi Delta Kappan*, vol. 90, no. 6, Feb. 2009, pp. 404-07. *JSTOR*, www.jstor.org/stable/20446131.

When our student writer had to read and take notes on the sources she found, she first made a set of bibliography cards with a notecard for every source. For the books, she recorded title, author or editor, city where published, publisher, and year of publication on each card; for the articles, she wrote down the article title, author, title of the magazine or journal, date of issue or volume and issue numbers, and page numbers on each card. Then she began to read her sources. She wrote only one idea or quotation per notecard, and she remembered to record on each notecard the author's name and the page number on which she found the information. She also made sure, as she took notes, to restate information in her own words or else put the author's exact words in quotation marks.

R-6.2 MAKING A WORKING OUTLINE

Before you begin your first draft, you might want to write an informal working outline as a guide. Such an exercise can help you see the range of your coverage and the order and development of your ideas. With an outline, you can readily determine where you need more information, less information, or more reliable sources. But be flexible; this outline may change dramatically as your essay develops.

If you are using notecards, you can simply rearrange them to create your outline. Start by putting all your notecards into small stacks of related ideas. Which ideas might work well together? Which should you put in the introduction? Which do you want to save for your conclusion? When you get all your notecards in stacks, label each group of cards according to its topic. These labels will then become the topics of your paper. You are now ready to start your working outline.

A good way to begin an outline is to write your tentative thesis statement at the top of a page and then list the topics you have developed. These topics should be arranged in a logical order that is easy to follow and will help you prove your main point. Each topic should directly support your thesis statement. Leave room in your outline to add subtopics and details throughout the paper. This outline then becomes a guide for your writing, one that will change and grow with every paragraph that you add.

Our student writer started developing her paper by putting related notecards into stacks. Next, she labeled her stacks of notecards and then organized these topics in different ways until they started making sense to her. Her list of topics, with her thesis statement at the top, became her working outline. She eventually turned these topics into topic sentences for her body paragraphs. The stack of cards for each topic became the content of her body paragraphs.

R-7 Writing a Documented Essay

Writing the first draft of a documented essay is your chance to discover new insights and to find important connections among ideas that you may not have previously been aware of. This draft is your opportunity to demonstrate that you understand your topic and your sources on three increasingly difficult levels—literal, interpretive, and analytical; that you can organize your material effectively; that you can integrate your sources (in the form of summaries, paraphrases, or quotations) with your opinions; and that you can document (that is, cite) your sources.

To begin this process, look again at your thesis statement and your working outline, and adjust them to reflect any new discoveries you have made as you read your sources and wrote in your research journal. Then, organize your research notes in a logical fashion.

When you begin to draft your paper, write the sections of the essay that you feel most comfortable with first. Throughout the essay, feature your own point of view by integrating your own analysis into the summaries, paraphrases, and quotations from other sources. Each point you make should be a section of your paper consisting of your sources (in the form of facts, examples, summaries, paraphrases, and quotations) and your own conclusions. Remember that the primary reason for doing such an assignment is to let you demonstrate your ability to synthesize material, analyze your sources and your reasoning, and draw your own conclusions.

R-7.1 WRITING THE INTRODUCTION

Construct an introduction that leads to your thesis statement. The introduction to a research paper is your chance to make a great first impression. Just like a firm handshake and a warm smile in a job interview, an essay's introduction should capture your readers' interest, set the tone for your essay, and state your specific purpose. Introductions often have a funnel effect: They typically begin with general information and then narrow the focus to your position on a particular issue. Regardless of your method, your introduction should "hook" your readers by grabbing their attention and letting them know what you are going to attempt to prove in your essay.

To lead up to the thesis statement, your introductory paragraph should stimulate your readers' interest. Effective ways of capturing your audience's attention and giving necessary background information are to (1) use a quotation; (2) tell a story that relates to your topic; (3) provide a revealing fact, statistic, or definition; (4) offer an interesting comparison; or (5) ask an intriguing question. Be sure your introduction gives readers all the information they will need to follow your logic through the rest of your paper.

Our student writer's introduction starts out with a statement about the relationship between the Internet and multitasking. The paragraph then introduces a quote about the recent attention that the academic community has given to the effects of Internet use. The last sentence of the first paragraph contains our student writer's thesis statement and ends the introduction.

R-7.2 WRITING THE SUPPORTING PARAGRAPHS

Develop as many supporting paragraphs or body paragraphs as you think necessary to explain your thesis statement. Following the introductory paragraph, a research paper includes body paragraphs that support and explain the essay's thesis statement. Each body paragraph covers a topic that is directly related to the thesis statement.

Supporting paragraphs, or body paragraphs, usually include a topic sentence, which is a general statement about the paragraph's contents, and examples or details that support the topic sentence.

To write your supporting paragraphs, you should first organize your notecards within each of your stacks. Next, add details from the notecards to your working outline. Finally, write your supporting paragraphs by following your working outline and your notecards. Make adjustments to your outline as you write so you can keep track of your ideas and make sure you are developing them in a logical fashion. The body of the paper and your outline should change and develop together with each sentence you draft.

After you write your body paragraphs, look at your thesis statement again to confirm that it introduces what you say in the rest of your paper. This is a good time to use an informal outline to check the logic of your paper. Your thesis statement should refer to all your topics, even if only indirectly, in the order you discuss them. It should also prepare your readers for the conclusions you will draw.

Our student writer's paper has ten body paragraphs that fall into three main categories:

Background

Para. 2	*The Internet and multitasking*

Opposition

Para. 3	*Multitasking as counterproductive and impossible*
Para. 4	*Problems with multitasking for young*
Para. 5	*Problems with multitasking for older adults*
Para. 6	*Detrimental effects of multitasking on social and learning skills*
Para. 7	*Multitasking and quality of life*

Positive Effects

Para. 8   *Multitasking and productivity*

Para. 9   *Multitasking and literacy*

Para. 10   *The effects of multitasking on people's views of the world*

Para. 11   *Other benefits of multitasking*

Like the foundation of a solid building, these paragraphs provide support for the position our student writer takes in her thesis statement. The stronger the supporting paragraphs are, the stronger the final paper will be.

In addition to strong topic sentences, you should also write concluding sentences in your body paragraphs that will reinforce your thesis statement or build a transition to the next paragraph. Concluding sentences bring a paragraph to a close just as a conclusion brings an essay to a close, and well-crafted concluding sentences also focus your readers on the highlights of your argument.

R-7.3 USING YOUR SOURCES

Make sure you use your sources as evidence for your argument.   Although your argument will evolve as you read your sources, you should decide on your general position before you begin to take notes. Be sure to find appropriate sources that help you develop your argument. The best way to do this is to tell your reader the significance of the direct quotations, paraphrases, or summaries that you use. Look, for example, at an excerpt from one of our student writer's paragraphs:

> *In a recent multitasking study involving older adults, researchers found that participants were unable to delete unnecessary information from their thoughts quickly after viewing several different items in rapid succession. The study demonstrated that adults had difficulty sorting through relevant and irrelevant information: "In the setting of distraction, the underlying deficit is suppressing irrelevant information that is present, and in the setting of interruption, the deficit is suppressing information that is no longer present and no longer relevant" (Clapp et al. 7215–16). In other words, multitasking can present the human mind with more than it can handle at once.*

Notice how our student writer does not stop with her source's remarks. Instead, she includes a point about the significance of what the source says. She reminds her readers that studies are not conclusive and that sometimes results show only one side of an issue.

If you simply provide a series of quotations and let them argue for you, you are not demonstrating your understanding of the quotations or showing how they fit into your argument. Be sure to use quotations as support for your argument rather than let them serve as the argument itself.

R-7.4 WRITING YOUR CONCLUSION

Write a concluding paragraph.   The concluding paragraph is the final paragraph of an essay. In its most basic form, it should summarize the main points of the essay and remind readers of the thesis statement.

The best conclusions expand on these two requirements and bring the essay to a close with one of four creative strategies. They can (1) ask a question that provokes thought on the part of the reader, (2) predict the future, (3) offer a solution to a problem, or (4) call the reader to action. Each of these options sends a specific message and creates a slightly different effect at the end of the paper. The most important responsibility of the last paragraph is to bring the essay to an effective close since it is the last information that readers see before they form their own opinions or take action.

Our student writer's conclusion gives a solution and calls the reader to action:

> *Although the arguments against multitasking on the Internet seem valid, they are not complete or conclusive. As several researchers have pointed out, multitasking online has unusual benefits that are often overlooked. We must respond to this discrepancy in theory by becoming smarter multitaskers. We will inevitably be more successful when attempting to multitask if we are aware of how we handle distraction and consciously make decisions to maintain intelligent Internet habits.*

Her concluding paragraph refocuses the reader's attention on the problem, offers a solution, and then calls the reader to action.

R-7.5 CREATING YOUR TITLE

Think of a catchy title.   Your title is what readers see first in any paper. A title is a phrase, usually no more than a few words, that suggests or sums up the subject, purpose, or focus of the essay. Some titles are very imaginative, drawing on different sources for their meaning. Others are straightforward, like the title of this chapter, "Writing a Documented Essay." Besides suggesting an essay's purpose, a good title should attract an audience's attention and make them want to read your paper. Our student writer's title, "Multitasking and the Internet: Doing More and Accomplishing Less?," will capture most readers' attention because of its relevant subject matter and the rhythm of its words.

R-7.6 A CHECKLIST FOR WRITING DOCUMENTED ESSAYS

Here is a checklist to guide you through the process of writing a documented essay.

WRITING DOCUMENTED ESSAYS

Preparing to Write
√ What is your purpose?
√ Who is your audience?

Writing

√ Do you have a thesis statement?

√ Have you organized your material effectively?

√ Have you avoided plagiarism and cited your sources correctly?

√ Do you use the appropriate documentation style?

Rewriting

√ Are the essay's assertions clear? Are they adequately supported?

√ Are other points of view recognized and examined?

√ Does the organization of your paper further your argument?

√ Are your summaries, paraphrases, or quotations presented accurately?

√ Do you introduce the sources in your paper when appropriate?

√ Are your sources in the proper format (MLA, APA, or another)?

√ Have you followed your instructor's guidelines for your title page, margins, page numbers, tables, and abstracts?

√ Do you have an alphabetical list of sources for the end of your paper?

R-8 Documenting

As you have already learned in this part of the text, you must document each source you use in your research paper with two types of citations that support each other: an in-text citation and an end-of-paper citation. Both kinds of citations are important, and both follow very strict guidelines based on the documentation style you use.

R-8.1 INTRODUCING YOUR SOURCES

Once you evaluate your sources and figure out which ones will help establish your argument, you then need to learn how to seamlessly integrate them into your paper. In other words, you should introduce them effectively while showing readers that they are credible and that they provide valuable evidence to back up your argument.

When you use a source for the first time, always (1) introduce the author(s) using the full name(s), (2) give the title of the source (use quotes for works inside larger works and italics or underlining for books), and (3) quote or paraphrase the information you need to build your argument. Here are some examples of good introductions of Fenella Saunders's "Multitasking to Distraction."

(1) Fenella Saunders, in "Multitasking to Distraction," explains that people may be motivated to multitask in order to gain more information about others.

(2) One problem, asserts Fenella Saunders in "Multitasking to Distraction," is that people may be motivated to multitask in order to gain more information about others.

(3) According to Fenella Saunders in "Multitasking to Distraction," people may be motivated to multitask in order to gain more information about others.

(4) People may be motivated to multitask in order to gain more information about others, explains Fenella Saunders in "Multitasking to Distraction."

These model sentences are only a few options for introducing Saunders's ideas; you can probably think of many more. The main words in the titles are capitalized; commas and periods as end punctuation go inside the quotation marks. In addition, the verbs in these examples each express a slightly different meaning. Finally, you should refer to the author by last name only—"According to Saunders"—each subsequent time you use the source.

R-8.2 DOCUMENTATION FORMAT

Documentation styles vary from discipline to discipline. As a result, you need to ask your instructor what documentation style he or she wants you to follow. Three of the major documentation styles are Modern Language Association (MLA), used in humanities courses; American Psychological Association (APA), used in social science courses; and *Chicago Manual of Style* (CMS), used in history, mathematics, and science classes. Even though documentation styles vary, the basic concept behind documentation is the same in all disciplines: You must give proper credit to other writers by acknowledging the sources of the summaries, paraphrases, and quotations that you use to support the ideas in your documented essay. Remember that you have two goals in any citation: (1) to acknowledge the author and (2) to help the reader locate the material. Once you grasp this basic concept, you will have no trouble avoiding plagiarism.

Because you may have to write a paper using any one of these documentation styles, you should have a basic understanding of their differences.

In-Text Citations

The major difference among in-text citations for MLA, APA, and CMS is that MLA and APA use parenthetical references whereas CMS uses a footnote or endnote system. Look at the differences in the following sentences:

MLA: Tyler Cowen contends that "multitasking is not a distraction from our main activity; it *is* our main activity" (56).

APA: Tyler Cowen contends that "multitasking is not a distraction from our main activity; it *is* our main activity" (2009, p. 56).

R-8

CMS: Tyler Cowen contends that "multitasking is not a distraction from our main activity; it *is* our main activity."[1]

MLA and APA furnish the page number for the source (APA with a "p." and MLA without a "p."). APA also includes the year the article was written. For CMS, a reader would find the publication information (including the page number of the source) in a numbered footnote or endnote.

In contrast, certain in-text features are similar in all three documentation styles:

- Citation information must appear directly after every quotation.
- Citation information must appear after a paraphrase of a source. (A paraphrase can be more than one sentence.)
- Punctuation must follow the parenthetical citation, not the quotation.
- Longer quotes should be indented in block form and do not require quotation marks.
- Blocked quotes should be double spaced in the same size font as the paper.

End-of-Paper Citations

One of the most obvious differences among MLA, APA, and CMS is how they list their sources at the end of the paper. MLA includes a "Works Cited" page; APA lists "References"; and CMS has a "Bibliography." Works Cited and References pages list only those sources cited in the paper. These sources are listed alphabetically. Your in-text citations tell the reader the name and page number of the source you are using, and the Works Cited/References pages provide readers with the full bibliographic information.

A bibliography lists every source you looked at while researching your paper. Documentation styles that include a bibliography use a separate page for notes to show which of the sources from the bibliography you actually cited in your paper. Pages for notes use a numbering system that corresponds to a number in the body of the paper. Writers using a bibliography have the advantage of showing their readers all the sources they read for the paper, even if they took no material directly from a source.

Regardless of which documentation style you use, the source lists at the end of the paper share common formatting features:

- The title is centered and is in regular font. It is not bolded, underlined, put in quotation marks, or italicized (unless you include another title within your own title).
- The page numbers are continuous from the body of the paper.
- The entries are all double-spaced.
- The entries all use a hanging indent (which can be accessed in Microsoft Word either through the "Paragraph" feature under "Format" or by

manipulating the hourglass on the ruler). Note: Some documentation styles prefer paragraph indenting.

- The entries are all alphabetized. Note: You do not rearrange authors' names in a single entry so that they are alphabetical. Leave the order as it appears in your source.

Regardless of the documentation style, the in-text citations, end-of-paper sources, and footnotes or endnotes (where applicable) all work together to give readers access to the bibliographic information of the sources you are using.

R-8.3 MLA VERSUS APA

Because MLA and APA are the most popular documentation styles, you should know the basic elements of each. The logic behind both styles is similar, but there are important differences between them.

In-Text Citations

MLA
- *Author's full names are used.*
- *Dates don't necessarily have to be mentioned.*
- *A parenthetical citation includes author's last name and a page number: (Cowen 56).*

APA
- *Author's last name and first initial are used.*
- *Dates must either follow the author's name in the sentence or appear in parentheses following the sentence.*
- *A parenthetical citation includes author's last name, date, and a page number: (Cowen, 2009, p. 56).*

Works Cited/References Page

MLA and APA both require similar information but in a different order.

MLA: Cowen, Tyler. "Three Tweets for the Web." *The Wilson Quarterly,* vol. 33, no. 4, Autumn 2009, pp. 54-58.

APA: Cowen, T. (2009). Three tweets for the web. *The Wilson Quarterly, 33,* 54-58.

R-8.4 SAMPLE STUDENT REFERENCES

Our student writer used the MLA format for her paper, which she wrote for an English class. English instructors usually have their students use MLA. The student includes a variety of sources in her paper, which we can use to illustrate the two types of citations. Listed here are some sample in-text citations, with the corresponding entries at the end of her paper.

R-8

Book—name of author, title of book, name of publisher, year

In-Text Citation: (Levitin 96)

Works Cited: Levitin, Daniel J. *The Organized Mind.*
                             Dutton, 2014.

Journal—name of author(s), title of article, name of journal, volume number, issue number, month or season (if applicable) and year, page number

In-Text Citation: (Saunders 455)

Works Cited: Saunders, Fenella. "Multitasking to Dis-
                             traction." *American Scientist*, vol. 97,
                             no. 6, Nov.-Dec. 2009, p. 455.

Online Database—name of author(s), title of article, name of journal, volume number, issue number, date of publication, page number, name of database, URL or DOI (digital object identifier)

In-Text Citation: (Cowen 56)

Works Cited: Cowen, Tyler. "Three Tweets for
                             the Web." *The Wilson Quarterly*,
                             vol. 33, no. 4, Autumn 2009,
                             pp. 54-58. *JSTOR*, www.jstor.org/
                             stable/20700628.

General-Circulation Magazine—name of author(s), title of article, name of magazine, volume number, date of publication, page number (for print magazines) or URL (for online magazines)

In-Text Citation: (Thompson)

Works Cited: Thompson, Derek. "If Multitasking Is
                             Impossible, Why Are Some People
                             So Good at It?" *The Atlantic*, 17 Nov.
                             2011, www.theatlantic.com/business/
                             archive/2011/11/if-multitasking-is-
                             impossible-why-are-some-people-so-
                             good-at-it/248648/.

Note: Because this online article does not have page numbers or numbered paragraphs, our student writer used only the author's last name in the in-text citation.

Every source is cited in a slightly different way, depending on the type of source and the documentation style. So when you have chosen your sources and determined that they are relevant, reliable, and recent (Remember the "3Rs" from R-4.1?), your last step is to consult an appropriate, current manual or website to make sure you cite each source correctly.

R-9 Revising and Editing a Documented Essay

Part of the process of writing any paper, including a documented essay, is revising and editing your work.

R-9.1 REVISING

To revise a research paper, you should play the role of your readers and impartially evaluate your argument and the sources you have used as evidence in that argument. To begin with, revise your thesis to represent all the discoveries you made as you wrote your first draft. Then, look for problems in logic throughout the essay; you might even revise your working outline at this point to help you check your reasoning:

- Are the essay's assertions clear? Are they adequately supported?
- Are other points of view recognized and examined?
- Does the organization of your paper further your argument?

Next, check your documentation style:

- Are your summaries, paraphrases, and quotations presented accurately?
- Do you introduce the sources in your paper when appropriate?
- Are your sources in the proper format (MLA, APA, or another)?

Logic

Look at the following excerpt from our student writer's first draft:

(1) If texting or talking on a phone can cause people to ignore something so obvious, it can surely distract them from the subtle social cues that they receive from others throughout the day. (2) Therefore, it stands to reason that multitasking can have detrimental effects on social life as well as on the ability to perform well. (3) Multitasking, however, is not always a negative activity; when done correctly, it can enhance the quality of our work and our lives.

In this excerpt, our student writer summarized the opposing arguments (sentences 1 and 2) and introduced her first point (sentence 3) in the same paragraph. Upon inspection, however, she realized that this paragraph needed to be revised. As a result, she kept the first two sentences in the first paragraph and started a new paragraph with sentence 3:

(1) If texting or talking on a phone can cause people to ignore something so obvious, it can surely distract them from the subtle social cues that they receive

from others throughout the day. (2) Therefore, it stands to reason that multitasking can have detrimental effects on social life as well as on the ability to perform well.

(3) Multitasking, however, is not always a negative activity; when done correctly, it can enhance the quality of our work and our lives.

By starting a new paragraph with sentence 3, our student writer makes the paragraphs better organized and clearer for the reader. These two paragraphs in their complete forms are in our student's revised essay in paragraphs 6 and 7.

Synthesis

When writers use more than one source in an essay, they *synthesize* their sources. In other words, they take pieces of information from different sources and weave them into their own argument. If you've written any papers using more than one source, you were synthesizing material. As you write a documented essay, your own argument establishes the order of your ideas. Then your sources provide evidence or proof for your argument.

Look at how our student writer uses sources. Here is a paragraph from her first draft:

(1) Furthermore, multitasking on the Internet promotes literacy and the open exchange of knowledge. (2) In her essay "Online Debate: Online, R U Really Reading?," Motoko Rich argues that "the Internet has created a new kind of reading, one that schools and society should not discount. (3) The Web inspires a teenager . . . who might otherwise spend most of her leisure time watching television, to read and write." (4) Time spent multitasking on the Internet is often more educational and productive than time spent watching television.

As our student writer was revising this paragraph, she realized she was forcing the reader to make connections between her sources and her argument because she was not providing explanations that made those connections. So she revised her paragraph, connecting her sources to her own ideas and making her argument clearer. Her changes are underlined in the following paragraph:

(1) Furthermore, multitasking on the Internet promotes literacy and the open exchange of knowledge. (2) <u>The more time people spend on different Web sites, the more they are reading, listening, learning, and experiencing.</u> (3) In her essay "Online Debate: Online, R U Really Reading?," Motoko Rich argues that "the Internet has created a new kind of reading, one that schools and society should not discount. (4) The Web inspires a teenager . . . who might otherwise spend most of her leisure time watching television, to read and write." (5) Time spent multitasking on the Internet is often more educational and

productive than time spent watching television. (6) <u>As Rich's article explains,</u> <u>*even distracted reading is better than no reading at all.*</u>

By adding sentence 2, our student writer introduces Rich's quote and ties it to her argument that multitasking can be beneficial. She strengthens her case by connecting Rich's quote to her own thoughts. Similarly, our student writer adds sentence 6 to emphasize her point that multitasking on the Internet promotes literacy and to conclude her paragraph. She shows that she understands Rich's quote as she incorporates it into her argument.

To better understand how our student writer's paragraph works as a combination of her ideas and sources, look at the following breakdown of her paragraph:

(1)	**Our student writer's** *introductory sentence*
(2)	**Introduction** *to Source A*
(3–4)	**Quotation/paraphrase** *of Source A*
(5)	**Our student writer's** *commentary, elaborating on Source A*
(6)	**Our student writer's** *conclusion to the paragraph*

This skeleton outline of our student writer's paragraph should help you see how she balances her opinions/observations and her sources so they work as one unit that supports her main argument. If you get stuck writing your own paragraphs, referring back to this outline might help you see where you need to add information.

R-9.2 EDITING

At the editing stage you must proofread carefully.

- Have you found and corrected all your grammar, usage, and syntax errors?
- Have you followed your instructor's guidelines for your title page, margins, page numbers, tables, and abstracts?
- Do you have an alphabetical list of your sources at the end of your paper?

After our student writer's revisions were complete, she edited her essay by correcting several grammar, usage, and syntax errors. First, she found a fragment in paragraph 6 that she had to correct:

> In addition to arguing against the effectiveness of multitasking. Some critics also suggest that the habit has detrimental effects on social skills.

She corrected her fragment by combining it with an independent clause:

In addition to arguing against the effectiveness of **multitasking, some** critics also suggest that the habit has detrimental effects on social skills.

Next, she found a comma splice in paragraph 7, punctuating two sentences as one:

Multitasking, however, is not always a negative activity, when done correctly, it can enhance the quality of our work and our lives.

She corrected the error by separating the two sentences with a semicolon:

Multitasking, however, is not always a negative **activity; when** done correctly, it can enhance the quality of our work and our lives.

As she reads further, she realizes she has a pronoun-antecedent agreement error in paragraph 8:

While critics of multitasking are quick to condemn this "destructive" habit, he or she fails to evaluate the quality of those distractions.

"Critics" is plural and needs a plural pronoun to refer to it:

While **critics** of multitasking are quick to condemn this "destructive" habit, **they fail** to evaluate the quality of those distractions.

Notice that the verb also has to be changed to agree with the pronoun "they."

R-9.3 STUDENT ESSAY: DOCUMENTATION AT WORK

The following documented essay uses sources to support its observations and conclusions about the connection between the Internet and multitasking. First, the writer discusses how the Internet encourages multitasking. She then goes on to explain why many researchers contend that multitasking is inefficient. Her next several paragraphs argue that, regardless of what many critics think, multitasking on the Internet can actually increase productivity. She concludes by suggesting constructive ways people can multitask at the computer. Throughout the essay, the student writer carefully supports her main points with summaries, paraphrases, and quotations from other sources. Notice that she uses the MLA documentation style and closes the paper with an alphabetical list of "Works Cited." Look also for her uses of different rhetorical modes, which are identified in the margins in brackets ([ ]).

Focused title

Multitasking and the Internet: Doing More and Accomplishing Less?

Background   The Internet is a modern-day breeding ground 1
for multitasking—offering videos, websites, hyperlinks, tabs, and many other seductive features. Since
most Internet users naturally do more than two tasks
at once, modern researchers have begun to examine
the effects of this habit. Tyler Cowen, a well-known
economist, professor, and blogger, has commented on
this research, noting:

Past research
> The arrival of virtually every new cultural medium
> has been greeted with the charge that it truncates
> attention spans and represents the beginning of cul-
> tural collapse—the novel (in the 18th century), the
> comic book, rock 'n' roll, television, and now the
> Web. (55)

Summary of research   While many scholars and researchers consider multitasking to be distracting and harmful, some think
there may still be undiscovered benefits to it. Internet
multitaskers have nearly unlimited information at their
fingertips, which they can access instantaneously. The
Internet has played a crucial role in promoting media   Thesis statement
multitasking, and, contrary to many claims, is the per-
fect venue for multitaskers to increase their productivity and enhance their lives, causing the benefits of
multitasking on the Internet to far outweigh its
disadvantages.

Background   The Internet promotes multitasking at every turn. 2
When people go online, as Nicholas Carr points out   Source of quotation
in "The Juggler's Brain," they are subject to a sensory
Quotation   assault: "The Net engages all of our senses—except,
In-text citation   so far, those of smell and taste—and it engages them
simultaneously" (10). A mouse and keypad occupy   Explanation
our hands; clicking, music, audio commentary, or
soundtracks entertain our ears; and brightly lit, often-
changing monitors stimulate our eyes. Additionally,
computers are usually plugged into power sources that
give life to many other electronic devices. Telephones,
fax machines, and printers, all of which can emit
noises and flashing lights, are frequently found near
laptop docking stations or computer desks. Multiple
tabs and windows offered by browsers provide users
the opportunity to keep several pages open at once,

and hyperlinks on Web sites facilitate faster navigation through the Internet. These stimuli encourage multitasking, making the Web a productive place to practice doing more than one activity at a time.

Many scientists and scholars, however, agree that **3** multitasking is not only counterproductive, but literally impossible, favoring the task-switching perspective that Allan Goldstein explains in his essay "'Our Brains Are Evolving to Multitask,' Not! The Illusion of Multitasking." In a variety of studies, researchers *Paraphrase* have found that multitaskers devote less attention to each task and are therefore less able to completely focus on any one of the tasks. According to Goldstein, "serialtasking" or "task-switching" may be better terms for multitasking. He finds that "neuroscientists are discovering that different parts of the brain are switching on and off. . . . This switching happens so fast that it appears we are performing multiple tasks *In-text citation* simultaneously" (Goldstein).

Transition Problems with multitasking affect people of all ages. **4** Young people, although accustomed to media multitasking, often become distracted while attempting it. *Opposition* In her article "Kids Really *Are* Different These Days," *Source of quotation* Diana D. Coyl argues:

> The human brain is not capable of focusing on more *Longer block quotation* than one thing at a time; the experience of media multitasking requires the brain to perform sequential processing, switching attention back and forth from one task to another. Research findings are clear that the quality of complex tasks (e.g., homework assignments) and depth of thought is [sic] reduced when *In-text citation* individuals' attention is divided. (405)

According to these authors, children who have grown up with the Internet may feel like they are successfully *Explanation* multitasking when they are really only switching rapidly between tasks, resulting in less-focused thought, often without producing speedier results. These critics argue that even adults, who have had their entire lives to practice multitasking, cannot effectively master the skill.

In a recent multitasking study involving older **5** *Opposition* adults, researchers found that participants were unable

Margin labels (left): Opposition, Quotation, Transition, Source of quotation, In-text citation, Opposition

R-9

to delete unnecessary information from their thoughts quickly after viewing several different items in rapid succession. The study demonstrated that adults had difficulty sorting through relevant and irrelevant information:

Paraphrase

Quotation

> In the setting of distraction, the underlying deficit is suppressing irrelevant information that is present, and in the setting of interruption, the deficit is suppressing information that is no longer present and no longer relevant. (Clapp et al. 7215-16)

In other words, multitasking can present the human mind with more than it can handle all at once. Neuroscientist Daniel J. Levitin reaches a similar conclusion. In *The Organized Mind*, Levitin writes that "multitasking . . . can overstimulate your brain and cause mental fog or scrambled thinking" (96). While seeming to advance the argument against multitasking, these researchers disregard the overall amount of information being absorbed. Although multitaskers may be less focused than non-multitaskers, they are presented with, and may learn, much more information than their counterparts.

In-text citation

Argument against opposition

In addition to arguing against the effectiveness of multitasking, some critics also suggest that the habit has detrimental effects on social skills. Referring to a recent study, behavioral psychologist Susan Weinschenk reports that "people talking on their cell phones while walking, ran into people more often and didn't notice what was going on around them." The subjects' lack of attention caused them to ignore major, as well as minor, events. Even when "the researchers had someone in a clown suit ride a unicycle," some multitaskers failed to notice (Weinschenk). If texting or talking on a phone can cause people to ignore something so obvious, it can surely distract them from the subtle social cues that they receive from others throughout the day. Therefore, it stands to reason that multitasking can have detrimental effects on social life as well as on the ability to perform well.

6

Opposition

Source of quotation

Quotation

In-text citation

Multitasking, however, is not always a negative activity; when done correctly, it can enhance the

7

First claim [Cause/ Effect]

quality of our work and our lives. As Maria Konnikova points out in her article titled "Multitasking Masters," it is possible to achieve greater productivity through multitasking. Since at least one team of experienced researchers found that, because multitaskers' brains "become less, not more, active with additional tasks," it can be concluded that "they are functioning more efficiently" (Konnikova). Critics would argue that the stimuli associated with multitasking are distracting, thus dismissing the potential benefits of media multitasking. But multiple Web sites allow users access to unprecedented amounts of information, and e-mail or instant messaging chats enrich our lives by keeping us in contact with friends and family.

Explanation

Quotation

In-text citation

Opposing argument

Argument against opposition

The amount of information and the speed at which we can access it are not the only positive side effects of multitasking on the Internet. According to Derek Thompson, multitasking, when done judiciously, can also increase productivity in the workplace:

Transition

8

Second claim [Cause/Effect]

Explanation/ Quotation

> Most of what we know about attention suggests that our focus comes with strict limits. . . . Short bursts of attention punctuated with equally deliberate breaks are the surest way to harness our full capacity to be productive.

Many multitasking critics fail to mention the importance of taking short breaks, which help people maintain focus when working for prolonged periods of time. Multitasking on the Internet can also help workers generate ideas that can increase productivity:

Argument against opposition

> The Web is perfect for indulging our multitasking, which is really nothing more than the rapid switching of tasks, because it promises something new and fast. Science suggests that the secret to thriving in an age of universal distraction isn't to avoid distractions, but to distract ourselves smartly. The National University of Singapore found that workers who spend 20 percent or less of their time browsing the Web are 9 percent more productive than those who never go online at all. (Thompson)

Longer block quotation

Statistics

In-text citation

While critics of multitasking are quick to condemn this "destructive" habit, they fail to evaluate the quality of those distractions. Fast-paced Web surfing can

Paraphrase/ Evidence

produce ideas that have the potential to enrich both our lives and our productivity.

Third claim [Cause/ Effect] Furthermore, multitasking on the Internet pro- **9** motes literacy and the open exchange of knowledge. The more time people spend on different Web sites, **Explanation** the more they are reading, listening, learning, and experiencing. In her essay "Literacy Debate: Online, **Source of** R U Really Reading?" Motoko Rich argues that **quotation**

> the Internet has created a new kind of reading, one that schools and society should not discount. The **Longer** Web inspires a teenager . . . who might otherwise **block**
> **Example** spend most of her leisure time watching television, **quotation** to read and write.

Time spent multitasking on the Internet is often more educational and productive than time spent watching television. As Rich's article explains, even distracted reading is better than no reading at all. **Summary**

Transition Finally, looking at multitasking from different per- **10** spectives can change preconceived notions about its **Source of** disadvantages. Tyler Cowen contends that "multitask- **Fourth** **quotation** ing is not a distraction from our main activity; it *is* **claim** **In-text** our main activity" (56). He continues by arguing that **[Cause/** **citation** doing several online chores at once helps people build **Effect]** their own unique narratives about the world; through **Explanation** multitasking, we are able to see multiple stories unfold simultaneously, which can give us varied perspectives on single events as we form our own opinions about **Source of** them. Offering a different line of reasoning, Jerome **quotation** Rekart's essay "Taking on Multitasking" claims:

> Today's student may be paying attention in a differ- **Longer** ent way, and so one must be careful not to assume **block** that the ramifications are entirely negative. One **quotation** effect of media multitasking is that students are paying attention to multiple stimuli rather than sustaining focus on just one stimulus. This has been referred to as a 'breadth approach,' and it may yield benefits that have yet to be uncovered **In-text** or realized. (63) **citation** These unusual but solid arguments in favor of multi- tasking dispute much of what researchers have claimed **Summary** about its detrimental consequences and point us **statement** toward new ways of looking at the issue.

Reflection/
Analysis

Regardless of the conflicting conclusions that mod- 11
ern writers have drawn about multitasking, many people
believe they can successfully do it. This brings up two
very interesting questions: Why are we driven to work
on several tasks at once, and why specifically are we
enticed to do them on the Internet? Fenella Saunders   Source of
proposes two different but viable motives: quotation

Longer
block
quotation

One possibility is that multitaskers have become so
habituated to an onslaught of information that they
operate on the assumption that any input is potentially relevant. Another idea is that it's much like why
humans now overindulge in unhealthful foods: Just
as we are wired to like sugar and fats, we are predis-
posed to seek out as much information as possible,
particularly about other humans. (455)   In-text
citation

The popularity and fast-paced nature of social networking Web sites clearly validates Saunders's argument. However, regardless of our motivation to

Source
of quotation

multitask, the practice can be improved. Craig Childs
of Lifehack.org suggests that we multitask with activities that are different from each other: "The example of   Quotation
listening to music while reading makes sense: you read
faster and clearer if the music you listen to has no lyrics."
Activities that allow large margins of error are also ideal   Summary
for multitasking, as the likelihood of mistakes increases   statement
with the decrease of focused attention.

Summary

Although the arguments against multitasking on the   12
Internet seem valid, they are not complete or conclusive. As several researchers have pointed out, multitasking online has unusual benefits that are often overlooked.
We must respond to this discrepancy in theory by   Conclusion
becoming smarter multitaskers. We will inevitably be
more successful when attempting to multitask if we are
aware of how we handle distraction and consciously
make decisions to maintain intelligent Internet habits.

Works Cited

Sources
referred
to in the
paper

Carr, Nicholas. "The Juggler's Brain." *Phi Delta
    Kappan*, vol. 92, no. 4, Nov. 2010-Dec. 2011,   Alphabetical
    pp. 8-14. *JSTOR*, www.jstor.org/stable/27922479.   order
Childs, Craig. "If You Must Multitask, Do It This
    Way." *Lifehack*, www.lifehack.org/articles/
    productivity/if-you-must-multitask-do-it-this-way
    .html. Accessed 9 Jan. 2016.

Clapp, Wesley C., et al. "Deficit in Switching between Functional Brain Networks Underlies the
Impact of Multitasking on Working Memory in
Older Adults." *Proceedings of the National Academy
of Sciences of the United States of America*, vol. 108,
no. 17, Apr. 2011, pp. 7212-17. *Academic Search
Elite*, doi:10.1073/pnas.1015297108.

Coyl, Diana D. "Kids Really *Are* Different These
Days." *Phi Delta Kappan*, vol. 90, no. 6, Feb. 2009,
pp. 404-07. *JSTOR*, www.jstor.org/stable/
20446131.

Cowen, Tyler. "Three Tweets for the Web."
The Wilson Quarterly, vol. 33, no. 4, Autumn
2009, pp. 54-58. *JSTOR*, www.jstor.org/
stable/20700628.

Goldstein, Allan. "'Our Brains Are Evolving to Multitask,' Not! The Illusion of Multitasking." *UCSD Center
for Mindfulness*, 1 July 2011, ucsdcfm.wordpress
.com/2015/04/10/our-brains-are-evolving-to-
multitask-not-the-ill-usion-of-multitasking/.

Konnikova, Maria. "Multitasking Masters." *The
New Yorker*, 7 May 2014, www.newyorker.com/
science/maria-konnikova/multitask-masters.

Levitin, Daniel J. *The Organized Mind*. Dutton, 2014.

Rekart, Jerome L. "Taking on Multitasking." *Phi
Delta Kappan*, vol. 93, no. 4, Dec. 2011-Jan.
2012, pp. 60-63. *Academic Search Elite*,
doi:10.1177/003172171109300415.

Rich, Motoko. "Literacy Debate: Online, R U
Really Reading?" *The New York Times*, 27 July
2008, nyti.ms/1Z1Odi6.

Saunders, Fenella. "Multitasking to Distraction."
American Scientist, vol. 97, no. 6, Nov.-Dec.
2009, p. 455.

Thompson, Derek. "If Multitasking Is Impossible,
Why Are Some People So Good at It?" *The
Atlantic*, 17 Nov. 2011, www.theatlantic.com/
business/archive/2011/11/if-multitasking-is-
impossible-why-are-some-people-so-good-
at-it/248648/.

Weinschenk, Susan. "The True Cost of Multitasking." *Psychology Today*, 18 Sept. 2012, www
.psychologytoday.com/blog/brain-wise/201209/
the-true-cost-multi-tasking.

Student Writer's Comments

From the moment this essay was assigned, I knew my topic would be multitasking with the Internet because I felt the key to a convincing argument was to select a subject I was interested in. Since I've been in college, I have been more tempted than ever to multitask, so it is a topic I can discuss passionately. I wanted to bring together ideas about media multitasking in a way that I thought would be new, and once I read Goldstein's essay on the topic, I knew I had an angle to attack: I could talk about how multitasking, while sometimes detrimental, is not always counterproductive, especially when done while using the Internet. This seemed especially important during a time when our country is so fast-paced and technologically inclined. I wanted to be honest as I appealed to the emotions, concerns, and ethics of my audience. Multitasking is definitely a part of our media-saturated society, and the Internet will always provide a temptation. Because of this, I felt like I needed to research and write about the relationship between the two.

I began the process of writing this paper by getting on the computer every chance I had (between classes, during lunch, and at night before I went home) and collecting information about the Internet and multitasking. I found plenty of material, and I also uncovered arguments that I really didn't expect to find. I was fascinated by the information—both facts and opinions—that I discovered. But the material wasn't taking any shape at all yet; so far, the only common denominators were the general topic and my interest level.

I was taking notes on notecards, so I had filled quite a stack of cards when I stopped to reread all my material to see if I could put it into any coherent categories. Happily, my notes fell quite naturally into four divisions: (1) how the Internet encourages multitasking, (2) the negative effects of multitasking while on the Internet, (3) the positive effects, and (4) what motivates people to multitask online. I could see right away that I had enough material from reputable sources on my topic. I had stray notes that didn't fit any of these categories, but I decided to worry about them later. I tried my hand at a thesis statement, which I think had been floating around in my head for days. Then I wrote the paper topic by topic over a period of several days. I didn't attempt the introduction and the conclusion until I began to rewrite. As I composed the essay, I was especially aware of the types of material I had on each of my topics, and I put my source and page numbers (or paragraph numbers) into my first draft. I also had several examples for each of my topics and a good blend of facts and opinions.

When I rewrote my essay, I kept in mind that I would be successful in arguing my case only if my words caused the readers to make a change, however small, in their own behavior. I reworked my research paper several times as I played different readers with various biases, paying special attention to word choice and sentence structure.

Overall, writing this paper gave me a great deal of pleasure. I feel even more strongly that multitasking is not innately detrimental to our learning abilities and personal relationships, but it should be done judiciously.

GLOSSARY OF USEFUL TERMS

Numbers in parentheses indicate pages in the text where the term is defined and/or examples are given. Numbers in brackets are paragraph numbers in the readings. Italicized terms within definitions are also defined in this glossary.

Abstract (143–144) nouns, such as "truth" or "beauty," are words that refer to general concepts, qualities, and conditions that summarize an entire category of experience. Conversely, *concrete* terms, such as "apple," "crabgrass," "computer," and "French horn," make precise appeals to our senses. Most good writers use *abstract* terms sparingly in their *essays,* preferring instead the vividness and clarity of *concrete* words and phrases.

Allusion is a reference to a well-known person, place, or event from life or literature. In "Summer Rituals," for example, Ray Bradbury alludes to Herman Melville's great novel *Moby Dick* when he describes an old man who walks on his front porch "like Ahab surveying the mild day" [para. 2].

Analogy (290) is an extended *comparison* of two dissimilar objects or ideas.

Analysis (3–4, 187–188, 536–537) involves examining and evaluating a topic by separating it into its basic parts and elements and studying it systematically.

Anecdote (95) is a brief account of a single incident.

Argumentation (443–458) is an appeal predominantly to *logic* and reason. It deals with complex issues that can be debated.

Attitude (100, 103) refers to the narrator's personal feelings about a particular subject. In "Excerpt from *Battle Hymn of the Tiger Mother,*" Amy Chua communicates her rigid, unforgiving attitude about raising children.

Audience (26–31, 37) refers to the person or group of people for whom an *essay* is written. The primary audience of Jay Walljasper's "Our Schedules, Our Selves," for example, is people who feel enslaved by their frantic daily routines.

Cause and effect (396–408) is a form of *analysis* that examines the causes and consequences of events and ideas.

Characterization is the creation of imaginary yet realistic persons in fiction, drama, and *narrative* poetry.

Chronological order (31, 35, 97, 103, 145, 151, 193, 194) is a sequence of events arranged in the order in which they occurred. Brent Staples follows this natural time sequence in his *example* essay entitled "A Brother's Murder."

Classification (237–248) is the analytical process of grouping together similar subjects into a single category or class; *division* works in the opposite fashion, breaking down a subject into many different subgroups. In "The Ways We Lie," Stephanie Ericsson classifies lies into ten distinct categories.

Clichés are words or expressions that have lost their freshness and originality through continual use. For example, "busy as a bee" "pretty as a picture," and "hotter than hell" have become trite and dull because of overuse. Good writers avoid clichés through vivid and original phrasing.

Climactic order (151) refers to the *organization* of ideas from one extreme to another— for example, from least important to most important, from most destructive to least destructive, or from least promising to most promising.

Cognitive skills (4) are mental abilities that help us send and receive verbal messages.

Coherence (151) is the manner in which an *essay* "holds together" its main ideas. A coherent *theme* will demonstrate such a clear relationship between its *thesis* and its logical structure that readers can easily follow the argument.

Colloquial diction consists of words appropriate for very informal conversation.

Comparison (289–302) is an *expository* writing technique that examines the similarities between objects or ideas, whereas *contrast* focuses on differences.

Conclusions (33, 37) bring *essays* to a natural close by summarizing the argument, restating the *thesis*, calling for some specific action, or explaining the significance of the topic just discussed. The conclusion should leave your reader satisfied that you have actually "concluded" your discussion.

Concrete: See *Abstract.*

Conflict is the struggle resulting from the opposition of two strong forces in the plot of a play, novel, or short story.

Connotation and Denotation (463) are two principal methods of describing the meanings of words. *Connotation* refers to the wide array of positive and negative associations that most words naturally carry with them, whereas *denotation* is the precise, literal *definition* of a word that might be found in a dictionary. See, for example, Amy Tan's description of the terms "broken" or "fractured" English in "Mother Tongue" (267).

Content and Form (33, 37) are the two main components of an *essay. Content* refers to the subject matter of an *essay,* whereas its *form* consists of the graphic symbols that communicate the subject matter (word choice, spelling, punctuation, paragraphing, etc.)

Contrast: See *Comparison.*

Deduction (452) is a form of logical reasoning that begins with a general assertion and then presents specific details and *examples* in support of that *generalization. Induction* works in reverse by offering a number of *examples* and then concluding with a general truth or principle.

Definition (345–355) is a process whereby the meaning of a term is explained. Formal definitions require (1) finding the general class to which the object belongs and (2) isolating the object within that class by describing how it differs from other elements in the same category. In "Beliefs about Families," Mary Pipher defines a family as "a collection of people who pool resources and help each other over the long haul" [para. 1].

Denotation: See *Connotation.*

Description (40–53) is a mode of writing or speaking that conveys the sights, sounds, tastes, smells, or feelings of a particular experience to its readers or listeners. Good descriptive writers, such as those featured in Chapter 4, are particularly adept at receiving, selecting, and expressing sensory details from the world around them. Along with *persuasion, exposition,* and *narration,* description is one of the four dominant types of writing.

Development (32) concerns the manner in which a *paragraph* of an *essay* expands on its topic.

Dialect is a speech pattern typical of a certain regional location, race, or social group that exhibits itself through unique word choice, pronunciation, and/or grammatical *usage.,* See, for example, Amy Tan's description of her mother's "fractured" English in "Mother Tongue" or John Tierney's parody of a nineteenth-century song in "A Generation's Vanity, Heard Through Lyrics."

Dialogue is a conversation between two or more people, particularly within a novel, play, poem, short story, or other literary work. See, for example, the *dialogue* between the author and Ricardo in Jessica Blau's "Red-Headed."

Diction (30-31) is word choice. If a vocabulary is a list of words available for use, then good *diction* is the careful selection of those words to communicate a particular subject to a specific *audience*. Different types of diction include *formal* (scholarly books and articles), *informal* (essays in popular magazines), *colloquial* (conversations between friends, including newly coined words and expressions), *slang* (language shared by certain social groups), *dialect* (language typical of a certain region, race, or social group), *technical* (words that make up the basic vocabulary of a specific area of study, such as medicine or law), and *obsolete* (words no longer in use).

Division: See *Classification.*

Documentation (568–572) refers to the process of acknowledging sources in a *documented essay* through in-text citations and end-of-paper citations.

Documented essay (536–537) is a research or term paper that integrates *paraphrases, summaries,* and *quotations* from secondary sources with the writer's own insights and conclusions. Such *essays* normally include bibliographic references within the paper and, at the end, a list of the books and articles cited. See Part III of this book: "Reference: Reading and Writing from Sources."

Dominant impression (43, 46) in *descriptive* writing is the principal effect the author wishes to create for the *audience.*

Editing (33–34, 37) is an important part of the *rewriting* process of an *essay* that requires writers to make certain their work observes the conventions of standard written English.

Effect: See *Cause and effect.*

Emphasis (102–103, 450) is the stress given to certain words, phrases, sentences, and/or *paragraphs* within an *essay* by such methods as repeating important ideas; positioning thesis and *topic sentences* effectively; supplying additional details or *examples;* allocating more space to certain sections of an *essay;* choosing words carefully; selecting and arranging details judiciously; and using certain mechanical devices, such as italics, underlining, capitalization, and different colors of ink.

Essay is a relatively short prose composition on a limited topic. Most *essays* are five hundred to one thousand words long and focus on a clearly definable question to be answered or problem to be solved. *Informal essays,* such as Wayne Norman's, "When Is a Sport Not a Sport," are generally brief, humorous, and loosely structured; *formal essays,* such as David Hanson's "Binge Drinking," are generally characterized by seriousness of *purpose,* logical organization, and dignity of language. *Essays* in this textbook have been divided into nine traditional *rhetorical* categories, each of which is discussed at length in its chapter introduction.

Etymology (350) is the study of the origin and development of words.

Evidence (444–445, 447, 451–454) is any material used to help support an *argument,* including details, facts, *examples,* opinions, and expert testimony. Just as a lawyer's case is won or lost in a court of law because of the strength of the evidence presented, so too does the effectiveness of a writer's essay depend on the evidence offered in support of its *thesis statement.*

Example (143–154) is an illustration of a general principle or *thesis statement.* Harold Krents's "Darkness at Noon," for instance, gives several different examples of prejudice against handicapped people.

Exposition is one of the four main *rhetorical* categories of writing (the others are *persuasion, narration,* and *description*). The principal purpose of expository prose is to "expose" ideas to your readers, meaning to explain, define, and interpret information through one or more of the following modes of exposition: *example, process analysis, division/classification, comparison/contrast, definition,* and *cause/effect.*

Figurative language (49, 454) is writing or speaking that purposefully departs from the literal meanings of words to achieve a particularly vivid, expressive, and/or imaginative image. When, for example, Jessica Mitford describes the skin of a corpse as composed of a "velvety softness" [para. 11], she is using *figurative language.* Other principal figures of speech include *metaphor, simile, hyperbole, allusion,* and *personification.*

Flashback (103) is a technique used mainly in *narrative* writing that enables the author to present scenes or conversations that took place prior to the beginning of the story. See, for example, Ray Bradbury's "Summer Rituals," in which the author chronicles several nostalgic events from his youth.

Focus (31–32, 34) is the concentration of a *topic* on one central point or issue.

Form: See *Content.*

Formal diction is language that is used principally in scholarly books and articles.

Formal essay: See *Essay.*

Free association (27) is a process of generating ideas for writing through which one thought leads randomly to another.

General words (143–144) are those that employ expansive categories, such as "animals," "sports," "occupations," and "clothing"; *specific* words are more limiting and restrictive, such as "koala," "lacrosse," "computer programmer," and "bow tie." Whether a word is *general* or *specific* depends at least somewhat on its context: "Bow tie" is more *specific* than "clothing," yet less *specific* than "the pink and green striped bow tie Aunt Martha gave me last Christmas." See also *Abstract.*

Generalization (143–144, 145, 146, 452–453) is a broad statement or belief based on a limited number of facts, *examples,* or statistics. A product of inductive reasoning, generalizations should be used carefully and sparingly in *essays.*

Hyperbole the opposite of *understatement,* is a type of *figurative language* that uses deliberate exaggeration for the sake of emphasis or comic effect. (For example, Kimberly Wozencraft refers to Lexington prison as a "country club" in her essay "Notes from the Country Club").

Hypothesis (536) is a tentative theory that can be proved or disproved through further investigation and analysis.

Idiom refers to a grammatical construction unique to a certain people, region, or class that cannot be translated literally into another language.

Illustration (143–144) is the use of *examples* to support an idea or *generalization.*

Imagery is *description* that appeals to one or more of our five senses. See, for example, Malcolm Cowley's description in "The View from 80" of one of the pleasures of old age: "simply sitting still, like a snake on a sun-warmed stone, with a delicious feeling of indolence that was seldom attained in earlier years" [para. 16]. *Imagery* is used to help bring clarity and vividness to descriptive writing.

Induction: See *Deduction.*

Inference is a *deduction* or *conclusion* derived from *specific* information.

Informal diction consists of language used principally in college essays and articles in popular magazines.

Informal essay: See *Essay.*

Introduction (33) refers to the beginning of an *essay.* It should identify the subject to be discussed, set the limits of that discussion, and clearly state the *thesis* or general *purpose* of the paper. A good introduction will generally catch the audience's attention by beginning with a quotation, a provocative statement, a personal *anecdote,* or a stimulating question that somehow involves its readers in the *topic* under consideration. See also *Conclusions.*

Irony is a figure of speech in which the literal, *denotative* meaning is the opposite of what is stated. In "How Lincoln and Darwin Shaped the Modern World," Adam

Gopnik actually refers to the "irony of history" when discussing Lincoln and Darwin [para. 2].

Jargon is the special language of a certain group or profession, such as psychological *jargon*, legal *jargon*, or medical *jargon*. When *jargon* is excerpted from its proper subject area, it generally becomes confusing or humorous, as in "I have a latency problem with my backhand" or "I hope we can interface tomorrow night after the dance."

Levels of thought (2–3) is a phrase that describes the three sequential stages at which people think, read, and write: literal, interpretive, and analytical.

Logic (444–454) is the science of correct reasoning. Based principally on *inductive* or *deductive* processes, *logic* establishes a method by which we can examine *premises* and *conclusions*, construct *syllogisms*, and avoid faulty reasoning.

Logical fallacy (398–399, 453–454) is an incorrect conclusion derived from faulty reasoning. See also *Post hoc, ergo propter hoc* and *Non sequitur.*

Metaphor (49, 454) is an implied *comparison* that brings together two dissimilar objects, persons, or ideas. Unlike a *simile,* which uses the words "like" or "as," a metaphor directly identifies an obscure or difficult subject with another that is easier to understand. For example, when Ray Bradbury describes a piano as "yellow-toothed" [para. 8], he is using a metaphor to explain how the piano keys are like stained human teeth.

Mood (99, 454) refers to the atmosphere or *tone* created in a piece of writing. The mood of Garrison Keillor's "Hoppers" is good-humored and sensible and of Jessica Mitford's "Behind the Formaldehyde Curtain," sarcastic and derisive.

Narration (95–108) is storytelling: the recounting of a series of events, arranged in a particular order and delivered by a narrator to a specific *audience* with a clear *purpose* in mind. Along with *persuasion, exposition,* and *description,* it is one of the four principal types of writing.

Narrative is a rhetorical mode based on story telling. See, for example, Russell Baker's "The Saturday Evening Post."

Non sequitur from a Latin phrase meaning "it does not follow," refers to a *conclusion* that does not logically derive from its *premises.*

Objective (41, 45, 48) writing is detached, impersonal, and factual; *subjective* writing reveals the author's personal feelings and attitudes. KarenLachtanski's "Match the Right Communication Type to the Occasion" is an *example* of objective prose, whereas Amy Tan's "Mother Tongue" is essentially *subjective* in nature. Most good college-level *essays* are a careful mix of both approaches, with lab reports and technical writing toward the *objective* end of the scale and personal *essays* in composition courses at the *subjective* end.

Obsolete diction refers to words no longer in use.

Organization (31, 33) refers to the order in which a writer chooses to present his or her ideas to the reader. Five main types of organization may be used to develop *paragraphs* or *essays:* (1) *deductive* (moving from general to specific), (2) *inductive* (from specific to general), (3) *chronological* (according to time sequence), (4) *spatial* (according to physical relationship in space), and (5) *climactic* (from one extreme to another, such as least important to most important).

Paradox is a seemingly self-contradictory statement that contains an element of truth. In "The View from 80," Malcolm Cowley paradoxically declares that the Ojibwa Indians were "kind to their old people" by killing them when they became decrepit [para. 1].

Paragraphs are groups of interrelated sentences that develop a central topic. Generally governed by a *topic sentence,* a paragraph has its own *unity* and *coherence* and is an integral part of the logical *development* of an *essay.*

Parallelism is a structural arrangement within sentences, *paragraphs,* or entire *essays* through which two or more separate elements are similarly phrased and developed. See the following sentence from Mary Pipher's "Beliefs About Families": "From the Greeks, to Descartes, to Freud and Ayn Rand, Westerners have valued the independent ego" [para. 16].

Paraphrase (557, 558, 559–561) is a restatement in your own words of someone else's ideas or observations.

Parody is making fun of a person, an event, or a work of literature through exaggerated imitation.

Person (103) is a grammatical distinction identifying the speaker or writer in a particular context: first person (I or we), second person (you), and third person (he, she, it, or they). The person of an *essay* refers to the voice of the narrator. See also *Point of view.*

Personification is *figurative language* that ascribes human characteristics to an abstraction, animal, idea, or inanimate object. Consider, for example, Robert Ramirez's description in "The Barrio" of the bakery that "sends its sweet messenger aroma down the dimly lit street, announcing the arrival of fresh, hot, sugary *pan dulce*" [para. 6].

Persuasion (443–458) is one of the four chief forms of *rhetoric.* Its main purpose is to convince a reader (or listener) to think, act, or feel a certain way. It involves appealing to reason, to emotion, and/or to a sense of ethics. The other three main *rhetorical* categories are *exposition, narration,* and *description.*

Plagiarism (557–561) is using someone else's phrasing or ideas as if they were your own. Students can protect themselves from plagiarizing by carefully documenting their *sources.* See also *Documentation.*

Point of view (49–50, 103) is the perspective from which a writer tells a story, including *person, vantage point,* and *attitude.* Principal *narrative* voices are first person, in which the writer relates the story from his or her own vantage point ("I think about Lexington almost daily. I will be walking up Broadway to shop for groceries, or maybe riding my bike in the original Central Park, and suddenly I'm wondering who's in there now, at this very moment, and for what inane violations, and what they're doing" [para. 30]. from "Notes from the Country Club" by Kimberly Wozencraft); omniscient, a third-person technique in which the narrator knows everything and can even see into the minds of the various characters; and concealed, a third-person method in which the narrator can see and hear events but cannot look into the minds of the other characters.

Post hoc, ergo propter hoc (398), a Latin phrase meaning "after this, therefore because of this," is a *logical fallacy* confusing *cause and effect* with *chronology.* Just because Carter wakes up every morning before the sun rises doesn't mean that the sun rises *because* Carter wakes up.

Premise (452) is a *proposition* or statement that forms the foundation of an *argument* and helps support a *conclusion.* See also *Logic* and *Syllogism.*

Prereading (11–12, 24) is thoughtful concentration on a topic before reading an *essay.* Just as athletes warm up their physical muscles before competition, so, too, should students activate their "mental muscles" before reading or writing *essays.*

Prewriting (26–31, 37), which is similar to *prereading,* is the initial stage in the composing process during which writers consider their topics, generate ideas, narrow and refine their *thesis statements,* organize their ideas, pursue any necessary research, and identify their *audiences.* Although prewriting occurs principally, as the name suggests, "before" an essay is started, writers usually return to this "invention" stage again and again during the course of the writing process.

Process analysis (187–198), one of the seven primary modes of *exposition,* either gives directions about how to do something (directive) or provides information on how something happened (informative).

Proofreading (33, 34, 37), an essential part of *rewriting,* is a thorough, careful review of the final draft of an *essay* to ensure that all errors have been eliminated.

Proposition is a proposal or statement.

Purpose (26, 30–31, 33, 37, 444, 446, 454) refers to the overall aim or intention of an *essay*: to entertain, inform, or persuade a particular *audience* with reference to a specific topic (to persuade an audience, for example, that violence on television and in video games is psychologically damaging our children in Dave Grossman's "We Are Training Our Kids to Kill"). See also *Dominant impression.*

Quotation is a phrase or passage that has been published or spoken elsewhere.

Refutation is the process of discrediting the *arguments* that run counter to your *thesis statement.*

Revision (33–34, 37), meaning "to see again," takes place during the entire writing process as you change words, rewrite sentences, and shift *paragraphs* from one location to another in your *essay*. It plays an especially vital role in the *rewriting* stage of the composing process.

Rewriting (33–34, 37) is a stage of the composing process that includes *revision, editing,* and *proofreading.*

Rhetoric is the art of using language effectively.

Rhetorical questions are intended to provoke thought rather than bring forth a specific answer. See, for example, the following question asked by Sara Gilbert: "What are the different ways of being smart?" (254).

Rhetorical strategy or mode is the plan or method whereby an *essay* is developed and/ or organized. Most writers choose from methods discussed in this book, such as *narration, example, comparison/contrast, definition,* and *cause/effect.*

Sarcasm is a form of *irony* that attacks a person or belief through harsh and bitter remarks that often mean the opposite of what they say. See, for example, Jessica Mitford's sarcastic praise of the funeral director in "Behind the Formaldehyde Curtain": "He . . . has revamped the corpse to look like a living doll, he has arranged for it to nap for a few days in a slumber room. He has done everything in his power to make the funeral a real pleasure for everybody concerned" [para. 27]. See also *Satire.*

Satire (340) is a literary technique that attacks foolishness by making fun of it. Most good satires work through a "fiction" that is clearly transparent. For example, in "A Generation's Vanity, Heard Through Lyrics," John Tierney makes a sarcastic comment about good values: "A sure sign something might not be the best value: Charlie Sheen talks about it a lot" [para. 21].

Setting refers to the immediate environment of a *narrative* or *descriptive* piece of writing: the place, time, and background established by the author.

Simile (49, 454) is a *comparison* between two dissimilar objects that uses the words "like" or "as." See, for example, Ray Bradbury's description of the women in "Summer Rituals," who appear "like ghosts hovering momentarily behind the door screen" [para. 10]. See also *Metaphor.*

Slang is casual conversation among friends; as such, it is inappropriate for use in formal and informal writing, unless it is placed in quotation marks and introduced for a specific rhetorical purpose: "Hey dude, whassup?" See, for example, the use of slang throughout Jessica Blau's "Red-Headed."

Sources (536–537, 551–557) are books, articles, journals, magazines, websites, interviews, blogs, discussion boards, emails, newsletters, and similar resources from which writers gather material for documented papers.

Spatial order (49, 52, 151) is a method of *description* that begins at one geographical point and moves onward in an orderly fashion. See, for example, the first two sentences of NASA's description of Mars (88).

Specific: See *General words.*

Style is the unique, individual way in which each author expresses his or her ideas. Often referred to as the "personality" of an *essay*, style is dependent on a writer's manipulation of *diction*, sentence structure, *figurative language, point of view, characterization, emphasis, mood, purpose, rhetorical strategy*, and all the other variables that govern written material.

Subjective: See *Objective.*

Summary (557, 558, 559–561) is a condensed statement of someone else's thoughts or observations.

Syllogism (452) refers to a three-step *deductive argument* that moves logically from a major and a minor *premise* to a *conclusion*. A traditional example is "All men are mortal. Socrates is a man. Therefore, Socrates is mortal."

Symbol refers to an object or action in literature that metaphorically represents something more important than itself. In Susan Tardanico's "Is Social Media Sabotaging Real Communication?" the golf course is a symbol of doing business on a personal level.

Synonyms are terms with similar or identical *denotative* meanings, such as "aged," "elderly," "older person," and "senior citizen."

Syntax describes the order in which words are arranged in a sentence and the effect that this arrangement has on the creation of meaning.

Technical diction involves words that compose the basic vocabulary of a specific and often highly specialized area of study. See, for example, the embalmer's *technical diction* in Jessica Mitford's "Behind the Formaldehyde Curtain."

Theme is another term for an *essay* or written assignment.

Thesis statement or thesis (30–31) is the principal *focus* of an *essay*. It is usually phrased in the form of a question to be answered, a problem to be solved, or an assertion to be argued. The word *thesis* derives from a Greek term meaning "something set down," and most good writers find that "setting down" their thesis in writing helps them tremendously in defining and clarifying their topic before they begin to write an outline or a rough draft.

Tone (99, 454) is a writer's *attitude* or *point of view* toward his or her subject. See also *Mood.*

Topic is the main subject of an *essay* or *argument.*

Topic sentence is the central idea around which a *paragraph* develops. A *topic sentence* controls a *paragraph* in the same way a *thesis statement* unifies and governs an entire *essay*. See also *Induction* and *Deduction.*

Transition (103) is the linking together of sequential ideas in sentences, *paragraphs*, and *essays*. This linking is accomplished primarily through word repetition, pronouns, parallel constructions, and such transitional words and phrases as "therefore," "as a result," "consequently," "moreover," and "similarly."

Understatement the opposite of *hyperbole*, is a deliberate weakening of the truth for comic or emphatic purpose. Commenting, for example, on the great care funeral directors take to make corpses look lifelike for their funerals, Jessica Mitford explains in "Behind the Formaldehyde Curtain," "This is a rather large order, since few people die in the full bloom of health" [para. 14].

Unity (151) exists in an *essay* when all ideas support a central *thesis statement.*

Usage (33–34, 37) refers to the customary rules that govern written and spoken language.

Vantage point (49–50, 103) is the frame of reference of the narrator in a story: close to the action, far from the action, looking back on the past, or reporting on the present. See also *Person* and *Point of view.*

CREDITS

INDEX OF AUTHORS AND TITLES